MATTHEW ~ II
(Chapters 16:13–28:20)

THE PREACHER'S OUTLINE & SERMON BIBLE®

MATTHEW ~ II
(Chapters 16:13–28:20)

THE PREACHER'S OUTLINE & SERMON BIBLE®

NEW TESTAMENT

KING JAMES VERSION

Leadership Ministries Worldwide
Chattanooga, TN

THE PREACHER'S OUTLINE & SERMON BIBLE® - MATTHEW II
KING JAMES VERSION

Copyright © 1996 by ALPHA-OMEGA MINISTRIES, INC.

All Rights Reserved

All other Bible study aids, references, indexes, reference materials
Copyright © 1991 by Alpha-Omega Ministries, Inc.

All rights reserved. No part of this publication may be reproduced, stored in a retrieval system, or transmitted in any form or by any means—electronic, mechanical, photo-copy, recording, or otherwise—without the prior permission of the copyright owners.

Previous Editions of **The Preacher's Outline & Sermon Bible®**,
New International Version NT   Copyright © 1998
King James Version NT   Copyright © 1991, 1996, 2000
by Alpha-Omega Ministries, Inc.

Please address all requests for information or permission to:
Leadership Ministries Worldwide
PO Box 21310
Chattanooga, TN 37424-0310
Ph.# (423) 855-2181   FAX (423) 855-8616   E-Mail info@outlinebible.org
http://www.outlinebible.org

Library of Congress Catalog Card Number: 96-75921
ISBN Softbound Edition: 1 978-1-57407-002-6
ISBN Deluxe 3-Ring Edition: 978-1-57407-027-9

LEADERSHIP MINISTRIES WORLDWIDE
CHATTANOOGA, TN

Printed in the United States of America

Leadership Ministries Worldwide

DEDICATED

To all the men and women of the world who preach and teach the Gospel of our Lord Jesus Christ and to the Mercy and Grace of God

&

- Demonstrated to us in Christ Jesus our Lord.

  "In whom we have redemption through His blood, the forgiveness of sins, according to the riches of His grace." (Ep.1:7)

- Out of the mercy and grace of God, His Word has flowed. Let every person know that God will have mercy upon him, forgiving and using him to fulfill His glorious plan of salvation.

  "For God so loved the world, that he gave His only begotten Son, that whosoever believeth in Him should not perish, but have everlasting life. For God sent not his son into the world to condemn the world, but that the world through him might be saved." (Jn.3:16-17)

  "For this is good and acceptable in the sight of God our Saviour; who will have all men to be saved, and to come unto the knowledge of the truth." (1 Ti.2:3-4)

The Preacher's Outline & Sermon Bible® is written for God's servants to use in their study, teaching, and preaching of God's Holy Word…

- to share the Word of God with the world.
- to help believers, both ministers and laypersons, in their understanding, preaching, and teaching of God's Word.
- to do everything we possibly can to lead men, women, boys, and girls to give their hearts and lives to Jesus Christ and to secure the eternal life that He offers.
- to do all we can to minister to the needy of the world.
- to give Jesus Christ His proper place, the place the Word gives Him. Therefore, no work of Leadership Ministries Worldwide—no Outline Bible Resources—will ever be personalized.

ACKNOWLEDGMENTS AND BIBLIOGRAPHY

Every child of God is precious to the Lord and deeply loved. And every child as a servant of the Lord touches the lives of those who come in contact with him or his ministry. The writing ministries of the following servants have touched this work, and we are grateful that God brought their writings our way. We hereby acknowledge their ministry to us, being fully aware that there are many others down through the years whose writings have touched our lives and who deserve mention, but whose names have faded from our memory. May our wonderful Lord continue to bless the ministries of these dear servants—and the ministries of us all—as we diligently labor to reach the world for Christ and to meet the desperate needs of those who suffer so much.

THE GREEK SOURCES

Expositor's Greek Testament, Edited by W. Robertson Nicoll. Grand Rapids, MI: Eerdmans Publishing Co., 1970.

Robertson, A.T. *Word Pictures in the New Testament*. Nashville, TN: Broadman Press, 1930.

Thayer, Joseph Henry. *Greek-English Lexicon of the New Testament*. New York: American Book Co.

Vincent, Marvin R. *Word Studies in the New Testament*. Grand Rapids, MI: Eerdmans Publishing Co., 1969.

Vine, W.E. *Expository Dictionary of New Testament Words*. Old Tappan, NJ: Fleming H. Revell Co.

Wuest, Kenneth S. *Word Studies in the Greek New Testament*. Grand Rapids, MI: Eerdmans Publishing Co., 1953.

THE REFERENCE WORKS

Cruden's Complete Concordance of the Old & New Testament. Philadelphia, PA: The John C. Winston Co., 1930.

Josephus' Complete Works. Grand Rapids, MI: Kregel Publications, 1981.

Lockyer, Herbert. *All the Men of the Bible*. Grand Rapids, MI: Zondervan Publishing House, 1958.

_____. *All the Miracles of the Bible*. Grand Rapids, MI: Zondervan Publishing House, 1961.

_____. *All the Parables of the Bible*. Grand Rapids, MI: Zondervan Publishing House, 1963.

_____. *The Women of the Bible*. Grand Rapids, MI: Zondervan Publishing House, 1967.

Nave's Topical Bible. Nashville, TN: The Southwestern Co., 1921.

The Amplified New Testament. (Scripture Quotations are from the *Amplified New Testament,* Copyright 1954, 1958, 1987 by the Lockman Foundation. Used by permission.)

The Four Translation New Testament (Including King James, New American Standard, Williams - New Testament in the Language of the People, Beck - New Testament in the Language of Today.) Minneapolis, MN: World Wide Publications, 1966.

The New Compact Bible Dictionary, Edited by T. Alton Bryant. Grand Rapids, MI: Zondervan Publishing House, 1967.

The New Thompson Chain Reference Bible. Indianapolis, IN: B.B. Kirkbride Bible Co., 1964,

THE COMMENTARIES

Barclay, William. *Daily Study Bible Series*. Philadelphia, PA: Westminster Press, 1958.

Bruce, F.F. *The Epistle to the Colossians*. Westwood, NJ: Fleming H. Revell Co., 1968.

_____. *The Epistle to the Hebrews*. Grand Rapids, MI: Eerdmans Publishing Co., 1964.

_____. *The Epistles of John*. Old Tappan, NJ: Fleming H. Revell Co., 1970.

Criswell, W.A. *Expository Sermons on Revelation*. Grand Rapids, MI: Zondervan Publishing House, 1962-66.

ACKNOWLEDGMENTS AND BIBLIOGRAPHY

Greene, Oliver. *The Epistles of John.* Greenville, SC: The Gospel Hour, Inc., 1966.

———. *The Epistles of Paul the Apostle to the Hebrews.* Greenville, SC: The Gospel Hour, Inc., 1965.

———. *The Epistles of Paul the Apostle to Timothy & Titus.* Greenville, SC: The Gospel Hour, Inc., 1964.

———. *The Revelation Verse by Verse Study.* Greenville, SC: The Gospel Hour, Inc., 1963.

Henry, Matthew. *Commentary on the Whole Bible.* Old Tappan, NJ: Fleming H. Revell Co., n.d.

Hodge, Charles. *Exposition on Romans & on Corinthians.* Grand Rapids, MI: Eerdmans Publishing Co., 1972-1973.

Ladd, George Eldon. *A Commentary on the Revelation of John.* Grand Rapids, MI: Eerdmans Publishing Co., 1972-1973.

Leupold, H.C. *Exposition of Daniel.* Grand Rapids, MI: Baker Book House, 1969.

Newell, William R. *Hebrews, Verse by Verse.* Chicago, IL: Moody Press, 1947.

Strauss, Lehman. *Devotional Studies in Philippians. Neptune, NJ: Loizeaux Brothers, 1959.*

———. *Colossians & 1 Timothy.* Neptune, NJ: Loizeaux Brothers, 1960.

———. *The Book of the Revelation.* Neptune, NJ: Loizeaux Brothers, 1964.

The New Testament & Wycliffe Bible Commentary, Edited by Charles F. Pfeiffer & Everett F. Harrison. New York: The Iverson Associates, 1971. Produced for Moody Monthly. Chicago Moody Press, 1962.

The Pulpit Commentary, Edited by H.D.M. Spence & Joseph S. Exell. Grand Rapids, MI: Eerdmans Publishing Co., 1950.

Thomas, W.H. Griffith. *Hebrews, A Devotional Commentary.* Grand Rapids, MI: Eerdmans Publishing Co., 1970.

———. *Studies in Colossians & Philemon.* Grand Rapids, MI: Baker Book House, 1973.

Tyndale New Testament Commentaries. Grand Rapids, MI: Eerdmans Publishing Co., Began in 1958.

Walker, Thomas. *Acts of the Apostles.* Chicago, IL: Moody Press, 1965.

Walvoord, John. *The Thessalonian Epistles.* Grand Rapids, MI: Zondervan Publishing House, 1973.

ABBREVIATIONS

&	=	and	O.T.	=	Old Testament
bc.	=	because	p./pp.	=	page/pages
concl.	=	conclusion	pt.	=	point
cp.	=	compare	quest.	=	question
ct.	=	contrast	rel.	=	religion
e.g.	=	for example	rgt.	=	righteousness
f.	=	following	thru	=	through
illust.	=	illustration	v./vv.	=	verse/verses
k.	=	Kingdom, K. of God, K. of Heaven	vs.	=	versus

THE BOOKS OF THE OLD TESTAMENT

Book	Abbreviation	Chapters	Book	Abbreviation	Chapters
GENESIS	Gen. or Ge.	50	Ecclesiastes	Eccl. or Ec.	12
Exodus	Ex.	40	The Song of Solomon	S. of Sol. or Song	8
Leviticus	Lev. or Le.	27	Isaiah	Is.	66
Numbers	Num. or Nu.	36	Jeremiah	Jer. or Je.	52
Deuteronomy	Dt. or De.	34	Lamentations	Lam.	5
Joshua	Josh. or Jos.	24	Ezekiel	Ezk. or Eze.	48
Judges	Judg. or Jud.	21	Daniel	Dan. or Da.	12
Ruth	Ruth or Ru.	4	Hosea	Hos. or Ho.	14
1 Samuel	1 Sam. or 1 S.	31	Joel	Joel	3
2 Samuel	2 Sam. or 2 S.	24	Amos	Amos or Am.	9
1 Kings	1 Ki. or 1 K.	22	Obadiah	Obad. or Ob.	1
2 Kings	2 Ki. or 2 K.	25	Jonah	Jon. or Jona.	4
1 Chronicles	1 Chron. or 1 Chr.	29	Micah	Mic. or Mi.	7
2 Chronicles	2 Chron. or 2 Chr.	36	Nahum	Nah. or Na.	3
Ezra	Ezra or Ezr.	10	Habakkuk	Hab.	3
Nehemiah	Neh. or Ne.	13	Zephaniah	Zeph. or Zep.	3
Esther	Est.	10	Haggai	Hag.	2
Job	Job or Jb.	42	Zechariah	Zech. or Zec.	14
Psalms	Ps.	150	Malachi	Mal.	4
Proverbs	Pr.	31			

THE BOOKS OF THE NEW TESTAMENT

Book	Abbreviation	Chapters	Book	Abbreviation	Chapters
MATTHEW	Mt.	28	1 Timothy	1 Tim. or 1 Ti.	6
Mark	Mk.	16	2 Timothy	2 Tim. or 2 Ti.	4
Luke	Lk. or Lu.	24	Titus	Tit.	3
John	Jn.	21	Philemon	Phile. or Phm.	1
The Acts	Acts or Ac.	28	Hebrews	Heb. or He.	13
Romans	Ro.	16	James	Jas. or Js.	5
1 Corinthians	1 Cor. or 1 Co.	16	1 Peter	1 Pt. or 1 Pe.	5
2 Corinthians	2 Cor. or 2 Co.	13	2 Peter	2 Pt. or 2 Pe.	3
Galatians	Gal. or Ga.	6	1 John	1 Jn.	5
Ephesians	Eph. or Ep.	6	2 John	2 Jn.	1
Philippians	Ph.	4	3 John	3 Jn.	1
Colossians	Col.	4	Jude	Jude	1
1 Thessalonians	1 Th.	5	Revelation	Rev. or Re.	22
2 Thessalonians	2 Th.	3			

HOW TO USE
The Preacher's Outline & Sermon Bible®
Follow these easy steps to gain maximum benefit from The POSB.

① **SUBJECT HEADING**

② **MAJOR POINTS**

③ **SUBPOINTS & SCRIPTURE**

④ **COMMENTARY**

---

1 CORINTHIANS 13:1-13

CHAPTER 13

D. The Most Excellent Quality of Life: Love, Not Gifts, 13:1-13^{DS1}

1. The great importance of love
   a. Verdict 1: Tongues without love are meaningless
   b. Verdict 2: Gifts without love are nothing
      1) Prophecy is nothing
      2) Understanding all mysteries & knowledge are nothing
      3) Faith is nothing
   c. Verdict 3: Giving without love profits nothing
      1) Giving one's goods
      2) Giving one's life—martyrdom

2. The great acts of love

Though I speak with the tongues of men and of angels, and have not charity, I am become *as* sounding brass, or a tinkling cymbal.
2 And though I have *the gift of* prophecy, and understand all mysteries, and all knowledge; and though I have all faith, so that I could remove mountains, and have not charity, I am nothing.
3 And though I bestow all my goods to feed *the poor*, and though I give my body to be burned, and have not charity, it profiteth me nothing.
4 Charity suffereth long, *and* is kind; charity envieth not; charity vaunteth not itself, is not puffed up,
5 Doth not behave itself unseemly, seeketh not her own, is not easily provoked, thinketh no evil;
6 Rejoiceth not in iniquity, but rejoiceth in the truth;
7 Beareth all things, believeth all things, hopeth all things, endureth all things.
8 Charity never faileth: but whether *there be* prophecies, they shall fail; whether *there be* tongues, they shall cease; whether *there be* knowledge, it shall vanish away.
9 For we know in part, and we prophesy in part.
10 But when that which is perfect is come, then that which is in part shall be done away.
11 When I was a child, I spake as a child, I understood as a child, I thought as a child: but when I became a man, I put away childish things.
12 For now we see through a glass, darkly; but then face to face: now I know in part; but then shall I know even as also I am known.
13 And now abideth faith, hope, charity, these three; but the greatest of these *is* charity.

3. The great permanence of love
   a. It never fails, never ceases, never vanishes
   b. It is perfect & complete
   c. It is maturity—mature behavior
   d. It is the hope of being face-to-face with God—possessing perfect consciousness & knowledge

4. The great supremacy of love

DIVISION VII

THE QUESTIONS CONCERNING SPIRITUAL GIFTS, 12:1–14:40

D. The Most Excellent Quality of Life: Love, Not Gifts, 13:1-13

(13:1-13) **Introduction**: there is no question, what the world needs more than anything else is love. If people loved each other, really loved each other, there would be no more war, crime, abuse, injustice, poverty, hunger, starvation, homelessness, deprivation, or immorality. Love is the one ingredient that could revolutionize society. Love is the greatest quality of human life. Love is the supreme quality, the most excellent way for a man to live.
1. The great importance of love (vv.1-3).
2. The great acts of love (vv.4-7).
3. The great permanence of love (vv.8-12).
4. The great supremacy of love (v.13).

DEEPER STUDY # 1

(13:1-13) **Love**: throughout this passage, the word used for love or charity is the great word *agape*. (See DEEPER STUDY # 4, *Love*—Jn.21:15-17 for more discussion.) The meaning of *agape love* is more clearly seen by contrasting it with the various kinds of love. There are essentially four kinds of love. Whereas the English language has only the word *love* to describe all the affectionate experiences of men, the Greek language had a different word to describe each kind of love.
1. There is *passionate love* or *eros love*. This is the physical love between sexes; the patriotic love of a person for his nation; the ambition of a person for power, wealth, or fame. Briefly stated, *eros love* is the base love of a man that arises from his own inner passion. Sometimes *eros love* is focused upon good and other times it is focused upon bad. It should be noted that *eros love* is never used in the New Testament.
2. There is *affectionate love* or *storge love*. This is the kind of love that exists between parent and child and between loyal citizens and a trustworthy ruler. *Storge love* is also not used in the New Testament.
3. There is an *endearing love*, the love that cherishes. This is *phileo love*, the love of a husband and wife for each other, of a brother for a brother, of a friend for the dearest of friends. It is the love that cherishes, that holds someone or something ever so dear to one's heart.
4. There is *selfless and sacrificial love* or *agape love*. Agape love is the love of the mind, of the reason, of the will. It is the love that goes so far…
   - that it loves a person even if he does not deserve to be loved
   - that it actually loves the person who is utterly unworthy of being loved

---

① Glance at the **Subject Heading**. Think about it for a moment.

② Glance at the **Subject Heading** again, and then the **Major Points** (1, 2, 3, etc.). Do this several times, reviewing them together while quickly grasping the overall subject.

③ Glance at **both** the **Major Points** and **Subpoints** together while reading the **Scripture**. Do this slower than Step 2. Note how these points sit directly beside the related verse and simply restate what the Scripture is saying—in Outline form.

④ Next read the **Commentary**. Note that the *Major Point Numbers* in the Outline match those in the Commentary. A small raised number (**DS1, DS2**, etc.) at the end of a Subject Heading or Outline Point, directs you to a related **Deeper Study** in the Commentary.

Finally, read the **Thoughts** and **Support Scripture** (not shown).

As you read and re-read, pray that the Holy Spirit will bring to your attention exactly what you should preach and teach. May God bless you richly as you study and teach His Word.

The POSB contains everything you need for sermon preparation:

1. **The Subject Heading** describes the overall theme of the passage, and is located directly above the Scripture (keyed *alphabetically*).

2. **Major Points** are keyed with an outline *number* guiding you to related commentary. Note that the Commentary includes *"Thoughts"* (life application) and abundant Supporting Scriptures.

3. **Subpoints** explain and clarify the Scripture as needed.

4. **Commentary** is fully researched and developed for every point.
   - **Thoughts** (in bold) help apply the Scripture to real life.
   - **Deeper Studies** provide in-depth discussions of key words.

"Woe is unto me, if I preach not the gospel"
(1 Co.9:16)

THE GOSPEL ACCORDING TO MATTHEW

INTRODUCTION

AUTHOR: Matthew. The Bible in no place says that Matthew is the author; however, the evidence for Matthew's authorship is strong.

1. Early writers have always credited the Gospel to Matthew. William Barclay quotes one of the earliest church historians, a man named Papias (A.D. 100), as saying, "Matthew collected the sayings of Jesus in the Hebrew tongue" (*The Gospel of Matthew*, Vol.1. "The Daily Study Bible." Philadelphia, PA: The Westminster Press, 1956, p.xxi). Irenaeus (about A.D. 175), the saintly bishop of Lyons, wrote: "Matthew also issued a written Gospel among the Hebrews in their own dialect, while Peter and Paul were preaching at Rome and laying the foundations of the church" (Irenaeus, *Against Heresies*, 3.1.1).

2. Matthew was qualified to write the Gospel. He had been a tax collector which means that he was involved in large business transactions. A study of the Gospel shows that the author had an interest in figures, large numbers (Mt.18:24; 28:12), and statistics (Mt.1:17). The detailed messages of Jesus point to a man experienced with shorthand which he had apparently used in his business. Very little is given in the Scripture about Matthew.
   a. He was one of the twelve apostles (Mk.2:14).
   b. He left all to follow Christ (Lu.5:27-28).
   c. He introduced his friends to Christ by inviting them to a feast which he gave in honor of Christ (Lu.5:29).

DATE: Uncertain. A.D. 50-70. It was written some years after Jesus' ascension, but before A.D. 70.

1. The fall of Jerusalem, A.D. 70, is prophetic (Mt.24:1f).
2. The statements such as "unto this day" (Mt.27:8) and "until this day" (Mt.28:15) suggest a date sometime after Jesus' ascension, but not too far in the distant future.
3. The scattering of the Jerusalem Church due to persecution (Ac.8:4) suggests a date sometime after the ascension. A Gospel would not have been necessary so long as the church and apostles were together.
4. The quote by Irenaeus points to Matthew's writing during Nero's reign, "while Paul and Peter were in Rome."

TO WHOM WRITTEN: The Gospel was written originally to the Jews. However, it breathes a message for all, a message proclaiming the Messianic hope of the world for the Great Deliverer.

PURPOSE: To show that Jesus is the Messiah, the Savior and King prophesied by the Hebrew prophets.

Matthew is a strong book, a book written to force belief in Jesus. Matthew sets out to prove that all the prophecies of the O.T. are fulfilled in Jesus, the carpenter from Nazareth. It has one recurring theme: "All this was done, that it might be fulfilled which was spoken by the prophets, saying...." This is repeated approximately sixteen times, and there are ninety-three O.T. quotations.

SPECIAL FEATURES:

1. Matthew is *The Ecclesiastical Gospel*. Down through the centuries, Matthew has been widely used by the church. Its material is arranged primarily by subjects, not by a strict chronological sequence. It is somewhat a topical arrangement of the ministry and teachings of Jesus. As such, it has been extremely useful to the church: as an apology to defend the faith, as a handbook of instructions for new believers, and as a book of worship to read in church services.

2. Matthew is *The Teaching Gospel*. Much of Jesus' teaching is arranged so that it can be easily taught and easily lived. This material is clearly seen in five sections.
   a. The Sermon on the Mount (Mt.5-7).
   b. The Messiah's messengers and their mission (Mt.9-10:42).
   c. The Messiah's parables (Mt.13).
   d. The Messiah's disciples and their behavior toward one another (Mt.18).
   e. The Messiah's prophecy of His return and the end of time: the great Olivet discourse (Mt.24-25).

3. Matthew is *The Royal Gospel* or *The Kingdom Gospel*. The heart of Matthew's Gospel is that Jesus is King. Jesus is the Son of David, the greatest of Israel's kings. He is the fulfillment of the Messianic prophecies that foretold the coming of a King like unto David.
   a. His genealogy shows Him to be David's son by birth (Mt.1:1-17).
   b. He was born King of the Jews (Mt.2:2).
   c. He was called the King of David time and time again (Mt.9:27; 15:22; 20:30; 21:9, 15; 22:42).
   d. He personally claimed the power of a king by over-riding the law: "I say unto you...." (Mt.5:21-22, 27-28, 31-32, 33-34, 38-39, 43-44).
   e. He dramatically showed Himself to be King by His triumphal entry into Jerusalem (Mt.21:1-11).
   f. He deliberately accepted the title of King before Pilate (Mt.27:11).
   g. His cross bore the title, "King of the Jews" (Mt.27:11).
   h. He claimed the supreme power of the King of Kings, "All power is given unto me" (Mt.28:18).
   i. The word "Kingdom" is used fifty four times and "Kingdom of Heaven" thirty-two times.

INTRODUCTION TO MATTHEW

4. Matthew is *The Apocalyptic Gospel*. Among the Gospels, it has the most comprehensive account of the Lord's return and of the end time (Mt.24-25).

5. Matthew is *The Gospel of the Church*. It is the only Synoptic Gospel that mentions the church (Mt.16:13-23; 18:17; see Mk.8:27-33; Lu.9:18-22).

6. Matthew is *The Gospel of the Jew*. Matthew never failed to show that Jesus fulfills O.T. prophecy. He makes more than one hundred allusions or quotations from the O.T. He is determined to compel the Jew to believe that Jesus is the Messiah.

OUTLINE OF MATTHEW

THE PREACHER'S OUTLINE AND SERMON BIBLE® is *unique*. It differs from all other Study Bibles and Sermon Resource Materials in that every Passage and Subject is outlined right beside the Scripture. When you choose any *Subject* below and turn to the reference, you have not only the Scripture, but you discover the Scripture and Subject *already outlined for you—verse by verse*.

For a quick example, choose one of the subjects below and turn over to the Scripture, and you will find this marvelous help for faster, easier, and more accurate use.

In addition, every point of the Scripture and Outline is *fully developed in a Commentary with supporting Scripture* at the bottom of the page. Again, this arrangement makes sermon preparation much easier and faster.

Note something else: The Subjects of *Matthew* have titles that are both Biblical and *practical*. The practical titles sometimes have more appeal to people. This *benefit* is clearly seen for use on billboards, bulletins, church newsletters, etc.

A suggestion: For the *quickest* overview of *Matthew*, first read *all the major titles* (I, II, III, etc.), then come back and read the subtitles.

OUTLINE OF MATTHEW

I. **THE BIRTH AND CHILDHOOD OF JESUS, THE MESSIAH, 1:1–2:23**

   A. Jesus' Genealogy: Interesting Roots, 1:1-17
   (see Lu.3:23-28)
   B. Jesus' Divine Birth: Unusual Events, 1:18-25
   (Lu.1:26-28; 2:1-7)
   C. Jesus' Acknowledgment as King by Wise Men or Magi: An Unexpected Worship, 2:1-11
   D. Jesus' Childhood: Facing Danger after Danger, 2:12-23

II. **THE PREPARATION FOR THE MESSIAH'S COMING, 3:1–4:11**

   A. Jesus' Forerunner, John the Baptist: A Message for All, 3:1-12
   (Mk.1:1-8; Lu.3:1-20; Jn.1:6-8, 15-37)
   B. Jesus' Baptism: What Baptism Is All About, 3:13-17
   (Mk.1:9-11; Lu.3:21-22; Jn.1:28-34)
   C. Jesus' Temptation: Overcoming All, 4:1-11
   (Mark 1:12-13; Lu.4:1-13)

III. **THE BEGINNING OF THE MESSIAH'S MINISTRY, 4:12-25**

   A. Jesus' Ministry: Going Forth with Purpose, 4:12-17
   B. Jesus' Disciples: The Kind of Person Called, 4:18-22
   (Mk.1:16-20; see Lu.5:1-11; Jn.1:35-51)
   C. Jesus' Dramatic Fame: A Successful Ministry, 4:23-25

IV. **THE TEACHINGS OF THE MESSIAH TO HIS DISCIPLES: THE GREAT SERMON ON THE MOUNT, 5:1–7:29** (Lu.6:20-49)

   A. The True Disciple (Part I): Who He Is and His Reward (the Beatitudes), 5:1-12
   (Lu.6:20-23)
   B. The True Disciple (Part II): The Salt of the Earth—Serving God, 5:13
   (Mk.9:50; see Lu.14:34-35; Col.4:6)
   C. The True Disciple (Part III): The Light of the World—Shining for God, 5:14-16
   (Mk.4:21-23; Lu.8:16-18; 11:33)
   D. The Law and Jesus: Breaking the Law of God, 5:17-20
   E. The Real Meaning of Murder, 5:21-26
   F. The Real Meaning of Adultery, 5:27-30
   (see Mt.19:3-11; Mk.10:2-12; Lu.16:18; 1 Co.7:1-16)
   G. The Real Meaning of Divorce, 5:31-32
   H. The Real Meaning of Oaths and Swearing, 5:33-37
   I. The Real Meaning of the Law Governing Injury, 5:38-42
   (Lu.6:29-30)
   J. The Real Meaning of Human Relationships, 5:43-48
   (Lu.6:27-36)

K. The Right Motive for Giving, 6:1-4
L. The Right Motive for Prayer, 6:5-6
M. The Three Great Rules for Prayer, 6:7-8
N. The Model Prayer, 6:9-13
   (Lu.11:2-4)
O. The Basic Principle of Prayer: Forgiveness, 6:14-15
   (Mk.11:25-26)
P. The Right Motive for Fasting, 6:16-18
Q. The Warning About Wealth and Materialism, 6:19-24
R. The Counsel on Worry and Anxiety, 6:25-34
S. The Warning About Judging and Criticizing Others, 7:1-6
   (Lu.6:37-42)
T. The Key to Prayer: Persevering in Prayer, 7:7-11
U. The Summit of Ethics: The Golden Rule and Two Choices in Life, 7:12-14
   (Lu.6:31; 13:23-24)
V. The Warning About False Prophets, 7:15-20
W. The Warning About False Pretenses: Who Will Enter the Kingdom of Heaven, 7:21-23
   (Lu.13:26-27)
X. The Wise and Foolish Builder, 7:24-27
   (Lu.6:47-49)
Y. The Teaching of Jesus and Its Impact, 7:28-29

V. THE MESSIAH'S GREAT AUTHORITY AND POWER REVEALED IN WORD AND WORK, 8:1–9:34

A. Jesus Heals a Leper: Cleansing the Most Unclean, 8:1-4
   (Mk.1:40-45; Lu.5:12-16)
B. Jesus Heals a Centurion's Servant: Receiving and Rejecting Men, 8:5-13
   (Lu.7:1-10)
C. Jesus Heals Peter's Mother-in-Law: Jesus' Power and Its Purpose, 8:14-17
   (Mk.1:29-34; Lu.4:38-41)
D. Jesus Attracts People: The Cost of True Discipleship, 8:18-22
   (Lu.9:57-62)
E. Jesus Calms a Storm: Conquering Fear and Nature, 8:23-27
   (Mk.4:35-41; Lu.8:22-25)
F. Jesus Casts Out Demons: Saving Men, 8:28-34
   (Mk.5:1-20; Lu.8:26-40)
G. Jesus Heals a Paralyzed Man: Forgiving Sin, 9:1-8
   (Mk.2:1-12; Lu.5:17-26)
H. Jesus Calls Matthew: Receiving Sinners, 9:9-13
   (Mk.2:14-17; Lu.5:27-32)
I. Jesus Answers the Question About Fasting: Ushering in a New Age and Covenant, 9:14-17
   (Mk.2:18-22; Lu.5:33-39)
J. Jesus Heals Several People: Meeting Man's Desperate and Helpless Needs, 9:18-34
   (Mk.5:21-43; Lu.8:41-56; 11:14-15)

VI. THE MESSIAH'S MESSENGERS AND THEIR MISSION, 9:35–10:42
(Mk.6:7-13; Lu.9:1-6)

A. The Mission of the Messiah, 9:35-38
B. The Messiah's Call to His Disciples, 10:1-4
   (Mk.3:13-19; Lu.6:13-19; Ac.1:13)
C. The Messiah's Commission to His Disciples, 10:5-15
D. The Messiah's Warning of Persecution, 10:16-23
E. The Messiah's Encouragement Not to Fear Persecution, 10:24-33
F. The Cost of Being the Lord's Disciple, 10:34-42

VII. THE MESSIAH'S VINDICATION OF HIS MESSIAHSHIP, 11:1-30

A. The Assurance: Given to a Questioning Disciple, John the Baptist, 11:1-6
   (Lu.7:18-23)
B. The Reminder: Given to a Forgetful and Fickle People, 11:7-15
   (Lu.7:24-28)
C. The Message: Given to a Childish Generation, 11:16-27
   (Lu.7:31-35; 10:12-15; 10:21-22)
D. The Great Invitation: Given to this Generation, 11:28-30

VIII. THE MESSIAH'S DEFENSE OF HIMSELF AGAINST OPPONENTS, 12:1-50

A. Defense 1: Messiah Is Greater than Religion, 12:1-8
   (Mk.2:23-28; Lu.6:1-5)
B. Defense 2: Man Is Greater than Religion, 12:9-13
   (Mk.3:1-6; Lu.6:6-11)
C. Defense 3: Messiah Is the Chosen Servant of God, 12:14-21
   (Mk.3:7-12)
D. Defense 4: Messiah Is of God's Kingdom and House, 12:22-30
   (Mk.3:22-30; Lu.11:14-23)
E. Defense 5: A Man's Words Determine His Destiny, 12:31-37
   (Mk.3:28-30; Lu.11:14-16)
F. Defense 6: Messiah's Answer to an Evil Generation or to Apostates, 12:38-45
   (Lu.11:29-32)
G. Defense 7: Messiah's Answer to Doubting Relatives, 12:46-50
   (Mk.3:31-35; Lu.8:19-21)

IX. THE MESSIAH'S PARABLES DESCRIBING THE KINGDOM OF HEAVEN, 13:1-52

A. The Parable of the Sower: How a Man Receives the Gospel, 13:1-9
   (see Mt.13:18-23; Mk.4:1-9; Lu.8:4-15)
B. The Messiah's Reasons for Speaking in Parables: Who Receives and Who Loses, 13:10-17
   (Mk.4:10-12; Lu.8:9-10; 10:23-24)
C. The Parable of the Sower Explained, 13:18-23
   (Mk.4:13-20)
D. The Parable of the Wheat and the Weeds: The Question of Evil—Why It Exists, 13:24-30
   (see Mt.13:36-43)
E. The Parable of the Mustard Seed: The Growth and Greatness of Christianity, 13:31-32
   (Mk.4:30-32; Lu.13:18-19)
F. The Parable of the Leaven: The Transforming Power of the Gospel, 13:33
   (Lu.13:20-21)
G. The Messiah's Purpose for Speaking in Parables, 13:34-35
   (Mk.4:33-34)
H. The Parable of the Wheat and the Weeds Explained, 13:36-43
I. The Parable of the Hidden Treasure: Giving Up All for Christ, 13:44
J. The Parable of the Merchant Man and the Pearl of Great Price: Giving Up All for Christ, 13:45-46
K. The Parable of the Dragnet: Separating the Bad from the Good, 13:47-50
L. The Parable of the Householder: Devotion, Study, and Sharing, 13:51-52

X. THE MESSIAH'S MINISTRY WHILE IN EXILE FROM HEROD, 13:53–16:12

A. The Messiah Was Rejected in His Hometown: Why Jesus Is Rejected, 13:53-58
   (Mk.6:1-6; see Lu.4:16-30)
B. The Messiah's Forerunner Is Murdered: A Godly vs. an Ungodly Man, 14:1-14
   (Mk.6:14-29; Lu.9:7-9)
C. The Messiah's Power to Feed Five Thousand: The Essentials for Ministry, 14:15-21
   (Mk.6:30-44; Lu.9:10-17; Jn.6:1-14)
D. The Messiah's Power to Calm a Storm: The Power of His Presence, 14:22-33
   (Mk.6:45-52; Jn.6:16-21)
E. The Messiah's Power Sought and Trusted: The Steps to Seeking and Being Made Whole, 14:34-36
F. The Messiah Teaches What Defiles a Person, 15:1-20
   (Mk.7:1-23; see Lu.11:37-41)
G. The Messiah Teaches What It Takes to Receive Things of God, 15:21-28
   (Mk.7:24-30)
H. The Messiah's Compassion for Man's Physical Need: How to Minister, 15:29-39
   (Mk.8:1-9)
I. The Messiah Warns Against the Yeast or Leaven of Religionists: A Warning Against Spiritual Blindness and False Teaching, 16:1-12
   (Mk.8:10-21)

XI. THE MESSIAH'S DRAMATIC REVELATION: HIS MESSIAHSHIP, HIS CHURCH, AND HIS CROSS, 16:13–17:27

A. The Messiah's Dramatic Revelation of Himself and His Church: Peter's Great Confession, 16:13-20
   (Mk.8:27-30; Lu.9:18-21; see Jn.6:68-69)
B. The Messiah Foretells His Death and Future Glory (First Time): Total Commitment, 16:21-28
   (Mk.8:31-9:1; Lu.9:22-27)
C. The Transfiguration: Strengthened to Bear the Cross, 17:1-13
   (Mk.9:2-13; Lu.9:28-36)

- D. The Powerless Disciples: A Great Lesson on Faith and Power, 17:14-21
  (Mk.9:14-29; Lu.9:37-42)
- E. The Messiah Foretells His Death and Resurrection (Second Time): Delivered Up by God, 17:22-23
  (Mk 9:30-32; Lu.9:43-45)
- F. The Messiah Reveals Himself through Good Citizenship, 17:24-27
  (see Mk.12:13-17)

XII. THE MESSIAH'S DISCIPLES AND THEIR BEHAVIOR TOWARD ONE ANOTHER, 18:1-35

- A. The Conditions for Greatness, 18:1-4
  (Mk.9:33-37; Lu.9:46-48)
- B. The Warning Against Offending, Mistreating a Child, 18:5-10
  (Mk.9:42-48)
- C. The Parable of the Lost Sheep: The Supreme Example of Caring, 18:11-14
  (Lu.15:1-7)
- D. The Steps to Correcting Offending Brothers, 18:15-20
  (Lu.17:3-4)
- E. The Parable of the Unmerciful Servant: The Spirit of Forgiveness, 18:21-35

XIII. THE MESSIAH'S TEACHINGS ON THE WAY TO JERUSALEM, 19:1–20:34

- A. The Sanctity of Marriage, 19:1-12
  (see Mt.5:31-32; Mk.10:1-12; Lu.16:18; 1 Co.7:10-16)
- B. The Acceptance of Children, 19:13-15
  (Mk.10:13-16; Lu.18:15-17)
- C. The Rich Young Ruler: How a Rich Man Enters the Kingdom of Heaven, 19:16-22
  (Mk.10:17-22; Lu.18:18-23; see Lu.10:25-37)
- D. The Danger of Riches, 19:23-26
  (Mk.10:23-27; Lu.18:24-27)
- E. The Reward for Believers, 19:27-30
  (Mk.10:28-31; Lu.18:28-30)
- F. The Parable of Workers in the Vineyard: God's Glorious Grace, 20:1-16
- G. The Messiah Foretells His Death and Resurrection (Third Time), 20:17-19
  (Mk.10:32-34; Lu.18:31-34)
- H. The Price and Meaning of Greatness, 20:20-28
  (Mk.10:35-45; see Lu.22:24-27)
- I. The Two Blind Men Healed: How the Desperate Can Be Saved, 20:29-34
  (Mk.10:46-52; see Lu.18:35-43)

XIV. THE MESSIAH'S LAST WEEK: HIS CLAIM CHALLENGED AND REJECTED, 21:1–23:39

- A. The Triumphal Entry: Jesus Deliberately Claimed to be the Messiah, 21:1-11
  (Mk.11:1-11; Lu.19:28-40; Jn.12:12-19)
- B. The Temple Cleansed: Authority over God's House, 21:12-16
  (Mk.11:15-19; Lu.19:45-46; see Jn.2:13-16)
- C. The Fig Tree Cursed: The Source of Power, 21:17-22
  (Mk.11:12-14, 20-26)
- D. The Questioning of the Messiah's Power: The Problem with Obstinate Unbelief, 21:23-27
  (Mk.11:27-33; Lu.20:1-8)
- E. The Parable of Two Sons: What It Takes to Enter God's Kingdom, 21:28-32
- F. The Parable of the Wicked Tenants: Israel's Rejection of Jesus' Messiahship, 21:33-46
  (Mk.12:1-12; Lu.20:9-19; see Is.5:1-7)
- G. The Parable of the Marriage Feast: Israel's Rejection of God's Great Invitation, 22:1-14
  (Lu.14:15-24)
- H. The Question About God and Caesar: The Two Citizenships, 22:15-22
  (Mk.12:13-17; Lu.20:20-26)
- I. The Question About The Resurrection: The Resurrection Denied, Yet Proven, 22:23-33
  (Mk.12:18-27; Lu.20:27-38)
- J. The Question About the Great Commandment: A Study of Love, 22:34-40
  (Mk12:28-34; Lu.10:25-37)
- K. The Questions Asked by Jesus: "What Do You Think About the Messiah?" 22:41-46
  (Mk.12:35-37; Lu.20:39-44)
- L. The Warning Against False Religion, 23:1-12
  (Mk.12:38-40; Lu.20:45-47)
- M. The Nine Accusations Against False Religionists, 23:13-36
  (Lu.11:39-50)
- N. The Great Lament of Jesus: Jesus' Love Rejected, 23:37-39
  (Lu.13:34-35)

XV. THE MESSIAH'S PROPHECY OF HIS RETURN AND THE END OF THE AGE: THE OLIVET DISCOURSE, 24:1–25:46

A. The Signs of the Last Days, 24:1-14
(Mk.13:1-13; Lu.21:5-11)
B. The Most Terrible Sign of the Last Days: The Abomination of Desolation and the Great Tribulation or Distress, 24:15-28
(Mk.13:14-27; Lu.21:20-28)
C. The Coming of the Son of Man: Five Events, 24:29-31
D. The Time of the Lord's Return, 24:32-41
(Mk.13:28-34; Lu.21:29-35)
E. The Lord's Return and the Believer's Duty: Watch—Be Ready—Be Faithful and Wise, 24:42-51
(Mk.13:35-37; Lu.21:36)
F. The Parable of the Ten Virgins: The Warning to Watch, 25:1-13
(see Lu.13:35-37)
G. The Parable of the Talents: The Believer's Duty to Work, 25:14-30
H. The Parable of the Sheep and Goats: The Final Judgment of Nations, 25:31-46

XVI. THE MESSIAH'S ARREST, TRIAL, AND CRUCIFIXION, 26:1–27:66

A. The Messiah's Death Explained and Plotted, 26:1-5
(Mk.14:1-2; Lu.22:1-2)
B. The Messiah Anointed for Death: A Picture of Sacrificial Love and Faith, 26:6-13
(Mk.14:3-9; Jn.12:1-8)
C. The Messiah Betrayed by Judas: The Picture of a Ruined Life, 26:14-16
(Mk.14:10-11; Lu.22:3-6)
D. The Messiah's Last Supper: The Lord's Supper Instituted, 26:17-30
(Mk.14:12-26; Lu.22:7-23; see Jn.13:1-30)
E. The Messiah Foretells the Disciples' Failure: Stumbling and Falling Away in Life, 26:31-35
(Mk.14:27-31; Lu.22:31-34; Jn.13:36-38)
F. The Messiah's Agony in Gethsemane: Confronting Death and the Terrifying Trials of Life, 26:36-46
(Mk.14:32-42; Lu.22:39-46; Jn.18:1; see He.5:7-8; 12:3-4)
G. The Messiah Betrayed, Arrested, and Deserted: Four Pictures of Commitment, 26:47-56
(Mk.14:43-52; Lu.22:47-53; Jn.18:3-11)
H. The Messiah's Trial Before Caiaphas and the Sanhedrin: Facing the Great Trials of Life, 26:57-68
(Mk.14:53-65; Lu.22:54, 63-71; see Jn.18:12-14, 19-24)
I. The Messiah Denied by Peter: A Look at Denying Christ, 26:69-75
(Mk.14:66-72; Lu.22:54-62; Jn.18:15-18, 25-27)
J. The Messiah's Traitor, Judas, and His End: A Picture of Wrong Repentance and Human Religion, 27:1-10
(see Ac.1:16-19)
K. The Messiah's Tragic Trial Before Pilate: The Tragedy of an Indecisive Man, 27:11-25
(Mk.15:1-15; Lu.23:1-25; Jn.18:28-40)
L. The Messiah's Suffering and Crucifixion: A Picture of the World's Treatment of God's Son, 27:26-44
(Mk.15:16-32; Lu.23:43; Jn.19:16-24)
M. The Messiah's Great Triumph: The Miraculous Events Surrounding the Cross, 27:45-56
(Mk.15:33-41; Lu.23:44-49; Jn.19:30-37)
N. The Messiah's Burial: Reactions to His Death, 27:57-66
(Mk.15:42-47; Lu.23:50-56; Jn.19:38-42)

XVII. THE MESSIAH'S TRIUMPHANT RESURRECTION, 28:1-20

A. The Messiah's Resurrection: Surrounding Events, 28:1-15
(Mk.16:1-13; Lu.24:1-49; Jn.20:1-23)
B. The Messiah's Final Commission to His Disciples, 28:16-20
(Mk.16:15-18; Lu.24:46-49; Jn.20:21; see Jn.17:18; Ac.1:8)

MATTHEW 16:13-20

	XI. THE MESSIAH'S DRAMATIC REVELATION: HIS MESSIAHSHIP, HIS CHURCH, & HIS CROSS, 16:13–17:27 A. The Messiah's Dramatic Revelation of Himself & His Church: Peter's Great Confession, 16:13-20 *(Mk 8:27-30; Lu 9:18-21; Jn 6:68-69)*	16 And Simon Peter answered and said, Thou art the Christ, the Son of the living God. 17 And Jesus answered and said unto him, Blessed art thou, Simon Barjona: for flesh and blood hath not revealed *it* unto thee, but my Father which is in heaven. 18 And I say also unto thee, That thou art Peter, and upon this rock I will build my church; and the gates of hell shall not prevail against it.	a. The second critical question: Whom do you say I am?, v.15 b. The true confession: A personal trust in Christ 4. **This confession is revealed by God alone** 5. **This confession is the foundation of the church**^{DS1} a. Fact 1: His church b. Fact 2: He builds c. Fact 3: He protects
1. **This confession was made at Caesarea Philippi** 2. **This confession is not the confession of the world** a. The first critical question: Whom do men say I am? b. The false confessions 3. **This confession declares one's trust in Christ**	13 When Jesus came into the coasts of Caesarea Philippi, he asked his disciples, saying, Whom do men say that I the Son of man am? 14 And they said, Some *say that thou art* John the Baptist: some, Elias; and others, Jeremias, or one of the prophets. 15 He saith unto them, But whom say ye that I am?	19 And I will give unto thee the keys of the kingdom of heaven: and whatsoever thou shalt bind on earth shall be bound in heaven: and whatsoever thou shalt loose on earth shall be loosed in heaven. 20 Then charged he his disciples that they should tell no man that he was Jesus the Christ.	6. **This confession assigns great responsibility to believers in the church** a. A responsibility to use the keys to the kingdom b. A responsibility to bind & loose on earth, to open & shut the door of heaven through the gospel 7. **This confession must be understood before being shared with others**

DIVISION XI

THE MESSIAH'S DRAMATIC REVELATION: HIS MESSIAHSHIP, HIS CHURCH, AND HIS CROSS, 16:13–17:27

A. The Messiah's Dramatic Revelation of Himself and His Church: Peter's Great Confession, 16:13-20

(16:13-20) **Introduction**: Jesus withdrew to be alone with His disciples. He was facing the end very, very soon. There was much to reveal and teach them. It was time for them to learn that He was *building a church*—an assembly of people who would be confessing Him to be the Messiah. The present passage is one of the most dramatic revelations ever made. It is also one of the most demanding questions ever asked. It is demanding because the answer given determines a person's eternal destiny. How a person answers the questions determines where he will spend eternity, with God in heaven or apart from God in hell. And note: there is only one answer to the question that can qualify a person for heaven: "Thou are the Christ, the Son of the living God." The importance of the question and its confession is clearly seen by glancing quickly at the points of the passage.
1. This confession was made at Caesarea Philippi (v.13).
2. This confession is not the confession of the world (vv.13-14).
3. This confession declares one's trust in Christ (vv.15-16).
4. This confession is revealed by God alone (v.17).
5. This confession is the foundation of the church (v.18).
6. This confession assigns great responsibility to believers in the church (v.19).
7. This confession must be understood before being shared with others (v.20).

1 (16:13) **Caesarea Philippi**: Christ was in the area of Caesarea Philippi. (See DEEPER STUDY # 1—Mk.8:27. This note will give the dramatic background for the Lord's pointed question. Jesus had withdrawn to be alone and to pray before this event and its profound revelation [see Lu.9:18].)

2 (16:13-14) **Profession, False**: Peter's confession is not the confession of the world. Note two significant points.

a. Jesus had asked a critical question: "Whom do men say that I the Son of Man am?" We must know what others say about Jesus, just who He is. What men think of Jesus...
- determines their destiny
- determines how we are to reach out to them
- determines their reaction to us as we witness to them
- determines to a large degree the morality and justice of a society

b. There were false confessions regarding Christ. The popular opinions show that Christ was highly esteemed and greatly respected. He was considered one of the greatest of men. It should be noted that these opinions were not only untrue, but they were dangerous in that they contained only half truths. The result was tragic: people were deceived and misled by them.

MATTHEW 16:13-20

1) Some people said Jesus was John the Baptist. These people were professing Jesus to be a great spirit of righteousness, a spirit that was willing to be martyred for its faith. Herod and others thought this (Mt.14:1-2). Upon hearing of Jesus' marvelous works, Herod fancied that either John had been revived or else his spirit indwelt the man about whom he was hearing.

The common people saw some similarity between John and Jesus: both were doing a unique and great work for God; both were divinely chosen and gifted by God; and both proclaimed the Kingdom of God and prepared men for it. Therefore, when some people looked at Jesus and His ministry, they did not consider Him to be the Messiah, but rather the promised forerunner of the Messiah (Mal.4:5).

2) Some people said Jesus was Elijah. Elijah was considered to be the greatest prophet and teacher of all time and was also predicted to be the forerunner of the coming Messiah (Mal.4:5). William Barclay points out that even today the Jews expect Elijah to return before the Messiah. In the celebration of the Passover, they always leave a chair vacant for him to occupy (*The Gospel of Matthew*, Vol.2, p.150). Elijah had also been used by God to miraculously feed a widow woman and her son (1 K.17:14). The people connected Elijah's miracle and Jesus' feeding of the multitude.

3) Some people said Jesus was Jeremiah. They were professing Jesus to be a prophet who was revealing some very important things about God and religion to men. It had always been thought that Jeremiah was going to return to earth right before the Messiah and bring with him the tabernacle, ark, and altar of incense. He was said to have taken these and hid them in Mount Nebo right before he died (2 Maccabees 2:1-12; 2 Esdras 2:18).

4) Some people said Jesus was one of the prophets. They were professing Jesus to be a great prophet who had been sent for their day and time. He was thought to be one of the great prophets brought back to life or one in whom the spirit of a great prophet dwelt (see De.18:15, 18).

It should be noted that the same false confessions about Christ exist in every generation.

⇒ There are some people who think that Jesus was only a great man of righteousness who was martyred for His faith. Therefore, He leaves us a great example of how to live and stand up for what we believe.

⇒ There are other people who think that Jesus was only one of the great teachers and prophets of history.

⇒ There are still others who think that Jesus was only a great man who revealed some very important things to us about God and religion. Therefore, He can make a significant contribution to every man in his search for God.

⇒ There are some others who think that Jesus was just a great man and prophet sent to the people (Jews) of His day. We can learn about Him by studying His life.

"Is not this the carpenter, the son of Mary, the brother of James, and Joses, and of Juda, and Simon? and are not his sisters here with us? And they were offended at him" (Mk.6:3).

"He was in the world, and the world was made by him, and the world knew him not. He came unto his own, and his own received him not" (Jn.1:10-11).

"Then said they unto him, Where is thy Father? Jesus answered, Ye neither know me, nor my Father: if ye had known me, ye should have known my Father also" (Jn.8:19).

"Who is a liar but he that denieth that Jesus is the Christ? He is antichrist, that denieth the Father and the Son. Whosoever denieth the Son, the same hath not the Father" (1 Jn.2:22-23).

"Every spirit that confesseth not that Jesus Christ is come in the flesh is not of God: and this is that spirit of antichrist, whereof ye have heard that it should come; and even now already is it in the world" (1 Jn.4:3).

Thought 1. Note three things about the world's opinions of Jesus Christ.

(1) The world is not unanimous in its opinion of Christ. There are many different opinions, yet there is only one *truth*. He either is or is not who He claimed to be: the Son of God. As long as the world does not hold to the truth, it shall wander around in a maze of opinions, following guess after guess and hypothesis after hypothesis.

(2) Most of the world's opinions of Christ see Him as a good and great man. The opinions are not accurate, but they at least elevate Christ above the average man.

(3) The world's opinions are false and inaccurate. There are two bases for this statement.

(a) If Christ should not be the Son of God, then He is not a good and great man. He is the worst deceiver and biggest hoax to ever arrive on the world scene. Why? Because He claimed to be the Son of God and the God of righteousness, and He built His following on the claim. If Jesus Christ is not the Son of God, then every true follower of His is living in a *dream world* of *false hope* and denying himself many of the world's goods. He is also teaching a deceptive lie to others. If Christ should not be the Son of God, then He is not worth following.

(b) Scripture emphatically declares: Jesus Christ is the Son of God. He is who He claimed to be.

3 (16:15-16) **Confession—Jesus Christ, Names and Titles**: Peter's confession was a personal trust in Christ.

a. Jesus asked a second critical question, and He asked this question much more emphatically in the Greek: "But you, who do you say that I am?" The answer to this question is critical; it is all-important. It determines a person's eternal destiny.

b. The true confession declares one's personal trust in Christ. Note Peter's words, "Thou art the Christ, the Son of the living God"—a simple and yet momentous confession arising from a personal conviction. It is the confession that saves the soul and the confession that lays the foundation for the church. The very life and survival of a man's soul and of the church as a whole rests upon this simple, yet profound conviction.

⇒ The *Christ*: the Messiah, the anointed One of God (see DEEPER STUDY # 2—Mt.1:18).

⇒ The *Son of God*: of the same being, the same substance; One with the Father (see note—Ph.2:6).

MATTHEW 16:13-20

⇒ The *Son of the Living God*: the source and being of life; possessing the source, energy, and power of life within Himself (Jn.5:26; 17:2-3; 1 Th.1:9).

Peter probably did not understand all that was involved in Christ's being the Son of God (the cross and resurrection had not yet taken place). But his confession was made in simple trust arising from a heart that was truly convicted that Jesus was the Christ, the Son of the living God. It is simple trust which God desires and longs for—nothing more and nothing less. Peter was simply confessing step by step, "I believe you are..."

- the true Messiah
- not a mere man
- but the Son of God
- sent by God
- to fulfill all that the prophets foretold

Thought 1. The question is personal. It is directed to every man: "Whom say ye that I am." Every man has to answer, and his eternal destiny depends upon his answer. But his answer is critical, for it is not a confession *about* Christ that Christ is after. He is after a belief, a confession in His deity, a trusting of His saving grace.

"Whosoever therefore shall confess me before men, him will I also confess before my Father which is in heaven. But whosoever shall deny me before men, him will I also deny before my Father which is in heaven" (Mt.10:32-33).

"Whosoever therefore shall be ashamed of me and of my words in this adulterous and sinful generation; of him also shall the Son of man be ashamed, when he cometh in the glory of his Father with the holy angels" (Mk.8:38).

"Also I say unto you, Whosoever shall confess me before men, him shall the Son of man also confess before the angels of God" (Lu.12:8).

"That if thou shalt confess with thy mouth the Lord Jesus, and shalt believe in thine heart that God hath raised him from the dead, thou shalt be saved. For with the heart man believeth unto righteousness; and with the mouth confession is made unto salvation" (Ro.10:9-10).

"He first findeth his own brother Simon, and saith unto him, We have found the Messias, which is, being interpreted, the Christ" (Jn.1:41).

"Philip findeth Nathanael, and saith unto him, We have found him [the Messiah], of whom Moses in the law, and the prophets, did write, Jesus of Nazareth, the son of Joseph" (Jn.1:45).

"Nathanael answered and saith unto him, Rabbi, thou art the Son of God; thou art the King of Israel" (Jn.1:49).

"Come, see a man, which told me all things that ever I did: is not this the Christ?" (Jn.4:29).

"And we believe and are sure that thou art that Christ, the Son of the living God" (Jn.6:69).

"She saith unto him, Yea, Lord: I believe that thou art the Christ, the Son of God, which should come into the world" (Jn.11:27).

"And Thomas answered and said unto him, My Lord and my God" (Jn.20:28).

"And as they went on their way, they came unto a certain water: and the eunuch said, See, here is water; what doth hinder me to be baptized? And Philip said, If thou believest with all thine heart, thou mayest. And he answered and said, I believe that Jesus Christ is the Son of God" (Ac.8:36-37).

4 (16:17) **Conviction—Holy Spirit, Work of**: Peter's confession was revealed by God alone. Only God can convict the soul of a man and lead a man to personally trust Christ as the Son of God. There are two reasons for this.

a. Man is only flesh and blood. A person cannot convict another person to trust Christ, not convict him in regenerating power. Conviction that leads a man to trust Christ—that leads to regeneration—is the work of God's Spirit (Jn.16:8-11).

b. The natural man cannot receive the things of the Spirit of God (1 Co.2:14). Man is of the earth; he is earthly. Christ is of heaven and of God; He is heavenly. God is Spirit, and they who worship Him must worship Him *in spirit* and in truth (Jn.4:23-24). Man cannot come to know Christ in a personal way through natural wisdom or study. Humanly, the fact is as clear as can be, man cannot *recreate* himself. If he is to be reborn, he has to be *recreated* by Someone other than himself. He has to be recreated by God (Jn.3:3, 5-6).

⇒ Man cannot *quicken* himself; he cannot give spiritual life to himself—only God can.
⇒ Man cannot *regenerate* himself—only God can.
⇒ Man cannot *transform* himself—only God can.
⇒ Man cannot *redeem* himself—only God can.
⇒ Man cannot *infuse* himself with eternal life—only God can.

"Which were born, not of blood, nor of the will of the flesh, nor of the will of man, but of God" (Jn.1:13).

"That which is born of the flesh is flesh; and that which is born of the Spirit is spirit" (Jn.3:6).

"For by grace are ye saved through faith; and that not of yourselves: it is the gift of God: not of works, lest any man should boast" (Ep.2:8-9).

"Not by works of righteousness which we have done, but according to his mercy he saved us, by the washing of regeneration, and renewing of the Holy Ghost" (Tit.3:5).

"Being born again, not of corruptible seed, but of incorruptible, by the word of God, which liveth and abideth for ever" (1 Pe.1:23).

"Whosoever believeth that Jesus is the Christ is born of God: and every one that loveth him that begat loveth him also that is begotten of him" (1 Jn.5:1).

MATTHEW 16:13-20

Thought 1. Natural man has been led away from the spiritual...
- by pride, power, fame, wealth, and glory
- by the prejudices of education, the philosophy of humanism, the limitations of scientific methodology, and the materialistic results of technology
- by the pull to disbelieve, the lack of courage to buck the crowd, and the hesitation to surrender all of self and possessions to Christ
- by the love of the flesh, the enjoyment of looking, the stimulation of touching, the sensation of experiencing, and the consumption of tasting
- by the deceptions of the evil one, the lusts of the human heart, and the sins of personal behavior

5 (16:18) **Church, Foundation**: Peter's confession is the foundation of the church (see DEEPER STUDY # 1, *Church*—Mt.16:18. Also see notes—Ep.2:20; 4:4-6 for more discussion.) Christ replied to Peter, "You are Peter [*petros*] and on this rock [*petra*] I will build my church." No matter how a person interprets this passage, one thing is sure: this was a tremendous compliment to Peter. But what did Jesus mean? Probably this: the rock was *Peter himself and his confession*, not simply Peter and not just his confession. The rock was *both*, but in a very special sense.

a. Peter himself was the rock in two senses.
  1) Peter was the first person to *fully* grasp who Jesus really was. He was the first to confess with *full* understanding that Jesus is the Christ, the Son of the living God. Others had made similar confessions before (Jn.1:41, 45, 49; 6:69), but they had not yet been with Jesus long enough to *fully* grasp what being "the Son of God" really meant. Their confessions had been the earthly confessions of a simple child-like faith. But now Peter understood more fully; he *fully* grasped who Jesus was. Therefore, he became the first man, the first rock, the foundation *upon* which the church and all other "living stones" were to be built.

  Great weight is given to this meaning in Ep.2:20. The apostles and prophets are said to be the foundation of the church upon which all future believers or "living stones" are built (1 Pe.2:5). Jesus Christ is said to be the chief cornerstone. The picture is unquestionably clear. From the human perspective, the apostles and prophets work and build the church, and upon their work and effort the church depends. From God's perspective, Christ's power and work establishes the church (see 1 Co.3:11; 1 Pe.2:4-8; see note—Mt.16:19).

  2) Peter was the one who launched and laid the foundation of the church. He was the early leader of the church who stood forth at Pentecost when three thousand souls were saved (Ac.2:41) and at Caesarea when the door of salvation was opened to the Gentiles (10:1f). Therefore, he was the rock and the foundation in that he was the first man who ever opened the doors of the church to both Jew and Gentile.

b. Peter's confession (or one might say, Christ Himself) was the rock. Christ said, "You are Peter and on this rock [I, Myself, the great truth of your confession] will I build my church." There is no question that the church is built upon Christ. He is unquestionably the builder of the church and the power behind its structure (1 Co.3:11). It is He who takes every believer, all the "living stones," and places him into the structure of His church (1 Pe.2:4-8). The church *depends* upon Christ, not upon Peter nor any other man or combination of men. It was first *built* by Peter after Pentecost; but it is *held up and held together* by Christ, the only foundation.

Note the exact words spoken by Christ.
  ⇒ Fact 1: "My church." The church is Christ's not man's.
  ⇒ Fact 2: "I will build." Christ builds the church.
  ⇒ Fact 3: "The gates of hell shall not prevail." Christ Himself protects the church.

"Therefore whosoever heareth these sayings of mine, and doeth them, I will liken him unto a wise man, which built his house upon a rock" (Mt.7:24).

"Jesus saith unto them, Did ye never read in the Scriptures, The stone which the builders rejected, the same is become the head of the corner: this is the Lord's doing, and it is marvellous in our eyes?" (Mt.21:42).

"For other foundation can no man lay than that is laid, which is Jesus Christ" (1 Co.3:11).

"And are built upon the foundation of the apostles and prophets, Jesus Christ himself being the chief corner stone" (Ep.2:20).

"To whom coming, as unto a living stone, disallowed indeed of men, but chosen of God, and precious, ye also, as lively stones, are built up a spiritual house, an holy priesthood, to offer up spiritual sacrifices, acceptable to God by Jesus Christ. Wherefore also it is contained in the scripture, Behold, I lay in Sion a chief corner stone, elect, precious: and he that believeth on him shall not be confounded" (1 Pe.2:4-6).

Thought 1. The *true* church is universal. It is made up of *all* who genuinely confess Jesus to be the Christ, the Son of the living God. But note: He is the Son of the *living* God. If God is living, then Christ is living. He is, therefore, "*My* Lord, *my* God." A genuine believer, that is, a true church member, becomes a person who has surrendered himself to be a servant of God's Son, of God's Lord.

Thought 2. We should go to Christ often and confess our trust and faith in Him. We should do so alone, demonstrating strength, devotion, tenderness, and warmth. He desires such strong and warm devotion, for we are the "living stones" of His church.

Thought 3. Note a fact often overlooked. Christ not only loved and died for us individually—He also loved and died for the church as a whole (universally). "Christ also loved the church, and gave Himself for it" (Ep.5:25).

MATTHEW 16:13-20

> **DEEPER STUDY # 1**
>
> (16:18) **Church** (ekklesia): the word means to call out a gathering, an assembly. In the Greek, there is no spiritual significance ascribed to the word itself. An example is the town meeting in Ephesus which was *called out* (ekklesia). It was only an official city-wide meeting (Ac.19:32, 39, 41).
>   What is the difference then between such secular gatherings and the church of God?
>   1. It is God who calls together and gathers His church. His church is the body of people "called out" from the world by Him. They are His body of people, a people sanctified or *set apart* by Him to form the church of the living God.
>   2. God dwells within the very presence of believers when they gather together (see note—1 Co.3:16-17).
>   3. The gathering of God meets together for two purposes—worship and mission. God is the object of worship, and His mission becomes the objective of the church. Therefore, God's church, the local assembly, gathers together to worship and to pool its resources in order to carry out the mission of God Himself. It should be noted that this is the first mention of the church in the New Testament. (See notes—Mt.16:18; Ep.2:20; 4:4-6 for more discussion.)

6 (16:19) **Christian Responsibility**: Peter's confession assigned great responsibility to believers for the church. The steward of the house is given the keys or the responsibility for the house. The steward has the responsibility to close (bind) and to open (loose) the house. The key is the gospel, the message of the Lord Jesus Christ Himself. It is the business of the steward to proclaim and teach the Gospel. By proclaiming and teaching, he opens the door; by not proclaiming and not teaching, he shuts the door.

Note: the keys are not the keys to the church but to the Kingdom of Heaven. It is entrance into the Kingdom of Heaven that is the point. Peter was the first man to preach the gospel and open the door to Israel at Pentecost (Ac.2:38-42) and to the Gentiles in the house of Cornelius (Ac.10:3-48).

Note another point of critical importance: Peter claimed no power or authority beyond preaching the gospel and opening the door to unbelievers (Ac.15:7-11). His epistles say nothing whatsoever about man's acting in God's behalf and determining who will and who will not enter the Kingdom of Heaven. Only God will determine who lives and who does not live in His presence. There is also this additional evidence: Peter claimed nothing more for himself than what other men claimed—to be gifted by God as an apostle (1 Pe.1:1) and an elder (1 Pe.5:1). This fact is clearly seen in his subservience to James. James presided over the Jerusalem Council, not Peter (Ac.15:19; Ga.2:11-14).

> **Thought 1.** The servants of God, ministers and laymen alike, have been given the gospel, the keys to the Kingdom of Heaven. It is every believer's responsibility to use the keys. The unbeliever who rejects the gospel in hostility and begins to persecute the believer is to be turned away from (Mt.10:11-14, 23). The one who receives the gospel and the believer is to have the door of the kingdom opened to him.
>
> "Go ye therefore, and teach all nations, baptizing them in the name of the Father, and of the Son, and of the Holy Ghost: teaching them to observe all things whatsoever I have commanded you: and, lo, I am with you alway, even unto the end of the world" (Mt.28:19-20).
>
> "And he said unto them, Go ye into all the world, and preach the gospel to every creature" (Mk.16:15).
>
> "Then said Jesus to them again, Peace be unto you: as my Father hath sent me, even so send I you" (Jn.20:21; see Mt.20:28; Lu.19:10).
>
> "But ye shall receive power, after that the Holy Ghost is come upon you: and ye shall be witnesses unto me both in Jerusalem, and in all Judaea, and in Samaria, and unto the uttermost part of the earth" (Ac.1:8).
>
> "And the things that thou hast heard of me among many witnesses, the same commit thou to faithful men, who shall be able to teach others also" (2 Ti.2:2).
>
> "But sanctify the Lord God in your hearts: and be ready always to give an answer to every man that asketh you a reason of the hope that is in you with meekness and fear" (1 Pe.3:15).

7 (16:20) **Witnessing**: Peter's confession must be understood before being shared with others. There were several reasons the disciples were forbidden to share that Jesus was the Son of God.

a. They still needed more preparation. They did not yet know the *full* gospel. The death and resurrection of Jesus, the very core of the gospel, had not yet taken place.

b. The disciples needed the indwelling power of the Holy Spirit if the message was to be effective, and the Spirit had not yet come. Pentecost had not yet taken place.

c. The people misunderstood the prophecies of the Messiah. If the disciples began preaching with force, the people might revolt against the Roman conquerors (see notes—Mt.1:1; Deeper Study # 2—1:18; Deeper Study # 3—3:11; notes—11:1-6; 11:2-3; Deeper Study # 1—11:5; Deeper Study # 2—11:6; Deeper Study # 1—12:16; note—Lu.7:21-23).

> **Thought 1.** Two things are essential before a believer can effectively proclaim the gospel.
> (1) He must understand the death and resurrection of Jesus Christ (1 Co.15:1-4).
> (2) He must be indwelt and infilled with the Spirit of God (Ac.1:8).

MATTHEW 16:21-28

	B. The Messiah Foretells His Death & Future Glory (First Time): Total Commitment, 16:21-28 (Mk 8:31–9:1; Lu 9:22-27)	24 Then said Jesus unto his disciples, If any *man* will come after me, let him deny himself, and take up his cross, and follow me.	2. His death demands total commitment on our part a. Must will to follow Christ b. Must deny self c. Must take up the cross d. Must follow Christ

1. His death required total commitment on His part
a. His death was necessary: He "must go" to suffer
  1) In Jerusalem^{DS1}
  2) To suffer many things^{DS2}
  3) To be killed
  4) To be raised
b. His death arouses natural man
 	
c. His death shows man to be an adversary of God
 	
d. His death reveals man's true nature
		21 From that time forth began Jesus to show unto his disciples, how that he must go unto Jerusalem, and suffer many things of the elders and chief priests and scribes, and be killed, and be raised again the third day.
		22 Then Peter took him, and began to rebuke him, saying, Be it far from thee, Lord: this shall not be unto thee.
		23 But he turned, and said unto Peter, Get thee behind me, Satan: thou art an offence unto me: for thou savourest not the things that be of God, but those that be of men.
			25 For whosoever will save his life shall lose it: and whosoever will lose his life for my sake shall find it.
			26 For what is a man profited, if he shall gain the whole world, and lose his own soul? or what shall a man give in exchange for his soul?
			27 For the Son of man shall come in the glory of his Father with his angels; and then he shall reward every man according to his works.
			28 Verily I say unto you, There be some standing here, which shall not taste of death, till they see the Son of man coming in his kingdom.
				3. His death offers four reasons for total commitment
				a. An abandonment of this life saves a man
				b. A man's soul is worth more than the whole world
				
				c. A day of judgment is coming
				
				d. A promise is given–the promise of never having to taste death

DIVISION XI

THE MESSIAH'S DRAMATIC REVELATION: HIS MESSIAHSHIP, HIS CHURCH, AND HIS CROSS, 16:13–17:27

B. The Messiah Foretells His Death and Future Glory (First Time): Total Commitment, 16:21-28

(16:21-28) **Introduction**: a new stage was now launched by Jesus. Note the words, "From that time forth." More plainly than ever before and without reserve, Christ revealed that *the Son of the living God* was going to be killed and raised again from the dead. Never before had so phenomenal an event happened, and never again would it happen. History would be made. "Jerusalem...that killed the prophets" was going to commit the ultimate crime—they were going to kill God's own Son (see Mt.23:27).

Note two facts.

1. Christ had already been telling His disciples about His death and resurrection for some time, but they had not understood. There were two primary reasons for their blindness. First, the idea of a suffering Messiah differed radically from their own idea of the Messiah (see notes—Mt.1:1; Deeper Study # 2—1:18; Deeper Study # 3—3:11; notes—11:1-6; 11:2-3; Deeper Study # 1—11:5; Deeper Study # 2—11:6; Deeper Study # 1—12:16; Deeper Study # 1—Mk.8:27; notes—8:30; Lu.7:21); and second, the revelation had been hidden in pictures and symbols.

> "Destroy this temple, and in three days I will raise it up" (Jn.2:19).
>
> "As Moses lifted up the serpent in the wilderness, even so must the Son of Man be lifted up" (Jn.3:14).
>
> "I am the living bread which came down from heaven: if any man eat of this bread, he shall live for ever: and the bread that I will give is my flesh, which I will give for the life of the world" (Jn.6:51).

Now, however, there was a significant switch in how Jesus went about preparing His disciples for His death. The difference was that Christ no longer spoke in pictures and symbols. He now taught them in simple and direct words (Mt.20:18-20; Lu.18:31-33). A new stage in the revelation of God's plan for the world was now taking place: God's Son was to die and be raised again for the sins of the world. God's plan for saving the world was to take place through a suffering Messiah, not a conquering Messiah. God's Messiah was not going to deliver a *materialistic* world into the hands of His followers. God's Messiah was going to die; and through death, He was going to usher in the Kingdom of God, making it possible for His followers to live eternally in the very presence of God Himself (see Deeper Study # 3—Mt.19:23-24; see Jn.3:16; 5:24f).

2. The disciples now understood *more fully* that Jesus was "the Messiah, the Son of the living God" (Mt.16:16). They had taken a great leap forward in their understanding of His nature, just who He really was. Now they needed to learn two things: that the real way into God's kingdom and glory was through death, sacrifice, and self-denial. The path of suffering had to be taken not only by God's Messiah but also by the followers of God's Messiah (vv.24-28).

Just imagine the radical difference between the two concepts...
- a suffering Messiah vs. a conquering Messiah
- a suffering believer vs. a conquering believer

MATTHEW 16:21-28

Seeing the radical difference helps a person understand Peter's behavior and the reason why the disciples were so slow to grasp what Christ was saying. In fact, they never completely understood until after the resurrection (see outlines and notes—Mt.17:22-23; 20:17-19; Mk.8:31-33; 9:30-32; 10:32-34).

The lesson of Christ is clear: God's plan to save the world is through the death of His Son, His sacrifice and self-denial, and the way of salvation for man is the same. Man must undergo personal sacrifice, self-denial, and death (Mt.16:24-26).

1. His death required total commitment on His part (vv.21-23).
2. His death demands total commitment on our part (v.24).
3. His death offers four reasons for total commitment (vv.25-28).

1 (16:21-23) **Jesus Christ, Death**: Jesus' death required total commitment on His part.

a. His death was necessary: He "must go to Jerusalem to suffer." The words *must* [dei] *go* are strong: a constraint, an imperative, a necessity was laid upon Christ. He had no choice. His death and resurrection had been planned and willed by God through all eternity. The prophets had predicted it; He must fulfill the will of God, for God had ordained His death (see Mt.26:54; Lu.24:26, 46).

The resurrection of Jesus Christ was also necessary. Jesus' prediction of His resurrection is clear to us because we can look back upon it, but it was never clear to His disciples. Why? Very simply, it was to be a new experience. No one had ever risen from the dead never to die again. It was unprecedented. The apostles believed perhaps somewhat like Martha—that there was to be a future resurrection of all men (Jn.11:24-26). Such a belief is an expression of the hope that is within every man, the hope to continue on in some form of existence. Such a belief is easy to hold, but to think of a resurrection now, to think of a person's arising from the dead today is difficult. The actual resurrection of a dead person would be inconceivable to those who had not been grounded in its teaching.

Just what they thought Christ meant by *being raised again* is not known. The fact that they did not fully understand is clear from the fact that their spirits were crushed when He was killed. However, some of His followers seemed to grasp more of *a real bodily* resurrection than others. This is clear by an immediate remembrance of His words after His resurrection. There was John who believed immediately (Jn.20:8-9). Mary Magdalene was shown that He had risen just "as He said" (Mt.28:6), and she understood after seeing Him. But others were slower to understand and believe (Mk.16:11; Jn.20:24-25).

> **"Destroy this temple, and in three days I will raise it up" (Jn.2:19).**
>
> **"As Moses lifted up the serpent in the wilderness, even so must the Son of Man be lifted up" (Jn.3:14).**
>
> **"I am the living bread which came down from heaven: if any man eat of this bread, he shall live for ever: and the bread that I will give is my flesh, which I will give for the life of the world" (Jn.6:51).**
>
> **"Having therefore obtained help of God, I continue unto this day, witnessing both to small and great, saying none other things than those which the prophets and Moses did say should come: that Christ should suffer, and that he should be the first that should rise from the dead, and should show light unto the people, and to the Gentiles" (Ac.26:22-23).**
>
> **"For I delivered unto you first of all that which I also received, how that Christ died for our sins according to the Scriptures; and that he was buried, and that he rose again the third day according to the scriptures" (1 Co.15:3-4).**
>
> **"[Christ] died for all, that they which live should not henceforth live unto themselves, but unto him which died for them, and rose again" (2 Co.5:15).**
>
> **"For Christ also hath once suffered for sins, the just for the unjust, that he might bring us to God, being put to death in the flesh, but quickened by the Spirit" (1 Pe.3:18).**

Thought 1. Christ revealed His death and resurrection in stages—revealed it only as the disciples were able to receive and bear the fact. Christ always teaches us gradually and moves us along as we are able to learn. There is great truth in the saying that He does not put more upon us than we can bear.

Thought 2. Note that Jesus spoke of His resurrection when He spoke of His death. It was for the joy that was set before Him that He endured the cross (He.12:2). The joy and hope of spending eternity with Christ and His followers is what encourages us to bear *our cross* while here on earth (see Lu.9:23).

b. His death arouses natural man. Natural man rebels at the idea of the cross. Natural man wants another way other than the cross. This is what Peter was doing: rebelling against the idea that *God's Son* was to die, that His blood had to be shed for the sins of the world (1 Pe.2:24). Peter could accept Jesus as "the Son of the living God" but not as the suffering Savior. Such an idea was repulsive and unacceptable to him. Therefore, he tried to stop the idea. Note the words, "Peter took Him" (proslabomenos). The Greek is strong; it means *caught hold of*. Peter took hold of Christ; he grabbed Christ and took Him aside for a conference.

Note also that Peter "began to rebuke [epitiman] Him." This again is strong. It is not just a wish but a forcible attempt to stop the idea of the suffering Savior. "This shall not be unto thee." *This must not and cannot happen to you. God forbid it* is the equivalent idea. The point is this: Peter was out to stop the cross. He was urging Christ to be the Messiah of power, fame, and sensation whom the Jews were expecting (see notes—Mk.8:27-9:50; 8:30; Mt.1:1; DEEPER STUDY # 2—1:18; DEEPER STUDY #3—3:11; notes—11:1-6; 11:2-3; DEEPER STUDY # 1—11:5; DEEPER STUDY # 2—11:6; DEEPER STUDY # 1—12:16; note—Lu.7:21-23). Peter was urging Christ to follow his own human schemes instead of God's way; and by such urging, he was tempting Christ with the very same compromises that Satan used to tempt Christ—the compromises of power,

MATTHEW 16:21-28

fame, and sensation (Mt.4:1-11). Peter was zealous for God, but he was mistaken and ignorant in his zeal. He did not understand that God was planning to save the world through the death of His Son (see note, pt.3—Mk.8:31).

Such behavior is the way of the world. It is the natural, carnal mind. Man rebels and recoils against the idea of a suffering Savior who had to die for the sins of the world—a Savior who demands the same sacrifice and denial of His followers. Such an idea is unacceptable and repulsive.

> **Thought 1.** The natural man's idea of God and of God's plan for man is seen in three concepts.
> (1) Some think the path of life is love, so they live showing interest and care for others. God is seen as a giving, loving, and indulgent *grandfather type* of person—the indulgent grandfather who tolerates even the worst behavior, no matter how much human suffering and devastation is wrought by the hands of a person. To think of the cross and *the blood* of Christ as an emblem of suffering is repulsive and repelling. The cross is viewed only as an emblem of love, not of sin and shame. The way of love is thought to be the path of life which man is to follow.
> (2) Some think that comfort and pleasure is the path of life. God again is viewed only as an indulgent *grandfather type* who gives man the good things of life and helps man when he gets in trouble. God's will for man is thought to be comfort and pleasure, ease and plenty, health and leisure. Again the cross is only an emblem of love and care for the world, not of suffering and sacrifice and self-denial. The shame, pain, and agony of the cross and its purpose of reconciling a world lost in sin and reeling in desperate need is over-looked.
>
> > "And that which fell among thorns are they, which, when they have heard, go forth, and are choked with cares and riches and pleasures of this life; and bring no fruit to perfection" (Lu.8:14).
> > "And I will say to my soul, Soul, thou hast much goods laid up for many years; take thine ease, eat, drink, and be merry" (Lu.12:19).
> > "But she that liveth in pleasure is dead while she liveth" (1 Ti.5:6).
> > "[They] shall receive the reward of unrighteousness, as they that count it pleasure to riot [party] in the day time. Spots they are and blemishes, sporting themselves with their own deceivings while they feast with you" (2 Pe.2:13).
> > "Therefore hear now this, thou that art given to pleasures, that dwellest carelessly, that sayest in thine heart, I am, and none else beside me; I shall not sit as a widow, neither shall I know the loss of children: but these two things shall come to thee in a moment in one day, the loss of children, and widowhood: they shall come upon thee in their perfection for the multitude of thy sorceries, and for the great abundance of thine enchantments" (Is.47:8-9).
>
> (3) Some feel that triumph, victory, position, authority, power, and reigning supreme is God's way. This was the idea of most Jews in Christ's day. It was Peter's concept of the Messiah (see notes—Mt.1:1; DEEPER STUDY #2—1:18; DEEPER STUDY #3—3:11; 11:1-6; 11:2-3; DEEPER STUDY #1—11:5; DEEPER STUDY #2—11:6; DEEPER STUDY #1—12:16; note—Lu.7:21-23). The concepts of power, position, and authority are clearly seen in movements that stress *self-image*, *self-improvement*, and *personality development*. Developing one's self-image as much as possible and achieving all that one can are said to be God's plan and path for man. However, the idea of suffering and sacrifice and self-denial is rejected.
>
> > "They that are great exercise authority upon them. But it shall not be so among you: but whosoever will be great among you, let him be your minister; and whosoever will be chief among you, let him be your servant" (Mt.20:25-27).
> > "How can ye believe, which receive honour one of another, and seek not the honour that cometh from God only?" (Jn.5:44).
> > "And if any man think that he knoweth any thing, he knoweth nothing yet as he ought to know" (1 Co.8:2).
> > "For all that is in the world, the lust of the flesh, and the lust of the eyes, and the pride of life, is not of the Father, but is of the world" (1 Jn.2:16).
> > "Thou art wretched, and miserable, and poor, and blind, and naked" (Re.3:17).
> > "Nevertheless man being in honour abideth not: he is like the beasts that perish" (Ps.49:12).
> > "Pride goeth before destruction, and a haughty spirit before a fall" (Pr.16:18).
> > "Seest thou a man wise in his own conceit? There is more hope of a fool than of him" (Pr.26:12).

c. His death shows man to be an adversary of God. The literal meaning of Satan in the words "*get thee behind me, Satan*" is "adversary" (see note—Re.12:7-9). Calling Peter "Satan" is stern, yet such sternness was necessary. Peter was tempting Christ with the very same temptation that Christ had faced in the wilderness (see notes—Mt.4:8-10). All the worldly glory that could be His flashed across His mind. The loyalty and allegiance of men without the cross was again being suggested to Him. How this must have cut Christ! This time the temptation was coming from one of His own disciples! When a man refuses to accept God's plan for life, he becomes an adversary to God. He opposes God's will. In essence, man says that he knows what is best; that he is *wiser* than God. Think! When a man does not accept God's plan for life, the crux of what he says to God is, "The cross is not necessary. Jesus' dying to save the world was a useless plan. It was not needed."

This is what Peter was doing and saying. He was opposing God's plan for life, that is, saving the world through the death of His Son. He was saying that he was wiser than God. Note: Christ abruptly turned to Peter before Peter could say anything else and stopped him in his tracks. He charged Peter with being Satan, with being under the authority of Satan, with speaking as Satan. He had become *as* Satan, an adversary to God and God's plan for His Son and for the salvation of the world.

"And said, O full of all subtilty and all mischief, thou child of the devil, thou enemy of all righteousness, wilt thou not cease to pervert the right ways of the Lord?" (Ac.13:10).

"Ye are of your father the devil, and the lusts of your father ye will do" (Jn.8:44).

"In time past ye walked according to the course of this world, according to the prince of the power of the air, the spirit that now worketh in the children of disobedience" (Ep.2:2).

"In this the children of God are manifest, and the children of the devil: whosoever doeth not righteousness is not of God, neither he that loveth not his brother" (1 Jn.3:10).

Thought 1. No man should instruct or counsel God. Our task is not to force our ideas upon God but to surrender to His will.

"For Who is he that condemneth? It is Christ that died, yea rather, that is risen again, who is even at the right hand of God, who also maketh intercession for us" (Ro.8:34).

d. His death reveals man's true nature. Note the words *Thou savorest not* [ou phroneis]. This means to think; to mind. Peter did not have his mind or his thoughts in line with God's mind and thoughts. His tastes were different from God's tastes. Peter's thoughts and tastes were worldly and self-pleasing, not spiritual and pleasing to God. He was using human reasoning not God's reasoning. The thought that God's Son had to die and shed His blood for the sins of the world was disgraceful to Peter. In his mind, such a concept was unfit for God.

Note how true Christ's words to Peter are! "Thou savourest not the things that be of God, but those that be of men." The death of Christ reveals man's true nature, a nature that uses natural and carnal reasoning instead of spiritual reasoning.

"For they that are after the flesh do mind the things of the flesh; but they that are after the Spirit the things of the Spirit. For to be carnally minded is death; but to be spiritually minded is life and peace. Because the carnal mind is enmity against God: for it is not subject to the law of God, neither indeed can be" (Ro.8:5-7).

"This I say therefore, and testify in the Lord, that ye henceforth walk not as other Gentiles walk, in the vanity of their mind" (Ep.4:17).

"For many walk, of whom I have told you often, and now tell you even weeping, that they are the enemies of the cross of Christ: whose end is destruction, whose God is their belly, and whose glory is in their shame, who mind earthly things" (Ph.3:18-19).

"And you, that were sometime alienated and enemies in your mind by wicked works, yet now hath he [God] reconciled in the body of his flesh through death, to present you holy and unblameable and unreproveable in his sight" (Col.1:21-22).

"Unto the pure all things are pure: but unto them that are defiled and unbelieving is nothing pure; but even their mind and conscience is defiled" (Tit.1:15).

"The LORD knoweth the thoughts of man, that they are vanity" (Ps.94:11).

"Wash thine heart from wickedness, that thou mayest be saved. How long shall thy vain thoughts lodge within thee?" (Je.4:14).

Thought 1. Man feels a little more humane, a little more civil by denying "the blood of Christ" for the sins of the world. To reject what is sometimes called a "blood religion" makes a person feel more acceptable in a so-called *civilized society*. Two things need to be noted.
(1) The cross should be viewed as repulsive. The cross is a symbol of sin and shame. Hanging upon the cross, God's *very own Son* bore our sins and the sins of the whole world (1 Jn.2:1-2). Sin and shame are always repulsive, and the fact that God's Son hung there *becoming sin for us* is abhorrent. Nothing could be any more distasteful than what actually happened.
(2) The cross should be viewed as glorious. The cross is a symbol of life and of forgiven sins (1 Pe.2:20). Through the cross, God gloriously reconciles man to Himself and to one another (see outline and notes—Ep.2:13-18). So much comes through the glorious work of the cross that Paul just exclaimed, "God forbid that I should glory, save in the cross of our Lord Jesus Christ" (Ga.6:14).

DEEPER STUDY # 1
(16:21) **Jesus Christ, Opposition**: note the three Jewish groups who were to take the lead in killing Jesus. These were the three groups who made up the Sanhedrin, the supreme court of Jewish justice. It was comprised of seventy members (see the historical basis for this structure, 2 Chr.19:5-11).

1. The elders: these were the older and most respected men of a community. The elders were judges of the civil courts and of temporal affairs (Ex.3:29; 12:21; 24:9; Nu.11:25; 1 S.16:4; Ezr.10:14; Mt.27:12).

2. The chief priests: these were primarily the leaders among the Sadducees. They held most of the high offices of Jewish government under Roman rule (see Deeper Study # 1—Ac.23:8). The chief priests were judges of religious affairs.

3. The Scribes: these were primarily Pharisees who held the teaching positions of the nation (see Deeper Study # 1—Lu.6:2).

Thought 1. Note that the three groups who opposed Jesus were the very people who should have been following Him, the very leaders who should have known God. They should have known God well enough to have recognized His Son the Messiah. But, as with so many in every generation, they were blinded by their own religion, power, wealth, fame, and position.

MATTHEW 16:21-28

> **DEEPER STUDY # 2**
> (16:21) **"Many things"**: the sufferings of Jesus are spelled out in some detail in two passages (Mt.20:18-19; Lu.18:31-33). (Also see DEEPER STUDY #1—Mt.27:26-44 for a detailed description of Jesus' death.)

2 (16:24) **Jesus Christ, Death—Cross—Commitment**: Jesus' death demands the total commitment of a man. Christ gives four steps that are involved in total commitment (see note—Mt.16:25-28. The note is adequate for stirring thoughts for application.)

a. A person must *will* to follow Christ. The word *wills* (thelei) means to desire, wish, design, purpose, resolve, determine. It is a deliberate willing, a deliberate choice, a determined resolve to follow Christ. If a person really wills and deliberately chooses to follow Christ, then he has to do the three things mentioned. Note: the choice is voluntary; it is made by the person. It is the individual who wills and chooses; therefore, it is the individual who must act and do the three things mentioned.

b. A person must deny self. The word *deny* (aparnesastho) means to disown, disregard, forsake, renounce, reject, refuse, restrain, disclaim, do without. It means to subdue, to disregard one's self and one's interest. Very simply, it means to say "no." But note: the call is not to say "no" to some behavior or thing but to *self*. A person is to *deny self*; and this means much more than just being negative, that is, giving up something and doing without something. It means that we are to act positively, to say "yes" to Christ and "no" to self. It means to let Christ rule and reign in our hearts and lives, to let Christ have His way completely. Of course, if a person allows Christ to rule in his life, all negative as well as positive behavior is taken care of (see note and DEEPER STUDY #1,2,3—Mk.8:34). In the Greek the word "deny" is an ingressive aorist which means that the person enters a new state or condition. It means, "Let him *at once begin* to deny self."

c. A person must take up the cross. (See note and DEEPER STUDY #1, *Self-denial*—Lu.9:23 for discussion.)

d. A person must follow Jesus. The word *follow* (akoloothei) means to be a follower or companion, to be a disciple. It has the idea of seeking to be in union with and in the likeness of. It is following Christ, seeking to be just like Him. Again, this is not a passive behavior but an active commitment and walk. It is energy and effort, action and work. It is going after Christ with zeal and energy, struggling and seeking to follow in His footsteps, no matter the cost. Note that the steps of Christ led to death before they led to glory (Mt.16:21).

3 (16:25-28) **Commitment**: Jesus' death offers four arguments for total commitment.

a. An abandonment of this life saves a person. What does it mean when Scripture says that a person saves his life by losing it and loses his life by finding it? The key is in the words "for my sake." Christ says that "whosoever will lose his life *for my sake* shall find it." The person who abandons this life—who sacrifices and gives all that he is and has for Christ—shall save his life. But the person who *keeps* his life and what he has and *seeks* more and more of this life, shall lose his life completely and eternally.

The person who "saves his life"...
- by seeking to avoid the aging of the body and death and yet denies Christ—that person shall lose his life eternally.
- by seeking to make his life more and more comfortable, easy, and secure (beyond what is necessary) and neglects Christ shall lose his life eternally.
- by seeking to gain wealth and power and fame by compromising Christ shall lose his life eternally.
- by seeking the thrills, excitement, and stimulation of this world by ignoring Christ shall lose his life eternally.

As said above, the person who loses his life for Christ—who sacrifices and gives all he is and has for Christ—saves his life, and he saves it eternally. The person who keeps his life and what he has for himself shall lose his life, and he loses it eternally. The call of Christ is just what He says: a life of denial that takes up the cross and follows in His steps.

> "Even as the Son of man came not to be ministered unto, but to minister, and to give his life a ransom for many" (Mt.20:28).
> "For the Son of man is come to seek and to save that which was lost" (Lu.19:10).
> "Then said Jesus to them again, Peace be unto you: as my Father hath sent me, even so send I you" (Jn.20:21).
> "We then that are strong ought to bear the infirmities of the weak, and not to please ourselves" (Ro.15:1).

b. A man's soul is worth more than the whole world. The word *soul* is the same word translated *life* (v.25). Christ uses the word *life* in two senses. There are *two stages*, two beings, two existences to the same life: the life that exists on this earth and the life that shall exist beyond this life. Once a person (life) is born into this world, he shall exist forever. It is just a matter of where he goes after this world: to be with God or to be apart from God.

No man can gain the whole world, but what if he could? All the pleasure and wealth and power and fame are nothing compared with his soul. There are four primary reasons why the soul is far superior to the things of this earth.

1) Everything fades and passes away. A person possesses something only for a short time.
2) Everything cannot be used all at once. Everything sits and remains unused most of the time.
   ⇒ Clothes sit.
   ⇒ A car sits.
   ⇒ Power goes unused.
   ⇒ Popularity and fame quickly pass and are forgotten.

3) The human soul is eternal. The soul never dies and never ceases to exist. It shall live forever either with God or apart from God.
4) The human soul is of more value than the whole world.

Once a man has lost his soul, it is lost. It cannot be bought back. The man forfeits and suffers the loss of it forever. Imagine! Even if a man possessed all the wealth of the world, he would not be able to buy back his soul. Why? Because it is gone; it has passed on forever. The man will never return to earth, not even for one day. He is gone forever.

> "What is a man advantaged, if he gain the whole world, and lose himself, or be cast away?" (Lu.9:25).
>
> "And I say unto you, That many shall come from the east and west, and shall sit down with Abraham, and Isaac, and Jacob, in the kingdom of heaven. But the children of the kingdom [false professions] shall be cast out into outer darkness: there shall be weeping and gnashing of teeth" (Mt.8:11-12).
>
> "And he saith unto him, Friend, how camest thou in hither not having a wedding garment [righteousness]? and he was speechless. Then said the king to the servants, Bind him hand and foot, and take him away, and cast him into outer darkness; there shall be weeping and gnashing of teeth" (Mt.22:12-13).
>
> "Ye have not chosen me, but I have chosen you, and ordained you, that ye should go and bring forth fruit, and that your fruit should remain: that whatsoever ye shall ask of the Father in my name, he may give it you" (Jn.15:16).
>
> "But I keep under my body, and bring it into subjection: lest that by any means, when I have preached to others, I myself should be a castaway" (1 Co.9:27).
>
> "And take heed to yourselves, lest at any time your hearts be overcharged with surfeiting, and drunkenness, and cares of this life, and so that day come upon you unawares" (Lu.21:34).

c. A day of judgment is coming. When Christ returns, the true value of sacrifice vs. self-satisfaction will be clearly seen. Sacrifice for Christ will be abundantly rewarded; self-satisfaction will be condemned. Man is to be judged according to his works. The word "works" means doing, working, acting. It is not isolated acts, but continuous behavior. A person is to be rewarded on the basis of his continuous behavior, not isolated acts.

> "And then will I profess unto them, I never knew you: depart from me, ye that work iniquity" (Mt.7:23).
>
> "But he answered and said, Verily I say unto you, I know you not" (Mt.25:12).
>
> "But he that denieth me before men shall be denied before the angels of God" (Lu.12:9).
>
> "But he shall say, I tell you, I know you not whence ye are; depart from me, all ye workers of iniquity" (Lu.13:27).

d. A promise is given—a promise of never having to taste death. This verse is much clearer when it is compared to Mark's account: "Verily, I say unto you, that there be some of them that stand here, which shall not taste of death, till they have seen the kingdom of God come with power" (Mk.9:1). It is the power of the kingdom to which Jesus refers; that is, His death and resurrection and Pentecost and to the many, many converts to His kingdom that resulted. After Pentecost the power of His Kingdom came—power beyond anything the disciples could have ever dreamed.

MATTHEW 17:1-13

CHAPTER 17

C. The Transfiguration: Strengthened to Bear the Cross, 17:1-13

(Mk 9:2-13; Lu 9:28-36)

Outline	Scripture

1. The struggle to be alone with God
  a. Jesus withdrew to a high mountain
  b. He took three witnesses^{DS1}
	And after six days Jesus taketh Peter, James, and John his brother, and bringeth them up into an high mountain apart,

2. The strength of God's glory
  a. His face shone as the sun
  b. His clothes gleamed
	2 And was transfigured before them: and his face did shine as the sun, and his raiment was white as the light.

3. The strength of great saints
  a. Moses: The lawgiver
  b. Elijah: The great prophet
	3 And, behold, there appeared unto them Moses and Elias talking with him.

4. The strength of a heavenly experience
  a. A taste of glory
  b. A staggering request by Peter
	4 Then answered Peter, and said unto Jesus, Lord, it is good for us to be here: if thou wilt, let us make here three tabernacles; one for thee, and one for Moses, and one for Elias.

5. The strength of God's presence
  a. The cloud: The Shekinah glory of God descended
  b. The voice of God: Proclaimed Jesus to be His Son–listen to Him
	5 While he yet spake, behold, a bright cloud overshadowed them: and behold a voice out of the cloud, which said, This is my beloved Son, in whom I am well pleased; hear ye him.

c. The disciples' reaction: They prostrated themselves–terrified	6 And when the disciples heard it, they fell on their face, and were sore afraid.
d. The Lord's intercession: His closeness & presence	7 And Jesus came and touched them, and said, Arise, and be not afraid.
e. The Lord's preeminence: They saw no one but Jesus	8 And when they had lifted up their eyes, they saw no man, save Jesus only.
6. The strength of the resurrection a. The prediction of the Messiah's resurrection	9 And as they came down from the mountain, Jesus charged them, saying, Tell the vision to no man, until the Son of man be risen again from the dead.
b. The misconception of the Messiah	10 And his disciples asked him, saying, Why then say the scribes that Elias must first come?

c. The misconception corrected
    1) Elijah had already come (in the person of John the Baptist, v.13)
    2) The people had killed him
	11 And Jesus answered and said unto them, Elias truly shall first come, and restore all things.
	12 But I say unto you, That Elias is come already, and they knew him not, but have done unto him whatsoever they listed. Likewise shall also the Son of man suffer of them.

d. The Messiah must also suffer	
e. The disciples finally understood	13 Then the disciples understood that he spake unto them of John the Baptist.

DIVISION XI

THE MESSIAH'S DRAMATIC REVELATION: HIS MESSIAHSHIP, HIS CHURCH, AND HIS CROSS, 16:13–17:27

C. The Transfiguration: Strengthened to Bear the Cross, 17:1-13

(17:1-13) **Introduction**: the transfiguration of Christ is a most unusual experience, but Christ and the disciples needed *unusual strength* to face the future. The future held the cross for both.

Christ had just entered the last stage of training for the disciples (see outline and notes—Mt.16:21-28). It was most important that they grasp God's plan for the world: He was the Messiah, and He was to save the world through death and not through earthly power and conquest (see notes—Mt.1:1; DEEPER STUDY # 2—1:18; DEEPER STUDY # 3—3:11; notes—11:1-6; 11:2-3; DEEPER STUDY # 1—11:5; DEEPER STUDY # 2—11:6; DEEPER STUDY # 1—12:16; note—Lu.7:21-23). He was to bear the cross for the sins of the world (1 Pe.2:24), but they too were to bear the cross if they were to follow Him. For some days now, He had been drilling this message into them. Soon He was to face the reality of the cross, and they were going to fully understand the thrust of what He meant by their "taking up the cross" (see outline and notes—Mt.16:24-28). They both needed a very special portion of strength to face what lay in front of them.

The transfiguration was God's answer to their need. God used five things to strengthen Christ and the disciples. The same five things are applicable to the great needs we face. God will use the same kinds of things to strengthen us.

1. The struggle to be alone with God (v.1).
2. The strength of God's glory (v.2).
3. The strength of great saints (v.3).
4. The strength of a heavenly experience (v.4).
5. The strength of God's presence (vv.5-8).
6. The strength of the resurrection (vv.9-13).

1 (17:1) **Devotion**: Jesus was on a high mountain. Note that this event took place six days after drilling His disciples with the fact of His coming death and resurrection. Christ needed to get all alone with God. He took three disciples, Peter, James and John, with Him and climbed a high mountain. The place chosen is important. It was *"an high mountain,"* an isolated place where they would not be interrupted. It was conducive, fitted for being alone with God. Four major things drove Christ to get alone with God. The same things should always cause us to get alone with God for an extended time:

⇒ pressure (from facing the cross)
⇒ a momentous decision (to bear the cross)
⇒ intensive training
⇒ the need for renewed strength

MATTHEW 17:1-13

> **DEEPER STUDY # 1**
> (17:1) **Peter, James, and John**: see Deeper Study # 1—Mk.9:2 for the reasons these three were chosen.

2 (17:2) **God's Glory**: there was the strength of God's glory. The word *transformed* (metamorphothe) means a change into another form; a transformation; a change of countenance; a complete change. Luke said, "the fashion of His countenance was altered" (Lu.9:29). Note how the gospel writers described what happened.

> "His face did shine as the sun and His raiment was white as the light" (Mt.17:2).
> "His raiment became shining, exceeding white as snow; so as no fuller on earth can white them" (Mk.9:3).
> "The fashion of His countenance was altered, and His raiment was white and glistening" (Lu.9:29).

Apparently *the glory* of His Godly nature was allowed to shine through His body. "The glory which [He] had with God before the world" shone through His body right on through His clothes (Jn.17:5). Peter said, "We were eyewitnesses of His majesty" (2 Pe.1:16). In John's vision of Christ in *The Revelation*, he described the glory of Christ as the sun that shines in its strength (Re.1:16).

The scripture says:

> "God is light" (1 Jn.1:5).
> "[God]...dwelling in the light which no man can approach" (1 Ti.6:16).
> "[God] who coverest thyself with light as with a garment" (Ps.104:2).

Thought 1. Believers experience some portion of the glory of the Lord.

> "But we all, with open face beholding as in a glass the glory of the Lord, are changed into the same image from glory to glory, even as by the Spirit of the Lord" (2 Co.3:18).

Of course, our sense of God's glory is very much dependent upon our doing what Christ did: getting alone with God in an intensive session of prayer and devotion. We are to be transformed into the image of Christ, transformed in all His moral excellence. But we must learn that the change is brought about only by the Spirit of God and only as we seek His face in prayer and genuine trust.

> "And be not conformed to this world: but be ye transformed by the renewing of your mind, that ye may prove what is that good, and acceptable, and perfect, will of God" (Ro.12:2).

3 (17:3) **Moses—Elijah**: there was the strength of great saints. Why did Moses and Elijah appear with Jesus? There seem to be two reasons.

a. To discuss Jesus' death (Lu.17:31). Jesus needed to be strengthened to bear the weight and pressure of the cross (see note—Mk.9:2-13. See the Garden of Gethesamane experience and His cry on the cross, Lu.22:39-46; see note—Mt.27:46-49.)

b. To show that Jesus was the true Messiah, the Son of God, the One who was superior to the Law and the prophets. Moses represented the law; and Elijah, who was considered the greatest of the prophets, represented the prophets. These two men were honoring and ministering to Christ. By such, they were symbolizing that the law and the prophets found their fulfillment in Christ.
 ⇒ Christ was the One of whom the law and the prophets spoke.
 ⇒ Christ was the One to whom the law and the prophets pointed. The old covenant was now to be fulfilled in and superseded by Christ who was to usher in the new covenant (see note—Mk.9:2-4. See outline and notes—2 Co.3:6-18; Mt.9:16-17.)

Thought 1. Christ was soon to fulfill His prophetic and priestly offices. Moses and Elijah were symbolically transferring the old prophetic and priestly offices to Him.

> "Then he took unto him the twelve, and said unto them, Behold, we go up to Jerusalem, and all things that are written by the prophets concerning the Son of man shall be accomplished" (Lu.18:31).
> "Of which salvation the prophets have enquired and searched diligently, who prophesied of the grace that should come unto you: searching what, or what manner of time the Spirit of Christ which was in them did signify, when it testified beforehand the sufferings of Christ, and the glory that should follow" (1 Pe.1:10-11).

Thought 2. Something very significant is seen here. Believers who have gone on before are as *alive*, if not more alive, than we are. They are living in a dimension other than our physical world, an eternal world that is perfect and free from all sin, suffering, and death. What a glorious hope!

> "We are confident, I say, and willing rather to be absent from the body, and to be present with the Lord" (2 Co.5:8).
> "For I am in a strait betwixt two, having a desire to depart, and to be with Christ; which is far better" (Ph.1:23).

MATTHEW 17:1-13

4 (17:4) **Spiritual Experiences—Glory**: there was the strength of a heavenly experience. The three disciples were tasting *glory*. They were in the very presence of God Himself and were tasting some of heaven's joy, peace, security, fulfillment, and perfection. They did not want to leave this hallowed ground.

Note what Peter did.

a. He offered to build three shelters (skenas) for Jesus and the two prophets. By this act, he hoped to extend the stay of the heavenly guests and the glorious experience. The shelters offered were the booths made of branches and grass which could be quickly built, the kind often built by travellers on their stops along the road night by night.

b. He said, "If thou wilt." Peter, even in a moment as glorious as this, would not act against his Lord's will. Imagine the devotion and loyalty!

Thought 1. There is a great need to learn something: God knows exactly how to meet every believer's need. He knows just what kind of experience is needed, and God will do whatever it takes to meet our need—if we truly seek Him.

However, we must remember something: our experiences must conform to God's Word. God will not go against His Word in order to give growth and experiences. The experiences that come from God are the experiences that conform to His Word. In fact, spiritual experiences and growth usually come about as a result of reading and studying God's Word.

Thought 2. A deep spiritual experience with God is always a glorious time. Nothing can compare to a session of deep communion with Christ, and there is always the wish that we could remain in His presence.

But such is not our calling, not now. Our present call is to bear the cross and its message, not to wallow around in deep spiritual experiences. Our spirits do occasionally need to be spiritually renewed, but they are always renewed for a purpose: to strengthen us for going out and bearing a much stronger witness for our Lord.

"Is it not [your purpose] to deal thy bread to the hungry, and that thou bring the poor that are cast out to thy house? when thou seest the naked, that thou cover him; and that thou hide not thyself from thine own flesh?" (Is.58:7).

"I have showed you all things, how that so labouring ye ought to support the weak, and to remember the words of the Lord Jesus, how he said, It is more blessed to give than to receive" (Ac.20:35).

"We then that are strong ought to bear the infirmities of the weak, and not to please ourselves" (Ro.15:1).

"Bear ye one another's burdens, and so fulfil the law of Christ" (Ga.6:2).

"Remember them that are in bonds, as bound with them; and them which suffer adversity, as being yourselves also in the body" (He.13:3).

"Pure religion and undefiled before God and the Father is this, To visit the fatherless and widows in their affliction, and to keep himself unspotted from the world" (Js.1:27).

"Finally, be ye all of one mind, having compassion one of another, love as brethren, be pitiful, be courteous" (1 Pe.3:8).

5 (17:5-8) **Spiritual Experience—Heaven**: there was the strength of God's presence. The cloud also covered the disciples. It and the voice of God terrified the disciples and caused them to fall immediately upon their faces, prostrated and unable to look up. As mortal men, they were crouched in fear and paralyzed in terror. Note four facts.

a. The cloud was *a bright cloud*. This was the Shekinah glory, the cloud that symbolized God's presence. It was the cloud that guided Israel out of Egypt and that rested upon the tabernacle (Ex.40:34-38) and above the Mercy Seat in the Most Holy Place. God dwells in unapproachable light upon which no man can look. The Shekinah glory is a light so glorious and brilliant that there is no need for a sun. It is a light that radiates splendor (see Re.21:11, 23). Peter later called it "the excellent glory" (2 Pe.1:17).

"[God] only hath immortality, dwelling in the light which no man can approach unto" (1 Ti.6:16).

The *bright cloud* overshadowing Christ was in contrast to the dark and threatening cloud that overshadowed the giving of the old covenant to Moses, that is, the law (Ex.19:18; 20:21). There is a point to be made here.

⇒ The law (old covenant) was dark and threatening (see Deeper Study # 2—Gal.3:10).

⇒ The new covenant (the love of Christ) is bright and is given to save and bless, not to threaten and condemn (He.12:18-24. See Heb.8:6-13.)

b. The voice speaking actually says in the Greek, "This is My Son, the Beloved One." Note the two facts stressed: Christ is God's Son, and He is the Beloved One. The idea is that Christ is the "only begotten Son" who was to be given for the world (Jn.3:16).

c. Note the disciples experienced a clear, intense sense of God's presence. They fell prostrate on their faces before the Lord.

d. The Lord stood there alone. The representatives of the Old Testament and covenant (law) had faded away. The bondage and darkness and terror of the law were now gone. Christ now stood in the law's place (see note—Mt.5:17-18). The new covenant was soon to take effect; the new covenant of light, love, and liberty was now replacing the old covenant of darkness, fear, and bondage.

The disciples' experience can be applied to the believer's future, to his appearance before God in *the great Day of Redemption*. In fact, that is just what is happening to Peter, James, and John. They find themselves in God's presence. The believer's experience when he meets Christ face to face will undoubtedly be very much like what they experienced.

MATTHEW 17:1-13

1. The believer will experience the Shekinah glory and see its full manifestation upon Christ.
2. The believer will hear the voice of God proclaiming Christ to be His Son; expressing perfect approval of His redemptive work; and rejoicing that He has been heard and is to be heard throughout all eternity.
3. The believer will fall upon his face, prostrating himself before Christ in awe and adoration and worship.
4. The believer will experience the Lord's intercessory work. He will feel the Lord's hand reaching out to touch him and to lift him up, and the believer will stand in the Lord's righteousness and perfection, living in a state of glory forever.

> **Thought 1.** How often God would grant a clear, intense sense of His presence—if we would only get alone with Him for long sessions of meditation and prayer! How much power would be present in our lives and ministries if we often got alone with God for long periods!

5. The believer will witness and experience the Lord's preeminence throughout all eternity.

> **Thought 1.** The message of God was, is, and ever will be...
> - this is my beloved Son,
> - in whom I am well pleased,
> - hear ye Him.

6 (17:9-13) **Jesus Christ, Resurrection**: there was the strength of the resurrection. The resurrection proves two things.
⇒ First, the resurrection proves that Jesus Christ is definitely the Son of God.
⇒ Second, the resurrection proves that the transfiguration actually happened—that it actually foreshadowed the supremacy of the new covenant and to some degree the believer's experience of heaven.

Jesus did not allow the three disciples to share their experience because it could not be understood. It was just too incredible to grasp until after the resurrection. This charge to keep silent baffled the disciples because the Scribes had always taught that Elijah was to come to proclaim the Messiah (see Mal.4:5). They had just seen Elijah with Christ. When would Elijah begin announcing Jesus to be the Messiah? And if he were going to proclaim the message, why should they keep silent about Jesus' Messiahship? Should they not also proclaim Him as Messiah? Jesus told them that John the Baptist was the prophesied prophet like Elijah who was to come. The people killed him, and the Messiah too was to suffer at the hands of the people.

> **Thought 1.** Jesus Christ is the Messiah, the Son of God. Belief in Him is absolutely essential.
>
> "I said therefore unto you, that ye shall die in your sins: for if ye believe not that I am he, ye shall die in your sins" (Jn.8:24).
> "The woman saith unto him, I know that Messiah cometh, which is called Christ: when he is come, he will tell us all things. Jesus saith unto her, I that speak unto thee am he" (Jn.4:25-26).
> "And we believe and are sure that thou art that Christ, the Son of the living God" (Jn.6:69; see Jn.11:25-27).
> "But Saul [Paul the apostle] increased the more in strength, and confounded the Jews which dwelt at Damascus, proving that this is very Christ" (Ac.9:22; see Ac.17:2-3).
> "Whosoever believeth that Jesus is the Christ is born of God: and every one that loveth him that begat loveth him also that is begotten of him" (1 Jn.5:1).

MATTHEW 17:14-21

	D. The Powerless Disciples: A Great Lesson on Faith & Power, 17:14-21 (Mk 9:14-29; Lu 9:37-42)	I suffer you? bring him hither to me.	b. His patience was limited
1. The availability of power		18 And Jesus rebuked the devil; and he departed out of him: and the child was cured from that very hour.	c. His power broke the power of Satan
a. Jesus joined the crowd: After the transfiguration	14 And when they were come to the multitude, there came to him a *certain* man, kneeling down to him, and saying,		
b. Was approached by a desperate man		19 Then came the disciples to Jesus apart, and said, Why could not we cast him out?	4. The clear reason for no power: Unbelief
2. The tragedy of no power		20 And Jesus said unto them, Because of your unbelief: for verily I say unto you, If ye have faith as a grain of mustard seed, ye shall say unto this mountain, Remove hence to yonder place; and it shall remove; and nothing shall be impossible unto you.	5. The great power of faith promised^{DS3}
a. A desperate need unmet	15 Lord, have mercy on my son: for he is lunatick, and sore vexed: for ofttimes he falleth into the fire, and oft into the water.		
b. A frantic disappointment^{DS1}	16 And I brought him to thy disciples, and they could not cure him.		
c. An embarrassing situation: Could not heal him			
3. The rebuke of no power^{DS2}	17 Then Jesus answered and said, O faithless and perverse generation, how long shall I be with you? how long shall		6. The two ways to secure great faith & power^{DS4, 5}
a. His presence will not always be available		21 Howbeit this kind goeth not out but by prayer and fasting.	a. By prayer b. By fasting

DIVISION XI

THE MESSIAH'S DRAMATIC REVELATION: HIS MESSIAHSHIP, HIS CHURCH, AND HIS CROSS, 16:13–17:27

D. The Powerless Disciples: A Great Lesson on Faith and Power, 17:14-21

(17:14-21) **Introduction**: this is an excellent study on *power and faith*. The points speak for themselves.
1. The availability of power (v.14).
2. The tragedy of no power (vv.15-16).
3. The rebuke of no power (vv.17-18).
4. The clear reason for no power: unbelief (vv.19-20).
5. The great power of faith promised (v.20).
6. The two ways to secure great faith and power (vv.20-21).

1 (17:14) **Devotion—Prayer**: Jesus after the transfiguration. What a contrast—the heavenly glory and the mountain-top experience of the transfiguration vs. the earthly problems and the valley experiences of the next day (Lu.9:37)! What a lesson for all of us! The glory of devotions is for the purpose of going out and meeting the multitudes in all their need. We do not stay on the mountain top; we come down to the valley, down to earth where people are.

No experience of Christ teaches the necessity for both devotions and ministry any more forcibly than this experience.
⇒ The transfiguration is an *end* in itself, but it is also a *means* to service.
⇒ The transfiguration calls us to a monastic life, but it also prepares us for going out and meeting the needs of a corrupt world.
⇒ The mount of prayer calls us to be renewed, but it also strengthens us to go forth and labor in a mixed up world.
⇒ God wants to meet us *daily* for our own soul's nourishment, but He also wants to send us out to meet the daily needs of a crying world.
⇒ God wants our private attention and fellowship, but He also wants to send us out to give attention and godly fellowship to a lost world.

2 (17:15-16) **Powerlessness—Unbelief**: the tragedy of no power (see Deeper Study # 1—Mt.17:16). The son's illness seems to have been both physical and spiritual. The description of the illness in *The Gospel of Mark* points toward what is known today as epilepsy and demon-possession (Mt.17:15; Mk.9:17-18; Lu.9:39). The demon-possession in particular seems to have heightened and aggravated the condition, perhaps causing some suicidal tendencies (Mt.17:15; Mk.9:22). Throughout the gospels, this seems to be one of the major works of evil spirits: to *heighten and aggravate* existing conditions. The great tragedy of the event was unbelief and having no power. These tragedies plague so many servants of God. But note: they plague us only because "we ask not" (Js.4:2). We fail to go up to the high mountain of transfiguration and receive the renewing of God's presence. Our lack of power too often results in three things.
  a. So many *desperate needs* going unmet.
  b. So many *frantic disappointments* being experienced.
  c. So many *embarrassing situations* happening.

MATTHEW 17:14-21

"He shall call upon me, and I will answer him: I will be with him in trouble; I will deliver him, and honour him" (Ps.91:15).

"Then shalt thou call, and the LORD shall answer; thou shalt cry, and he shall say, here I am. If thou take away from the midst of thee the yoke, the putting forth of the finger, and speaking vanity" (Is.58:9).

"Call unto me, and I will answer thee, and show thee great and mighty things, which thou knowest not" (Je.33:3).

Thought 1. Note two things.
(1) The father was seeking and interceding for his child.
(2) Christ's heart was tender and compassionate toward the child. There had been only one thing lacking—someone with faith and power to stand in the gap. There simply was no one.

How many children are gripped by desperate needs both physical and spiritual? How many are trapped by sin? Where are the parents who are concerned enough to seek Jesus, not half-heartedly and haphazardly, but genuinely? Where are the parents who seek Him, persevering until He answers? As in the above case, Jesus is willing to meet the needs of our children, but where are the parents who seek Jesus with the fervency of the father? And where are the servants of God who can lead parents to trust Christ?

DEEPER STUDY # 1
(17:16) **Power, Lack of**: Why do men lack power? (See DEEPER STUDY # 3—Mk.9:18 for discussion.)

---

3 (17:17-18) **Powerlessness—Unbelief**: the rebuke of no power. Christ rebuked the lack of power. A person with no power saddens and brings sorrow to His heart. What can He do to stir faith and power? He does all He can: He warns, yet He offers hope.
   a. He warns that His presence will not always be available (Ge.6:3. See note—Mt.12:14-16.)
   b. He warns that His patience is limited (see Pr.29:1. See note—Mt.12:31-32.)
   c. He assures that His power breaks the power of Satan. Note that it is the Word of Christ that breaks the devil's power. Satan cannot stand before God's Word. Christ has spoiled the principalities and powers under Satan's control (Col.2:15).

Thought 1. A *faithless* person...
- cannot receive the blessing which he *might have had*.
- cannot do the works which he *might have done*.

Note the tone and ache of Christ's heart and words. He aches for us to receive what we should have and to do the works which we should do. He longs for us to live an abundant life of power and fulfillment (Jn.10:10).

Thought 2. There is a critical point to remember: the longer Christ has to put up with our *faithless* and *powerless* behavior, the more He is displeased with us. We must learn and learn quickly. His presence will not always be with us, and His patience is limited.

Thought 3. Note the glorious message of the gospel proclaimed and illustrated in this event. When the faith and power of men fail, when all other hope and help fails, we can go to Christ and know that He will hear and help us. He will have compassion and use His power to meet our need—no matter how desperate.

DEEPER STUDY # 2
(17:17) **Perverse** (diastrepho): to distort, to twist; to turn aside or away; to be torn in two; to be corrupted (see Ac.20:30; Ph.2:15).

"That ye may be blameless and harmless, the sons of God, without rebuke, in the midst of a crooked and perverse nation, among whom ye shine as lights in the world" (Ph.2:15).

"Also of your own selves shall men arise, speaking perverse things, to draw away disciples after them" (Ac.20:30).

"Perverse disputings of men of corrupt minds, and destitute of the truth, supposing that gain is godliness: from such withdraw thyself" (1 Ti.6:5).

"The integrity of the upright shall guide them: but the perverseness of transgressors shall destroy them" (Pr.11:3).

"A man shall be commended according to his wisdom: but he that is of a perverse heart shall be despised" (Pr.12:8).

"A wholesome tongue is a tree of life: but perverseness therein is a breach in the spirit" (Pr.15:4).

"Better is the poor that walketh in his uprightness, than he that is perverse in his ways, though he be rich" (Pr.28:6).

---

4 (17:19-20) **Unbelief—Powerlessness**: the clear reason for no power was unbelief. What is unbelief? Why does faith weaken and turn into unbelief? The disciples had been given and promised unusual power earlier, and they had ministered effectively (Mt.10:1; Lu.10:17). But now the power seemed to be gone, and they were unable to minister. "Why?" they asked.

Pointedly, Jesus answered, "Because of your *unbelief*." Unbelief is four things, or to put it in the form of a question, "What is unbelief?"

a. Unbelief is doubting Christ Himself, the object of one's faith. It is questioning the power of Christ. Is He really strong enough to do what is needed: to save, deliver, heal, and help; and to remove evil empires, entrenched wickedness, destructive greed, and the threat of wars?

b. Unbelief is doubting the power of the Lord *within* oneself. It is questioning if one is close enough to Christ for Him to hear and answer or to grant enough power to meet the need.

c. Unbelief is doubting one's own faith. It is questioning the strength of one's own dependence and confidence in Christ.

d. Unbelief is doubting if the thing needed is God's will. It is questioning if one should be seeking such a thing or if God is willing to do what is needed.

"And he said unto them, Why are ye so fearful? how is it that ye have no faith?" (Mk.4:40).

"Afterward he appeared unto the eleven as they sat at meat, and upbraided them with their unbelief and hardness of heart, because they believed not them which had seen him after he was risen" (Mk.16:14).

"Then he said unto them, O fools, and slow of heart to believe all that the prophets have spoken" (Lu.24:25).

"He that believeth on him is not condemned: but he that believeth not is condemned already, because he hath not believed in the name of the only begotten Son of God" (Jn.3:18).

"He that believeth on the Son hath everlasting life: and he that believeth not the Son shall not see life; but the wrath of God abideth on him" (Jn.3:36).

"I said therefore unto you, that ye shall die in your sins: for if ye believe not that I am he, ye shall die in your sins" (Jn.8:24).

"And when he is come, he will reprove the world of sin, and of righteousness, and of judgment: of sin, because they believe not on me" (Jn.16:8-9).

"Take heed, brethren, lest there be in any of you an evil heart of unbelief, in departing from the living God" (He.3:12).

"Let us labour therefore to enter into that rest, lest any man fall after the same example of unbelief" (He.4:11).

The answer to unbelief is hungering and thirsting after God so much that we spend a great deal of time in God's presence—so much time that even food is forgotten. We do without in order to meet God (see note—Mt.6:16-18).

"Faith cometh by hearing [prayer], and hearing by the Word of God" (Ro.10:17).

"And he said unto them, Why are ye so fearful? how is it that ye have no faith?" (Mk.4:40).

"But without faith it is impossible to please him: for he that cometh to God must believe that he is, and that he is a rewarder of them that diligently seek him" (He.11:6).

"Art thou the Christ? tell us. And he said unto them, If I tell you, ye will not believe" (Lu.22:67).

"Verily, verily, I say unto thee, We speak that we do know, and testify that we have seen; and ye receive not our witness" (Jn.3:11).

"Then came the Jews round about him, and said unto him, How long dost thou make us to doubt? If thou be the Christ, tell us plainly. Jesus answered them, I told you, and ye believed not: the works that I do in my Father's name, they bear witness of me" (Jn.10:24-25).

"But though he had done so many miracles before them, yet they believed not on him" (Jn.12:37).

"Who hath believed our report? and to whom is the arm of the LORD revealed?" (Is.53:1).

Thought 1. When things are not going well and we are not successful in life or marriage or ministry, note two things.

(1) It tends to lead everyone to blame others:
- ⇒ spouse blames spouse
- ⇒ workman blames fellow workman
- ⇒ congregation blames minister
- ⇒ minister blames congregation

(2) The fault usually lies at our own feet (not always, of course, but usually), and the cause is our unbelief. We are not trusting and seeking God like we should, not diligently.

Thought 2. Something displeases God enormously: distrusting any power or gift given by Him. So many confuse personal strength and gifts with God's strength and gifts. To deny His power and gifts is not humility; it is distrust. His power and gifts are to be used to the utmost.

5 (17:20) **Faith—Power**: the great power of faith is promised. The Jews clearly understood what Jesus meant by "removing mountains." The phrase was a Jewish idiom or proverb meaning "to remove difficulties" (see Zec.4:7; 1 Co.13:2). The greatest difficulties in human life can be removed by faith. Prayer and faith can do anything for God. They can remove all kinds of mountains: fear, disappointment, depression, despair, sickness, temptation, guilt, weariness, loneliness, persecution, heartache. Such mountains loom ever so large as a barrier before man's path. Such mountains can really defeat life. How can they be overcome? By prayer and faith—praying and believing God even to the point of fasting (see Deeper Study # 3—Mt.17:20).

Thought 1. Every believer has two strengths and two gifts to offer the world. He has both his own strength and gifts (talents) and God's strength and gifts. (See Ro.12:6f; 1 Co.12:4-11; Ep.4:11.)
(1) God's strength and gifts are as high as the heavens above our strength and gifts.
(2) Our call is to learn to use God's strength and gifts.

Thought 2. An *active* faith can remove mountains (see note and Deeper Study # 1—He.11:6).

DEEPER STUDY # 3
(17:20) **Faith—Power—Mustard Seed**: what does Christ mean by "faith as a grain of mustard seed"? The mustard seed was known for its small size, the smallest of all plants; yet it grew to be one of the largest bushes (see note—Mt.13:32). Picture a mustard seed lying in a person's hand. It is *real* and it is *small*. Just imagine the potential for *growth and use*. So it is with faith: faith is "as a grain of mustard seed." It is real and small, yet it has enormous power for growth, for use, and for ministry.

"And all things, whatsoever ye shall ask in prayer, believing, ye shall receive" (Mt.21:22).
"Jesus said unto him, If thou canst believe, all things are possible to him that believeth" (Mk.9:23).

[6] (17:20-21) **Faith—Power**: the two ways to secure great faith and power.
a. The first way to secure great faith and power is to pray (see note, *Prayer*—Mt.7:7-11; see Ep.6:18).
b. The second way to secure great faith and power is to fast (see note, *Fasting*—Mt.6:16-18).

DEEPER STUDY # 4
(17:20-21) **Faith**: see notes and Deeper Study # 1—He.11:6; see Mk.11:23; He.10:38; Jn.2:23-24.

DEEPER STUDY # 5
(17:20-21) **Power**: see 2 Ti.1:7; Ep.3:20.

MATTHEW 17:22-23

	E. The Messiah Foretells His Death & Resurrection (Second Time): Delivered Up by God, 17:22-23
	(Mk 9:30-32; Lu 9:43-45)
1. He foretold His betrayal 2. He foretold the guilty party	22 And while they abode in Galilee, Jesus said unto them, The Son of man shall be betrayed into the hands of men:
3. He foretold His death 4. He foretold His resurrection	23 And they shall kill him, and the third day he shall be raised again. And they were exceeding sorry.

DIVISION XI

THE MESSIAH'S DRAMATIC REVELATION: HIS MESSIAHSHIP, HIS CHURCH, AND HIS CROSS, 16:13–17:27

E. The Messiah Foretells His Death and Resurrection (Second Time): Delivered Up by God, 17:22-23

(17:22-23) **Introduction**: the death and resurrection of Jesus Christ cannot be overstressed. They are of paramount importance: a person's destiny is determined by his response to the death and resurrection of Jesus Christ. His death and resurrection are the pivotal points of human history, the hub of God's plan for eternity. History itself revolves around the death and resurrection of God's dear Son. God works all things out for good to the praise of His dear Son. Even the evil and devastation of men are turned around and worked out for the good of Christ and for those for whom He died and arose again.

All that the Scripture says about the death and resurrection of Jesus Christ speaks to every generation of men. (See outline and notes—Mt.16:21-23; 20:17-19; Mk.8:31-33; 9:30-32; 10:32-34.)
1. He foretold His betrayal (v.22).
2. He foretold the guilty party (v.22).
3. He foretold His death (v.23).
4. He foretold His resurrection (v.23).

1 (17:22) **Jesus Christ, Death**: Christ foretold His betrayal. Note two facts.

a. The phrase *while they abode* (anastrephomenon) means went to and fro. The point is this: while Jesus and the disciples went all about Galilee, He was drilling into them the fact that He was to be killed and raised from the dead.

Jesus had been in the extreme northern country for several weeks (see notes—Mt.15:21-22; 15:29; 16:13). At some point He returned to the country of Galilee, but quietly (Mk.9:30). Apparently He just kept moving about rather secretly so that He could indoctrinate His disciples to the fact of His impending death and resurrection (see notes—Mt.15:21-22; 15:29; 16:21-28). Interestingly, this fact is referred to by the angels in announcing His resurrection: "Remember how he spake unto you when He was yet in Galilee, Saying, The Son of man must be delivered into the hands of sinful men, and be crucified, and the third day rise again" (Lu.24:6-7).

Jesus had to continue talking about His death and resurrection because it was so hard to understand. There were three primary reasons why the disciples had difficulty in grasping the fact.
1) The Messiah's death and resurrection were new experiences, new happenings. History was to be made. The talk of a literal death and resurrection was bound to be understood in symbolic and spiritual language (see note—Mt.18:1-2). (How like so many to spiritualize the two events—even though the events really took place and are so strongly proclaimed by the disciples.) (See 1 Co.15:3-8. See notes—Mk.9:32; 9:34.)
2) The Messiah's death and resurrection were thought to be impossible. How could God die? Most men proclaim that God cannot die. Of course, the disciples had not yet seen what death really is—basically separation from God (see DEEPER STUDY # 1—Heb.9:27). They had to learn that God was dealing with spiritual and eternal life (and death), not just with physical and temporal life (and death) on this earth.
3) The Messiah's death and resurrection were contrary to all their hopes and expectations. It was just different from all the disciples had ever heard or been taught. The Messiah was thought to be a Messiah of power and sovereign rule not a Messiah who had to suffer and die in order to save man. (See notes—Mt.1:1; DEEPER STUDY # 2—1:18; DEEPER STUDY # 3—3:11; notes—11:1-6; 11:2-3; DEEPER STUDY # 1—11:5; DEEPER STUDY # 2—11:6; DEEPER STUDY # 1—12:16; notes—22:42; Lu.7:21-23.)

b. The word *betrayed* is actually *delivered up* (paradidosthai) which means that His death was ordained. Christ was saying that He was about to be *delivered up* to death—it was ordained, that is, determined in the counsel and plan of God. Christ was delivered up to death by three persons.

MATTHEW 17:22-23

1) God delivered Christ up to be betrayed.

"For God so loved the world, that he gave his only begotten Son, that whosoever believeth in him should not perish, but have everlasting life" (Jn.3:16).

"Him, being delivered by the determinate counsel and foreknowledge of God, ye have taken, and by wicked hands have crucified and slain" (Ac.2:23).

"He that spared not his own Son, but delivered him up for us all, how shall he not with him also freely give us all things?" (Ro.8:32).

"For he hath made him to be sin for us, who knew no sin; that we might be made the righteousness of God in him" (2 Co.5:21).

"Thanks be unto God for his unspeakable gift" (2 Co.9:15).

2) Christ delivered Himself up to be crucified.

"Who gave himself for our sins, that he might deliver us from this present evil world, according to the will of God and our Father" (Ga.1:4).

"And walk in love, as Christ also hath loved us, and hath given himself for us an offering and a sacrifice to God for a sweetsmelling savour....Husbands, love your wives, even as Christ also loved the church, and gave himself for it" (Ep.5:2, 25).

"Who gave himself for us, that he might redeem us from all iniquity, and purify unto himself a peculiar people, zealous of good works" (Tit.2:14).

"Hereby perceive we the love of God, because he laid down his life for us: and we ought to lay down our lives for the brethren" (1 Jn.3:16).

3) Judas betrayed and delivered Christ up to be crucified (see notes—Mt.26:21-25; 27:3-5; Mk.14:10-11; Lu.22:4-6; Jn.13:18; 13:21-26).

"And as they did eat, he said, Verily I say unto you, that one of you shall betray me" (Mt.26:21).

"And Judas Iscariot, one of the twelve, went unto the chief priests, to betray him unto them" (Mk.14:10).

"I speak not of you all: I know whom I have chosen: but that the scripture may be fulfilled, He that eateth bread with me hath lifted up his heel against me" (Jn.13:18).

2 (17:22) **Jesus Christ, Death**: Christ foretold the guilty party. Jesus had already named the men who would kill Him (see DEEPER STUDY # 1—Mt.16:21). The order of the betrayal would be *Judas*, who identified Him for the *elders*, *chief priests*, and *Scribes*, who in turn would deliver Him to the *Gentiles* or Romans for execution (Mt.20:19).

Peter, in preaching to the Jews right after Pentecost, accused the Jews: "Him, being delivered by the determinate counsel and foreknowledge of God, ye have taken, and by wicked hands have crucified and slain" (Ac.2:23).

Thought 1. Men killed Jesus—men who so desperately needed Him.
(1) The men who plotted and caused His death were the Jews. They were His own people by race and by God's choice. They were even expecting the Messiah, yet they did not know Him (Jn.1:11). They did not want the kind of Messiah He was claiming to be. They wanted a Messiah of power and fame and wealth that would give Israel the glory of an international government or theocracy (see notes—Mt.1:1; DEEPER STUDY # 2–1:18; DEEPER STUDY # 3–3:11; notes—11:1-6; 11:2-3; DEEPER STUDY # 1—11:5; DEEPER STUDY # 2—11:6; DEEPER STUDY # 1—12:16; note—Lu.7:21-23).
(2) The men who carried out His death were the Romans. They were the very ones for whom He had come to open the door of salvation. Salvation had been closed to them. Now in Him, they could be saved and live eternally. They should have been grateful and received Him with open arms, yet they too rejected His claims. They tried and executed Him—all for political purposes.

"For God so loved the world, that he gave his only begotten Son, that whosoever believeth in him should not perish, but have everlasting life. For God sent not his Son into the world to condemn the world; but that the world through him might be saved. He that believeth on him is not condemned: but he that believeth not is condemned already, because he hath not believed in the name of the only begotten Son of God. And this is the condemnation, that light is come into the world, and men loved darkness rather than light, because their deeds were evil" (Jn.3:16-19).

3 (17:23) **Jesus Christ, Death**: Christ foretold His death. As simply as possible, Jesus Christ was killed for two reasons.
a. The religionists delivered Him up to the Gentiles because He was a threat to them (see notes and DEEPER STUDY # 1—Mt.12:10; see 12:1-8. These are important notes for understanding just why the religionists killed Jesus.) Three passages will show this clearly.

"Then the Jews took up stones again to stone him. Jesus answered them, Many good works have I showed you from my Father; for which of those works do ye stone me? The Jews answered him,

MATTHEW 17:22-23

saying, For a good work we stone thee not; but for blasphemy; and because that thou, being a man, makest thyself God" (Jn.10:31-33).

"Ye men of Israel, hear these words; Jesus of Nazareth, a man approved of God among you by miracles and wonders and signs, which God did by him in the midst of you, as ye yourselves also know: Him, being delivered by the determinate counsel and foreknowledge of God, ye have taken, and by wicked hands have crucified and slain" (Ac.2:22-23).

"...the Jews: who both killed the Lord Jesus, and their own prophets, and have persecuted us" (1 Th.2:14-15).

b. God delivered Him up to die for the sins and the life of the world. Most of the passages in the New Testament dealing with the death of Christ follow (see *JESUS CHRIST*, Death—Master Subject Index, for additional information on the death of Christ).

"As Jonas was three days and three nights in the whale's belly: so shall the Son of man be three days and three nights in the heart of the earth" (Mt.12:40).

"A wicked and adulterous generation seeketh after a sign; and there shall no sign be given unto it, but the sign of the prophet Jonas...From that time forth began Jesus to show unto his disciples, how that he must go unto Jerusalem, and suffer many things of the elders and chief priests and scribes, and be killed, and be raised again the third day" (Mt.16:4, 21; see Lu.11:30; Lu.9:22).

"But I say unto you, That Elias is come already, and they knew him not, but have done unto him whatsoever they listed. Likewise shall also the Son of man suffer of them. Then the disciples understood that he spake unto them of John the Baptist" (Mt.17:12-13).

"And while they abode in Galilee, Jesus said unto them, The Son of man shall be betrayed into the hands of men" (Mt.17:22).

"And Jesus going up to Jerusalem took the twelve disciples apart in the way, and said unto them, Behold, we go up to Jerusalem; and the Son of man shall be betrayed unto the chief priests and unto the scribes, and they shall condemn him to death, And shall deliver him to the Gentiles to mock, and to scourge, and to crucify him: and the third day he shall rise again" (Mt.20:17-19).

"The Son of man came not to be ministered unto, but to minister, and to give his life a ransom for many" (Mt.20:28; see Mk.10:32, 34).

"But last of all he [God] sent unto them his son, saying, They will reverence my son. But when the husbandmen saw the son, they said among themselves, This is the heir; come, let us kill him, and let us seize on his inheritance. And they caught him, and cast him out of the vineyard, and slew him" (Mt.21:37-39).

"After two days is the feast of the passover, and the Son of man is betrayed to be crucified" (Mt.26:2).

"The Son of man goeth as it is written of him: but woe unto that man by whom the Son of man is betrayed! it had been good for that man if he had not been born" (Mt.26:24).

"This is my blood of the new testament, which is shed for many for the remission of sins" (Mt.26:28).

"O my Father, if it be possible, let this cup pass from me: nevertheless not as I will, but as thou wilt" (Mt.26:39).

"O my Father, if this cup may not pass away from me, except I drink it, thy will be done" (Mt.26:42).

"Thinkest thou that I cannot now pray to my Father, and he shall presently give me more than twelve legions of angels? But how then shall the scriptures be fulfilled, that thus it must be?" (Mt.26:53-54; see Mk.14:24, 36, 39).

"And he began to teach them that the Son of man must suffer many things, and be rejected of the elders, and of the chief priests, and scribes, and be killed, and after three days rise again" (Mk.8:31).

"For he taught his disciples, and said unto them, The Son of man is delivered into the hands of men, and they shall kill him; and after that he is killed, he shall rise the third day" (Mk.9:31).

"Behold, we go up to Jerusalem; and the Son of man shall be delivered unto the chief priests, and unto the scribes, and they shall condemn him to death, and shall deliver him to the Gentiles: And they shall mock him, and shall scourge him, and shall spit upon him, and shall kill him: and the third day he shall rise again" (Mk.10:33-34; see Mt.20:18, 19; Lu.18:31-33).

"Saying, The Son of man must suffer many things, and be rejected of the elders and chief priests and scribes, and be slain, and be raised the third day" (Lu.9:22).

"When the time was come that he should be received up, he stedfastly set his face to go to Jerusalem" (Lu.9:51).

"I have a baptism to be baptized with: and how am I straitened till it be accomplished!" (Lu.12:50; see Lu.22:15).

"First must he suffer many things, and be rejected of this generation" (Lu.17:25).

"With desire I have desired to eat this passover with you before I suffer....He took bread, and gave thanks, and brake it, and gave unto them, saying, This is my body which is given for you: this do in remembrance of me. Likewise also the cup after supper, saying, This cup is the new testament in my blood which is shed for you" (Lu.22:15, 19-20).

"This that is written must yet be accomplished in me, And he was reckoned among the transgressors: for the things concerning me have an end" (Lu.22:37).

"Father, if thou be willing, remove this cup from me: nevertheless not my will, but thine, be done" (Lu.22:42).

"Behold the Lamb of God, which taketh away the sin of the world" (Jn.1:29).

"As Moses lifted up the serpent in the wilderness, even so must the Son of man be lifted up: That whosoever believeth in him should not perish, but have eternal life. For God so loved the world, that he gave his only begotten Son, that whosoever believeth in him should not perish, but have everlasting life. For God sent not his Son into the world to condemn the world; but that the world through him might be saved" (Jn.3:14-17).

"I am the living bread which came down from heaven: if any man eat of this bread, he shall live for ever: and the bread that I will give is my flesh, which I will give for the life of the world" (Jn.6:51).

"I am the good shepherd: the good shepherd giveth his life for the sheep....I lay down my life for the sheep...I lay down my life, that I might take it again. No man taketh it from me, but I lay it down of myself. I have power to lay it down, and I have power to take it again...And I give unto them eternal life; and they shall never perish, neither shall any man pluck them out of my hand. My Father, which gave them me, is greater than all; and no man is able to pluck them out of my Father's hand. I and my Father are one. Then the Jews took up stones again to stone him" (Jn.10:11, 15, 17-18, 28-31).

"Consider that it is expedient for us, that one man should die for the people, and that the whole nation perish not. And this spake he not of himself: but being high priest that year, he prophesied that Jesus should die for that nation; and not for that nation only, but that also he should gather together in one the children of God that were scattered abroad" (Jn.11:50-52).

"Except a corn of wheat fall into the ground and die, it abideth alone; but if it die, it bringeth forth much fruit...Now is the judgment of this world: now shall the prince of this world be cast out. And I, if I be lifted up from the earth, will draw all men unto me. This he said, signifying what death he should die" (Jn.12:24, 31-33).

"He that eateth bread with me hath lifted up his heel against me. Now I tell you before it come, that, when it is come to pass, ye may believe that I am he....Verily, verily, I say unto you, that one of you shall betray me" (Jn.13:18-19, 21; see Mt.26:21; Mk.14:18; Lu.22:21).

"Let not your heart be troubled: ye believe in God, believe also in me. In my Father's house are many mansions: if it were not so, I would have told you, I go to prepare a place for you. And if I go and prepare a place for you, I will come again, and receive you unto myself; that where I am, there ye may be also" (Jn.14:1-3).

"Yet a little while, and the world seeth me no more" (Jn.14:19).

"Ye have heard how I said unto you, I go away, and come again unto you. If ye loved me, ye would rejoice, because I said, I go unto the Father: for my Father is greater than I. And now I have told you before it come to pass, that, when it is come to pass, ye might believe. Hereafter I will not talk much with you: for the prince of this world cometh, and hath nothing in me. But that the world may know that I love the Father; and as the Father gave me commandment, even so I do. Arise, let us go hence" (Jn.14:28-31).

"Greater love hath no man than this, that a man lay down his life for his friends" (Jn.15:13).

"Ye shall weep and lament, but the world shall rejoice: and ye shall be sorrowful, but your sorrow shall be turned into joy" (Jn.16:20).

"The cup which my Father hath given me, shall I not drink it?" (Jn.18:11).

"Jesus answered, Thou couldest have no power at all against me, except it were given thee from above: therefore he that delivered me unto thee hath the greater sin" (Jn.19:11).

"And now, brethren, I wot [know] that through ignorance ye did it, as did also your rulers. But those things, which God before had showed by the mouth of all his prophets, that Christ should suffer, he hath so fulfilled. Repent ye therefore, and be converted, that your sins may be blotted out, when the times of refreshing shall come from the presence of the Lord; And he shall send Jesus Christ, which before was preached unto you: Whom the heaven must receive until the time of restitution of all things, which God hath spoken by the mouth of all his holy prophets since the world began" (Ac.3:17-21).

"The God of our fathers raised up Jesus, whom ye slew and hanged on a tree. Him hath God exalted with his right hand to be a Prince and a Saviour, for to give repentance to Israel, and forgiveness of sins" (Ac.5:30).

"The church of God, which he hath purchased with his own blood" (Ac.20:28).

"Having therefore obtained help of God, I continue unto this day, witnessing both to small and great, saying none other things than those which the prophets and Moses did say should come: That Christ should suffer, and that he should be the first that should rise from the dead, and should show light unto the people, and to the Gentiles" (Ac.26:22-23).

"When we were yet without strength, in due time Christ died for the ungodly. Scarcely for a righteous man will one die: yet peradventure for a good man some would even dare to die. But God commendeth his love toward us, in that, while we were yet sinners, Christ died for us. Much more than, being now justified by his blood, we shall be saved from wrath through him. For if, when we were enemies, we were reconciled to God by the death of his Son, much more, being reconciled, we shall be saved by his life. We also joy in God through our Lord Jesus Christ, by whom we have now received the atonement" (Ro.5:6-11).

"Know ye not, that so many of us as were baptized into Jesus Christ were baptized into his death? Therefore we are buried with him by baptism into death, that like as Christ was raised up from the dead by the glory of the Father, even so we also should walk in newness of life. For if we have been planted together in the likeness of his death, we shall be also in the likeness of his resurrection" (Ro.6:3-5).

"Christ being raised from the dead dieth no more; death hath no more dominion over him. For in that he died, he died unto sin once" (Ro.6:9-10).

"God sending his own Son in the likeness of sinful flesh, and for sin, condemned sin in the flesh" (Ro.8:3).

"He that spared not his own son, but delivered him up for us all, how shall he not with him also freely give us all things?" (Ro.8:32).

"Who is he that condemneth? It is Christ that died, yea rather, that is risen again, who is even at the right hand of God, who also maketh intercession for us. Who shall separate us from the love of Christ? shall tribulation, or distress, or persecution, or famine, or nakedness, or peril, or sword?" (Ro.8:34-35).

"Nay, in all these things we are more than conquerors through him that loved us. For I am persuaded, that neither death, nor life, nor angels, nor principalities, nor powers, nor things present, nor things to come, nor height, nor depth, nor any other creature, shall be able to separate us from the love of God, which is in Christ Jesus our Lord" (Ro.8:37-39).

"To this end Christ both died, and rose, and revived, that he might be Lord both of the dead and living" (Ro.14:9).

"For Christ sent me not to baptize, but to preach the gospel: not with wisdom of words, lest the cross of Christ should be made of none effect. For the preaching of the cross is to them that perish, foolishness; but unto us which are saved, it is the power of God" (1 Co.1:17).

"For I determined not to know anything among you, save Jesus Christ, and him crucified" (1 Co.2:2).

"Even Christ our passover is sacrificed for us" (1 Co.5:7).

"Ye are bought with a price: therefore glorify God in your body, and in your spirit, which are God's" (1 Co.6:20).

"Through thy knowledge shall the weak brother perish, for whom Christ died" (1 Co.8:11).

"For I delivered unto you first of all that which I also received, how that Christ died for our sins according to the scriptures; And that he was buried, and that he rose again the third day according to the scriptures" (1 Co.15:3-4).

"[We are] always bearing about in the body the dying of the Lord Jesus, that the life also of Jesus might be made manifest in our body. For we which live are always delivered unto death for Jesus' sake, that the life also of Jesus might be made manifest in our mortal flesh" (2 Co.4:10-11).

"The love of Christ constraineth us; because we thus judge, that if one died for all, then were all dead: and that he died for all, that they which live should not henceforth live unto themselves, but unto him which died for them, and rose again" (2 Co.5:14-15).

"To wit, that God was in Christ, reconciling the world unto himself, not imputing their trespasses unto them; and hath committed unto us the word of reconciliation. Now then we are ambassadors for Christ, as though God did beseech you by us: we pray you in Christ's stead, be ye reconciled to God. He hath made him to be sin for us, who knew no sin; that we might be made the righteousness of God in him" (2 Co.5:19-21).

"Ye know the grace of our Lord Jesus Christ, that, though he was rich, yet for your sakes he became poor, that ye through his poverty might be rich" (2 Co.8:9).

"[Christ] who gave himself for our sins, that he might deliver us from this present evil world, according to the will of God and our Father" (Ga.1:4).

"I am crucified with Christ: nevertheless I live; yet not I, but Christ liveth in me: and the life which I now live in the flesh I live by the faith of the Son of God, who loved me, and gave himself for me" (Ga.2:20).

"Christ hath redeemed us from the curse of the law, being made a curse for us: for it is written, Cursed is every one that hangeth on a tree" (Ga.3:13).

"When the fulness of the time was come, God sent forth his Son, made of a woman, made under the law, to redeem them that were under the law, that we might receive the adoption of sons" (Ga.4:4-5).

"He hath made us accepted in the beloved. In whom we have redemption through his blood, the forgiveness of sins, according to the riches of his grace" (Ep.1:6-7).

"Now in Christ Jesus ye who sometimes were far off are made nigh by the blood of Christ. He is our peace, who hath made both one, and hath broken down the middlewall of partition between us" (Ep.2:13-14).

"And that he might reconcile both unto God in one body by the cross, having slain the enmity thereby" (Ep.2:16).

"For through him we both have access by one Spirit unto the Father" (Ep.2:18).

"Christ also hath loved us, and hath given himself for us an offering and a sacrifice to God for a sweetsmelling savour" (Ep.5:2).

"Christ also loved the church, and gave himself for it" (Ep.5:25).

"Who, being in the form of God, thought it not robbery to be equal with God: But made himself of no reputation, and took upon him the form of a servant, and was made in the likeness of men: And being found in fashion as a man, he humbled himself, and became obedient unto death, even the death of the cross" (Ph.2:6-8).

"In whom we have redemption through his blood, even the forgiveness of sins" (Col.1:14).

MATTHEW 17:22-23

"Having made peace through the blood of his cross, by him to reconcile all things unto himself; by him, I say, whether they be things in earth, or things in heaven. And you, that were sometime alienated and enemies in your mind by wicked works, yet now hath he reconciled. In the body of his flesh through death, to present you holy and unblameable and unreproveable in his sight" (Col.1:20-22).

"[Christ] blotting out the handwriting of ordinances that was against us, which was contrary to us, and took it out of the way, nailing it to his cross; And having spoiled principalities and powers, he made a show of them openly, triumphing over them in it" (Col.2:14-15).

"Whom he raised from the dead, even Jesus, which delivered us from the wrath to come" (1 Th.1:10).

"For if we believe that Jesus died and rose again, even so them also which sleep in Jesus will God bring with him" (1 Th.4:14).

"God hath not appointed us to wrath, but to obtain salvation by our Lord Jesus Christ, Who died for us, that, whether we wake or sleep, we should live together with him" (1 Th.5:9-10).

"This is a faithful saying, and worthy of all acceptation, that Christ Jesus came into the world to save sinners; of whom I am chief. Howbeit for this cause I obtained mercy, that in me first Jesus Christ might show forth all long-suffering, for a pattern to them which should hereafter believe on him to life everlasting" (1 Ti.1:15-16).

"For this is good and acceptable in the sight of God our Savior; Who will have all men to be saved, and to come unto the knowledge of the truth. For there is one God, and one mediator between God and men, the man Christ Jesus; Who gave himself a ransom for all, to be testified in due time" (1 Ti.2:3-6).

"[God] Who hath saved us, and called us with a holy calling, not according to our works, but according to his own purpose and grace, which was given us in Christ Jesus before the world began, But is now made manifest by the appearing of our Savior Jesus Christ, who hath abolished death, and hath brought life and immortality to light through the gospel" (2 Ti.1:9-10).

"For the grace of God that bringeth salvation hath appeared to all men. Teaching us that, denying ungodliness and worldly lusts, we should live soberly, righteously, and godly, in this present world; Looking for that blessed hope, and the glorious appearing of the great God and our Savior Jesus Christ; Who gave himself for us, that he might redeem us from all iniquity, and purify unto himself a peculiar people, zealous of good works" (Tit.2:11-14).

"But after that the kindness and love of God our Savior toward man appeared, Not by works of righteousness which we have done, but according to his mercy he saved us, by the washing of regeneration, and renewing of the Holy Ghost; Which he shed on us abundantly through Jesus Christ our Savior; That being justified by his grace, we should be made heirs according to the hope of eternal life" (Tit.3:4-7).

"Hath in these last days spoken unto us by His Son, whom he hath appointed heir of all things, by whom also he made the worlds; Who being the brightness of his glory, and the express image of his person, and upholding all things by the word of his power, when he had by himself purged our sins, sat down on the right hand of the Majesty on high" (He.1:2-3).

"But we see Jesus, who was made a little lower than the angels for the suffering of death, crowned with glory and honour; that he by the grace of God should taste death for every man. For it became him, for whom are all things, and by whom are all things, in bringing many sons unto glory, to make the captain of their salvation perfect through sufferings" (He.2:9-10).

"As the children are partakers of flesh and blood, he also himself likewise took part of the same; that through death he might destroy him that had the power of death, that is, the devil; And deliver them who through fear of death were all their lifetime subject to bondage. For verily he took not on him the nature of angels; but he took on him the seed of Abraham. Wherefore in all things it behooved him to be made like unto his brethren, that he might be a merciful and faithful high priest in things pertaining to God, to make reconciliation for the sins of the people. For in that he himself hath suffered being tempted, he is able to succor them that are tempted" (He.2:14-18).

"Who in the days of his flesh, when he had offered up prayers and supplications with strong crying and tears unto him that was able to save him from death, and was heard in that he feared; Though he were a Son, yet learned he obedience by the things which he suffered; And being made perfect, he became the author of eternal salvation unto all them that obey him" (He.5:7-9).

"Wherefore he is able also to save them to the uttermost that come unto God by him, seeing he ever liveth to make intercession for them. For such a high priest became us, who is holy, harmless, undefiled, separate from sinners, and made higher than the heavens; Who needeth not daily, as those high priests, to offer up sacrifice, first for his own sins, and then for the people's: for this he did once, when he offered up himself" (He.7:25-27).

"Neither by the blood of goats and calves, but by his own blood he entered in once into the holy place, having obtained eternal redemption for us. For if the blood of bulls and of goats, and the ashes of an heifer sprinkling the unclean, sanctifieth to the purifying of the flesh: How much more shall the blood of Christ, who through the eternal Spirit offered himself without spot to God, purge your conscience from dead works to serve the living God? And for this cause he is the mediator of the new testament, that by means of death, for the redemption of the transgressions that were under the first testament, they which are called might receive the promise of eternal inheritance. For where a testament is, there must also of necessity be the death of the testator. For a testament is of force after men are dead: otherwise it is of no strength at all while the testator liveth" (He.9:12-17).

"Nor yet that he should offer himself often, as the high priest entereth into the holy place every year with the blood of others; For then must he often have suffered since the foundation of the world:

but now once in the end of the world hath he appeared to put away sin by the sacrifice of himself. And as it is appointed unto men once to die, but after this the judgment: Christ was once offered to bear the sins of many" (He.9:25-28).

"For then must he often have suffered since the foundation of the world: but now once in the end of the world hath he appeared to put away sin by the sacrifice of himself" (He.9:26).

"We are sanctified through the offering of the body of Jesus Christ once for all" (He.10:10).

"This man, after he had offered one sacrifice for sins for ever, sat down on the right hand of God" (He.10:12).

"By one offering he hath perfected for ever them that are sanctified. Whereof the Holy Ghost also is a witness to us: for after that he had said before, This is the covenant that I will make with them after those days, saith the Lord; I will put my laws into their hearts, and in their minds will I write them; and their sins and iniquities will I remember no more. Now where remission of these is, there is no more offering for sin. Having therefore, brethren, boldness to enter into the holiest by the blood of Jesus, By a new and living way, which he hath consecrated for us, through the veil, that is to say, his flesh" (He.10:14-20).

"Looking unto Jesus the author and finisher of our faith; who for the joy that was set before him endured the cross, despising the shame, and is set down at the right hand of the throne of God" (He.12:2).

"To Jesus, the mediator of the new covenant, and to the blood of sprinkling, that speaketh better things than that of Abel" (He.12:24).

"The bodies of those beasts, whose blood is brought into the sanctuary by the high priest for sin, are burned without the camp. Wherefore Jesus also, that he might sanctify the people with his own blood, suffered without the gate" (He.13:11-12).

"Elect according to the foreknowledge of God the Father, through sanctification of the spirit, unto obedience and sprinkling of the blood of Jesus Christ" (1 Pe.1:2).

"Ye know that ye were not redeemed with corruptible things, as silver and gold, from your vain conversation received by tradition from your fathers; But with the precious blood of Christ, as of a lamb without blemish and without spot: Who verily was foreordained before the foundation of the world, but was manifest in these last times for you, Who by him do believe in God, that raised him up from the dead, and gave him glory; that your faith and hope might be in God" (1 Pe.1:18-21).

"Christ also suffered for us, leaving us an example, that ye should follow his steps" (1 Pe.2:21).

"Who his own self bare our sins in his own body on the tree, that we, being dead to sins, should live unto righteousness: by whose stripes ye were healed" (1 Pe.2:24).

"Christ also hath once suffered for sins, the just for the unjust, that he might bring us to God, being put to death in the flesh, but quickened by the Spirit" (1 Pe.3:18).

"Forasmuch then as Christ hath suffered for us in the flesh, arm yourselves likewise with the same mind" (1 Pe.4:1).

"The blood of Jesus Christ his son cleanseth us from all sin" (1 Jn.1:7).

"He is the propitiation for our sins: and not for ours only, but also for the sins of the whole world" (1 Jn.2:2).

"Hereby perceive we the love of God, because he laid down his life for us" (1 Jn.3:16).

"Herein is love, not that we loved God, but that he loved us, and sent his Son to be the propitiation for our sins" (1 Jn.4:10).

"Unto him that loved us, and washed us from our sins in his own blood, And hath made us kings and priests unto God and his Father" (Re.1:5-6).

"Thou wast slain, and hast redeemed us to God by thy blood out of every kindred, and tongue, and people, and nation; And hast made us unto our God kings and priests: and we shall reign on the earth...Saying with a loud voice, Worthy is the Lamb that was slain to receive power, and riches, and wisdom, and strength, and honour, and glory, and blessing" (Re.5:9-10, 12).

"And all that dwell upon the earth shall worship him, whose names are not written in the book of life of the Lamb slain from the foundation of the world" (Re.13:8).

4 (17:23) **Jesus Christ, Resurrection**: Christ foretold His resurrection. God raised Christ for several reasons (see outline and notes—Ac.2:29-31; Col.3:1-4).
 a. He was raised to reign with God.
 b. He was raised to deliver His soul from hell.
 c. He was raised to deliver His flesh from corruption.
 d. He was raised to do seven wonderful things for us (see note—Col.3:1-4 for discussion).

(See *JESUS CHRIST*, Resurrection—Master Subject Index, for additional information on the resurrection of Christ.)

Most of the passages in the New Testament dealing with the resurrection follow. One of the most precious and profitable studies a person can make is to place each passage under some subjects such as: Purpose, Results, Meaning, Importance, Power of, Effects, Object of, Predicted or Prophesied, Proof of, Necessity of, Sign of, Fact, etc.

"As Jonas was three days and three nights in the whale's belly; so shall the Son of man be three days and three nights in the heart of the earth" (Mt.12:40).

"From that time forth began Jesus to show unto his disciples, how that he must go unto Jerusalem...and be killed, and be raised again the third day" (Mt.16:21; see Mt.17:23; Lu.9:22, 31; 24:7).

MATTHEW 17:22-23

"[They] shall deliver him to the Gentiles to mock, and to scourge, and to crucify him: and the third day he shall rise again" (Mt.20:19; see Mk.10:34).

"After I am risen again, I will go before you into Galilee" (Mt.26:32; see Mk.14:28).

"And as they came down from the mountain, he charged them that they should tell no man what things they had seen till the Son of man were risen from the dead. And they kept that saying with themselves, questioning one with another what the rising from the dead should mean" (Mk.9:9-10).

"And they shall scourge him, and put him to death: and the third day he shall rise again" (Lu.18:33).

"Thus it is written, and thus it behooved Christ to suffer, and to rise from the dead the third day" (Lu.24:46).

"Jesus answered and said unto them, Destroy this temple, and in three days I will raise it up....He spake of the temple of his body" (Jn.2:19, 21; see Mk.14:58).

"A little while, and ye shall not see me: and again, a little while, and ye shall see me, because I go to the Father" (Jn.16:16).

"[The apostles] to whom also he showed himself alive after his passion by many infallible proofs, being seen of them forty days, and speaking of the things pertaining to the kingdom of God" (Ac.1:3).

"[Must] one be ordained to be a witness with us of his resurrection" (Ac.1:22).

"Whom God hath raised up, having loosed the pains of death: because it was not possible that he should be holden of it. For David speaketh concerning him, I foresaw the lord always before my face; for he is on my right hand, that I should not be moved: therefore did my heart rejoice, and my tongue was glad; moreover also my flesh shall rest in hope: because thou wilt not leave my soul in hell, neither wilt thou suffer thine Holy One to see corruption. Thou hast made known to me the ways of life; thou shalt make me full of joy with thy countenance" (Ac.2:24-28).

"This Jesus hath God raised up, whereof we all are witnesses. Therefore being by the right hand of God exalted, and having received of the Father the promise of the Holy Ghost, he hath shed forth this, which ye now see and hear....Therefore let all the house of Israel know assuredly, that God hath made that same Jesus, whom ye have crucified, both Lord and Christ....Repent, and be baptized every one of you in the name of Jesus Christ for the remission of sins, and ye shall receive the gift of the Holy Ghost" (Ac.2:32-33, 36, 38).

"And killed the Prince of life, whom God hath raised from the dead; whereof we are witnesses" (Ac.3:15).

"Be it known unto you all, and to all the people of Israel, that by the name of Jesus Christ of Nazareth, whom ye crucified, whom God raised from the dead, even by him doth this man stand here before you whole" (Ac.4:10).

"And with great power gave the apostles witness of the resurrection of the Lord Jesus: and great grace was upon them all" (Ac.4:33).

"The God of our fathers raised up Jesus, whom ye slew and hanged on a tree. Him hath God exalted with his right hand to be a Prince and a Saviour, for to give repentance to Israel, and forgiveness of sins. And we are his witnesses of these things; and so is also the Holy Ghost, whom God hath given to them that obey him" (Act.5:30-32).

"Him God raised up the third day, and showed him openly; Not to all the people, but unto witnesses chosen before of God, even to us, who did eat and drink with him after he rose from the dead" (Ac.10:40-41).

"But God raised him from the dead: And he was seen many days of them which came up with him from Galilee to Jerusalem, who are his witnesses unto the people. And we declare unto you glad tidings, now that the promise which was made unto the fathers, God hath fulfilled the same unto us their children, in that he hath raised up Jesus again; as it is also written in the second psalm, Thou art my Son, this day have I begotten thee, And as concerning that he raised him up from the dead, now no more to return to corruption, he said on this wise, I will give you the sure mercies of David. Wherefore he saith also in another psalm, Thou shalt not suffer thine Holy One to see corruption. For David, after he had served his own generation by the will of God, fell on sleep, and was laid unto his fathers, and saw corruption: But he, whom God raised again, saw no corruption" (Ac.13:30-37).

"And Paul, as his manner was, went in unto them, and three sabbath days reasoned with them out of the scriptures, Opening and alleging, that Christ must needs have suffered, and risen again from the dead; and that this Jesus, whom I preach unto you, is Christ...He will judge the world in righteousness by that man whom he hath ordained; whereof he hath given assurance unto all men, in that he hath raised him from the dead" (Ac.17:2-3, 31).

"Having therefore obtained help of God, I continue unto this day, witnessing both to small and great, saying none other things than those which the prophets and Moses did say should come: That Christ should suffer, and that he should be the first that should rise from the dead, and should show light unto the people, and to the Gentiles. And as he thus spake for himself, Festus said with a loud voice, Paul, thou art beside thyself; much learning doth make thee mad. But he said, I am not mad, most noble Festus; but speak forth the words of truth and soberness" (Ac.26:22-25).

"[Christ] declared to be the Son of God with power, according to the spirit of holiness, by the resurrection from the dead" (Ro.1:4).

"...it shall be imputed, if we believe on him [righteousness] that raised up Jesus our Lord from the dead; Who was delivered for our offences, and was raised again for our justification" (Ro.4:24-25).

MATTHEW 17:22-23

"If, when we were enemies, we were reconciled to God by the death of his son, much more, being reconciled, we shall be saved by his life" (Ro.5:10).

"Christ was raised up from the dead by the glory of the Father. If we have been planted together in the likeness of his death, we shall be also in the likeness of his resurrection....Christ being raised from the dead dieth no more; death hath no more dominion over him. For in that he died, he died unto sin once: but in that he liveth, he liveth unto God" (Ro.6:4-5, 9-10).

"But if the Spirit of him that raised up Jesus from the dead dwell in you, he that raised up Christ from the dead shall also quicken your mortal bodies by his Spirit that dwelleth in you" (Ro.8:11).

"Who is he that condemneth? It is Christ that died, yea rather, that is risen again, who is even at the right hand of God" (Ro.8:34).

"If thou shalt confess with thy mouth the Lord Jesus, and shalt believe in thine heart that God hath raised him from the dead, thou shalt be saved" (Ro.10:9).

"God hath both raised up the Lord, and will also raise up us by his own power" (1 Co.6:14).

"For I delivered unto you first of all that which I also received, how that Christ died for our sins according to the scriptures....And that he was buried, and that he rose again the third day according to the scriptures" (1 Co.15:3-4).

"Now is Christ risen from the dead, and become the firstfruits of them that slept. For since by man came death, by man came also the resurrection of the dead. For as in Adam all die, even so in Christ shall all be made alive. But every man in his own order: Christ the firstfruits; afterward they that are Christ's at his coming" (1 Co.15:20-23).

"[We are] always bearing about in the body the dying of the Lord Jesus, that the life also of Jesus might be made manifest in our body. For we which live are alway delivered unto death for Jesus' sake, that the life also of Jesus might be made manifest in our mortal flesh" (2 Co.4:10-11).

"Knowing that he which raised up the Lord Jesus shall raise up us also by Jesus, and shall present us with you" (2 Co.4:14).

"And that he died for all, that they which live should not henceforth live unto themselves, but unto him which died for them, and rose again" (2 Co.5:15).

"Though he was crucified through weakness, yet he liveth by the power of God" (2 Co.13:4).

"Paul, an apostle, (not of men, neither by man, but by Jesus Christ, and God the Father, who raised him from the dead)" (Ga.1:1).

"[Power] which he wrought in Christ, when he raised him from the dead, and set him at his own right hand in the heavenly places" (Ep.1:20).

"That I may know him, and the power of his resurrection" (Ph.3:10).

"[He is] the firstborn from the dead; that in all things he might have the preeminence" (Col.1:18).

"[Ye are] buried with him in baptism, wherein also ye are risen with him through the faith of the operation of God who hath raised him from the dead" (Col.2:12).

"And to wait for His Son from heaven, whom he raised from the dead, even Jesus, which delivered us from the wrath to come" (1 Th.1:10).

"For if we believe that Jesus died and rose again, even so them also which sleep in Jesus will God bring with him" (1 Th.4:14).

"Remember that Jesus Christ of the seed of David was raised from the dead according to my gospel" (2 Ti.2:8).

"Wherefore he is able also to save them to the uttermost that come unto God by him, seeing he ever liveth to make intercession for them" (He.7:25).

"For Christ is not entered into the holy places made with hands... but into heaven itself, now to appear in the presence of God for us" (He.9:24).

"Now once in the end of the world hath he appeared to put away sin by the sacrifice of himself. And as it is appointed unto men once to die, but after this the judgment: So Christ was once offered to bear the sins of many; and unto them that look for him shall he appear the second time without sin unto salvation" (He.9:26-28).

"But this man, after he had offered one sacrifice for sins for ever, sat down on the right hand of God" (He.10:12).

"Accounting that God was able to raise him up, even from the dead; from whence also he received him in a figure" (He.11:19).

"The God of peace, that brought again from the dead our Lord Jesus" (He.13:20).

"Blessed be the God and Father of our Lord Jesus Christ, which according to his abundant mercy hath begotten us again unto a lively hope by the resurrection of Jesus Christ from the dead, To an inheritance incorruptible, and undefiled, and that fadeth not away, reserved in heaven for you" (1 Pe.1:3-4).

"By him do [we] believe in God, that raised him up from the dead, and gave him glory" (1 Pe.1:21).

"For Christ also hath once suffered for sins, the just for the unjust, that he might bring us to God, being put to death in the flesh, but quickened by the Spirit" (1 Pe.3:18).

"Baptism doth also now save us (not the putting away of the filth of the flesh, but the answer of a good conscience toward God,) by the resurrection of Jesus Christ: Who is gone into heaven, and is on the right hand of God; angels and authorities and powers being made subject unto him" (1 Pe.3:21-22).

"Jesus Christ, who is the faithful witness, and the first begotten of the dead...I am he that liveth, and was dead; and behold, I am alive for evermore, Amen; and have the keys of hell and of death" (Re.1:5, 18).

MATTHEW 17:24-27

	F. The Messiah Reveals Himself Through Good Citizenship, 17:24-27 *(Mk 12:13-17)*		
1. Jesus was visited by tax collectors 　a. They questioned Peter instead of Jesus 　b. They asked if Jesus was a tax-dodger 2. Jesus demonstrated good citizenship: He paid taxes 3. Jesus made a unique claim about His own citizenship	24 And when they were come to Capernaum, they that received tribute *money* came to Peter, and said, Doth not your master pay tribute? 25 He saith, Yes. And when he was come into the house, Jesus prevented him, saying, What thinkest thou, Simon? of whom do the kings of the	earth take custom or tribute? of their own children, or of strangers? 26 Peter saith unto him, Of strangers. Jesus saith unto him, Then are the children free. 27 Notwithstanding, lest we should offend them, go thou to the sea, and cast an hook, and take up the fish that first cometh up; and when thou hast opened his mouth, thou shalt find a piece of money: that take, and give unto them for me and thee.	a. He is the Son of a King (God) & of a different kingdom than the earth b. He is free of the earthly kingdom 4. Jesus set the standard for citizenship: Paid the tax to keep others from stumbling 5. Jesus demonstrated His citizenship & Messiahship: He paid the tax miraculously

DIVISION XI

THE MESSIAH'S DRAMATIC REVELATION: HIS MESSIAHSHIP, HIS CHURCH, AND HIS CROSS, 16:13–17:27

F. The Messiah Reveals Himself Through Good Citizenship, 17:24-27

(17:24-27) **Introduction**: Jesus had been carrying His disciples through intensive training for some time now. He had been zeroing in on His death and resurrection (see notes—Mt.16:21-28; 17:1-13; 17:22-23). In this passage, Jesus showed just how capable a teacher He really was. He was able to take the visit by a tax collector and continue to make the unique claims of Messiahship and at the same time teach the importance of good citizenship. He is God's Son, and every believer is responsible to be a good citizen.

1. Jesus was visited by tax collectors (v.24).
2. Jesus demonstrated good citizenship: He paid taxes (v.25).
3. Jesus made a unique claim about His own citizenship (vv.25-26).
4. Jesus set the standard for citizenship: paid the tax to keep others from stumbling (v.27).
5. Jesus demonstrated His citizenship and Messiahship: He paid the tax miraculously (v.27).

1 (17:24) **Tax, Temple**: Jesus was visited by a tax collector. Perhaps Jesus was behind in His tax payments because He had been away for so long. The tax collectors approached Peter instead of Jesus because it was Jesus' habit to lodge in Peter's house when in Capernaum or perhaps because they feared Jesus.

The tax spoken of is the temple tax. The temple was an extremely expensive building to maintain just as any large building is. Time deteriorates furnishings, even stone and mortar, and all has to be replaced. In addition, there was the upkeep of the priests, their shelter, food, and clothing. There was the provision of the animals, incense, wine, flour, and oil used in the sacrifices which had to be offered every day—and the list could go on and on. Upkeep of the temple was so expensive that a nation-wide tax had to be imposed upon every male Jew over twenty years old. It was just a small tax (one half-shekel) for each man, amounting to about two days work; nevertheless, it had to be paid. It was collected annually by the tax collectors setting up their *tax collecting* booths in strategic locations throughout the country. (See Ex.30:13-16.)

2 (17:25) **Citizenship—Taxes**: Jesus demonstrated good citizenship. He paid taxes. It was His practice to pay taxes, and Peter knew this. Therefore, Peter was able to answer, "Yes, the master pays taxes."

Note a point which really strikes out at those who say they do not attend church because the church has too many hypocrites in it. In Christ's day, the temple was *a den of thieves,* and much of its worship was hypocritical and corrupt; yet Christ supported it (Mt.21:13; Mk.11:17). Why? There are at least three reasons.

　a. Despite its corruptions, the temple was still the house of God and the house of prayer.
　b. Christ benefited from the temple. When He entered the temple, His spirit was right with God, so He was able to worship and minister within its walls despite the hypocrisy of so many and the corruption of so much.
　c. The temple was where God's people were thought and expected to be. The world expected God's people to be in the temple and not somewhere else when it was time for worship. Christ could be nowhere else "lest He should offend them" (v.27). (See outlines and notes—Mt.22:15-22; Mk.12:13-17; Lu.20:19-26 for more discussion.)

> "Not forsaking the assembling of ourselves together, as the manner of some is; but exhorting one another: and so much the more, as ye see the day approaching" (He.10:25).

3 (17:25-26) **Jesus Christ, Deity**: Jesus made a unique claim by sharing an illustration. The illustration is brief and yet forceful. Jesus asked Peter a simple question: "From whom do kings collect their taxes? from their own children or from the citizens?" The answer is obvious: "He collects taxes from the citizens, not from his own children." And then Jesus made the phenomenal claim: "Then the children are free."

MATTHEW 17:24-27

The tax was the temple tax. The temple was God's, and Jesus was the Son of God. As the Son of God, He was free from the tax. He did not owe the tax.

Christ was not trying to keep from paying taxes. His point was to make a unique claim, a threefold claim.

a. He was the Son of a King, the Son of God Himself. (See notes—Jn.1:1-2; 1:34. See Deeper Study # 1—Jn.1:39; note—3:16-18; Deeper Study # 1—5:25; notes 6:38-40, 44, 57; Deeper Study # 1—8:32; notes—9:35; 10:32-33, 36-38; 1 Jn.5:5, 9-12.)

He was of another kingdom—the Kingdom of Heaven (see note and Deeper Study # 1—Jn.3:31; notes—6:33; 6:38; 6:41-51; Deeper Study # 2—8:23; 16:28).

b. He was free of the earthly kingdom. He had no obligation to pay taxes. If He paid them, it was because He willingly and voluntarily paid them.

There is more than meets the eye to the fact that Christ is free of the earthly kingdom. He is free of it because He is of God. His citizenship is of heaven; therefore, He has no obligation to the earth. The world and man neither merit nor deserve any attention from God. Man has forfeited his right to God's attention by his sin—by his degradation, depravity, evil, rebellion, and treason—all manifesting themselves in daily acts ranging from thoughts of selfishness to the slaughter of human life. Whatever God does for man and the world is of grace and mercy; it is because He loves man and the world. It is not because He is obligated or in bondage to serve man by meeting his need.

The above truth, however, is not true of the believer. When the believer trusts Christ as his Savior, he receives the divine nature of God. He becomes a new man and a new citizen of heaven; however, he is still of the earth. He is a new creature born from heaven above, but he is still flesh—still of the earth as well (2 Pe.1:1; see Deeper Study # 3—Ep.4:24; note—Ph.3:20). Therefore, he has an obligation not only to be a good citizen of heaven but also of the earth. God expects him to live for heaven by living a pure life and to live for the earth by sharing the good news of salvation with the rest of the world.

Thought 1. The three claims made by Christ are eye catching (glance at the outline points). There is a sense in which the same claims become the claims of the believer.
(1) Even as Christ is the Son of a King, the Son of God, so the believer is adopted as a child of the King (see Deeper Study # 2—Ga.4:5-6).
(2) Even as Christ is of another kingdom and of another world—of heaven itself—so the believer is made a citizen of heaven (Ph.3:20; 1 Pe.1:4; see Lu.22:30).
(3) Even as Christ is free of the earthly kingdom, so the believer is made free of the earthly kingdom. But remember: he is free only in a very special sense (Ro.6:18, 22; 8:2; Gal.5:1). He is free of the sin, bondage and death of this world, not free of the responsibility for this world. Even after being saved and made a citizen of heaven, he is still a citizen of this earth. He is a citizen of both earth and heaven, and as such he is obligated to care for the earth (see Mt.22:15-22; Mk.12:13-18; Lu.20:19-26. See outline and notes—Ro.13:1-7; 1 Ti.2:1-4; Tit.3:1-2; 1 Pe.2:13-17. See 1 Co.9:19; 1 Pe.2:16.)

"Then saith he unto them, Render therefore unto Caesar the things which are Caesar's; and unto God the things that are God's" (Mt.22:21).

"Let every soul be subject unto the higher powers. For there is no power but of God: the powers that be are ordained of God" (Ro.13:1).

"Put them in mind to be subject to principalities and powers, to obey magistrates, to be ready to every good work" (Tit.3:1).

"Submit yourselves to every ordinance of man for the Lord's sake: whether it be to the king, as supreme; or unto governors, as unto them that are sent by him for the punishment of evildoers, and for the praise of them that do well" (1 Pe.2:13-14).

4 (17:27) **Citizenship**: Jesus set the standard for citizenship—to keep others from stumbling. Note the word *offend* (skandalizo, verb; or skandalon, noun). When used as a verb the word *offend* means to put a snare or stumbling block in someone's way; to cause someone to trip or fall. When used as a noun the word *offend* means something that causes someone to stumble, trip, fall, or slip back. It is anything that arouses prejudice within others; anything that is a roadblock or a hindrance to others; anything that causes others to fall by the wayside. It is important to note that the stumbling block is sometimes good, and those who stumble are the ones in the wrong. For example, Christ is said to be a "rock of offense" (Ro.9:33) and His cross is said to *offend some;* that is, it is a stumbling block to some (Ga.5:11).

Christ was saying that He must not set a bad example by not paying His taxes. He was not obligated to pay them, but if He refused, then He would be encouraging poor citizenship. Therefore, He would forego His freedom in order to keep from causing others to stumble. He must not offend others, cause them to slip, stumble, or fall—under any circumstances.

Note two things.

a. Christ *never did* anything that would cause others to minimize or think less of their duty toward others (whether individuals, groups, or government). He did the very opposite. He always encouraged others to fulfill their duty so long as the duty was a legitimate act.

b. Christ never did anything that would cause others to stumble. Even when He was allowed or had the right to do something, He refused to do it if it would offend or hurt someone.

Thought 1. Many things may be lawful for us, but they may offend others. In such cases, abstinence is our Lord's command.

"[Let] no man put a stumblingblock or an occasion to fall in his brother's way. I know, and am persuaded by the Lord Jesus, that there is nothing unclean of itself: but to him that esteemeth any thing to be unclean, to him it is unclean. But if thy brother be grieved with thy meat [act], now walkest thou not charitably. Destroy not him with thy meat for whom Christ died. Let not then your good be evil spoken of" (Ro.14:13-16).

"We then that are strong ought to bear the infirmities of the weak, and not to please ourselves. Let every one of us please his neighbor for his good to edification. For even Christ pleased not himself; but, as it is written, The reproaches of them that reproached thee fell on me" (Ro.15:1-3).

5 (17:27) **Citizenship**: Jesus demonstrated His citizenship and Messiahship. He paid the tax miraculously. This miracle demonstrated beyond question the three claims Christ had just made. His knowing (omniscience) that a coin was in the mouth of a fish showed Peter that He...
- was of royalty, the Son of God.
- was of another kingdom that was superior to this earth and its seas.
- was free of the earth and its restrictions and obligations. How could Christ better demonstrate His Messiahship and Deity?

Why would Jesus Christ pay taxes if He were really of heaven? Why would He who did not belong to this earth subject Himself to civil and religious law?

There seem to be several reasons.

a. Christ was made (born) under the law (Ga.4:4). He was exactly who Peter had confessed Him to be: "the Christ, the Son of the living God" (Mt.16:16). Yet, He had deliberately subjected His glory and humbled Himself to become a man. He was the God-Man. As God, He was not obligated to the earth; but as Man, He was willingly subjecting Himself to the laws of men. The disciples needed to know this. What He and the Father were doing for man was not out of obligation but out of love and care.

b. Christ wished to foreshadow the atonement that He was soon to make for man. The temple tax was called "an atonement for the soul" (Ex.30:15. See Ex.30:13-16.) Atonement means *a covering* for a person's sins, a covering that makes reconciliation between man and God possible. The tax was paid as an atonement for a person's sin. It was to be paid in an act of faith, believing that one's sins would be covered and forgiven and that one would be reconciled and accepted by God anew and afresh. It was intended by God to be a renewed dedication of life.

Christ was made "in the likeness of sinful flesh" (Ro.8:3), and He became sin for us (2 Co.5:21). But Christ was not sinful. He had no sins for which to atone. Therefore, He had to declare to the disciples that He was free of the tax; for He was truly the Son of God, and He was truly free of sin. His payment of the tax was an entirely willing and voluntary act. As such, it foreshadowed the *voluntary atonement* He was to bear for man.

c. Christ wished to reinforce that He was the Son of God. He could have paid the taxes without comment, but by declaring that He was free of the tax because He was God's Son, He reinforced who He was to the disciples.

d. Christ wished to set an example for man. Every person is to "fulfill all righteousness" (Mt.3:15). Since Christ proved to be a good citizen, so must all who follow Him.

e. Christ held both the temple and government in high regard (see outline and notes—Ro.13:1-7). While on earth He had benefited from the temple: He had worshipped and ministered there, and He had reaped benefits from the temple. Therefore, He was now setting an example of how man is to return a portion of his income to help in the temple's (church's) support.

f. Christ did not wish to offend or to be a stumbling block to anyone. If He refused to pay the taxes, He would offend some. They would feel He was not carrying His load, and He would be a stumbling block to others. He would be setting an example of rebellion and lawlessness. If He refused to support the government and temple and everyone followed His example, then all governments and temples would collapse and cease to exist. Therefore, Christ demonstrated good citizenship for a very solid reason.

> **Thought 1.** What is it that makes us pay attention to Christ and do what He taught? The fact that He proved His Messiahship and that He is truly the Son of the living God. It is because of who He is that we are driven to trust Him and to be the very best citizens we can.

> "A new commandment I give unto you, That ye love one another; as I have loved you, that ye also love one another. By this shall all men know that ye are my disciples, if ye have love one to another" (Jn.13:34-35).
>
> "For all the law is fulfilled in one word, even in this; Thou shalt love thy neighbour as thyself" (Ga.5:14).
>
> "If ye fulfil the royal law according to the scripture, Thou shalt love thy neighbour as thyself, ye do well" (Js.2:8).
>
> "And this is his commandment, That we should believe on the name of his Son Jesus Christ, and love one another, as he gave us commandment" (1 Jn.3:23).

MATTHEW 18:1-4

	CHAPTER 18 XII. THE MESSIAH'S DISCIPLES & THEIR BEHAVIOR TOWARD ONE ANOTHER, 18:1-35 A. The Conditions for Greatness, 18:1-4 *(Mk 9:33-37; Lu 9:46-48)* At the same time came the disciples unto Jesus, saying, Who is the greatest	in the kingdom of heaven? 2 And Jesus called a little child unto him, and set him in the midst of them, 3 And said, Verily I say unto you, Except ye be converted, and become as little children, ye shall not enter into the kingdom of heaven. 4 Whosoever therefore shall humble himself as this little child, the same is greatest in the kingdom of heaven.	b. Second, there are degrees of greatness c. Jesus used a child to illustrate the truth 2. **Condition 1: Conversion** a. How: By turning & becoming as a child b. Why: Will be rejected if not converted 3. **Condition 2: Humility** a. How: Live as a child b. The result: Will be the greatest in heaven
1. **Two assumptions** a. First, a person is great if he is in the kingdom			

DIVISION XII

THE MESSIAH'S DISCIPLES AND THEIR BEHAVIOR TOWARD ONE ANOTHER, 18:1-35

A. The Conditions for Greatness, 18:1-4

(18:1-4) **Introduction—Greatness**: the disciples argued over who should hold the highest positions in the kingdom of God. This conflict arose on several occasions (see outlines and notes—Mt.20:20-28; Mk.9:33-37; Lu.22:24-30). Their desire was for recognition and honor in an earthly kingdom. Jesus had to reeducate their thinking. The disciples' struggle for position and power should not surprise us, for all men have the same needs, the needs for...

- some recognition
- some position
- some prestige
- some money
- some authority
- some esteem
- some challenge
- some physical satisfaction

There is nothing wrong with these needs. They are human and legitimate needs and they must be met. But men allow their hearts to be overtaken with *selfishness* and begin to want more and more to the point of lusting and consuming and hoarding. They become prideful, covetous, worldly, ambitious, envious, and hurtful even to the point of destroying and killing.

What Christ sets out to do is to change the lives of men and reeducate men in their concept of greatness.
1. Two assumptions (vv.1-2).
2. Condition 1: conversion (v.3).
3. Condition 2: humility (v.4).

1 (18:1-2) **Children—Jesus Christ, Nature—Greatness**: note the two assumptions in the question of the disciples. First, a person is great if he is in the Kingdom of Heaven. Second, there are degrees of greatness. Christ did not refute or deny these assumptions. On the contrary, He taught both: a person is great if he is in the Kingdom of Heaven. Everything and everyone in heaven is great, even perfected. As Christ says, a person can be *the greatest* in the Kingdom of Heaven (v.4. See scripture and notes—Mt.13:8, 23; 25:20-30; Lu.12:41-48; 16:10-12; 19:15-23). The question is not "who shall be the greatest" but how does one become *great* in God's kingdom? How does one prove that he is trustworthy and responsible before God? How does one show God that he can be trusted and depended upon and should be rewarded with responsibility in heaven (see notes—Mt.25:20; Lu.19:15; 22:28-29)?

Note several things about the question asked by the disciples.
 a. Note what they meant. By "the greatest in the kingdom of heaven," they did not mean the greatest in quality or character but in name and position. They were thinking in terms of power, fame, wealth, position, and name (see notes—Mt.1:1; DEEPER STUDY # 2—1:18; DEEPER STUDY # 3—3:11; notes—11:1-6; 11:2-3; DEEPER STUDY # 1—11:5; DEEPER STUDY # 2—11:6; DEEPER STUDY # 1—12:16; note—Lu.7:21-23 for a picture of their concept of the Messiah).
 b. Note the reasons why they asked the question.
  1) They sensed that Christ was about to set up His kingdom, that He was about to assume His throne. They were looking forward to becoming chiefs of state in His kingdom.
  2) They had seen three of them honored in special ways (Peter, James, and John—Mt.17:1-13), and one of them in particular had been distinguished (Peter, Mt.16:17-19). Who were the leaders to be in the Lord's kingdom? They were apparently gripped with jealousy, envy, ambition, and some rivalry.
  3) They had just been arguing among themselves about who the greatest was going to be. Mark says that the argument had begun immediately after Christ began to intensify His teaching on His death and resurrection (Mk.9:33-34; see 9:30-37). They misinterpreted what He was saying, spiritualizing it instead of taking His Word at face value (see note—Mt.17:22). Apparently they connected the thought of *rising from the dead* with the setting up of His kingdom and began to argue over the top positions of leadership.

MATTHEW 18:1-4

c. Note: they did not yet understand what the Kingdom of Heaven is. They still saw an earthly, temporal kingdom and not a spiritual, eternal kingdom. It is interesting what Christ said in v.3. He was speaking to the disciples, and He *actually said* that they would not enter the kingdom of heaven unless they became as little children.

Christ gave a living demonstration of greatness. He "*called* a little child unto him." The child was not an infant, for he was personally *called* to come to Christ. Note how the child immediately demonstrated several traits of children. He *trusted* Christ enough to respond (trustfulness) and did what Christ requested (submission, humility, and obedience).

This says something about the nature and character of Christ as well. He demonstrated enough warmth and openness for the child to feel free to respond and to enter a group of adults who were sitting together in a formal session.

> **Thought 1.** The thoughts of the average person focus upon appearance, personal image, self-esteem, possessions, privileges, position, and glory, and he spends much time in thinking of these things. He imagines and fancies himself to be the center of attention, the *hero* of the game or play, the main attraction, the one considered most honorable and esteemed. It is such thoughts and ambitions that Christ wants to change. Our thoughts and minds are to be centered on Christ and others and upon things that are true, not on self (Ro.12:2; 2 Co.10:5; Ph.4:8).

> **Thought 2.** How often we think in terms of *earthly and fleshly greatness*. If we are asked who are the *greatest* people in a city or country, we answer by naming the famous, the prestigious, the wealthy, the powerful, and the educated. We think little, if any, of those who serve and minister.

2 (18:3) **Greatness—Conversion**: the first condition for greatness is conversion. The word *conversion* (straphete) means to turn, to turn around; to be converted; to turn from one thing to something else (1 Th.1:9, "how ye turned to God from idols"). (See repentance for the same idea.)

The meaning here is that the disciples must *turn*; they must turn completely around. Christ warned them: "Unless ye turn." Turn from what? Their sins were many, sins that are so common to men as they walk in selfishness day by day.

Note that they were possessed by a selfish desire for...
- position
- power
- prestige
- fame
- wealth
- fleshly stimulation

Note that they were possessed by a spirit of...
- pride
- covetousness
- ambition
- jealousy
- worldliness
- envy
- rivalry

Conversion is one of the great subjects of the Bible. The reason is made clear by Christ: "Except ye be converted...ye shall not enter into the kingdom of heaven" (v.3). Whether or not a person is converted determines his eternal destiny.

   a. How is a person converted? By turning and becoming as a little child. What does it mean "to become as a little child"? When Christ *called* the child to Him, the child demonstrated exactly what Christ meant.
      1) The child *trusted Christ*. The child responded to the call of Christ. He sensed the openness, warmth, tenderness, care, and love of Christ; so he felt free to respond and to trust Christ's call.
      2) The child *surrendered* himself to Christ. He was willing to give up what he was doing and go to Christ, willing to surrender whatever it was that was occupying his thoughts and behavior.
      3) The child was *obedient* to Christ. He obeyed and did exactly what Christ requested, and it was probably difficult to do so. There were at least thirteen adult men standing or sitting there, and the child was being asked to walk into the midst of these men. Note that he obeyed despite the difficulty and obeyed simply because Christ asked him.
      4) The child was *humble* before Christ. All the above traits show humility. However, there is something often overlooked and abused by the adult world. Little children do not push themselves forward. They are not interested in prominence, fame, power, wealth, or position. They do not want to be placed in the midst of a group of adults, for they prefer to be in the background, away from staring, gawking eyes. Such embarrasses them and makes them feel self-conscious. Therefore, they prefer to be left in their obscure world. They are by nature humble, knowing little if anything of the competitive world that surrounds them; that is, they know little of it until they are brought into it by adults.
   b. Why is a person to be converted? Because non-conversion brings rejection and loss of greatness. Note that the warning is severe: "Except ye be converted...ye shall not enter into the kingdom of heaven." And Christ is speaking to the disciples. "Unless they are converted and become as little children, they shall not enter into the kingdom of heaven."

If the disciples were warned, how much more are we and everyone else warned! The absolute necessity of conversion is hereby stressed.

> "And said, Verily I say unto you, Except ye be converted, and become as little children, ye shall not enter into the kingdom of heaven" (Mt.18:3).
> "Repent ye therefore, and be converted, that your sins may be blotted out, when the times of refreshing shall come from the presence of the Lord" (Ac.3:19).
> "Brethren, if any of you do err from the truth, and one convert him. Let him know, that he which converteth the sinner from the error of his way shall save a soul from death, and shall hide a multitude of sins" (Js.5:19-20).

MATTHEW 18:1-4

"The law of the LORD is perfect, converting the soul: the testimony of the LORD is sure, making wise the simple" (Ps.19:7).

"Restore unto me the joy of thy salvation; and uphold me with thy free spirit. Then will I teach transgressors thy ways; and sinners shall be converted unto thee" (Ps.51:12-13).

"Let the wicked forsake his way, and the unrighteous man his thoughts: and let him return unto the LORD, and he will have mercy upon him; and to our God, for he will abundantly pardon" (Is.55:7).

"But if the wicked will turn from all his sins that he hath committed, and keep all my statutes, and do that which is lawful and right, he shall surely live, he shall not die" (Eze.18:21).

Thought 1. Note that the very traits possessed by a child are the essentials for conversion or salvation: trust, surrender, obedience, and humility.

Thought 2. What Christ is after is the total conversion of a person, a conversion that is complete and thorough: a conversion of heart, life, and thoughts. Our thoughts make us what we are. And, oh, how they are centered on self, making ourselves the center of attention.

"Lord, my heart is not haughty, nor mine eyes lofty: neither do I exercise myself in great matters, or in things too high for me. Surely I have behaved and quieted myself, as a child that is weaned of his mother: my soul is even as a weaned child" (Ps.131:1-2).

"Repent therefore of this thy wickedness, and pray God, if perhaps the thought of thine heart may be forgiven thee" (Ac.8:22).

"Casting down imaginations, and every high thing that exalteth itself against the knowledge of God, and bringing into captivity every thought to the obedience of Christ" (2 Co.10:5).

3 (18:4) **Humility**: the second condition for greatness is humility.

a. How does a person become humble? By living as a child. The child had humbled himself to come to Christ. Christ said so.
   1) The child had given up what he was doing. Whatever it was that was occupying his thought and time, he walked away from it. He humbled himself in order to come to Christ.
   2) The child had obeyed Christ. He went to Christ. Obedience always demands humility, a humbling of oneself (thoughts, energy, time, effort) in order to do whatever another asks.
   3) The child overcame feelings he had in order to respond to Christ. Because of the twelve men surrounding Christ, there was bound to be some hesitation, dread, apprehension, or fear; yet he humbled himself and went to Christ despite all. Humility has always been one of the most *insignificant* traits among men, yet it determines whether a man enters heaven or not. It is of critical importance.

b. The result of humility is greatness. The greatest persons in the Kingdom of Heaven will be the persons who have been converted and walked most humbly among men. First Cor.13 says exactly what Christ is demonstrating.

"Charity suffereth long, and is kind; charity envieth not; charity vaunteth not itself, is not puffed up, doth not behave itself unseemly, seeketh not her own, is not easily provoked, thinketh no evil; rejoiceth not in iniquity, but rejoiceth in the truth; beareth all things, believeth all things, hopeth all things, endureth all things...And now abideth faith, hope, charity, these three; but the greatest of these is charity" (1 Co.13:4-7, 13).

Thought 1. Men fear humility. They feel that *humility* is a sign of weakness and cowardice. They fear humility will make them the object of contempt and abuse. They fear humility may cause them to be passed over, but the very opposite is true. Humility leads a person to Christ and to conversion. It leads a person to realize his full potential. It causes a person to evaluate himself and to work at improving himself. It leads a person to become all that he can and should be. It also leads to better and more healthy relationships and to a stronger and more productive community and world.

When men consider others (humble themselves), they win friends and influence people. They build and strengthen everyone and everything involved.

"Whosoever therefore shall humble himself as this little child, the same is greatest in the kingdom of heaven" (Mt.18:4).

"But ye shall not be so: but he that is greatest among you, let him be as the younger; and he that is chief, as he that doth serve" (Lu.22:26).

"For I say, through the grace given unto me, to every man that is among you, not to think of himself more highly than he ought to think; but to think soberly, according as God hath dealt to every man the measure of faith" (Ro.12:3).

"Let nothing be done through strife or vainglory; but in lowliness of mind let each esteem other better than themselves. Look not every man on his own things, but every man also on the things of others" (Ph.2:3-4).

"Humble yourselves in the sight of the Lord, and he shall lift you up" (Js.4:10).

"Likewise, ye younger, submit yourselves unto the elder. Yea, all of you be subject one to another, and be clothed with humility: for God resisteth the proud, and giveth grace to the humble" (1 Pe.5:5).

MATTHEW 18:5-10

	B. The Warning Against Offending, Mistreating a Child, 18:5-10 (Mk 9:42-48)	8 Wherefore if thy hand or thy foot offend thee, cut them off, and cast *them* from thee: it is better for thee to enter into life halt or maimed, rather than having two hands or two feet to be cast into everlasting fire.	c. The way to handle the sin of being a stumblingblock 1) Cut off the hand that sins 2) Cut off the foot that sins
1. The child represents Christ	5 And whoso shall receive one such little child in my name receiveth me.		

2. Offense 1: Leading a child astray
  a. A child who believes
  b. The worst conceivable sin
  c. The severe judgment
	6 But whoso shall offend one of these little ones which believe in me, it were better for him that a millstone were hanged about his neck, and *that* he were drowned in the depth of the sea.	9 And if thine eye offend thee, pluck it out, and cast *it* from thee: it is better for thee to enter into life with one eye, rather than having two eyes to be cast into hell fire.	3) Pluck out the eye that sins
			d. The escaping of the punishment is worth any price
			  1) It will be eternal fire[DS1]
			  2) It will be the fire of hell

3. Offense 2: Being a stumbling block
  a. The certainty of sin in a sinful world
  b. The warning to the sinner
	7 Woe unto the world because of offences! for it must needs be that offences come; but woe to that man by whom the offence cometh!	10 Take heed that ye despise not one of these little ones; for I say unto you, That in heaven their angels do always behold the face of my Father which is in heaven.	4. Offense 3: Despising, degrading a child
			  a. A caution: Take heed
			  b. The reason: Children have direct access to God[DS2]

DIVISION XII

THE MESSIAH'S DISCIPLES AND THEIR BEHAVIOR TOWARD ONE ANOTHER, 18:1-35

B. The Warning Against Offending, Mistreating a Child, 18:5-10

(18:5-10) **Introduction—Christians—Responsibility**: Christ used *the child* (see Mt.18:1-4) as an object lesson to teach that believers have an awesome responsibility for watching over one another. The Jews used the word *child* in two ways. It referred either to a small child or to a disciple of some teacher, a beginner in the faith. In this passage, Jesus used the word *child* to refer to three persons (see note and DEEPER STUDY # 1,2—Mk.9:42).

  1. It means a small child.

  2. It means a beginner in the faith, someone who has just been converted and become a newborn child of God. This person is a new Christian; therefore, he knows little about the Lord and about how he is to live. Hence he is very impressionable, and he can be easily misled or confused.

  3. It means any believer who has a childlike spirit and character. This childlike spirit is the very spirit about which Christ has just spoken (Mt.18:3-4). It is the spirit He desires and expects in every follower of His.

Christ cares deeply for children, for all who have the childlike spirit and character. He calls those who follow Him "little ones" (18:6; 10:42). The depth of His care is clearly seen in this passage, a passage that lays a terrible responsibility upon all men—a responsibility that is unmistakably clear and so desperately needed. Christ gives three terrible warnings against offending a child, and He spells out the three terrible offenses against a child, "little ones who believe in" Him (v.6).

  1. The child represents Christ (v.5).
  2. Offense 1: leading a child astray (v.6).
  3. Offense 2: being a stumbling block (vv.7-9).
  4. Offense 3: despising, degrading a child (v.10).

1 (18:5) **Children**: the child represented Christ. The word for *shall receive* (dechetai) means to receive a child in every way possible.

⇒ It means to receive the child as a *person*: with tenderness, warmth, care, affection and love—no matter how low or unimportant or poor. Christ is contrasting *the child* with *the greatest person*, the person over whom the disciples had just been arguing (see notes—Mt.18:1-4; 18:1-2).

⇒ It means to receive the child when he is in need *physically* or *materially*: to feed, cloth, shelter, visit, and help him (Mt.25:35f; Js.1:27).

⇒ It means to receive the child *spiritually*: to help him grow, build him up, encourage, and motivate him to follow Christ and to share his faith.

Note two reasons why we are to receive the child.

1. The child represents Christ. To receive a child is to receive Christ. Whatever is done for the child is done for Christ.

2. Christ cared for each child, every single one. He said, "one such little child"; that is, that single child is important to Christ. Christ does not want that child...

- left out, feeling like a non-person, uncared for and unloved
- left in need physically or materially, having to scrap and scrounge around, surviving all alone
- left alone, not knowing how to follow Christ and how to grow spiritually

Christ clearly said: to receive and help "one such child" is to receive and help Him (see Mt.25:35f).

MATTHEW 18:5-10

Thought 1. Welcoming and being receptive and open to people and their needs are of utmost importance to Christ (see outline and notes—Mt.10:40-42).

Thought 2. There is an unbelievable lesson here, a lesson that is so often unheard of among men: to minister to people is much more important than "being the greatest" in an earthly kingdom (see notes—Mt.18:1-4; 18:1-2). The point is simply this: *to receive another person is to receive Christ*, and receiving Christ is much more important than *being the greatest*.

2 (18:6) **Sin, Leading Others**: the first warning is against leading a child astray. Leading a child, a follower of Christ, astray is the worst conceivable sin. There is nothing worse than leading another person into sin. In fact, it would be better to hang a millstone about one's neck and cast oneself into the depths of the sea than to lead another person astray. This sounds severe, very severe. And it is. But note: Christ meant what He said and said what He meant. How do we know this? From three facts.

a. The *millstone* (mulos) spoken of by Christ was the huge millstone, the one that the oxen or donkey pulled around to grind the grain. It was not the small hand millstone used by the women to grind a little grain at a time. The very fact that Christ chose the huge millstone to illustrate His point shows just how great this sin is. The person would be held at the bottom of the sea by the most awful and terrible weight. The sin of leading a child astray is the worst imaginable sin; therefore, its condemnation shall be the worst punishment imaginable.

b. Drowning was a form of criminal punishment used by the Romans but never by the Jews. The Jews saw drowning as a symbol of *utter destruction and annihilation*. They feared it. Even the Romans reserved it only for the worst criminals.

c. Christ *added to the fear* of His audience. He painted the picture of a stone around the offender's neck so that the body could never rise to the top and be recovered for proper burial. And then He added even more to the fear. He pictured the huge millstone, not the small one. Why? Why did He strike fear into the hearts of His hearers? The answer is clear: the sin of leading another person astray is terrible, and the offender must know the fate that is awaiting him.

There are several ways we cause others to sin.

⇒ By leading them into sin and teaching them to sin: "Oh, come on, no one will know. It's not going to hurt you."
⇒ By example; by the things we do. Example is not a direct proposition, so we are not necessarily aware that *the child* sees or is observing us. Nevertheless, he sees and learns from what we do: "If it's all right for him, then it is bound to be all right for me." "If he can do it and still work and play and get by as well as he does, then I can too."
⇒ By overlooking or passing over wrong; by giving soft names to it; by considering some sins to be merely *white sins*: "Oh, that's all right. There's not that much to it. It isn't going to hurt anyone. Don't pay any attention to it. Just forget it."
⇒ By ridiculing and poking fun at, or joking and sneering at a person's attempt to do right: "Oh, don't be a fuddy-duddy. You're acting like a fanatic. You and your religion."
⇒ By looking, touching, and tasting some things that are socially acceptable but sinful to God. They are harmful and habit forming and physically stimulating when they should not be: "Wow, look at that." "Taste that." "Man! What a stir!"
⇒ By persecuting and threatening *a child* or a believer. The threat can range all the way from loss of promotion, job, friendship, or acceptance, to abuse, imprisonment, and death.

Thought 1. A genuine believer, no matter how young or immature as a Christian, has "obtained like precious faith with us." Standing before God, a believer is on equal footing with all other believers. Of course, this does not mean they are to be given positions of leadership while they are young believers (1 Ti.3:6, 10). It simply means that they are to be focused upon and taught and developed in Christ, not ignored and overlooked because they cannot yet contribute much to the work of God's kingdom.

Thought 2. There are some things that seem innocent enough, yet they can lead others astray (1 Co.8:10-11). A mature believer is not to abuse the young believer by his liberty (see outline and notes—Ro.14:1-23).

3 (18:7-9) **Stumbling Block—World, Sinful**: the second warning is against being a stumbling block. Note the outline points of the Scripture.

a. There is the certainty of sin in a sinful world. This is a sinful world, full of evil behavior. No one can walk out into the world without facing temptation after temptation and pull after pull to look, touch, and taste—to experience the *good life* of physical gratification and earthly comfort and personal fulfillment. We are tempted, seduced, and influenced by it at every turn. There is no escape (see Ro.3:9-18).

> "The whole world lieth in wickedness" (1 Jn.5:19).
> "For all have sinned and come short of the glory of God" (Ro.3:23).

b. There is the warning to the sinner. Every man is personally responsible for his sin. The fact of a sinful world does not lessen a man's personal responsibility. He cannot blame the world, society, or others; for man...
- has free will
- has the knowledge of much good
- has the pull to do good (at least initially)
- usually has examples of goodness
- can choose to do good
- can work to overcome and strengthen his weakness

MATTHEW 18:5-10

Most of all, man has God who provides a way to escape temptation (1 Co.10:13). The sinner is personally responsible. Every sin becomes a stumbling block to others! The man who sins becomes the stumbling block over which others can fall!

   c. There is the way to handle the sin of being a stumbling block. Again, the severity of the language shows the severity of the sin. There is no greater sin than being a stumbling block to one of God's dear children.
      1) Christ says "cut off the hand that sins": force the hand away, pull it back, push it aside. Let the hand that sins have no part of you. Deny the hand's presence, its existence.

> "**Wherefore come out from among them, and be ye separate, saith the Lord, and touch not the unclean thing; and I will receive you, and will be a Father unto you, and ye shall be my sons and daughters, saith the Lord Almighty**" (2 Co.6:17-18).

      2) Christ says "cut off the foot that sins": Remove it, take it away from the sin. Make the foot of no use and the body will be immobilized for you. Remove the foot and your body cannot go to the sin; take the foot far enough away that you will have time to think of the consequences. Deny the foot's presence, its existence.

> "**See then that ye walk circumspectly, not as fools, but as wise**" (Ep.5:15).
> "**As ye have therefore received Christ Jesus the Lord, so walk ye in him**" (Col.2:6).
> "**He that saith he abideth in him ought himself also so to walk, even as he walked**" (1 Jn.2:6).

      3) Christ says "pluck out the eye": Turn away from the sight; leave it; don't look. In fact, make sure you cannot look upon sin. Deny the eye's presence, its existence.

> "**Whosoever looketh on a woman to lust after her hath committed adultery with her already in his heart**" (Mt.5:28).
> "**All that is in the world, the lust of the flesh, and the lust of the eyes, and the pride of life, is not of the Father, but is of the world**" (1 Jn.2:16).
> "**He that winketh with the eye causeth sorrow**" (Pr.10:10).
> "**The eye is not satisfied with seeing, nor the ear filled with hearing**" (Ec.1:8).
> "**Neither is his eye satisfied with riches**" (Ec.4:8).

Note that it is the *hand that touches* the sin, the *foot that takes* one to the sin or to the place of sin, and the *eye that looks* upon the sin and leads to the desire and lust for the sin. The way to escape is to deny self (see notes and DEEPER STUDY #1—Lu.9:23; see outline—Ro.6:11-13) and to draw nigh to God (see outline—Js.4:7-10).

   d. There is the escaping of the punishment, which is worth any price. The most horrible death imaginable is death by fire. Just imagine burning and burning in everlasting fire. There is no more terrible punishment than that described by Christ. How horrible eternity apart from God must be. The severity of hell again stresses the severity of the sin in God's eyes.

> "**Then said he unto the disciples, It is impossible but that offences will come: but woe unto him, through whom they come! It were better for him that a millstone were hanged about his neck, and he cast into the sea, than that he should offend one of these little ones**" (Lu.17:1-2).
> "**Let us not therefore judge one another any more: but judge this rather, that no man put a stumblingblock or an occasion to fall in his brother's way**" (Ro.14:13).
> "**But if thy brother be grieved with thy meat, now walkest thou not charitably. Destroy not him with thy meat, for whom Christ died**" (Ro.14:15).
> "**It is good neither to eat flesh, nor to drink wine, nor any thing whereby thy brother stumbleth, or is offended, or is made weak**" (Ro.14:21).
> "**Give none offence, neither to the Jews, nor to the Gentiles, nor to the church of God**" (1 Co.10:32).
> "**Giving no offence in any thing, that the ministry be not blamed**" (2 Co.6:3).
> "**He that loveth his brother abideth in the light, and there is none occasion of stumbling in him**" (1 Jn.2:10).

Thought 1. The world is full of people who are stumbling blocks, people who are...
- bad examples
- tempters
- false guides
- seducers
- deceivers
- persecutors

Thought 2. Note several logical facts.
(1) *A righteous God* knows unmistakably who is a stumbling block to the *little child*.
(2) *A righteous God* knows exactly at whose feet to lay the guilt for causing a *little child* to stumble.
(3) *A righteous God* knows precisely who ruins the precious soul of a child, preventing the child from being saved.
(4) *A righteous God* will reckon with the man who causes a *little child* to stumble—severely and eternally. He is righteous; therefore, He has to deal severely, matching the punishment to the evil.

Thought 3. Note a critical fact: the hand, the foot, and the eye are the sinner's own hand, foot, and eye. He is sinning as well as causing another to sin. He is damaging and destroying his own life as well as the life of a child. He is dooming himself to hell as well as the child.

Thought 4. This is strong language, very descriptive and severe in its point. But honesty and thought are called for in seeing the point of Christ. What on earth is more horrible than leading a child astray and being a stumbling block to his salvation, dooming him to what Christ calls *hell fire* and *everlasting fire*. If God really loves the *little child* as Christ says, and if *hell fire* is real, then strong and severe language is needed to awaken the world to the truth.

MATTHEW 18:5-10

DEEPER STUDY # 1
(18:8-9) **Hell Fire—Everlasting Fire** (to pur to aionion): this is the first time the words *everlasting fire* are used. The words point to an awful fate, a terrible and horrible eternity. Everlasting means for the duration, on and on without end. The fact that the unforgiven sinner is to suffer so great a punishment should cause all sinners to cease being stumbling blocks. It should stir them to become stepping stones to God (see Deeper Study # 2—Mt.5:22; Deeper Study # 3—Lu.16:23; Deeper Study # 4—16:24).

"Whose fan is in his hand, and he will throughly purge his floor, and gather his wheat into the garner; but he will burn up the chaff with unquenchable fire" (Mt.3:12).

"And shall cast them into a furnace of fire: there shall be wailing and gnashing of teeth" (Mt.13:42).

"Wherefore if thy hand or thy foot offend thee, cut them off, and cast them from thee: it is better for thee to enter into life halt or maimed, rather than having two hands or two feet to be cast into everlasting fire" (Mt.18:8).

"Then shall he say also unto them on the left hand, Depart from me, ye cursed, into everlasting fire, prepared for the devil and his angels" (Mt.25:41).

"But the fearful, and unbelieving, and the abominable, and murderers, and whoremongers, and sorcerers, and idolaters, and all liars, shall have their part in the lake which burneth with fire and brimstone: which is the second death" (Re.21:8).

"The sinners in Zion are afraid; fearfulness hath surprised the hypocrites. Who among us shall dwell with the devouring fire? who among us shall dwell with everlasting burnings?" (Is.33:14).

"And they shall go forth, and look upon the carcases of the men that have transgressed against me: for their worm shall not die, neither shall their fire be quenched; and they shall be an abhorring unto all flesh" (Is.66:24).

4 (18:10) **Children, Sins Against—Despite**: the third warning is against despising a child. There are several ways that a child or a believer is despised.

a. By considering the child unimportant. He is not considered as competent as others; therefore, he is neglected, ignored, or pushed aside. As a result, his growth and potential for life and service are untapped, or stifled and stunted.

b. By doing unbecoming things in the child's presence; by disregarding the child's presence and going ahead with one's *off-color* language and jokes, *little white lies*, and socially acceptable but sinful habits.

c. By twisting the child's mind or body into evil behavior and sin. This can range all the way from sinful ambition and self-seeking to child abuse through sexual deviation and murder.

"Behold, ye despisers, and wonder, and perish: for I work a work in your days, a work which ye shall in no wise believe, though a man declare it unto you" (Ac.13:41).

"Or despisest thou the riches of his goodness and forbearance and longsuffering; not knowing that the goodness of God leadeth thee to repentance?" (Ro.2:4).

"This know also, that in the last days perilous times shall come. For men shall be lovers of their own selves, covetous, boasters, proud, blasphemers, disobedient to parents, unthankful, unholy, without natural affection, trucebreakers, false accusers, incontinent, fierce, despisers of those that are good" (2 Ti.3:1-3).

"He that despised Moses' law died without mercy under two or three witnesses: of how much sorer punishment, suppose ye, shall he be thought worthy, who hath trodden under foot the Son of God, and hath counted the blood of the covenant, wherewith he was sanctified, an unholy thing, and hath done despite unto the Spirit of grace?" (He.10:28-29).

"The Lord knoweth how to deliver the godly out of temptations, and to reserve the unjust unto the day of judgment to be punished: but chiefly them that walk after the flesh in the lust of uncleanness, and despise government [discipline]. Presumptuous are they, selfwilled, they are not afraid to speak evil of dignities [authorities]" (2 Pe.2:9-10).

Thought 1. Children have a most favored position before God. The fact that their guardian angels *"do always behold"* God's face shows this. There could be no greater privilege than to be before God always "beholding His face." Children are very, very precious to God. For this reason alone, we should do all we can to rid ourselves and the world of evil.

DEEPER STUDY # 2
(18:10) **Angels**: see Deeper Study # 1—He.1:4-14. We must always remember that Christ came from (ek, out of) the spiritual world, out of the dimension of heaven, to reveal heaven to us. He taught the reality of angels, that is, heavenly messengers. Here He teaches that children have "guardian angels" who have direct access to God. This fact is a warning to the offender: every sin and stumbling block placed before His children (believer, v.6) is brought before Him, so no offense will go unpunished. It is also an encouragement to every child of His: the child will be vindicated and can depend upon God Himself to vindicate Him.

"Are they not all ministering spirits, sent forth to minister for them who shall be heirs of salvation?" (He.1:14).

"I say unto you, that likewise joy shall be in heaven over one sinner that repenteth, more than over ninety and nine just persons, which need no repentance....Likewise, I say unto you, there is joy in the presence of the angels of God over one sinner that repenteth" (Lu.15:7, 10).

"The angel of the lord encampeth round about them that fear him, and delivereth them" (Ps.34:7).

"For he shall give his angels charge over thee, to keep thee in all thy ways" (Ps.91:11).

MATTHEW 18:11-14

	C. The Parable of the Lost Sheep: The Supreme Example of Caring, 18:11-14 *(Lu 15:1-7)*	and nine, and goeth into the mountains, and seeketh that which is gone astray? 13 And if so be that he find it, verily I say unto you, he rejoiceth more of that *sheep,* than of the ninety and nine which went not astray. 14 Even so it is not the will of your Father which is in heaven, that one of these little ones should perish.	c. The sheep was sought: In the mountains^{DS1}
1. Jesus came to save the lost	11 For the Son of man is come to save that which was lost.		3. Jesus may or may not find the lost one

2. Jesus seeks every single one
  a. The sheep wandered away
  b. The sheep was sought: By the shepherd
	12 How think ye? if a man have an hundred sheep, and one of them be gone astray, doth he not leave the ninety		4. Jesus forgives & rejoices over the recovered one

			5. Jesus declares a wonderful truth: God wills that not a single soul be lost

DIVISION XII

THE MESSIAH'S DISCIPLES AND THEIR BEHAVIOR TOWARD ONE ANOTHER, 18:1-35

C. The Parable of the Lost Sheep: The Supreme Example of Caring, 18:11-14

(18:11-14) **Introduction**: this is one of the most famous parables shared by Jesus—the parable of "The Lost Sheep" or the parable of "The Seeking Shepherd." It holds a great message for both the believer and the unbeliever, and Jesus applies it to both. Two things show this.

1. The words "these little ones" refer to genuine Christian believers, and the word "perish" refers to the lost (see note—Mt.18:5-10).
2. On this particular occasion, Jesus was speaking to His disciples (Mt.18:1). In Luke Jesus shared the same parable with a different audience and directed it more toward the lost.

Some believers are weak, never having grown in the Lord; others cool off and wander away; still others backslide into sin and shame. Some are stubborn toward the Lord, and some become self-centered because of hurt and neglect. Others allow the hurt and neglect to develop into bitterness and hostility against a person, and go out and sin in anger. There are innumerable reasons for sinning, but believers do sin, and some sin rather seriously.

The one who strays and the one who is lost are always with us. The thing to remember is this...

> "For the Son of man is come to save that which was lost" (Mt.18:11).
> "Even so it is not the will of your Father which is in heaven, that one of these little ones should perish" (Mt.18:14).

1. Jesus came to save the lost (v.11).
2. Jesus seeks every single one (v.12).
3. Jesus may or may not find the lost one (v.13).
4. Jesus forgives and rejoices over the recovered one (v.13).
5. Jesus declares a wonderful truth: God wills that not a single soul be lost (v.14).

1 (18:11) **Jesus Christ, Savior—Man, Lost**: Jesus came to save the lost. This is the Messiah's great statement of purpose; this is why He came to earth. He came to save the lost. There is a world of meaning in this great statement.

a. It means that Christ willingly and deliberately *left* the glory of heaven and His equality with God and "emptied Himself" of that glory and equality (see notes—Ph.2:6; 2:7).

b. It means that both the world as a whole and man as an individual have gone astray. Each person has strayed away from God, is lost, and is wandering about in a wilderness of sin; and each person is doomed to be destroyed by that wilderness unless he is reached and saved by Christ. Everyone needs to be saved (Ro.3:10-18, 23; 10:13; Jn.3:16; Ac.10:43; 1 Jn.5:1).

c. It means that *God lost man.* God lost man's worship and service and life. Not only has man *gone astray*, not only is man *not seeking* after God and gone out of the way—but he has become unprofitable, *lost to God* (Ro.3:11-12). While man remains lost *in the wilderness*, God has no hope of fellowship with man. Man's worship, service, and life are lost to God as long as man remains lost. The words *that which was lost* should be noted. They are in the Greek neuter participle. This means that the person lost is not only man (masculine) but woman (feminine) as well. "That [neuter] which was lost" and sought after is both man and woman. The point is to show the span of Jesus' love: He loves all who are lost, both man and woman. No one is outside the scope of His love and seeking. He loves and seeks after all.

> **Thought 1.** Note a striking truth: not only is man lost, but God has lost man and man has lost God. Both lose out and suffer when man chooses to wander out into the wilderness of the world and sin. Man has so much to gain from following God (Jn.5:24; Ga.5:22-23), and God has so much to gain by man's choosing to follow God (worship and service eternally).

MATTHEW 18:11-14

2 (18:12) **Jesus Christ, Seeking—Shepherd**: Jesus seeks every single sheep that is lost. Christ made three significant points.
  a. The sheep went astray (see DEEPER STUDY # 1—Mt.18:12).
  b. The sheep was sought by the shepherd. Note several facts.
  1) The Shepherd takes care of the whole flock, the ninety-nine, in a very special way. While seeking the lost sheep, He leads the flock *into the mountains or hills* where the pasture is thick with grass and safe and secure. He makes sure that they are secure (Jn.10:27-29).
  2) The Shepherd's concern is for the individual, no matter how large the flock. He loves the individual. He is unwilling to lose a single one.
  3) The Shepherd is the One who does the seeking. He does not hire or send another person after the lost sheep. Neither does He wait for the sheep to return, and most interesting, He does not even allow the care of the ninety-nine to keep Him from going after the one lost sheep. The fact that the sheep is lost is so important a matter to Him that He personally goes after the sheep—no matter the cost.
  4) The Shepherd is patient and enduring. He seeks and seeks after the sheep until He has either found it or else He knows there is no hope of the sheep's being alive.
  5) The Shepherd seeks every path, ridge, and crevice; He uses every means at His disposal to find the lost sheep.
  ⇒ The Shepherd depends upon the hardness, danger, trials, and sufferings of the wilderness and the heart, conscience, and memory of the sheep to turn it around and begin seeking a way out.
  ⇒ The Shepherd depends upon his own knowledge of the sheep and wilderness to search for the sheep. The Shepherd knows every ridge and crevice of the wilderness. It is just a question of finding the sheep soon enough. Has the lost sheep gone too far out on a ridge, too far down into a crevice to be found? Has the lost sheep already been killed by enemies or the roughness of the wilderness?
  ⇒ The Shepherd depends rather heavily upon His voice to reach the ears and the heart of the lost sheep. By calling and calling, He hopes the lost sheep will hear Him. Whether He hears or not depends upon two things. (1) How far out into the wilderness the lost sheep has wandered? Can the sheep hear the voice of the Shepherd? (2) Does the sheep still have strength enough to answer (respond) even if he hears the voice of the Shepherd? Is the sheep so drained and sapped by the wilderness that he cannot answer? Or is the sheep injured or dying, unable to answer the call of the Shepherd?

> "How think ye? if a man have an hundred sheep, and one of them be gone astray, doth he not leave the ninety and nine, and goeth into the mountains, and seeketh that which is gone astray?" (Mt.18:12).
> "For the Son of man is come to seek and to save that which was lost" (Lu.19:10).
> "Jesus heard that they had cast him out; and when he had found him, he said unto him, Dost thou believe on the Son of God?" (Jn.9:35).

  c. The sheep was sought in the mountains (see note 3—Lu.15:4 for the reasons a sheep goes astray. The reasons are simply stated here.)
  ⇒ The sheep is attracted by something "out in the wilderness" away from the flock and shepherd.
  ⇒ The sheep is aimless, not paying attention to what is going on.
  ⇒ The sheep refuses to heed the shepherd's warnings and the other sheep's example.
  ⇒ The sheep is not attached enough to the shepherd or to the other sheep.

Thought 1. The Shepherd knew "the lost sheep." He had a large flock to tend, but He knew every single one. When "the lost sheep" got lost, the Shepherd knew it. He missed the sheep, and He went after it.

Thought 2. When a child is lost, a family stops everything to seek for the lost child. It does not matter how large the family is, the child is sought.

DEEPER STUDY # 1
(18:12) **World—Wilderness**: see note 4—Lu.15:4 for a picture of the wilderness.

---

3 (18:13) **Lost—Unsaved**: Jesus may or may not find the lost sheep. Finding the sheep is not a sure thing. It depends on so much...
  • How far astray has the lost sheep wandered? Can the lost sheep hear the voice of the Shepherd? Or is it too far off?
  • Is the lost sheep willing to respond when it hears the Shepherd's voice?
  • Is the lost sheep *going on and on*, farther and farther into the wilderness?
  • Has the lost sheep been so careless and unconcerned that it has been injured by falling into a deep crevice?
  • Is the mind of the lost sheep so numb that it is unconscious of the Shepherd's presence and voice?
  • Is the lost sheep aware that it is lost? If so, how concerned is it over being lost?
  • Is the lost sheep concerned enough to begin searching for a way out of the wilderness?
  • Has the patience of the Shepherd ended? Has he given up? Has so much time passed that He knows there is no longer any hope?

MATTHEW 18:11-14

Thought 1. A person may resist the spirit of God so long and wander so far into the wilderness of the world that he can never be found (see thought 1—Mt.12:14-16).

"And the Lord said, My spirit shall not always strive with man" (Ge.6:3).
"He, that being often reproved hardeneth his neck, shall suddenly be destroyed, and that without remedy" (Pr.29:1).

4 (18:13) **Joy—Salvation**: Jesus forgives and rejoices over the recovered sheep. The extreme joy is not because the lost sheep means more than the other sheep. The safe sheep have always filled the Shepherd with joy and peace, but there is a special moment of joy and celebration when a lost sheep is found. There are at least two reasons for this.
   a. The lost sheep was almost *lost forever*, never to be known again or to share in and contribute to the life of the flock. All that the lost sheep meant and was capable of contributing was almost lost forever. There is bound to be great joy and glory over his being snatched out of the claws of danger and death.
   b. The lost sheep cost so much of the Shepherd's life: His thoughts, energy, effort, time, and sufferings. There is great joy and glory when the trial is over and the task is successful. The effort was well worth the price.
   Note the great appeal to the lost sheep to return to the Shepherd. There is...

- no grudging
- no contempt
- no lecture
- no rebuke
- no threat
- no punishment
- only love
- only concern
- only seeking

"And when he cometh home, he calleth together his friends and neighbours, saying unto them, Rejoice with me; for I have found my sheep which was lost. I say unto you, that likewise joy shall be in heaven over one sinner that repenteth, more than over ninety and nine just persons, which need no repentance" (Lu.15:6-7).
"And he that reapeth receiveth wages, and gathereth fruit unto life eternal: that both he that soweth and he that reapeth may rejoice together" (Jn.4:36).
"For what is our hope, or joy, or crown of rejoicing? Are not even ye in the presence of our Lord Jesus Christ at his coming? For ye are our glory and joy" (1 Th.2:19-20).
"Looking unto Jesus the author and finisher of our faith; who for the joy that was set before him endured the cross, despising the shame, and is set down at the right hand of the throne of God" (He.12:2).
"He that goeth forth and weepeth, bearing precious seed, shall doubtless come again with rejoicing, bringing his sheaves with him" (Ps.126:6).

5 (18:14) **God, Will of—Salvation**: God wills that not a single sheep should perish. In verse ten Jesus had said "My Father," but here He switched to "your Father." This is significant: when the Savior *finds* each of us, we become a member of *our Father's* family. As a member, He expects our help in reaching the lost sheep and in caring for the flock. Being a member of the family carries with it the responsibilities of reaching the lost and of helping to care for the other members of the family.
   Note two things.
   a. The Father is not willing that any should perish.

"Who will have all men to be saved, and to come unto the knowledge of the truth" (1 Ti.2:4).
"The Lord is not slack concerning his promise, as some men count slackness; but is longsuffering to us-ward, not willing that any should perish, but that all should come to repentance" (2 Pe.3:9).

   b. Christ died for the weak brother as well as for the lost.

"But if thy brother be grieved with thy meat, now walkest thou not charitably. Destroy not him with thy meat, for whom Christ died" (Ro.14:15).
"And through thy knowledge shall the weak brother perish, for whom Christ died?" (1 Co.8:11).

Thought 1. This is critical: God cares for every single person. What a contrast with our lack of concern when just one or two wander off. What a lesson for us! The concern of God for a single soul!

MATTHEW 18:15-20

	D. The Steps to Correcting Offending Brothers, 18:15-20 (Lu 17:3-4)	church: but if he neglect to hear the church, let him be unto thee as an heathen man and a publican. 18 Verily I say unto you, Whatsoever ye shall bind on earth shall be bound in heaven: and whatsoever ye shall loose on earth shall be loosed in heaven. 19 Again I say unto you, That if two of you shall agree on earth as touching any thing that they shall ask, it shall be done for them of my Father which is in heaven. 20 For where two or three are gathered together in my name, there am I in the midst of them.	brother^{DS2} a. The earthly discipline: Expel him
1. Step 1: Attempt reconciliation^{DS1} a. Go to the brother alone	15 Moreover if thy brother shall trespass against thee, go and tell him his fault between thee and him alone: if he shall hear thee, thou hast gained thy brother.		b. The heavenly support of God in clearing or in correcting a brother
b. Go to the brother with witnesses	16 But if he will not hear *thee, then* take with thee one or two more, that in the mouth of two or three witnesses every word may be established.		3. Step 3: The essential step— bathe the matter in prayer^{DS3} a. Seeking agreement b. Seeking God's will & approval
c. Go before the church	17 And if he shall neglect to hear them, tell *it* unto the		c. Seeking unity in God's name
2. Step 2: Discipline the			d. Result: God's presence

DIVISION XII

THE MESSIAH'S DISCIPLES AND THEIR BEHAVIOR TOWARD ONE ANOTHER, 18:1-35

D. The Steps to Correcting Offending Brothers, 18:15-20

(18:15-20) **Introduction—Division—Church Discipline**: sinning against a brother is a matter of great concern to God. It is so serious that if the offending brother refuses to rectify the matter, he is to be severely disciplined (v.17). However, when dealing with discipline, two critical points are to be noted.

1. The sinning brother *is a brother*, a *genuine* believer. He sins against another brother. The breach is between two genuine believers who are *in the church*.
2. The trespass is a personal offense; that is, the wrong and harm are done against another person. A fellow Christian believer is injured, hurt, and damaged in some way.

God has one great concern: He wants peace restored. He wants peace between the brothers, and He wants peace within the church. The disturbance caused by two offending brothers is so damaging that God lays down very specific steps as to how the matter is to be handled; and if the sinning brother refuses to be reconciled and to rectify the wrong, God says the disturbance is not to be tolerated any longer.

1. Step 1: attempt reconciliation (vv.15-16).
2. Step 2: discipline the brother (vv.17-18).
3. Step 3: the essential step—bathe the matter in prayer (vv.19-20).

1 (18:15-16) **Believers, Sin Against—Reconciliation**: the first step in correcting an offending brother is to attempt reconciliation (see DEEPER STUDY # 1—Mt.18:15). Note when a brother disturbs or offends us, we do not wait on the *offending brother* to come to us. We are to go immediately to him. There are three specific steps to be taken.

a. Go to the brother alone and "tell him his fault." This seems to indicate that he may not know that he has done wrong and offended us. If we do not go to him, he may never know or be able to correct his behavior. If he does know he has offended us and we do not approach him, then the breach remains, and the guilt of the sin continues. The division and damaging effects of the division can only grow and deepen.

Something else can happen: our own heart and mind can brood, be poisoned, become resentful, even bitter and grudging and revengeful. We desperately need to do all we can to resolve the matter.

1) He is to be approached alone. We are not to share the matter with anyone else, nor are we to openly rebuke him. This only deepens and hardens the feelings and division, causing bitterness and hostility.
2) The words "between thee and him alone" hint at how he is to be approached:
   ⇒ humbly; searching our own hearts (to see if we did anything to cause the offending behavior—knowing that we too can offend others ever so easily).
   ⇒ being soft spoken and gentle.
   ⇒ expressing our desire for understanding and straightening out the matter so that we may be reconciled.

> "Leave there thy gift before the altar, and go thy way; first be reconciled to thy brother, and then come and offer thy gift" (Mt.5:24).
> "Let nothing be done through strife or vainglory; but in lowliness of mind let each esteem other better than themselves" (Ph.2:3).
> "Of these things put them in remembrance, charging them before the Lord that they strive not about words to no profit, but to the subverting of the hearers" (2 Ti.2:14).
> "And the servant of the Lord must not strive; but be gentle unto all men, apt to teach, patient" (2 Ti.2:24).

MATTHEW 18:15-20

Thought 1. When a brother offends us, our response becomes critical to Christ. There are four responses common to human flesh that we are to guard against with all diligence.
(1) *A self-centered response*: acting babyish, innocent, or as a martyr; brooding, hatching, and pondering the evil and hurt done to us; being consumed with the wrong done; keeping our minds on the personal injury until the whole divisive affair poisons our hearts and minds. Remember: this is common to human flesh, a tendency among us all.
(2) *A withdrawing response*: avoiding the brother; being apprehensive, perhaps even fearing to face or associate with him; showing displeasure or getting back at him by ignoring or neglecting him.
(3) *A gossiping response*: a self-justifying sharing; a self-vindicating sharing; a tendency to share hurt and evil and wrong done, to share with close friends in order to picture ourselves as blameless. The problem with sharing the division with others is that Christ says we are to go to the person first. Then if he does not respond to our appeal, we are to seek loving and wise counsel.
(4) *A retaliating response*: becoming embroiled in the divisiveness and wrongdoing ourselves; reacting and lowering ourselves to the level of the wrongdoer; getting back at the wrongdoer.

Thought 2. When a brother offends us, the most important response (after prayer, of course) is to go to the brother alone. There is great wisdom in this instruction, wisdom that teaches both brothers to subject the flesh and to give prominence to the spirit.
(1) Wisdom for the *offended brother*. Human nature tends to react, brood, share the evil, and seek retaliation—whether simply withdrawing or attacking. Christ demands that we conquer the urges of the flesh to react and that we control the situation through the Spirit. We are to keep quiet and pray. Then we are to go to the brother and discuss the matter, seeking reconciliation. Simply put, we are to be spiritually minded.
(2) Wisdom for the *offending brother*. Human nature avoids and is slow in admitting wrong. A humble, loving, and caring visit to seek reconciliation is *an encouragement* for a brother to confess, apologize, and be reconciled.

Thought 3. Note just how wise the Lord's instruction really is. Just think what enormous lessons and qualities are learned and developed by three brothers' sitting down to seek reconciliation—the very qualities of the Spirit's fruit...
- love
- joy
- peace
- long-suffering
- gentleness
- goodness
- faith
- meekness
- self-control

Thought 4. Think what a different world this would be if this step alone was practiced by all: the difference in human relationships personally, nationally, and internationally; the difference in health emotionally and physically (ulcers, blood pressure, heart attacks, etc.).

b. Go to the brother with witnesses. Some Christian brothers are stubborn; others are immature; still others are gripped by selfish and sinful motives and behavior. Therefore an offending brother may not be willing to be reconciled nor willing to admit his wrong. In such cases, one or two loving and wise brothers are to be taken with us to the offending brother. This act does several things.
1) It shows the brother that there is deep concern; a number of people do care and want to help.
2) It also shows that the offense is known by more than one or two people. At least several know.
3) It also provides objective and wise counsel between the two differing parties. Agreement and reconciliation are more likely to arise from this.
4) It helps to prevent bias, selfish reaction, and partial interest.

Thought 1. This step should never be taken until the brother has been approached alone. We are not to talk about or share a brother's wrong with anyone else—not ever—not until we have sat down with him personally in the love of Christ.
However, this step *is* to be taken if he persists in his divisiveness. But it is always to be done in a spirit of humility, love, care, and personal unworthiness.

Thought 2. There is sometimes a tendency to give up after a divisive brother refuses reconciliation—to let him suffer whatever punishment follows. However, Christ says, "Keep on; stay after him. Don't give up." Note: this is the demand of Christ throughout the whole course of discipline. Christ never gives up reaching out to the sinning brother. Therefore, the church is never to give up (see Deeper Study # 2—Mt.18:17). The divisiveness of the Galatian church and its personal attack upon Paul are prime examples of this fact. Paul was constantly reaching out to those who were so imperfect and ever failing (see Gal.4:19f).

c. Go before the church (see Deeper Study # 2—Mt.18:17 for discussion).

DEEPER STUDY # 1
(18:15) **Believers, Sin Against—Reconciliation**: how does a Christian brother trespass or offend another brother? There are many ways.
1. By his behavior and Christian liberty: doing that which is allowed but is offensive and misunderstood by a weaker brother. (See Ro.14:1-23; 1 Co.8:12.)
⇒ offending his conscience
⇒ grieving his spirit
⇒ being a stumbling block
⇒ being a bad example

MATTHEW 18:15-20

> 2. By confronting him face to face.
>   - ⇒ insulting
>   - ⇒ abusing
>   - ⇒ humiliating
>   - ⇒ degrading
>   - ⇒ arguing
>   - ⇒ showing disrespect
>   - ⇒ showing bitterness
>   - ⇒ being angry
>   - ⇒ being hostile
>
> 3. By tearing him down behind his back.
>   - ⇒ talking about
>   - ⇒ lying
>   - ⇒ gossiping
>   - ⇒ murmuring
>   - ⇒ criticizing
>   - ⇒ spreading rumors
>
> 4. By encroaching on his rights or property.
>   - ⇒ deceiving
>   - ⇒ cheating
>   - ⇒ stealing
>   - ⇒ lying
>   - ⇒ envying
>   - ⇒ bypassing

2 (18:17-18) **Church Discipline**: the second step in correcting an offending brother is to discipline the brother. Christ discusses two points in dealing with the actual disciplining of an offending brother.

a. The earthly discipline. If the offending brother refuses to be reconciled after the appeal by two or three believers, then the matter is to be carried to the church. Why would Christ say that personal offenses are to be taken before the church and made public?

1) The offending brother has already refused two humble and loving appeals: the first appeal of the offended person, and the second appeal by one or two loving and wise witnesses.

2) The offending brother's refusal to be reconciled is a serious threat and danger. If the breach continues unresolved, it will cause more division and harm both within and without the church. Other lives will be seriously affected, both among the saved and the lost. The testimony of the church and of those involved in the division will be weakened, and the interest of the almost saved will be soured and dampened, perhaps extinguished. The tongues of the carnal believers and of the lost will be set aflame. A brother who trespasses against another brother and causes division within the church (and who refuses to be reconciled) commits a serious offense that affects many lives. Because of this, the matter has to be dealt with step by step. It cannot be ignored and left unresolved.

Taking a person's behavior before the church, whether the church as a whole or some official committee of the church, is a very serious matter. It is as serious a matter as can be imagined. But what Christ is after must be kept in mind: Christ wants to keep the sin, division, and devastation from spreading and destroying the lives and testimonies of others.

3) Christ wants the two brothers to be reconciled with each other and with God, and He wants the offending brother to be restored into the care and fellowship of the church.

4) Christ wants to keep the sin, division, and devastation from spreading and destroying the interest of the *nearly saved*, perhaps causing them to be lost forever.

5) Christ wants to prevent giving the world a reason for setting their tongues on fire and spreading rumors that damage the image and work of His church.

6) Christ wants the two brothers and their close friends and fellow church members to build a strong witness, not a divisive witness. He is not willing for a single person to perish. He wants the world saved, every person in the world (2 Pe.3:9), and two things are essential for a church to reach the maximum number of people which it should be reaching:
   ⇒ Love—brother loving brother in the Lord (Jn.13:33-34).
   ⇒ A strong witness and testimony by the brothers of the church.

7) Christ wants differences and divisiveness settled among His people and not by the world's legal system of carnal or godless philosophies and arguments. The atmosphere of law settles nothing; it only produces more trouble and deeper feelings and rifts. Among God's people, disputed relationships and differences are to be settled between the two involved persons *alone*. If that fails, then one or two loving and wise persons are to be called in. Then and only then, if these fail to settle the matter, is the matter to be taken before a number of official representatives from the church. This procedure is clearly the wish of our Lord (Mt.18:15-17. See outline and notes—1 Co.6:1-8.)

8) Christ wants every member to work and build, not destroy the church. The church exists for worship, fellowship, ministry, and witness. Harmony, peace, love, and purpose build the church; sin and divisiveness destroy the church. For this reason alone, divisiveness must not be allowed to prevail within the church. It has to be dealt with if the church is to remain the church and be the Lord's.

What is said above bears repeating. Taking a person's behavior before the church is a very serious matter. It is as serious a matter as can be imagined. Several facts make it extremely serious.

a. A person's life is involved. The person can be damaged, turned off and pushed away from the Lord and God's people forever.

b. Public discussion of personal behavior is a very, very sensitive subject. It can easily arouse emotions and cause more division. It can even turn some of the spiritually minded away from the church.

c. Personal behavior and *juicy news* are what the carnal nature of man enjoys discussing. It is the subject of which rumors are made. It sets aflame the tongues and imaginations of most people. Few are spiritually free of the urge to talk about the faults and rumors surrounding others. The very nature of man enjoys knowing and sharing the faults of others with close friends. Why? It is the downing of others that elevates self and gives some justification (excuse) to sinful behavior and flesh-feeding habits. And most follow and revel in sinful flesh, not in God's Spirit. This is true even among many professing believers.

MATTHEW 18:15-20

  d. Few can keep confidences. Few can keep quiet. Even the most trusted and loving and wise do not keep confidences. A person who will keep confidences is more rare than a precious gem that takes many lifetimes to discover. Therefore, when a matter is shared, it must always be remembered and understood that it will be spread around. What will the effects be as it spreads around? The effects must always be measured as one considers sharing personal behavior and differences with others, whether with just another individual, or with the church as a whole.
  e. The world—both the public and the lost within and without the local community—will hear about personal behavior being carried before the church. Again, the effect upon the world's thoughts, talk, attitudes, and openness of heart to the gospel must be carefully considered before rushing before the church with matters that concern personal behavior.

Now, when should a personal matter and difference be taken before the church? (Perhaps a more appropriate question would be, when should a personal matter concerning a brother ever be discussed with another individual?)
  a. When we are *absolutely sure* that God does not want us to continue bearing the hurt and injury any longer as a learning experience. When we are absolutely sure there is no more need for us to be...
  - learning more trust
  - learning more patience
  - learning more endurance
  - learning more humility
  - learning more love
  - learning more experience
  - learning more hope
  - learning more conformity to His image (or suffering)
  - learning more glory
  b. When we are *absolutely sure* that the Lord's Spirit is leading us to share the matter of personal behavior.
  c. When we are *ready to acknowledge* our own failures and sinfulness and potential for failing (Ro.14:4; 1 Co.10:12).
  d. When we are gripped by a spirit of prayer, softness, tenderness, warmth, love, and humility.
  e. When we are gripped by the spirit of "bearing one another's burdens" (Ga.6:1-3).
  f. When we are *absolutely sure* that we have followed the steps spelled out by Christ (Mt.18:15-17).

  b. The heavenly support of the discipline. Note that heaven's discipline of the divisive brother is the same as the earthly or church discipline. What does this mean? One thing is sure—it cannot mean that any man or any church has the power to forgive or not forgive sins. No man or church has the power to doom or save and set free a person.
  What it probably means is this: when a brother chooses sin and refuses to be reconciled after the church reaches and reaches out after him, he is lost to the church. There is no relationship between him and the church. The church failed to reach him; therefore he is *bound to the earth* and to being treated as an outsider. Thus heaven—God Himself—will reckon him to be bound by sin as an outsider just as the church binds (reckons) him. Similarly, if he is ever reached by the church and "loosed" from the bondage of sin, heaven will reckon him loosed. God will receive him back as a redeemed brother, as an insider.

   Thought 1. In the final analysis, divisiveness and those who cause divisiveness have to be confronted and handled. "A house divided against itself cannot stand" (Mt.12:25).
   Christ insists that a divisive brother be disciplined and treated as an outsider. (But we must *always* remember: this action is to be taken only after reconciliation has been attempted at least three times.) Why must divisiveness and the brother who caused the divisiveness be handled?
   (1) Divisiveness threatens survival. A body, an organization, even the church itself can stand only if it is unified and functioning in peace and harmony.
   (2) Divisiveness threatens purity and character. The church is seen as corrupt and weak if such things as divisiveness and grumbling are allowed.
   (3) Divisiveness threatens order and mission and ministry. Divisiveness can threaten and cause failure of any purpose, mission, or ministry. Disorder assures defeat and failure.

   Thought 2. This passage is a wonderful thing: Christ Himself, our wonderful Lord, has given us the very procedure (steps) to take in dealing with divisive brothers. How much we need to follow His instructions!

   Thought 3. Discipline of a divisive brother is necessary in order to preserve the church and all that it stands for.

DEEPER STUDY # 2
(18:17) **Discipline, Church**: the outlines and preceding notes of this Scripture should be read before reading this note in order to have a complete picture (Mt.18:15-20).
  A brother who has a personal quarrel with another brother is to be disciplined if three things exist.
  ⇒ If he continues in open rebellion against the Lord.
  ⇒ If he continues to be gripped by the selfishness, covetousness, and worldliness of this earth.
  ⇒ If he refuses reconciliation with his brother after three attempts at reconciliation have been made as spelled out by Christ.

  What is the discipline? The divisive brother is to be treated just as he is acting: as an outsider—just as a heathen and a publican. The heathen or sinners and publicans were the very people for whom Christ reached out. They were outside the fold, but they were reachable. The divisive brother is acting as an outsider: he will not listen and respond to the humble and loving appeals for reconciliation. Therefore, he is to be left alone and not bothered until he is ready to listen and be reconciled. He is refusing reconciliation and living as an outsider, just as the lost live. Accordingly, the church can do nothing but treat him as an outsider.

MATTHEW 18:15-20

> 1. The offending brother himself made the choice not to be reconciled. He stood at the crossroads of reconciliation on three specific occasions. He is personally responsible for his decision.
> 2. The church reached and reached out for the dear brother. It made every attempt to lead the brother to stop the divisiveness and to be reconciled.
> 3. The life the brother has chosen to live is his discipline. It is his decision to be an outsider instead of being reconciled to his brother and his church. It is his decision to live in the world of "sinners and publicans" instead of living in the presence and reconciliation of God's people.
> 4. The discipline of the brother is a discipline which allows the church to continue to reach out for the backslidden brother. *Sinners and publicans* are the very people to whom Christ went and to whom the church is to go. The discipline of the brother is: "Let him be unto thee as a heathen and a publican." Apparently Christ is saying this: the church is to continue seeking after him *as it deems wise*, just as they seek after all outsiders. Realistically, however, the attempts at future reconciliation would probably be much less often. The dear brother's heart will have fewer opportunities to be stirred by those who love and care for him so deeply.
>
> "And whosoever shall offend one of these little ones that believe in me, it is better for him that a millstone were hanged about his neck, and he were cast into the sea" (Mk.9:42).
> "Let us not therefore judge one another any more: but judge this rather, that no man put a stumbling block or an occasion to fall in his brother's way" (Ro.14:13).
> "But if thy brother be grieved with thy meat, now walkest thou not charitably. Destroy not him with thy meat, for whom Christ died" (Ro.14:15).
> "It is good neither to eat flesh, nor to drink wine, nor any thing whereby thy brother stumbleth, or is offended, or is made weak" (Ro.14:21).
> "Giving no offence in any thing" (2 Co.6:3).
> "He that loveth his brother abideth in the light, and there is none occasion of stumbling in him" (1 Jn.2:10).

3 (18:19-20) **Prayer**: the third step in correcting an offending brother is the essential step—to bathe the matter in prayer. The words, "Again, I say unto you," stress the importance of this step. The matter must be *bathed in prayer*, but how we go about praying is critical.

a. We must seek agreement about the matter of correcting a brother (v.19). The matter of correction is an awesome responsibility. It is not to be left in the hands of a single person. There are always to be at least two persons involved.

b. We must seek God's will and approval, making sure correction is His will (v.19). No correction should ever be attempted that is not God's will and is not according to the explicit statement of His Word. Any correction of an offending brother must demonstrate God's love, compassion, and mercy.

c. We must seek unity "in Jesus' name," not just human agreement, not just following human thoughts and rules governing discipline. The unity must be "in His name," brought about by His Spirit and in accordance with the whole counsel of God's Word (not just a section taken out of context or interpreted without considering all of God's teaching about a matter) (v.19).

If these steps are truly pursued, the Lord promises His presence in the decision made and in the correction of an offending brother.

> "Ask, and it shall be given you; seek, and ye shall find; knock, and it shall be opened unto you" (Mt.7:7).
> "And all things, whatsoever ye shall ask in prayer, believing, ye shall receive" (Mt.21:22).
> "Praying always with all prayer and supplication in the Spirit, and watching thereunto with all perseverance and supplication for all saints" (Ep.6:18).
> "Seek the LORD and his strength, seek his face continually" (1 Chr.16:11).

DEEPER STUDY # 3

(18:19-20) **Prayer**: this passage shows us the power of united prayer—even if the number praying is only two persons.
1. Christ says, "Anything that they shall ask, it shall be done for them" (v.19).
2. Christ also says, "There am I in the midst of them" (v.20). Note: Christ did not say, "I will be there." He is already there. This is a very special presence, the real, actual presence of Christ. It is equivalent to the Shekinah glory, the very special presence of God that dwelt in the tabernacle and temple. It is a deep sense, a consciousness, an intense awareness of God's Spirit communing with our spirit. God manifests His presence in a very special way to the believer (see note—Jn.14:21-22; 2 Co.3:17-18).

However, two things are absolutely essential to experience the power of united prayer.
1. "If two of you *shall agree* [sumphonesosin]": the words *shall agree* mean to be in complete accord; to harmonize together like that of a symphony; to sound together; to act together in each other's nature. It is the very opposite of wandering thoughts, half-hearted commitment, disconnected purpose, disjointed and misplaced understanding, unsynchronized spirits, and incomplete and piecemeal knowledge.
2. If "two or three are gathered together *in my name* [eis to emon unoma]": literally this says "into my name." The idea is close and intimate union with Christ. It is a "getting into" the Spirit of Christ; a longing to be in union with Him and to act only for His glory. It is a depth of *spiritual union* demonstrated by so few. Note: it comes not only from private prayer but from prayer with others.

This says something of critical importance. We should never attempt to correct a brother unless we first have a deep spiritual union with Christ—a union so deep that we can act only for His glory. We must be free of all fleshly urges to *get at a brother*. We must act only for God's glory.

MATTHEW 18:21-35

	E. The Parable of the Unmerciful Servant: The Spirit of Forgiveness, 18:21-35		unforgiveness

1. **The spirit & practice of forgiveness**
a. Peter asked about forgiving a brother: Is forgiveness limited?
b. Jesus answered: Forgiveness is unlimited^{DS1}
c. Jesus illustrated: Is like the Kingdom of Heaven
2. **The spirit of God's forgiveness: Like a king who settles his accounts with his servants**
a. All must give account
b. One was brought to him
c. The servant owed a huge debt
d. The servant was bankrupt
  1) He was to be sold
  2) He was to lose all
e. The servant faced him
f. The servant cried for mercy
  1) Worshipped the king
  2) Made a commitment
g. The servant experienced the compassion of a loving king: Was freed & forgiven
3. **The servant's spirit of**
	21 Then came Peter to him, and said, Lord, how oft shall my brother sin against me, and I forgive him? till seven times?
	22 Jesus saith unto him, I say not unto thee, Until seven times: but, Until seventy times seven.
	23 Therefore is the kingdom of heaven likened unto a certain king, which would take account of his servants.
	24 And when he had begun to reckon, one was brought unto him, which owed him ten thousand talents.
	25 But forasmuch as he had not to pay, his lord commanded him to be sold, and his wife, and children, and all that he had, and payment to be made.
	26 The servant therefore fell down, and worshipped him, saying, Lord, have patience with me, and I will pay thee all.
	27 Then the lord of that servant was moved with compassion, and loosed him, and forgave him the debt.
	28 But the same servant
		went out, and found one of his fellowservants, which owed him an hundred pence: and he laid hands on him, and took *him* by the throat, saying, Pay me that thou owest.
		29 And his fellowservant fell down at his feet, and besought him, saying, Have patience with me, and I will pay thee all.
		30 And he would not: but went and cast him into prison, till he should pay the debt.
		31 So when his fellowservants saw what was done, they were very sorry, and came and told unto their lord all that was done.
		32 Then his lord, after that he had called him, said unto him, O thou wicked servant, I forgave thee all that debt, because thou desiredst me:
		33 Shouldest not thou also have had compassion on thy fellowservant, even as I had pity on thee?
		34 And his lord was wroth, and delivered him to the tormentors, till he should pay all that was due unto him.
		35 So likewise shall my heavenly Father do also unto you, if ye from your hearts forgive not every one his brother their trespasses.
			a. He faced a fellow servant who owed him: In comparison, a very small sum
			b. He reacted severely
			c. He heard his servant's cry for mercy: Rejected the cry & refused to forgive
			d. He acted materialistically & selfishly–according to law & justice
			e. He grieved the other servants: They carried the matter to their Lord
			4. **The great day of accounting**
			a. Two bases of judgment
			  1) God's forgiveness: Offered in Christ
			  2) The servant's wickedness: He lacked compassion & mercy
			b. The judgment
			  1) The Lord's anger
			  2) The Lord's justice: The man was condemned & punished
			5. **The point: An unforgiving person will be judged**

DIVISION XII

THE MESSIAH'S DISCIPLES AND THEIR BEHAVIOR TOWARD ONE ANOTHER, 18:1-35

E. The Parable of the Unmerciful Servant: The Spirit of Forgiveness, 18:21-35

(18:21-35) **Introduction**: How often are we to forgive a person? Does God expect us to forgive and forgive—no matter the abuse and number of times the wrong is done? Christ answered these and many other questions in this discussion.
1. The spirit and practice of forgiveness (v.21-22).
2. The spirit of God's forgiveness: like a king who settles his accounts with his servants (vv.23-27).
3. The servant's spirit of unforgiveness (vv.28-31).
4. The great day of accounting (vv.32-34).
5. The point: an unforgiving person will be judged (v.35).

1 (18:21-22) **Forgiveness**: there is the spirit and practice of forgiveness. Note exactly what happened between Peter and Jesus.
   a. Peter asked about forgiving a brother. Is forgiveness limited? Peter's concern was forgiving another Christian brother, a fellow disciple (see notes—Mt.18:5-10; 18:5). Christ also placed the discussion in the context of "the kingdom of heaven," that is, the Christian community or church (see DEEPER STUDY #3—Mt.19:23-24). Peter was very generous in his concept of forgiveness. To forgive a person seven times for having wronged oneself is very generous, far more generous than what most do.
   b. Jesus answered that forgiveness is unlimited (see DEEPER STUDY #1—Mt.18:22).
   c. Jesus illustrated the spirit of forgiveness by referring to the kingdom of heaven. The kingdom of heaven in its present form includes some people who are servants of God, but they are servants in profession only. The servant in this parable professes faith in God, but his profession is false. He is in the church walking among God's people. In a desperate moment of dire need, God has met him and offered mercy and forgiveness, but he has not personally learned anything about God's compassion and forgiveness (see note—Mt.18:35).

MATTHEW 18:21-35

> **DEEPER STUDY # 1**
>
> **(18:22) Forgiveness—Relationship—Brotherhood—Unity:** seventy times seven is four hundred and ninety, but this is not the point Jesus is making. The question is how often should we forgive a brother?
> ⇒ Peter: "Till seven times?"
> ⇒ Jesus: "No. Until seventy times seven."
>
> What Jesus meant is seventy times seven, times seventy times seven—and on and on through eternity. Forgiveness is a matter of the heart, not of the mind. The mind will only keep a record of wrongs. A spirit of forgiveness does not measure and limit the number of times it will forgive. A spirit of forgiveness will tolerate being wronged and hurt time after time. Why?
>
> There are several reasons why the spirit of forgiveness knows no limit, no measure, no number of times that it will forgive.
>
> 1. Forgiveness is a thing of the spirit, a quality of the spirit. All spiritual things, substances and realities—such as love, mercy, grace, joy, forgiveness—cannot be measured or limited. They are by their very nature spiritual and not physical. Therefore, they are without measure or limit, so they are to be known and practiced without limit or measure. We are to experience and practice love at every opportunity. We are to experience and practice forgiveness at every opportunity. Forgiveness is a reality of the spirit; therefore it is to be a spirit of life. The spirit of forgiveness is to forgive seventy times seven—*ad infinitum*.
>
> 2. Good human relationships are impossible without a forgiving spirit. Offending others is common to us all. We are all sinful and we all offend—much too often. None of us walks perfectly or anywhere close to what he should. If we kept score, there would be little time to do anything else. To keep relationships healthy, we need to know at least four things.
>
>   a. Coming short and sinning, failing and offending are common to us all. We all offend by failing...
>   - to smile
>   - to greet
>   - to speak
>   - to love
>   - be believe
>   - to recognize
>   - to acknowledge
>   - to word things properly
>   - to be gentle
>   - to be joyful
>   - to be good
>   - to be humble
>   - to be controlled
>   - to be generous
>   - to be pleasant
>   - to be calm
>   - to be long-suffering
>   - to be victorious
>
>   b. Offending others is usually unintentional and unknown. All of us offend others, but we are often unaware that we have offended them. The reasons we fail others are innumerable, but common causes are preoccupation of thought, heavy hearts and minds, and trials and problems that consume our thoughts. Keeping this in mind will help us to forgive others when they offend us.
>
>   c. We offend others as much as they offend us. We are as human as the next person, and we need forgiveness as much as the next person. Remembering this will do as much to maintain healthy relationships as any other single fact.
>
>   d. The common response to being offended is to react: react by withdrawing, taking vengeance, or wallowing around in self-pity and in a spirit of unforgiveness. Many revel in the attention secured by being the subject of abuse instead of handling the matter quietly in a true spirit of reconciliation.
>
> 3. An unforgiving spirit shows that a person is basically ill-natured, self-centered, and spiritually immature. Unforgiveness reveals that a person has not grown to be like Christ in his nature of understanding, compassion, and love. A forgiving spirit understands the nature of man (sinful and offending) and the nature of God (spiritual and forgiving, pt. 1 above).
>
> 4. Peace and health can be preserved only through a forgiving spirit. An unforgiving spirit causes as much disturbance and division as the offender. An unforgiving spirit has stooped to the level of the offender and has, in fact, become an offender. Think: as long as there is an unforgiving spirit, there can never be peace. Disturbance, conflict, and division prevail. An unforgiving spirit also affects a person's emotions and mind and body. It is the lack of peace, the lack of a good relationship with God and man, that disturbs the normal functioning of the body, mind, and emotions. Ulcers, high blood pressure, disturbed thoughts and emotions, and on and on—all can and often do come from an unforgiving spirit.
>
> **"And above all things have fervent charity among yourselves: for charity shall cover the multitude of sins" (1 Pe.4:8).**
>
> **"Peace I leave with you, my peace I give unto you: not as the world giveth, give I unto you. Let not your heart be troubled, neither let it be afraid" (Jn.14:27).**

2 **(18:23-27) Forgiveness:** there is God's spirit of forgiveness. He is just like a king who takes account of his servants.

The parable is simple, yet very descriptive and full of meaning. God is the King, but He is a very unusual King. He is a King who rules justly as all kings should. But He is more. He is loving, compassionate, and forgiving; and He is even more than these. He is consumed with love and compassion—so much so that He forgives enormous debts, debts so enormous that they are inconceivable.

The King takes account of His servants. He takes account at varying times. An accounting is required at conversion and on those occasions when God leads us to evaluate our lives. Note how the seven steps related by Christ can be applied to either of these times.

a. All must give an account (v.24). The word *reckon* (sunairein) means to take account; to make a reckoning; to settle accounts. This is the same word that is translated "take account" in v.24. The king began to check the province and the

MATTHEW 18:21-35

ledgers of his province: receipts and expenditures and the capital improvements. The king had a critical interest in what his servant had received through gifts and what he had used in the ministry.

b. We are all brought to the King by the Spirit, the Word, or some Christian witness (v.24).

c. We are all led to see our huge debt of sin and service that we owe God (v.24. See Ps.19:12; 40:12.) The debt of the servant was huge. It was millions of dollars. It was probably the gross revenues of a province or state in that day. The servant was the high official placed over the province who was held responsible for its administration. The point is that God has given us life and made us overseer of that life. To sin is to mismanage that life and to cause loss; therefore, sin puts us in debt to God. The debt is infinite, beyond anything we can ever pay.

d. We are all bankrupt (unable to pay) before God (v.25). Sin bankrupts man and puts him in debt to God. We are so bankrupt by sin that nothing can pay our debt.

⇒ Silver and gold, no amount of wealth, can pay our debt.
⇒ Neither a brother nor any other family member can pay our debt.

> "They that trust in their wealth, and boast themselves in the multitude of their riches; none of them can by any means redeem his brother, nor give to God a ransom for him" (Ps.49:6-7).

⇒ Good works cannot pay our debt.

> "Not by works of righteousness which we have done, but according to his mercy he saved us, by the washing of regeneration, and renewing of the Holy Ghost; which he shed on us abundantly through Jesus Christ our Saviour" (Tit.3:5-6).

⇒ Making sacrifice and giving offerings cannot pay our debt.

> "And Samuel said, Hath the LORD as great delight in burnt offerings and sacrifices, as in obeying the voice of the LORD? Behold, to obey is better than sacrifice, and to hearken than the fat of rams" (1 S.15:22).

Note that the man's debts affected his family. His enslavement and loss would have meant their enslavement and loss. A man's sins always affect both him and his family (see note—Ro.1:24; note and DEEPER STUDY # 1—Ep.1:7. See Ro.7:14-20.)

e. We face the justice of a just God (v.25).

f. We cry for mercy (v.26). Our only hope is that God loves us enough that He will simply forgive us in compassion and mercy.

> "But God, who is rich in mercy, for his great love wherewith he loved us, even when we were dead in sins, hath quickened us together with Christ, (by grace ye are saved)" (Ep.2:4-5).

g. We hear the love and forgiveness of a loving God (v.27).

Thought 1. Some of the things that bring us to God and cause us to evaluate and take account of our lives are trials, trouble, sickness, disease, a sermon or witness, tragedy, parents, friends, or special days or occasions (for example, the New Year).

Thought 2. Note that the false servant had not cried out for mercy until he was brought face to face with the king. We are often careless about sin until we are called to account. How fewer trials, sufferings, and temptations we would face if we turned from sin immediately.

3 (18:28-31) **Unforgiveness**: there was the servant's spirit of unforgiveness. The very steps taken by the servant are the steps involved in an unforgiving spirit.

a. He faced a person who owed him, that is, who *had offended* him in some way (v.28). In comparison, the debt or offense was very small. It was not a millionth of the debt owed by the unforgiving servant. The proportion was over 1 to 1,250,000—an enormous difference (A. Lukyn Williams. *St. Matthew*. "The Pulpit Commentary," Vol. 15, ed. by HDM Spense and Joseph S. Exell. Grand Rapids, MI: Eerdmans, 1950, p.215). This shows the enormous difference between our sin against a brother and our brother's sin against us. When we really see this, an unforgiving spirit toward a brother is inexcusable. We can forgive anything.

b. He reacted severely (v.28). He attacked the debtor; that is, he exercised his authority over the debtor and attempted to squeeze the payment out of him. He got angry and showed malice. There was no need for this kind of behavior; it was inexcusable. Remember the king's mercy to him. The king had not pressed charges against him; the king had even forgiven his debt. How we need to remember the love and forgiveness of God! God's love and forgiveness need to become the controlling factors of all our relationships.

c. He rejected the cry for mercy and refused to forgive (v.29).

d. He acted selfishly and worldly, according to law and justice (v.30). The man really owed the servant. The debt was a just and legal debt. The servant had every right to demand and force payment. Such was justice, but again, remember the point Christ was making. The King, God, does not act toward us legally, executing justice. He has compassion and mercy upon us and forgives us, wiping out all our debts.

The question is, how often should we forgive our brother? "Seventy times seven," Christ said. "Have compassion and mercy; do not demand justice. Do not execute the law against a man. Do not trample him underfoot. Do not act cruelly,

MATTHEW 18:21-35

swallowing him up and destroying his spirit. Love him and forgive him 'even as God for Christ's sake hath forgiven you'" (Ep.4:32).

Thought 1. Note what it is that made this servant go to law and demand justice: money. He was materialistic and worldly minded. The debt was owed, so it was a true debt. It was money that made him selfish. How often money, materialism, and worldliness destroy a person!

Thought 2. Note another point: he had just gone through a frightening experience himself—an experience that had carried him into the depths of insecurity. Such an experience was bound to affect him. He would thereafter want to make sure he had enough to care for himself and his family. Humanly speaking, he had every right to demand payment of those who owed him. No man would object to his demand in light of his experience. However, there was something objectionable, something missing in his heart and life. He was hard, not soft. He was exacting, not understanding. He was just, not compassionate. He was legal, not loving; He was the very opposite of God. God is loving, compassionate, merciful, and forgiving; and God expects His servants to be as He is.

e. He grieved others (v.31). Note the words "they were very sorry." God's true servants are always grieved to see people mistreated, abused, and trampled upon. Cruel and mean treatment always troubles God's people. Suffering, pain, hurt, and death cut the heart of God's people.
 1) They feel for the afflicted: their suffering, pain, and hurt.
 2) They feel for the just but sinful man: sinful in that he is unmerciful and uncompassionate. His strict justice causes more and more trouble and disturbance and oppression of people. God's people took the only recourse; they did the only thing they could. They took the matter to God. They could not remain silent and allow the license of oppression and legalism to destroy a human spirit.

4 (18:32-34) **Death—Judgment—Wickedness**: there was the great day of accounting. This is a day that lies out in the future for every man. It is both the summons of death and the summons to stand before God to be judged. It is the death and the day of judgment that every man must face (He.9:26).
 a. Note the two bases for judgment.
  1) The first basis of judgment is God's forgiveness. God's forgiveness is provided in Christ and is always available. Christ "is the propitiation for our sins: and not for ours only, but also for the sins of the whole world" (1 Jn.2:2).

> "God so loved the world, that he gave his only begotten Son, that whosoever believeth in him should not perish, but have everlasting life...He that believeth on him is not condemned: but he that believeth not is condemned already, because he hath not believed in the name of the only begotten Son of God" (Jn.3:16, 18).

  2) The second basis of judgment is man's wickedness. It is important to understand what wickedness and sin are. Wickedness and sin are primarily coming "short of God's glory," coming short of what God is. This is clearly illustrated by this wicked servant (church member). He was a just and lawful man. He was a high official in government and politics, serving directly under the king. He was well respected and honored, an outstanding citizen, but he was not like God. He was not compassionate and merciful, loving and forgiving in his dealings with others. There are two great commandments that a servant of the King must obey. This servant tried to obey the first one, "Thou shalt love the Lord thy God...."; but he ignored the second one, "Thou shalt love thy neighbor as thyself" (Mt.22:39).
   Very simply put, a wicked man is a man who does not honestly believe God nor diligently seek to live as God lives (He.11:6). He is a man who does not believe that God is, does not believe to the point that it changes his life. His life is not compassionate, merciful, and forgiving. Because of this, he shall face the judgment of the King and be condemned.

> "Or despisest thou the riches of his goodness and forbearance and longsuffering; not knowing that the goodness of God leadeth thee to repentance?" (Ro.2:4).

 b. Note the judgment and condemnation that man is to experience.
  1) Man shall experience the Lord's anger. Two things are extremely detestable to God and arouse His anger: not believing Him and not being compassionate and merciful nor loving and forgiving toward others.

> "For if we sin wilfully after that we have received the knowledge of the truth, there remaineth no more sacrifice for sins, but a certain fearful looking for of judgment and fiery indignation, which shall devour the adversaries" (He.10:26-27).
> "But the LORD is the true God, he is the living God, and an everlasting king: at his wrath the earth shall tremble, and the nations shall not be able to abide his indignation" (Je.10:10).

  2) Man shall experience justice. Note two critical things about the justice executed.
   a) The unmerciful servant received perfect justice. He received exactly what was due him. He had to *pay*; he was punished only for what he owed—no more, no less. He received the exact penalty, the exact punishment due him.

MATTHEW 18:21-35

    b) The King, God, was perfectly just. He merely executed perfect justice. He executed what the servant himself had chosen: due payment for due debt.

        "**Seeing it is a righteous thing with God to recompense tribulation to them that trouble you**" **(2 Th.1:6).**

        "**For if the word spoken by angels was stedfast, and every transgression and disobedience received a just recompence of reward; how shall we escape, if we neglect so great salvation; which at the first began to be spoken by the Lord, and was confirmed unto us by them that heard him?**" **(He.2:2-3).**

        "**And as for me also, mine eye shall not spare, neither will I have pity, but I will recompense their way upon their head**" **(Eze.9:10).**

        "**But as for them whose heart walketh after the heart of their detestable things and their abominations, I will recompense their way upon their own heads, saith the Lord GOD**" **(Eze.11:21).**

5 (18:35) **Judgment**: this is the point—an unforgiving person shall be judged. The point is clear and critical. It is critical because it determines our eternal destiny. We must not only forgive, we must live a life of forgiveness and mercy. We must develop a nature of forgiveness and compassion and mercy and love toward others. If we do not forgive *from our hearts*, neither will God forgive us. Note three things.

    a. Forgiveness comes from the heart, from a new nature wrought in Christ.

    b. Christ says "*My* Father," *not* "*your* Father." God was not the servant's Father. The servant was not a genuine follower of God. He only professed to be.

    c. The person who does not forgive others does not know the forgiveness of God. Having a spirit of forgiveness is so important that Christ taught it time and again.

        "**Blessed are the merciful: for they shall obtain mercy**" **(Mt.5:7).**

        "**But I say unto you, Love your enemies, bless them that curse you, do good to them that hate you, and pray for them which despitefully use you, and persecute you....Be ye therefore perfect, even as your Father which is in heaven is perfect**" **(Mt.5:44, 48; see Lu.6:35-36).**

        "**And forgive us our debts, as we forgive our debtors....For if ye forgive men their trespasses, your heavenly Father will also forgive you: But if ye forgive not men their trespasses, neither will your Father forgive your trespasses**" **(Mt.6:12, 14-15).**

        "**For he shall have judgment without mercy, that hath showed no mercy; and mercy rejoiceth against judgment**" **(Js.2:13).**

MATTHEW 19:1-12

CHAPTER 19

XIII. THE MESSIAH'S TEACHINGS ON THE WAY TO JERUSALEM, 19:1–20:34

A. The Sanctity of Marriage,DS1 19:1-12

(Mt 5:31-32; Mk 10:1-12; Lu 16:18; 1 Co 7:10-16)

1. The contrast between two attitudes toward Jesus
   a. Jesus left Galilee & entered Jordan
   b. Attitude 1: The seeking of help by large crowds
   c. Attitude 2: The testing & questioning by religionists–questioned Him about marriage
2. The creation of male & female
3. The creation of a new family
4. The creation of one bodyDS2
   a. God joins the two persons into one body
   b. Man is not to separate the body of marriage
5. The ideal of permanence in marriage
   a. The question of legal divorceDS3
   b. Divorce was only a concession
   c. The cause: Hard heartsDS4
   d. Divorce was never intended by God
6. The allowance for divorce: Marital unfaithfulnessDS5
7. The supernatural power needed for marriage
   a. Disciples questioned the hard & fast rule
   b. Christ replied: Only believers can receive this truthDS6
8. The highest ideal in marriage: Total devotion to God's kingdom

And it came to pass, *that* when Jesus had finished these sayings, he departed from Galilee, and came into the coasts of Judaea beyond Jordan;

2 And great multitudes followed him; and he healed them there.

3 The Pharisees also came unto him, tempting him, and saying unto him, Is it lawful for a man to put away his wife for every cause?

4 And he answered and said unto them, Have ye not read, that he which made *them* at the beginning made them male and female,

5 And said, For this cause shall a man leave father and mother, and shall cleave to his wife: and they twain shall be one flesh?

6 Wherefore they are no more twain, but one flesh. What therefore God hath joined together, let not man put asunder.

7 They say unto him, Why did Moses then command to give a writing of divorcement, and to put her away?

8 He saith unto them, Moses because of the hardness of your hearts suffered you to put away your wives: but from the beginning it was not so.

9 And I say unto you, Whosoever shall put away his wife, except *it be* for fornication, and shall marry another, committeth adultery: and whoso marrieth her which is put away doth commit adultery.

10 His disciples say unto him, If the case of the man be so with *his* wife, it is not good to marry.

11 But he said unto them, All *men* cannot receive this saying, save *they* to whom it is given.

12 For there are some eunuchs, which were so born from *their* mother's womb: and there are some eunuchs, which were made eunuchs of men: and there be eunuchs, which have made themselves eunuchs for the kingdom of heaven's sake. He that is able to receive *it*, let him receive *it*.

DIVISION XIII

THE MESSIAH'S TEACHINGS ON THE WAY TO JERUSALEM, 19:1–20:34

A. The Sanctity of Marriage, 19:1-12

(19:1-12) **Introduction—Marriage—Divorce**: the questions regarding marriage and divorce are always burning questions, extremely controversial within societies heavily influenced by Christian teaching. Opinions vary and interpretations differ. There is always the closed view that says divorce is never allowed by God no matter the cruelty and meanness that may exist. And there is always the more open view that says divorce is allowed if the rift between a couple is not reconciled and causes more damage than good.

⇒ The former view says that Christ gave a complete exposition on marriage and divorce; the latter says He gave guidelines.
⇒ The former view sometimes treats divorce in such a spirit that it appears to be the unpardonable sin; the latter view sometimes treats it in such a spirit that it appears to be the escape route to do as a person likes (ranging from minor selfish ends to licentious pleasures).

In Christ's day, the two schools of thought were the Shammai School (conservative) and the Hillel School (liberal). (See DEEPER STUDY # 1—Mt.19:1-12.) As in every generation, there were those within each school that would have nothing to do with anyone who held another opinion. A person's view was made a matter of fellowship.

It was because of these strong feelings that the religionists (Pharisees) thought they could entrap and discredit Jesus. No matter what He said, a great number of people would differ, and they would stop supporting His ministry. He would be discredited and His ministry destroyed.

Note several things.

1. There is always a reluctance to express a different opinion when a great number hold a particular position. Compare for example, slavery, smoking, over-eating, mixed bathing, gambling, playing cards, movies, television, and divorce.

2. It is wrong not to face the issues of marriage and divorce, no matter the different opinions and practices of society. Why?

a. There are always a large number of divorced people. Many of these need help, desperately need help. Their faith, hope, security, children, and whole lives have been drastically affected. If believers, God's people, do not open their hearts to them, then a great opportunity to reach out and help them grow in Christ is missed.
b. There are always a large number of marriages (perhaps most) experiencing difficulty, some serious difficulty. Hardness and cruelty, ranging from mild withdrawal to physical abuse, just tear and tear away at the marriage commitment. Sometimes it is the fault of one; sometimes it is the fault of both. In either case, great need exists. Again, if God's people do not reach out and help, a great opportunity is lost for Christ.

Note what Christ did: He spoke up and taught about the issue, and the issue was as controversial in His day as it has been in succeeding generations. (Also see outlines and notes—Mt.5:31-32; 1 Co.7:1-7; 7:8-16.)
1. The contrast between two attitudes toward Jesus (vv.1-3).
2. The creation of male and female (v.4).
3. The creation of a new family (v.5).
4. The creation of one body (vv.5-6).
5. The ideal of permanence in marriage (vv.7-8).
6. The allowance for divorce: marital unfaithfulness (v.9).
7. The supernatural power needed for marriage (vv.10-11).
8. The highest ideal in marriage: total devotion to God's Kingdom (v.12).

DEEPER STUDY # 1
(19:1-12) **Marriage—Divorce—Shammai—Hillel**: the Pharisees came to Jesus tempting Him and saying, "Is it lawful for a man to put away his wife for every cause?"
There is a background to this question. The society of Jesus' day was very lax in its morals. Marriage was considered nothing more than a piece of paper: if it worked, fine; if it did not work, fine. One could always divorce (see note—Mt.5:31).
There were two positions or schools of thought on divorce. Moses had said that any man could divorce his wife if "she find no favor in his eyes, because he has found some uncleanness in her" (De.24:1).
1. The school of Shammai said that the words *some uncleanness* meant adultery only. A wife could be as loose and mean as Jezebel, but she was not to be divorced unless she committed adultery.
2. The school of Hillel said that the words *some uncleanness* meant anything that was not pleasing to the man. One should remember that women were counted as nothing but *property* to be possessed by men. They had no rights whatsoever except as a man might wish to give. Of course, this was the position followed by society, for it was the position that allowed human nature to run loose. Women were abused: used and discarded, neglected and violated. They were nothing but chattel property of men and were often considered of less value than property, whether animals or things. Therefore, divorce ran rampant in Christ's day.

The Pharisees wished to embroil Jesus in the controversy between the conservative (Shammai) and liberal view (Hillel). They were simply asking Jesus if He agreed with the school of Hillel: "Is it lawful for a man to put away his wife for every cause?" (v.3). No matter which position He took, He would offend and stir up a large number of people, becoming embroiled in a mean controversy.

1 (19:1-3) **Divorce**: there are two attitudes toward Jesus, and there is a sharp contrast between the two attitudes. Christ was making His final journey toward Jerusalem where He was to be killed. He would not return to Galilee until after His resurrection (Mt.28:7).
The same two attitudes toward Christ prevail in every generation: there are those who sincerely seek the help of Christ; and there are those who are always testing and questioning Him, stretching every inch they can out of the world and the flesh. They question and question; and, by their questioning, they are able to create uncertainty and doubt over right and wrong. They are able to live as they wish.
Note the question asked, "Is it lawful for a man to put away his wife for every cause?" The flesh says no matter how frivolous—if there is displeasure, disgust, dislike—then divorce is allowed. But is it? That is what Christ is answering.

2 (19:4) **Marriage—Divorce**: Christ said there is the creation of male and female: "God made them [Adam and Eve] male and female" (v.4). He did not make them males and females, as He did animals, but He made one male and one female. Each one was made for the other. They were not made for anyone else, for there was no one else.

Thought 1. Creation is the root basis for marriage: one male for one female; one female for one male. There was no one else, just Adam and Eve. This was not so with the creation of other animals. They were created *en masse*; a large number were created simultaneously. There is also the added fact that male and female were created spiritual beings, created for much higher purposes. Since there were no others like them, they were sharing their purposes together in constant fellowship with God.

3 (19:5) **Marriage—Divorce**: Christ said there is the creation of a new family: "A man [shall] leave father and mother, and shall cleave to his wife" (v.5). One man shall cleave to his wife and create a new family distinct from the family of his parents. He says *a man*, not men, and *his wife*, not wives. Note that a man leaves his father and mother. The union between husband and wife is to gain primacy over the union between parent and child. The union of *cleaving* is wrought by God and appointed by God. Therefore marriage is a divine institution. Just as parents and children are not to divorce one another, neither are the husband and wife to divorce each other.

> **Thought 1.** Father, mother, and child comprise a unit, a family. However, Christ said father and mother are there when the child leaves. And the child (man) leaves to "cleave to his wife." There is no thought, not even a hint of separation in this statement. It is unquestionably a statement of God's purpose for father, mother, and child. The structure of the family is the means by which man is to carry out the purposes of God on earth. Divorce, tearing down the structure of the family, is not the purpose of God. The structure of a family—father, mother, and child—is the purpose of God.

> **Thought 2.** Note: Christ said the relation between father and mother is to be closer and more intimate, longer and more durable than that between parent and child. The day comes when the child (man) leaves the parent, and the parents are left with each other *all alone*. This says much to both husband and wife. They must not neglect their life together, for the day comes when they will be all alone and have the company *only of one another*.

4 (19:5-6) **Marriage—Divorce**: Christ said there is the creation of one body: "A man...shall cleave to his wife and they twain [two] shall be one flesh" (v.5). There is the molding into one person. The man and the wife cleave to each other: "Wherefore they are no more twain, but one flesh." What is it that makes them one flesh? *Cleaving*. They are one body, one flesh, one person. They are not joined to two or three or four other persons, but they cleave only to one other person.

Christ also says that a marriage joined together by Him is not to be destroyed by any man. "A man...shall cleave to his wife...wherefore [cleaving] they are no more twain, but one flesh [joined together by God]. What therefore God hath joined together, let not man put asunder" (v.5-6).

The points are clear.
   a. The cleaving husband and wife are joined together by God.
   b. No one is to cut asunder what God joins together. Neither the husband nor wife nor anyone else is to step in between the two and cause separation.

> "And Adam said, This is now bone of my bones, and flesh of my flesh: she shall be called Woman, because she was taken out of Man. Therefore shall a man leave his father and his mother, and shall cleave unto his wife: and they shall be one flesh" (Ge.2:23-24).
> "Let thy fountain be blessed: and rejoice with the wife of thy youth" (Pr.5:18).
> "Live joyfully with the wife whom thou lovest all the days of the life of thy vanity, which he hath given thee under the sun, all the days of thy vanity: for that is thy portion in this life, and in thy labor which thou takest under the sun" (Ec.9:9).
> "Husbands, love your wives, even as Christ also loved the church, and gave himself for it" (Ep.5:25).
> "Likewise, ye husbands, dwell with them according to knowledge, giving honour unto the wife, as unto the weaker vessel, and as being heirs together of the grace of life; that your prayers be not hindered" (1 Pe.3:7).

Thought 1. Note something of critical importance. By *cleaving* Christ does not mean what is often thought or pictured: cleaving does not mean taking hold of a wife by civil contract, embracing, or sexual union.
Note the words...
- *cleaving*
- *one flesh*
- *what God hath joined together*

Spouses who are *obedient* to Christ by *cleaving* to each other—in all of their being and life, not only physically, but also spiritually—are the ones who become one flesh. They are the ones whom God joins together. A civil contract does not bind people together, neither does embracing and neither does sex. Only God can bind a couple together *spiritually*, and He does so because a couple is obedient to Him. He rewards and blesses obedience, not disobedience.

Thought 2. Note how the power of God is infused into a couple who obeys Him. He causes their cleaving to bind them so closely together they are as one person.

Thought 3. Note a significant point: "They are no more twain, but one flesh." "No man ever yet hated his own flesh; but nourisheth and cherisheth it"—he does not cut it off (Ep.5:29).

DEEPER STUDY # 2

(19:5) **Cleave** (kollao; proskollao): to join fast together; to glue together; to cement together; to be joined in the closest union possible; to be bound together; to be so totally united together that two become one. Therefore, to cleave means a spiritual union. It is a union higher and stronger than the union of parent and child. It is a union that means more than living together, more than having sex and bearing offspring. Animals do this. It is a union that can be wrought by God alone (v.11). It is a spiritual union that places man above the physical plane of animals. It is a spiritual fullness, a spiritual sharing of life together: a dedication, a consecration, a completeness, a satisfaction that makes a person the exclusive possession of God and of the spouse. As said, such a cleaving or spiritual union is wrought by God alone. Both husband and wife

MATTHEW 19:1-12

must be willing and submissive for God to bring about such a cleaving in their lives. "Submitting yourselves one to another in the fear [trust] of God" (Ep.5:21; see outlines and notes—Ep.5:22-33).

There are three unions within a true marriage, that is, a marriage that *really cleaves* and is really *joined together* by God (Mt.19:6).

1. There is the physical union: the sharing of each other's body (1 Co.7:2-5). But note: physical sharing cannot reach its ultimate fullness unless it is experienced while conscious of God's warm and tender mercies (Ep.5:25-33).

2. There is the mental union: the sharing of each other's life and dreams and hopes and the working together to realize those dreams and hopes. It is important to note that this union still deals only with the physical and material world.

3. There is the spiritual union: the sharing and melting and molding of each other's spirit (see Ep.5:25-33). This can be wrought only by God. Therefore, there has to be a sharing together with God for there to be a *nourishing* and *nurturing* of the spirit.

Now here is the point: the greatest thing in the world is to know God personally and to be perfectly assured that we shall live now and eternally—to have life abundant with all the love, significance, meaning, and purpose humanly possible. But a man and a woman cannot experience abundant life of and by themselves. They can only nurture the mind and mesh themselves together mentally and physically. To be meshed together spiritually, the couple must share God and His saving grace together. When a couple shares God together day by day, God works supernaturally within their spirits, *melting* their beings and *molding* them into what He calls *one flesh*. They actually become as *one person*. This is what is meant by "God hath joined together." The Greek word for "joined together" (sunzeugen) actually means to *yoke together*. It is God's yoking, God's joining, God's binding the couple together into a spiritual union that causes them to become one person.

A couple who is spiritually united does two very practical things.

1. The couple "submits themselves one to the other in the fear of God" (Ep.5:21). They submit, yield, surrender, sacrifice, give themselves up to the other as they live day by day in the fear (trust) of God. Day by day, they deliberately set out to nourish and cherish the other, even as the Lord nourishes and cherishes the church (Ep.5:29). They work to become part of each other—so deliberately that they seek to become part of each other's body, each other's flesh, each other's bones (Ep.5:30). They seek to be joined "as one flesh," no matter the surrender and sacrifice required. The meshing together is done by God. God takes such deliberate purpose and behavior, such a melting of one's being, and molds it into the flesh of the other—so much so the two actually become as one, not only physically and mentally but spiritually as well.

2. The couple shares the presence of God and His saving grace together. As a result, God gives them a spiritual assurance and strength which they share together throughout life. They share the knowledge and confidence...
- that God shall care for and look after them now and forever.
- that God shall carry them through the devastating trials of life that confront every human being every so often.
- that God shall bless them with all that is necessary as they walk through life together.
- that God shall give them an abundant entrance into the everlasting kingdom of the Lord Jesus Christ—forever and ever.

Again, the point is this: God takes such deliberate sharing of spiritual things and melts and molds the man and woman into *one flesh* spiritually—so much so that they actually become one. A man and a woman being spiritually united by God as one person is what cleaving means. Cleaving to one another in God's Spirit is true marriage—the glorious gift of God.

---

5 (19:7-8) **Marriage—Divorce**: there is the ideal of permanence in marriage. The Pharisees had entrapped Jesus, or so they thought. Jesus had given four reasons why there was to be no divorce. He was standing against Moses. In their view, Moses had given a commandment that allowed divorce (v.7). Jesus says three things about the ideal of marriage.

> "Moses, because of the hardness [sinfulness] of your heart suffered you [allowed, made a concession for you] to put away your wives: but from the beginning [Adam and Eve] it was not so [not intended, not willed by God]" (v.8).

a. Moses made a concession (De.24:1-4).
b. The reason: man's hard, sinful hearts.
c. Divorce was never willed and was not the purpose of God.

Thought 1. Note three important facts.
(1) God's will for marriage was permanence. Divorce was permitted under Moses, but it was not God's will. It was sin, short of God's will and purpose.
(2) The cause for divorce is said to be *hardness of heart*—a very serious indictment.
(3) The union of marriage is not brought about by a natural law but by God. Marriage is not a law of nature, inherent within man. It is not something that operates by nature, that just happens because two people agree to live together and sign a civil contract. A true union or marriage that is joined together by God is a blessing, a gift of God. It is brought about because a couple is obedient to God. They live in and for each other *under God* (acknowledging God in all things), just as He says to live ("cleaving"). Therefore, God blesses them by joining them together in the most binding of spiritual unions.

It bears repeating: marriage is not a natural law; it is not a law of nature; it is a spiritual law that operates only if each spouse walks in the Spirit.

MATTHEW 19:1-12

DEEPER STUDY # 3
(19:7) **Old Testament Reference**: see De.24:1-4.

DEEPER STUDY # 4
(19:8) **Hardness, of Heart—Marriage**: many are living together, both within and without marriage, who are not joined together by God. As Jesus said, "All cannot receive this saying" (see DEEPER STUDY # 6—Mt.19:11). The world is corrupted; all are frail, selfish, and sinful. Many become hard of heart; and many, because of the hardness of heart, *wish* silently or vocally to divorce. Some do.

What is it that causes hardness of heart?

1. Many have not received God into their lives and marriages (Jn.1:12; Re.3:20); therefore, God and His power are foreign, unknown to them (Ep.3:20).

2. Some are not *cleaving* (see DEEPER STUDY # 2—Mt.19:5). One or both hearts are hard toward the other. Pride and hurt and barrier after barrier have grown between them. Therefore, one or both withdraw and have little to do with the other, avoiding daily contact and relationships as much as possible.

3. Some think sex is all cleaving means. Many come short in thinking that the physical union is the unique feature that glues a marriage together. Sex is important, of course, as any well-adjusted couple knows. But when the newness of the experience passes and life settles into responsibility, there has to be more than the physical cleaving to prevent barriers and hardness of heart. The unique feature is God, not sex (Mt.19:11; see outlines and DEEPER STUDY # 2—Mt.19:5; notes—Ep.5:22-24; 5:25-33).

4. Many are living only humanistic lives. They have no more than animals have: living together, being physically united, bearing offspring, and protecting and providing for each other. But that is all. They are not spiritually alive; they have not received God into their lives and marriage. They have *hard hearts* or *no heart* toward God. Therefore, some live on no higher plane than some animals live, and others do not even have the order and respect for one another that some animals have within their packs.

How do we prevent hardness of heart and divorce? There are four very basic requirements.

1. "Wives, submit yourselves unto your own husbands, as unto the Lord. For the husband is the head of the wife, even as Christ is the head of the church: and he is the saviour of the body. Therefore as the church is subject unto Christ, so let the wives be to their own husbands in every thing" (Ep.5:22-24).

2. "Husbands, love your wives, even as Christ also loved the Church, and gave himself for it....So ought men to love their wives as their own bodies. He that loveth his wife loveth himself. For no man ever yet hated his own flesh; but nourisheth and cherisheth it, even as the Lord the church" (Ep.5:25, 28-29).

3. "Nevertheless let every one of you in particular so love his wife even as himself; and the wife see that she reverence her husband" (Ep.5:33).

4. "And be ye kind one to another, tenderhearted, forgiving one another, even as God for Christ's sake hath forgiven you" (Ep.4:32).

6 (19:9) **Marriage—Divorce**: there is the allowance for divorce—fornication. Christ says, "Whosoever puts away his wife, except it be for fornication, and shall marry another committeth adultery...." (v.9).
- There is one clear reason for divorce: adultery.
- Remarriage commits adultery.

Before Christ came into the world, adultery was punishable by death. Since Christ has come, the penalty has been changed. Divorce itself is to be the punishment, not death. (What an impact this change of law has made on societies in the past! How much it is needed in some parts of the world even today! Compassion is the answer to sin, not anger and wrath.)

Note the importance and high esteem that Christ places upon sex within marriage. It is so intimate and meaningful and important an experience that if it is violated, divorce is allowed. Note however: Christ did not say that divorce must take place. It is only *allowed*. If the couple has been living in Him and blessed by Him and the violated spouse cannot emotionally accept the unfaithfulness, divorce can take place. But if the offended spouse can forgive—if he or she can be emotionally controlled and forgiving enough to forgive—then the spouse should forgive.

> "Therefore shall a man leave his father and his mother, and shall cleave unto his wife: and they shall be one flesh" (Ge.2:24).
>
> "Ye have heard that it was said by them of old time, Thou shalt not commit adultery: but I say unto you, That whosoever looketh on a woman to lust after her hath committed adultery with her already in his heart" (Mt.5:27-28).
>
> "But I say unto you, That whosoever shall put away his wife, saving for the cause of fornication, causeth her to commit adultery: and whosoever shall marry her that is divorced committeth adultery" (Mt.5:32).
>
> "What therefore God hath joined together, let not man put asunder" (Mk.10:9).
>
> "For the woman which hath an husband is bound by the law to her husband so long as he liveth; but if the husband be dead, she is loosed from the law of her husband. So then if, while her husband liveth, she be married to another man, she shall be called an adulteress: but if her husband be dead, she is free from that law; so that she is no adulteress, though she be married to another man" (Ro.7:2-3).

"Know ye not that the unrighteous shall not inherit the kingdom of God? Be not deceived: neither fornicators, nor idolaters, nor adulterers, nor effeminate, nor abusers of themselves with mankind" (1 Co.6:9).

"And unto the married I command, yet not I, but the Lord, Let not the wife depart from her husband" (1 Co.7:10).

"And shall receive the reward of unrighteousness, as they that count it pleasure to riot in the day time. Spots they are and blemishes, sporting themselves with their own deceivings while they feast with you" (2 Pe.2:13-14).

DEEPER STUDY # 5
(19:9) **Fornication—Adultery**: a person, especially a Christian believer, needs to think of the meaning of adultery here. Adultery is the turning away from a spouse to another person. Many a person would never think of turning away from their spouse to a third person, yet they readily and willingly turn toward self and toward other things. As God said of the nation Israel, "I saw, when for all the causes whereby backsliding Israel committed adultery I had put her away, and given her a bill of divorce" (Je.3:8). Many a person has done just as Israel did. They refused to surrender to God. They lived in a backslidden state, and day by day they turned more and more away from their spouse and, in many cases, from their children.

Day by day a person can take a spouse and children and...
- be mean and ugly.
- be nagging and mentally cruel.
- be neglectful and unthoughtful.
- be physically abusive and life-threatening.
- be deliberately withdrawn and separated.

And the truth of the matter is that many live selfishly that way.
⇒ Some are cruel; others sadistic.
⇒ Some are critical; others sarcastic; still others *demonic and hellish*.
⇒ Some are mentally abusive; others physically abusive, *even* to the point of murdering spouse and children—the unthinkable.

The truth of a marriage is known only to God. A husband or a wife can use his or her personality to present a front to the world. Yet within the heart, there can be such a hardness toward a spouse, such an unwillingness to truly cleave, that God just cannot join them together as one flesh. Hardness, very simply, wrecks a marriage. It wrecks a marriage by causing a person to turn away and separate from his or her spouse. If a spouse is not with the other spouse, then the two are separate, not cleaving. There can be no cleaving if there are not *two* persons together; and as pointed out earlier, cleaving is the blessing and gift of God. Cleaving is only possible as each allows God to "join them together."

---

[7] (19:10-11) **Marriage**: there is the supernatural power needed for marriage. The disciples were shocked, for Jesus was saying that divorce is not God's will: "From the beginning [from Adam and Eve] it was not so," that is, not intended by God (v.8). Thus the disciples exclaimed: "It is not good to marry"—one can be caught in a bad situation.

"But [Jesus] said unto them, All men cannot receive this saying, save they to whom it is given" (v.11); that is, only a God-given power can make a marriage what it should be so that a person will not want out. It is necessary for God to be in the center of a marriage. God has to join the two together. (See outline and notes—Ep.5:22-24; 5:25-33.)

Thought 1. Men rebel at the strictness of Christ in marriage. The disciples rebelled to such an extent that they were ready to say that it is better not to marry. But note: they, as so many, had not yet grasped what Christ was saying. Marriage is to be a spiritual union joined together by God. It is to be a union ever so precious, tender, warm, supportive, meaningful, and significant—a union seldom heard of and known in experience, even among believers.

Thought 2. How many can truly *cleave*, submitting wholly (100 percent, not 50-50)? How many can truly love the other completely as oneself? Not everyone can receive this saying. Only they who will surrender to one another *under God* can receive a true marriage, a true joining together from God. It is not a matter of not marrying. It is a matter of obeying God and living as He wills.

Thought 3. There is *death to self* required in marriage in order to *cleave* and to be as *one flesh*. But there are also the blessings of *a new life*, the glory and excitement of two persons' living as *one flesh* and being joined together in all of life.

DEEPER STUDY # 6
(19:11) **Marriage, Essentials**: "All cannot receive this saying." What saying?
1. The saying that a man and wife are "to cleave to one another." They are to be (1) totally united together as *one flesh*: "Wherefore they are no more twain, but one flesh" (v.5-6).
2. The saying that it is God and God alone who can *join together* a man and a wife (v.6; see DEEPER STUDY # 2—Mt.19:5).

MATTHEW 19:1-12

> These two things, cleaving and God Himself, are the two essentials for a true marriage. Many are living together who refuse *to cleave* and refuse to let God join them together. They are not willing to cleave, nor are they willing to let God make them as *one flesh*. They are not willing to let God join them together.
>
> (Note: man and woman can only cleave and join themselves together physically. God is not needed for a purely physical union. If a married couple wishes more than a physical union, they must turn to God. He alone can "join together" a couple spiritually.)

8 (19:12) **Marriage—Eunuchs**: there is the highest ideal in marriage—total devotion to God's Kingdom. The very highest ideal for a man is total concentration upon God and His Kingdom (see 1 Co.7:1f). This is so whether a person is married or not married. Christ was not downgrading marriage nor was He saying that being unmarried is preferable to being married. He was simply answering the disciples' question, "Yes, some men have chosen not to marry and chosen to be eunuchs. Some are born eunuchs; others are enslaved and made eunuchs; and still others choose to devote themselves only to the Kingdom of Heaven." Then He said the very same thing He said in v.11, "He that is able to receive it [be a eunuch] receive it." Christ spoke first to the married; then in answer to the disciples He spoke to the unmarried:

⇒ To the married, He said that it takes God in a person's life for the person to receive a true marriage, to cleave and be joined together with a spouse (see DEEPER STUDY #6—Mt.19:11).

⇒ To the unmarried, He said that it takes God to be a eunuch, to dedicate one's life to the Kingdom of Heaven (v.12).

Thought 1. Some can live more for God if they remain single. They should, therefore, commit themselves to remain single (see note—1 Co.7:1).

Thought 2. Some choose to remain single in order to have the freedom to live lustful, sensual lives. Christ deals with sexual sins in other passages. He is not condoning such here by approving the single life. The single state is to be chosen for the purpose of serving God more diligently, and it is to be chosen for that purpose only.

MATTHEW 19:13-15

	B. The Acceptance of Children, 19:13-15 *(Mk 10:13-16; Lu 18:15-17)*

1. Children were brought to Jesus: To touch & pray for
2. Parents cared & believed: Brought their children
3. The disciples rebuked the parents: Jesus was too busy
4. Jesus rebuked those who disregarded the children
   a. He received the children
   b. He said the kingdom belonged to children
   c. He touched the children
	13 Then were there brought unto him little children, that he should put *his* hands on them, and pray: and the disciples rebuked them.
	14 But Jesus said, Suffer little children, and forbid them not, to come unto me: for of such is the kingdom of heaven.
	15 And he laid *his* hands on them, and departed thence.

DIVISION XIII

THE MESSIAH'S TEACHINGS ON THE WAY TO JERUSALEM, 19:1–20:34

B. The Acceptance of Children, 19:13-15

(19:13-15) **Introduction**: children are very dear to God. People in Jesus' day considered children to be insignificant and unimportant. It was this that Jesus was combating in this experience. Children are as important as any other persons to God, and they are not to be disregarded or discouraged from coming to God. They are to be welcomed and accepted with open arms.
 1. Children were brought to Jesus: to touch and pray for (v.13).
 2. Parents cared and believed: brought their children (v.13).
 3. The disciples rebuked the parents: Jesus was too busy (v.13).
 4. Jesus rebuked those who disregarded the children (vv14-15).

1 (19:13) **Children—Parents**: children were brought to Jesus for Him to touch and to pray for. Note four facts about the little children.
 a. The children were so little that they had to be brought to Jesus for. Luke called them *infants* (Lu.18:15).
 b The children were brought for Jesus to touch and to pray for. This was the purpose for their being brought to Him. The laying on of hands was a symbol of special blessing and dedication (Ge.48:14; Nu.27:23). It demonstrated a belief in God, in His love and power to bless. Therefore, the laying on of hands during special moments has always been very meaningful to God's people.
 c. The children were brought despite threatening opposition. At this particular time, Jesus was being greatly opposed by the religious and political leaders. They were seeking to kill Jesus (Mt.12:14; see note—Mt.12:7; note and DEEPER STUDY #1—12:10). The parents knew this, but they still wanted Jesus to bless their children. His blessing was so important to the parents that they brought their children to Him despite the danger.

> "And that their children, which have not known any thing, may hear, and learn to fear the LORD your God, as long as ye live in the land whither ye go over Jordan to possess it" (De.31:13).

 d. The children were too young to understand what was happening. They knew nothing about the importance of being blessed by Christ, but their age made no difference. They were brought to Him anyway.

> "And, ye fathers, provoke not your children to wrath: but bring them up in the nurture and admonition of the Lord" (Ep.6:4).
> "And thou shalt teach them diligently unto thy children, and shalt talk of them when thou sittest in thine house, and when thou walkest by the way, and when thou liest down, and when thou risest up" (De.6:7).
> "Train up a child in the way he should go: and when he is old, he will not depart from it" (Pr.22:6).

Thought 1. Think of the children who are not brought to Christ. The result is tragic: they never come to know Christ and the life and security He brings to the human heart.

Thought 2. The benefits of bringing children to Christ are innumerable. Just a few major ones are as follows.
(1) A child who is brought to Christ grows up learning love: that he is loved by God and by all who trust God. He matures year by year knowing that no matter how evil some people may act, he is to love even those who do wrong. He learns that he is to help sow the seed of love upon earth.

MATTHEW 19:13-15

(2) A child who is brought to Christ grows up learning power and triumph: that God will help His followers through all; that there is a supernatural power available to help, a power to help when mother and dad and loved ones have done all they can.

(3) A child who is brought to Christ grows up learning hope and faith: that no matter what happens, no matter how great a trial, he can still trust God and hope in Him. God has provided a very special strength to carry him through the trials of this life (no matter how painful). God has provided a very special place called heaven where He will carry him and his loved ones when he faces death.

(4) A child who is brought to Christ grows up learning the truth of life and endurance (service): that God has given him the privilege of life and of living in a beautiful earth and universe; that the evil and bad which exist in the world are caused by evil and bad people; that despite such evil, he is to serve in appreciation for life and for the beautiful earth upon which God has placed him. He is to work and work diligently, making the greatest contribution he can.

(5) A child who is brought to Christ grows up learning trust and endurance: that life is full of temptations and pitfalls which can easily rob him of joy and destroy his life and the fulfillment of his purposes; that the way to escape the temptations and pitfalls is to follow Christ and endure in his work and purpose.

(6) A child who is brought to Christ grows up learning peace: that there is an inner peace despite the turbulent waters of this world; that peace is knowing and trusting Christ.

2 (19:13) **Parents—Children**: the parents cared for their children, and they believed Jesus could help them. Therefore, they brought their children to Jesus. Note three facts about the parents.

a. The parents cared for their children, cared enough that they wanted the very best for them. Jesus Christ was claiming to be the Messiah, the very Son of God; so they wanted their children to be blessed by Him instead of an ordinary religious leader.

b. The parents believed in Jesus, in His love and power to bless. They believed that Jesus' blessing was meaningful to their children—very, very meaningful. They also believed that He cared and loved enough that He would bless them.

c. The parents' concern for their children was strong and persistent. They brought their children to Jesus despite strong religious opposition and despite the disciples' public rebuke (see note—Mt.12:7; note and DEEPER STUDY # 1—12:10). They did not turn around and leave. They were determined to have their children blessed by Jesus.

Thought 1. Life is given by God, so children belong to God. In a very special sense, children are *bundles of trust* that God puts into the care of parents for a short time. Parents are *the trustees* of God's property, of the little lives that God has given. Parents are responsible for caring enough to trust God's power and blessing for their children.

Thought 2. Children should be presented to God as "living sacrifices" for His care and purposes.

> "I beseech you therefore, brethren, by the mercies of God, that ye present your bodies a living sacrifice, holy, acceptable unto God, which is your reasonable service. And be not conformed to this world: but be ye transformed by the renewing of your mind, that ye may prove what is that good, and acceptable, and perfect, will of God" (Ro.12:1-2).

Thought 3. Most parents have *the true love of a parent* for their children. The greatest gift of love they can show is to bring their children to Christ. They should also seek to bring other children to Christ.

Thought 4. There are several reasons why parents do not bring their children to Christ.

(1) Some parents (in civilized as well as uncivilized parts of the world) are not aware of the only living and true God. Therefore, they are blind; they just do not know. Christians have failed to take the gospel to the whole world.

(2) Some parents have heard the truth, but they have rejected Christ. They are agnostics or atheists, or else they love the world and the things of the world more than they love the news of the living God who gives eternal life. They do not care about anything beyond comfort of self and the benefits of this world.

(3) Some parents believe, at least mentally, but they are complacent and lethargic. They are not concerned enough to make the effort to come to Christ nor to bring their children to Christ.

(4) Some parents are believers; but, unfortunately, they are immature and inconsistent in their religious lives. Their own Christian lives and worship are weak and neglected, sometimes up and sometimes down. Their children are thereby taught that Christ is not really all that important.

(5) Some parents are liberal-minded. They are not willing to influence and mold their children's thinking spiritually. They want their children to make their own choices. They are willing to teach them what foods to eat and books to read, anything that will teach them how to care for themselves physically, but they leave the care of the spiritual up to them after they become adults.

Thought 5. There are two great errors committed by parents who do not bring their children to Christ.

(1) Any parent who does not bring his child to Christ is following a false philosophy of life and reality.

> "But without faith it is impossible to please him: for he that cometh to God must believe that he is, and that he is a rewarder of them that diligently seek him" (He.11:6).
>
> "Jesus saith unto him, I am the way, the truth, and the life: no man cometh unto the Father, but by me" (Jn.14:6).
>
> "For there is one God, and one mediator between God and men, the man Christ Jesus" (1 Ti.2:5).

MATTHEW 19:13-15

(2) A child's mind is molded by those with whom he associates. His mind is either molded by the loose and immoral or the disciplined and moral. If the child's mind is not molded by *godly parents*, it will be molded by the world and its selfish and corrupt ways.

3 (19:13) **Parents—Disciples**: the disciples rebuked the parents. Note several facts about the disciples.

a. The disciples thought they knew the mind of Christ. They were good men, and they were leaders among the followers of Christ. But they did not know the mind of Christ, not in this instance. They did not fully understand the ways of God, but they were acting as though they did. They were determining who could and who could not approach to be blessed by Christ.

b. The disciples rebuked the parents for bringing the children to Jesus. There are several possible reasons for their action.

1) The parents' frivolous pride over their children. The disciples may have thought the parents just wanted to show off their children and have Jesus make over them.
2) A misunderstanding about the importance of children. The disciples may have thought the children were just not important or significant enough to merit the attention of so important a person as Jesus. He was just too busy, and His work was too important to be interrupted by those who really did not need Him.
3) An immature concept of the blessing and power of God. By rebuking the parents, the disciples definitely showed they were guilty of this. To them blessing and praying for little children were not important enough to merit the attention of Jesus. They could not understand how small infants, who were not yet old enough to believe, could receive any good from being blessed by Christ.

Thought 1. There are two attitudes toward children that are critical mistakes, both of which are sometimes adopted by parents and society.

(1) There is the attitude that children are not as important as adults. They are, therefore, often neglected, ignored, by-passed, and pushed aside without much attention or training. Such, of course, leads to a *squashed*, weak personality, making the child shy, and instilling a sense of inferiority. To say that children are as important as adults does not mean that they are to be given the rights of an adult. Such would only indulge and pamper the child. But it does mean that they are to be treated as *real persons* with needs and rights—the needs and rights of a child, not of an adult.
(2) There is the attitude that children are to be unrestrained and allowed to develop their own desires, urges, wills, and personalities. The feeling is that few, if any, restrictions should be placed upon children. They are to have what they desire and go without nothing. Such an attitude, of course, leads to an indulged, pampered, and selfish personality. (See note—Ep.6:4.)

Thought 2. Children's questions about Jesus are often ignored or quickly and unthoughtfully answered. They are considered too young and too unimportant to merit much of our time. No one should ever be stopped from coming to Christ, no matter who they may be.

Thought 3. Too many *important persons* are unavailable to the small and less important persons of the world. The time of the *important* person is thought to be too valuable. There is some truth to this. Many of the less important could dominate the time of the more important to such an extent that the more important would not have time to function. But the demand of the important to be left alone is often a selfish and sinful demand.

4 (19:14-15) **Children**: Jesus rebuked those who stopped and disregarded the children. Note several things about Jesus.

a. Jesus rebuked those who stopped and disregarded the children. He said that such action was wrong. We are not to stop little children from coming to Him. Contrariwise, we are to bring them to Him. He is God; and as God, He is providential, doing as He wills. Therefore, He is the One who determines whom He will bless. No man determines for Him. No matter the tender age and lack of reason, children are not to be kept from coming to Him. No obstacle is to be put in their way.

b. Jesus called for and received the children. Children were welcomed even if they were so little they had to be brought. Children may be too little to understand, but Christ is big enough to bless them and to see that the blessing sticks all through eternity. He is, after all, God; and as God, He is omnipotent, all-powerful, and able to exercise His power as He wills. Children will in no way be rejected by Him.

c. Jesus said that the Kingdom of Heaven belongs to children. He was saying two things.

1) Children are citizens of His kingdom, at least until their minds mature enough to personally choose or reject Him. Such a time is usually referred to as the *age of accountability*.
2) Children demonstrate the traits needed to enter heaven (see outline and notes—Mt.18:3. This passage will help greatly in understanding just what Christ was saying.)

d. Jesus touched the children. He was not influenced by the objections. He went ahead and blessed the children. There is a great truth here that we often overlook. It is not so much that we come and touch God as it is that He comes and touches us. It is not so much that we apprehend God as it is that we are apprehended by Him (Ph.3:12-13).

> "But as many as received him, to them gave he power to become the sons of God, even to them that believe on his name: Which were born, not of blood, nor of the will of the flesh, nor of the will of man, but of God" (Jn.1:12-13).

MATTHEW 19:13-15

God's blessing is not so much due to how rational and capable we are as to His purpose and will. God can choose to touch and bless whom He wills, and He demonstrates beyond all question that He chooses to touch and bless the children brought to Him.

"**But Jesus said, Suffer little children, and forbid them not, to come unto me: for of such is the kingdom of heaven**" (Mt.19:14).

"**As arrows are in the hand of a mighty man; so are children of the youth. Happy is the man that hath his quiver full of them: they shall not be ashamed, but they shall speak with the enemies in the gate**" (Ps.127:4-5).

"**Thy wife shall be as a fruitful vine by the sides of thine house: thy children like olive plants round about thy table**" (Ps.128:3).

"**Children's children are the crown of old men; and the glory of children are their fathers**" (Pr.17:6).

Thought 1. Jesus never refused to receive a person. We are...
- not to be too important to receive people
- not to be too busy or tired to receive people
- not to regard a person as too young or too old to receive
- not to be unavailable to people

MATTHEW 19:16-22

	C. The Rich Young Ruler: How a Rich Man Enters the Kingdom of Heaven,^{DS1} 19:16-22 (Mk 10:17-22; Lu 10:25-37; 18:18-23) 16 And, behold, one came and said unto him, Good Master, what good thing shall I do, that I may have eternal life? 17 And he said unto him, Why callest thou me good? *there is* none good but one, *that is,* God: but if thou wilt enter into life, keep the commandments. 18 He saith unto him, Which? Jesus said, Thou shalt do no murder, Thou	shalt not commit adultery, Thou shalt not steal, Thou shalt not bear false witness, 19 Honour thy father and *thy* mother: and, Thou shalt love thy neighbour as thyself. 20 The young man saith unto him, All these things have I kept from my youth up: what lack I yet? 21 Jesus said unto him, If thou wilt be perfect, go *and* sell that thou hast, and give to the poor, and thou shalt have treasure in heaven: and come *and* follow me. 22 But when the young man heard that saying, he went away sorrowful: for he had great possessions.	Especially needed by the rulers & the rich of the world

1. Step 1: Seek eternal life^{DS2}
  a. Approach Christ
  b. Confess your need
 	
2. Step 2: Know that God alone is good
  a. The wrong concept of man's nature: Man is good
  b. The right concept: God alone is good
3. Step 3: Obey the commandments
  a. The commandments dealing with our neighbor:
			b. The wrong concept of God's law: A tragic sense of self-righteousness
			
			4. Step 4: Give all you are & have to Christ
			  a. Result: Will receive heaven & treasures in heaven
			  b. Demand: Must follow Christ
			  c. Reaction: Rejection by the young ruler
			    1) Unbelief, v.17
			    2) Self-righteousness, v.20
			    3) Love of the world, v.21

DIVISION XIII

THE MESSIAH'S TEACHINGS ON THE WAY TO JERUSALEM, 19:1–20:34

C. The Rich Young Ruler: How a Rich Man Enters the Kingdom of Heaven, 19:16-22

(19:16-22) **Introduction**: the Lord's approach to this young man has often seemed perplexing. There are three reasons for the perplexity.

1. The young man called Christ "Good Master," but Christ denied that He was good. How can Christ, who claims to be God, deny that He is good?
2. The young man asked how he might receive eternal life. Christ said nothing about believing but told the young man to keep certain laws.
3. The third perplexity is shocking. Christ told the young man that he had to sell all that he had and give it to the poor in order to receive eternal life. The question immediately arises, does Christ really demand that a person give all he is and has in order to be saved?

These three facts are puzzling. However, when we study the passage and understand what was happening, the puzzle fades. Christ led the young man through the steps that are needed to receive eternal life.
1. Step 1: seek eternal life (v.16).
2. Step 2: know that God alone is good (v.17).
3. Step 3: keep the commandments (vv.18-20).
4. Step 4: give all you are and have to Christ (vv.21-22).

DEEPER STUDY # 1
(19:16-22) **Young People**: this man is known as "the rich young ruler." He is so called because of the composite picture gleaned from all three gospels.
⇒ He was rich (Mt.19:22; Mk.10:22; Lu.18:23).
⇒ He was young (Mt.19:20).
⇒ He was a ruler (Lu.18:18).
He was a rare young man among the young people of his day. He was conscientious, responsible, dependable—so much so that he had already been placed in a responsible position and made a ruler.

1 (19:16) **Eternal Life**: the first step to entering God's kingdom is to seek eternal life. The rich young ruler demonstrated how we should seek eternal life. He did exactly what we must do when we wish anything: seek it. We are to seek eternal life just as the rich young ruler did. But in seeking, there is a critical step to be taken: we must go to the right source. This is exactly what the rich young ruler did: (a) he approached Christ, the Source of eternal life; and (b) he asked, that is, confessed his need.

Note two things about the rich young ruler's seeking eternal life.
  a. He believed that eternal life existed, that there was a thing such as eternal life. He believed there was life in another world, and he was sincere and eager (perhaps desperate) to receive it. He "came running and kneeled" before Jesus (Mk.10:17).
  b. He did a rare thing. He openly confessed his eager concern for eternal life. Few of the rich would ever confess an open concern as he did, and few of the young would ever consider it important enough at their stage of life. He lacked

and had need, and he knew it and confessed it openly. He was seeking for inner peace and a sense of completeness, for a satisfaction which his wealth and position had not given him.

Thought 1. Note: a person does not secure eternal life; he receives it. And...
(1) A man does not receive eternal life until he seeks it.

"That they should seek the Lord, if haply they might feel after him, and find him, though he be not far from every one of us" (Ac.17:27).
"Seek the LORD and his strength, seek his face continually" (1 Chr.16:11).
"The LORD is nigh unto them that are of a broken heart; and saveth such as be of a contrite spirit" (Ps.34:18).
"Be merciful unto me, O God, be merciful unto me: for my soul trusteth in thee: yea, in the shadow of thy wings will I make my refuge until these calamities be overpast" (Ps.57:1).
"Seek the LORD, and his strength: seek his face evermore" (Ps.105:4).
"The LORD is nigh unto all them that call upon him, to all that call upon him in truth" (Ps.145:18).
"Seek ye the LORD while he may be found, call ye upon him while he is near" (Is.55:6).

(2) A man does not receive eternal life until he approaches Christ, the Source of life.

"Come unto me, all ye that labour and are heavy laden, and I will give you rest" (Mt.11:28).
"And the Spirit and the bride say, Come. And let him that heareth say, Come. And let him that is athirst come. And whosoever will, let him take the water of life freely" (Re.22:17).
"Come now, and let us reason together, saith the LORD: though you sins be as scarlet, they shall be as white as snow; though they be red like crimson, they shall be as wool" (Is.1:18).
"Ho, every one that thirsteth, come ye to the waters, and he that hath no money; come ye, buy, and eat; yea, come, buy wine and milk without money and without price" (Is.55:1).

(3) A man does not receive eternal life until he confesses his need.

"Whosoever therefore shall confess me before men, him will I confess also before my Father which is in heaven" (Mt.10:32).
"Also I say unto you, Whosoever shall confess me before men, him shall the Son of man also confess before the angels of God" (Lu.12:8).
"That if thou shalt confess with thy mouth the Lord Jesus, and shalt believe in thine heart that God hath raised him from the dead, thou shalt be saved" (Ro.10:9).
"Whosoever denieth the Son, the same hath not the Father: he that confesseth the Son hath the Father also" (1 Jn.2:23).
"Whosoever shall confess that Jesus is the Son of God, God dwelleth in him, and he in God" (1 Jn.4:15).

DEEPER STUDY # 2
(19:16) **Eternal Life**: note the different words that are used interchangeably throughout this passage. (Also see DEEPER STUDY # 3—Mt.19:23-24; DEEPER STUDY # 1—Jn.17:2-3; see DEEPER STUDY # 2—Jn.1:4; DEEPER STUDY # 1—10:10.)
⇒ Eternal life: "That I may have *eternal life*" (v.16).
⇒ Life: "If thou wilt *enter into life*" (v.17).
⇒ Heaven: "Thou shalt have treasure in *heaven*" (v.21).

The way Christ dealt with the subjects of eternal life, life, and heaven is meaningful. In essence, what He was saying is threefold.

1. He was making a distinction between life and existence. To receive eternal life is to enter life; to really live as one should live; to live just as God intended life to be lived; to live full of love, joy, and peace (Ga.5:22-23). He was saying what Scripture proclaims time and again—that man without Christ does not have life. He is not living; he is only existing. He is in a state of death (always dying) and is separated from God, the Source of real life (Ep.2:1; 1 Jn.5:12).

2. He was teaching eternal existence. Man does not cease to be; he continues on and on. The only question is, does he continue on in a state of life, living eternally, or of death, being separated from God eternally? To receive eternal life means that a man "*enters* life," a continuation of life. To remain as he is means that a person continues on just existing, existing in a state of death, that is, being without God in this world and existing without eternal life (see DEEPER STUDY # 1—He.9:27).

3. He was teaching that heaven is another world—a real world in another dimension of being, an eternal dimension. It is wholly different from the physical and temporal dimension of this world. Note: there is to be "treasure *in* heaven" for following Christ, eternal treasure.

---

2 (19:17) **Man, Misconceptions of**: the second step to entering God's kingdom is to know that God alone is good. The rich young ruler failed at one critical point: he lived a self-righteous life. He did not know that the only good person was God and God alone. This is what Christ was saying to him. The rich young ruler had a wrong concept about the nature of man and saw Christ only as a man. To him man could be good.

MATTHEW 19:16-22

a. He called Jesus "Good Master." By *Master* he meant *Good teacher, good Rabbi,* acknowledging that Jesus was an honorable person to be highly regarded. But he saw Jesus only as a highly regarded teacher. He did not consider Jesus to be the Son of God. He perceived Jesus to be only a mere man, not God. He thought Jesus was a man who had achieved unusual moral goodness and by such had become a *Good Master,* one capable of teaching the truths of God and life.

b. He asked, "What *good thing* shall I do?" He had a religion of works not of faith. He thought he could secure eternal life by being good. If he could just keep some great rule and live a clean life, then God would accept him. He believed that his acts of morality and good works piled up a balance sheet, making him acceptable to God.

Christ had to correct these two errors. He attempted to do so by asking a pointed question, "Why callest thou me good? there is none good, but one, that is, God." He was saying to the young man, "God alone is good. No man is good, not in comparison to God, not even good enough to stand before God in righteousness. If I am but a mere man, a good teacher, then I am not good and do not have the words to eternal life. But if I am God, then you can address me as good, and I do have the words to eternal life."

Note two things.

1. Christ told the young man how to enter life, that is, how to receive eternal life. Therefore, Christ was claiming to be God.

2. Christ was correcting the young man. He was speaking these words forcefully: "Why callest thou me good? there is none good but one, that is, God." Christ would not have the young man's thinking of Him only as a man, no matter how preeminent a teacher the young man thought Him to be. He was God, God's very own Son, and He was to be called the Son of God. Therefore, Christ tried to lead the young man to acknowledge Him as God. It was the only way the young man could ever receive eternal life.

> "For God so loved the world, that he gave his only begotten Son, that whosoever believeth in him should not perish, but have everlasting life" (Jn.3:16).
>
> "Jesus saith unto him, I am the way, the truth, and the life: no man cometh unto the Father, but by me. If ye had known me, ye should have known my Father also: and from henceforth ye know him, and have seen him" (Jn.14:6-7).
>
> "That if thou shalt confess with thy mouth the Lord Jesus, and shalt believe in thine heart that God hath raised him from the dead, thou shalt be saved. For with the heart man believeth unto righteousness; and with the mouth confession is made unto salvation" (Ro.10:9-10).
>
> "For whosoever shall call upon the name of the Lord shall be saved" (Ro.10:13).
>
> "For there is one God, and one mediator between God and men, the man Christ Jesus" (1 Ti.2:5).

Thought 1. The great misconception of man is that man is good—that the basic core and the raw nature of man is good—that man...
- can be good enough to secure God's approval.
- can do enough good works to make himself acceptable to God.

There are at least two basic faults with the position of self-righteousness.

(1) Self-righteousness lowers God, makes God less than perfect. It says that God will accept less than perfection. It almost makes man as high as God. In fact, theoretically and mathematically, if we can become better, gain more goodness, then we can work ourselves up to perfection. It says we can become as high as God, become as gods unto ourselves. Of course, such a theory and position are foolish. It fails to face up to the reality of the world, to the presence of evil and death and to the need to be transformed into a new creature capable of living eternally and perfectly.

(2) Self-righteousness pollutes the area surrounding God with evil and imperfection. No matter how much good we do, we cannot make ourselves perfect. Bad and evil always lie in our background and roots. If God accepts us as bad and evil and wrong, then we would stand on the ground before Him imperfect, contaminating that ground and the atmosphere surrounding Him. Heaven would be contaminated and imperfect. Heaven would no longer be heaven, no longer perfect and free of sin.

There has to be a change, a complete and thorough change, of our being—a transformation, a new birth—before we can enter God's presence. Realistically, no man nor anything else can transform man so that his body becomes perfect and his acts become only good. No man has or ever will have the power to perfect his body and behavior to live perfectly, permanently and eternally. In our present bodies, we come short of God's glory and we die (Ro.3:23; 5:12; 6:23).

If we are going to be transformed, then God Himself will have to do it, and He will have to do it out of pure and perfect love. He will simply have to love us so much that he will transform us. And the glorious news is that He does love us that much. He loves us so much...
- that He gave His only Son to pay the penalty for our sins, which is death (1 Pe.2:24. This means, of course, that if the penalty has been paid, then we do not have to die.)
- that He gave His only Son to show us His great love and to lead us to believe in His love (Jn.5:24. This means, of course, that if we believe, then God will accept us and transform us.)

Thought 2. God alone is perfectly good. He is the Fountain, the Pattern, the Ideal of all goodness. All goodness is to be measured by Him.

The problem with the rich young ruler was that he had not thought deeply enough. His thinking was shallow. How could he ever measure up enough to become acceptable to God? Is God so low? If so, if God is less than perfect, then how could He be God?

MATTHEW 19:16-22

Thought 3. Self-righteousness (a person who thinks that he can be good enough and do enough good to make God accept him) commits a terrible fault. It makes God's love less than perfect. How?

The person who walks in self-righteousness waters down God's love; he makes God's love less than perfect and disallows God the right to express His love perfectly.

⇒ A perfect love must express itself perfectly: it must, from its height of perfection, reach down to the lowest depth of imperfection and give itself for that imperfection. A perfect love reaches from the highest height to the lowest depth. And the lowest depth of imperfection is man, a being who (of all things) rebels against God Himself and lives a self-willed life instead of a God-centered life. (Just picture the terrible scene: a being, a man rebelling against the God of the universe, the Creator and Lord of all things.)

This is exactly what God did for man. He reached down from the highest height and gave His only Son, the highest and most perfect Being, for man who had reached the lowest depth in rebelling against God (Jn.3:16; 2 Co.5:21; 1 Pe.2:24).

Thought 4. The rich young ruler failed in two areas.
(1) He failed to face the reality of man's nature and the way of an imperfect world (Ro.3:10-20).
(2) He failed to understand that Christ was more than a great and good man (see note—Mt.19:17).

3 (19:18-20) **Law—Commandments—Brotherhood**: the third step to entering God's kingdom is to keep the commandments. Once Christ had led the young man to trust Him as God, then Christ had to lead him to love his neighbor. This, too, was a critical weakness in the man. Because of his low concept of God and his inaccurate concept of man's nature, he would claim that he had loved his neighbor; that he had kept the commandments dealing with his neighbor. But Christ would prove that he had not loved his neighbor, not as he should. He had kept the commandments only in a superficial sense. He had not kept them within, not in his spirit. He had not loved his neighbor from the heart. If he had, he would have helped his neighbor more, much more (see vv.21-22).

Christ told the young man very simply, "Keep the commandments." The young man asked, "Which?" By asking, the man revealed an inadequate concept of God's law. He thought some were more important than others. He wanted to know which ones would give him life.

Christ struck at the man's real problem. The man was failing to love his neighbor as himself, so Christ quoted five of the ten commandments, five that have to do with his duty toward his neighbor (Ex.20:12-16).
1. Murder: concerns our neighbor's life.
2. Adultery: concerns our neighbor's chastity and purity. To commit adultery does two things.
   ⇒ Adultery takes the body of our neighbor to ourselves and gives our body to another.
   ⇒ Adultery takes the body of our neighbor's spouse away from our neighbor and takes our own body away from our spouse.

3. Stealing: concerns our neighbor's property.
4. False witness: concerns our neighbor's name, reputation, and understanding of the truth.
5. Honoring parents: concerns our duty to the closest neighbors we have, our own family.

Note: Christ summed up all five commandments by saying, "Thou shalt love thy neighbor as thyself" (Le.19:18). This is what James called the "royal law" (Js.2:8). The person who loves his neighbor will have excellent relations with all and will experience love, joy, and peace—the abundance of life. He will experience exactly what Christ says: he will "enter into life."

The man made the phenomenal claim that he had kept all five of the commandments that Christ quoted. Of course, as is true with all men, he had not kept them—not perfectly, not in God's eyes, not in the spirit in which God intended them to be kept. He was not generous enough with others, not giving and helping like he should. Christ was ready to show him this.

In essence, Christ had said to the rich young ruler: keep the commandments.
a. Keep the commandments dealing with your neighbor: the ones especially needed by the rulers and the rich of the world—the commandments which are so often misunderstood and neglected by rulers and the rich.
b. However, the rich young ruler misunderstood God's law: he had a tragic sense of self-righteousness.
   1) He thought that some commandments were more important than others.
   2) He thought that man could keep the commandments and build up a balance sheet against God, securing God's acceptance.

> "Whosoever believeth that Jesus is the Christ is born of God: and every one that loveth him that begat loveth him also that is begotten of him. By this we know that we love the children of God, when we love God, and keep his commandments" (1 Jn.5:1-2).

Thought 1. Note two extremely important facts.
(1) The first thing Jesus told the young man was the very commandment of God.

> "And this is his commandment, That we should believe on the name of His Son Jesus Christ, and love one another, as he gave us commandment" (1 Jn.3:23).

MATTHEW 19:16-22

(2) Christ summed up the law in two commandments. The first has to do with our love for God which sums up the first five commandments, and the second is the one He used to sum up the second group of commandments which He quoted to this young man.

"Thou shalt love thy neighbor as thyself" (Mt.22:39).

Thought 2. Note that the very commandments quoted by Christ are the commandments needed by the rich, the powerful, the famous, and the wise. They are the commandments so often ignored, neglected, and denied by the achiever. In fact, the achiever sometimes uses and steps upon his neighbor to secure what he seeks.

4 (19:21-22) **Self-Denial**: the fourth step to enter God's kingdom is to give all you are and have to Christ. Christ knew exactly what the young man needed. His rejection of Christ showed this. He was hoarding wealth instead of distributing it. God had given to him that he might have to give to others (Ep.4:28), but he was failing to love and help his neighbor anywhere close to what he should.

a. What the young man needed was just what Christ said: "If thou wilt be perfect [that is, really keep the commandments and receive heaven], then demonstrate to all publicly and without question that you love your neighbor: go and sell *all* you have, and give to the poor...and come *follow* me."

b. In our struggle to protect the glorious truth that man is saved by grace and grace alone, we often forget and neglect another great truth: to follow Christ is to serve and minister to our neighbor. To follow Christ is to deny self completely, all that we are as well as all that we have (see note and Deeper Study # 1—Lu.9:23). When we love our neighbor as ourselves, then we show that we truly love God. If we do not love and minister to our neighbor (above self), then we do not love God.

When we deny self by giving all we are and have (1 Jn.4:20), then and only then do we receive heaven and the treasures of heaven. To deny self, to give all we are and have, is a hard saying; but Christ demands it. Our attempts to soften it do not annul His demand (see note and Deeper Study # 1—Lu.9:23; Deeper Study # 1—Ro.3:3).

c. The young man rejected Christ for three reasons.
1) Unbelief: he was not willing to entrust his life to Christ. There was some lack of belief that Jesus Christ was really God's very own Son standing before him.
2) Self-righteousness and pride: his concept of religion was keeping laws and doing good in order to secure God's acceptance. He felt that he had the power and goodness to make God approve and accept him.
3) Love of the world: he was rich and was unwilling to give up the comfort and possessions he had obtained. He made the fatal mistake that so many make with wealth, power, and fame.
   a) He loved the things of the world more than he loved people. He preferred hoarding and extravagance, preferred living sumptuously and comfortably to helping those who were so desperately in need: the hungry, thirsty, poor, diseased, suffering, orphans, widows, widowers, empty, lonely, and the lost.
   b) He loved the things of the world more than he loved the hope of eternal life.
   c) He loved the position and recognition and esteem and power of the earth more than he loved Christ.

"Then Peter began to say unto him, Lo, we have left all, and have followed thee" (Mk.10:28).
"And he said to them all, If any man will come after me, let him deny himself, and take up his cross daily, and follow me" (Lu.9:23).
"If any man come to me, and hate not his father, and mother, and wife, and children, and brethren, and sisters, yea, and his own life also, he cannot be my disciple. And whosoever doth not bear his cross, and come after me, cannot be my disciple" (Lu.14:26-27).
"So likewise, whosoever he be of you that forsaketh not all that he hath, he cannot be my disciple" (Lu.14:33).

MATTHEW 19:23-26

	D. The Danger of Riches, 19:23-26 (Mk 10:23-27; Lu 18:24-27)	needle, than for a rich man to enter into the kingdom of God. 25 When his disciples heard *it*, they were exceedingly amazed, saying, Who then can be saved? 26 But Jesus beheld *them*, and said unto them, With men this is impossible; but with God all things are possible.	than for a rich man to enter the kingdom

1. The fact: Wealth pulls a person from the kingdom^{DS1, 2, 3}
  a. Creates the big "I," vv. 16, 20
  b. Makes one hoard, v. 21
  c. Attaches to the world, v. 22
2. The great difficulty illustrated: It is easier for a camel to go through the eye of a needle
	23 Then said Jesus unto his disciples, Verily I say unto you, That a rich man shall hardly enter into the kingdom of heaven.
	24 And again I say unto you, It is easier for a camel to go through the eye of a
			3. The shock: Who is saved if wealth is not God's blessing & a blessing of righteousness?
			4. The reality: The only hope for the rich
			  a. To turn away from trusting in men
			  b. To turn to God & His power^{DS4}

DIVISION XIII

THE MESSIAH'S TEACHINGS ON THE WAY TO JERUSALEM, 19:1–20:34

D. The Danger of Riches, 19:23-26

(19:23-26) **Introduction**: the words "then said Jesus" connect this passage to the experience of the rich young ruler. Jesus took the rich young ruler's rejection and *warned* all men about the dangers of wealth. Wealth is fraught with dangers and pitfalls...
- for the man who is seeking to be rich
- for the man who is already rich

The dangers are many, and they are entangling and enslaving—so much so that Christ made the shocking statement that it was extremely difficult for a rich man to be saved.

The words are strong; the idea is shocking. However, Christ loves and cares for all men including the rich, so He had to be truthful. It is extremely difficult for a rich man to enter heaven. The dangers that face the rich are real and terrible, so the warning must be real and truthful.

1. The fact: wealth pulls a person from the kingdom (v.23).
2. The great difficulty illustrated: it is easier for a camel to go through the eye of a needle than for a rich man to enter the kingdom (v.24).
3. The shock: Who is saved if wealth is not God's blessing and a blessing of righteousness (v.25)?
4. The reality: the only hope for the rich (v.26).

1 (19:23) **Wealth—Materialism—Pride—Worldliness**: wealth pulls a person away from the Kingdom of Heaven. It is difficult for a rich person to enter heaven. Christ made this statement because of the things that *pulled* the rich young ruler away. Wealth does pull a person away from heaven. There is a lure, an attraction, a force, a power, a pull that reaches out to draw us when we look at or possess wealth. There are pulls so forceful that they will enslave and doom any rich man who fails to turn and embrace God.

a. *Wealth creates the big "I"* (see v.16, 20). The wealthy are usually esteemed, honored, and envied. Wealth brings comfort, possessions, position, power, and recognition. It boosts *ego* and makes a person self-sufficient and independent in this world. As a result, there is a tendency for the rich to feel independent and self-sufficient, to live as though they need nothing; and in such an atmosphere and world of thought, God is forgotten. A person forgets that there are things that money cannot buy and events from which money cannot save. Peace, love, joy—all that really matters within the spirit of man—can never be bought. Neither can money save a person from trouble, disaster, disease, accident, or death—the trials that are sure to come upon all.

b. *Wealth tends to make a person hoard* (see v.21). The Bible lays down the principle for handling money for all men, even for the poor:

> "Let him labor...that he may have to give to him that needeth" (Ep.4:28).
> "Thou shalt love thy neighbor as thyself" (Mt.19:19; 22:39).

The world reels in desperate need. People are starving, sick, unhoused, unclothed, and suffering by the millions; and teeming millions are spiritually lost and without God in this world and doomed to die without ever knowing Him. When any of us sit still and objectively look at the world in its desperate plight, we ask: "How in this world can any man hoard and not help—even to the last available penny? Why would any man keep more than what he needs for himself and his family?"

As God looks at the rich, He is bound to ask the same questions. In fact, His questions are bound to be more pointed and forceful. This is exactly what Christ said to the rich young ruler:

> "Go and sell that thou hast; and give to the poor, and thou shalt have treasure in heaven: and come and follow me" (Mt.19:21).

c. *Riches tend to make a man selfish*. For some unexplainable reason, the more we get, the more we want. When we taste the things of this world and become comfortable, we tend to fear losing our possessions. We struggle to keep what we have and to get more. True, many are willing to make contributions—but only a certain amount, an amount that will not lower their overall estate, or standing, or level of comfort and possessions. There are few who give all they are and have to Christ in order to meet the needs of the world.

As Christ said, "It is difficult, very difficult for the rich [meaning those who have anything in comparison with most of the world] to enter heaven." If we do not have compassion and take care of our brothers (fellow-man) when they are in desperate need, how can we expect God to have compassion and take care of us when we face the desperate need for heaven? It is foolish for us to think that a loving and just God will meet our need for life when we would not meet the need of our fellow man for life. The rich (all of us who have anything in comparison with the rest of the world) have the means to help and to reach the world with the gospel if they just would.

d. *Wealth attaches a person to the world* (see v.22). Wealth enables a person to buy things that...
- make him comfortable
- please his taste
- stir his ego
- expand his experience
- challenge his mental pursuit
- stimulate his flesh
- stretch his self-image

If a man centers his life upon the things of the world, his attention is on the world and not on God. He tends to become wrapped up in securing more and in protecting what he has. Too often, he gives little if any time and thought to heavenly matters. Wealth and the things it can buy can and usually do consume the rich.

DEEPER STUDY # 1
(19:23) **Hardly** (duskolos): the word means barely or with great difficulty. It is difficult, very difficult for a rich man to enter heaven. Why? In one simple sentence, it is difficult for a rich man to give all that he has to help the needy—to give all that has been so pleasing, so comfortable, so ego boosting, and so rewarding in possessions and position and self-esteem.

DEEPER STUDY # 2
(19:23) **Rich**: Who are the rich? This question seriously needs to be asked of every individual in light of the great and desperate needs of the world. Every one of us needs to compare what we have with what the vast majority of the world has. The rich are persons who have anything to put back beyond meeting the needs of their own family (and by needs is meant *real* needs). This is exactly what Christ and the Bible say time and again (see also Mk.12:41-44; Lu.21:1-4; Ac.4:34-35).

In a summary statement, who are the rich? The rich are any of us who have anything beyond what we need. What Christ demands is that we give all that we *are and have* to meet the needs of those in such desperate need, holding back nothing. This is often the great complaint against Christians, that we just do not believe, not to the point that we are willing to follow the sacrificial example of Christ. The evidence of our unbelief is seen in Christ's insistence that we give all we have to feed the starving and to meet the desperate needs of the world, and yet we do not do it. Gandhi, the great leader of India's independence, is said to have never embraced Christianity for this very reason. How many others have rejected Christ because of our hypocrisy?

"Go and sell that thou hast, and give to the poor, and thou shalt have treasure in heaven: and come and follow me" (Mt.19:21).

"And every one that hath forsaken houses, or brethren, or sisters, or father, or mother, or wife, or children, or lands, for my name's sake, shall receive an hundredfold, and shall inherit everlasting life" (Mt.19:29).

"For where your treasure is, there will your heart be also" (Mt.6:21).

"Thou shalt love thy neighbor as thyself" (Mt.22:39).

"Seek ye the kingdom of God; and all these things shall be added unto you. Fear not, little flock; for it is your Father's good pleasure to give you the kingdom. Sell that ye have, and give alms; provide yourselves bags which wax not old, a treasure in the heavens that faileth not, where no thief approacheth, neither moth corrupteth. For where your treasure is, there will your heart be also" (Lu.12:31-34).

"And Zacchaeus stood, and said unto the Lord; Behold, Lord, the half of my goods I give to the poor; and if I have taken any thing from any man by false accusation, I restore him fourfold" (Lu.19:8).

"By this shall all men know that ye are my disciples, if ye have love one to another" (Jn.13:35).

"If ye keep my commandments, ye shall abide in my love; even as I have kept my Father's commandments, and abide in his love" (Jn.15:10).

"Let love be without dissimulation. Abhor that which is evil; cleave to that which is good" (Ro.12:9).

"Even as I please all men in all things, not seeking mine own profit, but the profit of many, that they may be saved" (1 Co.10:33).

"For ye know the grace of our Lord Jesus Christ, that, though he was rich, yet for your sakes he became poor, that ye through his poverty might be rich" (2 Co.8:9).

"Let him that stole steal no more: but rather let him labour, working with his hands the thing which is good, that he may have to give to him that needeth" (Ep.4:28).

"And the Lord make you to increase and abound in love one toward another, and toward all men, even as we do toward you" (1 Th.3:12).

"Let your conversation [life, behavior] be without covetousness; and be content with such things as ye have: for he hath said, I will never leave thee, nor forsake thee" (He.13:5).

MATTHEW 19:23-26

DEEPER STUDY # 3
(19:23-24) **Kingdom of Heaven**: the Kingdom of Heaven evidently means the same thing as the Kingdom of God, eternal life, and salvation. The Kingdom of Heaven and the Kingdom of God are interchanged when Jesus says, "a rich man shall hardly enter into the Kingdom of Heaven" (Mt.19:23) or "Kingdom of God" (Mt.19:24). Eternal life (Mt.19:26) and salvation (Mt.19:25) belong to the very same concept. Eternity and salvation, the Kingdom of God and the Kingdom of Heaven, is the very subject being discussed in Mt.19:16-30. Having eternal life, being saved, or entering into the Kingdom of God or of Heaven is more difficult for a rich man than for a camel to go through the eye of a needle.

The Kingdom of Heaven and of God is revealed in four different stages throughout history.

1. There is the spiritual kingdom that is at hand; it is present right now (Mt.4:17; 12:28).
   a. The present kingdom refers to God's rule and reign and authority in the lives of believers.

   > "The eyes of your understanding being enlightened; that ye may know what is the hope of his calling, and what the riches of the glory of his inheritance in the saints, and what is the exceeding greatness of his power to us-ward who believe, according to the working of his mighty power, which he wrought in Christ, when he raised him from the dead, and set him at his own right hand in the heavenly places, far above all principality, and power, and might, and dominion, and every name that is named, not only in this world, but also in that which is to come: and hath put all things under his feet, and gave him to be the head over all things to the church, which is his body, the fulness of him that filleth all in all" (Ep.1:18-23).

   > "Let this mind be in you, which was also in Christ Jesus: who, being in the form of God, thought it not robbery to be equal with God: but made himself of no reputation, and took upon him the form of a servant, and was made in the likeness of men: and being found in fashion as a man, he humbled himself, and became obedient unto death, even the death of the cross. Wherefore God also hath highly exalted him, and given him a name which is above every name: that at the name of Jesus every knee should bow, of things in heaven, and things in earth, and things under the earth; and that every tongue should confess that Jesus Christ is Lord, to the glory of God the Father" (Ph.2:5-11).

   > "Who hath delivered us from the power of darkness, and hath translated us into the kingdom of his dear Son" (Col.1:13).

   b. The present kingdom is offered to the world and to men in the person of Jesus Christ.
   c. The present kingdom must be received as a little child.

   > "But when Jesus saw it, he was much displeased, and said unto them, Suffer the little children to come unto me, and forbid them not: for of such is the kingdom of God" (Mk.10:14-15).

   d. The present kingdom is experienced only by the new birth.

   > "Jesus answered and said unto him, Verily, verily, I say unto thee, Except a man be born again, he cannot see the kingdom of God" (Jn.3:3).

   e. The present kingdom is entered now and must be received now.

   > "Whether of them twain did the will of his father? They say unto him, The first. Jesus saith unto them, Verily I say unto you, That the publicans and the harlots go into the kingdom of God before you" (Mt.21:31).
   > "Verily I say unto you, Whosoever shall not receive the kingdom of God as a little child, he shall not enter therein" (Mk.10:15).

   f. The present kingdom is a spiritual, life-changing blessing.

   > "For the kingdom of God is not meat and drink; but righteousness, and peace, and joy in the Holy Ghost" (Ro.14:17).

   g. The present kingdom is to be the first thing sought by believers.

   > "But seek ye first the kingdom of God, and his righteousness; and all these things shall be added unto you" (Mt.6:33).

2. There is the professing kingdom that is also in this present age. It refers to people who profess Christianity in every generation. It pictures the imperfect state of the Kingdom of Heaven or professing Christianity, what professing Christianity is like between Christ's first coming and His return. This imperfect state is what is called "the mysteries of the kingdom of heaven" (Mt.13:1-52, esp.11).

   > "Another parable put he forth unto them, saying, The kingdom of heaven is likened unto a man which sowed good seed [good men] in his field: but while men slept, his enemy came and sowed tares [evil men] among the wheat, and went his way" (Mt.13:24-25).

3. There is the millennial kingdom that is future. It is the actual rule of Christ or the government of Christ that is to come to this earth for a thousand years.
   a. The millennial kingdom is the kingdom predicted by Daniel.

> "And in the days of these kings shall the God of heaven set up a kingdom, which shall never be destroyed: and the kingdom shall not be left to other people, but it shall break in pieces and consume all these kingdoms, and it shall stand for ever" (Da.2:44).

> "But the saints of the most High shall take the kingdom, and possess the kingdom for ever, even for ever and ever....Until the Ancient of days came, and judgment was given to the saints of the most High; and the time came that the saints possessed the kingdom....And the kingdom and dominion, and the greatness of the kingdom under the whole heaven, shall be given to the people of the saints of the most High, whose kingdom is an everlasting kingdom, and all dominions shall serve and obey him" (Da.7:18, 22, 27).

   b. The millennial kingdom is the kingdom promised to David.

> "And when thy days be fulfilled, and thou shalt sleep with thy fathers, I will set up thy seed after thee, which shall proceed out of thy bowels, and I will establish his kingdom....And thine house and thy kingdom shall be established for ever before thee: thy throne shall be established for ever" (2 S.7:12, 16).

> "I have made a covenant with my chosen, I have sworn unto David my servant, thy seed will I establish for ever, and build up thy throne to all generations" (Ps.89:3-4).

> "In that day shall the LORD defend the inhabitants of Jerusalem; and he that is feeble among them at that day shall be as David; and the house of David shall be as God, as the angel of the LORD before them" (Zec.12:8).

   c. The millennial kingdom is the kingdom pictured by John.

> "And I saw thrones, and they sat upon them, and judgment was given unto them: and I saw the souls of them that were beheaded for the witness of Jesus, and for the word of God, and which had not worshipped the beast, neither his image, neither had received his mark upon their foreheads, or in their hands; and they lived and reigned with Christ a thousand years. But the rest of the dead lived not again until the thousand years were finished. This is the first resurrection. Blessed and holy is he that hath part in the first resurrection: on such the second death hath no power, but they shall be priests of God and of Christ, and shall reign with him a thousand years" (Re.20:4-6).

4. There is the perfect kingdom of the new heaven and earth that is future.
   a. The eternal kingdom is the rule and reign of God in a perfect universe for all eternity.

> "Let not your heart be troubled: ye believe in God, believe also in me. In my Father's house are many mansions: if it were not so, I would have told you. I go to prepare a place for you. And if I go and prepare a place for you, I will come again, and receive you unto myself; that where I am, there ye may be also" (Jn.14:1-3).

> "Then cometh the end, when he shall have delivered up the kingdom to God, even the Father; when he shall have put down all rule and all authority and power" (1 Co.15:24).

> "But the day of the Lord will come as a thief in the night; in the which the heavens shall pass away with a great noise, and the elements shall melt with fervent heat, the earth also and the works that are therein shall be burned up. Seeing then that all these things shall be dissolved, what manner of persons ought ye to be in all holy conversation and godliness, looking for and hasting unto the coming of the day of God, wherein the heavens being on fire shall be dissolved, and the elements shall melt with fervent heat? Nevertheless we, according to his promise, look for new heavens and a new earth, wherein dwelleth righteousness" (2 Pe.3:10-13).

> "And I saw a new heaven and a new earth: for the first heaven and the first earth were passed away" (Re.21:1).

   b. The eternal kingdom is the perfect state of being for the believer in the future.

> "Now this I say, brethren, that flesh and blood cannot inherit the kingdom of God; neither doth corruption inherit incorruption" (1 Co.15:50).

> "And God shall wipe away all tears from their eyes; and there shall be no more death, neither sorrow, nor crying, neither shall there be any more pain: for the former things are passed away. And he that sat upon the throne said, Behold, I make all things new. And he said unto me, Write: for these words are true and faithful" (Re.21:4-5).

   c. The eternal kingdom is an actual place into which believers are to enter sometime in the future.

> "And I say unto you, That many shall come from the east and west, and shall sit down with Abraham, and Isaac, and Jacob, in the kingdom of heaven" (Mt.8:11).

MATTHEW 19:23-26

> d. The eternal kingdom is a gift of God that will be given in the future.
>
> "Fear not, little flock; for it is your Father's good pleasure to give you the kingdom" (Lu.12:32).

2 (19:24) **Riches—Camel—Needle**: it is extremely difficult for a rich man to enter into the Kingdom of God. It is so difficult that Jesus says, "It is easier for a camel to pass through the eye of a needle, than for a rich man to enter into the kingdom of God."

There have been various interpretations of *camel* and *needle* in an attempt to soften the words of Jesus. For example, some have said that the "needle" was a small gate in the wall surrounding Jerusalem, a small gate which sat right beside the large gate. It is thought that the large gate was closed at night to protect the city from marauders and enemies, and the small gate was used by the travelling public. The small gate is said to have been called "the Needle's Eye" because it was so small that it was difficult for even a single person to pass through.

Others have said that the Greek word Christ used was *kamilos* (a ship's rope or cable) not *kamelos* (camel). Note: the only difference between the two words is that the letter *i* is an *e* in the word for camel (*kamelos*).

Three things need to be noted about these interpretations.

a. There is no doubt that Jesus means a literal *needle*. He as much as says so in v.26, "With men this is impossible." What He does is use a proverbial saying *for an impossibility*. Most countries have proverbs that express the impossibility of some things. The camel was the largest animal among the Jews, so Christ either used a well known proverb among the Jews or else created one. There is also this point, when Christ chose to speak in parables, He chose the most common and ordinary thing to express His meaning.

b. Attempts to soften the Lord's point are just that: attempts to soften. But nothing can be softened with v.26, "With men this is impossible." No man, not even the rich man himself, can save a rich man. The danger of riches is very real and terrible. Wealth entangles and enslaves a man so much that it is extremely difficult for a rich man to let go and give his wealth to help the desperate needs of the world. He just cannot accept the fact that he is to "labor so that he may have to give to others" (Ep.4:28). If a man is rich, it is difficult not to live in personal luxury and to build large estates. Heavy and fancy meals, full and fashionable wardrobes, a fine and large house, recognition and attention, position and power—so much is so difficult to let go. It is the ego that refuses to let go.

c. It is just as difficult for the softening interpretations to be performed as it is for the literal interpretation. How does a camel's trying to get through a gate made only for a man soften anything? It would be impossible. And how does threading a needle with a ship's cable soften anything? Again, it is impossible.

> **Thought 1.** In the illustration given by Christ, there are some comparisons between a camel and a rich man.
>
> (1) A camel is *too big* to go through the eye of a needle; a rich man is too big to go through the gate of heaven.
>
> "Charge them that are rich in this world, that they be not highminded, nor trust in uncertain riches, but in the living God, who giveth us richly all things to enjoy" (1 Ti.6:17).
>
> (2) A camel *never thinks* about going through the eye of a needle; a rich man seldom, if ever, thinks about going into heaven.
>
> "And I will say to my soul, Soul, thou hast much goods laid up for many years; take thine ease, eat, drink, and be merry. But God said unto him, Thou fool, this night thy soul shall be required of thee: then whose shall those things be, which thou hast provided?" (Lu.12:19-20).
> "The rich man's wealth is his strong city, and as a high wall in his own conceit" (Pr.18:11).
> "And when thy herds and thy flocks multiply, and thy silver and thy gold is multiplied, and all that thou hast is multiplied; then thine heart be lifted up, and thou forget the LORD thy God, which brought thee forth out of the land of Egypt, from the house of bondage" (De.8:13-14).
>
> (3) A camel was *not made* to go through the eye of a needle; a man was not made for wealth, not made to be possessed and enslaved by the *things* and *possessions* of this world.
>
> "And the cares of this world, and the deceitfulness of riches, and the lusts of other things entering in, choke the word, and it becometh unfruitful" (Mk.4:19).
> "But they that will be rich fall into temptation and a snare, and into many foolish and hurtful lusts, which drown men in destruction and perdition" (1 Ti.6:9).
>
> (4) A camel *works* for its master; a man is to work for his Master (God).
>
> "No man can serve two masters: for either he will hate the one, and love the other; or else he will hold to the one, and despise the other. Ye cannot serve God and mammon" (Mt.6:24).
> "Servants, obey in all things your masters according to the flesh; not with eyeservice, as menpleasers; but in singleness of heart, fearing God: and whatsoever ye do, do it heartily, as to the Lord, and not unto men; knowing that of the Lord ye shall receive the reward of the inheritance: for ye serve the Lord Christ" (Col.3:22-24).

MATTHEW 19:23-26

3 (19:25) **Wealth—Salvation**: the disciples were shocked, thoroughly dismayed. Christ was saying something diametrically opposed to what they and everyone else had always thought. They had been taught (as have succeeding generations, even the church)...
- that prosperity (wealth, comfort, and things) is God's blessing
- that a person receives and has because God is blessing him
- that prosperity is the reward of righteousness and obedience
- that God blesses a person with the things of this earth if they are righteous and obedient

However, Christ was saying the very opposite: that a prosperous person would most likely never enter heaven; that prosperity posed such a dangerous threat to a person that his eternal doom was almost assured. The disciples knew that God would never put a person in such a precarious and dangerous position. They knew that Christ was attacking the world's most cherished and ardent belief: be good (righteous) and you will be blessed by God (and the thought of blessing is always of material blessing. See note—Ep.1:3 for more discussion.)

They were shocked, thoroughly dismayed: Who then could be saved? The vast majority of people were threatening their own eternal destiny. They were dooming themselves. Since prosperity is not the reward (sign) for righteousness, and the rich are barred from heaven, that means that the poor, too, are barred; for they are spending most of their time dreaming and seeking prosperity!

The idea that prosperity is the reward for righteousness, that God blesses a person with the things of this earth if they are righteous and obedient, is so prevalent a view that a comment is needed at this point.

a. God's concern is spiritual blessings, not material blessings. God promises a man the necessities of life (food, clothing, shelter) if he seeks God first (Mt.6:33; see Mt.6:25-34). God can, if He chooses, bless any of us with whatever and however much He wishes for special purposes, for the purposes of having in order "to give to him that needeth." But just because a man is prosperous does not mean the man is righteous, and just because a person is righteous does not mean that he is going to be blessed materially. Righteousness and prosperity have nothing to do with each other. In fact, "A rich man shall hardly enter into the kingdom of heaven."

b. Wealth is seldom a good thing. As Christ taught in this passage, wealth is fraught with dangers that make it extremely difficult for the rich to enter heaven. Nevertheless the whole world, rich and poor alike, puts its primary attention upon securing more and more.

c. Wealth is secured by man himself, by his own energy and effort. Man secures wealth by dreaming how to make it (a vision, perspective) and having the initiative to make it (acting and timing). A man may trust God to help him secure wealth, but a man may have nothing to do with God and secure wealth on his own. There is a sense in which a man's strength and mind are from God, but that has nothing to do with a personal or active relationship with God. Most rich men control their own lives and go about securing their treasure on this earth *without God* (Mt.6:21).

On the other hand, a man may trust God to bless him so that he may help others, and God may choose to bless him. But God's choosing to bless him is for the purpose of helping others, not to hoard and live above what is needed (extravagantly and sumptuously). In fact what Christ teaches is that the rich are *to live just as sacrificially* as the poor. (See DEEPER STUDY # 1,2—Mt.19:23; Mk.12:42. See outline—Lu.21:1-4.)

> **Thought 1.** Something is usually forgotten: man was not made for things (money, wealth, possessions), but things were made for man. Yet man allows himself to become enslaved to things, ever lusting after more and more.
>
> Wealth (money, possessions, things) is only a commodity—a means, a tool—to help man carry out his purpose and service upon earth. At least, that is what wealth is supposed to be. But most men become the tool and the commodity of money. Few men know why God put them on earth.
>
> "It is better to trust in the LORD than to put confidence in princes" (Ps.118:9).
> "Cease ye from man, whose breath is in his nostrils: for wherein is he to be accounted of?" (Is.2:22).
> "Thus saith the LORD; cursed be the man that trusteth in man, and maketh flesh his arm, and whose heart departeth from the LORD" (Je.17:5).

4 (19:26) **Wealth—Salvation—Repentance**: there is one hope for the rich man—God.

a. A rich man must turn away from men. No man can save a rich man nor any other man for that matter.
  1) No man has the strength or know-how to break the power of *seeking things* that hold sway over a rich man. The natural urge within man is to seek more and more comfort and ease and possessions. No man has the power to break that *natural urge*. The entanglements are too pleasing and enslaving
  2) No man can recreate the soul of a man, change it so that he seeks "those things which are above" and sets his "affection on things above, *not on things on the earth*" (Col.3:1-2). No philosophy, no psychology, no medicine, no education, no politics, no social movement can change the soul of a man.

> "A rich man shall hardly enter into the kingdom of heaven...Who then can be saved [for even the poor dream and seek]?...With men this [salvation] is impossible" (vv.23, 26).

b. A rich man must turn to God and His power. God is the only hope for a rich man. Only God can break a rich man's enslavement to this earth—only God can convert and change, turn and save the rich man from the danger and doom of wealth.

MATTHEW 19:23-26

How? Very simply. The words of Christ to the rich young ruler tell the rich what to do: "...go and sell that thou hast, and give to the poor, and thou shalt have treasure in heaven: and come and follow me" (Mt.19:21).

This is a hard saying, a difficult thing for any of us to do—so difficult that we try to escape from its stringent demand, softening it and explaining it away. *But it is what Christ said. The disciples understood it perfectly* (v.25-27).

In very practical terms, to receive eternal life, we must *give all we are and have*. Naturally, this is more difficult for the rich, for "he has great possessions" (v.22).

There are four practical steps that will help a rich man be saved.

1. He must listen and heed immediately the inner voice, the pricking of conscience to give his life and possessions to God. He must turn immediately to God and never turn away.

2. He must study God's Word daily for direction, and talk to and trust God to keep his heart free from the lure and deceptions of possessions.

3. He must use his wealth to help the desperate needs of others. He must *realize, know, and acknowledge* that the vast majority of the world is hungry, hurting, and needing help—desperately so—and that God expects him to use all he has to meet those needs. He must not hoard and live extravagantly in the midst of so much need.

4. He must develop a strong desire for heaven, knowing that his sojourn on earth is ever so short, as brief as the lily of the field.

> "For with God nothing shall be impossible" (Lu.1:37).
>
> "I know that thou canst do every thing, and that no thought can be withholden from thee" (Jb.42:2).
>
> "Charge them that are rich in this world, that they be not highminded, nor trust in uncertain riches, but in the living God, who giveth us richly all things to enjoy; that they do good, that they be rich in good works, ready to distribute, willing to communicate; laying up in store for themselves a good foundation against the time to come, that they may lay hold on eternal life" (1 Ti.6:17-19).
>
> "For other foundation can no man lay than that is laid, which is Jesus Christ" (1 Co.3:11).
>
> "By faith Moses, when he was come to years, refused to be called the son of Pharaoh's daughter; choosing rather to suffer affliction with the people of God, than to enjoy the pleasures of sin for a season; esteeming the reproach of Christ greater riches than the treasures in Egypt: for he had respect unto the recompence of the reward" (He.11:24-26).

DEEPER STUDY # 4

(19:26) **Rich, The**: some rich persons did turn to Christ. They serve as excellent examples for the rich to follow in turning to God (also see outline—Lu.8:2-3).

⇒ James and John (Mk.1:20; see note—Mk.10:36-37).
⇒ Matthew (see note and DEEPER STUDY # 1—Mt.9:9-13).
⇒ Zacchaeus (Lu.19:1-10).
⇒ Joseph of Arimathaea (Mt.27:57).
⇒ Nicodemus (Jn.20:39 see 3:1f. He may or may not have been saved.)
⇒ Lydia (Ac.16:14-15).
⇒ Manaen, a foster brother of Herod, who was probably wealthy (Ac.13:1).
⇒ Some women who supported Jesus (see outline and notes—Lu.8:2-3).

MATTHEW 19:27-30

	E. The Reward for Believers, 19:27-30 *(Mk 10:28-31; Lu 18:28-30)*	throne of his glory, ye also shall sit upon twelve thrones, judging the twelve tribes of Israel.	

1. The two essentials for reward
  a. Must leave everything behind
  b. Must follow Christ
	27 Then answered Peter and said unto him, Behold, we have forsaken all, and followed thee; what shall we have therefore?	29 And every one that hath forsaken houses, or brethren, or sisters, or father, or mother, or wife, or children, or lands, for my name's sake, shall receive an hundredfold, and shall inherit everlasting life.	3. The believer's reward: Will receive great benefits
			  a. Reason: Left all–supreme allegiance
			  b. The present reward: A hundred times as much
			  c. The future reward: Eternal life

2. The apostles' reward: Will reign & rule with Christ
  a. When: In the new age
  b. Purpose: To judge–rule, govern–the 12 tribes of Israel^{DS1}
	28 And Jesus said unto them, Verily I say unto you, That ye which have followed me, in the regeneration when the Son of man shall sit in the	30 But many *that are* first shall be last; and the last *shall be* first.	4. The believer's judgment: A shocking surprise–execution of perfect justice

DIVISION XIII

THE MESSIAH'S TEACHINGS ON THE WAY TO JERUSALEM, 19:1–20:34

E. The Reward for Believers, 19:27-30

(19:27-30) **Introduction**: Peter's question is often misunderstood. Peter was not being mercenary; he needed assurance. He wanted to make sure that he and the other disciples were *really saved*. Anyone would need assurance after what Jesus had just said: "If thou wilt be perfect, go and sell that thou hast, and give to the poor, and thou shalt have treasure in heaven: and come and follow me" (Mt.19:21).

Few sell everything and give it all away (v.21), and few, whether rich or poor, control their dreams and urges to have more (see note—Mk.10:25). The disciples, as all honest men, knew this. They also knew the extreme demands Christ was making to be a true follower of Christ. They, unlike so many of us in our attempts to soften His words, understood exactly what He was saying. The extremity of His words was shocking. They could not see how anyone could be saved, and the answer Christ gave to their question about salvation said nothing to give them *personal* assurance: "With men this is impossible; but with God all things are possible" (v.26).

The disciples sensed a deep need for assurance. Had they done enough and given up enough? They thought so and were almost sure they had, but had they? Somewhat meekly Peter said, "Lord, behold [look] we have forsaken all, and followed thee. We have surrendered all to you. What shall we have therefore? Shall we receive eternal life...?" Christ used Peter's question to teach a wonderful truth. They and all who followed Him could rest assured—they would be enormously rewarded.

Note the Lord's assuring words: "I say *unto you*, that *ye*...shall sit in the throne of [My] glory....And everyone that hath forsaken [all]...shall inherit everlasting life" (vv.28-29).
1. The two essentials for reward (v.27).
2. The apostle's reward: will reign and rule with Christ (v.28).
3. The believer's reward: will receive great benefits (v.29).
4. The believer's judgment: a shocking surprise—execution of perfect justice (v.30).

1 (19:27) **Rewards—Believers—Self-Denial**: there are two essentials for reward.

a. A person must forsake all. What is meant by this? Peter and some of the other disciples had families, and they readily met the needs of their families (Mt.8:14). Therefore, *forsaking all* does not mean deserting and shirking our day-to-day responsibilities to our families. What *forsaking all* means is to renounce and to relinquish all—to give up all unreservedly. It means that a person takes care of his family, yes; but beyond that, he uses what he has to meet the needs of a desperate world. It means that a person serves and puts Christ before all, including family and friends. It means that a person *forsakes all sinful behavior* such as dirty habits, evil associations, crooked ways, off colored jokes and curse words. It means that we allow nothing to interfere with serving Christ. It means to put *following Christ* first. When we put Him first, we discover a wonderful truth: life becomes balanced. All other things, including family, fall into their proper place; and life becomes a most enriching experience (even if a person's family rejects him).

b. A person must follow Christ (see note and DEEPER STUDY # 1—Lu.9:23). A person who really follows Christ has no sense of regret and no desire to complain. He is truly a new creature: "old things are passed away; behold all things are become new" (2 Co.5:17). He is satisfied and complete (Col.2:10).

"Then Peter began to say unto him, Lo, we have left all, and have followed thee" (Mk.10:28).

"And after these things he went forth, and saw a publican, named Levi, sitting at the receipt of custom: and he said unto him, Follow me" (Lu.5:27).

"And he said to them all, If any man will come after me, let him deny himself, and take up his cross daily, and follow me, For whosoever will save his life shall lose it: but whosoever will lose his life for my sake, the same shall save it" (Lu.9:23-24).

"So likewise, whosoever he be of you that forsaketh not all that he hath, he cannot be my disciple" (Lu.14:33).

"And he said unto them, Verily I say unto you, There is no man that hath left house, or parents, or brethren, or wife, or children, for the kingdom of God's sake. Who shall not receive manifold more in this present time, and in the world to come life everlasting" (Lu.18:29-30).

MATTHEW 19:27-30

"Yea doubtless, and I count all things but loss for the excellency of the knowledge of Christ Jesus my Lord: for whom I have suffered the loss of all things, and do count them but dung, that I may win Christ" (Ph.3:8).

Thought 1. We face two great dangers that can lower our reward.
(1) Not forsaking all for Christ: hanging on to some things whether behavior, habit, relationship, or possession.
(2) Super-spirituality: after forsaking all for Christ, there is always the danger of thinking that we have given up and sacrificed more than others. Several areas in particular lend themselves to spiritual pride...
- suffering
- service and works
- financial and benevolent gifts
- talents and spiritual gifts
- ministry and ministerial position
- being saved from the depth of sin

Thought 2. Some attempt to bargain with God. This is not to be. We are to go ahead and forsake all, trusting and following Christ (2 Co.6:17-18; 1 Jn.2:15-16).

2 (19:28) **Reward—Apostles—Regeneration**: the apostles were to be wonderfully rewarded. They were to receive a great honor—the honor of ruling and reigning with Christ Himself. Note that Christ told them three things. (See DEEPER STUDY # 1—Mt.19:28 for a discussion of these three points.)
⇒ When they would reign with Him.
⇒ Why they would reign with Him.
⇒ Whom they would govern and direct in their reign.

The word *regeneration* (paliggenesia) means recreation, restoration, renovation, renewal, new birth. The word is used one other time in the New Testament referring to the new birth of an individual (Tit.3:5). Here Christ uses the word to refer to the "restoration of all things" (Ac.3:21), a period of time in the future when He will set up the new order of things under His personal rule and reign (see Ro.8:19-23; Is.11:6-9). That day is often called the day of redemption or referred to as the Kingdom of God. (See note and DEEPER STUDY # 1—Ep.1:7; DEEPER STUDY # 3—Mt.19:23-24.)

Note several things.

a. The *restoration of all things* is in the future. Christ did not say "ye which have followed me in the regeneration" but "ye which have followed me, in the regeneration *when* the Son of Man shall...." The comma is to be placed after "followed me." The period of time is "when the Son of man shall sit in the throne of His glory"—a time out in the future.

b. Christ said that the apostles would be rewarded with twelve thrones, each one governing one of the twelve tribes of Israel. When were they to govern? "In the regeneration," when the new order of things is set up under the rule and reign of Christ. But when is the new order of things to be? There are two possible answers: either during the millennial reign of Christ (see DEEPER STUDY # 3—Mt.19:23-24; DEEPER STUDY # 2—Re.20:4-6) or during the new heavens and earth (Re.21:1f; see 1 Co.15:23-28).

There are three passages in which Christ deals with the regeneration as predicted here.

"Ye which have followed me, in the regeneration when the Son of man shall sit in the throne of his glory, ye also shall sit upon twelve thrones, judging the twelve tribes of Israel" (Mt.19:28).

The request of James and John's mother: "Grant that these my two sons may sit, the one on thy right hand, and the other on the left, in thy kingdom...And he saith unto them, Ye shall drink indeed of my cup, and be baptized with the baptism that I am baptized with: but to sit on my right hand, and on my left, is not mine to give, but it shall be given to them for whom it is prepared of my Father" (Mt.20:21, 23).

"Ye are they which have continued with me in my temptations. And I appoint unto you a kingdom, as my Father hath appointed unto me; That ye may eat and drink at my table in my kingdom, and sit on thrones judging the twelve tribes of Israel" (Lu.22:28-30).

The fulfillment of this promise seems to be the Messianic kingdom or millennial reign of Christ on earth. This seems to be the way Christ's promise to Israel will be fulfilled.

"And I will restore thy judges as at the first, and thy counsellors as at the beginning: afterward thou shalt be called, the city of righteousness, the faithful city" (Is.1:26).

c. It should be noted, however, that some find great difficulty in saying there is *ever again to be a distinction between Jew and Gentile*. They say that Christ came to bring peace to all men and between all men, breaking down the wall of partition between all. They say that the great weight of Scripture is opposed to there ever again being a distinction between Jew and Gentile. This interpretation simply says that when Christ returns, that is it; the end of time will be at hand. When He returns, He sets up His *eternal* reign and rules forever. Therefore, the apostles' rule and reign refers to the church, that is, to spiritual Israel or to the true Israel of God (Ga.6:15-16; see Ro.2:28-29).

d. Christ said He would reward the apostles with *a particular honor*. Why? The apostles believed and followed Christ in the embryonic or beginning stage of Christianity. They clung to their belief and endured in the face of unbelievable odds. Just imagine!
⇒ Imagine standing before a man who looks just like all other men, merely a man, and believing that man to really be the *Son of God*.
⇒ Imagine clinging to and continuing to follow Christ when everyone else had turned away from Him (see Jn.6:67).
⇒ Imagine following immediately upon the heels of the risen Lord and being instantly responsible for reaching the world. (No wonder God had to plan for His Spirit to infill the disciples as He did on Pentecost and to live within our bodies as He does. See notes—1 Co.3:16; 6:19-20.)
⇒ Imagine continuing on and on, trying to be obedient and to reach more and more despite unbelievable odds and having to constantly face the harassment of their fellow citizens, the Judaizers or religionists.

⇒ Imagine confronting and enduring through unbelievable threats and persecution launched from both an immoral government and a man-corrupted religion that reacted fiercely against those who differed with it.

The apostles not only were responsible for more and faced more than most of us will ever know but they also were responsible for and faced more than we can ever imagine (see 1 Co.4:9-13; 2 Co.11:24-28).

Thought 1. There are two regenerations.
(1) The regeneration of a person's life: a rebirth, a recreation of a person's nature and life (see Deeper Study # 1—Jn.3:1-15).
(2) The regeneration of the universe: a remaking of heaven and earth (Ro.8:21-23; 2 Pe.3:10-13; 21:1).

DEEPER STUDY # 1
(19:28) Judging (Krino)—Eternal Life: to judge, govern, direct; to administer affairs, supervise, and oversee. The assignment of responsibility, of duties, of work to be done is being taught here. There is to be *judging*, that is, governing, giving direction and supervision and oversight throughout eternity. Christ told the apostles that they would govern and oversee Israel. Paul said that believers would direct and oversee the world and angels (1 Co.6:2-3). All this activity and responsibility, of course, is under the direction of Christ.

For some unknown reason we so often picture *eternal life* as some dreamy sleep or semi-conscious type of existence. We think of it as some future existence that puts us on a fluffy cloud upon which we float in an eternal state of inactivity. Why man cannot accept the simple statement of Christ that life is to be eternal is difficult to understand. Eternal life is life that goes on and on. There is, however, one basic difference: life will be perfected—perfected in body, mind, and spirit. It is life lived in the midst of a new heavens and earth (perfected)—life lived before Christ and responsible to Christ in all that it is assigned (Jn.3:16; 5:24; Ro.8:19-23; 2 Pe.3:9-18; 1 Jn.5:11-13; Re.21:1).

---

3 (19:29) **Reward**: the apostles are not the only ones to be rewarded. Every true follower of *Christ* will be greatly rewarded. Christ said three things about the reward of the believer in this verse.
a. The reason for the reward: the believer is to be rewarded because he has left all; he has given his supreme allegiance to Jesus Christ (see note—Mt.19:27, the two essentials for reward).

Note that the two closest things to a man are named by Christ: his immediate family and his possessions (honor and lands). These are by far the most difficult things to surrender to Christ. Hobbies, habits, pleasures, friends—all can be given up (subjected to Christ) quicker than family or possessions. Note also that Christ began and ended the list with material possessions. How enslaving they are, even more so than family for some persons!

b. The present reward: an hundredfold. The Gospel of Mark makes it clear that Christ was speaking of present reward (Mk.10:21). No true follower of Christ has ever forsaken anyone or anything and been left alone and destitute by Christ. Christ rewards His true follower manyfold. Note: the reward is both human and material.
1) The human reward is a real and true fellowship among genuine believers. Christ knows when a follower of His has been turned against by those whom Christ loves ever so deeply. Christ knows when to send someone into the life of His own, when to meet the aching need of His follower for true friendship. He more than abundantly meets the need.

> "That which we have seen and heard declare we unto you, that ye also may have fellowship with us: and truly our fellowship is with the Father, and with his Son Jesus Christ" (1 Jn.1:3).
> "But if we walk in the light, as he is in the light, we have fellowship one with another, and the blood of Jesus Christ his Son cleanseth us from all sin" (1 Jn.1:7).
> "And they continued stedfastly in the apostles' doctrine and fellowship, and in breaking of bread, and in prayers" (Ac.2:42).
> "For where two or three are gathered together in my name, there am I in the midst of them" (Mt.18:20).
> "So we, being many, are one body in Christ, and every one members one of another" (Ro.12:5).
> "I am a companion of all them that fear thee, and of them that keep thy precepts" (Ps.119:63).
> "Then they that feared the LORD spake often one to another: and the LORD hearkened, and heard it, and a book of remembrance was written before him for them that feared the LORD, and that thought upon his name" (Mal.3:16).

2) The material reward is the meeting of necessities and whatever else God wants us to have left over so that we can help meet the needs of others.

The idea Christ was conveying is that of perfect material care and security. The very reason we seek and seek is because we are basically insecure and have a basic urge to crave more and more. Craving, greediness, fear, and insecurity are most unhealthy and destabilizing. When we forsake all, genuinely following Christ, He gives us the greatest peace and security possible: Himself and His power to provide for our necessities. We never have to worry or be anxious again (see notes—Mt.6:25-34; Lu.16:10-12. See Mk.10:29-30; Lu.18:28-30; Ep.4:28.) There is much more happiness, joy, peace, security, assurance, confidence, satisfaction, completeness, and fulfillment in Christ than in any amount of possessions or worldly companionship and friendship.

> "But seek ye first the kingdom of God, and his righteousness; and all these things shall be added unto you" (Mt.6:33; see Mt.6:25-34).
> "The thief cometh not, but for to steal, and to kill, and to destroy: I am come that they might have life, and that they might have it more abundantly" (Jn.10:10).

MATTHEW 19:27-30

"And God is able to make all grace abound toward you; that ye, always having all sufficiency in all things, may abound to every good work" (2 Co.9:8).

"Now unto him that is able to do exceeding abundantly above all that we ask or think, according to the power that worketh in us" (Ep.3:20).

"But my God shall supply all your need according to his riches in glory by Christ Jesus" (Ph.4:19).

"For so an entrance shall be ministered unto you abundantly into the everlasting kingdom of our Lord and Saviour Jesus Christ" (2 Pe.1:11).

"Thou preparest a table before me in the presence of mine enemies: thou anointest my head with oil; my cup runneth over" (Ps.23:5; see Ps.36:8).

"Blessed be the Lord, who daily loadeth us with benefits, even the God of our salvation" (Ps.68:19).

"Then shall he give the rain of thy seed, that thou shalt sow the ground withal; and bread of the increase of the earth, and it shall be fat and plenteous: in that day shall thy cattle feed in large pastures" (Is.30:23).

"And ye shall eat in plenty, and be satisfied, and praise the name of the Lord your God, that hath dealt wondrously with you: and my people shall never be ashamed" (Joel 2:26).

"Bring ye all the tithes into the storehouse, that there may be meat in mine house, and prove me now herewith, saith the LORD of hosts, if I will not open you the windows of heaven, and pour you out a blessing, that there shall not be room enough to receive it" (Mal.3:10).

c. The future reward is everlasting life (see DEEPER STUDY # 1—Jn.17:2-3; see DEEPER STUDY # 2—Jn.1:4; note and DEEPER STUDY # 1—Mt.19:28. See Ro.8:16-18.)

"Then Jesus beholding him loved him, and said unto him, One thing thou lackest: go thy way, sell whatsoever thou hast, and give to the poor, and thou shalt have treasure in heaven: and come, take up the cross, and follow me" (Mk.10:21).

"That whosoever believeth in him should not perish, but have eternal life" (Jn.3:15).

"He that believeth on the Son hath everlasting life: and he that believeth not the Son shall not see life; but the wrath of God abideth on him" (Jn.3:36).

"And he that reapeth receiveth wages, and gathereth fruit unto life eternal: that both he that soweth and he that reapeth may rejoice together" (Jn.4:36).

"Verily, verily, I say unto you, He that heareth my word, and believeth on him that sent me, hath everlasting life, and shall not come into condemnation; but is passed from death unto life" (Jn.5:24).

"And this is life eternal, that they might know thee the only true God, and Jesus Christ, whom thou hast sent" (Jn.17:3).

"For he that soweth to his flesh shall of the flesh reap corruption; but he that soweth to the Spirit shall of the Spirit reap life everlasting" (Ga.6:8).

Thought 1. Christ promises to reward His followers presently, reward them with an unbelievable Christian community, fellowship, and security. He founded the church to fulfill this promise. The church has a high calling. Imagine, the local church and its genuine believers are to be as close to one another as families are. The church is to provide a precious fellowship for the alienated, lonely, shy, friendless, and stranger. It is to meet the needs where families fail.

A pointed question: how many churches provide a true fellowship (see DEEPER STUDY # 3—Ac.2:42)? How often does God have to turn away from local congregations to others in order to meet the needs of a disciple of His?

4 (19:30) **Reward—Judgment**: the Lord's words are clear. There is to be a severe judgment of believers—the execution of perfect justice. Our judgment, human judgment, is often inaccurate. *Many persons* will be switched around: many whom we esteemed and rewarded the highest will be placed last, and many whom we thought weakest and lowest will be placed first. Only God knows the true heart of His servants. We judge and reward...
- by visible works
- by visible morality
- by age and seniority
- by friendliness
- by years as a Christian
- by recognition
- by esteem or influence
- by ability and skill
- by position

However, God sees into the heart of His dear followers, into the heart of every single one; and He will straighten out the misjudgments of all our dear brothers and sisters in Christ. Christ leaves no doubt: the most humble on earth will be elevated to be the greatest in heaven. It may be a shocking surprise, but there is to be judgment, a just realignment and positioning of believers (see DEEPER STUDY # 1—2 Co.5:10; note—1 Jn.3:1-2).

"For we must all appear before the judgment seat of Christ; that every one may receive the things done in his body, according to that he hath done, whether it be good or bad" (2 Co.5:10).

"Every man's work shall be made manifest: for the day shall declare it, because it shall be revealed by fire; and the fire shall try every man's work of what sort it is. If any man's work abide which he hath built thereupon, he shall receive a reward. If any man's work shall be burned, he shall suffer loss: but he himself shall be saved; yet so as by fire" (1 Co.3:13-15).

"He hath put down the mighty from their seats, and exalted them of low degree" (Lu.1:52).

"Woe unto you that are full! for ye shall hunger. Woe unto you that laugh now! for ye shall mourn and weep" (Lu.6:25).

"Son, remember that thou in thy lifetime receivedst thy good things, and likewise Lazarus evil things: but now he is comforted, and thou art tormented" (Lu.16:25).

MATTHEW 20:1-16

1. God's grace provides work for man–a field to tend^{DS1}	**CHAPTER 20** F. The Parable of Workers in the Vineyard: God's Glorious Grace, 20:1-16 For the kingdom of heaven is like unto a man *that is* an householder, which went out early in the morning to hire labourers into his vineyard.	8 So when even was come, the lord of the vineyard saith unto his steward, Call the labourers, and give them *their* hire, beginning from the last unto the first.	3. God's grace pays the promised wages: At the appointed time, at the end of the day a. Paid through His foreman
2. God's grace seeks & calls men to work^{DS2, 3, 4, 5} a. The early call: To the willing & eager 1) Shown grace: Promised a full wage 2) Sent into the field		9 And when they came that were hired about the eleventh hour, they received every man a penny. 10 But when the first came, they supposed that they should have received more; and they likewise received every man a penny.	b. Paid out of a heart of care & grace 1) Mercy shown to the latecomers: A full wage 2) Justice shown to the eager workers: A full wage
b. The latecomer call: To the idle, slothful, self-seeking, complacent 1) Shown grace: A forceful challenge & the promise of a just wage 2) Some responded	2 And when he had agreed with the labourers for a penny a day, he sent them into his vineyard. 3 And he went out about the third hour, and saw others standing idle in the marketplace, 4 And said unto them; Go ye also into the vineyard, and whatsoever is right I will give you. And they went their way.	11 And when they had received it, they murmured against the goodman of the house, 12 Saying, These last have wrought *but* one hour, and thou hast made them equal unto us, which have borne the burden and heat of the day.	c. Pay is not based on works & energy: Illustrated by the eager workers who murmured over the same pay being given to all workers
c. The persistent call: To all–shows constant grace d. The final call: The eleventh hour call–to the idle 1) He strongly rebuked 2) They excused themselves 3) He showed grace: A forceful challenge & the promise of a just wage	5 Again he went out about the sixth and ninth hour, and did likewise. 6 And about the eleventh hour he went out, and found others standing idle, and saith unto them, Why stand ye here all the day idle? 7 They say unto him, Because no man hath hired us. He saith unto them, Go ye also into the vineyard; and whatsoever is right, *that* shall ye receive.	13 But he answered one of them, and said, Friend, I do thee no wrong: didst not thou agree with me for a penny? 14 Take *that* thine *is*, and go thy way: I will give unto this last, even as unto thee. 15 Is it not lawful for me to do what I will with mine own? Is thine eye evil, because I am good? 16 So the last shall be first, and the first last: for many be called, but few chosen.	1) Pay is gracious & just: A full wage as promised 2) Pay is based on God's care for all: For the last as well as for the first d. Pay is not as man sees (evil, selfish eyes): Pay is as God wills–He is good 4. God's justice will pay exactly what He promised^{DS6}

DIVISION XIII

THE MESSIAH'S TEACHINGS ON THE WAY TO JERUSALEM, 19:1–20:34

F. The Parable of Workers in the Vineyard: God's Glorious Grace, 20:1-16

(20:1-16) **Introduction**: the parable of workers in the vineyard is one of the most meaningful parables in Scripture, yet the meaning is sometimes missed. Christ was continuing His discussion of salvation (Mt.19:25) and everlasting life (Mt.19:29). (See note—Mt.19:27-30.) What He now wished to do was show *the marvelous grace of God* in salvation, in giving eternal life. This He did by sharing a parable—a parable which demonstrates God's marvelous grace as few other lessons do.

1. God's grace provides work for man—a field to tend (v.1).
2. God's grace seeks and calls men to work (vv.1-7).
3. God's grace pays the promised wages: at the appointed time, at the end of the day (vv.8-15).
4. God's justice will pay exactly what He promised (v.16).

1 (20:1) **Work—Labor—Grace—Purpose**: God's grace provides work for man, a field to tend. Two significant facts are being stressed.

a. It is God who provides work for man, who gives a field to be tended. The great Householder is God. The vineyard or field can be either the world or the church. The world, the church, and man himself are all due to God's grace. It is God's grace that has created man. It is God's grace that has provided the field (the world and church) for man to work in. Without God there would be nothing (Ro.11:36; Col.1:16f).

b. It is God who goes out to seek and call men to work. It is not the workers who come to Him. God's going out after man is grace, marvelous grace (Lu.19:10; Jn.3:16; 15:16). Every step involved in the call of God is of grace: the call itself, the challenge to go and work, the promise of wages (reward), the acceptance of the responses, and the sending forth into the field. God did not have to issue a call or take any of the steps taken. Each step is a marvelous demonstration of God's care and grace.

MATTHEW 20:1-16

Note another matter: the soul of man serves something. It either serves self and sin or God and righteousness. Man either works for the world and its end or for heaven and its end (Ro.6:16-22). It is for this reason that God issues call after call (see outline above and notes for each of the calls).

> "Then saith he unto his disciples, The harvest truly is plenteous, but the labourers are few; pray ye therefore the Lord of the harvest, that he will send forth labourers into his harvest" (Mt.9:37-38).
>
> "Say not ye, There are yet four months, and then cometh harvest? behold, I say unto you, Lift up your eyes, and look on the fields; for they are white already to harvest. And he that reapeth receiveth wages, and gathereth fruit unto life eternal: that both he that soweth and he that reapeth may rejoice together" (Jn.4:35-36).
>
> "And the Lord said, Who then is that faithful and wise steward, whom his lord shall make ruler over his household, to give them their portion of meat in due season? Blessed is that servant, whom his lord when he cometh shall find so doing" (Lu.12:42-43).
>
> "He said therefore, A certain nobleman went into a far country to receive for himself a kingdom, and to return. And he called his ten servants, and delivered them ten pounds, and said unto them, Occupy till I come" (Lu.19:12-13).

DEEPER STUDY # 1
(20:1) **Kingdom of Heaven**: see Deeper Study # 3—Mt.19:23-24.

---

2 (20:1-7) **Call—Purpose—Reward**: the early call is God's very first call to a person. It is directed at a person when there is a special willingness and eagerness to serve God. The first call is God's beginning to speak to the heart of a person. There is a tug, a pull, a voice, a thought, a movement in one's heart to listen and turn to God.

Note two things.

a. The householder promised the workers a full wage. If the willing workers believed his promise, they would go into the fields and work. If they did not believe his promise, they would not go. Their belief preceded their work. He promised, and they believed and served.

God's call is by grace, not by works. The fact that Christ speaks of work and wages does not in any sense mean that salvation is earned, that it is of works. We are saved by God's grace through faith (Ro.4:3-5; Ep.2:8-10).

b. The time of service was a day, which symbolizes a lifetime. When the day (life) ended, the willing workers would receive the promise of the householder. They would be rewarded with exactly what he had promised, and the reward would be theirs forever. The day was but a brief period of time in comparison with having their needs met. They could withstand any trial (burden or heat, v.12) for just a day, for it would soon end.

They had two things to encourage them to remain with the work: they had only a short period of time to work, only one day, and they had the presence of the householder himself. He was constantly encouraging them, fellowshipping with them and reminding them of his promise.

> "Go ye therefore into the highways, and as many as ye shall find, bid" (Mt.22:9).
>
> "Who will have all men to be saved, and to come unto the knowledge of the truth" (1 Ti.2:4).
>
> "See, I have set before thee this day life and good, and death and evil" (De.30:15).

DEEPER STUDY # 2
(20:3-4) **Call—Purpose**: the latecomer's call is a call made for more workers after the first or early call. Every city has its labor market hangout. Any of us who have dealt with the labor market know that an employer often finds that he needs more workers as the day progresses. So he returns to call for more workers. Each time he returns it is, so to speak, an act of grace—he meets the need of more men.

An employer who asks workers to join his working force meets all kinds of responses.

1. There are the *willing and eager* workers. These are always out early, needing and looking for work. They realize and know their need, and they are extremely responsible in doing all they can to provide for their needs. Often they are men who want purpose, meaning, and significance as much as they want physical provision.

2. There are what Christ calls *the idle*. They have little if any interest in work at all. They are there simply because it is a gathering place where they can find company and pass time away.

3. There are the *self-seeking* or *pleasure workers*. These move around questioning each employer about what kind of work is to be done. If the work sounds too difficult or not enjoyable and pleasing, they refuse, choosing to wait for something more pleasing and enjoyable. However, later on in the day, after nothing else more satisfying has come along, they are willing to heed the call of the earlier employer.

4. There are the *slothful workers*. These are just lazy, not interested in a full-day's work. They prefer lying around, being loose and unobligated rather than exerting the energy and effort required by work. They choose to live with less rather than to work a full day. Thus, they show up at the marketplace only when they need a little work.

5. There are the *complacent workers*, the slow-movers. They sleep late, move slow, and are always late in getting to the marketplace. They could care less if they miss the better opportunities, just so they are able to get enough to meet their immediate needs.

6. There are the workers who are *weak failures*. These go to work at jobs that appeal to them, but they discover the jobs are hard and difficult. So they walk away from their commitment and return to the marketplace for something easier.

The parallel with God's latecomer call is easily seen. Note two things about the latecomer call that is different from the early call.

MATTHEW 20:1-16

1. The call to work is more forceful: "Go ye." It has to be more forceful. All of these have already rejected the early call or else were not present to hear the call. Some of the day (of their life) has already passed and can never be recovered. It takes more force and more convincing to stir most of the latecomers.

2. The promise of a wage (reward) is promised but not an amount. The Lord merely said, "Whatsoever is right, I will give you." A latecomer, the person who does not respond to God until later in life, must simply trust God to be fair and just. The promise is that He will give *a just reward*.

> "For we hear that there are some which walk among you disorderly, working not at all, but are busybodies" (2 Th.3:11).
> "That ye be not slothful, but followers of them who through faith and patience inherit the promises" (He.6:12).
> "He also that is slothful in his work is brother to him that is a great waster" (Pr.18:9).
> "I went by the field of the slothful, and by the vineyard of the man void of understanding; and, lo, it was all grown over with thorns and nettles had covered the face thereof, and the stone wall thereof was broken down" (Pr.24:30-31).

DEEPER STUDY # 3

(20:5) **Call—Purpose**: the constant call is the occasional movement of God in the heart of man. There is nothing so tragic as a person who is unemployed, that is, not serving God in this world and in the church. God cares and God has plenty of work for every man to do. Therefore, He tries and tries to reach the heart of man, calling at every hour He can. Note three things about the constant call of God.

1. It is God's great compassion for all of us that keeps His calling to us.
2. The calls of God are limited; they are only periodic. In the parable, only four calls have been issued up to this point. There is only one more call to go, only five calls in a day and in a life. God's movement, His Spirit does not always strive with us (Ge.6:3). We know this by experience. When *the striving* begins in our heart or mind (whether through reading, hearing a message, or whatever) and we ignore it and do not make a decision immediately, it diminishes and finally quits. It leaves us, and we continue on just as we always have.
3. The calls of God become dimmer and dimmer and less forceful with the rejection of each call.
   ⇒ Our conscience becomes harder; our minds less impressionable.
   ⇒ Our hearts become less sensitive; our ego more self-centered.
   ⇒ Our thoughts become more worldly; our lives more encumbered.
   ⇒ Our wills become more sluggish (Pr.29:1).

> "And if it seem evil unto you to serve the LORD, choose you this day whom ye will serve; whether the gods which your fathers served that were on the other side of the flood, or the gods of the Amorites, in whose land ye dwell: but as for me and my house, we will serve the LORD" (Jos.24:15).
> "And Elijah came unto all the people, and said, How long halt ye between two opinions? if the LORD be God, follow him: but if Baal, then follow him. And the people answered him not a word" (1 K.18:21).
> "I have sent also unto you all my servants the prophets, rising up early and sending them, saying, Return ye now every man from his evil way, and amend your doings, and go not after other gods to serve them, and ye shall dwell in the land which I have given to you and to your fathers: but ye have not inclined your ear, nor hearkened unto me" (Je.35:15).
> "Say unto them, As I live, saith the LORD God, I have no pleasure in the death of the wicked; but that the wicked turn from his way and live: turn ye, turn ye from your evil ways; for why will ye die, O house of Israel?" (Eze.33:11).
> "Come, and let us return unto the Lord: for he hath torn, and he will heal us; he hath smitten, and he will bind us up" (Ho.6:1).

DEEPER STUDY # 4

(20:5) **Time, Jewish**: a Jewish day began at 6 a.m. and ended at 6 p.m. The early call was issued before 6 a.m., the hour that work would begin. The latecomer call would have been issued at 9 a.m. when a fourth of the day (a life) had already passed. The sixth hour was 12 noon; the ninth hour was 3 p.m., and the eleventh hour was 5 p.m.

DEEPER STUDY # 5

(20:6-7) **Call—Purpose—Decision**: the final call is the last call of God to a man—it is the eleventh-hour call. Note what happens with the persons who wait until the eleventh hour.

1. God strongly rebukes them, much more forcibly than any of the others: Why stand ye here *all day* idle? There is no excuse for such behavior.
2. They excuse themselves: no man has hired us. Such is not the case; they lie, deceiving their own hearts.
3. God shows grace despite their deceptive excuse: He issues a forceful call and a promise of a just wage.

But note something: nothing is said about how many responded. Just think. How many actually would respond to go out for just one hour's work? How many would be willing to trust after rejecting four other offers during a single day? Realistically, not many would respond.

Three very practical things work strongly against a person who waits until the eleventh hour to accept God's call.

MATTHEW 20:1-16

> 1. A man does not often know when the eleventh hour is. Few know when they are to die, much less when God shall call for the last time.
> 2. A man in the eleventh hour has little time to serve. A man who has failed to capture an opportunity that has passed tends to accuse and condemn himself. He senses unworthiness. There is little likelihood that he will sense God's call to the point of responding.
> 3. A man in the eleventh hour who has rejected call after call is hard, very hard. There is little softness and sensitivity left to respond to God's call—no matter how forceful.
>
> "And sent forth his servants to call them that were bidden to the wedding: and they would not come" (Mt.22:3).
> "And ye will not come to me, that ye might have life" (Jn.5:40).
> "But to Israel he saith, All day long I have stretched forth my hands unto a disobedient and gainsaying people" (Ro.10:21).
> "And now, because ye have done all these works [evil], saith the LORD, and I spake unto you, rising up early and speaking, but ye heard not; and I called you, but ye answered not" (Je.7:13).
> "My God will cast them away, because they did not hearken unto him: and they shall be wanderers among the nations" (Ho.9:17).

3 (20:8-15) **Reward—Grace—Death**: God's grace pays the promised wages to those who have worked for Him. He will pay at the appointed time. When is the appointed time? In the evening, at death, when all work ends. This is the meaning of *the evening*, of *the appointed time*. There are two *evenings*, two appointed times for the servant of God.

First, there is the evening or the time of death when the servant passes from this life into God's presence. He receives his reward of eternal life. God transports him into the Lord's presence, and the believer is transformed into the image of Christ (see note—1 Jn.3:2). This is the reward of wages referred to in this parable.

Second, there is the evening or the appointed time of judgment when the servants' works are to be judged (see DEEPER STUDY #1—2 Co.5:10). This evening of judgment *is not* what this parable is about.

  a. The steward is Christ, God's Son, to whom God has committed all judgment (Jn.5:22; 2 Co.5:10).
  b. God pays everyone out of a heart of grace and care. This is so critical to understand: God is love and He cares. He cares for all servants, no matter how old or how long they have been serving Him. He cares, wanting the workers to have enough to meet their needs. A day's wage (the reward of eternal life) was necessary to meet their need. He would have no servant go away without at least that much. Therefore, He pays *even the latecomers* a full wage (eternal life).

Note another point: when we speak of eternal life and perfection, that is, of being conformed to the nature and image of Christ, God shows no preference. We shall all be made just like Christ, perfected in nature.

⇒ We shall have different responsibilities and, apparently, varying degrees of glory; but we shall all be perfected in nature.
⇒ We shall all face the Judgment Seat of Christ. We shall all receive different duties in heaven because of good and bad service here on earth, but we shall all be perfectly happy and joyful in what we do.
⇒ We shall all be judged for our faithfulness on this earth. Some shall be set up as large vessels and others as smaller vessels, but we shall all be perfectly complete and filled to the brim (2 Ti.2:20-21).
⇒ We shall all give an account for the trust and gifts put into our keeping. We shall all be rewarded accordingly, but we shall all be perfectly fulfilled.
⇒ We shall all stand before Christ for what fruit we have borne on earth, but we shall all be perfectly satisfied and fruitful.

> "...Go out into the highways and hedges, and compel them to come in, that my house may be filled" (Lu.14:23).
> "...many shall come from the east and west, and shall sit down with Abraham, and Isaac, and Jacob, in the kingdom of heaven" (Mt.8:11).

  c. God's pay (reward) is not based on works and energy. It is based on God's grace and justice, and it is based on God's concern and care for all.
   1) Note that God is gracious and just and caring. God's grace and care do not annul or erase His justice. God is not unjust (see Ro.4:5-6).
    ⇒ When God gives work to a man who is desperate for work, it is a caring and gracious act. Such was the case with the early call to the eager worker. Not to take advantage of the man's desperation is an act of grace. To offer and pay a full wage and not take advantage of the man is not unjust but the very opposite. It is a just and gracious act, a very caring act.
    ⇒ Similarly, when God pays a man more than what he earned because God cares that the man has enough to live, it is a gracious and caring act. It is not an unjust act against the first or earlier worker. It is simply a gracious act that reveals God to be an enormously caring Person.
    ⇒ If God gives us what He promised us, He is not unjust if He gives something to someone else. He is not even unjust to us if He gives an enormous gift to another person. He is just, and He is enormously caring and gracious by keeping His Word and giving to us *and to the other person*.

   2) Note that the complaining by the earlier workers causes some to apply the parable to the relationship between God and the Jews and the Gentiles. The earlier workers, representing the Jews, complain because God gives an equal pay (reward and position in His kingdom) to the Gentiles. Almost any commentary will give insight into this interpretation if the reader wishes to pursue it.

MATTHEW 20:1-16

d. God's pay (reward) is not as man sees but as God knows and wills. Our eyes are evil because we are of an evil world. Therefore, we judge and understand from an imperfect and selfish stance. God is good; He cares and is full of mercy and grace. Therefore, He gives eternal life to all who come, no matter when they come, at the early call or the eleventh-hour call.

> "But we believe that through the grace of the Lord Jesus Christ we shall be saved, even as they" (Ac.15:11).
> "Being justified freely by his grace through the redemption that is in Christ Jesus" (Ro.3:24).
> "For by grace are ye saved through faith; and that not of yourselves: it is the gift of God: not of works, lest any man should boast" (Ep.2:8-9).
> "For the grace of God that bringeth salvation hath appeared to all men" (Tit.2:11).
> "That being justified by his grace, we should be made heirs according to the hope of eternal life" (Tit.3:7).

4 (20:16) **Justice—Reward**: this is the very statement that caused Christ to share the parable—"So the last shall be first, and the first last" (see Mt.19:30; 20:16). Remember that the disciples needed assurance of their salvation. Christ gave them assurance and promised the reward of ruling and reigning with Him and living forever (see Mt.19:27-30. See note—Mt.19:27-30.) But Christ wanted them to know that they could not judge others, for they could not tell what was within a man, not for sure. They did not know who was to be highly rewarded and who was not.

For example, who would have ever thought that the willing and eager workers who immediately responded to the Lord would expose a grumbling, jealous spirit? To prevent His servants from judging and showing preference among themselves, Christ closes His discussion of eternal life and salvation with two warnings.

a. The last shall be first; that is, many of the last (latecomers) will outstrip us unless we are fervent and zealous in serving God. We may have professed and served Christ for years before others did; yet we may...
- fail to worship Christ day by day as consistently as the later workers
- fail to grow in the knowledge of Christ as eagerly as the later workers
- fail to study the Scriptures and pray as much as the later workers
- fail to use our gifts as faithfully as the later workers
- fail to witness as boldly as the later workers
- fail to give all that we are and have as willingly and sacrificially as the later workers
- fail to love as meekly as the later workers
- fail to respond as kindly as the later workers
- fail to live as unselfishly as the later workers
- fail to relate as lovingly as the later workers
- fail to endure as patiently as the later workers
- fail to look for the return of Christ as hopefully as the later workers

Note: Christ seems to switch from discussing the gift of eternal life to warning His servant that there will be a judgment of works—a judgment that will determine degrees of glory and position and responsibility (See Deeper Study # 1, *Judgment Seat of Christ*—2 Co.5:10).

> "He hath put down the mighty from their seats, and exalted them of low degree" (Lu.1:52).
> "Woe unto you that are full! for ye shall hunger. Woe unto you that laugh now! for ye shall mourn and weep" (Lu.6:25).
> "But Abraham said, Son, remember that thou in thy lifetime receivedst thy good things, and likewise Lazarus evil things: but now he is comforted, and thou art tormented" (Lu.16:25).
> "But God is the judge: he putteth down one, and setteth up another" (Ps.75:7).
> "The LORD lifteth up the meek: he casteth the wicked down to the ground" (Ps.147:6).

b. Many are called, but few are chosen. The servant must not be judging others (as the willing and eager servant did), for he has enough to do in making sure of his own calling and election (2 Pe.1:10). God's servant needs to be *working out his own salvation*. Outwardly it may appear that a man is a true servant, but inwardly he may be unchanged. Note that Christ says "many are called, but few are chosen." Many are counterfeit, *not willing to give all* they are and have. They are as the rich young ruler, just unwilling. The price of discipleship is too great. In all reality, how many are honestly following Christ as He demands throughout this discussion? (Mt.19:21, 29-30, 16. See note and Deeper Study # 1—Lu.9:23.)

> "Then Peter began to say unto him, Lo, we have left all, and have followed thee" (Mk.10:28).
> "And after these things he went forth, and saw a publican, named Levi, sitting at the receipt of custom: and he said unto him, Follow me" (Lu.5:27).
> "So likewise, whosoever he be of you that forsaketh not all that he hath, he cannot be my disciple" (Lu.14:33).

DEEPER STUDY # 6

(20:16) **Justice**: this footnote is placed last because it deals with a different subject than the outline above. *Is God unjust in His treatment of men?* This is the charge levelled against God by the willing and eager servant (vv.10-15). Men often question and charge God with being unjust. Such an unholy charge is caused by religious and theological discussions and by wrong belief and unbelief. The charge is also levelled against God when a crisis arises and we question, "How could God do that or let that happen?"

The New Testament discusses the question of God's being unjust in three passages (see note, pts. 3 and 4—Mt.20:8-15; also see notes—Ro.3:5-8; Ro.9:14-33).

	G. The Messiah Foretells His Death & Resurrection (Third Time), 20:17-19
	(Mk 10:32-34; Lu 18:31-34)
1. Jesus took the disciples aside 　a. While on the way 　b. To prepare them for His death **2. Jesus was to be betrayed & delivered for prosecution**^{DS1} 　a. The betrayer or deliverer was not named 　b. The prosecutors: The Jews or religionists **3. Jesus was to be delivered for execution** 　a. To the Gentiles 　b. By crucifixion **4. Jesus was to be raised from the dead**	17 And Jesus going up to Jerusalem took the twelve disciples apart in the way, and said unto them, 18 Behold, we go up to Jerusalem; and the Son of man shall be betrayed unto the chief priests and unto the scribes, and they shall condemn him to death, 19 And shall deliver him to the Gentiles to mock, and to scourge, and to crucify *him:* and the third day he shall rise again.

DIVISION XIII

THE MESSIAH'S TEACHINGS ON THE WAY TO JERUSALEM, 19:1-20:34

G. The Messiah Foretells His Death and Resurrection (Third Time), 20:17-19

(20:17-19) **Introduction**: this is the third time that Matthew stresses the death and resurrection of Jesus Christ. Christ had warned His disciples time and again that He was to die and be raised on the third day (see outline and notes—Mt.16:21-23; 17:22-23; Mk.8:31-33; 9:30-32; 10:32-34. These passages should be studied with this passage. Matthew 17:22-23 includes most, if not all, of the New Testament passages on the death and resurrection of Christ. There is an abundance of material in these references.)

Jesus Christ had to get three facts across to His disciples.
1. Jesus took the disciples aside (v.17)
2. Jesus was to be betrayed and delivered for *prosecution* (v.18).
3. Jesus was to be delivered for *execution* (v.19).
4. Jesus was to be raised from the dead (v.19).

1 (20:17) **Jesus Christ, Death**: Jesus took the disciples aside to get all alone. The word *took* (parelaben) means that He took His disciples "apart to Himself." There is great meaning in these words.

　a. There is tenderness and warmth and intimacy. He needed and wanted them close to Him, right by His side. He needed to feel and know their presence, in particular that they were with Him as He *went up to Jerusalem* to face death. They also needed His presence, to have Him right beside them and to feel what He felt. Such memories would help them as they faced the trials that lay ahead of them.

　b. There is tremendous pressure and tension (also see note—20:19). The very air surrounding them was tight. There seemed to be a heavy weight hanging over the Lord's head. He seemed to be consumed in deep thought—the kind of thought that quickens a person's pace, tightens the muscles of the body, and strains the expressions of the face. The pressure and tension cannot be overstated. Mark expressed it well: "They were in the way going up to Jerusalem; and Jesus went before [walked ahead of] them. And they were amazed [bewildered, perplexed]; and as they followed, they were afraid [seized with alarm]" (Mk.10:32).

　Two events show just how much the pressure must have been building at this time:
　　⇒ the experience in the garden of Gethsemane where the pressure was so great that Christ sweated great drops of blood (Lu.22:44)
　　⇒ the experience of the cross where Christ was to suffer for the sins of the world, bearing to the ultimate degree all the pain possible for a heart, mind, and body to bear (1 Pe.2:24; see Mt.27:46; 2 Co.5:21)

　c. There is purpose and encouragement. This is seen in two facts.
　　1) Jesus was deliberately "going up to Jerusalem." He did not have to go. He was fully Man, and as Man, He could choose what to do (He.2:16-18; 4:15). He knew what lay ahead, yet He would not shirk God's purpose.
　　2) Jesus deliberately took the disciples apart to prepare them for His coming death. They were to face the most shocking event of their lives—an event so shocking that it could potentially devastate their lives and hinder God's plan for the ages. Christ had to prepare them to withstand the shock of His death (see note—Mt.16:21-28).

There are at least two reasons why Jesus could not reveal His death by crucifixion to the public.
　a. Many would have become discouraged from following Him. They would have feared the Romans who were to be the executioners of Christ. The fervor of the crowds would have cooled, and they would have forsaken Him. Seeing

multitudes desert Christ could have discouraged the disciples tremendously, and this was not what they needed at this time. They needed encouragement and preparation for facing the cross.

b. Some of the people would be tempted to defend Christ, perhaps striking first. Some of the disciples, perhaps all, could be caught up in the fervor of such an ill-advised reaction.

Thought 1. Christ wants to draw all of us "apart to Himself."
(1) He wants moments of tenderness and warmth with us, many such moments (Re.3:20; see Ps.145:18; Lu.18:1; 1 Jn.1:3).
(2) He wants us to draw near to Him in times of pressure and tension (Ph.4:6-7; Heb.4:15-16; Ps.34:18).
(3) He wants us to draw near to Him for purpose and encouragement (Is.43:10; Mt.11:28-30; Js.4:8-10). He wants us to guard against *shirking* God's purpose and to be more and more prepared to proclaim His death. He wants us fortified against the shock of being rejected, ridiculed, abused, and even persecuted as we go about fulfilling the purpose of God.

Thought 2. There are times to minister to the multitudes and times not to minister to them. The multitude was not yet ready to hear about the death of Christ. People have to be fed progressively. All have not reached the same level of spiritual growth and spiritual maturity.
(1) Some are new in Christ. They are not yet grounded in the basics. They are not ready for the *meat* of the Word (1 Pe.2:2-3).
(2) Some live carnal lives. They are not spiritually minded. They would not have the interest nor would they understand (1 Co.3:1-2; Heb.5:11-14).
(3) Some are unregenerate. They are in the church but are not followers of Christ. They have no interest in Christ and would be offended by the cross of Christ.

2 (20:18) **Jesus Christ, Death**: Christ was to be betrayed and delivered for prosecution.

a. The betrayer is not named. However, note the words *shall be betrayed* (paradothesetai). The phrase means *shall be delivered*. It is the same Greek word translated *delivered* in the next verse. Who delivered Jesus up to be prosecuted and executed? Jesus did not name the person. Scripture teaches that three persons delivered Jesus to be crucified (see note—Mt.17:22 for discussion).

b. The prosecutors of Jesus are named. They were the Jews, in particular the leaders among the Jews, the chief priests and Scribes and elders (see Deeper Study # 1,2—Mt.16:21; note—1 Th.2:15-16). But note: they were to be only the prosecutors not the executioners. They were forbidden by law to execute anyone (Jn.18:31). They had to deliver Him over to the Gentiles for execution. There is symbolism seen in this fact:
1) Both Jew and Gentile (the world) are guilty of the death of God's Son.
2) Christ was to bear the sin of both Jew and Gentile in His death. He was to reconcile both, that is, reconcile the whole world to God. (See outline and notes—Ep.2:14-18.)

"For God so loved the world, that he gave his only begotten Son, that whosoever believeth in him should not perish, but have everlasting life" (Jn.3:16).

" And that he might reconcile both unto God in one body by the cross, having slain the enmity thereby" (Ep.2:16).

"And, having made peace through the blood of his cross, by him to reconcile all things unto himself; by him, I say, whether they be things in earth, or things in heaven" (Col.1:20).

"And he is the propitiation [sacrifice] for our sins: and not for ours only, but also for the sins of the whole world" (1 Jn.2:2).

Thought 1. There is a truth that is seldom thought about: we are to *think often about death* even as Christ was obsessed with His death. There are three reasons we are not to shun and deny the thought.
(1) Death is an eternal matter even as life is an eternal matter (2 Co.10:5).
(2) Death is no longer to be feared (He.2:14-15; 2 Ti.1:7).
(3) We are to live—dying daily, constantly denying self (see note and Deeper Study # 1—Lu.9:23; see Ro.8:36; Tit.3:12-15).

DEEPER STUDY # 1
(20:18) **Jesus Christ, Death**: the pain of suffering reached its summit in the sufferings of Jesus Christ. He suffered pain to the ultimate degree, in an absolute sense. Yet in the midst of such terrible suffering, there is something that is very precious—a thought, a truth that should be very, very precious to us. It is this: *Jesus' death was dear to His own heart*—dear despite the terrible suffering He was to endure. In a way unknown to man and which can never be understood by man, Jesus set His heart and face toward the cross. He was consumed and obsessed with the cross. Why? Because the cross was the focus of God's purpose throughout all eternity.

1. The cross was dear to His heart because it was His Father's will. In dying, He could please His Father, and pleasing His Father was the supreme objective of His life (see note—Ep.5:2).
2. The cross was dear to His heart because it was the means by which He was to gain many brothers (see note—Ro.8:29).
3. The cross was dear to His heart because through death He was to be made *the captain* of man's salvation (He.2:9-10).

MATTHEW 20:17-19

> 4. The cross was dear to His heart because by death He was to destroy the power of the devil over man, that is, death (He.2:14-15).
> 5. The cross was dear to His heart because by the cross He was to reconcile all men, reconcile them both to God and to one another (see outline and notes—Ep.2:13-18).
> 6. The cross was dear to His heart because through death He was to return to His former glory which He had possessed with the Father before the foundation of the world (Jn.17:1-5).

3 (20:19) **Jesus Christ, Death**: Christ was to be delivered to the Gentiles for torture and execution. Note the three forms of torture mentioned.

⇒ Mock: to ridicule, scorn, insult, humiliate, defy, jeer.
⇒ Scourge: to beat with a rod or a whip weighted with either jagged metal or bone chips. Thirty nine or forty
⇒ Lashes were inflicted. The whole purpose of scourging was to inflict severe pain.
⇒ Crucify (see DEEPER STUDY # 1—Mt.27:26-44 for the terrible suffering of the cross).

Jesus bore the sins of man, suffering the ultimate degree of pain. He suffered pain in an absolute sense.

a. Mentally: while He was being tortured, His mind was bound to be upon why He was suffering. He was thinking about the sin of man and the problem sin had caused God. Imagine the world's sin, all of it, the enormity and awfulness of it consuming His mind. He was suffering mentally to the ultimate degree.

> "For he hath made him to be sin for us, who knew no sin; that we might be made the righteousness of God in him" (2 Co.5:21).
> "And he is the propitiation for our sins: and not for ours only, but also for the sins of the whole world" (1 Jn.2:2).

b. Spiritually: His heart was being broken. Those whom He loved so much were committing a sin so horrendous it defied imagination. They were rebelling against God so much that they were killing God's own Son.

In addition and even more terrible, His own Father, God Himself, was to turn His back upon Him. God was to separate Himself from His very own Son (see notes—Mt.27:46-49; Mk.15:34). He was beginning to bear, and was going to bear, the judgment, condemnation, and punishment due man—He was going to bear spiritual pain in an absolute sense. The wrath of God's holiness against sin was to be cast against Him.

> "All we like sheep have gone astray; we have turned every one to his own way; and the LORD hath laid on him the iniquity of us all" (Is.53:6).
> "And at the ninth hour Jesus cried with a loud voice, saying, Eloi, Eloi, lama sabachthani? which is, being interpreted, My God, my God, why hast thou forsaken me?" (Mk.15:34).
> "And being in an agony he prayed more earnestly: and his sweat was as it were great drops of blood falling down to the ground" (Lu.22:44).
> "For it became him, for whom are all things, and by whom are all things, in bringing many sons unto glory, to make the captain of their salvation perfect through sufferings" (He.2:10).
> "Though he were a Son, yet learned he obedience by the things which he suffered" (He.5:8).
> "Wherefore Jesus also, that he might sanctify the people with his own blood, suffered without the gate" (He.13:12).
> "Who his own self bare our sins in his own body on the tree, that we, being dead to sins, should live unto righteousness: by whose stripes ye were healed" (1 Pe.2:24).
> "For Christ also hath once suffered for sins, the just for the unjust, that he might bring us to God, being put to death in the flesh, but quickened by the Spirit" (1 Pe.3:18).

c. Physically: His pain was to be more severe because of the mental and spiritual pressure He was having to bear at the same time. There is also truth to the fact that the more ridicule within a persecutor's heart, the more he tortures his victim (see the crown of thorns, royal robe, and excessive mockery of the soldiers). The fact that Christ claimed to be the Son of God aroused the persecutors to inflict more scorn and torture. (See Mt.27:1f.)

> "I gave my back to the smiters, and my cheeks to them that plucked off the hair: I hid not my face from shame and spitting" (Is.50:6).
> "And one shall say unto him, What are these wounds in thine hands? Then he shall answer, Those with which I was wounded in the house of my friends" (Zec.13:6).
> "And when they had platted a crown of thorns, they put it upon his head, and a reed in his right hand: and they bowed the knee before him, and mocked him, saying, Hail, King of the Jews!" (Mt.27:29).
> "And they crucified him, and parted his garments, casting lots: that it might be fulfilled which was spoken by the prophet, They parted my garments among them, and upon my vesture did they cast lots" (Mt.27:35).
> "And they that passed by reviled him, wagging their heads" (Mt.27:39).
> "And they that passed by railed on him, wagging their heads, and saying, Ah, thou that destroyest the temple, and buildest it in three days" (Mk.15:29).

MATTHEW 20:17-19

Thought 1. Jesus suffered the ultimate degree of pain, and He did it *for us*. This fact should break our hearts, yet it seldom does. Why? Because so few of us spend time meditating upon His death—and, among us who do, an even smaller percentage spend anywhere close to the time that should be spent.

4 (20:19) **Jesus Christ, Resurrection**: Christ was to be raised from the dead. Covering the resurrection in the same discussion with His death does three major things.

a. The prediction of the resurrection drove the point of the resurrection into the mind of the disciples again. They must forever remember the resurrection. The death of Christ was not the final word.

"Remember that Jesus Christ of the seed of David was raised from the dead according to my gospel" (2 Ti.2:8).

b. The prediction of the resurrection foreshadowed the power of God. After the Lord's resurrection, the disciples would remember, and the glorious truth of God's power would be reinforced in their minds and hearts forever.
  1) The power of God is victorious.

"O death, where is thy sting? O grave, where is thy victory?...But thanks be to God, which giveth us the victory through our Lord Jesus Christ" (1 Co.15:55, 57).

  2) The power of God does triumph.

"And having spoiled principalities and powers, he made a show of them openly, triumphing over them in it" (Col.2:15).

  3) The power of God does conquer.

"Nay, in all these things we are more than conquerors through him that loved us. For I am persuaded, that neither death, nor life, nor angels, nor principalities, nor powers, nor things present, nor things to come, nor height, nor depth, nor any other creature, shall be able to separate us from the love of God, which is in Christ Jesus our Lord" (Ro.8:37-39).
"Forasmuch then as the children are partakers of flesh and blood, he also himself likewise took part of the same; that through death he might destroy him that had the power of death, that is, the devil" (He.2:14-15).

c. The prediction of the resurrection foreshadowed the stirring that God's power was going to work in their lives.
  1) The power to encourage and motivate.

"The eyes of your understanding being enlightened; that ye may know what is the hope of his calling, and what the riches of the glory of his inheritance in the saints, and what is the exceeding greatness of his power to us-ward who believe, according to the working of his mighty power" (Ep.1:18-19).
"For God hath not given us the spirit of fear; but of power, and of love, and of a sound mind" (2 Ti.1:7).

  2) The power to assure and build confidence.

"And after eight days again his disciples were within, and Thomas with them: then came Jesus, the doors being shut, and stood in the midst, and said, Peace be unto you. Then saith he to Thomas, Reach hither thy finger, and behold my hands; and reach hither thy hand, and thrust it into my side: and be not faithless, but believing" (Jn.20:26-29).

  3) The power to give courage and boldness.

"And being let go, they went to their own company, and reported all that the chief priests and elders had said unto them. And when they heard that, they lifted up their voice to God with one accord, and said, Lord, thou art God, which hast made heaven, and earth, and the sea, and all that in them is" (Ac.4:23-24).
"Be not thou therefore ashamed of the testimony of our Lord, nor of me his prisoner: but be thou partaker of the afflictions of the gospel according to the power of God; who hath saved us, and called us with an holy calling, not according to our works, but according to his own purpose and grace, which was given us in Christ Jesus before the world began" (2 Ti.1:8-9).

	H. The Price & Meaning of Greatness, 20:20-28 (Mk 10:35-45; Lu 22:24-27)	baptism that I am baptized with: but to sit on my right hand, and on my left, is not mine to give, but *it shall be given to them* for whom it is prepared of my Father.	e. The price of unshakeable loyalty: To Christ^{DS3, 4}

1. What the sin of false ambition is: Selfishly seeking personal greatness^{DS1}
a. Is self-seeking
 	
b. Is deceptive & uses people
c. Misuses influence, position, & power
d. Arises from pride & contempt
e. Misunderstands true greatness
	20 Then came to him the mother of Zebedee's children with her sons, worshipping *him,* and desiring a certain thing of him.
	21 And he said unto her, What wilt thou? She saith unto him, Grant that these my two sons may sit, the one on thy right hand, and the other on the left, in thy kingdom.
		24 And when the ten heard *it,* they were moved with indignation against the two brethren.
		25 But Jesus called them *unto him,* and said, Ye know that the princes of the Gentiles exercise dominion over them, and they that are great exercise authority upon them.
			3. What greatness is
			a. Eternal greatness is of God
			b. Greatness is not dominion over people
			  1) The disciples' misconception
			  2) The world's traits

2. What greatness requires: Is a person willing to pay the price?
a. The price of contemplation: Understanding greatness
b. The price of suffering: The cup^{DS2}
c. The price of death: Baptism
d. The price of determination: "We can," v. 22
	22 But Jesus answered and said, Ye know not what ye ask. Are ye able to drink of the cup that I shall drink of, and to be baptized with the baptism that I am baptized with? They say unto him, We are able.
	23 And he saith unto them, Ye shall drink indeed of my cup, and be baptized with the
		26 But it shall not be so among you: but whosoever will be great among you, let him be your minister;
		27 And whosoever will be chief among you, let him be your servant:
		28 Even as the Son of man came not to be ministered unto, but to minister, and to give his life a ransom for many.
			c. Greatness is serving others
			  1) The great: Are servants
			  2) The greatest: Are slaves
			
			d. True greatness is demonstrated by Christ^{DS5}

DIVISION XIII

THE MESSIAH'S TEACHINGS ON THE WAY TO JERUSALEM, 19:1–20:34

H. The Price and Meaning of Greatness, 20:20-28

(20:20-28) **Introduction**: Jesus was on His way to Jerusalem. This was to be a momentous visit to the capital. This was the visit when the crisis was to take place, the crisis of His death and resurrection. He had just shared the fact of the crisis again (vv.17-19). For months His death and resurrection had consumed His attention and private messages to the disciples (Mt.16:13-20; 16:21-28; 17:1-13; 17:22; 17:24-27; 20:17). There was no question in the disciples' minds: this visit to Jerusalem was the momentous event for which they had long looked. Jesus was about to free Israel and set up His kingdom on earth.

We who live today know what Christ meant by His death and resurrection. He was to die for our sins, and He was to be raised again to impart new life to us, but the disciples did not know this. Christ had not yet died nor been raised from the dead. To them, He was speaking of an earthly and material kingdom. If He were about to set up His kingdom, now was the time to seize the promise of position and power in His kingdom. Now was the time to secure the positions of rule and authority. (See notes—Mt.1:1; Deeper Study # 2—1:18; Deeper Study # 3—3:11; notes—11:1-6; 11:2-3; Deeper Study # 1—11:5; Deeper Study # 2—11:6; Deeper Study # 1—12:16; note—Lu.7:21-23.)

This is what James and John were doing. They were assuring themselves of key positions in Christ's government. (See outlines and notes—Mt.18:1-4; Lu.22:24-30.)

1. What the sin of false ambition is: selfishly seeking personal greatness (vv.20-21).
2. What greatness requires: Is a person willing to pay the price (vv.22-23)?
3. What greatness is (vv.23-28).

1 (20:20-21) **Ambition, False—Greatness**: note the sins of false ambition and of seeking personal greatness. They are fivefold.

a. False ambition is self-seeking. James and John were interested in position for honor only, not for the purpose of serving. Pomp and ceremony, position and recognition, power and authority were on their minds, not ministering to and serving people.

b. False ambition is deceptive and uses people. Note how deceptively James and John and their mother came to Jesus. The sons persuaded their mother to use her influence with Jesus. She was a tool for their ambition. By her having taken the lead, they hoped Christ would think the request originated with her and not with them. He had already rebuked them for self-ambition (see outline and notes—Mt.18:1-4). Ambition often causes us to use people. Too often we put desire for things, position, power, and influence before and over people. Some even deceive and use others to achieve their ends.

c. False ambition misuses influence, position, and power. James and John along with Peter formed the inner circle around Christ. Christ gave them opportunities to witness several events the others were not permitted to see. They felt more favored and felt that their position was superior to the other disciples (see Deeper Study # 1—Mk.9:2). This became especially true when James and John used their family's position to influence Jesus (see Deeper Study # 1—Mt.20:20-21).

MATTHEW 20:20-28

d. False ambition arises from pride. They felt more honored, more special, more preferred; and they were showing their conceit. They fully expected their request to be granted. Their kneeling with their mother (probably behind their mother) showed this. There is always contempt for others in pride. Feeling more honored and more preferred elevates one over others and treats them as inferior.

e. False ambition misunderstands the facts. James and John did not understand Jesus' death and resurrection. They misinterpreted it. They made the same mistake that man so often makes: they spiritualized God's Word.

When Christ said that He was to die, they probably thought He was referring to the conflict that was going to take place as He overthrew Roman domination. When Christ said that He was to arise, they probably thought it referred to the rising of God's kingdom to power. They thought only in terms of an earthly or temporal power. They missed the point entirely—missed the literal death and resurrection of God's Son which was to save man spiritually and eternally. The point is this: false ambition centers attention on securing things now, not eternally. It interprets life and the values of life only in terms of earthly power, position, recognition, and wealth. It fails to see that such is ever so brief and does not last. It misunderstands the facts entirely.

Thought 1. There is good, healthy ambition; and there is bad, unhealthy ambition. Good ambition gives purpose, meaning, and significance to life; it builds drive, initiative, self-esteem, and much, much more. All such qualities are healthy and needed by every human being. We must all feel worthwhile, yet true inner health comes only from serving others, not from position and power. This is what James and John were missing.

Bad ambition is false ambition. It is deceptive in every conceivable way. It may lead to exaltation and power, but it corrupts and destroys. It eats away at a person's body as well as a person's spirit and consumes and misuses people. Sin corrupts and destroys, so false ambition is sin.

Thought 2. There is nothing wrong with high positions of responsibility and authority. Leadership and organization, government and law, teachers and learners, parent and child—all are essential. However, all positions should exist not to *lord it over people* but to serve people. We are to seek to serve people, not seek to rule people. Our ambition should not be to *lead* but to serve. This was James' and John's error. It is often ours. There is a tremendous difference between leading and serving.

Thought 3. There is something very commendable about James and John in this experience: their strong faith in Jesus and His kingdom. They were wrong in their ambition, but they were right about Jesus Himself. He was the true Messiah who had come to rule over the works and lives of men. They were just wrong about His method. He was going to do it spiritually not militarily.

Thought 4. James and John had left all for Christ (Mt.19:27-29). They had travelled about the country and suffered with Him for three years. Now they thought their trials were about over. Christ was going to change things and raise them up above the sufferings, and He was to reward their trust. They were so wrong. Like so many of us, they misunderstood what following Christ really meant. Christ does not remove our trials; He carries us through them. He does not take suffering away; He delivers us through suffering. Our rest from labor and trials and our crown come in the next world, not this world.

DEEPER STUDY # 1
(20:20-21) **Salome**: the mother of James and John was named Salome (Mt.27:56; see Mk.15:40; 16:1). An interesting fact is that Salome was probably the sister of Mary, the mother of Jesus, which means that James and John were first cousins of Jesus. We see this in Mark's and John's accounts of the crucifixion. Mark says that Salome was at the cross with Mary, Jesus' mother (Mk.15:40). John simply says, "Jesus' mother, His mother's sister...." (Jn.19:25).

---

2 (20:22-23) **Greatness**: What does greatness require, and, is a person willing to pay the price? Christ told James and John how to become great; greatness in His kingdom requires five things.

a. The price of contemplating suffering and death. A person must understand that greatness involves the suffering of discipline and obedience and the death of self and comfort, of indulgence and extravagance. The person must think about, contemplate, and understand what he is seeking. Thinking takes time; it takes concentration, energy, and effort. It means many long and tiring hours and days of concentration in study and learning. It means knowing and understanding what one asks. It means knowing where one is, has been, and should be going in life.

b. The price of bearing the cup of suffering. It means a willingness to die to self daily and to give one's life in bearing whatever has to be borne in order to serve Christ (see Deeper Study # 2, *Cup*—Mt.20:22-23; note and Deeper Study # 1—Lu.9:23).

c. The price of being baptized into death. It means paying any price to achieve one's God-given purpose—even if it means death (see Deeper Study # 2, *Baptism*—Mt.20:22-23).

d. The price of determination. James and John answered Christ: "We are able." Greatness is accepting the challenge because one loves the Lord and is willing to share in His sufferings and death no matter the cost.

e. The price of unshakable loyalty to Christ. Greatness is enduring and persevering no matter the suffering or denial demanded. James and John both drank the cup and were baptized with the baptism of Christ (see Deeper Study # 3,4—Mt.20:23).

> "So likewise, whosoever he be of you that forsaketh not all that he hath, he cannot be my disciple" (Lu.14:33).

"And he said to them all, If any man will come after me, let him deny himself, and take up his cross daily, and follow me. For whosoever will save his life shall lose it: but whosoever will lose his life for my sake, the same shall save it" (Lu.9:23-24).

"If any man come to me, and hate not his father, and mother, and wife, and children, and brethren, and sisters, yea, and his own life also, he cannot be my disciple. And whosoever doth not bear his cross, and come after me, cannot be my disciple" (Lu.14:26-27).

"For if ye live after the flesh, ye shall die: but if ye through the Spirit do mortify the deeds of the body, ye shall live" (Ro.8:13).

"And they that are Christ's have crucified the flesh with the affections and lusts" (Ga.5:24).

"Yea doubtless, and I count all things but loss for the excellency of the knowledge of Christ Jesus my Lord: for whom I have suffered the loss of all things, and do count them but dung, that I may win Christ" (Ph.3:8).

Thought 1. Christ pulls no punches. If we desire greatness, there is a price to pay, a tremendous price. If we wish to have the crown He gives, there is a bitter cup to be drunk and a baptism in which to be immersed (see note—Mt.20:22).

Thought 2. When we say "yes" to Christ, we have to mean it. There has to be an iron determination to follow Him. We must be able to say with James and John, "We are able"—no matter the cup and the baptism. However, we must always remember that *we are able* only through the strength of His resurrected power.

Thought 3. Note that Christ did not write James and John off because they were wrong and had committed a terrible sin. He did not give up on them, cast them aside as useless. He simply corrected them, taught them the truth, and continued to use them. Note something else: Christ trusted them. He knew their hearts deep within, knew they would come through and, in the final analysis, pay any price for Him.

There is a tremendous lesson here. Christ believes in us and counts us trustworthy (1 Ti.1:12; see Ro.8:28f). Even when we fail and begin to dislike and hate ourselves, He loves and cares for us, wanting to correct us, teach us, and set us back on our feet on the path of usefulness.

DEEPER STUDY # 2
(20:22-23) **Cup—Baptism**: there is a difference between drinking the cup of suffering and being baptized with suffering. The cup refers more to what a person takes into himself and bears within himself. It is more internal suffering and agony. The baptism refers more to what is put upon a person from the outside. It is more external sufferings.

The cup means drinking the bitterness and agony of trials, pain, hurt, sorrow, heartbreak, suffering, disappointment, and tears (see Christ's experience in the Garden of Gethsemane, Mt.26:36-46; His sufferings, Mt.20:19; 27:46-49; and John's experience on Patmos, Re.1:9; see INTRODUCTION—Date). The cup is associated with suffering and with God's wrath (see Ps.11:6; Is.51:17; Eze.23:33).

The baptism of suffering means being immersed in the rapids of affliction, rejection, abuse, ridicule, opposition, persecution, and martyrdom.

The Christian believer who truly lives and witnesses for Christ will drink His cup and be baptized with His baptism. Just think for a moment. Christ demands all we *are* and *have* in order to help people and to carry the message of salvation to a lost world. If we should be serious and give all we *are* and *have*, just imagine the cost to us. Imagine how different we would be from the world. Imagine the world's reaction to us. That is the reason Christ and the apostles met with so much opposition so often. They gave all they *were* and *had* to live so differently. They lived for God instead of living for self and the world; therefore, the world could not understand them. Some ignored and others ridiculed, abused, persecuted, and even killed them. They had the Lord's cup and baptism of suffering and sacrifice to bear, and so do all who truly follow Him. (See outlines and notes—Mt.10:16-23; 10:24-33; 10:34-42; 19:23-26; 19:27-30. See Mt.10:22; Ph.1:29; 2 Ti.3:12; 1 Pe.2:21; 4:1-5; 5:10; Mt.19:29; Ro.8:16-17.)

DEEPER STUDY # 3
(20:23) **James**: was killed by Herod. He was the first apostle to drink the cup of martyrdom.

DEEPER STUDY # 4
(20:23) **John**: lived to be around one hundred years old and died in bed as far as we know. However, he drank the cup and was baptized with suffering in a most distressful way:
⇒ He witnessed the sufferings of Christ's death.
⇒ He lived through the murder and deaths of all the other apostles.
⇒ He lived a long life of banishment and exile on the island of Patmos (see Introduction, Revelation—Date).

---

3 (20:23-28) **Greatness**: What is true greatness? It is four things.

a. Greatness that is eternal is of God. There is no greatness other than that of God, not a greatness that brings eternal position and honor. The greatness conceived by men is superficial; it fades away. Note two things Christ seemed to be saying.

MATTHEW 20:20-28

1) Christ said that some will sit on His right hand and some on His left hand. God is preparing to bestow such honor upon some. This seems to point toward degrees of glory in heaven (see vv.26-27).
2) Christ was saying that the right to reign with Him was to be determined by God alone (that is, His absolute justice). He also made a distinction between *the great* who only commit themselves to minister, and the *chief* (greatest) who commit themselves to be *bond-slaves* (v.26; see v.27).

> "What I tell you in darkness, that speak ye in light: and what ye hear in the ear, that preach ye upon the housetops" (Mt.10:27).
> "If any man serve me, let him follow me; and where I am, there shall also my servant be: if any man serve me, him will my Father honour" (Jn.12:26).
> "If I then, your Lord and Master, have washed your feet; ye also ought to wash one another's feet" (Jn.13:14).
> "He saith to him again the second time, Simon, son of Jonas, lovest thou me? He saith unto him, Yea, Lord; thou knowest that I love thee. He saith unto him, Feed my sheep" (Jn.21:16).
> "For ye are bought with a price [Christ's blood]: therefore glorify God in your body, and in your spirit, which are God's" (1 Co.6:20).
> "For he that is called in the Lord, being a servant, is the Lord's freeman: likewise also he that is called, being free, is Christ's servant" (1 Co.7:22).
> "Knowing that of the Lord ye shall receive the reward of the inheritance: for ye serve the Lord Christ" (Col.3:24).

b. Greatness is not dominion over people. The disciples still thought the Messiah's kingdom would be the restoration of Israel as an earthly nation and power. The ten other disciples were indignant because they desired the highest positions themselves. They would have been worried, not angered, by such evil and selfish behavior if they had not had the same feelings. The world's view of greatness is twofold.
1) The external view is measured by power, fame, recognition, influence, authority, dominion, and position.
2) The internal view is measured by wealth, buildings, vehicles, and machines, and the ability to work and achieve goals. The world seeks after these things; individuals as well as nations seek after them. In fact, most men are caught up to some degree in *worldly greatness*, seeking some recognition, position, influence, fame, and wealth. Few are void of *worldly greatness*.

> "He loveth transgression that loveth strife: and he that exalteth his gate seeketh destruction" (Pr.17:19).
> "It is not good to eat much honey: so for men to search their own glory is not glory" (Pr.25:27).
> "And whosoever shall exalt himself shall be abased; and he that shall humble himself shall be exalted" (Mt.23:12).
> "How can ye believe, which receive honour one of another, and seek not the honour that cometh from God only?" (Jn.5:44).

c. Greatness is serving others. The great are they who minister. The greatest, the chief among all, are they who are bond-slaves (see note—Ro.1:1). Note the two words *chief* (protos) and *servant* (doulos, bond slave). Christ made a significant distinction between what He said in v.26 and v.27. The difference is striking and challenging. There is...
- the *great* (v.26) vs. the *chief* (v.27).
- the *minister* (v.26) vs. the *bond-slave* (v.27).

Another way to see the difference is...
- the *great* are they who *minister*.
- the *chief* are they who are *bond-slaves*.

What Christ was saying is this: among His disciples, the person who ministers is great, but the person who is a bond-slave is the chief. The idea of the person who ministers is that of occasional service; whereas the bond-slave is a person who is bound to the Lord every moment of life, always serving, regardless of the hour or call or difficulty.

The idea that there are degrees of service is unquestionably in mind. Not every believer serves with the same fervor or commitment. The idea of *degrees of reward* for work is conveyed by our Lord time and again (see note, *Reward*—Lu.16:10-12 for a complete list).

> "And whosoever shall give to drink unto one of these little ones a cup of cold water only in the name of a disciple, verily I say unto you, he shall in no wise lose his reward" (Mt.10:42).
> "Even so it is not the will of your Father which is in heaven, that one of these little ones should perish" (Mt.18:14).
> "But ye shall not be so: but he that is greatest among you, let him be as the younger; and he that is chief, as he that doth serve" (Lu.22:26).
> "If I then, your Lord and Master, have washed your feet; ye also ought to wash one another's feet" (Jn.13:14).
> "With good will doing service, as to the Lord, and not to men" (Ep.6:7).
> "Wherefore we receiving a kingdom which cannot be moved, let us have grace, whereby we may serve God acceptably with reverence and godly fear" (He.12:28).
> "By humility and the fear of the LORD are riches, and honor, and life" (Pr.22:4).

"He hath showed thee, O man, what is good; and what doth the LORD require of thee, but to do justly, and to love mercy, and to walk humbly with thy God?" (Mi.6:8).

    d. True greatness was demonstrated by Christ in three supreme acts.

      1) The act of coming to earth: "The Son of Man *came.*" The incarnation is the Son of God becoming man. Most men look upon mankind as the summit of creation on this earth. But within the span and scope of the universe and the dimension of the spiritual world, and in particular before God, man is nothing—not to an honest and thinking man. He is only as a speck of sand on the beach or a drop of water in the ocean. At most, he lasts only about seventy years *if he can*.

        In all reality, for God to become a member of so low a race of beings is unimaginable. It is the most humiliating act possible.

      2) The act of ministering: "[He] came not to be ministered unto, but to minister." Furthermore, He was treated as the lowest of creatures by the men to whom He came. Impossible, yet true! They gave Him no place to lay His head (Mt.8:20; Lu.9:58) and, only three years after publicly announcing that He had come to save them, they killed Him. Now note: Jesus is the King of kings and Lord of lords, yet He secured His kingdom by becoming a minister and a servant to all. He did not *lord it* over men. He ministered to and served men, and because He became the servant to all, God has now highly exalted Him (Ph.2:8).

      3) The act of giving His life "a ransom for many" (see note—Mt.20:28).

DEEPER STUDY # 5

(20:28) **Ransom for many** (lutron anti pollon): a ransom in exchange (anti) for many; a ransom for many; a ransom instead of many.

Ransom is a means of setting loose in the Old Testament. It is the setting loose of a life or the ransom for a life (Ex.21:30). It is the setting loose, the ransom price, the redemptive price for something, for example...
- it is the price paid for the setting loose or freeing of a slave (Le.19:20).
- it is the redemptive price paid for land (Le.25:24).
- it is the ransom price paid for a captive (Is.45:13).

The Greek word for ransom (anti) is significant. There is no question that the idea of *exchange* is present. Christ gave His life in *exchange*, that is, in the place of or as a substitute for many. (See DEEPER STUDY # 2, *Justification*—Ro.4:22; note—5:1.)

The word is used two other times in the New Testament (Mk.10:45; 1 Ti.2:6). In 1 Ti.2:6, the words are "a substitutionary ransom for all" (antilutron huper panton). *Huper* is the preposition for the idea of substitution. It is a substitution in behalf of all. However, note two things.

1. All do not receive the offer. Paul said, "[Christ] gave Himself a ransom for all" (1 Ti.2:5). John said, "He is the propitiation...for the sins of the whole world" (1 Jn.2:2). And He is—potentially. Christ has met the need and provided the ransom price for every man and woman, but everyone has to accept the offer of the ransom in their own behalf. Christ has made provision, but anyone can reject the offer of ransom. And some do. Therefore, Scripture speaks of Christ's dying "for all" and also "for many." He died for *all* in that He has made *provision* for all to be saved, but He died for *many* in that only some receive the offer of the ransom.

2. There is the idea of sacrifice in the word ransom. In fact, that is just what *ransom* is. It is the exchange, the sacrifice, the giving up of something for something else. Something is substituted and sacrificed for something else. This is exactly what Christ did for us. He sacrificed and gave Himself up as a ransom for us (Ep.1:7; 1 Jn.2:1-2). (See the Old Testament sacrifices; they were a picture of what Christ was to do for us.)

    "Unto Him that loved us, and washed [loosed] us from our sins in His blood" (Re.1:5).

    "Ye were not redeemed with corruptible things, as silver and gold...but with the precious blood of Christ, as of a lamb without blemish and without spot" (1 Pe.1:18-19).

    "Christ hath redeemed us from the curse of the law, being made a curse for us" (Ga.3:13).

    "And that he died for all, that they which live should not henceforth live unto themselves, but unto him which died for [huper] them, and rose again" (2 Co.5:15).

    "For he hath made him to be sin for [huper] us, who knew no sin; that we might be made the righteousness of God in him" (2 Co.5:21).

    "Who needeth not daily, as those high priests, to offer up sacrifice, first for his own sins, and then for [huper] the people's: for this he did once, when he offered up himself" (He.7:27).

    "For if the blood of bulls and of goats, and the ashes of an heifer sprinkling the unclean, sanctifieth to the purifying of the flesh: how much more shall the blood of Christ, who through the eternal Spirit offered himself without spot to God, purge your conscience from dead works to serve the living God?" (He.9:13-14).

    "Nor yet that he should offer himself often, as the high priest entereth into the holy place every year with blood of others; for then must he often have suffered since the foundation of the world: but now once in the end of the world hath he appeared to put away sin by the sacrifice of himself" (He.9:25-26).

    "By the which will we are sanctified through the offering of the body of Jesus Christ once for all" (He.10:10).

    "But this man, after he had offered one sacrifice for sins for ever, sat down on the right hand of God....For by one offering he hath perfected for ever them that are sanctified" (He.10:12, 14).

    "Who his own self bare our sins in his own body on the tree, that we, being dead to sins, should live unto righteousness" (1 Pe.2:24; see 1 Co.5:7; Ep.5:2).

MATTHEW 20:29-34

	I. The Two Blind Men Healed: How the Desperate Can Be Saved, 20:29-34
	(Mk 10:46-52; Lu 18:35-43)
		buked them, because they should hold their peace: but they cried the more, saying, Have mercy on us, O Lord, *thou* Son of David.	mercy
			  a. In the face of opposition
			
			  b. Until Jesus responds

1. Step 1: Knowing that Jesus saves multitudes
  a. The crowd followed Him
  b. Two blind men sat nearby
2. Step 2: Seizing the chance when Jesus passes by
3. Step 3: Crying for mercy^{DS1}
4. Step 4: Continuing to cry for
	29 And as they departed from Jericho, a great multitude followed him.
	30 And, behold, two blind men sitting by the way side, when they heard that Jesus passed by, cried out, saying, Have mercy on us, O Lord, *thou* Son of David.
	31 And the multitude re-
		32 And Jesus stood still, and called them, and said, What will ye that I shall do unto you?
		33 They say unto him, Lord, that our eyes may be opened.
		34 So Jesus had compassion *on them,* and touched their eyes: and immediately their eyes received sight, and they followed him.
			5. Step 5: Asking great things of Jesus
			
			6. Step 6: Receiving the compassion & touch of Jesus
			7. Step 7: Following Jesus

DIVISION XIII

THE MESSIAH'S TEACHINGS ON THE WAY TO JERUSALEM, 19:1–20:34

I. The Two Blind Men Healed: How the Desperate Can Be Saved, 20:29-34

(20:29-34) **Introduction**: we live in a desperate world full of desperate people. Many hurt because of emptiness, loneliness, disease, death, accidents, problems, conflicts, difficulties, poverty, hunger, no purpose, no meaning, no significance, hopelessness, and helplessness. The two blind men show how the desperate can be saved and helped.

1. Step 1: knowing that Jesus saves multitudes (vv.29-30).
2. Step 2: seizing the chance when Jesus passes by (v.30).
3. Step 3: crying for mercy (v.30).
4. Step 4: continuing to cry for mercy (vv.31-32).
5. Step 5: asking great things of Jesus (v.33).
6. Step 6: receiving the compassion and touch of Jesus (v.34).
7. Step 7: following Jesus (v.34).

1 (20:29-30) **Multitudes—Jesus Christ**: as Jesus left Jericho there was also a host of pilgrims on their way to Jerusalem to celebrate the passover feast. The famous Jewish historian Josephus estimated that two to three million attended this feast every year. An enormous crowd would have been following Christ at this time.

There were several reasons why the crowds followed Christ in such numbers throughout His ministry.

  a. Some followed Christ because they had great need. They truly believed He could help them.

  b. Some followed Christ for what they could get out of Him. Following Him met, to some degree, their material and physical desires (Jn.6:26).

  c. Some followed Christ out of curiosity.

  d. Some followed Christ because they thought He was the answer to utopia, to personal and national fulfillment. They thought He might possibly be the Messiah who was to free Israel and meet the needs of its people forever (see DEEPER STUDY #2—Mt.1:18).

  e. Some few followed Christ because they honestly believed He was the true Messiah and had the words of eternal life. They desired to be a true disciple of His (Jn.6:67-68; see Jn.1:29, 34, 40-41, 45, 49; Mt.16:16).

As Jesus was walking out of the city, two blind men were sitting on the side of the road. There are three things said about these two men.

⇒ They were desperate. They were both blind and suffering the same physical infirmity.

⇒ They were together. They were companions who found some fellowship together. They sat and talked together, and as this event shows, acted together.

⇒ They were sitting where Christ passed by. Some may call it fate or chance, others destiny, and still others purpose; but the fact is, they were exactly where Christ passed by.

Thought 1. The two men suffered together and acted together. There is great benefit in our sharing together with someone who has a common experience, not to moan over our common plight but to encourage one another.

Note another fact: Christ encourages praying together. Every friendship among Christians should include praying together. These two men approached Christ together, and they could not even see. Christ should be made a significant part of our fellowship (Mt.18:20).

Thought 2. Note two things.

(1) The needy and desperate need to put themselves where Christ is. They need to go and sit where they know they can hear Christ.

(2) The needy and desperate can have great hope, but there is a condition. They must be where they can hear Christ. If these two had been elsewhere, they would have missed Christ. It is critical to find out where Christ can be heard.

MATTHEW 20:29-34

2 (20:30) **Salvation—Need**: first, the desperate can be saved by seizing the chance when Christ passes by, but alertness and sensitivity are essential. These two men were both alert and sensitive. They heard the feet and the conversation of the crowd as they passed by. Hearing the feet of the crowd alerted them, and hearing the conversation told them exactly what was going on.

Thought 1. The desperate can find where Jesus is by being alert to where God's people go and by listening to where God's people say He is. The feet and voice of the followers of Christ will direct the desperate to Christ.

Thought 2. One thing is critical for the desperate: to seize the opportunity. They must not let it pass. When we see or hear where Jesus is we must go to Him. If we do not put ourselves where He is, we increase the chance that we will miss Him forever. There are three reasons why our chances diminish.
(1) We become more dull, hardened, insensitive, unconcerned, and inactive; and we begin to accept conditions as they are.
(2) A more convenient time will never present itself. Intentions are good, but an immediate decision is needed. Paul preached and many listened. A few said, "We will hear thee again of this matter" (Ac.17:32). But they never did.
(3) Christ may never come our way again. If He does, He may not return with such force.

"That they should seek the Lord, if haply they might feel after him, and find him, though he be not far from every one of us" (Ac.17:27).
"Seek the LORD, and his strength: seek his face evermore" (Ps.105:4).
"Seek ye the LORD, all ye meek of the earth, which have wrought his judgment; seek righteousness, seek meekness: it may be ye shall be hid in the day of the LORD's anger" (Zep.2:3).
"Seek ye the LORD while he may be found, call ye upon him while he is near" (Is.55:6).

3 (20:30) **Salvation—Mercy**: second, the desperate can be saved by crying for mercy. Three things need to be noted about the two blind men's crying out for mercy.
a. They had an imperfect knowledge of Christ. They were blind; therefore, they could not travel about and learn of Him. Their knowledge of Him was based upon what they had heard *about* Him.
b. They believed what they had heard: that He was the Messiah, the promised Son of David. They believed in His power to help and deliver them.
c. They stirred themselves up and cried out for mercy. Imagine the obstacles: the crowd was large, the noise was loud. They were blind, and their chance of getting to Christ and being heard by Him was slim. But two things made the difference. They were desperate and they believed. So they stirred themselves up and cried out. *They acted on what knowledge and faith* they had.

There are two important facts about their cry for mercy.
⇒ They cried out for mercy themselves. They did not ask someone else to approach Christ for them.
⇒ They asked for mercy and only mercy. They did not ask for anything else. They were poor and they were beggars, but they did not ask for housing or clothing or even for food. They asked for their most basic need to be met—for mercy.

"And his mercy is on them that fear him from generation to generation" (Lu.1:50).
"And the publican, standing afar off, would not lift up so much as his eyes unto heaven, but smote upon his breast, saying, God be merciful to me a sinner. I tell you, this man went down to his house justified" (Lu.18:13-14).
"But God, who is rich in mercy, for his great love wherewith he loved us, even when we were dead in sins, hath quickened us together with Christ, (by grace ye are saved)" (Ep.2:4-5).
"Have mercy upon me, O LORD; for I am weak: O LORD, heal me; for my bones are vexed: my soul is also sore vexed: but thou, O LORD, how long?" (Ps.6:2-3).
"Hear, O LORD, when I cry with my voice: have mercy also upon me, and answer me" (Ps.27:7).
"Have mercy upon me, O God, according to thy lovingkindness: according unto the multitude of thy tender mercies blot out my transgressions" (Ps.51:1).
"Show us thy mercy, O LORD, and grant us thy salvation" (Ps.85:7).
"Let thy tender mercies come unto me, that I may live: for thy law is my delight" (Ps.119:77).
"And rend your heart, and not your garments, and turn unto the LORD your God: for he is gracious and merciful, slow to anger, and of great kindness, and repenteth him of the evil" (Joel 2:13).
"Rejoice not against me, O mine enemy: when I fall, I shall arise; when I sit in darkness, the LORD shall be a light unto me" (Mi.7:8).

DEEPER STUDY # 1
(20:30) **Son of David**: see notes—Mt.1:1; DEEPER STUDY # 2—1:18; DEEPER STUDY # 3—3:11; notes—11:1-6; 11:2-3; DEEPER STUDY # 1—11:5; DEEPER STUDY # 2—11:6; DEEPER STUDY # 1—12:16; note—Lu.7:21-23.

---

4 (20:31-32) **Salvation—Persistence**: third, the desperate can be saved by persisting in their cry for mercy.

a. The desperate must persist even in the face of opposition. A person who really wants Christ is to persevere; he is to fight against all obstacles until Christ responds.

These two men teach us perseverance. The crowd rebuked and tried to stop them from reaching Christ, but they would not be stopped. Note the Scripture: "They cried the more." A stream of fervency and sensation vibrated through their

MATTHEW 20:29-34

bodies. They were in dead earnest; nothing was going to keep them back. They were desperate—this opportunity might never come again—so they struggled, wrestled, and fought against the crowd, crying at the top of their voices, "Have mercy on us, thou son of David."

Thought 1. Note two things.
(1) There are many hindrances to our seeking after Christ—hindrances within and without. Sometimes we stand in the way, sometimes another person, sometimes circumstances. The hindrances are always there.
(2) Hindrances are to be struggled against and overcome. We are not to give in to hindrances, but we are to use them to learn endurance and experience (victorious living) and hope. Trials are to be used to sharpen, to increase, and to grow our faith. It is for this reason that we not only "rejoice in hope for the glory of God....but we glory in tribulations also" (Ro.5:2-4).

b. The desperate are to persist until Jesus responds. Persistence always grabs the Lord's attention (see outline and notes—Mt.7:7-11. See Lu.18:1.) Note the question Jesus asked. He already knew what the blind men wanted. He had probably heard their crying out as well, but He wanted them to experience persistence. Why? Why does Christ teach persistence and perseverance instead of just meeting our needs immediately? There are at least five reasons.

⇒ Having to persevere sharpens and grows our faith. It teaches endurance, experience (victorious living), and hope (Ro.5:2-4).
⇒ Having to persevere sharpens and makes us more aware of our minds. It gives us more time for thought, meditation, and searching for the truth of ourselves and our needs. It zeros in on real needs.
⇒ Having to persevere teaches us to pray and to seek God more and more. It creates more awareness of our helplessness and our need for His presence and help. It necessitates more fellowship and deep communion with Him.
⇒ Having to persevere gives us more part in His work and worship. It creates a sense within us of having a greater part. This is not a need on God's part, but a need on our part. Serving Him is a great privilege which He allows us.
⇒ Having to persevere allows more time for a greater number of people to be reached with God's power. Perseverance is a greater witness for God. When God answers and moves, more people are aroused to observe God's working.

"Ask, and it shall be given you; seek, and ye shall find; knock, and it shall be opened unto you" (Mt.7:7).
"But if from thence thou shalt seek the LORD thy God, thou shalt find him, if thou seek him with all thy heart and with all thy soul" (De.4:29).
"Seek ye me, and ye shall live" (Am. 5:4).

Thought 1. This is an important lesson for the church. Often the poor and most needful are pushed back, ignored, neglected, rebuked, and not wanted by the church. They are thought to be lazy or lacking in initiative or unable to contribute much. The church rationalizes that the poor and needy would feel uncomfortable and not want to be a part of the fellowship anyway.
Our Lord never rejected a person. He never planned for the church to meet the needs only of a certain class. What is *class* anyway? Is it a certain amount of money? Is it a certain *number* of dresses? Of suits? Of shoes? Of watches? Is it a certain *size* of house? Of car? Of office? Of desk? Of chair? Is it stature? Hairstyle? Is it a certain location in town? In a suburb? Beside a golf course? A lake? How foolish can we be? How long will we play the fool while the world around us cries out in desperation? Is there anyone anywhere who will think and see and feel as God thinks and sees and feels? Where is the person who will stand in the gap for God and reach out to help the lost and poor of this world?

5 (20:33) **Prayer**: fourth, the desperate can be saved by asking great things of Christ. Note what a great request they asked of Christ.
a. They were beggars, ever so poor. There was nothing appealing about them at all.
b. Society rejected them. Even the crowd surrounding Jesus pushed them away and tried to silence their search for God.
c. They had never followed Christ. They had never heard Him preach even once. They knew very little about Him.
d. They had an unbelievable request to make: for Christ to heal their blindness.

"And all things, whatsoever ye shall ask in prayer, believing, ye shall receive" (Mt.21:22).
"And whatsoever ye shall ask in my name, that will I do, that the Father may be glorified in the Son" (Jn.14:13).
"If ye abide in me, and my words abide in you, ye shall ask what ye will, and it shall be done unto you" (Jn.15:7).
"Hitherto have ye asked nothing in my name: ask, and ye shall receive, that your joy may be full" (Jn.16:24).
"And this is the confidence that we have in him, that, if we ask any thing according to his will, he heareth us: and if we know that he hear us, whatsoever we ask, we know that we have the petitions that we desired of him" (1 Jn.5:14-15).
"And it shall come to pass, that before they call, I will answer; and while they are yet speaking, I will hear" (Is.65:24).
"Call unto me, and I will answer thee, and show thee great and mighty things, which thou knowest not" (Je.33:3).

MATTHEW 20:29-34

Thought 1. Many come to Christ only when they are in physical trouble (blindness). However, their real problem is spiritual blindness. They are spiritually blind and do not know it (Jn.9:41).

Thought 2. There is a lesson here on being specific in our requests. At first, the blind men asked for mercy without identifying just where they needed mercy. Christ asked for them to be specific: "What will ye that I shall do unto you?"

6 (20:34) **Decision**: fifth, the desperate can be saved by receiving the compassion and touch of Jesus. Note what happens.
  a. Jesus had compassion. They no sooner asked than Jesus' compassion was immediately aroused. He cared and felt for them.
  b. Jesus touched their eyes. He did more than express compassion and feelings; He reached out to them and touched them. He let them feel His touch and care. He reached out and gave Himself to them. What a lesson for ministry!
  c. Jesus healed them. They *immediately* experienced the love and power of God. They were healed.

> "Wherefore he is able also to save them to the uttermost that come unto God by him, seeing he ever liveth to make intercession for them" (He.7:25).
> "But without faith it is impossible to please him: for he that cometh to God must believe that he is, and that he is a rewarder of them that diligently seek him" (He.11:6).
> "Commit thy way unto the LORD; trust also in him; and he shall bring it to pass" (Ps.37:5).
> "Trust in the LORD with all thine heart; and lean not unto thine own understanding" (Pr.3:5).
> "Trust ye in the LORD for ever: for in the LORD JEHOVAH is everlasting strength" (Is.26:4).

Thought 1. The men had their prayer and cry answered; they had their need met for two reasons.
(1) They believed in Christ, the Messiah, and His power to meet their need.
(2) They persisted in that belief. They were not quitters. They did not allow other people and circumstances to prevent them from seeking Jesus.

7 (20:34) **Discipleship**: sixth, the desperate can be saved by following Jesus. Note the simple words: "And they followed Him." He had shown mercy, and they became His disciples. Being a disciple meant two things.
  a. They followed Him to learn of Him.

> "And he said to them all, If any man will come after me, let him deny himself, and take up his cross daily, and follow me" (Lu.9:23).
> "My sheep hear my voice, and I know them, and they follow me" (Jn.10:27).
> "If any man serve me, let him follow me; and where I am, there shall also my servant be: if any man serve me, him will my Father honour" (Jn.12:26).
> "Be ye therefore followers of God, as dear children" (Ep.5:1).
> "As ye have therefore received Christ Jesus the Lord, so walk ye in him" (Col.2:6).
> "For even hereunto were ye called: because Christ also suffered for us, leaving us an example, that ye should follow his steps" (1 Pe.2:21).
> "He that saith he abideth in him ought himself also so to walk, even as he walked" (1 Jn.2:6).

  b. They followed Him to be witnesses to Him and His power.

> "Let your light so shine before men, that they may see your good works, and glorify your Father which is in heaven" (Mt.5:16).
> "That ye may with one mind and one mouth glorify God, even the Father of our Lord Jesus Christ" (Ro.15:6).
> "For ye are bought with a price: therefore glorify God in your body, and in your spirit, which are God's" (1 Co.6:20).
> "That the name of our Lord Jesus Christ may be glorified in you, and ye in him, according to the grace of our God and the Lord Jesus Christ" (2 Th.1:12).
> "By him therefore let us offer the sacrifice of praise to God continually, that is, the fruit of our lips giving thanks to his name" (He.13:15).
> "But ye are a chosen generation, a royal priesthood, an holy nation, a peculiar people; that ye should show forth the praises of him who hath called you out of darkness into his marvellous light" (1 Pe.2:9).
> "Sing praises to the LORD, which dwelleth in Zion: declare among the people his doings" (Ps.9:11).
> "Let the people praise thee, O God; let all the people praise thee" (Ps.67:3).

Thought 1. There is a lesson here on gratitude. The men expressed their appreciation in the greatest way possible. They became witnesses to His benevolence, love, mercy, and power. Many never express gratitude at all. Too many get what they want then soon forget that it came from God.

MATTHEW 21:1-11

CHAPTER 21

XIV. THE MESSIAH'S LAST WEEK: HIS CLAIM CHALLENGED & REJECTED, 21:1–23:39

A. The Triumphal Entry: Jesus Deliberately Claimed to Be the Messiah,DS1 21:1-11

(Mk 11:1-11; Lu 19:28-40; Jn 12:12-19)

1. **He deliberately began His last week in Jerusalem**
   a. In a suburb of BethphageDS2
   b. Sent two disciples on a special mission
2. **He deliberately fulfilled prophecy**
   a. The disciples' special mission: To secure a donkey & her colt
   b. The point: A deliberate fulfillment of prophecy–a picture of Zec.9:9

And when they drew nigh unto Jerusalem, and were come to Bethphage, unto the mount of Olives, then sent Jesus two disciples,
2 Saying unto them, Go into the village over against you, and straightway ye shall find an ass tied, and a colt with her: loose *them,* and bring *them* unto me.
3 And if any *man* say ought unto you, ye shall say, The Lord hath need of them; and straightway he will send them.
4 All this was done, that it might be fulfilled which was spoken by the prophet, saying,
5 Tell ye the daughter of Sion, Behold, thy King cometh unto thee, meek, and sitting upon an ass, and a colt the foal of an ass.
6 And the disciples went, and did as Jesus commanded them,
7 And brought the ass, and the colt, and put on them their clothes, and they set *him* thereon.
8 And a very great multitude spread their garments in the way; others cut down branches from the trees, and strawed *them* in the way.
9 And the multitudes that went before, and that followed, cried, saying, Hosanna to the Son of David: Blessed *is* he that cometh in the name of the Lord; Hosanna in the highest.
10 And when he was come into Jerusalem, all the city was moved, saying, Who is this?
11 And the multitude said, This is Jesus the prophet of Nazareth of Galilee.

    1) A warning to Jerusalem
    2) The King comes
    3) He comes gently
    4) He comes upon a coltDS3

3. **He deliberately received the homage of the disciples**
   a. They did as He requested
   b. They used their own clothes for a saddle

4. **He deliberately received the homage of the people**
   a. Many received Him as King: Spread cloaks & branches before Him

   b. Many received Him as Messiah
      1) As the Son of David

      2) As the Lord
      3) As the Highest

5. **He deliberately stirred the people to ask the key question of life**
   a. Question: Who is this?
   b. Answer: Jesus the prophet of NazarethDS4

DIVISION XIV

THE MESSIAH'S LAST WEEK: HIS CLAIM CHALLENGED AND REJECTED, 21:1–23:39

A. The Triumphal Entry: Jesus Deliberately Claimed to Be the Messiah, 21:1-11

(21:1-11) **Introduction—Jesus Christ, Last Week**: Jesus began the last week of His life. He had spent the night before (the Sabbath evening) in Bethany with Lazarus, Mary, and Martha (Jn.12:1f). He was now going to deliberately demonstrate that He was the Messiah, the One prophesied to be the Savior of the world. He pictured without question that He was the fulfillment of prophecy, the One for whom all righteous men had longed and looked.
1. He deliberately began His last week in Jerusalem (v.1).
2. He deliberately fulfilled prophecy (vv.2-5).
3. He deliberately received the homage of the disciples (vv.6-7).
4. He deliberately received the homage of the people (vv.8-9).
5. He deliberately stirred the people to ask the key question of life (vv.10-11).

DEEPER STUDY # 1
(21:1-11) **Holy Week—Palm Sunday**: the last week of our Lord's life has been known as Holy Week since the earliest of times. The Triumphal Entry was the first event of the week, taking place on the first day. It was and still is called Palm Sunday.

1 (21:1) **Jesus Christ, Poverty**: He deliberately began His last week in Jerusalem. Note the lowliness of Jesus. He had to depend upon friends for lodging. Up to the very end, "the Son of Man hath not where to lay His head" (Mt.8:20; Lu.9:58).
    He also "drew nigh unto Jerusalem" by foot. He had no stallion, no donkey, no camel—no means of transportation. He had only what God had given Him as He entered the world, His feet, to get Him where He wished to go. How God's heart must be cut to the core by our concern for material comfort and ease. Jesus' face was always set toward saving and helping the world. Up to the very end, He went about His purpose untainted and unswerved by the world. What a lesson for us!
    a. Christ began His last week in Bethphage (see DEEPER STUDY # 2—Mt.21:1).
    b. Christ sent two disciples on a special mission.

DEEPER STUDY # 2
(21:1) **Bethphage**: the name of the city means "House of figs." It was a suburb of Jerusalem, lying toward the Mount of Olives. Note that Jesus arrived in Bethphage by foot, indicating that He had no means of travel except walking.

MATTHEW 21:1-11

2 (21:2-5) **Prophecy**: the Lord deliberately fulfilled prophecy.

    a. Christ sent two disciples into the city to secure a donkey and her young colt. He borrowed the two animals from another man, probably another disciple. One of three things happened that led the man to loan the animals.
        1) The man was a disciple who would allow *the Lord* to borrow his animals. The emphasis, "The *Lord* hath need of them," points rather strongly to this fact's being at least part of what happened. The Lord (o kurios) would be a strong expression to use with an unbeliever. It was equivalent to Jehovah.
        2) The Lord had made previous arrangements with the owner to borrow the animals. This was, or course, possible; but the possibility that the disciples would be questioned about borrowing the animals makes this unlikely.
        3) The Lord demonstrated His Divine omniscience to further validate His claim of Messiahship. As God, He knew exactly where the animals would be, the questioning about loaning them, and the fact that the owner would loan them. This could easily be part of what happened.

The important thing to note is the strength and authority of Christ throughout this whole event. He assumed the position of Messiah, the Lord God (Jehovah) of all men, of their will and their property, even of their animals.

Thought 1. Every mission of the Lord—every task, no matter how small—is important. Going to fetch the animals was a small task, yet it was critically important in the proclamation of Christ as King. No task should ever be thought too small in the service of our Lord.

Thought 2. Note two things.
(1) Jesus encourages and comforts us with the presence of others. He seldom sends us out alone.
(2) How often has Christ had a mission to be done and there was no one present to do it, especially the small and insignificant missions such as this one?

Thought 3. The colt was borrowed. Again, Jesus had nothing of this world's goods. In order to fulfill the Scripture that the Messiah was to enter the city riding a colt, Jesus had to borrow the colt. How materialistic we become, thinking we must have things in order to live! We even think we *cannot minister* effectively without the latest *material things* of the world (machines, equipment, methods). How unlike Christ!

      "For ye know the grace of our Lord Jesus Christ, that though he was rich, yet for your sakes he became poor, that ye through his poverty might be rich" (2 Co.8:9).

Thought 4. Note a significant fact: when the proclamation of His Messiahship was at stake, Christ let nothing stand in the way. It was essential that the people know that He was the Messiah. He did not own a donkey to fulfill the prophecy, so He went out to find one. Such determination and unswerving purpose should grip us in proclaiming that He is the Messiah.

    b. Christ had a reason for making such detailed preparations to enter Jerusalem. He was deliberately fulfilling the prophecy of Zec.9:9. The prophecy said four things.
        1) "Tell ye the daughter of Sion [that is, Jerusalem]": Jerusalem was to be told, given a threefold warning. Why must she be warned? Because what she expected was not going to happen, not like she anticipated.
        2) "Behold, thy King cometh unto thee": this was the first warning. Jerusalem's King was coming, coming just as Jerusalem had expected. The people were correct in this part of their expectation. But there is danger in expectation, the danger of being so fervent in our own ideas that we miss what really happens. Fervent expectation can miss the event when the event occurs a little differently than what was expected. "Thy King cometh," but He comes somewhat differently than expected.
        3) "Thy King cometh...*meek*": this was the second warning. The Messiah was coming in meekness not as a reigning monarch. He was coming to win men's hearts and lives spiritually and eternally, not physically and materially (see notes—Mk.11:1-11; Ep.1:3; see Mt.11:29).
        4) "Thy King cometh...sitting upon an ass [donkey], and a colt": this was the third warning. The Messiah was coming not as a conqueror riding a white stallion but as a King of peace riding a donkey. He was coming to save the world through peace, to reconcile the world to the God of love, not to the God of hate and retaliation and war. He was not going to kill men and overthrow their governments (the Romans and Gentiles). He was coming to win men's hearts and lives through the glorious news (gospel) that God loves and reconciles (see outline and notes—Ep.2:13-18).

Note the prophecy and the careful preparation Christ made to fulfill the prophecy. This is significant, for it means that Christ was dramatizing His Messiahship—dramatizing it so clearly that men could not fail to see that He was God's Messiah. This was God's will prophesied generations before Christ came. God wanted His Son to proclaim His Messiahship so clearly that the people could not mistake what He was doing.

Thought 1. Jesus claimed to be the Messiah, God's very own Son. The great pains He took to fulfill this prophecy clearly showed what He was claiming. He was deliberately working out God's will. He was doing exactly what God said He wanted His Son to do centuries before (Zec.9:9). He was making the claim to be God's Messiah in a dramatic way. He was painting a picture so clearly that man could not fail to see what He was claiming. A deliberate decision is now required of us. We either accept His claim or not. As He *deliberately* fulfilled the prophecy, so we now *deliberately accept or deliberately reject* His claim.

MATTHEW 21:1-11

"Through the tender mercy of our God; whereby the dayspring from on high hath visited us, to give light to them that sit in darkness and in the shadow of death, to guide our feet into the way of peace" (Lu.1:78-79).

"And suddenly there was with the angel a multitude of the heavenly hosts praising God, and saying, Glory to God in the highest, and on earth peace, good will toward men" (Lu.2:13-14).

"Peace I leave with you, my peace I give unto you: not as the world giveth, give I unto you. Let not your heart be troubled, neither let it be afraid" (Jn.14:27).

"These things I have spoken unto you, that in me ye might have peace. In the world ye shall have tribulation: but be of good cheer; I have overcome the world" (Jn.16:33).

"The word which God sent unto the children of Israel, preaching peace by Jesus Christ: (he is Lord of all)" (Ac.10:36).

"Therefore being justified by faith, we have peace with God through our Lord Jesus Christ" (Ro.5:1).

"For the kingdom of God is not meat and drink; but righteousness, and peace, and joy in the Holy Ghost" (Ro.14:17).

"For he is our peace, who hath made both one, and hath broken down the middle wall of partition between us" (Ep.2:14).

"And, having made peace through the blood of his cross, by him to reconcile all things unto himself; by him, I say, whether they be things in earth, or things in heaven" (Col.1:20).

"The LORD will give strength unto his people; the LORD will bless his people with peace" (Ps.29:11).

Thought 2. Note two very significant things.
(1) Christ did not come to execute justice but to save men spiritually through the forgiveness of sin. Christ came not as a judge to judge men for ignoring, neglecting, rejecting, and misinterpreting God; but He came as the Messenger of Peace to reconcile men to God by the cross (see outline and notes—Ep.2:13-18; Col.1:20).
(2) Christ is coming again, coming as Judge to execute justice among all men, both the saved and unsaved (DEEPER STUDY # 1—He.9:27; see Mt.25:31-46; 2 Co.5:10).

DEEPER STUDY # 3
(21:5) **Ass - Colt**: see DEEPER STUDY # 4—Mk.11:7.

---

3 (21:6-7) **Homage—Obedience**: Christ deliberately received the homage of the disciples. The disciples paid Him homage (reverence, recognition). They did exactly what He asked despite the uncertainty of the matter. They had no money to buy or rent the animals, and they were to be questioned about why they wanted the animals. Yet they obeyed—not questioning, not doubting.

Note the other act of homage: there was no saddle for their Lord. They cared about Him and His comfort, so they took their own outer garments and threw them across the animals. Again, this was an act of homage (reverence and recognition). In following Christ, the two men had lived a life of poverty, so they had little clothing. It cost them to use their clothing for such a humble act. The clothing would be soiled and smelly, but they cared and they worshipped through this act.

The point is that Christ was now unmistakably claiming the dignity and rights of a King. He was not washing feet now; He was deliberately accepting their homage and reverence.

But note something of critical importance. In claiming the dignity and rights of a King, He was doing it in the most humble practice of His day: entering the city as a King of Peace. This was symbolized by riding a young colt, instead of riding the conqueror's stallion. He was disclaiming all ideas of an earthly and material kingdom. He had come to save Jerusalem and the world through peace, not war.

Thought 1. There are three clear lessons in this event.
(1) We are to give homage to the Lord by obeying His commands. They may sometimes be difficult to understand and somewhat embarrassing, yet we are to trust and obey just as the two disciples did—not doubting or questioning.

"He that hath my commandments, and keepeth them, he it is that loveth me: and he that loveth me shall be loved of my Father, and I will love him, and will manifest myself to him" (Jn.14:21).

"If ye keep my commandments, ye shall abide in my love; even as I have kept my Father's commandments, and abide in his love....Ye are my friends, if ye do whatsoever I command you" (Jn.15:10, 14).

"And whatsoever we ask, we receive of him, because we keep his commandments, and do those things that are pleasing in his sight" (1 Jn.3:22).

"And Samuel said, Hath the LORD as great delight in burnt offerings and sacrifices, as in obeying the voice of the LORD? Behold, to obey is better than sacrifice, and to hearken than the fat of rams" (1 S.15:22).

(2) We are to give homage to the Lord by giving Him the best we have. He is worthy of all and due all, so we are to do as the disciples did, give Him all—even the very best of our clothing if needed.

MATTHEW 21:1-11

"Jesus said unto him, If thou wilt be perfect, go and sell that thou hast, and give to the poor, and thou shalt have treasure in heaven: and come and follow me" (Mt.19:21).

"Then Peter began to say unto him, Lo, we have left all, and have followed thee" (Mk.10:28).

"And after these things he went forth, and saw a publican, named Levi, sitting at the receipt of custom: and he said unto him, Follow me. And he left all, rose up, and followed him" (Lu.5:27-28).

"So likewise, whosoever he be of you that forsaketh not all that he hath, he cannot be my disciple" (Lu.14:33).

"Yea doubtless, and I count all things but loss for the excellency of the knowledge of Christ Jesus my Lord: for whom I have suffered the loss of all things, and do count them but dung, that I may win Christ" (Ph.3:8).

(3) We worship and pay homage to Christ when we give the clothes off our back. Such is a most noble ministry and assures great reward.

"Come, ye blessed of my Father, inherit the kingdom prepared for you...For I was...naked, and ye clothed me...." (Mt.25:34-36. See 25:31-46).

But note: there is a difference in giving old unusable clothes and in buying new clothes, or else giving the clothes off our backs. In order to minister, the disciples gave what they had to minister. They gave the clothes they were wearing (see the widow's mite, Lu.21:1-4).

4 (21:8-9) **Homage—Messiah**: Christ deliberately received the homage of the people. And note: it was a "very great multitude" (v.8). Apparently what happened was this. The multitude had begun to gather since early morning, excitedly looking for Him who had raised Lazarus from the dead. John told us this. In fact, he said there were so many people that the Pharisees said, "the world is gone after Him" (Jn.12:17-19). There was the crowd of disciples already accompanying Him and the pilgrims on their way to the Passover Feast who had joined His caravan. There were also the residents of Bethany and Bethphage who had heard of His presence and the miracles, and those who were already in Jerusalem, citizens and pilgrims who were rushing out to search for Him.

We are led to imagine an enormous crowd of teeming thousands lining the roadway as Christ was helped atop the donkey to begin His triumphal entry into Jerusalem. There are several facts that point toward this conclusion.

a. Two or more million pilgrims gathered in Jerusalem every year for the Passover Feast (see DEEPER STUDY # 1—Mt.26:2). Thousands upon thousands were strict religionists, believing in the Jewish Messiah.

b. The news being spread throughout the city and surrounding area concerned the miracles Christ had performed, a concentration of miracles for some days now which included the raising of Lazarus from the dead (Jn.11:1f; 11:55-56). The very atmosphere was electric with the exciting news that Jesus was God's promised Messiah. Multitudes had heard that He was in Bethany and Bethphage (Mk.14:1-9). As said above, there was the multitude who had turned around from Jerusalem to meet Him (Jn.12:17-19); there was the multitude already travelling with Him (Mt.21:29); and there was the multitude of citizens in Bethany and Bethphage who had begun gathering around Him (Mk.14:1-9; Jn.12:1f). The whole thrust of the picture points to teeming thousands searching for Him and rushing out to welcome Him when they heard He was coming. (Note the words of Matthew, "the multitudes that went before, and that followed" v.9.)

The multitudes did two things.
1. They received Him as King. This is shown by two acts which were always done for Kings' entering a city. They stripped off their cloaks and cut down tree branches, and they spread both out on the roadway before Him. They wished to honor and pay Him the homage of a King. They wished to show Him that they received Him as the promised King of Israel.
2. They received Him as Messiah. This is seen in what they shouted about Christ.
   ⇒ They shouted out, "Hosanna," which means save now, or save, we pray.
   ⇒ They called Him "the Son of David," which was the title of the Messiah (see notes—Mt.1:1; DEEPER STUDY # 2—1:18; DEEPER STUDY # 3—3:11; notes—11:1-6; 11:2-3; DEEPER STUDY # 1—11:5; DEEPER STUDY # 2—11:6; DEEPER STUDY #1—12:16; note—Lu.7:21-23).
   ⇒ They shouted out, "Blessed is He that cometh in the name of the Lord." This means blessed is He who is sent by God to save His people; blessed is He who is sent with the authority of God.
   ⇒ They shouted out, "Hosanna in the Highest" which means "God save, we pray. Thou who art in the Highest, save now through Him whom You have sent."

Thought 1. There are several critical lessons in this point.
(1) We must proclaim Christ as our King. He is to be the King of our hearts and lives, to rule and reign over us. But note the critical question: What do we mean by King? The people of Christ's day were willing to accept him as an earthly King; that is, they were willing to accept what authority and power He would use in their behalf. The farthest thought from their minds was the spiritual rule and reign of their lives. They wanted earthly and material benefits. How much like so many of us! We want His kingly power when in need (physically or materially), but we want nothing to do with His kingly authority over our lives.
(2) We must welcome Christ as God's true Messiah, the One who has come to truly save us. But again, what we mean by *save* is critical. We should not presume upon His earthly care and deliverance unless we are first willing to receive His spiritual care and deliverance (salvation and rebirth, the surrendering of all we are and have).
(3) Every man should cry out, "Hosanna, save now, I pray O Lord."

MATTHEW 21:1-11

"Behold, now is the accepted time; behold, now is the day of salvation" (2 Co.6:2).

(4) We must make two confessions.
- ⇒ Christ is *the Blessed* (who) comes in the name of the Lord.
- ⇒ "Hosanna in the highest": salvation is "in the highest"; it is in Christ whom God has sent.

"Nathanael answered and saith unto him, Rabbi, thou art the Son of God; thou art the King of Israel" (Jn.1:49).

"For God so loved the world, that he gave his only begotten Son, that whosoever believeth in him should not perish, but have everlasting life" (Jn.3:16).

"Pilate therefore said unto him, Art thou a king then? Jesus answered, Thou sayest that I am a king. To this end was I born, and for this cause came I into the world, that I should bear witness unto the truth. Every one that is of the truth heareth my voice" (Jn.18:37).

"For he saith, I have heard thee in a time accepted, and in the day of salvation have I succoured thee: behold, now is the accepted time; behold, now is the day of salvation" (2 Co.6:2).

"Which in his times he shall show, who is the blessed and only Potentate, the King of kings, and Lord of lords" (1 Ti.6:15).

"For the grace of God that bringeth salvation hath appeared to all men, teaching us that, denying ungodliness and worldly lusts, we should live soberly, righteously, and godly, in this present world" (Tit.2:11-12).

(5) We must lay all that we are and have before Christ, not only our clothes.

5 (21:10-11) **Jesus Christ, Response to**: He deliberately stirred the people to ask the key question of life. All the city was *moved* (eseisthe), that is, shaken. John reported that "the world is gone after him" (Jn.12:19).
- ⇒ The Romans sensed that a popular uprising might be in the making.
- ⇒ The Herodians, who were the Jewish ruling party, feared they would be overthrown, losing their power.
- ⇒ The Pharisees were stirred to new depths of envy and malice.
- ⇒ The common people were convinced that their day of liberation had finally arrived in Jesus of Nazareth.

DEEPER STUDY # 4
(21:11) **Prophet**: this was definitely a reference to the Messiah, the One who was sent from God (see Jn.1:21; 6:14; 9:17).

MATTHEW 21:12-16

	B. The Temple Cleansed: Authority Over God's House,DS1 21:12-16 (Mk 11:15-19; Lu 19:45-46; Jn 2:13-16)	14 And the blind and the lame came to him in the temple; and he healed them.	3. The temple (church) is to be a place for ministry
1. The temple (church) is to be a place where people are not exploited	12 And Jesus went into the temple of God, and cast out all them that sold and bought in the temple, and overthrew the tables of the moneychangers, and the seats of them that sold doves,	15 And when the chief priests and scribes saw the wonderful things that he did, and the children crying in the temple, and saying, Hosanna to the Son of David; they were sore displeased,	4. The temple (church) is to be a place where wonderful things are done
		16 And said unto him, Hearest thou what these say? And Jesus saith unto them, Yea; have ye never read, Out of the mouth of babes and sucklings thou hast perfected praise?	5. The temple (church) is to be a place where Christ is praised a. Children praised Him b. Some objected c. Christ commanded the children's praiseDS2
2. The temple (church) is to be a house of prayer	13 And said unto them, It is written, My house shall be called the house of prayer; but ye have made it a den of thieves.		

DIVISION XIV

THE MESSIAH'S LAST WEEK: HIS CLAIM CHALLENGED AND REJECTED, 21:1-23:39

B. The Temple Cleansed: Authority Over God's House, 21:12-16

(21:12-16) **Introduction**: the cleansing of the temple took place on Monday, the day after the triumphal entry into Jerusalem. Mark told us this.

> "And Jesus entered into Jerusalem, and into the temple: and when he had looked round about upon all things, and now the eventide was come, he went out unto Bethany with the twelve" (Mk.11:11).

The scene was this: teeming thousands had lined the roadway for Jesus' triumphal entry. As He rode along to the shouts of welcome from the multitudes, He was led right up to the steps of the temple. He entered the temple, as Mark said, "looked round about upon all things," and observed all that was going on. He stood off to the side observing all the corruption. After some time, heartbroken and weary, He left and returned to Bethany to spend Sunday night. When He arose on Monday morning, He returned to the temple to cleanse it of those who profaned its sacredness.

Four things should be noted about the temple during the last week of our Lord's life.

1. Jesus was ending His ministry in the temple, His Father's house of prayer, the place where God's presence dwelt in a very, very special way. He is about to complete His life upon earth, a glorious ministry fulfilling the will of God perfectly. The night before, as He stood off by Himself in the temple observing all that was taking place, His thoughts are very contemplative: thoughts that were meditating upon His Father; upon His life now about completed; upon the great sacrifice He was to pay for man's sins; upon the corruption of the temple taking place all around Him; upon the worshipping that should be taking place; and upon so much more. His heart was drawn ever so close to God, yet it was broken and weeping within. Right before Him was a picture of the terrible sin for which He was to die. The temple itself, the place where men should be able to draw close to God, was corrupted by men. It had become anything but a house of prayer. It was a place for commercialism, for man's greed.

2. Jesus was revealing who He was by cleansing the temple. He was proclaiming to all generations that He had the right to determine how the temple was to be used and to purge it of corruptions. As God's Son, the temple was His dwelling place, the place where the worship of God was to be especially known.

3. Jesus was revealing how men were to treat and use the temple of God.

4. Jesus began and ended His ministry by cleansing the temple. The two cleansings were separate events which marked the opening and closing of His ministry. The importance of the temple as God's house of prayer and worship was thereby demonstrated.

When our Lord entered Jerusalem, He did not go up to the palace of the King nor to the courts of the rulers, but He went up to the temple, the House of God. His kingdom was not of this world, not physical, but of heaven and spiritual. His authority and rule were in the temple of God and in the hearts of men. Therefore, He went up to the temple of God to cleanse it and to teach men how the temple was and is to be used.

1. The temple (church) is to be a place where people are not exploited (v.12).
2. The temple (church) is to be a house of prayer (v.13).
3. The temple (church) is to be a place for ministry (v.14).
4. The temple (church) is to be a place where wonderful things are done (v.15).
5. The temple (church) is to be a place where Christ is praised (vv.15-16).

MATTHEW 21:12-16

DEEPER STUDY # 1
(21:12-16) **Temple**: one must understand the layout of the temple in order to see what was happening in this event. The temple sat on top of Mt. Zion and was thought to have covered about thirty acres of land. It consisted of two parts, the temple building itself and the temple precincts or courtyards. The Greek language has two different words to distinguish which is meant.
   1. *The temple building* (naos) was a small ornate structure which sat in the center of the temple property. It was called the Holy Place or Holy of Holies, and only the High Priest could enter its walls, and he could enter only once during the year, on the Day of Atonement.
   2. *The temple precincts* (hieron) were four courtyards which surrounded the temple building, each decreasing in their importance to the Jewish mind. It is critical to remember that great walls separated the courts from each other.
      a. First, there was the Inner Court of the Priests. Only the priests were allowed to enter this court. Within the courtyard stood the great furnishings of worship: the Altar of Burnt Offering, the Brazen Laver, the Seven Branched lampstand, the Altar of Incense, and the Table of Showbread.
      b. The Court of the Israelites was next. This was a huge courtyard where Jewish worshippers met together for joint services on the great feast days. It was also where worshippers handed over their sacrifices to the priests.
      c. The Court of the Women was the third Courtyard. Women were usually limited to this area except for worship. They could, however, enter the Court of the Israelites when they came to make sacrifice or worship in a joint assembly on a great feast day.
      d. The Court of the Gentiles was the last courtyard. It covered a vast space, surrounding all the other courtyards, and was the place of worship for all Gentile converts to Judaism.

Three facts need to be noted about the Court of the Gentiles.
   1. It was the courtyard farthest removed from the center of worship, the Holy of Holies which represented God's very presence (see note—Ep.2:14).
   2. A high wall separated the Court of the Gentiles from the other courts, disallowing any Gentile a closer approach into God's presence. There were, in fact, tablets hanging all around the wall threatening death to any Gentile who went beyond his own courtyard.
   3. It was in the Court of the Gentiles where so much commercialism took place. There was a regular commercial market within its walls. How did a commercial market ever get into the temple of God? Very simply, greed. Worshippers needed animals, (oxen, sheep, doves), incense, meal, wine, oil, salt, and other items for their sacrifices and offerings. Pilgrims from foreign nations needed money exchanged. At some point in the history of the temple, the priests had decided to take advantage of the market themselves instead of letting retailers on the outside reap all the profits. So the priests began to set up booths within the court of the Gentiles and to lease out space to *outside* retailers. These often turned out to be family members. The owner of the booths or space was the High Priest or Annas. The courtyard was filled with booth-like spaces where worshippers could find any kind of service they needed. The atmosphere was one of commercial traffic and commotion, not of worship and prayer.

Remembering the teeming thousands who attended the great feasts, we can imagine the loudest commotion and our picture would still come short of the actual scene. Who can picture thousands of animals with their peculiar noises, wastes, and smells within the temple of God? And for what? What would cause men to so abuse the worshipping center of God? As said above, money, the greed of men. It is no wonder Christ did what He did. He could not do otherwise, for He was the Son of God, the Messiah sent into the world to bring about a true worship of God. And there was no hope of worship within the Court of the Gentiles. Prayer and worship were impossible.

1 (21:12) **Temple—Church**: the temple or church is not to be a place where people are exploited. Note what Jesus did to show this.
   a. He went into the temple (Court of the Gentiles) where God's presence was to be and where He and others should be able to worship in quietness and meditation. But what He found was the very opposite: commotion, commercial selling, and buying.
   b. He reacted in the power and cleansing judgment of God—the kind of power and cleansing judgment that causes men to tremble before God (Ph.2:9-11).
   c. He ran through the temple doing three things: (a) He chased out *all* who were buying and selling; (b) He threw over the tables of the moneychangers; and (c) He threw over the chairs of the dove dealers.

> "And said unto them that sold doves, Take these things hence; make not my Father's house an house of merchandise" (Jn.2:16).
>
> "What? have ye not houses to eat and to drink in [businesses to buy and sell in]? or despise ye the church of God, and shame them that have not? What shall I say to you? shall I praise you in this? I praise you not" (1 Co.11:22).
>
> "Ye shall keep my sabbaths, and reverence my sanctuary: I am the LORD" (Le.19:30).
>
> "Keep thy foot when thou goest to the house of God, and be more ready to hear, than to give the sacrifice of fools: for they consider not that they do evil" (Ec.5:1).
>
> "For the children of Judah have done evil in my sight, saith the LORD: they have set their abominations in the house which is called by my name, to pollute it" (Je.7:30).
>
> "Her [the temple, the churches] prophets are light and treacherous persons: her priests have polluted the sanctuary, they have done violence to the law" (Zep.3:4).

MATTHEW 21:12-16

Thought 1. There is serious warning here. The temple was corrupted for money; the church can be. People who came to worship were taken advantage of; they were used for material gain. Note something that should really speak to the church. The people were sold items that were necessary for their worship. They were not just items that would help them in their spiritual growth and their worship; they were essential items. Without them, the people were not able to worship.

Now think for a moment. If the items were necessary for their worship and growth, what was wrong with what they did? The words of v.12 tell us: "Jesus...cast out all them that sold and bought *in the temple*." The buying and selling of the items for worship and growth were necessary and good, but *not within* the temple. They were to be done outside the temple walls, off the temple grounds. The temple and church are not the place for commercialism.

Thought 2. People's desire for worship and spiritual growth is not to be used for material gain, not by the church nor within the church. Church leadership has to be responsible for protecting its worshippers from abusing the hallowed ground set apart for the worship of God.

Thought 3. Legitimate things, such as buying and selling items that help us grow, can be used wrongly. *Where* something is done is critical. Buying and selling is not to take place in God's church. The point is: worship should be the preoccupation of a person's mind when he is within the church.

Thought 4. Jesus' anger can be fierce. Note who aroused such fierce anger in Him.
(1) Those who abused God's temple (church).
(2) Those who exploited others.
(3) Those who made it impossible for others to truly worship God.

Thought 5. Note what happens to the man who abuses God's temple and exploits others: he is "cast out."

2 (21:13) **Temple—Church**: Jesus proclaimed the temple to be a house of prayer. This was an Old Testament quotation from two passages.

> "Mine house shall be called an house of prayer for all people" (Is.56:7).
> "Is this house, which is called by my name, become a den of robbers in your eyes?" (Je.7:11).

Christ made two points.

a. The temple was to be a house of prayer *for all people*. This included the Gentiles as well as the Jews. All people should have been able to worship in quietness and peace within God's temple. No one should have been barred, separated, or discouraged from worshipping God in His temple. All should have been welcomed.

Note something else. The temple (church) was called a house of prayer, not a house of sacrifice, offerings, teaching, prophecy, or preaching. Everything done within the House of God was to lead to prayer, the *worship and communion* of the Father.

b. The temple was not to be used for commercial purposes. It was not to be a place of buying and selling, marketing and retailing, stealing, and cheating. It was not to be profaned. The temple was the House of God, God's House of prayer. It was to be a place of sanctity, refined and purified by God Himself. It was to be a place of quietness and meditation, a place set aside for worship, not for buying and selling where man gets gain.

> "Surely goodness and mercy shall follow me all the days of my life: and I will dwell in the house of the LORD for ever" (Ps.23:6).
> "For a day in thy courts is better than a thousand. I had rather be a doorkeeper in the house of my God, than to dwell in the tents of wickedness" (Ps.84:10).
> "I was glad when they said unto me, Let us go into the house of the LORD" (Ps.122:1).

Thought 1. The temple or church is a piece of ground and a structure that is set apart for the worship of God. This is the very difference between it and all other grounds and structures. It is specifically set apart and dedicated for the sole purpose of worshipping God. It should, therefore, be used for that purpose. Once it is set apart for Him and His worship, God expects it to be His and to be used for that purpose alone.

Thought 2. There are plenty of markets surrounding the church, places where all services involving buying and selling can take place. The church is to be the house of prayer, not a market place, not a place where man is to get gain. It is not to be profaned, either to a minor degree or to a major degree, by becoming a "den for thieves."

Thought 3. A person's thoughts are to be centered upon God when he first steps on the hallowed ground of God's temple. While he is on the grounds of God's temple, He is to be praying and meditating upon His Lord. There should be nothing to distract his thoughts until he steps off God's property. Just think! How revered would God's temple, our churches, be if we really brought them back to God's original purpose? How far away have we really gotten from true worship centers, from the house of prayer?

3 (21:14) **Church—Ministry**: the temple or church is to be a place for ministry. Jesus used the temple as a place for ministry, and by such, He demonstrated that it was to be a place of ministry for all men.

Two wonderful things happened when the temple was cleansed of its corruptions.

a. The worshippers, those in need (symbolized by the blind and lame), were able to come to Christ to worship and have their needs met quietly.

MATTHEW 21:12-16

 b. Christ was able to take His rightful position within the temple. He was able to become the prominent figure and to receive the worshippers and to minister to those who had need.

> **Thought 1.** People are barred, kept away from the church, when corruption is within its walls. It may not be only buying and selling; it may be divisiveness, grumbling, complaining, gossiping, and a host of other sins. But nothing will keep people away from the church quicker than sin within the church.
> When such sins are removed and the church is purified, then Christ can and will be known to have His rightful place in the church. People can then come and be helped. They can worship and have their needs met.
>
> **Thought 2.** The needy are often barred, cut off, and unwelcomed by society. Such is not to be true of the church. The church is to have open arms and a pure heart, welcoming all, no matter how poor and needy. In fact, the church is to be the very worship center for ministry.

4 (21:15) **Temple, Purpose:** the temple is to be a place where wonderful things are done. The term *wonderful things* (Ta Thaumasia) means wonders, wonderful things, wonderful works. It refers to all the things Christ was doing in the temple. This is the only time the word is used in the New Testament. What a beautiful description of what the church is to be: a place where wonderful things are to be done for God.

> "Now unto him that is able to do exceeding abundantly above all that we ask or think, according to the power that worketh in us" (Ep.3:20)

5 (21:15-16) **Temple—Church:** The temple is to be a place where Christ is praised. Note three things that happen in this scene.
 a. Children are in the temple (Court of the Gentiles) crying, "Hosanna to the Son of David." Apparently, these children had participated with their parents in the Triumphal Entry the day before and were now witnessing the ministry of Christ to the lame and blind. They pick up the chorus which they had either sung along with their parents or heard sung the day before. The chorus, of course, proclaims Jesus to be the Messiah. It is most unlikely that the children were playing, as some suggest. Two facts suggest a seriousness in what the children were saying: Christ's clearing out all the commotion and noise and the extreme seriousness and hallowedness of His ministry to the people coming to Him. It is very difficult to picture too much commotion allowed by Christ in His serious moments of ministry; and He certainly would not have allowed the commotion and disturbance of His meeting by a group of children playing around. He would have dismissed them along with the others if they had not been serious in their worship and praise. It would be particularly difficult to picture Christ's allowing commotion after what He had just been through.
 b. The religionists (chief priests and scribes) are displeased and object to what they see and hear. They do not like the *wonderful things* being done in the temple, nor do they like Jesus' being praised in the temple. They object for at least three reasons.
  1) They are angered. Their own establishment and procedures for handling things have been disrupted and, in their minds, declared "no good" or else "less good" than what they should be.
  2) They do not like Jesus' being proclaimed the Messiah of God.
  3) They do not like the unseemly behavior occurring: ministering to the needs of common men, healing the lame and blind (v.14), and teaching (see Mk.11:18; Lu.19:47).
 Note that these are the very reasons people often become disturbed in the church today.
 c. Christ insists that He is to be praised. He simply replies to the objections, "God Himself has taken the mouths of these children and provided (brought forth) the praise you hear. And it is perfect praise because it is brought forth by God Himself and heaped upon His Son. The church is to be a place where God's Son is to be praised."

> **Thought 1.** Self-examination is called for. Is Christ really praised in our church? Really acknowledged and proclaimed as the Messiah, the Son of God?
>
> **Thought 2.** Children should be encouraged to praise God.
> (1) Note how the children were in attendance when Christ taught and ministered (Mk.11:18; Lu.19:47). They were welcomed by Him and felt comfortable around Him.
> (2) Note how Christ stood up for the children against the leadership (priests).
>
> **Thought 3.** The children follow the example of their parents. They had seen and participated with their parents in praising Christ the day before. Now they praise Him on their own as they witness His ministry and teaching.
>
> **Thought 4.** Some leaders make the same three tragic objections in churches today.
> (1) They object to the old way being changed, especially if it affects one's position, recognition, or authority.
> (2) They object to Christ's being proclaimed the Messiah, the Son of God. Some are willing to acknowledge Him as a great teacher and only as a great teacher. They deny Him as the Savior of the world who died for the sins of men.
> (3) They object to a public praising of God and to a ministry that helps the needy within the church walls.
>
> **Thought 5.** Note something. Christ says that God Himself raised up these children to praise Him and His ministry within the church. If a church ceases to praise Him, the likelihood is that God will raise up another to fill its voices with the praise and ministry of His Son.

DEEPER STUDY # 2
(21:16) **Old Testament Reference** See Ps.8:2.

MATTHEW 21:17-22

	C. The Fig Tree Cursed: The Source of Power, 21:17-22 (Mk 11:12-14, 20-26)		
1. Jesus' lodging in Bethany a. He returned to Jerusalem the next morning^{DS1} b. He was hungry 2. Jesus' great power over the physical world^{DS2} a. His expectation: Fruit^{DS3} b. His disappointment: No fruit c. His absolute power demonstrated	17 And he left them, and went out of the city into Bethany; and he lodged there. 18 Now in the morning as he returned into the city, he hungered. 19 And when he saw a fig tree in the way, he came to it, and found nothing thereon, but leaves only, and said unto it, Let no fruit grow on thee henceforward for ever. And	presently the fig tree withered away. 20 And when the disciples saw *it*, they marvelled, saying, How soon is the fig tree withered away! 21 Jesus answered and said unto them, Verily I say unto you, If ye have faith, and doubt not, ye shall not only do this *which is done* to the fig tree, but also if ye shall say unto this mountain, Be thou removed, and be thou cast into the sea; it shall be done. 22 And all things, whatsoever ye shall ask in prayer, believing, ye shall receive.	3. Jesus' great source of power: Faith a. The power of Christ stirred questioning b. The great source of power 1) Faith 2) Not doubting at all 3) God's authority: Given to those who speak the Word 4. Jesus' great promise of power to the disciples: Through prayer & faith

DIVISION XIV

THE MESSIAH'S LAST WEEK: HIS CLAIM CHALLENGED AND REJECTED, 21:1–23:39

C. The Fig Tree Cursed: The Source of Power, 21:17-22

(21:17-22) **Introduction—Power—Judgment**: Jesus destroyed the fig tree. Why? Some have said such destruction is out of character for Christ. He would never destroy a tree for not bearing fruit.

Why did Jesus destroy the tree?

⇒ He destroyed it for the same reason that He angrily ran through the temple casting out all who bought and sold (Mt.21:12-16).
⇒ He destroyed it for the same reason that He lashed out at the Pharisees for being hypocritical (Mt.23:13-39).
⇒ He destroyed it for the same reason that He cast the evil spirits into a herd of swine, killing them (Mt.8:28-34).
⇒ He destroyed it for the same reasons that He became indignant (angry) with the disciples for keeping little children from coming to Him (see DEEPER STUDY # 4—Mk.10:14).
⇒ He destroyed it for the same reason that He deliberately demanded uncompromising loyalty despite family or personal needs (Mt.8:18-22; 10:34-39).

Why did Jesus act with such force in destroying the tree? For the same reason He acted with such force in all of the above. Jesus always acted either to teach man or to save and help man. In destroying the fig tree, He was teaching man a much needed lesson.

The lesson: the Messiah has absolute power over all the physical universe. The unfruitful among men (symbolized in the fig tree) do not have such power. Contrariwise, He alone has such enormous power. He alone has the power to judge and to determine fruitfulness and unfruitfulness, life and death, salvation and condemnation. He alone laid down His life; no man took it from Him (Jn.10:11, 15-18, esp.18).

Remember this was Jesus' last week. It was Tuesday, just three days before He was to be killed by unfruitful men. Jesus had to do all He could to prepare His disciples for His onrushing death and for all they were to bear through the ensuing years. He had only two days left, so He had to undergird them all He could. He was hungry and He saw a fig tree full of leaves. He walked up to pluck some fruit, but He found no fruit. He saw an object lesson in the event—a lesson that could be uniquely used in teaching and preparing the disciples.

In destroying the tree, Jesus was showing the disciples (in an unmistakable way) that He had absolute power over all the physical world, even the power to keep from being killed. He was not dying out of weakness, not dying because He was not the Messiah, not dying because of the plots and intrigues of men. Men may be judging Him to be unfruitful and unworthy of life, but He was not dying because of them. He was dying because the death of God's Son was the way of salvation (Jn.3:16; 2 Co.5:19-20; 1 Pe.2:24). He was not being judged by unfruitful men or events; rather, unfruitful men and events were being judged by Him upon the cross (1 Pe.2:24; see Ep.2:13-22).

Very simply put, Jesus was picturing that He was truly God's Son with omnipotent power, picturing it in a way that we can never forget. He had the power to save Himself and to destroy the unfruitful men who would take His life. But He of course could not—not then. Right then He was sent into the world to die for men and to save men, including the very ones who were judging and condemning Him to be unfruitful and unworthy of life. However, the day is coming when He will judge the unfruitful just as He judged the fig tree. But that day is out in the future, for the present He was to save men.

Note: the lesson of *power through prayer and faith* was the lesson Christ drew from His action (vv.20-22).
1. Jesus' lodging in Bethany (vv.17-18).
2. Jesus' great power over the physical world (v.19).
3. Jesus' great source of power: faith (vv.20-21).
4. Jesus' great promise of power to the disciples: through prayer and faith (v.22).

MATTHEW 21:17-22

Thought 1. Jesus returned to Jerusalem despite the threat to His life. He returned because it was God's will. He would not be stopped from doing God's will. So it should be with us. We should never allow opposition and threats to stop us from doing God's will. Note that like Christ, Paul did not shirk from God's will, from setting his face toward Jerusalem despite the bonds and trials that awaited him there (Ac.21:13-15).

1 (21:17-18) **Bethany**: Jesus lodged in Bethany, which was a suburb of Jerusalem. It lay about two miles east of the great city. Bethany was the home of Lazarus, Mary, and Martha. Jesus stayed with the family when ministering in and around Jerusalem. We must remember that Jesus apparently had no home of His own, which was partly due to the fact that His immediate family did not believe in Him (Jn.7:1-5, esp.5). He Himself had said, "The foxes have holes, and the birds of the air have nests, but the Son of man hath not where to lay his head" (Mt.8:20). The only housing He had was the homes of others such as Mary and Martha (Jn.11:1f; see Lu.11:1f; Lu.10:38-42; 19:29f; Jn.12:1f).

DEEPER STUDY # 1
(21:18) **In the morning** (proias): means early morning, very early, the fourth or last watch of the previous night (Mk.1:35). Jesus began the events of Tuesday so early it was in the wee hours of the morning, or according to Jewish time, in the last hours of the previous day.

2 (21:19) **Jesus Christ, Power**: Jesus had great power over the physical world. He demonstrates His great power by three acts. These same acts are applicable to a human life.
  a. His expectation: fruit. The tree looked healthy and full of leaves. It was time for Him to feast, and He had the right to expect fruit on such a *mature* looking fruit tree. It professed fruit.
  b. His disappointment: no fruit. The tree had life; it was living. It had the sap to produce a rich foliage of leaves and it was professing fruit, but it had none. Its very purpose was to bear fruit, but it did not. It failed at three points.
    1) It had an empty profession.
    2) It had an unfulfilled purpose.
    3) It deceived instead of served.
  c. His absolute power over the physical world demonstrated. Christ demonstrated that He has the right and the power to execute judgment as He wills. He can deliver or He can destroy. His disciples needed to have this lesson fresh on their minds. His omnipotent power, the enormous power available to them, would encourage them as they experienced His death and as they faced the trials that lay ahead of their own witness. (See note—Mt.21:17-22.)

Thought 1. The fig tree is a clear picture of hypocrisy, of false profession (see DEEPER STUDY # 2—Mt.21:19).

Thought 2. If a tree is living, it is expected to bear fruit. That is its purpose for living. If it does not bear fruit, it is useless and good for nothing but to be cut down and burned (see Lu.13:7). Note another fact: the more alive a tree is, the fuller it appears and the more fruit it is expected to bear. If we give the appearance of righteousness, then God expects us to bear righteousness.

Thought 3. There are two times in particular when Christ looks for fruit within a person.
(1) There are the times of deep sensitivity wrought by life's great trials and great opportunities. These times cause a person to think of God, of his need for God, and of his obligation to use his life for good (for example, feeding, clothing, and giving to others). Christ expects us to bear fruit in a very special way during these times: to turn to Him in trial and to help and bear witness when great opportunities arise.
(2) There will be the time of eternal judgment. There is a day coming at the end of the world when Christ will judge all men, both believers and unbelievers. Fruit will be expected (see DEEPER STUDY # 1—2 Co.5:10; see Ga.5:22-23).

Thought 4. Christ has absolute power over the universe. He did not die at the hands of men. He died purposefully for the sins of the world just as God willed. He had the power to keep from dying, but He chose to lay down His life for the sake of men (Ro.5:8).

Thought 5. There is no question, the cursing of the fig tree shows the enormous power of Christ to do three things.
(1) It shows the power of Christ to deliver His disciples out of great trial.
(2) It shows the power of Christ to determine when His disciples should depart out of this world (see 2 Ti.4:6-8).
(3) It shows the power of Christ to judge and condemn. The great day of His wrath is not yet come (Re.6:17), but the day will come. When the day does come, then all unfruitfulness of men shall be judged by His absolute power. (See the parable of the fig tree, Lu.13:6-9.)

Thought 6. Some things will doom us: hypocrisy, false profession, uselessness, purposelessness, and no fruit. The cursed fig tree symbolizes all this.

DEEPER STUDY # 2
(21:19) **Fig Tree Cursed**: there are some who say the fig tree represented Israel. The fig tree was full of leaves, appearing fruitful; but it had no fruit. So Israel appeared to be full, that is, to be religious. The nation professed spiritual fruit, yet the nation bore no fruit. Its religion was barren, legalistic, and fruitless ceremony. Thus, the tree was a sign of God's disappointment and of the justice and punishment to be executed upon Israel.

We must note, however, that this is not the lesson drawn by Christ. There may be many lessons drawn from the event, including Israel's experience; but the application made by Christ is clearly power, power that comes through faith and prayer (vv.20-22).

DEEPER STUDY # 3
(21:19) **Fig tree**: some claim that late-bearing fruit would bear late in the fall and remain on the tree until the next spring. When the sap returned to the tree and began producing its leaves, the fruit would ripen. A tree in full leaf would therefore be expected to have some early fruit. Whatever the case, this much is known: the fig tree is unusual in that its fruit *appears* before the leaves. Therefore, when the tree is full of developed foliage, a person could expect the earliest fruit to be either ripe or close to ripening. Perhaps at least some fruit would be tasty enough to be edible to a hungry traveller.

Remember also that the word *Bethphage* means *House of Figs*. It is possible that the latest methods of fruit growing had grafted an early developing variety. Who knows? Early, mid, and late varieties are a common practice today. There are certainly indications that the people of old were astonishingly advanced in some areas.

3 (21:20-21) **Power—Faith**: the demonstration of Jesus' great power did just what He had wanted. It stirred the disciples to marvel and question. In amazement they asked, "How did the fig tree *immediately* wither away?" (This is a better understanding of the Greek.)

Jesus had them just where He wanted them: they were asking about His great power. He wanted to teach them that He had absolute power over the physical world and that the same power was available to them in the future as they served Him. He had demonstrated His absolute power; now they were asking about the source of that power.

Note how Jesus shared the source of His power. He said in essence, "Here is the source of my power, and the same power source is available to you." He was explaining the source of His power in the *second person* which makes it applicable to all His disciples. He was answering their question about His power, but He was doing it in such a way that they would know the same power was available to them.

What is the source of Christ's great power? Or, we may ask, what is the source of great power for the disciple of Christ? It is three things. (All the notes referred to in the following points give an excellent study on faith. Also see complete outline and notes—Mt.17:14-21.)

    a. Faith (see notes—Mk.11:22-23; He.11:1; note and Deeper Study # 1—11:6).

    b. Not doubting at all. This means never having a thought as to whether a thing can be done or not. It means not hesitating, not wondering, not questioning, not considering, not being concerned at all. Realistically, only God Himself could ever know whether or not something would happen—know so perfectly that no wondering thought would ever cross His mind. What Christ is after is that we grow in belief and trust. He wants us to believe that all things are possible through Christ who strengthens us (Ph.4:13). (See outlines and notes—Mt.17:15-16; 17:17-18; 17:19-20; Mk.9:18.)

    c. God's authority: given to those who speak the Word. Note the phrase "Shall say" (see note—Mt.17:20). The power of Christ came from the authority of God. All He had to do was *say*, that is, speak the Word, and it was done. That is the very point He is making to us. If we believe, not doubting, then we stand in the authority of God. We may *say*, that is, speak the Word, and it shall be done.

> "Then came the disciples to Jesus apart, and said, Why could not we cast him out? And Jesus said unto them, Because of your unbelief: for verily I say unto you, If ye have faith as a grain of mustard seed, ye shall say unto this mountain, Remove hence to yonder place; and it shall remove; and nothing shall be impossible unto you" (Mt.17:19-20).
>
> "And all things, whatsoever ye shall ask in prayer, believing, ye shall receive" (Mt.21:22).
>
> "For verily I say unto you, That whosoever shall say unto this mountain, Be thou removed, and be thou cast into the sea; and shall not doubt in his heart, but shall believe that those things which he saith shall come to pass; he shall have whatsoever he saith. Therefore I say unto you, What things soever ye desire, when ye pray, believe that ye receive them, and ye shall have them" (Mk.11:23-24).
>
> "If ye abide in me, and my words abide in you, ye shall ask what ye will, and it shall be done unto you" (Jn.15:7).
>
> "Now faith is the substance of things hoped for, the evidence of things not seen" (He.11:1).
>
> "But without faith it is impossible to please him: for he that cometh to God must believe that he is, and that he is a rewarder of them that diligently seek him" (He.11:6).
>
> "Even so faith, if it hath not works, is dead, being alone" (Js.2:17).

4 (21:22) **Prayer**: Jesus' promise of power to us is through prayer and faith. Christ drives home two striking points.

    a. His promise is comprehensive: "all things." It is all inclusive, much beyond the sphere of what we can ask or even think (Ep.3:20).

    b. His promise is conditional: "in prayer, believing." We have to *pray and believe* to receive.

        1) Prayer is to be constant. The person who receives answers from God knows God personally. He is in constant, unbroken fellowship and sharing with God. A person cannot come every now and then to God and expect answers. This is not what Christ means.

> "They all continued with one accord in prayer and supplication" (Ac.1:14).
>
> "Continuing instant in prayer" (Ro.12:12).
>
> "Give yourselves to fasting and prayer" (1 Co.7:5. Refer to this whole verse for a graphic picture.)

MATTHEW 21:17-22

"Praying always with all prayer and supplication in the Spirit, and watching thereunto with all perseverance and supplication for all saints" (Ep.6:18).

"Continue in prayer, and watch in the same with thanksgiving" (Col.4:2).

2) Believing is, of course, essential. Mark says it well: "Whosoever shall say...and shall not doubt in his heart, but shall believe that those things which he saith shall come to pass" (Mk.11:23). (See note—He.11:1.)

Thought 1. see note—Mt.21:22. See outline and notes—Mt.7:7-11.

Thought 2. God's supernatural power is available to us, but it is conditional. We do not possess supernatural power within ourselves. God's power comes only through prayer and faith.

Thought 3. Prayer is the vehicle; faith is the energy. It takes both to reach the desired destination.

Thought 4. Faith stirs prayer and communion with God. A person who really *believes*, who has real faith in God, is driven to pray and commune with God.

Thought 5. This great promise should stir us to pray and believe God, to ask and ask.

MATTHEW 21:23-27

	D. The Questioning of the Messiah's Power: The Problem with Obstinate Unbelief, 21:23-27 *(Mk 11:27-33; Lu 20:1-8)*	you by what authority I do these things.	
1. Unbelief can be obstinate
2. Unbelief treats Christ with disdain: They disturbed His teaching & the people's worship
3. Unbelief questions the authority of Christ
4. Unbelief must face the personal interrogation of Christ
a. Must face His right to question	23 And when he was come into the temple, the chief priests and the elders of the people came unto him as he was teaching, and said, By what authority doest thou these things? and who gave thee this authority?
24 And Jesus answered and said unto them, I also will ask you one thing, which if ye tell me, I in like wise will tell	25 The baptism of John, whence was it? from heaven, or of men? And they reasoned with themselves, saying, If we shall say, From heaven; he will say unto us, Why did ye not then believe him?
26 But if we shall say, Of men; we fear the people; for all hold John as a prophet.
27 And they answered Jesus, and said, We cannot tell. And he said unto them, Neither tell I you by what authority I do these things.	b. The question: Was John's ministry from heaven or from men?
5. Unbelief causes a threefold sin & guilt
a. A deliberate denial
b. A deliberate cowardice
c. A deliberate ignorance or concern for self
6. Unbelief results in Christ's silence: He refuses to reveal Himself to unbelievers

DIVISION XIV

THE MESSIAH'S LAST WEEK: HIS CLAIM CHALLENGED AND REJECTED, 21:1–23:39

D. The Questioning of the Messiah's Power: The Problem with Obstinate Unbelief, 21:23-27

(21:23-27) **Introduction—Jesus Christ, Opposition**: from this passage to the end of chapter 23, Jesus deals with His opponents, self-righteous religionists and civil leaders (the elders). All the events of this section as well as the Olivet discourse (Mt. 24-25) seem to have taken place on Tuesday (see Mt.22:23; 25:1; 26:1-2). A quick reading of this section is an eye-opener into the great tragedy and problem with self-righteousness and unbelief. Christ was forceful, very forceful, in attacking self-righteousness and unbelief. He delivered a *sustained attack*, leaving no doubt that a person who continues in self-righteousness, even a religionist, is unworthy of God's kingdom. Obstinate unbelief is doomed.
1. Unbelief can be obstinate (v.23).
2. Unbelief treats Christ with disdain: They disturbed His teaching and the people's worship (v.23).
3. Unbelief questions the authority of Christ (v.23).
4. Unbelief must face the personal interrogation of Christ (vv.24-25).
5. Unbelief causes a threefold sin and guilt (vv.25-27).
6. Unbelief results in Christ's silence: He refuses to reveal Himself to unbelievers (v.27).

1 (21:23) **Unbelief, Obstinate—Sanhedrin**: the obstinate unbelief of leaders. This event continues the Lord's final ministry in the courtyards of the temple. Pilgrims from all over the world were in Jerusalem. A large number had gathered in the temple and were surrounding Christ. They were listening to Him teach. Matthew said, "the chief priests and elders" became extremely upset and confronted Christ. Mark and Luke tell us that the Scribes were also present. This indicates that the leaders were an official delegation representing the ruling body of the Jews, the Sanhedrin (see notes—Mt.26:57; 26:59). All that had happened naturally created a crisis for the ruling body: the triumphal entry, Christ's acceptance of the people's homage, the cleansing of the temple, the disruption of the priests' profits from those who sold and bought, the healing of the blind and lame, and the worship of the children. What Christ was doing simply infuriated them, sending them into a rage. It aroused them to question: "Who does Jesus of Nazareth think He is?" (Mt.21:10-11).

But note: the question was one of contempt, not of seeking. The question was an attempt to discredit, not to learn the truth. The question was aroused because their own position, esteem, and gain were disturbed, not because they wanted to really know if He were the Messiah. Their minds were closed or shut to His claims. They had many claims and many proofs of His Messiahship, but they wilfully ignored and denied His divine mission. They had plenty of opportunities to learn the truth, yet they allowed nothing to change them (see note—Jn.3:2). They were gripped with obstinate unbelief (see notes—Mt.12:1-8; note and DEEPER STUDY # 1—12:10; note—15:1-20; DEEPER STUDY # 2—15:6-9. These notes will give some background to the opposition against Christ.)

Thought 1. See notes—Mt.21:23. See DEEPER STUDY # 4—Mt.12:24; note—12:31-32.

Thought 2. These things often happen to a person who has position, esteem, and wealth and who seeks more gain.
(1) He fears the truth lest it threaten what he has.
(2) He is forced to continue in unbelief and denial. The person fears facing the issue honestly lest he has to confess he has been wrong. Such would be too embarrassing and humiliating, causing more ridicule than he is willing to bear.

2 (21:23) **Unbelief**: unbelief treats Christ with disdain. Christ was teaching and people were worshipping. Nevertheless, in utter rudeness, the unbelievers walked right in, interrupting His teaching and the people's worship.

Thought 1. Unbelief treats Christ with contempt. Unbelief pays no attention to what Christ says and does. Imagine how serious the contempt is. Christ, the Son of God...
- has left the glory of heaven and come to earth
- has spoken, revealing the truth about God, man, and the world
- has secured salvation and everlasting life for man

Yet despite all that Christ has done, man denies Christ. He prefers a few years of human esteem and pleasure to believing and committing his hope upon the fact that life continues on forever. Speaking of contempt—there is no greater contempt than to deny the Son of God. Unbelief definitely treats Christ with disdain.

Thought 2. Unbelief always interrupts. What God wants is a free flow for the spirit of belief. When one unbelieving person is present, he disrupts the spirit of belief. There is not a free flow of the spirit of belief. The more unbelief present, the more the free flow is hindered. Unbelief hinders, hampers, disrupts, and disturbs belief.

"And they that passed by reviled him, wagging their heads, and saying, Thou that destroyest the temple, and buildest it in three days, save thyself. If thou be the Son of God, come down from the cross" (Mt.27:39-40).

"Likewise also the chief priests mocking said among themselves with the scribes, He saved others; himself he cannot save. Let Christ the King of Israel descend now from the cross, that we may see and believe. And they that were crucified with him reviled him" (Mk.15:31-32).

"And the people stood beholding. And the rulers also with them derided him, saying, He saved others; let him save himself, if he be Christ, the chosen of God" (Lu.23:35).

"And the scribes and the Pharisees began to reason, saying, Who is this which speaketh blasphemies? Who can forgive sins, but God alone?" (Lu.5:21).

"Therefore the Jews sought the more to kill him, because he not only had broken the sabbath, but said also that God was his Father, making himself equal with God" (Jn.5:18).

"Art thou greater than our father Abraham, which is dead? and the prophets are dead: whom makest thou thyself?" (Jn.8:53).

"The Jews answered him, saying, For a good work we stone thee not; but for blasphemy; and because that thou, being a man, makest thyself God" (Jn.10:33).

3 (21:23) **Unbelief**: unbelief strikes at the very core of Christ's nature; it questions His authority, who He really is. The Sanhedrin (chief priests, elders and Scribes) were the leaders of the nation and the chief priests were the guardians and rulers of the temple. They wanted to know who gave Christ the right to do what He was doing. He was interfering with their management and had no right to interfere.

They asked two questions: "By what authority doest thou these things? And who gave thee this authority?" They were questioning the authority for His works (first question) and for His person (second question). Unbelief always questions both works and person: *by what* authority "these things are done" and "who gave thee" such authority. Christ can give one of three possible answers: by the authority of Himself, of God, or of one of the temple authorities. His questioners knew that no temple authority had given Him authorization to do what He was doing; thus, by the questioning, they hoped to discredit Him.

If He said His authority came from God, they could demand a sign from heaven and accuse Him of blasphemy (see note—Mt.12:38-40; see Mt.26:65). If He said His authority was of Himself, the people would probably turn away from Him.

Thought 1. Unbelief strikes at the very core of Christ's nature. A man may say He believes in Christ but show no sign that he has committed his life to Him. Such belief is not biblical, not what the Bible means by belief. Such belief is only mental acceptance of an historical person. Belief that does not commit one's life is nothing more than thoughtless, mental acceptance. If a person really knows that Jesus is God's Son, that person will commit His life to Christ. Unbelief, whatever its claim or thoughts, questions and denies that Christ is truly the Son of God.

Thought 2. Unbelief always questions a person's genuineness and works. Unbelievers are always around watching for a chance to justify their position when a believer falls into sin. Therefore, every believer should know by whose authority he acts. Is he acting because of self or because of God? Minister and congregation alike need to be sure their action and behavior are of God and not of self. Living a life of righteousness is acting under God's authority. Righteousness is the only thing that will silence unbelief.

4 (21:24-25) **Unbelief**: unbelief must face the personal interrogation of Christ. Christ has as much right to question unbelievers as unbelievers do Him. He asked only one question: "Is John's ministry from heaven or of men?"

If John's ministry were from heaven, then Christ was God's Son. Why? Because John bore testimony: "Behold the Lamb of God, which taketh away the sin of the world...and I saw, and *bore record* that this is the Son of God" (Jn.1:29, 34).

If John's ministry were of men, then how can we account for so many changed lives and marvelous works? This one question shows the absurdity and sin of unbelief, not only of unbelievers in Jesus' day but of unbelievers in our day as well. (See outline and notes—Mt.3:1-17; Lu.7:29-31.)

Thought 1. Is John's ministry from heaven or of men? The very same question is applicable to our day. The question forces confession or denial, and denial is totally absurd and ridiculous. How can so many changed lives and wonderful works throughout the world and history be accounted for apart from Christ? There is an abundance of witnesses.

Thought 2. Think for a moment. Was John's ministry really of himself, from his own mind? How could so many down through history minister from their own minds? Imagine—an unbeliever has to say unbelievable things:
(1) That every believer who has ever ministered created his own ministry (works) out of his own mind.
(2) That every believer who has ever ministered was mistaken about Christ (knowing Him personally as the Son of God and being called and gifted by Him).

"And all the people that heard him [John] and the publicans, justified God, being baptized of John" (Lu.7:29).

"Jesus answered them, I told you, and ye believed not: the works that I do in my Father's name, they bear witness of me" (Jn.10:25).

"Say ye of him, whom the Father hath sanctified, and sent into the world, Thou blasphemest; because I said, I am the Son of God? If I do not the works of my Father, believe me not. But if I do, though ye believe not me, believe the works: that ye may know, and believe, that the Father is in me, and I in him" (Jn.10:36-38).

"And many resorted unto him, and said, John did no miracles: but all things that John spake of this man were true. And many believed on him there" (Jn.10:41-42).

"Believest thou not that I am in the Father, and the Father in me? the words that I speak unto you I speak not of myself: but the Father that dwelleth in me, he doeth the works" (Jn.14:10).

5 (21:25-27) **Unbelief**: unbelief causes a threefold sin and guilt. The words *they reasoned with themselves* (par eantois) mean they discussed their answer among themselves. They did not just reason in (en) themselves, each left to his own thoughts. This was a planned attack against Christ, a deliberate rejection of Christ.

The Lord's questioners immediately knew their predicament. If they replied that John's ministry was of God, then Christ would ask them why they did not believe John's testimony about the Messiah. If they replied that John's ministry was of men, they would arouse the people against themselves, for the people believed strongly that John was a true prophet from God.

Note how the questioners reasoned among themselves. Their concern was not to discover the truth but to save face and protect their position, esteem, and security. They committed a threefold sin.

a. They deliberately denied Christ. To confess that John was of God would force them to acknowledge Christ, and they just were not willing to confess Him. They feared the loss of all they possessed (position, power, wealth, esteem, image, security).

"If we suffer, we shall also reign with him: if we deny him, he also will deny us" (2 Ti.2:12).

"But there were false prophets also among the people, even as there shall be false teachers among you, who privily shall bring in damnable heresies, even denying the Lord that bought them, and bring upon themselves swift destruction" (2 Pe.2:1).

"Who is a liar but he that denieth that Jesus is the Christ? He is antichrist, that denieth the Father and the Son" (1 Jn.2:22).

b. They feared men; they were deliberately cowardly. They feared the reactions of men (abuse, ridicule, persecution).

"Whosoever therefore shall be ashamed of me and of my words in this adulterous and sinful generation; of him also shall the Son of man be ashamed, when he cometh in the glory of his Father with the holy angels" (Mk.8:38).

c. They chose expediency, to deliberately be ignorant. They feared being shamed, embarrassed, and ridiculed. To confess Christ would mean confessing they had been wrong all along. It would mean denying self completely and doing so publicly. Most men...
- choose expediency rather than principle
- choose to play it safe rather than to stand up for the truth
- choose to say, "I don't know," rather than to speak the truth

"Jesus answered them, I told you, and ye believed not: the works that I do in my Father's name, they bear witness of me" (Jn.10:25).

"Say ye of him, whom the Father hath sanctified, and sent into the world, Thou blasphemest; because I said, I am the Son of God? If I do not the works of my Father, believe me not. But if I do, though ye believe not me, believe the works: that ye may know, and believe, that the Father is in me, and I in him" (Jn.10:36-38)

"Believest thou not that I am in the Father, and the Father in me? the words that I speak unto you I speak not of myself: but the Father that dwelleth in me, he doeth the works" (Jn.14:10).

Thought 1. It is the duty of every thinking man to know whether or not Christ is true. For a thinking man to say, "I do not know," is unacceptable. A *thinking man* ought to know, for he has the capability to know. He is to think, determining the true from the false. If he fails to do this, he condemns himself.

MATTHEW 21:23-27

Thought 2. Two things are absurd.
(1) It is absurd to acknowledge a truth and then reject it. An unbeliever cannot acknowledge that John and Christ *are of God* and then not confess them. To say that they are *of God* and then deny them is the height of absurdity.
(2) It is absurd not to confess Christ. Denial is the height of absurdity. The evidence is overwhelming.

Thought 3. At least two things cause a man to reject and oppose the truth.
(1) Sin: a man loves sin too much to give it up. His sin may be such things as the flesh, pride, fame, power, wealth, self will, position, property. He is just too possessed to turn to Christ.
(2) Fear: men fear two things.
   (a) They fear God. If they confess Christ, they fear God will make demands upon them and they will have to give some things up. They fear the loss of whatever they have and enjoy: position, wealth, pleasure.
   (b) They fear men. If they confess Christ, they fear ridicule, embarrassment, persecution, shame, abuse, rejection, being passed over. These things and so many more cause men to commit the threefold sins of unbelief.

6 (21:27) **Decision—Unbelief**: unbelief results in Christ's silence. His questioners said, "We cannot tell." They lied. They knew perfectly well that John's baptism was of God. They just were not willing to run the risk of losing their position, livelihood and security. They loved the world more than God and the hope He extended toward them. Thus they denied, acted cowardly, and chose the route of expediency.

Thought 1. The point is this: these unbelievers would not be convinced of the truth. It is not that they *could not* be convinced, but they *would not*. Such obstinate unbelief seldom, if ever, sees the truth of Christ. Even if Christ openly revealed the truth to them, they would reject it.

> "If they hear not Moses and the prophets, neither will they be persuaded though one rose from the dead" (Lu.16:31).

Thought 2. When the sins of unbelief are pointed out, men are often provoked and retaliate. They act with malice, often legally and legitimately within society's rules. Sometimes they attempt to denounce and discredit, sometimes persecute.

Thought 3. The judgment of Christ stands against obstinate unbelief. What judgment? The judgment of silence; Christ will honor unbelief, honor it by not revealing Himself to the unbeliever. Unbelief is doomed.

> "If they hear not Moses and the prophets, neither will they be persuaded though one rose from the dead" (Lu.16:31).
> "And ye will not come to me, that ye might have life" (Jn.5:40).
> "[God] sent forth his servants to call them that were bidden to the wedding: and they would not come" (Mt.22:3).
> "And now, because ye have done all these works, saith the LORD, and I spake unto you, rising up early and speaking, but ye heard not; and I called you, but ye answered not....And I will cast you out of my sight" (Je.7:13, 15).
> "I call heaven and earth to record this day against you, that I have set before you life and death, blessing and cursing: therefore choose life, that both thou and thy seed may live: that thou mayest love the LORD thy God, and that thou mayest obey his voice, and that thou mayest cleave unto him: for he is thy life, and the length of thy days" (De.30:19-20).
> "For he saith, I have heard thee in a time accepted, and in the day of salvation have I succoured thee: behold, now is the accepted time; behold, now is the day of salvation" (2 Co.6:2).

MATTHEW 21:28-32

	E. The Parable of Two Sons: What It Takes to Enter God's Kingdom, 21:28-32	sir: and went not. 31 Whether of them twain did the will of *his* father? They say unto him, The first. Jesus saith unto them, Verily I say unto you, That the publicans and the harlots go into the kingdom of God before you. 32 For John came unto you in the way of righteousness, and ye believed him not: but the publicans and the harlots believed him: and ye, when ye had seen *it*, repented not afterward, that ye might believe him.	2) He never goes c. The first son did what his father wanted 2. **The point: Sinners enter the kingdom before religionists (the self-righteous & those who make a false profession)** 3. **The reason: Religionists do not believe John–that Jesus is the Son of God** a. John preached righteousness b. Sinners believed John c. The religionists' saw changed lives but still did not repent & believe
1. **The parable: A man & his two sons** a. The father commands the first son to go work in his vineyard 1) He says, "I will not" 2) He later changes his mind & goes b. The father also commands the second son to work 1) He says, "I will, sir"	28 But what think ye? A *certain* man had two sons; and he came to the first, and said, Son, go work to day in my vineyard. 29 He answered and said, I will not: but afterward he repented, and went. 30 And he came to the second, and said likewise. And he answered and said, I go,		

DIVISION XIV

THE MESSIAH'S LAST WEEK: HIS CLAIM CHALLENGED AND REJECTED, 21:1–23:39

E. The Parable of Two Sons: What It Takes to Enter God's Kingdom, 21:28-32

(21:28-32) **Introduction**: the words "what think ye?" tie this parable to the Jewish leaders who had just confronted Christ and tried to discredit Him. The Lord wanted to convey a critical message to them, a message that would determine their eternal destiny.

What does it take to enter God's Kingdom? Not only profession and righteousness, but also repentance and belief.
1. The parable: a man and his two sons (vv.28-31).
2. The point: sinners enter the kingdom before religionists (the self-righteous and those who make a false profession) (v.31).
3. The reason: religionists do not believe John—that Jesus is the Son of God (v.32).

1 (21:28-31) **Parable—Work—Service**: the parable is simple and clear. It concerns a man who had two sons. Note several facts.

1. The command "go work" is an emphatic imperative. The father meant what he said: "You go! You work!" There is no other choice in the father's mind; no other alternative. The sons were to work and serve their father.
2. Note the word "today." Today is the day to go. Today is the day to work, not tomorrow. Tomorrow may be too late. The harvest will rot in the field. The night will come when no man can work (Jn.9:4). The sons could also die (He.9:27). They had to go today while they had a chance to help their father.

> "...behold, now is the accepted time; behold, now is the day of salvation" (2 Co.6:2).
> "Today if ye will hear His voice, harden not your heart" (Ps.95:7-8).

3. The first son said, "*I will not*." This was disrespectful rebellion. It was the refusal of a son who wished to go his own way in life, who rebelled at being told what to do. He was selfish, worldly, carnal, fleshly, materialistic, and prideful. He would have his own way and do his own thing regardless. However, note that the first son *repented and went*. The word *repent* means to change, to turn. (See note and DEEPER STUDY # 1, *Repent*—Acts 17:29-30.) The first son changed and turned from his self-chosen life of rebellion and worldliness—turned back to his father and went into his father's vineyard to work. He did exactly what his father commanded him to do.
4. The second son said "*I go, sir*." Note: his response indicates that he will go immediately and serve zealously in the father's work. He said I go to work *for you*. But he failed; he *never* did go to work for his father. He went to work, but not for his father. He was just like the first son: selfish, disregarding the father and his needs. He went about his own life, living and working for *himself*. The only difference between the two sons is that the second son *professed* respect for the father and *professed* to work for the father, but he *never* went into the father's vineyard. He never did the father's work. (This implies that what he did day by day was his own work, his own labor. He worked and lived as he wished, disregarding the father entirely. It was a life of religion and moral strictness as we shall see.)
5. Christ asked the religionists standing around which of the two sons did the father's will. The religionists did not see the point of the parable yet, so they gave the obvious answer: the first son did the father's will.

Their immediate response to Christ is interesting. They demonstrated just how much religion and self-righteousness can blind a person, giving a sense of false security. A person, clergyman and layman alike, who sincerely lives a life of religion and moral purity has great difficulty understanding why he is not acceptable to God and cannot enter God's kingdom.

2 (21:31) **Salvation—Self-righteousness—Labor**: Jesus gave the point of the parable. Sinners enter the kingdom before religionists (the self-righteous and professors only). Note what Jesus did.

MATTHEW 21:28-32

  a. Jesus identified the man and the two sons in the parable.
    1) The man who owned the vineyard was God. God is the Person who possesses the kingdom (see Deeper Study #3—Mt.19:23-24).
    2) The first son represents the non-religious and worldly of this earth. These do not profess religion, and they do not know they are lost. They desire to go their own way, wanting nothing to do with God. The publicans or tax collectors represented the rejected and worldly-minded, those more interested in money and in the things of this world than in God. The harlots represented the immoral and sensual, those more interested in pleasure than God.
    3) The second son represents the religious of this earth (the self-righteous and those who make a false profession). These were either reared in church from earliest childhood or else came into the church sometime in later life. They professed religion and righteousness to be the way a person should live.
  b. Jesus identified the vineyard and work that was to be done. The vineyard is the Kingdom of God and the work is "Go into the kingdom of God"—serve God within His kingdom (see Deeper Study #3—Mt.19:23-24). Note two things:
    1) Both sons (all men) receive the same command and obligation: "Go into the vineyard."
    2) God respects both sons. He does not force either son to work, neither the son who rebels nor the son who makes a commitment but fails to work in God's vineyard. The sons' wills are honored. They may go and work wherever they wish.
  c. Jesus clearly stressed the point of the parable.
    1) He said emphatically "Verily, I say unto you." Verily means surely, truly, sit up and take notice. The word "I" means the Messiah, the Son of God Himself. The Messiah is revealing a critical truth.
    2) He said in unmistakable terms: sinners "go into the kingdom of God before you," before the self-righteous and false religionist and false professor. It is important to pay close attention to the Lord's words. He said, "before you." He was not shutting the door of heaven to the religionists. They just could not enter as they presently were. As Christ said in the next verse, they lacked one thing, and they must do that thing in order to enter God's kingdom.
  d. Jesus shocked His audience. He declared that man's idea of religion is wrong. Religion and righteousness are not enough to enter God's kingdom. It takes more. Religion is not enough (worship services, ceremony, ritual, profession, and ordinance). Righteousness is not enough (morality, virtue, law, rules and regulations, good works, and commitment). Christ shockingly declared to the religionist and to the righteous: "Sinners go into the kingdom *before you*. What *you* have is not enough; it takes more. Something else is needed."

> **"For I say unto you, That except your righteousness shall exceed the righteousness of the scribes and Pharisees, ye shall in no case enter into the kingdom of heaven" (Mt.5:20).**
> **"For they being ignorant of God's righteousness, and going about to establish their own righteousness, have not submitted themselves unto the righteousness of God" (Ro.10:3).**
> **"Awake to righteousness, and sin not; for some have not the knowledge of God: I speak this to your shame" (1 Co.15:34).**

3 (21:32) **Salvation—Rejection**: the reason sinners enter God's kingdom and religionists do not is clearly stated: religionists do not believe John's message that Jesus is the Messiah, the Son of God. Note that Christ said three things.
  a. John was righteous. John came in "the way of righteousness," the very righteousness that religionists say is necessary to live for God. John was godly and lived just like religionists said he should live, yet religionists did not believe John; that is, they did not believe his ministry and witness—that Jesus was the Messiah, the Son of God.
  Christ said to the religionists standing around Him: "You are contradictory. John came to you in 'the way of righteousness' which you profess. He was godly, yet you did not receive his ministry and witness":

> **"Behold the Lamb of God, which taketh away the sin of the world" (Jn.1:29 see Jn.1:29-36).**
> **"And I saw, and bare record that this is the Son of God" (Jn.1:34).**
> **"But the Pharisees and lawyers rejected the counsel of God against themselves, being not baptized of Him (John) (Lu.7:30).**

Thought 1. The great tragedy of religionists is this: they stand aloof. They reject the counsel of God; they do not go and work in His vineyard.

  b. Sinners believed John's witness: "The publicans and harlots believed him." The first son did exactly what John said to do: he repented of his loose life and believed that Jesus was the Son of God (see note—Mt.21:31).
  c. Religionists saw the evidence, but they rejected it. They saw the evidence of John's righteousness and of the changed lives of sinners ("when ye had seen it"). But the religionists still denied the facts. Note: a religionist commits two gross errors that are seen in this passage.
    1) The religionist lives a strict religious life, but he does not repent of coming short. He tells God he will *go and work in His vineyard*, that is, *His kingdom*, but he does not go into *God's* vineyard. However, note: he does work. In fact, he is very strict in his work, but he works in the vineyard of his own *religion* and righteousness and rules. He never enters God's vineyard (kingdom) to serve the Father.
    What happened is what Jesus said. The religionists rejected the Scriptural witness, which began with John's ministry and witness. This witness said that the only way to get into God's vineyard is through faith in Christ, and the only way to serve God adequately is through the indwelling power of Christ (Jn.14:6; 1 Ti.2:5).

> **"I am the vine, ye are the branches: He that abideth in me, and I in him, the same bringeth forth much fruit: for without me ye can do nothing" (Jn.15:5).**

MATTHEW 21:28-32

> "Now unto him that is able to do exceeding abundantly above all that we ask or think, according to the power that worketh in us" (Ep.3:20).

2) The religionist does not believe John's personal witness: that Jesus is the Messiah, the Son of God. The religionist most likely accepts Jesus as a great teacher, but not as the Lamb of God who sacrificed Himself for the sins of the world (1 Pe.2:24).

> "No man taketh it from me, but I lay it down of myself. I have power to lay it [my life] down, and I have power to take it again. This commandment have I received of my Father" (Jn.10:18).

> "Who his own self bare our sins in his own body on the tree, that we, being dead to sins, should live unto righteousness: by whose stripes ye were healed" (1 Pe.2:24).

> "For Christ also hath once suffered for sins, the just for the unjust, that he might bring us to God, being put to death in the flesh, but quickened by the Spirit" (1 Pe.3:18).

Thought 1. John's witness is the standard by which Jesus is measuring religionists. It is not enough to be religious and righteous, that is, a good, moral, outstanding citizen. A person has to do more.

(1) He has to repent for not going into *God's* vineyard or God's kingdom. The religionist created his own vineyard of religion and righteousness, but his vineyard was not God's vineyard. God's vineyard is the vineyard of faith.

(2) He has to believe in God's Son, Jesus Christ. He has to enter the vineyard of faith, and he has to work within the vineyard of faith.

> "For by grace are ye saved through faith; and that not of yourselves: it is the gift of God: not of works, lest any man should boast. For we are his workmanship, created in Christ Jesus unto good works, which God hath before ordained that we should walk in them" (Ep.2:8-10).

MATTHEW 21:33-46

	F. The Parable of the Wicked Tenants: Israel's Rejection of Jesus' Messiahship, 21:33-46 *(Mk 12:1-12; Lu 20:9-19; Is 5:1-7)*	and slew *him*. 40 When the lord therefore of the vineyard cometh, what will he do unto those husbandmen?	f. God is to judge the tenants^{DS6} 1) God is coming
1. The parable: Israel's history as God sees it a. God planted a vineyard (the nation of Israel)^{DS1}	33 Hear another parable: There was a certain householder, which planted a vineyard, and hedged it round about, and digged a winepress in it, and built a tower,	41 They say unto him, He will miserably destroy those wicked men, and will let out *his* vineyard unto other husbandmen, which shall render him the fruits in their seasons.	2) God will miserably destroy the wicked 3) God will trust His vineyard to others (to believers, v. 43; see Ro. 10:12-13)
b. God entrusted His vineyard to the cultivators, tenants^{DS2}	and let it out to husbandmen, and went into a far country:	42 Jesus saith unto them, Did ye never read in the scriptures,	2. The three claims of Jesus a. Christ is the Head cornerstone^{DS7}
c. God sent messengers to gather the fruit^{DS3} 1) Fruit was expected	34 And when the time of the fruit drew near, he sent his servants to the husbandmen, that they might receive the fruits of it.	The stone which the builders rejected, the same is become the head of the corner: this is the Lord's doing, and it is marvellous in our eyes?	1) At first, He is rejected 2) But He becomes the Head cornerstone
2) The tenants rebelled & rejected God's messengers	35 And the husbandmen took his servants, and beat one, and killed another, and stoned another.	43 Therefore say I unto you, The kingdom of God shall be taken from you, and given to a nation bringing forth the fruits thereof.	b. God will take His kingdom away from Israel & give it to another people^{DS8}
d. God showed patience—He continued to send messengers^{DS4} e. God finally sent His Son: Christ was claiming to be God's Son^{DS5} 1) They saw God's Son 2) They plotted His death 3) They planned to seize His inheritance	36 Again, he sent other servants more than the first: and they did unto them likewise. 37 But last of all he sent unto them his son, saying, They will reverence my son. 38 But when the husbandmen saw the son, they said among themselves, This is the heir; come, let us kill him, and let us seize on his inheritance.	44 And whosoever shall fall on this stone shall be broken: but on whomsoever it shall fall, it will grind him to powder. 45 And when the chief priests and Pharisees had heard his parables, they perceived that he spake of them.	c. Some people are doomed^{DS9,10} 1) Those who stumble over the stone 2) Those who oppose the stone 3. The results of the parable a. The religionists saw that Christ spoke to them
4) They murdered the Son	39 And they caught him, and cast *him* out of the vineyard,	46 But when they sought to lay hands on him, they feared the multitude, because they took him for a prophet.	b. The religionists reacted instead of repenting c. The people saw Christ as a prophet, not as the Messiah

DIVISION XIV

THE MESSIAH'S LAST WEEK: HIS CLAIM CHALLENGED AND REJECTED, 21:1–23:39

F. The Parable of the Wicked Tenants: Israel's Rejection of Jesus' Messiahship, 21:33-46

(21:33-46) **Introduction**: this is one of the most interesting parables ever told by Christ. It is interesting because it is both historical and predictive. Christ covered the history of Israel from God's perspective, just as God sees it (vv.33-36). Then He predicted or revealed exactly what was going to happen to Israel: they were going to reject God's own Son (vv.37-39, 42), and because of their rejection and cruelty, God was going to reject them by giving the Kingdom of God to another people (v.43).

What is said throughout this passage is applicable to all nations as well as to Israel. God has entrusted the vineyard of the church and of the world to us (Mt.28:19-20), the new nation, the new creation of God (see notes—Ep.2:11-18; pt.4, 2:14-15; 4:17-19). Every point covered in Israel's history should, therefore, be a dynamic message speaking loudly and clearly to our hearts.

There are three major points in this passage.
1. The parable: Israel's history as God sees it (vv.33-41).
2. The three claims of Jesus (vv.42-44).
3. The results of the parable (vv.45-46).

1 (21:33-41) **Israel**: Israel's history as God sees it. The householder is God. The vineyard is Israel, true Israel, the people of God. The cultivators are the religious leaders of Israel; the servants are the prophets; and the Son is Jesus Christ, the Messiah (see Is.5:1-7). (The subpoints of this point are so important they are discussed in separate notes. See DEEPER STUDY # 1,2,3,4,5,6—Mt.21:33-41.)

125

MATTHEW 21:33-46

DEEPER STUDY # 1

(21:33) **God—Care—Provision—World—Church—Israel**: God planted a vineyard. The vineyard can be looked upon in several ways.

1. The vineyard is Israel, that is, true Israel, a people for God (Is.5:7).
2. The vineyard is the Kingdom of God which Israel was to look after. This is probably the most accurate understanding of what Christ meant and what actually happens in God's dealing with men. He entrusts His kingdom or church (vineyard) into our hands and expects us to cultivate it (see v.43. See Deeper Study # 3—Mt.19:23-24.)
3. The vineyard can also be applied to the earth itself, to which Israel was to minister (see Deeper Study # 1—Jn.4:22).

Note three marvelous things that God did for His vineyard. He provided every conceivable thing needed to take care of His vineyard and the cultivators. Everything was provided to assure growth and fruitfulness. The cultivators had no excuse for not producing.

1. God *hedged it round about*. This was a wall built around the vineyard to keep the animals away from the grapes. The hedge or wall *assured* growth and fruitfulness.

> "Ye have not chosen me, but I have chosen you, and ordained you, that ye should go and bring forth fruit, and that your fruit should remain: that whatsoever ye shall ask of the Father in my name, he may give it you" (Jn.15:16).
>
> "Being filled with the fruits of righteousness, which are by Jesus Christ, unto the glory and praise of God" (Ph.1:11).
>
> "That ye might walk worthy of the Lord unto all pleasing, being fruitful in every good work, and increasing in the knowledge of God; strengthened with all might, according to his glorious power, unto all patience and longsuffering with joyfulness" (Col.1:10-11).

2. God dug a winepress. This was a trough or vat into which the wine was pressed. The trough was sometimes dug in rock, sometime built out of wood. The trough stands for the equipment which God provides to get His work done.

> "And unto one he gave five talents, to another two, and to another one; to every man according to his several ability; and straightway took his journey" (Mt.25:15).
>
> "But ye shall receive power, after that the Holy Ghost is come upon you: and ye shall be witnesses unto me both in Jerusalem, and in all Judaea, and in Samaria, and unto the uttermost part of the earth" (Ac.1:8).
>
> "Having then gifts differing according to the grace that is given to us" (Ro.12:6).
>
> "Now there are diversities of gifts, but the same Spirit" (1 Co.12:4).

3. God built a tower. This was a watchtower used to guard and protect the vineyard from thieves. The tower stands for the assurance and security of God's care which He gives to His cultivators (see Mt.6:25-34).

> "Therefore take no thought, saying, What shall we eat? or, What shall we drink? or, Wherewithal shall we be clothed? (For after all these things do the Gentiles seek:) for your heavenly Father knoweth that ye have need of all these things" (Mt.6:31-32).
>
> "But even the very hairs of your head are all numbered. Fear not therefore: ye are of more value than many sparrows" (Lu.12:7).
>
> "Casting all your care upon him; for he careth for you" (1 Pe.5:7).
>
> "But my God shall supply all your need according to his riches in glory by Christ Jesus" (Ph.4:19).

DEEPER STUDY # 2

(21:33) **Labor—Responsibility—Ministry**: God entrusted His vineyard to cultivators. The cultivators were the nation and people of Israel, in particular the leaders (both religious and civil). Everyone was responsible to take care of the whole nation, looking after everyone else, thereby contributing to the welfare and provision of all. (See the whole body of the church and every member's responsibility to labor in the vineyard, 1 Co.12:12f.)

Note two things.

1. God puts trust in men. Think what a glorious privilege it is to be trusted by God! Imagine how dear God's vineyard is to Him, and then think about how He entrusts its care to us and not to angels nor to some other higher form of being. What a wonderful and marvelous thing that God would trust us with His most precious vineyard!
2. God gives freedom to man. God left the cultivators to care for His vineyard as they wished. They were to exercise their will and energy in caring for the vineyard. They had the glorious privilege of freedom, of being free to use their own ingenuity and ideas and not have someone looking over their shoulders forcing behavior.

> "So God created man in his own image, in the image of God created he him; male and female created he them. And God blessed them, and God said unto them, Be fruitful, and multiply, and replenish the earth, and subdue it: and have dominion over the fish of the sea, and over the fowl of the air, and over every living thing that moveth upon the earth" (Ge.1:27-28).
>
> "Thou madest him to have dominion over the works of thy hands; thou hast put all things under his feet" (Ps.8:6).
>
> "For the kingdom of heaven is as a man travelling into a far country, who called his own servants, and delivered unto them his goods" (Mt.25:14).

MATTHEW 21:33-46

> "Moreover it is required in stewards, that a man be found faithful" (1 Co.4:2).
>
> "Keep that which is committed to thy trust, avoiding profane and vain babblings, and oppositions of science falsely so called" (1 Ti.6:20).
>
> "And he called his ten servants, and delivered them ten pounds, and said unto them, Occupy till I come" (Lu.19:13).

DEEPER STUDY # 3

(21:34-35) **Man—Rebellion—Rejection—Persecution**: God sent messengers to gather the fruits of His vineyard. The messengers would be the prophets and the good and godly leaders throughout Israel's history (judges, kings, and priests).

Note three things.

1. Fruit was expected. Every cultivator, that is, every person was responsible for the vineyard; everyone was expected to labor and produce.

2. A day of accountability came. Every man was expected to pay his dues and to make his contribution for the wonderful privilege of living in the beautiful vineyard and being blessed by it. (The Kingdom of God, the world, the church—however one applies this passage—all are wonderful vineyards for which we are responsible to contribute what fruit we can.)

> "He spake also this parable; A certain man had a fig tree planted in his vineyard; and he came and sought fruit thereon, and found none" (Lu.13:6).
>
> "Every branch in me that beareth not fruit he taketh away: and every branch that beareth fruit, he purgeth it, that it may bring forth more fruit" (Jn.15:2).
>
> "I am the vine, ye are the branches: He that abideth in me, and I in him, the same bringeth forth much fruit: for without me ye can do nothing. If a man abide not in me, he is cast forth as a branch, and is withered; and men gather them, and cast them into the fire, and they are burned" (Jn.15:5-6).

3. The cultivators rebelled and refused to pay the Master. In fact, their rebellion led to the persecution and murder of God's servants.

   a. Man deliberately rebels against God. Man wants to rule the vineyard himself. He wants to be the king of the kingdom, the ruler of the earth, and even the head of the church. He wants things to go his way, to rule and reign as he desires and wills. He wants no authority above himself; he wants to live as he wishes and do things as he wishes. He wants to claim the fruit for himself.

   b. Man wants his own way so much that he ridicules, slanders, persecutes, and even murders the true servants of God.

   > "Which of the prophets have not your fathers persecuted? and they have slain them which showed before of the coming of the Just One; of whom ye have been now the betrayers and murderers" (Ac.7:52. See Mt.23:34-37; He.11:36-38.)

   c. The servant of God must understand that he is called to suffer (see DEEPER STUDY # 4—Mt.21:36. See note and DEEPER STUDY # 2—Mt.20:22-23).

DEEPER STUDY # 4

(21:36) **Persecution**: God showed patience—He continued to send messengers. All through Israel's history God loved and showed His loving-kindness by not reacting and rejecting the nation. God has given us chance after chance. He sends messengers across our path time after time. He loves us and longs for us to pay our dues. He longs for us to bear fruit and live as we should.

Tragically, most cultivators continue as always: rebelling and claiming all rights to the vineyard and to their own lives. Therefore, they continue to react against God's messengers.

Thought 1. How many believers, laymen and ministers alike, are mistreated by the world!

> "For unto you it is given in the behalf of Christ, not only to believe on him, but also to suffer for his sake" (Ph.1:29).
>
> "Yea, and all that will live godly in Christ Jesus shall suffer persecution" (2 Ti.3:12).
>
> "Beloved, think it not strange concerning the fiery trial which is to try you, as though some strange thing happened unto you: but rejoice, inasmuch as ye are partakers of Christ's sufferings; that, when his glory shall be revealed, ye may be glad also with exceeding joy" (1 Pe.4:12-13; see 1 Pe.2:21; 4:5-6; Mt.19:29; Ro.8:16-17).

DEEPER STUDY # 5

(21:37-39) **Jesus Christ, Deity—Death**: God finally sent His Son. God wanted to speak to man Himself. Perhaps they would listen to His voice and reverence His rights. He condescended and asked His Son to leave the glory of eternity and to bring His Word to earth, speaking face to face with man.

Note five facts.

1. Christ claimed to be God's Son. He was different from all the servants sent before. He was more than another man-servant; He was God's very own Son. There is no question that Christ was making this unique claim for Himself.

2. The cultivators saw God's Son. There were all kinds of evidence: Old Testament prophecies; the testimony of John the Baptist; Jesus' own claim and the miraculous works; the signs of the times (Ga.4:4); the feeling that He was the promised Messiah, even among those who now opposed Him (see note—Jn.3:1-2; see Jn.11:47-52). This is the tragic indictment against the Jews. Down deep within they had a sense that Jesus really was the Messiah, but sin and greed for position, esteem, power, and security kept them from acknowledging Him. Their unbelief was deliberate and obstinate (see outline and notes—Mt.21:23-27).

3. The cultivators plotted His death (see Mt.12:14; Jn.11:53).

4. The cultivators planned to seize His inheritance. Man wants to possess the kingdom, nation, property, power, rule, reign, position, esteem, fame, recognition, and wealth. Whatever the possession is, man wants the possession himself; and he will deny, deceive, lie, cheat, steal, and even kill to get it. (See notes—Mt.12:1-8; note and DEEPER STUDY # 1—12:10; note—15:1-20; DEEPER STUDY # 2—15:6-9.)

5. The cultivators murdered the Son. They committed the worst crime in human history. They killed the Son of God Himself. Note that Christ's death was being prophesied. He was predicting His death Himself, and His death was to be a willing act on His part. He knew death lay ahead and could have escaped, but He chose to die. It was in "the determinate counsel of God" (Ac.2:23).

"For God so loved the world, that he gave his only begotten Son, that whosoever believeth in him should not perish, but have everlasting life" (Jn.3:16).

"But God commendeth his love toward us, in that, while we were yet sinners, Christ died for us" (Ro.5:8).

"But God, who is rich in mercy, for his great love wherewith he loved us, even when we were dead in sins, hath quickened us together with Christ, (by grace ye are saved)" (Ep.2:4-5).

DEEPER STUDY # 6

(21:40-41) **Judgment—Church**: God is to judge the cultivators. There are three important points here.

1. Christ said that the Lord of the vineyard is coming. He is coming to revenge the death of His only Son.

2. God is coming to destroy the wicked. The destruction is to be miserable (kakos) and terrible. Note: it was both the rulers and the people who said that justice would be executed. Man, by his very nature, expects injustice to be punished.

3. God is going to trust His vineyard to others. Again, it was the crowd who said this. Even man knows that a vineyard will not lie unkept. It will be cultivated by someone. God will raise up a new people to care for it (the church, the new creation of God. See DEEPER STUDY # 8—Mt.21:43; notes—Ep.2:11-18; pt.4, 2:14-15; 4:17-19.)

"And now also the axe is laid unto the root of the trees: therefore every tree which bringeth not forth good fruit is hewn down, and cast into the fire" (Mt.3:10).

"If a man abide not in me, he is cast forth as a branch, and is withered; and men gather them, and cast them into the fire, and they are burned" (Jn.15:6).

"But that which beareth thorns and briers is rejected, and is nigh unto cursing: whose end is to be burned" (He.6:8).

2 (21:42-44) **Jesus Christ, Cornerstone**: Christ made three astounding claims in these verses, claims that affect both world history and the personal destiny of everyone who ever lives in the world.
  a. He is the Head Cornerstone. (See DEEPER STUDY # 7—Mt.21:42 for discussion.)
  b. God shall turn away from Israel to another nation. (See DEEPER STUDY # 8—Mt.21:43 for discussion.)
  c. A man's rejection of Christ will cause that man to be crushed.

DEEPER STUDY # 7

(21:42) **Jesus Christ, Head Cornerstone**: Christ is the Head cornerstone (see note—Lu.2:34). This is a quotation from Ps.118:22-23 which was recognized as a Messianic prophecy. The Messiah was to be the Head Cornerstone who was to begin building the Kingdom of God and who was to support all other stones or leaders who came later. The religious leaders standing around Christ would know that He was referring to the Messiah (Is.28:16; Dan.2:34; Zec.3:9).

But note the prophecy: the stone is to be rejected at first. It is considered unsuitable, useless for the building, so the builders do not allow the stone to be a part of the building. It is cast aside and treated as undesirable.

However, the great Architect overrules the builders. He raises the stone from the graveyard of rejected stones and exalts it to the position of Head cornerstone, the stone which supports all other stones and which holds the building of God's kingdom together (see Ph.2:9-11. See notes—Ep.2:20.)

The symbolism of the Head cornerstone says at least two significant things.

1. The cornerstone is the first stone laid. All other stones are placed after it. It is the *preeminent* stone in time. So it is with Christ; He is *the first* of God's new movement.

⇒ Christ is the *captain* of salvation. All others are crew members who follow Him.

"For it became him, for whom are all things, and by whom are all things, in bringing many sons unto glory, to make the captain of their salvation perfect through sufferings" (He.2:10).

⇒ Christ is the *author* of eternal salvation, of our faith. All others are the readers of the story.

"And being made perfect, he became the author of eternal salvation unto all them that obey him" (He.5:9).
"Looking unto Jesus the author and finisher of our faith; who for the joy that was set before him endured the cross, despising the shame, and is set down at the right hand of the throne of God" (He.12:2).

⇒ Christ is the *beginning and the ending*. All others come after Him and are in between Him.

"I am Alpha and Omega, the beginning and the ending, saith the Lord, which is, and which was, and which is to come, the Almighty" (Re.1:8; see 21:6; 22:13).

⇒ Christ is the *forerunner* into the very presence of God. All others enter God's presence after Him.

"Which hope we have as an anchor of the soul, both sure and stedfast, and which entereth into that within the veil; whither the forerunner is for us entered, even Jesus, made an high priest for ever after the order of Melchisedec" (He.6:19-20).

2. The cornerstone is the supportive stone. All other stones are placed upon it and held up by it. They all rest upon it. It is the preeminent stone in position and power. So it is with Christ; He is the support and power, the Foundation of God's new movement.
⇒ Christ is *the Head cornerstone*, the only true foundation upon which man can build. All who are not laid upon Him will crumble.

"For other foundation can no man lay than that is laid, which is Jesus Christ" (1 Co.3:11).

⇒ Christ is *the chief cornerstone* upon which all others are fitly formed together. All who wish to be fitly formed together have to be laid upon Him.

"And are built upon the foundation of the apostles and prophets, Jesus Christ himself being the chief corner stone; in whom all the building fitly framed together groweth unto an holy temple in the Lord: in whom ye also are builded together for an habitation of God through the Spirit" (Ep.2:20-22).

⇒ Christ is *the living stone* upon which all others are built. It is upon Him that we are built up into a spiritual house. All others have to be built upon Him if they wish to live and have their spiritual sacrifice accepted by God.

"To whom coming, as unto a living stone, disallowed indeed of men, but chosen of God, and precious, ye also, as lively stones, are built up a spiritual house, an holy priesthood, to offer up spiritual sacrifices, acceptable to God by Jesus Christ" (1 Pe.2:4-5).

DEEPER STUDY # 8
(21:43) **Israel—Gentiles—Church—New Creation**: God shall take away His kingdom and give it to another nation. Christ gave a prophecy that dramatically affects world history: His vineyard or kingdom is going to be taken away from Israel and given to another nation.
There are several important facts that need to be understood at this point in order to grasp the significance of the Lord's prophecy.
1. Israel was the nation of people raised up by God to be His witness to the world (see DEEPER STUDY # 1—Jn.4:22).
   a. Israel bore up the name of God in the world.

"In Judah is God known: his name is great in Israel. In Salem [Jerusalem] also is his tabernacle, and his dwelling place in Zion" (Ps.76:1-2).

   b. Israel was given the oracles of God, that is, the Word of God, the revelation of God to the world.

"What advantage then hath the Jew?...chiefly, because that unto them were committed the oracles of God" (Ro .3:1-2).

   c. Israel was a greatly privileged people in spiritual things.

"[They] are Israelites; to whom pertaineth the adoption, and the glory, and the covenants, and the giving of the law, and the service of God, and the promises; whose are the fathers, and of whom as concerning the flesh Christ came, who is over all, God blessed for ever" (Ro.9:4-5. See notes—Ro.9:3-5 for a discussion of their great privileges.)

   d. Israel was given the glorious plan of salvation.

"Ye worship ye know not what: we know what we worship: for salvation is of the Jews" (Jn.4:22).

   e. Israel was given the glorious privilege of being God's witnesses upon the earth.

"Ye are my witnesses, saith the Lord, and my servant whom I have chosen: that ye may know and believe me, and understand that I am he: before me there was no God formed, neither shall there be after me" (Is.43:10).

2. Israel failed God in its God-given mission and failed God miserably. Therefore, God took His kingdom away from them. As Christ points out in this parable, they "took [God's] servants, and beat one, and killed another, and stoned another" (vv.35-36). Then they committed the most atrocious crime of history: they rejected and killed God's very own Son (v.39). All through its history Israel was unfruitful except for a bright spot here and there. They opposed the reins of God upon their lives, and in the final step of rebellion, they rejected and opposed the gospel of Christ. Therefore, they forfeited their Godly privileges. The Kingdom of God was taken from them and given to another nation.
   a. God turned from Israel because they killed His Son.

"And they caught Him [God's son], and cast Him out of the vineyard, and slew Him.... [Therefore] God will let out His vineyard to other husbandmen, which shall render Him the fruits in their seasons" (Mt.21:39, 41).

   b. God turned from Israel because they were unfruitful.

"Therefore say I unto you, The kingdom of God shall be taken from you, and given to a nation bringing forth the fruits thereof" (Mt.21:43).

   c. God turned from Israel because they sought after righteousness by law and not by faith.

"But Israel, which followed after the law of righteousness, hath not attained to the law of righteousness. Wherefore? Because they sought it not by faith, but as it were by the works of the law. For they stumbled at that stumblingstone; As it is written, Behold, I lay in Sion a stumblingstone and rock of offence: and whosoever believeth on him shall not be ashamed" (Ro.9:31-33).

   d. God turned from Israel because they would not submit themselves to the righteousness of God.

"They [Israel] have a zeal of God, but not according to knowledge. For they being ignorant of God's righteousness, and going about to establish their own righteousness, have not submitted themselves unto the righteousness of God (Ro.10:2-3).

   e. God turned from Israel because they did not obey the gospel.

"But they have not all obeyed the gospel. For Esaias saith, Lord, who hath believed our report?" (Ro.10:16).

   f. God turned from Israel because they were a disobedient and obstinate people.

"But to Israel he saith, All day long I have stretched forth my hands unto a disobedient and gainsaying [obstinate] people" (Ro.10:21).

   g. God turned from Israel because of unbelief.

"Well; because of unbelief they were broken off, and thou standest by faith. Be not highminded, but fear: For if God spared not the natural branches, take heed lest he also spare not thee. Behold therefore the goodness and severity of God: on them which fell, severity; but toward thee, goodness, if thou continue in his goodness: otherwise thou also shalt be cut off" (Ro.11:20-22).

3. Israel as a nation was never saved. Not all citizens believed in God. When God chose Israel to be His people, He did not mean *national salvation*. God knew that not all the citizens of Israel would believe. Not all citizens of any nation believe. What God meant, very simply, was that Israel as a nation was to be the *primary recipient and messenger* of His Kingdom and gospel (see the special privileges of Israel above—point 1). Salvation was never a national matter, not a matter of race or heritage. It was always a matter of personal belief. There was never a moment in Israel's history when every Jew believed in the promises of God.

"Not as though the word of God hath taken none effect. For they are not all Israel, which are of Israel: Neither, because they are the seed of Abraham, are they all children: but, in Isaac shall thy seed by called. That is, they which are the children of the flesh, these are not the children of God: but the children of the promise are counted for the seed" (Ro.9:6-8).

MATTHEW 21:33-46

"Esaias also crieth concerning Israel, Though the number of the children of Israel be as the sand of the sea, a remnant shall be saved...And as Esaias said before, Except the Lord of Sabaoth had left us a seed, we had been as Sodom, and been made like unto Gomorrha" (Ro.9:27, 29).

"For he is not a Jew, which is one outwardly; neither is that circumcision, which is outward in the flesh: But he is a Jew, which is one inwardly; and circumcision is that of the heart, in the spirit, and not in the letter; whose praise is not of men, but of God" (Ro.2:28-29).

"For the promise, that he should be the heir of the world, was not to Abraham, or to his seed, through the law, but through the righteousness of faith" (Ro.4:13).

"For what saith the scripture? Abraham believed God, and it was counted unto him for righteousness. Now to him that worketh is the reward not reckoned of grace, but of debt. But to him that worketh not, but believeth on him that justifieth the ungodly, his faith is counted for righteousness. Even as David also describeth the blessedness of the man, unto whom God imputeth righteousness without works, Saying, Blessed are they whose iniquities are forgiven, and whose sins are covered. Blessed is the man to whom the Lord will not impute sin" (Ro.4:3-8).

4. Israel did, however, always have a remnant, a small number of genuine believers (see outline and notes—Ro.11:1-10; see 9:27-29).

"Esaias also crieth concerning Israel, Though the number of the children of Israel be as the sand of the sea, a remnant shall be saved....And as Esaias said before, Except the Lord of Sabaoth had left us a seed, we had been as Sodom, and been made like unto Gomorrha" (Ro.9:27, 29).

"I say then, Hath God cast away his people? God forbid. For I also am an Israelite, of the seed of Abraham, of the tribe of Benjamin. God hath not cast away his people which he foreknew. Wot [know] ye not what the scripture saith of Elias? how he maketh intercession to God against Israel, saying, Lord, they have killed thy prophets, and digged down thine altars; and I am left alone, and they seek my life. But what saith the answer of God unto him? I have reserved to myself seven thousand men, who have not bowed the knee to the image of Baal. Even so then at this present time also there is a remnant according to the election of grace" (Ro.11:1-5).

5. God turned to a new nation and gave His kingdom to them.

"Therefore say I unto you, The kingdom of God shall be taken from you, and given to a nation bringing forth the fruits thereof" (Mt.21:43).

"As he saith also in Osee [Hosea], I will call them my people, which were not my people; and her beloved, which was not beloved. And it shall come to pass, that in the place where it was said unto them, Ye are not my people; there shall they be called the children of the living God" (Ro.9:25-26).

"What shall we say then? That the Gentiles, which followed not after righteousness, have attained to righteousness, even the righteousness which is of faith. But Israel, which followed after the law of righteousness, hath not attained to the law of righteousness. Wherefore? Because they sought it not by faith, but as it were by the works of the law. For they stumbled at that stumblingstone; As it is written, Behold, I lay in Sion a stumblingstone and rock of offence: and whosoever believeth on him shall not be ashamed" (Ro.9:30-33).

"But Esaias is very bold, and saith, I was found of them that sought me not; I was made manifest unto them that asked not after me" (Ro.10:20).

"For as ye in times past have not believed God, yet have now obtained mercy through their unbelief" (Ro.11:30).

6. God's new nation was to be a new creation; that is, it was not to be an existing nation. Just as God had created Israel to be a new nation through one man, Abraham, so God was to create another new nation through one Man, Jesus Christ.
Two things need to be noted about God's new nation.
   a. The land or inheritance of this new nation is not of this earth but of heaven. The inheritance is of the spiritual dimension of being; it is heavenly and eternal. It is not of the physical dimension of being; it is not worldly and temporal.
   b. The citizens of this new nation are people from all earthly nations who truly believe in the Lord Jesus Christ. When a person from any nation of the earth believes in Christ, God takes that person and gives him a new birth spiritually, (Jn.3:3-17; 1 Pe.1:23; 1 Jn.5:1, 4-5). The person becomes a new creature and a new man (2 Co.5:17; Ep.4:24; Col.3:10).

All believers counted together are said to comprise...
- the citizens of the new nation (Ep.2:19; 1 Pe.2:9).
- the family and household of God (Ep.2:19; 5:1, 8; see Ro.8:16-17).
- a new body of believers (1 Co.12:12-14; Ep.2:16).
- a holy temple (Ep.2:21-22).
- a new race (Ep.4:17).
- a spiritual house (1 Pe.2:5).
- a holy priesthood (1 Pe.2:5).
- a chosen generation (1 Pe.2:9).

- a royal priesthood (1 Pe.2:9).
- a peculiar people (1 Pe.2:9).
- the people of God (1 Pe.2:10).
- strangers and pilgrims on earth (1 Pe.2:11).

7. God is going to restore Israel; that is, He is going to have mercy upon Israel and turn them from ungodliness. Why? That He might have mercy upon all, both Gentile and Jew (Ro.11:32). (See outlines and notes—Ro.11:25-36. See Ro.11:11-16. God's historical dealings with the Jews and Gentiles are covered in detail in Romans, chapters 9, 10, and 11. Also see outline and notes—Rev.11:3-13 for more discussion.)

DEEPER STUDY # 9
(21:44) **Judgment—Stone, Stumbling—Stone, Crushing**: Christ said two types of people are doomed.
1. The people who stumble over Christ, the Head cornerstone of God, are doomed. Many who stood around Christ in that day stumbled and many stumble today. Many cannot believe that God actually sent His Son into the world. The idea that God would humiliate Himself that much is beyond understanding, so they refuse to believe. The belief that Christ was a great teacher is acceptable to them; but acknowledging Him to be more than a man, to be the Son of God who was to die for the sins of the world, is beyond them. Therefore, they stumble over the cornerstone, the very foundation which God has laid for the salvation of man. They stumble and fall over who He is, and they are shattered and broken (see note—Lu.2:34).
2. The men who oppose Christ over His being the Head cornerstone are doomed. Some actively oppose Christ and His kingdom. They say and teach that He is not really the Son of God. Neither He nor any other human being could ever be the Son of God. A good man, yes, but never the Son of God who has been exalted to the right hand of God. Christ says the Son (He Himself) will crush those who oppose Him, those who lead others astray trying to stamp out belief in Him and His kingdom. Severe judgment, holy vengeance shall straighten out all the injustices and sins of men.

DEEPER STUDY # 10
(21:44) **Jesus Christ, Names—Titles**: there are four pictures of Christ as the Stone given in Scripture. Each shows how the coming of Christ affects the world (see note—Lu.2:34).
1. Christ is the Head or Chief Cornerstone, the Foundation Stone. He is the Foundation and Cornerstone upon which every man must build his life. There is no other Foundation upon which man can build and be secure. In addition, Christ is the Foundation and Cornerstone of the church (see DEEPER STUDY # 7—Mt.21:42. See 1 Co.3:11; Ep.2:20-22; 1 Pe.2:4-5.)
2. Christ is the Stumbling Stone and the Rock of Offense. Some cannot understand the fact that Jesus is the Son of God. Others are repulsed by the cross and His blood. They stumble and are offended by His deity and death for sins. Israel was the first to stumble and multitudes have stumbled ever since (see DEEPER STUDY # 9—Mt.21:44. See Is.8:14-15; Ro.9:32-33; 1 Co.1:23; 1 Pe.2:8.)
3. Christ is the Crushing Stone or the Smiting Stone of Destruction (Mt.21:44; Dan.2:34). Christ rules and reigns at the right hand of God now. However, with so much evil and destruction in the world, it may appear as though He is not ruling; but He is. He is just waiting until more and more persons believe, not willing that any should perish. But the day of redemption for the believer and of destruction for the unbeliever is coming. He shall become the Crushing Stone, the Smiting Stone of Destruction to all who *oppose* Him. He shall crush and smite, destroying all who stand in opposition to Him. This apparently refers both to individuals and to world powers who oppose Him (DEEPER STUDY # 9—Mt.21:44. See Dan.2:34; Rev.16:13; 19:17.)
4. Christ is the Living Stone (1 Pe.2:4-5). He was disallowed by men but chosen by the Chief Architect, God Himself, and counted as the most Precious of Stones. All men who come to Him are laid upon Him, and they are built up into a spiritual house to offer up spiritual sacrifices (see DEEPER STUDY # 7—Mt.21:42).

3 (21:45-46) **Jesus Christ, Response**: the results of the parable are threefold.

a. The religionists saw that Christ was speaking directly to them, but their consciences were seared by obstinate unbelief (1 Ti.4:2). They were insensitive to His warnings (Mt.21:41-44).

b. The religionists reacted instead of repenting. They should have heeded the Lord's warning, but they did not. They were set against Him, seeking to destroy Him and to silence His claim.

c. The people saw Christ only as a prophet (a great teacher) and not as the Messiah. This too is tragic, but God was able to use their respect to protect Christ until the appointed time of His death.

CHAPTER 22

G. The Parable of the Marriage Feast: Israel's Rejection of God's Great Invitation, 22:1-14

(Lu 14:15-24)

1. Jesus again shared a parable
   a. Of the Kingdom of Heaven
   b. Of a marriage prepared by God for His Son

2. God's invitation to Israel
   a. God invited Israel, but they rejected
   b. God showed great mercy
      1) Extended a second invitation
      2) Prepared an abundance
   c. God saw His second invitation rejected
      1) By a busy farmer
      2) By a hurried businessman
      3) By the religionist & the worldly: Who denied, scoffed, & persecuted
   d. God judged Israel for rejecting His invitation
      1) Destroyed the abusers & murderers
      2) Rejected the rejecters

3. God's invitation to any & all
   a. God then invited all
      1) Those who were out on the street corners
      2) Those who were both good & bad
   b. God's invitation was accepted

4. God's confrontation with the guests
   a. God entered to see the guests
      1) He saw a man without wedding clothes
      2) He asked only one question
      3) The man was speechless
   b. God judged the man who was not clothed properly
      1) Was bound
      2) Was taken away
      3) Was cast into the darkness **DS1,2,3**
   c. God calls & invites many, but few are chosen

And Jesus answered and spake unto them again by parables, and said,

2 The kingdom of heaven is like unto a certain king, which made a marriage for his son,

3 And sent forth his servants to call them that were bidden to the wedding: and they would not come.

4 Again, he sent forth other servants, saying, Tell them which are bidden, Behold, I have prepared my dinner: my oxen and *my* fatlings *are* killed, and all things *are* ready: come unto the marriage.

5 But they made light of *it,* and went their ways, one to his farm, another to his merchandise:

6 And the remnant took his servants, and entreated *them* spitefully, and slew *them.*

7 But when the king heard *thereof,* he was wroth: and he sent forth his armies, and destroyed those murderers, and burned up their city.

8 Then saith he to his servants, The wedding is ready, but they which were bidden were not worthy.

9 Go ye therefore into the highways, and as many as ye shall find, bid to the marriage.

10 So those servants went out into the highways, and gathered together all as many as they found, both bad and good: and the wedding was furnished with guests.

11 And when the king came in to see the guests, he saw there a man which had not on a wedding garment:

12 And he saith unto him, Friend, how camest thou in hither not having a wedding garment? And he was speechless.

13 Then said the king to the servants, Bind him hand and foot, and take him away, and cast *him* into outer darkness; there shall be weeping and gnashing of teeth.

14 For many are called, but few *are* chosen.

DIVISION XIV

THE MESSIAH'S LAST WEEK: HIS CLAIM CHALLENGED AND REJECTED, 21:1–23:39

G. The Parable of the Marriage Feast: Israel's Rejection of God's Great Invitation, 22:1-14

(22:1-14) **Introduction—Lord's Great Marriage Feast**: several things need to be noted about this parable.

1. This parable should be compared with the parable in Luke 14:15-24. There are many similarities, but they do differ. Matthew's parable is *The Great Marriage Feast*; Luke's parable is *The Great Supper*. Luke's parable was told at a much earlier date. Matthew's parable was shared during the last week of Christ's life. Each parable had a different purpose and was shared in a different place. Some details also differ.

It is important not to confuse the two parables with each other. Each has its own lesson and truths. Christ is bound to have repeated His parables and teachings often, for all trials are common to all men (1 Co. 10:13). All men need the same lessons and the same truth. Christ just varied the details to apply to various congregations and their particular needs.

2. This parable, the Great Marriage Feast, deals with the *Kingdom of Heaven* (v.2). This is important. Although the parable tells how God dealt with Israel and turned from Israel, its major point is God's dealings with His new people, the church (the new nation. See DEEPER STUDY # 8—Mt.21:43; esp. pt.6.)

3. The meaning of the various points of the parable is clear.
   ⇒ The King is God.
   ⇒ The Son is Christ Himself. Note that He again claims to be the Son of God, distinctive from the servants of the King. This is a critical point to see. There is no question about Christ's understanding just who He is (see DEEPER STUDY # 5—Mt.21:37-39).
   ⇒ The Great Marriage Feast is the glorious day of redemption. It is the glorious day when the church will see Christ for the very first time and be joined with Him forever (see 1 Th.4:13-18).
   ⇒ Those "that were bidden" to the marriage refers to Israel. They were called by God from the very first, beginning with Abraham. However, this point can be applied to any of us—the farmer, the merchant, the religionist, the worldly—any who scoff, abuse, persecute and deny that Christ is the Son of God.
   ⇒ Those in "the highways" are the Gentiles, people from all other nations who are willing to accept God's glorious invitation to His dear Son's wedding.
   ⇒ The wedding garment is righteousness. No guest is acceptable for the wedding unless he is properly clothed, and the only proper clothing is righteousness, the righteousness of the Lord Jesus Christ.

MATTHEW 22:1-14

The parable has both an historical and personal meaning. That is to say, its points can be applied to any of us. A quick glance at its points, both major and minor, will show this.
1. Jesus again shared a parable (vv.1-2).
2. God's invitation to Israel (vv.3-7).
3. God's invitation to any and all (vv.8-10).
4. God's confrontation with the guests (vv.11-14).

1 (22:1-2) **The Great Marriage Feast**: Jesus again shared a parable about the Kingdom of Heaven. God has prepared a Great Marriage Feast for His Son and His true followers. The intimate relationship between Christ and His Church are often compared to a marriage (see Mt.9:15; Jn.3:29; 2 Co.11:2; Ep.5:23-32).

> "Let us be glad and rejoice, and give honor to him: for the marriage of the Lamb is come, and his wife hath made herself ready" (Re.19:7).
> "And there came unto me one of the seven angels which had the seven vials full of the seven last plagues, and talked with me, saying, Come hither, I will show thee the bride, the Lamb's wife" (Re.21:9).

The covenant of faith is like a covenant of marriage. When a person believes, Christ promises an eternal relationship with Himself. The relationship or union is forever, once and for all.

2 (22:3-7) **Israel—Invitation**: God's invitation to Israel is both historical and prophetic. This is clearly seen as we see the various events covered by Christ in verses 3-7. The various invitations sent out by the King were the practice of Jewish custom. The King would announce the upcoming occasion and then send out reminders as the day approached (see Esth.5:8 with 6:14). Note four points.
  a. God invited Israel, but they rejected.
   1) The words "them which are bidden" refer to the fact that Israel had *already* been invited. From the very first, beginning with Abraham himself (Ge.12:1f), God had invited Israel to the great feast of His Son.
   2) The servants "sent forth" with this particular invitation were those living during the life of Christ. In relation to time, this parable picks up the story of God's dealing with Israel during the life of Christ. The servants would, therefore, be John the Baptist, the twelve apostles (Mt.10:5f), and the seventy who were sent out into every city to prepare the people for the coming of Christ (Lu.10:1f).
   3) "They [Israel] would not come." The words are few and simply stated, yet the fact is so tragic. This was the first invitation, and they would not accept it. Why would anyone not accept the first invitation of a King to the marriage celebration of His only Son? (See Lu.13:34-35.) A person...
   - can be too busy
   - can set aside the invitation to accept later
   - can be committed to something else
   - can not care enough for the King
   - can prefer some other festivity
   - can wish to show personal dislike
   - can not trust, not believe that the King will actually have a feast
   - can not believe in the Son
   - can dislike the Son

> "For I bear them record that they have a zeal of God, but not according to knowledge. For they being ignorant of God's righteousness, and going about to establish their own righteousness, have not submitted themselves unto the righteousness of God" (Ro.10:2-3).
> "But to Israel he saith, All day long I have stretched forth my hands unto a disobedient and gainsaying people" (Ro.10:21).
> "But my people would not hearken to my voice; and Israel would none of me" (Ps.81:11).
> "And now, because ye have done all these works, saith the LORD, and I spake unto you, rising up early and speaking, but ye heard not; and I called you, but ye answered not" (Je.7:13).

  b. God showed great mercy. He had been spurned and rejected with all the disrespect and disgrace imaginable. Yet He did not react—despite the people's disregarding the invitation of the King the way they had. He acted with mercy and grace, still asking the people to attend the Great Marriage Feast of His only Son.
   1) God extended a second invitation. The servants who carried this invitation were the witnesses who went forth immediately after the Lord's resurrection and the coming of the Holy Spirit.
      Note that the dinner was now said to be ready: "all things are [now] ready." The great sacrifice necessary to prepare the meal had taken place. They were to come now, come immediately to the feast that *preceded* the marriage itself. Everyone was still invited (2 Co.5:11, 20; 2 Co.6:1).
   2) God prepared an abundance.
      ⇒ It was time for all dislikes and differences to be laid aside. The day for the King's only Son to be married had arrived.
      ⇒ It was time for joy: the only Son of the King was about to be married. The Feast was to be the greatest feast ever held. It was to be the most joyful of all occasions.
      ⇒ It was time for feasting.

MATTHEW 22:1-14

Thought 1. The very fact that God calls and calls reveals how His heart is *ready* to receive us. He longs for us to be present and prepared for His Son's Great Marriage.

   c. God saw His second invitation rejected. The people treated it lightly. The word for *made light* (amelesantes) means to care little if any; to be careless. In the Greek, this is an aorist participle: they were *making light of it*. They were *definite* in their decision not to attend the Great Marriage Feast. They were *careless and negligent* about it. They were *too busy* to be concerned with the King's invitation, too busy with the world and making a living and getting more and more for pleasure and comfort (see Js.4:13).

     1) Some were busy farmers. Property and crops needed to be looked after. Note the words *His farm* (ton idion agron). It was his *own* farm or property. The idea seems to be that of selfish enjoyment. The man went to the selfish enjoyment of his own property. He was *wrapped up* in the possessions of this world.

> "For what is man profited, if he shall gain the whole world, and lose his own soul? or what shall a man give in exchange for his soul?" (Mt.16:26).
>
> "And that which fell among thorns are they, which, when they have heard, go forth, and are choked with cares and riches and pleasures of this life, and bring forth fruit with patience" (Lu.8:14).
>
> "And seek not ye what ye shall eat, or what ye shall drink, neither be ye of doubtful mind" (Lu.12:29).
>
> "Surely every man walketh in a vain show: surely they are disquieted in vain: he heapeth up riches, and knoweth not who shall gather them" (Ps.39:6).
>
> "Therefore I went about to cause my heart to despair of all the labor which I took under the sun" (Ec.2:20).

     2) Some were busy merchants (city dwellers). They were engaged in commerce, business, trade. They were wrapped up in the business of the world.

> "Go to now, ye that say, To day or to morrow we will go into such a city, and continue there a year, and buy and sell, and get gain" (Js.4:13).
>
> "No man that warreth entangleth himself with the affairs of this life; that he may please him who hath chosen him to be a soldier" (2 Ti.2:4).
>
> "And they all with one consent began to make excuse. The first said unto him, I have bought a piece of ground, and I must needs go and see it: I pray thee have me excused. And another said, I have bought five yoke of oxen, and I go to prove them: I pray thee have me excused" (Lu.14:18-19.)

     3) Some were worldly-minded and religious. They were so attached to the world that they wanted nothing to do with the King. He disturbed their interests and their lives. He was a threat to their position, prestige, wealth, and security. Therefore, they were hostile to Him. In fact, they would have overthrown His reign and taken His kingdom for themselves. They persecuted and slayed His servants, anyone who reminded them of their obligation to keep the Marriage Feast of the King (see Acts 4:3; 5:40; 7:58; 9:2; 12:2f; 14:19; 16:23; 2 Co.11:23-25).

Thought 1. Men are always rejecting God's invitation. Why? *Not because* they *have* to but because they *want* to.

> "Ye will not come to me, that ye might have life" (Jn.5:40).

Thought 2. What a paradox! If anyone should ever be received with open arms, it is the messenger who brings the invitation to the King's Great Marriage Feast for His Son. Yet, the very opposite is too often true. The King's messengers are often unwelcomed, ridiculed, criticized, mistreated, abused, cursed, persecuted, murmured against, and sometimes killed.

> "Being defamed, we intreat: we are made as the filth of the world, and are the offscouring of all things unto this day" (1 Co.4:13).

   d. God judged Israel for rejecting His invitation. Some interpret this verse to refer to the destruction of Jerusalem in 70 A.D. by Titus. Perhaps such an application can be made, but it would mean that the death referred to is only physical death and destruction. Such an interpretation comes far short of what Christ meant. He was primarily referring to the eternal judgment which will take place in the future. Wrath will come upon all rejectors to the uttermost (1 Th.2:15-16). This is a parable, so the reference to armies and the burned city is parabolic language. Israel had the privilege of attending the Great Marriage Feast of God's only Son, but the people of Israel abused their privilege by rejecting the invitation and killing the messengers of the King. They have, therefore, lost their witness as God's people and are to be judged eternally just as all rejectors of God's invitation are to be judged.

Note the words, "They which were bidden were not worthy." They were not worthy to attend the Feast and wedding. And they shall not attend.

Thought 1. Note the two sins that bring the judgment of God upon our heads.
  (1) Ridiculing and abusing God's servants. Note that God "destroyed those murderers" (v.7), the people who had persecuted His messengers.
  (2) Rejecting God's invitation. Note the words: "not worthy." The thing that made them unworthy was rejecting God's most gracious invitation. It is the rejection of the invitation that caused their judgment, not the act of God. When we reject God, it is our rejection that causes us to be condemned. Rejection equals condemnation.

MATTHEW 22:1-14

"He that believeth on him is not condemned: but he that believeth not is condemned already, because he hath not believed in the name of the only begotten Son of God" (Jn.3:18).

"And now also the axe is laid unto the root of the trees: every tree therefore which bringeth not forth good fruit is hewn down, and cast into the fire" (Lu.3:9).

"And to you who are troubled rest with us, when the Lord Jesus shall be revealed from heaven with his mighty angels, in flaming fire taking vengeance on them that know not God, and that obey not the gospel of our Lord Jesus Christ: who shall be punished with everlasting destruction from the presence of the Lord, and from the glory of his power" (2 Th.1:7-9).

3 (22:8-10) **Invitation—Gentiles—Man**: God's invitation is now given to any and all. This is what is meant by the word *highways*. God's servants are to go out into the highways of the world to invite any and all to the Great Wedding Feast of His Son.

Note several things.

a. God's servants are to invite as many as they can find. The invitation is no longer just to the few. It is universal: to the Jew and Gentile, the rich and poor, the high and low, the free and slave, the moral and immoral, the religious and irreligious. Note an important point. Few, if any, out in the highway would ever expect an invitation to a King's wedding.

"Then Peter opened his mouth, and said, Of a truth I perceive that God is no respecter of persons: but in every nation he that feareth him, and worketh righteousness, is accepted with him" (Ac.10:34-35).

"For there is no difference between the Jew and the Greek: for the same Lord over all is rich unto all that call upon him" (Ro.10:12).

"Who will have all men to be saved, and to come unto the knowledge of the truth" (1 Ti.2:4).

b. God's servants are to invite both good and bad, that is, both the moral and thoughtful (for example, Cornelius, Ac.10:1f; the devout Greeks, Ac.17:4), and the immoral and irreligious (1 Co.6:9-11). This could also mean that some bad do presently accept the invitation, but never really dress for the occasion (vv.11-14). The visible church contains both bad and good (see Mt.13:1f).

"But go ye and learn what that meaneth, I will have mercy, and not sacrifice: for I am not come to call the righteous, but sinners to repentance" (Mt.9:13).

"For the Son of man is come to seek and to save that which was lost" (Lu.19:10).

c. God's servants are to fill the wedding with guests *from the highways*. God assures His Son: His wedding will have guests; but note, only as many as they can "find" (v.9), and only as many as they "found" (v.10).

"Come unto me, all ye that labour and are heavy laden, and I will give you rest" (Mt.11:28).

"And the Spirit and the bride say, Come. And let him that heareth say, Come. And let him that is athirst come. And whosoever will, let him take the water of life freely" (Re.22:17).

"Ho, every one that thirsteth, come ye to the waters, and he that hath no money; come ye, buy, and eat; yea, come, buy wine and milk without money and without price" (Is.55:1).

4 (22:11-14) **Judgment—Great Wedding Feast**: God's confrontation with the guests was a momentous occasion. However, note the emphasis of this parable. The emphasis was not on the joy and festivity of the Marriage Feast but on a guest who came improperly dressed for the occasion. A man tried to attend the wedding without the proper clothing. He was not clothed in the righteousness of Jesus Christ.

Christ said three things.

a. God entered the Feast to see the guests. Upon entering, He immediately saw the man without a wedding garment. The words "to see" (theasasthai) mean to view attentively; to carefully look over; to closely look upon and contemplate and inspect. The stress is upon the person who is seeing. He beholds and inspects. The idea is that God entered the banqueting feast *for the purpose* of looking over and inspecting the guests. He wanted to make sure everyone and everything was in order for His Son's great celebration. No one can be allowed to detract from His Son by being improperly dressed or clothed. (See notes and DEEPER STUDY # 2—*Righteousness*, Ro.13:14; note—2 Co.5:21. See DEEPER STUDY # 2, *Justification*—Ro.4:22; note—5:1.)

1) The guests did not know that the man lacked the proper garment, but the King did. The man deceived the other guests, but the King knew the kind of dress He had spelled out for all His guests to wear. And observe: the man was showing disrespect and dishonor by not following the King's request for proper dress.

2) He asked only one question, and He asked the question before the feast began: "Friend, why have you come not wearing a wedding garment?" He could not allow an eyesore to detract from the joyful occasion. He had to deal with the detraction. The man had been invited, and he was responsible for wearing a *proper* and *clean* garment (see Ep.4:24f; see Ep.4:1; Ph.1:27).

"For I say unto you, That except your righteousness shall exceed the righteousness of the scribes and Pharisees, ye shall in no case enter into the kingdom of heaven" (Mt.5:20).

"And that ye put on the new man, which after God is created in righteousness and true holiness" (Ep.4:24).

"Being filled with the fruits of righteousness, which are by Jesus Christ, unto the glory and praise of God" (Ph.1:11).

"And have put on the new man, which is renewed in knowledge after the image of him that created him" (Col.3:10).

MATTHEW 22:1-14

3) The man was speechless (ephimothe). The word means muzzled, muted, silenced, tongue-tied, closed-mouthed. He had no excuse. He stood guilty of disrespect and dishonor for wearing the wrong garment, a garment that was not right for a kingly occasion. The garment was unclean.

b. God judged the man who was not clothed properly. Note that God called His servants together. The *servants* (diakonois) were not the same servants who delivered the invitations. They were not the disciples (vv.3, 4) and preachers (vv.8, 10) of the Lord. They were the angelic guardians of heaven who minister to the Godhead (see Mt.13:41-43, 49-50). Three things were done.
 1) The man was bound hand and foot. The hand and foot are usually the bodily parts used by man to sin. The hands are bound so there is no resistance. The feet are bound so there is no escape. Whatever the King says is done in the Great Day of the Feast. No man can resist or flee.
 2) The man was taken away, out of the King's presence and out of the presence of His Son and of the other guests. He was not allowed to share in the joy and bounty of the occasion.
 3) He was cast into outer darkness, far, far away from everyone else. He was not only cut off from the sharing of the occasion but from ever seeing the occasion. Whatever light and brilliance there was in the Great Wedding Feast, he was cast into the *outer* regions of darkness, never to glimpse the light.

c. God calls many, but few are chosen. Christ had said this before (Mt.20:16). In the context of this parable, there were several calls of God to the Great Wedding Feast of His Son.
 1) There was God's call to the Jews, but few responded.
 2) There is God's call to the Gentiles, but few are responding.
 3) There is God's call to all those who enter in, but few wear the wedding garment. The only garment they have is that of hypocrisy and false profession.

What Christ was saying becomes clear if we look at the church and consider all who are in the church...
- There are those within the church who care more for the things and possessions of this world than they do for Christ.

 "And seek not ye what ye shall eat, or what ye shall drink, neither be ye of doubtful mind. For all these things do the nations of the world seek after: and your Father knoweth that ye have need of these things" (Lu.12:29-30).
 "For we brought nothing into this world, and it is certain we can carry nothing out. And having food and raiment let us be therewith content. But they that will be rich fall into temptation and a snare, and into many foolish and hurtful lusts, which drown men in destruction and perdition. For the love of money is the root of all evil: which while some coveted after, they have erred from the faith, and pierced themselves through with many sorrows....Charge them that are rich in this world, that they be not highminded, nor trust in uncertain riches, but in the living God, who giveth us richly all things to enjoy; that they do good, that they be rich in good works, ready to distribute, willing to communicate" (1 Ti.6:7-10, 17-18).

- There are those within the church who do not deny self nor sacrifice all they are and have to follow Christ (see note and DEEPER STUDY # 1—Lu.9:23).

 "And he said to them all, If any man will come after me, let him deny himself, and take up his cross daily, and follow me" (Lu.9:23).

- There are those within the church who are still conformed to the world.

 "And be not conformed to this world: but be ye transformed by the renewing of your mind, that ye may prove what is that good, and acceptable, and perfect, will of God" (Ro.12:2).

- There are those within the church who are careless in their conversation.

 "Neither filthiness, nor foolish talking, nor jesting, which are not convenient: but rather giving of thanks" (Ep.5:4).
 "But shun profane and vain babblings: for they will increase unto more ungodliness. And their word will eat as doth a canker: of whom is Hymenaeus and Philetus; who concerning the truth have erred, saying that the resurrection is past already; and overthrow the faith of some" (2 Ti.2:16-18).
 "For in many things we offend all. If any man offend not in word, the same is a perfect man, and able also to bridle the whole body....Even so the tongue is a little member, and boasteth great things. Behold, how great a matter a little fire kindleth! And the tongue is a fire, a world of iniquity: so is the tongue among our members, that it defileth the whole body, and setteth on fire the course of nature; and it is set on fire of hell. For every kind of beasts, and of birds, and of serpents, and of things in the sea, is tamed, and hath been tamed of mankind: but the tongue can no man tame; it is an unruly evil, full of deadly poison. Therewith bless we God, even the Father; and therewith curse we men, which are made after the similitude of God" (Js.3:2, 5-9).

- There are those within the church who demonstrate spirits other than the spirit of love.

 "Little children, yet a little while I am with you. Ye shall seek me: and as I said unto the Jews, Whither I go, ye cannot come; so now I say to you. A new commandment I give unto you, That ye love one another; as I have loved you, that ye also love one another" (Jn.13:33-34).

MATTHEW 22:1-14

- There are those within the church who live after the flesh instead of living for Christ.

   "Love not the world, neither the things that are in the world. If any man love the world, the love of the Father is not in him. For all that is in the world, the lust of the flesh, and the lust of the eyes, and the pride of life, is not of the Father, but is of the world" (1 Jn.2:15-16).

- There are those within the church who do not worship God consistently, either daily or weekly.

   "Not forsaking the assembling of ourselves together, as the manner of some is; but exhorting one another: and so much the more, as ye see the day approaching" (He.10:25).

- There are those within the church who profess Christ, but live hypocritical lives.

   "Therefore when thou doest thine alms, do not sound a trumpet before thee, as the hypocrites do in the synagogues and in the streets, that they may have glory of men. Verily I say unto you, They have their reward" (Mt.6:2).

The warning of Christ was clear and should cause thought and concern.

"Many are called, but few chosen" (Mt.22:14; 20:16).
"Many, I say unto you, will seek to enter in, and shall not be able" (Lu.13:24).
"Strait is the gate, and narrow is the way, which leadeth unto life, and few there be that find it" (Mt.7:14).
"Not every one that saith unto me, Lord, Lord, shall enter into the kingdom of heaven; but he that doeth the will of my Father which is in heaven" (Mt.7:21).

Thought 1. The Lord walks among the churches. He knows how much or how little we work, labor, endure, and love (Re.2:1-2).

Thought 2. Note that God in particular sees the hypocrite. The hypocrite stands out like a cancerous sore in God's eyes, and God is forced to treat the hypocrite as the master physician treats a cancerous sore.

Thought 3. The Great Feast Day is first of all a Great Inspection Day. Before God presents us to Christ, He is going to cast out all who do not wear the garment of righteousness (see outline and notes—1 Co.3:10-17).

Thought 4. The wedding garment which the man lacked was righteousness. The man did not possess the righteousness of Christ nor did he live righteously (see note—Mt.5:6).

(1) The man had not trusted the righteousness of Christ to make him acceptable to God. (See note, *Justification*—Ro.5:1 for more discussion.)

   "For they being ignorant of God's righteousness, and going about to establish their own righteousness, have not submitted themselves unto the righteousness of God. For Christ is the end of the law for righteousness to every one that believeth" (Ro.10:3-4).

   "For he hath made him to be sin for us, who knew no sin; that we might be made the righteousness of God in him" (2 Co.5:21).

(2) The man had not lived a moral and self-denying life (see note—Lu.9:23). He was not what he had professed to be.

   "And he said to them all, If any man will come after me, let him deny himself, and take up his cross daily, and follow me" (Lu.9:23).

DEEPER STUDY # 1
(22:13) **Outer darkness**: see note—Mt.8:12 for discussion.

DEEPER STUDY # 2
(22:13) **Weeping**: see note—Mt.8:12 for discussion.

DEEPER STUDY # 3
(22:13) **Gnashing of Teeth**: see note—Mt.8:12 for discussion.

MATTHEW 22:15-22

	H. The Question About God & Caesar: The Two Citizenships, 22:15-22 (Mk 12:13-17; Lu 20:20-26)	18 But Jesus perceived their wickedness, and said, Why tempt ye me, *ye* hypocrites? 19 Show me the tribute money. And they brought unto him a penny. 20 And he saith unto them, Whose *is* this image and superscription? 21 They say unto him, Caesar's. Then saith he unto them, Render therefore unto Caesar the things which are Caesar's; and unto God the things that are God's. 22 When they had heard *these words,* they marvelled, and left him, and went their way.	**3. The truth: There are two citizenships** a. Christ sees through false concepts & evil motives b. An earthly citizenship: There are things that belong to Caesar c. A heavenly citizenship: There are things that belong to God
1. The false concepts of citizenship a. Religion is supreme: The Pharisees^{DS1} b. The state is supreme: The Herodians^{DS2} **2. The sins common to a flawed view of citizenship** a. Selfish ambition: Leads to compromise b. Deception: Leads to insincere flattery & destruction c. Closed-mindedness & obstinate unbelief: Leads to the rejection of truth & self-condemnation^{DS3}	15 Then went the Pharisees, and took counsel how they might entangle him in *his* talk. 16 And they sent out unto him their disciples with the Herodians, saying, Master, we know that thou art true, and teachest the way of God in truth, neither carest thou for any *man*: for thou regardest not the person of men. 17 Tell us therefore, What thinkest thou? Is it lawful to give tribute unto Caesar, or not?		

DIVISION XIV

THE MESSIAH'S LAST WEEK: HIS CLAIM CHALLENGED AND REJECTED, 21:1–23:39

H. The Question About God and Caesar: The Two Citizenships, 22:15-22

(22:15-22) **Introduction**: this is the second challenge or attack by the leaders against Christ. The words "took council" indicate that the ruling body of the Jews, the Sanhedrin, held an official meeting. They plotted how they might deal with this man who was claiming to be the Messiah. They feared Christ, for He was gathering the loyalty of the people so strongly around Himself.

Their plot was to ask Him a question about a person's citizenship. The question was supposed to "entangle him in his talk" (v.15); that is, it was supposed to be impossible for Christ to answer without discrediting Himself either with the people or with the Roman authorities. If He discredited Himself with the people, they would react and desert Him; if He discredited Himself with the Romans, they would arrest Him.

Christ *is* the Messiah, the Son of God Himself; therefore, He saw through their plot. Christ used the occasion to teach the truth about citizenship, a truth which was both astounding and earth-shaking to the people of that day—earth-shaking because the Jews believed that the loyalty of a citizen belonged only to God, and the rest of the world believed that loyalty belonged to the ruling monarch of their territory.

Christ astounded the world of His day by declaring there was an earthly, physical citizenship to which some things are to be given; and there was a spiritual, heavenly citizenship to which some things are to be given.

1. The false concepts of citizenship (vv.15-16).
    a. Religion is supreme: the Pharisees.
    b. The state is supreme: the Herodians.
2. The sins common to a flawed view of citizenship (vv.16-17).
    a. Selfish ambition: leads to compromise.
    b. Deception: leads to false flattery and destruction.
    c. A closed mind and obstinate unbelief: Leads to the rejection of truth and self-condemnation
3. The truth: there are two citizenships (vv.18-22).
    a. Christ sees through false concepts and evil motives.
    b. An earthly citizenship: There are things which belong to Caesar
    c. A heavenly citizenship: There are things which belong to God

1 (22:15-16) **Citizenship**: these two false concepts of citizenship are seen in the Pharisees and Herodians. However, it must be remembered, the world did not know the concepts were false until this experience.

a. The first false concept is that *religion is supreme*. This is seen in the view of the Pharisees (see Deeper Study # 3—Ac.23:8). They believed strongly in the heavenly world, so much so they believed that all obedience and loyalty were due God and God alone. In fact, all things on earth were due God. The state and all other power and authority were to be subject to religious rule. Therefore, they were strongly against paying taxes to a foreign king. Such was an infringement upon God's right.

b. The second false concept is that *the state is supreme*. This is seen in the view of the Herodians (see Deeper Study # 2—Mt.22:16 for discussion).

Picture the scene and how strange it was. The Pharisees held that religion was dominant over government, and they despised Roman authority and taxation. The Herodians held that government was dominant over religion; consequently, they would agree that taxes must be paid to Caesar rather than to God. The Herodians and the Pharisees were bitter enemies. To find them together was strange indeed, but their hatred of Jesus brought them together against One whom they considered a common enemy. (See notes—Mk.3:6; Deeper Study # 3—Ac.23:8.)

MATTHEW 22:15-22

Thought 1. The world's concept of citizenship is still the same as it was in Christ's day, despite His teaching. The vast majority of the world would be humanists and secularists, that is, worldly-minded citizens and unbelieving politicians. They would hold that the state is supreme. On the other hand, there would be some who would hold that religion is supreme and is to dominate the state. However, the position of religious supremacy is very difficult to practice in an educated and industrialized society. To a large degree, it can be held only theoretically.

"For all flesh is as grass, and all the glory of man as the flower of grass. The grass withereth, and the flower thereof falleth away" (1 Pe.1:24).

"For when he dieth he shall carry nothing away: his glory shall not descend after him" (Ps.49:17).

"Therefore hell hath enlarged herself, and opened her mouth without measure: and their glory, and their multitude, and their pomp, and he that rejoiceth, shall descend into it" (Is.5:14).

"Hear the word of the LORD, ye that tremble at his word; Your brethren that hated you, that cast you out for my name's sake, said, Let the LORD be glorified: but he shall appear to your joy, and they shall be ashamed" (Is.66:5).

"Also, thou son of man, shall it not be in the day when I take from them their strength, the joy of their glory, the desire of their eyes, and that whereupon they set their minds, their sons and their daughters" (Eze.24:25).

"As they were increased, so they sinned against me: therefore will I change their glory into shame" (Ho.4:7).

DEEPER STUDY # 1
(22:15) **Pharisees**: see DEEPER STUDY # 3—Ac.23:8.

DEEPER STUDY # 2
(22:16) **Herodians**: the Herodians were not a religious party but a political party of Herod, the King of Galilee. They were supportive of Rome, compromising wherever they could in order to preserve their own power and influence. They had compromised to such a point that they gave some degree of consent to pagan temples. Religiously, they were mainly Sadducees who gave their first loyalty to the state (see DEEPER STUDY # 2—Acts 23:8). Thus, they opposed all Messianic claims because of the disturbance the claims caused among the people. They would agree that taxes must be paid to Caesar rather than to God.

---

2 (22:16-17) **Citizenship**: there are sins that are often committed by those who hold a flawed view of citizenship. Some of these sins are seen in the plot of the Pharisees and Herodians against Christ.

a. There is *selfish ambition,* which often leads to compromise and intrigue. Nothing could have been more surprising than to see the Pharisees and Herodians working together. They stood diametrically opposed to one another. The Pharisees thought the Herodians no better than the heathen doomed for hell, yet they were seen working with the Herodians against Christ. What was it that brought them together? Selfish ambition. They feared the loss of their position, influence, power, wealth, and security (see notes—Mt.12:1-8; note and DEEPER STUDY # 1—12:10; note—15:1-20; DEEPER STUDY # 2—15:6-9. These notes will help considerably in understanding why the rulers feared Christ so much.) A man who lives for this world will become a bedfellow with almost anyone to protect his security. The degree or strange appearance of the compromise will seldom matter.

The depth of the sin in selfish ambition is also seen here. The primary plotters were religious leaders; and they were not only willing to plot evil, they were trying to cause a man, Christ Himself, to be put to death. Just how evil government and religion can be in their ambition is clearly seen in this passage.

b. There is *deception,* which usually leads to insincere flattery and destruction. This is seen in two facts.
   1) The Pharisees themselves did not go to Christ. They sent "their disciples with the Herodians." The disciples were learners or students who would actually be seeking the answer to such a question themselves. The Herodians were along to give the appearance that the disciples had asked them first, but the disciples were not satisfied with their answer. It would seem that the disciples of the Pharisees wanted to know what Christ, One who claimed to be the Messiah, would answer. Thus, Christ would think the question was the legitimate question of a student, never suspecting a plot to entrap Him.
   2) The lowest kind of deception is seen in the insincere words of flattery that were used in approaching Christ.
      ⇒ "Master...
      ⇒ "We know that thou art true...
      ⇒ "And teachest the way of God in truth...
      ⇒ "Neither carest thou for any man...
      ⇒ "...for thou regardest not the person of men."

Note that everything they said about Christ was true.
   ⇒ He was Master: a rabbi, a teacher. He was even more: He was the Master and Lord of the universe.
   ⇒ He was true or truthful: a teacher from God. (Contrast their hypocritical approach with the sincerity of Nicodemus, Jn.3:2.)
   ⇒ He did teach the way of God: how a man is to live and behave if he wishes to please God.
   ⇒ He did not care what men said about Him: it did not influence Him or His action.
   ⇒ He did not regard man's person: show partiality or favoritism.

The problem is that they did not mean what they were professing, not in their hearts. What they were professing about Him was coming from an evil motive. They wanted to use Him to secure their own selfish purposes. In the end, they were successful; they were able to do what they were plotting and to have Him destroyed. As always, deception destroys that which is truthful and strong and lovely.

"For thy mouth uttereth thine iniquity, and thou choosest the tongue of the crafty" (Jb.15:5).
"For there is no faithfulness in their mouth; their inward part is very wickedness; their throat is an open sepulcher; they flatter with their tongue" (Ps.5:9).
"A man shall not be established by wickedness: but the root of the righteous shall not be moved" (Pr.12:3).
"A man that flattereth his neighbor spreadeth a net for his feet" (Pr.29:5).

c. There is *close-mindedness and obstinate unbelief,* which leads to rejection of the truth and self-condemnation. The question asked of Christ was simple: "Is it lawful to give tribute to Caesar, or not?"
⇒ The Pharisees, sincere Jewish religionists, would shout, "No."
⇒ The Herodians (and those securing position and wealth by Roman rule) would say, "Yes."

Standing there, the questioners thought they had entrapped Christ. If He said, "No, taxes should not be paid to Caesar," then the authorities would arrest and remove Him. The people would then know that His claim to Messiahship was false.

If He said, "Yes, taxes should be paid to Caesar," then He would be denying the Sovereignty of God; and the people, who strongly opposed Roman rule and taxes, would rise up against Him. Both the Pharisees and Herodians were close-minded. They saw nothing beyond themselves and the threat to their position and wealth. They were steeped in obstinate unbelief. Thus, they rejected the truth; and, as results from all rejection of the truth, they condemned themselves (see Jn.3:18-21).

Thought 1. Selfish ambition can, and too often does, penetrate the very heart of those who are called to serve. The halls of government and the sanctity of religion are not exempt. Regardless of who a man is, he can crave and be corrupted by position, influence, power, wealth, and security.

Thought 2. Too many will compromise anything to hang on to their earthly possessions.

Thought 3. Any man who loves the things of this world will turn away from Jesus, and any man who feels threatened by Jesus and His claims will react against Jesus (1 Jn.2:15-16).

Thought 4. Note the testimony Jesus had even among His enemies. He was true, teaching the way of God, self-denying and courageous, and completely impartial toward others. Knowing and professing the truth about Jesus is not enough. Those who opposed Christ knew the truth about Him. They were just not willing to surrender to the truth.

Thought 5. Obstinate unbelief, pride, and haughtiness will cause us to be condemned by the Lord. (See DEEPER STUDY #4—Mt.12:24; note—12:31-32 for a discussion of their obstinate unbelief.)

DEEPER STUDY # 3
(22:17) **Tribute—Tax**: the tax asked about is the poll tax. It was a tax that had to be paid by every person between the ages of twelve or fourteen to sixty-five. The poll tax amounted to about one day's wage in that time (see DEEPER STUDY # 1—Ro.13:6).

---

3 (22:18-22) **Citizenship**: the truth about citizenship. A man has two citizenships. A man is a citizen of this world; this is clearly evident. Therefore, he owes to the earthly powers what belongs to them. But a man is also a citizen of heaven, of the spiritual world; therefore, he owes to God what belongs to Him.
Note three things.

a. Christ saw through the false concepts of these men. He was the Son of God, so He naturally knew that their view of citizenship was flawed. Moreover, as the Son of God, He also saw that they had an evil motive.
Christ was pointed and forceful: "Why tempt ye me, ye hypocrites?" He knew their hearts...
• their selfish ambition with every act of compromise and intrigue.
• their deception with all the flattery and destructive poison of their tongues.
• their close-mindedness and obstinate unbelief that led them to reject Him and to condemn themselves.

Note the words *their wickedness* and *ye hypocrites* (v.18). They were wicked and they were hypocrites. They were pretending something that was not so.
⇒ They were pretending to be something they were not.
⇒ They were pretending to seek the truth when they were not really after the truth.
⇒ They were pretending to honor Him when they really did not.

b. There is something which belongs to Caesar: an earthly citizenship. Christ was brilliant and brief as He dealt with the Pharisees and their false concept of citizenship. "Show me the tribute money...Whose is this image and superscription," He simply asked.
Note two things.
1) He forced the Pharisees (religion is supreme concept) to admit that some things belonged to an earthly power. The image was Caesar's; the superscription was Caesar's; and the coin had been made or coined by Caesar's government. Therefore, the coin was Caesar's if Caesar said it was due him. The point was clear: since the religionists, as citizens, *used what was owned and provided by Caesar,* then they owed to Caesar what was due him. Christ said strikingly, "Render therefore unto Caesar the things that are Caesar's."

2) He revealed a very important truth for believers of all time: they *have a double citizenship*. They are citizens of heaven, yes, but they are also citizens of this world. They have an obligation to the government under which they live. They receive the benefits of government just as *the worldly-minded* do: for example, roads, sewage, water, protection, public transportation, and on and on. Therefore, believers are to pay their due share. (See note—Ro.13:1-7. This note is a thorough discussion of citizenship.)

"Let every soul be subject unto the higher powers. For there is no power but of God: the powers that be are ordained of God" (Ro.13:1).

"Notwithstanding, lest we should offend them, go thou to the sea, and cast an hook, and take up the fish that first cometh up; and when thou hast opened his mouth, thou shalt find a piece of money: that take, and give unto them for me and thee" (Mt.17:27).

"Put them in mind to be subject to principalities and powers, to obey magistrates, to be ready to every good work" (Tit.3:1).

"Submit yourselves to every ordinance of man for the Lord's sake: whether it be to the king, as supreme; or unto governors, as unto them that are sent by him for the punishment of evildoers, and for the praise of them that do well. For so is the will of God, that with well doing ye may put to silence the ignorance of foolish men" (1 Pe.2:13-15; see 1 Pe.2:17).

"And whosoever will not do the law of thy God, and the law of the king, let judgment be executed speedily upon him, whether it be unto death, or to banishment, or to confiscation of goods, or to imprisonment" (Ezr.7:26).

"I counsel thee to keep the king's commandment, and that in regard of the oath of God" (Ec.8:2).

c. There is something which belongs to God: a heavenly citizenship. Christ was just as brilliant in dealing with the Herodians and their false concept of citizenship as He had been with the Pharisees. The Herodians not only subjected religion to the state, but they were worldly minded and denied much of the supernatural, including life after death and the spiritual dimension of being.

Note two things.

1) Christ declared unequivocally to the Herodians: there is a spiritual world. God is; God exists, and there are some things which belong to God. "Render therefore...unto God the things that are God's." Again, the point is clear. Since the Herodians (the state is supreme concept) as citizens of the world and of life itself, used what was owned and provided by God, then they owed God what was due Him.

2) Christ revealed a very important truth to all men. They are beings of God as well as of this world, spiritual as well as physical beings. Therefore, they are responsible to live as citizens of God as well as citizens of this world. All men have received much from God:

⇒ life that was made to exist with God forever; therefore man owes God his life.
⇒ a spirit that can be "born again" and live a self-denying life of love, joy, and peace for the sake of all men everywhere (Ga.5:22-23).
⇒ a mind and body that have the power to enjoy the aesthetic beauty of the earth, learning to reason and produce for the betterment and service of all mankind.

All men receive these benefits and many more from God. Therefore, they are to pay their due share to God.

"But seek ye first the kingdom of God, and his righteousness; and all these things shall be added unto you" (Mt.6:33).

"And he said to them all, If any man will come after me, let him deny himself, and take up his cross daily, and follow me" (Lu.9:23).

"I beseech you therefore, brethren, by the mercies of God, that ye present your bodies a living sacrifice, holy, acceptable unto God, which is your reasonable service. And be not conformed to this world: but be ye transformed by the renewing of your mind, that ye may prove what is that good, and acceptable, and perfect, will of God" (Ro.12:1-2).

"What? know ye not that your body is the temple of the Holy Ghost which is in you, which ye have of God, and ye are not your own? For ye are bought with a price: therefore glorify God in your body, and in your spirit, which are God's" (1 Co.6:19-20).

"And ye shall serve the LORD your God, and he shall bless thy bread, and thy water; and I will take sickness away from the midst of thee" (Ex.23:25).

"But thou shalt remember the LORD thy God: for it is he that giveth thee power to get wealth, that he may establish his covenant which he sware unto thy fathers, as it is this day" (De.8:18).

"And it shall come to pass, if ye shall hearken diligently unto my commandments which I command you this day, to love the LORD your God, and to serve him with all your heart and with all your soul, that I will give you the rain of your land in his due season, the first rain and the latter rain, that thou mayest gather in thy corn, and thy wine, and thine oil. And I will send grass in thy fields for thy cattle, that thou mayest eat and be full" (De.11:13-15).

Thought 1. See notes—Ro.13:1-7; 13:8-10; 1 Pe.2:13-17. These notes are sufficient to stir thoughts for application. One may also wish to refer to the Master Subject Index for a complete study on citizenship.

Thought 2. The truth that Christ covers in this passage is just what He says: there are two citizenships—an earthly and a heavenly citizenship. A man is to be a good citizen of both.

"Fear God. Honor the King" (1 Pe.2:17).

MATTHEW 22:23-33

1. The Sadducees tried to discredit Christ
2. The resurrection was denied & scoffed at
  a. Moses' law: The Levirate law or law of the brother-in-law
    1) Was to marry the wife of a dead brother
    2) Purpose: To carry on the family & property
  b. The logical situation: A childless widow married seven brothers
  c. The logical question suppos-
	I. The Question About the Resurrection: The Resurrection Denied, yet Proven, 22:23-33
	(Mk 12:18-27; Lu 20:27-38)
	
	23 The same day came to him the Sadducees, which say that there is no resurrection, and asked him,
	24 Saying, Master, Moses said, If a man die, having no children, his brother shall marry his wife, and raise up seed unto his brother.
	25 Now there were with us seven brethren: and the first, when he had married a wife, deceased, and, having no issue, left his wife unto his brother:
	26 Likewise the second also, and the third, unto the seventh.
	27 And last of all the woman
		died also.
		28 Therefore in the resurrection whose wife shall she be of the seven? for they all had her.
		29 Jesus answered and said unto them, Ye do err, not knowing the scriptures, nor the power of God.
		30 For in the resurrection they neither marry, nor are given in marriage, but are as the angels of God in heaven.
		31 But as touching the resurrection of the dead, have ye not read that which was spoken unto you by God, saying,
		32 I am the God of Abraham, and the God of Isaac, and the God of Jacob? God is not the God of the dead, but of the living.
		33 And when the multitude heard *this*, they were astonished at his doctrine.
			edly shows the absurdity of the resurrection: Whose wife is she in eternity?
			
			3. The resurrection was denied for two reasons
			  a. Did not know Scripture
			  b. Did not know the power of God
			4. The resurrection exceeds earthly relationships
			  a. Exceeds marital relationships
			  b. Will be equal to angels
			5. The resurrection has four basic proofs
			  a. God has spoken & revealed the resurrection in His Word
			  b. God is; God exists
			  c. God is the God of Abraham, Isaac, & Jacob
			  d. God is not the God of the dead but of the living
			6. The resurrection causes astonishment

DIVISION XIV

THE MESSIAH'S LAST WEEK: HIS CLAIM CHALLENGED AND REJECTED, 21:1–23:39

I. The Question About the Resurrection: The Resurrection Denied, yet Proven, 22:23-33

(22:23-33) **Introduction**: it was still Tuesday of the Lord's last week. (Note the statement, "the same day.") On this day, the challenges to His authority had been pressing in ever so heavily upon Him.

First, the chief priests and lay leaders (elders) had challenged His authority (see outline and notes—Mt.21:23-27). Christ had met the challengers head on and routed them. In so doing, His mind had been focused upon His death and Israel's rejection. The very thought that Israel, in whom God had put so much trust, was failing God by putting His Son to death was bound to be ripping out the heart of Christ (see outline and notes—Mt.21:33-46; 22:1-14).

Second, the Pharisees and Herodians (Herod's political party) had attempted to discredit Christ by pitting Him either against the government or the people (see outlines and notes—Mt.22:15-22). Again, Christ had met and routed His challengers; but again, the struggle had been tiring and pressuring, hard and heavy.

Now, for a third time, the Lord was confronted and challenged; and again, it was a different group who tried to outargue and discredit Him. His challengers were the Sadducees, the religious and political liberals of the day. As Matthew pointed out, "[They] say that there is no resurrection" (v.23). Luke added, "The Sadducees say there is no resurrection, neither angel, nor spirit" (see Deeper Study # 3—Mt.16:12; Deeper Study # 2—Ac.23:8). Their liberal position caused two things.

1. It caused them to stumble at the spiritual and supernatural. They ridiculed and scorned both. In their minds, the teachings of Christ lacked philosophical analysis and natural or scientific proof; therefore, they were the teachings of an unthinking and illogical man.

2. Their liberal position caused them to feel threatened and to oppose Christ. The people were flocking to Christ and soaking up His teachings. This meant the Sadducees were losing their grip on the people; their position and wealth were being jeopardized. Therefore, they were compelled to attack and discredit Him before the people.

It was their liberal belief—their denial of the spirit and of a spiritual world, of life after death and of the resurrection—that they used to attack Christ.
1. The Sadducees tried to discredit Christ (v.23).
2. The resurrection was denied and scoffed at (vv.23-28).
3. The resurrection was denied for two reasons (v.29).
4. The resurrection exceeds earthly relationships (v.30).
5. The resurrection has four basic proofs (vv.31-32).
6. The resurrection causes astonishment (v.33).

1 (22:23) **Sadducees**: this sect had already been seen on two other occasions. They had already opposed John the Baptist (Mt.3:7f) and Christ (Mt.16:1-12. See Deeper Study # 3—Mt.16:12; Deeper Study # 2—Ac.23:8.)

MATTHEW 22:23-33

2 (22:23-28) **Resurrection—Sadducees**: the resurrection was denied and scoffed at by the Sadducees. Down through the centuries many liberal-minded men have continued in their steps (see 1 Co.15:12-58; 2 Pe.3:3-18). Note the argument of the Sadducees.

a. They used Moses' law, the levirate law, as the basis of their argument (De.25:5-6). When a husband died without a son, the levirate law said that his brother was to marry his wife and bear a son. By law, the son was considered the firstborn son of the deceased brother. This assured two things: (1) that the family name continued, and (2) that the property holdings were kept in the family. This was a law that had been given to help preserve and to enlarge the nation of Israel (see Ru.4:5).

b. The Sadducees then suggested a logical situation that could have arisen. Note the words, "There were *with us* seven brethren." The first brother married, but he died before bearing children. Each of the other brothers obeyed the law, but each died before bearing a child. Finally, the woman died also.

c. The logical question was now asked, the question which in the Sadducees' mind showed the absurdity of the resurrection. They asked, "Whose wife shall she be in eternity?" Note three things by reading through verses 23-28 several times.

1) The situation was logical; but the spirit of questioning was cold and coarse, egotistical and unbelieving, regrettable and revolting. The unbelievers's spirit is often self-incriminating and self-condemning.
2) The argument was thought to be irrefutable by the Sadducees. They believed it pointed out just how foolish the idea of another world was to the thinking person.
3) The Sadducees were thinking that the spiritual world would be just like the physical world, that it would be nothing more than a continuation of this world, both in *its nature and in its relationships*.

As this point is closed, a picture of what the Scripture says about the natural man is clearly seen.

> "But the natural man receiveth not the things of the Spirit of God: for they are foolishness unto him: neither can he know them, because they are spiritually discerned" (1 Co.2:14).

Thought 1. Every generation has its Sadducees, those who are liberal minded and who scoff at the idea of the resurrection and of a spiritual world. God knows this. He has always known that many would scoff and ridicule, so He has dealt with the issue in at least two extensive passages of Scripture (1 Co.15:12-58; 2 Pe.3:3-18).

> "Now if Christ be preached that he rose from the dead, how say some among you that there is no resurrection of the dead?" (1 Co.15:12).
>
> "Knowing this first, that there shall come in the last days scoffers, walking after their own lusts, And saying, Where is the promise of his coming? for since the fathers fell asleep, all things continue as they were from the beginning of the creation" (2 Pe.3:3-4).

Thought 2. Today's arguments against the existence of a spiritual world and resurrection arise from...
- logical and rational thought
- philosophical positions
- a natural and scientific hypothesis
- humanistic beliefs
- an unwillingness to change one's lifestyle
- a fear of rejection and ridicule by one's peers
- a refusal to admit that one's former position was wrong

Thought 3. Most unbelief in the spiritual world arises not from a thinking position, but from a worldly position. Few study through both the natural and spiritual positions. Most just love the world and the things of the world so much that they wish to reject the restraints which the spiritual world puts upon them.

3 (22:29) **Resurrection—Spiritual World—Scripture—God, Power of**: Christ said very pointedly to the Sadducees and to all who followed their liberal position: "You are in error. You deny the resurrection for two erroneous reasons."

a. "You do not know the Scriptures." The Scriptures are plain and clear. They leave no doubt that there is a spiritual world—that there is to be a resurrection into the spiritual world or spiritual dimension of being.

> "For I know that my Redeemer liveth, and that he shall stand at the latter day upon the earth: and though after my skin worms destroy this body, yet in my flesh shall I see God: whom I shall see for myself, and mine eyes shall behold, and not another; though my reins be consumed within me" (Jb.19:25-27).
>
> "Thy dead men shall live; together with my dead body shall they arise. Awake and sing, ye that dwell in dust: for thy dew is as the dew of herbs, and the earth shall cast out the dead" (Is.26:19).
>
> "And many of them that sleep in the dust of the earth shall awake, some to everlasting life, and some to shame and everlasting contempt" (Da.12:2).
>
> "Verily, verily, I say unto you, The hour is coming, and now is, when the dead shall hear the voice of the Son of God: and they that hear shall live" (Jn.5:25).
>
> "Marvel not at this: for the hour is coming, in the which all that are in the graves shall hear his voice, and shall come forth; they that have done good, unto the resurrection of life; and they that have done evil, unto the resurrection of damnation" (Jn.5:28-29).

MATTHEW 22:23-33

"And this is the will of him that sent me, that every one which seeth the Son, and believeth on him, may have everlasting life: and I will raise him up at the last day" (Jn.6:40).

"Jesus said unto her, I am the resurrection, and the life: he that believeth in me, though he were dead, yet shall he live" (Jn.11:25).

"And have hope toward God, which they themselves also allow, that there shall be a resurrection of the dead, both of the just and unjust" (Ac.24:15).

"But if the Spirit of him that raised up Jesus from the dead dwell in you, he that raised up Christ from the dead shall also quicken your mortal bodies by his Spirit that dwelleth in you" (Ro.8:11).

"For as in Adam all die, even so in Christ shall all be made alive" (1 Co.15:22).

"Knowing that he which raised up the Lord Jesus shall raise up us also by Jesus, and shall present us with you" (2 Co.4:14).

"For the Lord himself shall descend from heaven with a shout, with the voice of the archangel, and with the trump of God: and the dead in Christ shall rise first" (1 Th.4:16).

"But God will redeem my soul from the power of the grave: for he shall receive me" (Ps.49:15; see Ps.71:20; Ho.13:14).

Thought 1. There are three reasons why a person may not know the Scriptures.
(1) He simply has not *studied* the Scriptures, not *really studied*.
(2) He does not believe the Scriptures. He rejects the Scripture as God's Word.
(3) He does not take the Scriptures for what they say. He spiritualizes or allegorizes them.

b. "You do not know the power of God." There are three reasons why a person does not know the power of God.
1) He is ignorant of God. He knows nothing about God and seldom, if ever, gives any thought to God and His power.
2) He does not believe in God or His power. He refuses to acknowledge God's eternal power and Godhead seen in creation and goes about *creating* gods of his own (both mental and physical images). (See Ro.1:20-32.) He refuses to acknowledge the picture of nature that clearly illustrates the resurrection:

   "**Thou fool, that which thou sowest is not quickened, except it die: and that which thou sowest, thou sowest not that body that shall be, but bare grain, it may chance of wheat, or of some other grain: But God giveth it a body as it hath pleased him**" (1 Co.15:36-38).

3) He believes, but his belief in God and His power is weak. He cannot picture much happening beyond the physical world and the power of natural laws.

Thought 1. The idea of a spiritual world is perplexing to the natural man. Just imagine! While we are sitting here surrounded by all that we see...
- there is another world, a spiritual world, an unseen spiritual dimension of being that actually exists.
- there is a spirit, the real life within our bodies, that is destined to exist forever.
- there is to be a resurrection of all the dead bodies that have been lying scattered and decaying in the graves for ages and ages. God shall *call* all the parts of decayed bodies back together again, no matter where they are scattered, and these bodies shall be perfected and glorified to live and work again. How can He do such a thing? By the Word of His power *as God*.

Thought 2. When we really think about the facts of the resurrection, two confessions have to be made by every man, believer and unbeliever.
(1) The natural man, that is man within himself and his world, *can never know* about a spiritual world. He is bound by the physical and material world of which he is a part. He can only think and guess and theorize that a spiritual world exists and speculate on details such as a resurrection. Man cannot, while living in this world, penetrate the spiritual world with his body to scientifically prove the existence of the spiritual world.
(2) God alone can reveal the reality of the spiritual dimension and the fact that a resurrection will take place. Such can be known and experienced only by the power of God. No man has the power to bring it about. If a resurrection is to take place, God's power will have to do it.

Thought 3. By its very nature of permanence, the spiritual world supersedes and becomes much more important than the physical and dying world. Therefore, the spiritual world demands that man give preeminence to it. It is these demands that man rebels against. Therefore...
- a scientific society questions what it cannot prove
- a materialistic society questions what it cannot use to satisfy its lust for more
- an immoral society questions what it fears will correct its behavior
- a worldly society questions what it fears will restrain its pleasure
- a power society questions what it fears will loosen its grip and lessen its authority

4 (22:30) **Resurrection—Spiritual Dimension**: Christ said that the resurrection exceeded earthly relationships. The Sadducees did not know the Scriptures nor the power of God. When they thought of being resurrected into another world, they simply saw life continuing on as it does now. They pictured heaven as being just a continuation of this world. Very simply, they could not conceive that the qualities of life would be changed and that man would be given a totally new environment in which to live.

Christ said two things.

a. Future life and relationships shall exceed earthly relationships—even the bond of marital relationships. The strong union and bond of marriage will not be less, it will be greater and stronger.

b. Future life and relationships shall be equal to that experienced by the angels and God. This means at least two things. (Note: Christ had just admitted the existence of angels, refuting the disbelief of the liberal minded Sadducces.)

1) Heavenly life and relationships will be perfect. In heaven our relationships will not cease to be. They will be changed in that selfishness and sin will not affect our love and lives. Our love will be perfected; thus, we shall love everyone perfectly. A wife on this earth will not be loved as she was on this earth—imperfectly. She shall be loved more and loved perfectly. Everyone will love everyone else perfectly. God will change all relationships into perfection, even as the relationships between angels and God are perfected.

2) Heavenly life and relationships shall be eternal. There will be no ending of relationships. A man and wife will always have the other to love. One shall not cease to be (die) before the other (as is the case now). Everyone will always have everyone else to love. God will change the brief time we have with each other now into an eternal relationship. We shall enjoy the presence of each other eternally, even as the relationship between angels and God is enjoyed eternally.

Thought 1. Two warnings must always be issued when thinking of heaven and eternal life.

(1) A person can *materialize* heaven and *humanize* eternal life; that is, we can conceive heaven to be nothing more than a *glorified* world and eternal life to be nothing more than physical life plus a little more. This was the mistake of the Sadducees and is often the concept pictured by liberal thinkers when they hear about the resurrection.

(2) A person can *idealize* heaven and *allegorize* eternal life. We can think of heaven as little more than an ideal land for which we should seek and toward which we should direct our lives. And we can think of eternal life as little more than a utopian state of being, a utopian dream of an indefinite quality, or of floating around and being free of trouble and trials.

The teaching of Scripture or of God's revelation must always be kept in mind when thinking of heaven and eternal life. Scripture teaches that the very nature of things will be changed.

1. Heaven is said to be a spiritual dimension, a real world of being, and Scripture declares that the heavens and earth shall one day be transformed into that spiritual dimension of being. There will be a new heavens and earth, a perfect and eternal heavens and earth (2 Pe.3:3-13; Re.21:1, 5).

2. Eternal life is said to be life that shall exist forever in the spiritual dimension of being. The Scripture says:

> "So also is the resurrection of the dead. It is sown in corruption; it is raised in incorruption: It is sown in dishonour; it is raised in glory: it is sown in weakness; it is raised in power: It is sown a natural body: it is raised a spiritual body. There is a natural body, and there is a spiritual body" (1 Co.15:42-44. See 1 Th.5:13-18.)

> "As we have borne the image of the earthy, we shall also bear the image of the heavenly. Now this I say, brethren, that flesh and blood cannot inherit the kingdom of God; neither doth corruption inherit incorruption. Behold, I show you a mystery; We shall not all sleep, but we shall all be changed, in a moment, in the twinkling of an eye, at the last trump: for the trumpet shall sound, and the dead shall be raised incorruptible, and we shall be changed. For this corruptible must put on incorruption, and this mortal must put on immortality. So when this corruptible shall have put on incorruption, and this mortal shall have put on immortality, then shall be brought to pass the saying that is written, Death is swallowed up in victory" (1 Co.15:49-54).

(See notes and DEEPER STUDY # 1—Mt.19:28; DEEPER STUDY # 1—Jn.17:2-3; DEEPER STUDY # 1—2 Ti.4:18. See Jn.1:4.)

5 (22:31-32) **Resurrection**: Jesus said the resurrection had four basic proofs.

a. God had spoken and revealed the truth of the resurrection in His Word (see Jb.19:26; Eze.37:1f; Da.12:2). The Sadducees held only to the first five books of Moses as God's Word, that is, Genesis through Deuteronomy (see DEEPER STUDY # 2—Ac.23:8). Therefore, Christ used this Scripture to prove the resurrection.

Note three facts about what Christ said: "Have ye not *read* that which was spoken to you by God" (v.31).

1) Christ said that God had spoken to man; God had revealed the truth to man in the Scripture.
2) Christ said the Scripture *is* God's Word.
3) Christ questioned why they had not read what God had spoken. "Have ye not read" hints that they were without excuse. They should have read and understood; therefore, they should have known the truth of the resurrection (and all other truths) as God had revealed it.

b. God is; God exists. The fact that *God is* proves the resurrection. The Greek (ego eimi) means the self-existent, eternal One (see DEEPER STUDY # 1—Jn.6:20; 18:4-6).

> "I am the God...." (Mt.22:32).
> "He that cometh to God must believe that He is" (He.11:6).

Since God is, He possesses omnipotent power—power that is perfect and eternal. God can do anything, and He can do it perfectly and eternally. He can call the elements of a decayed body back together again and raise it up to live in the spiritual world both perfectly and eternally.

MATTHEW 22:23-33

Note carefully: the argument for *God's being* (living) is irrefutable. Note carefully the great passage in Ephesians dealing with the spiritual blessings that are ours in Christ: "We have obtained an inheritance...*that we should be*" (Ep.1:11-12).

The resurrection is a fact. It will be experienced by all men of all ages because *God is*. God has willed to give us an inheritance to *be*, that is, to live eternally with Him. We shall undergo a transformation of nature, a transformation of perfection and permanency. For this reason, we need to pay close attention to what Scripture says: "But without faith it is impossible to please him: for he that cometh to God must believe that *he [God] is*, and that he is a rewarder of them that diligently seek him" (He.11:6).

We must believe that God is, and that He is a rewarder of those who diligently seek after Him; that is, He rewards all who seek to live eternally with Him.

> "If by any means I might attain unto the resurrection of the dead" (Ph.3:11).

c. God is the God of Abraham, Isaac, and Jacob. Christ meant at least two things in this point.
  1) God's relationships are active relationships not inactive. God says, "I am the God of...," not "I was the God of...." His relationships with His people are continuous. They are maintained. God is eternal; therefore, He creates and maintains eternal, active relationships. God's people enter into the spiritual realm of His presence and actively relate to Him. The resurrection is a fact.
  2) God's relationships are good and rewarding. The patriarchs of old were promised rewards, personal rewards (see He.11:13-16). There has to be a resurrection if our relationship with God is good and rewarding. To die and be left dead as a decayed corpse is not good nor rewarding. Abraham, Isaac, and Jacob have a good and rewarding relationship with God. They are alive, more alive than they were while on earth, for they are now perfected and eternal. They are with God Himself. And so shall we be. The resur-rection is a fact.

d. God is not the God of the dead, but of the living. God is the God of Abraham, Isaac, and Jacob, not the God of dead, decayed corpses. When Moses wrote these words, the three patriarchs had been dead for many years. If they were dead, God was not their God. Since He was their God, they were alive, living in God's presence and living in relationship to Him, perfect and eternal. There is to be a resurrection.

> "For none of us liveth to himself, and no man dieth to himself. For whether we live, we live unto the Lord; and whether we die, we die unto the Lord: Whether we live therefore, or die, we are the Lord's. For to this end Christ both died, and rose, and revived, that he might be Lord both of the dead and living" (Ro.14:7-9).

Christ makes one point, and makes it very clearly: *since God is*, God is not the God of the dead, but of the living.

> "Why should it be thought a thing incredible with you, that God should raise the dead?" (Ac.26:8).
>
> "There shall be a resurrection of the dead, both of the just and unjust" (Ac.24:15).

Note what Scripture says about the resurrection (see notes—Mt.17:23; Acts 2:29-31; Col.3:1-4. See Related Subjects, General Subject Index.)

1. Note the emphatic statements of Christ:

> "[All that are in the graves] shall come forth; they that have done good, unto the resurrection of life; and they that have done evil, unto the resurrection of damnation" (Jn.5:29).
>
> "And this is the Father's will which hath sent me, that of all which he hath given me I should lose nothing, but should raise it up again at the last day. And this is the will of him that sent me, that every one which seeth the Son, and believeth on him, may have everlasting life: and I will raise him up at the last day...No man can come to me, except the Father which hath sent me draw him: and I will raise him up at the last day...Whoso eateth my flesh, and drinketh my blood, hath eternal life; and I will raise him up at the last day" (Jn.6:39-40, 44, 54).
>
> "Jesus said unto her, I am the resurrection, and the life: he that believeth in me, though he were dead, yet shall he live: And whosoever liveth and believeth in me shall never die. Believest thou this?" (Jn.11:25-26).

2. Note the personal testimony of Paul.

> "But when Paul perceived that the one part were Sadducees, and the other Pharisees, he cried out in the council, Men and brethren, I am a Pharisee, the son of a Pharisee: of the hope and resurrection of the dead I am called in question" (Ac.23:6).
>
> "But this I confess unto thee, that after the way which they call heresy, so worship I the God of my fathers, believing all things which are written in the law and in the prophets: And have hope toward God, which they themselves also allow, that there shall be a resurrection of the dead, both of the just and unjust...Touching the resurrection of the dead I am called in question by you this day" (Ac.24:14-15, 21).

3. Note the unquestionable teaching of Scripture.

> "For if we have been planted together in the likeness of his death, we shall be also in the likeness of his resurrection" (Ro.6:5).

"But if the Spirit of him that raised up Jesus from the dead dwell in you, he that raised up Christ from the dead shall also quicken your mortal bodies by his Spirit that dwelleth in you" (Ro.8:11).

"And God hath both raised up the Lord, and will also raise up us by his own power" (1 Co.6:14).

"Now if Christ be preached that he rose from the dead, how say some among you that there is no resurrection of the dead? But if there be no resurrection of the dead, then is Christ not risen: And if Christ be not risen, then is our preaching in vain, and your faith is also vain" (1 Co.15:12-14; see 1 Co.15:12-58).

"Knowing that he which raised up the Lord Jesus shall raise up us also by Jesus, and shall present us with you" (2 Co.4:14).

"If by any means I might attain unto the resurrection of the dead" (Ph.3:11).

"For the Lord himself shall descend from heaven with a shout, with the voice of the archangel, and with the trump of God: and the dead in Christ shall rise first: Then we which are alive and remain shall be caught up together with them in the clouds, to meet the Lord in the air: and so shall we ever be with the Lord. Wherefore comfort one another with these words" (1 Th.4:16-18).

"...others were tortured, not accepting deliverance; that they might obtain a better resurrection" (He.11:35).

"...This is the first resurrection. Blessed and holy is he that hath part in the first resurrection: on such the second death hath no power, but they shall be priests of God and of Christ, and shall reign with him a thousand years" (Re.20:5-6).

4. Note the reactions of men to the resurrection (see 2 Pe.3:3-18).

"And as they spake unto the people, the priests, and the captain of the temple, and the Sadducees, came upon them, Being grieved that they taught the people, and preached through Jesus the resurrection from the dead" (Ac.4:1-2).

"Then certain philosophers of the Epicureans, and of the Stoics, encountered him. And some said, What will this babbler say? other some, He seemeth to be a setter forth of strange gods: because he preached unto them Jesus, and the resurrection" (Ac.17:18).

"Now if Christ be preached that he rose from the dead, how say some among you that there is no resurrection of the dead?" (1 Co.15:12).

"But what things were gain to me, those I counted loss for Christ....If by any means I might attain unto the resurrection of the dead" (Ph.3:7, 11).

6 (22:33) **Resurrection**: the glorious hope of the resurrection not only caused amazement in Christ's day, it causes amazement today.

a. The believer is amazed that God would love him so much.
b. The unbeliever is amazed at such an idea as the resurrection, that anyone could believe such a thing.

MATTHEW 22:34-40

	J. The Question About the Great Commandment: A Study of Love, 22:34-40
	(Mk 12:28-34; Lu 10:25-37)
		great commandment in the law?
		37 Jesus said unto him, Thou shalt love the Lord thy God with all thy heart, and with all thy soul, and with all thy mind.
		38 This is the first and great commandment.
		39 And the second *is* like unto it, Thou shalt love thy neighbour as thyself.
		40 On these two commandments hang all the law and the prophets.
			Which is the greatest commandment?^{DS2}
			2. **First: Love God**^{DS3}
			  a. Love as your own God
			  b. Love with all your being: Your heart, soul, & mind^{DS4,5,6}
			  c. Love is man's chief duty
			3. **Second: Love your neighbor**^{DS7}
			  a. Love self
			  b. Love neighbor as self
			4. **The conclusion: Love includes & embraces all the commandments**

1. **The Pharisees plotted against Jesus**
  a. They gathered together
 	
  b. They appointed a brilliant lawyer, an expert in the law, to challenge Christ^{DS1}
 	
  c. They questioned Christ:
	34 But when the Pharisees had heard that he had put the Sadducees to silence, they were gathered together.
	35 Then one of them, *which was* a lawyer, asked *him a* question, tempting him, and saying,
	36 Master, which *is* the		

DIVISION XIV

THE MESSIAH'S LAST WEEK: HIS CLAIM CHALLENGED AND REJECTED, 21:1–23:39

J. The Question About the Great Commandment: A Study of Love, 22:34-40

(22:34-40) **Introduction—Jesus Christ, Challenged**: Jesus had just met His third group of challengers, the Sadducees. He had *silenced* and routed them. The Pharisees, the strict religionists of that day, heard about Christ's conquering His challengers again. In their minds, His threat to their security had increased. All three attempts to discredit Him had failed. They felt that they must somehow discredit Him before the people in order to break His hold on them. There was a very live possibility that the people might follow through with their proclaiming Him to be the Messiah by rising up against the Roman authorities. The responsibility for such action, of course, would lie at their feet as Jewish leaders; and they would be replaced as the ruling body of the Sanhedrin, losing their position, authority, esteem, and livelihood.

They met together to plan and plot again. This time they took a different approach. They had, over the last few hours, challenged Christ as a body of questioners; now they chose from among their body one who was most brilliant and versed in the law, a lawyer or a Scribe.

However, there was something about this brilliant lawyer that the others did not know. Apparently, his heart had been touched by Christ. There are two indications of this. First, Mark tells us that the man was present when Christ was "reasoning together" with the Sadducees (Mk.12:28), and he perceived "that [Christ] had answered them well." Second, at the conclusion of his own discussion with Christ, Christ said to the man, "Thou art not far from the kingdom of God" (Mk.12:34). This indicates that the lawyer had been in deep thought about Christ and was under conviction.

Something about Christ struck a chord within this man. His heart was touched and stirred rather deeply. True, he was being put forward by the official body to challenge Christ; but personally, the spirit, the wisdom, the self-consciousness, the authority—something about Christ when He was answering the Sadducees—had stirred his heart to wonder and to want to search more into Christ.

Christ used the occasion to teach man the greatest *provision* and *duty* of human life: love. Love will provide for every need man has; therefore, love is the greatest duty of man.

1. The Pharisees plotted against Jesus (vv.34-36).
2. First: love God (vv.37-38).
3. Second: love your neighbor (v.39).
4. The conclusion: love includes and embraces all the commandments (v.40).

1 (22:34-36) **Religionists**: the Pharisees plotted against Jesus. The word *"they"* seems to indicate that the Pharisees and Sadducees met together when the Pharisees heard about the Sadducees being *silenced* or routed by Christ. They met together in the council (Sanhedrin) to determine the next step to take (see note—Mt.22:34-40).

DEEPER STUDY # 1

(22:35) **Lawyer** (nomikos): a profession of laymen who studied, taught, interpreted, and dealt with the practical questions of Jewish law. They were a special group within the profession commonly called Scribes (see Mark 12:28). They functioned both in the court and synagogues (see Lu.7:30; 10:25; 11:45, 46, 52; 14:3; Tit.3:13). They apparently dealt more with the study and interpretation of the law.

DEEPER STUDY # 2

(22:36) **Commandment**: note the question, "Which is the great commandment in the law?" Through the years, Jewish teachers had set up six hundred commandments. No person could keep them all, so the question was often asked and discussed: Which commandment or commandments must be absolutely obeyed? Which ones are important and which ones are not? Can the failure to obey some be condoned or not? Which commandments are heavy and which are light? If a person keeps the greatest of the precepts, can he be excused for his failure to keep others (see Mt.19:16f)?

Note two things about the tendency to count some of God's laws important and some not.
1. This was the sin which James attacked.

> "For whosoever shall keep the whole law, and yet offend in one point, he is guilty of all" (Js.2:10).

2. Christ taught that some laws are all inclusive and broader than others.

> "Woe unto you, scribes and Pharisees, hypocrites! for ye pay tithe of mint and anise and cummin, and have omitted the weightier matters of the law, judgment, mercy, and faith: these ought ye to have done, and not to leave the other undone" (Mt.23:23).

The Pharisees were trying to turn the people against Jesus. People differed as to what the greatest commandment was. Some believed that it had to do with circumcision, others with sacrifices, and still others with the Sabbath. The Pharisees hoped that by stating His opinion, Christ would disturb the people who held a position different from His. He would thereby lose their following. There was the strong possibility that a man's giving his judgment would seem to be lessening the weight of other very important commandments.

Thought 1. All of God's laws are important—equally important. One is first and *weightier* only because it includes and embraces other laws. This means several things.
(1) We may think in terms of supreme laws and lesser laws—that if we keep the greater laws, we do not have to pay much attention to the lesser. We may think that if we break the lesser laws we can be excused, but such thinking is false.

> "For whosoever shall keep the whole law, and yet offend in one point, he is guilty of all" (Js.2:10).

(2) Just because we may deny the importance of some laws does not make them unimportant. Our unbelief and denial do not void the law, not a single one. They still condemn us. Each law, in the force of its pronouncement, strikes out at our violation. It condemns us—no matter how little value we may place upon it.

This is a common deception of man: unbelief makes a thing ineffective and voids it. A man thinks, "If I deny something, ignore it, refuse to accept it, push it out of my mind, it will not be, nor will it come to pass." Many treat God's Word and some commandments in this way, especially if they wish some sensual or stimulating pleasure. Too many conform their religion and their principles, their beliefs and the laws they obey to their behavior. They want the right to do as they wish, so they make all things fit their wishes, including their principles. They follow only the commandments that allow them to satisfy their desires, and because they obey some standards, they feel acceptable and secure.

Thought 2. This passage is a profitable passage for lawyers and for other professionals, in particular if they are open and honest as this man seems to have been. Just a passing thought—in the day of judgment it will be interesting to see if this lawyer is one of the converts mentioned in Acts 6:9.

[2] (22:37-38) **Commandment**: first, love God. Which is the great commandment in the law? (See De.6:5.) Christ's answer was powerful; it is an eye opener to people steeped in man-made religions.
  a. Love God: "Love the Lord *thy* God." Love God as *your* very own God. The word *your* is a personal relationship, not a distant relationship. God is not impersonal, far out in space someplace, distant and removed. God is personal, ever so close, and we are to be personally involved with God on a face-to-face basis. Note another fact: the command is to "love the Lord thy God." *Loving* God is an act that is alive and active, not dead and inactive. We are, therefore, to maintain a personal relationship with God that is alive and active.
  b. Love God with all your being. Christ breaks our being into three parts: the heart, the soul, and the mind (see DEEPER STUDY # 4,5,6—Mt.22:37).
  c. Love is man's chief duty. Man is responsible to maintain a loving relationship with God. Very practically, loving God involves the very same factors that loving a person involves (see outlines and notes—Ep.5:22-33).
    1) A loving relationship involves *commitment and loyalty*. True love does not allow lustful behavior with others. True love does not covet; it does not care for a carnal definition of love that allows fleshly acts and sensual relationships with others.
      True love is commitment and loyalty to one another. This is very significant. The first commandment deals with *commitment and loyalty*. God strikes out at the very core of man's carnal and fleshly behavior, at his tendency to define love in terms that allow him to satisfy his lust. God irrevocably says, "Thou shalt have no other gods" (Ex.20:3). God demands our total commitment and loyalty.
    2) A loving relationship involves *trust and respect* for the person loved. It is loving the person just for who he is. So it is when we love God. We love God because of Himself, because He is who He is. We love Him because...
      • He is the Creator and Sustainer of life.
      • He is the Savior and Redeemer of our souls.
      • He is the Lord and Owner of our lives.
    3) A loving relationship involves the *giving and surrendering* of oneself. The drive is to give oneself, to surrender oneself to the other, not to take and conquer. We are to so love God, to give and surrender ourselves to Him.
    4) A loving relationship involves *knowing and sharing*. The desire is to know and to share, learning, growing, working, and serving ever so closely together. We are to know and share with God, learning, growing, working, and serving ever so closely with Him

MATTHEW 22:34-40

Thought 1. The importance of a personal relationship with God cannot be overstated.
(1) It is the greatest, the sum and substance of all commandments.
(2) God demands that He be loved. It is His first commandment, and to love is both personal and active.
(3) The commandment to love God is given by Christ, the Son of God Himself.

Thought 2. A personal relationship can be maintained only through communication: we must talk to God and allow God to talk to us through prayer, His Word, and the presence of His Spirit.

Thought 3. A person's heart, soul, and mind are focused upon something: self, possessions, the world, the flesh, power, fame, a person. God demands that we focus our whole being upon Him.

DEEPER STUDY # 3
(22:37) **Love:** see De.6:5. See note—Jn.21:15-17.

DEEPER STUDY # 4
(22:37) **Heart:** the *seat* of man's affection and will (devotion). The heart attaches and focuses our will and devotion. The heart causes us to give either good things or bad things. The heart causes us to devote ourselves to either good or bad. Therefore, Christ says we are to love God "with all our heart." We are to focus our heart, our affection, and our will (devotion) upon God. We are to love God supremely.

"For where your treasure [object of affection] is, there will your heart be also" (Mt.6:21).
"...for out of the abundance of the heart the mouth speaketh. A good man out of the good treasure of the heart bringeth forth good things: and an evil man out of the evil treasure bringeth forth evil things" (Mt.12:34-35; see Mt.15:18-19).

DEEPER STUDY # 5
(22:37) **Soul** (psuche): the seat of man's breath and life or consciousness. The soul is the life of a man, the consciousness, the breath, the essence, the being of a man. The soul is the *animal life* of a man. The soul is the breath and consciousness that distinguishes man and other animals from vegetation. The world of vegetation lives and man and animals live, but there is a difference in their living. Man and animals are *breathing* and *conscious* beings. The essence of their being is breath and consciousness. They are living souls. This is clearly pointed out in the Hebrew language of Ge.1:20: "Let the waters bring forth abundantly '*living souls*' [nephesh] that hath life." The "living souls" that God created were different from the vegetation He had just created. The "living souls" were creatures (fish) that breathed and possessed consciousness.

Christ said we are to love God "with all our soul," that is, with all our life, our breath, our consciousness. We are to love God with all the breath and consciousness, all the life and awareness, we have.

DEEPER STUDY # 6
(22:37) **Mind:** the seat of reasoning and understanding. God has given intellectual powers to man. Man thinks, reasons, and understands. Christ says that our minds and thoughts are to be centered upon God. We are to love God "with all our mind."

"And be not conformed to this world: but be ye transformed by the renewing of your mind, that ye may prove what is that good, and acceptable, and perfect, will of God" (Ro.12:2).
"And that ye put on the new man, which after God is created in righteousness and true holiness" (Ep.4:24).
"Finally, brethren, whatsoever things are true, whatsoever things are honest, whatsoever things are just, whatsoever things are pure, whatsoever things are lovely, whatsoever things are of good report; if there be any virtue, and if there be any praise, think on these things" (Ph.4:8).
"And have put on the new man, which is renewed in knowledge after the image of him that created him" (Col.3:10).
"Casting down imaginations, and every high thing that exalteth itself against the knowledge of God, and bringing into captivity every thought to the obedience of Christ" (2 Co.10:5).

---

3 (22:39) **Love—Brotherhood—Neighbor:** Christ gave a second commandment: "Thou shalt love thy neighbor as thyself." (See Le.19:18.) The lawyer had not asked for the second greatest commandment, but the first commandment is abstract. It cannot be seen or understood standing by itself. There has to be a *demonstration, an act, something done* for love to be seen and understood. A profession of love without demonstration is empty. It is profession only. Love is not known without showing it.

Several important things need to be said about love at this point.

a. Love is an active experience, not inactive or dormant. That is what Christ is pointing out. Love for God *acts*. Love acts by showing and demonstrating itself. It is foolish for a man to say, "I love God," and then be inactive and do nothing for God. If he truly loves God, he will demonstrate his love for God through his actions. Anyone who loves another person will do things for the loved one.

b. The primary *thing* God wants from us is genuine love for our neighbors, not *religious rituals*. Performing *religious rituals* can be beneficial, but it is not the first thing God wants. God wants us to make loving our neighbor the first order of our lives. Religious rituals, observances, ordinances, and laws are lifeless, unfeeling, and unresponsive. They are not helped by our doing them; we alone are helped. They make us feel good and religious, which is beneficial to our growth, but performing *religious rituals* is not what demonstrates our love for God. Loving our neighbor is what proves our love for God. A man may say he loves God, but if he hates and acts unkindly and spitefully toward his neighbor, everyone knows his religion is profession only.

> "A new commandment I give unto you, That ye love one another; as I have loved you, that ye also love one another. By this shall all men know that ye are my disciples, if ye have love one to another" (Jn.13:34-35).
>
> "If a man say, I love God, and hateth his brother, he is a liar: for he that loveth not his brother whom he hath seen, how can he love God whom he hath not seen? And this commandment have we from him, That he who loveth God love his brother also" (1 Jn.4:20-21).

c. The great commandment to love God flows downward into another great commandment—to love our neighbor as ourselves. This fact is inescapable.

> "God commendeth [demonstrated] His love toward us, in that, while we were yet sinners, Christ died for us" (Ro.5:8).

When a man really sees the love of God for him, he cannot help but love God and share the love of God with his neighbors. It is the love of Christ for us, His death and sacrifice, that compels us to go and love all men everywhere.

> "We love him, because he first loved us....and this commandment have we from him, That he who loveth God love his brother also" (1 Jn.4:19, 21).
>
> "For the love of Christ constraineth us; because we thus judge, that if one died for all, then were all dead: And that he died for all, that they which live should not henceforth live unto themselves, but unto him which died for them, and rose again" (2 Co.5:14-15).

d. We are to love ourselves, but it must be a godly love, not a selfish one.
1) There is a corrupt love of self that feels the world should revolve around oneself. This self-love...
- wants all attention focused on oneself
- pushes self forward
- insists on one's own way
- demands and revels in recognition
- shows conceit and ignores others

2) There is a godly love for self that is natural and pleasing to God. It is a love that stirs a strong self-image, confidence, and assurance. It is a love that even helps in preventing some illnesses such as ulcers, tension, and high blood pressure. The godly love of self comes from knowing three things.
⇒ That one is actually the creation of God: the highest creation possible.
⇒ That one is actually the object of God's love: the most supreme love possible.
⇒ That one is actually the trustee of God's gifts: the greatest gifts possible.

3) The godly love of self has three traits that are clearly seen.
⇒ It esteems others better than self. It does esteem self ever so highly as God's glorious creation, but it esteems others more highly.

> "Let nothing be done through strife or vainglory; but in lowliness of mind let each esteem other better than themselves" (Ph.2:3).

⇒ It looks on the things of others. It looks on one's own things as a trustee of God's gifts, but it also looks on the things of others.

> "Look not every man on his own things, but every man also on the things of others" (Ph.2:4).

⇒ It walks humbly before others.

> "But he that is greatest among you shall be your servant. And whosoever shall exalt himself shall be abased; and he that shall humble himself shall be exalted" (Mt.23:11-12).
>
> "...all of you be subject one to another, and be clothed with humility: for God resisteth the proud, and giveth grace to the humble" (1 Pe.5:5).

e. We are to love our neighbor as ourselves. Note three very specific things about this second great commandment.
1) To love our neighbor is a command, not an option. If the commandment is not obeyed, God is displeased and we stand guilty of having broken the law of God.
2) To love our neighbor arouses the question: Who is our neighbor? Christ answers the question Himself in the Parable of the Good Samaritan.
⇒ A good neighbor is *he that shows mercy on any who need mercy*—even if the needy person is socially despised (Lu.10:25-37, esp. 36-37).

Therefore our neighbor is everyone in the world, no matter his status, condition, or circumstances. Every man is to be esteemed ever so highly and helped no matter who he is. No man is to be injured or wronged. Every man is to be esteemed better than oneself (Ph.2:3).

3) To love our neighbor is a very practical command. It involves some very practical acts that are spelled out in Scripture.
⇒ Love suffereth long (endures long, is patient).
⇒ Love is kind.
⇒ Love envies not (is not jealous).
⇒ Love vaunts not itself (does not brag; does not boast).
⇒ Love is not puffed up (vainglorious, arrogant, prideful).
⇒ Love does not behave itself unseemingly (unbecomingly, rudely, indecently, unmannerly).
⇒ Love seeks not her own (is not selfish or self-seeking; does not insist on one's own right and way).
⇒ Love is not easily provoked (not touchy, angry, fretful, resentful).
⇒ Love thinks no evil (harbors and plans no evil thought; takes no account of a wrong done it).
⇒ Love rejoices not in iniquity (wrong, sin, evil, injustice), but rejoices in the truth (justice and righteousness).
⇒ Love bears all things.
⇒ Love believes all things (exercises faith in everything; is ready to believe the best in everyone).
⇒ Love hopes all things (keeps up hope in everything, under all circumstances).
⇒ Love endures all things (without weakening; it gives power to endure).

Thought 1. *Religious things* can enslave a person. A person can be so engrossed in religion, buildings, ritual, ceremony, rules, and regulations that he neglects and ignores people, in particular the poor and downtrodden.

Thought 2. The church and *religious things* are the picture of religion among men. Therefore, a man feels *good* and *religious* when he attends church and does *religious things*.

Thought 3. A man loves God when he loves his neighbor. In fact, a man loves God only if he truly loves his neighbor (1 Jn.4:20-21; see Jn.13:34-35).

DEEPER STUDY # 7
(22:39) **Love**: see Le.19:18. See note—1 Co.13:4-7.

---

4 (22:40) **Love**: Christ says that love includes and embraces all the commandments. In fact, the term *the law and the prophets* is a term often used to refer to all Scripture. What Christ really says is that all Scripture hangs on love for God and love for one's neighbor. Christ actually paints a picture by using the word "hang." He says that love for God is a *hanger* and love for neighbor is a *hanger*. Upon these two hangers hang all that God has ever said, whether commandments or revelation of truth or practice of ceremony and ritual. The sum and substance of all that God has said and done is love. And the sum and substance of all that God wants of man is love: love of God and love of neighbor.

> **"Love is the fulfilling of the law" (Ro.13:10).**
> **"Now the end of the commandment is love out of a pure heart" (1 Ti.1:5).**
> **"Therefore all things whatsoever ye would that men should do to you, do ye even so to them: for this is the law and the prophets" (Mt.7:12).**

	K. The Question Asked by Jesus: What Do You Think About the Messiah? 22:41-46 *(Mk 12:35-37; Lu 20:39-44)*	43 He saith unto them, How then doth David in spirit call him Lord, saying,	4. Scripture's claim: He is Lord–the Lord of David^{DS1}
		44 The LORD said unto my Lord, Sit thou on my right hand, till I make thine enemies thy footstool?	a. Fact: David called Him Lord–by the Spirit 1) Said He is exalted with God 2) Said He will subject all enemies
1. Jesus questioned men	41 While the Pharisees were gathered together, Jesus asked them,	45 If David then call him Lord, how is he his son?	b. Question: How can He be David's Lord & Son?
2. The critical question: What do you think about the Messiah? 3. Man's idea: He is the Son of a man–of David	42 Saying, What think ye of Christ? whose son is he? They say unto him, *The Son* of David.	46 And no man was able to answer him a word, neither durst any *man* from that day forth ask him any more *questions*.	5. Conclusion: The question silenced the critics of Jesus

DIVISION XIV

THE MESSIAH'S LAST WEEK: HIS CLAIM CHALLENGED AND REJECTED, 21:1–23:39

K. The Question Asked by Jesus: What Do You Think About the Messiah? 22:41-46

(22:41-46) **Introduction**: it was still Tuesday of the Lord's last week on earth. He had just been challenged four different times by four different opponents. He had met each group and questioner in a unique way. He had answered the questions and turned them around to teach a much needed truth (see 21:23f; 22:15f; 22:23f; 22:34f). Christ had silenced those who opposed His claim to be the Messiah.

Now it was His turn; He questioned His opponents. But Christ did not stand against them as an opponent. Christ questioned them as men who were in error and needed to see the truth. He was reaching out to them in hope. He hoped that some would receive the truth of His Messiahship and accept Him as the Son of God. The spirit of His questioning is seen in the discussion He had with them. Note the question He asked: it is the all important question which He asks of every man: "What think ye of Christ, the Messiah?"

1. Jesus questioned men (v.41).
2. The critical question: What do you think about the Messiah (vv.41-42)?
3. Man's idea: He is the son of a man—of David (v.42).
4. Scripture's claim: He is Lord—the Lord of David (vv.43-45).
5. Conclusion: The question silenced the critics of Jesus (v.46).

1 (22:41) **Jesus Christ, Questions**: Jesus questioned and questioned men, and there are reasons why He questioned them. These are clearly seen in His dealing with these men.

a. Christ is long-suffering and tender. These men had challenged Christ time and again trying to discredit and embarrass Him before the crowd, yet He never reacted once. He answered their questions honestly and in such a way that He opened up new truths which they desperately needed to know. He questioned them because He was patient and long-suffering. He wanted to open up further truth to them. He longed for them to see and surrender to His Messiahship.

b. Christ questioned and questioned in order to reach people *with* the truth. In the case of these men, Christ was making a last-ditch effort, a last appeal to them. They had rejected and rejected until there was little hope. But Christ was still hoping, still reaching out to them. He questioned them in order to lead them to see that He is the Messiah, the Lord, the Son of God Himself.

While considering the Lord's questioning, there is another fact to consider, a critical fact. There is an end to His questioning, a time when He knows there is no hope and no chance that a man will repent and believe. There is a time when He begins to pronounce judgment. This question of Christ was His last question; after asking it, He began to pronounce judgment. Christ discussed and questioned the truth with these men time and again, but after they continually rejected it and became steeped in their unbelief, Christ ceased the discussion and began to pronounce judgment (see Mt.23:1-39).

Thought 1. Most people, at one time or another, think and wonder who Christ is. God uses such things as preaching, teaching, events, circumstances, situations, and tragedies to cause us to think about Christ and who He is. He tries to stir us to reason with Him so that we might be led to believe.

Thought 2. Man can become obstinate in unbelief, reject and reject until he becomes so hardened that he will not believe. These men (leaders) demonstrate such obstinate unbelief (see Ge.6:3; Pr.29:1).

2 (22:41-42) **Messiah**: Jesus asked the critical question. "What think ye of the Messiah?" This is the critical question for all men. Note two things about the question.

a. The Greek uses the definite article "*the* Messiah" (tou Christou). Jesus was trying to stir these men to think about the Messiah. He did not ask them what they thought of Him but what they thought about *the Messiah*. A man's destiny is determined by what he thinks about the Messiah.

b. Jesus asked a specific question about the Messiah: "Whose son is he?" Think about the Messiah. What is His origin? Who is to give birth to Him? In practical day-to-day terms, Christ was asking three things.

MATTHEW 22:41-46

1) Where does your deliverance come from? The Messiah is to deliver man from all the evil and enslavements of the world. Where will such a One come from?
2) Where does your Lord come from—the person you are to follow? The Messiah is to be the Lord who is to rule and reign and govern all lives, executing perfect justice and care. Where will He come from—from earthly parents or from God?
3) Where does your utopia come from—the person who is to bring about the perfect world and all that is good and beneficial? Where will the One come from who is to bring utopia, the Kingdom of God to earth? Will He come from earth or heaven?

Thought 1. It is not enough to ask this question: "What do you think of the Messiah?" True, it must be asked; but standing alone, the question will not lead a man to the truth. This is clearly seen in the experience of these religionists. Christ asked them the critical question, yet they did not come to the truth. Two things are necessary before answering the question.
(1) A man must think. He must be willing to study and think through the question of the Messiah.
(2) A man must be honest. He must rid himself of bias and presuppositions. He must approach the subject of the Messiah with a willingness to see and confess the truth.

Thought 2. There are three critical questions which need to be asked by each of us.
(1) Where does my deliverance come from? From the son of a mere man like myself or from God?
(2) Where does my Lord come from—the person I am willing to follow as long as I exist? From the son of a mere man like myself or from God?
(3) Where does my utopia come from—the person who is to bring about the perfect world and all that is good and beneficial? From a man who is like myself or from God?

Thought 3. In all honesty, are there parents anywhere who can give birth to a son...
- who can deliver us?
- who can be a true Lord to us?
- who can bring about a world that is nothing but good and beneficial to all?

3 (22:42) **Messiah**: the Pharisees answered Jesus' question by giving the common idea of man—the Messiah is the son of a man, the son of David.
  Note two facts about their answer.
  a. The common title for the Messiah was "the Son of David." The Old Testament definitely said the Messiah was to come from the line of David. It was from such passages as these that the Messiah was known as "the Son of David." (See note—Lu.3:24-31 for the Davidic promises and their fulfillment.)

> "Once have I sworn by my holiness that I will not lie unto David. His seed shall endure for ever, and his throne as the sun before me" (Ps.89:35-36).
> "For unto us a child is born, unto us a son is given: and the government shall be upon his shoulder: and his name shall be called Wonderful, Counselor, The mighty God, The everlasting Father, The Prince of Peace. Of the increase of his government and peace there shall be no end, upon the throne of David, and upon his kingdom, to order it, and to establish it with judgment and with justice from henceforth even for ever. The zeal of the Lord of hosts will perform this" (Is. 9:6-7).
> "And there shall come forth a rod out of the stem of Jesse, and a Branch shall grow out of his roots: And the spirit of the Lord shall rest upon him, the spirit of wisdom and understanding, the spirit of counsel and might, the spirit of knowledge and of the fear of the Lord; And shall make him of quick understanding in the fear of the Lord: and he shall not judge after the sight of his eyes, neither reprove after the hearing of his ears: But with righteousness shall he judge the poor, and reprove with equity for the meek of the earth: and he shall smite the earth with the rod of his mouth, and with the breath of his lips shall he slay the wicked. And righteousness shall be the girdle of his loins, and faithfulness the girdle of his reins" (Is.11:1-5).

  The Messiah was to do four specific things. (See notes—Mt.1:1; DEEPER STUDY # 2—1:18; DEEPER STUDY # 3—3:11; notes—11:1-6; 11:2-3; DEEPER STUDY # 1—11:5; DEEPER STUDY # 2—11:6; DEEPER STUDY # 1—12:16; notes—22:42; Lu.7:21-23. These notes are important for the full concept of the Messiah.)
  1) He was to free Israel from all enslavement. Enslavement was to be abolished and all men set free under God's domain.
  2) He was to give victory over all enemies, and Israel was to be established as the seat of His rule. This, of course, meant Israel was to be the leading nation of the world.
  3) He was to bring peace to earth. All people were to serve God under the government established by the Messiah.
  4) He was to provide plenty for all. The Messiah was to see that all men had the benefits of God's rule and care.
  b. The common idea of the Messiah's origin was that He was to be human, born of a man. The idea that he might be of divine origin, of God Himself, was just unacceptable to men.

  Thought 1. Note two striking points about man's common concept of the Messiah.
  (1) Man thinks of deliverance and plenty in terms of power...
  - national power
  - military power
  - personal power
  - political power
  - institutional power
  - monetary power

MATTHEW 22:41-46

(2) Man thinks that deliverance and plenty come from human ability and fame, from...
- a national leader
- a military leader
- a business leader
- a political leader
- an institutional leader

4 **(22:43-45) Messiah**: Jesus then pointed out the claim of Scripture—the Messiah is Lord, the Lord of David. Scripture says that the Messiah is the Son of David, but it also says that He is the *Lord* of David.
The Scripture is strong in its statement.

a. David called the Messiah Lord *in the Spirit*; that is, David's words were spoken under the inspiration of the Holy Spirit. God was directing Him (see 2 Pe.1:21 and 1 Co.12:3).

b. David said that "the Lord [Jehovah God] said to *my* Lord [the Messiah]." David unquestionably called the Messiah, "*My Lord*."

c. David said that *my* Lord sits on the right hand of God. The Messiah is *Lord*, for He is *exalted* by God.

> "Which he wrought in Christ, when he raised him from the dead, and set him at his own right hand in the heavenly places" (Ep.1:20).
> "Wherefore God also hath highly exalted him, and given him a name which is above every name" (Ph.2:9).
> "Now of the things which we have spoken this is the sum: We have such an high priest, who is set on the right hand of the throne of the Majesty in the heavens" (He.8:1).

d. David said that my Lord's "enemies are to be made His footstool." The Messiah is Lord, for all His enemies are to be subjected under Him.

> "That at the name of Jesus every knee should bow, of things in heaven, and things in earth, and things under the earth; and that every tongue should confess that Jesus Christ is Lord, to the glory of God the Father" (Ph.2:10-11).

After quoting the Scripture, Christ asked the pointed question: How can the Messiah be both David's Lord and Son? Jesus is doing at least two things in this question.

1. Jesus was saying this: man's concept of the Messiah as being only human is inadequate—totally inadequate. It is not enough to think in terms of earthly power, of national and political, military and institutional leadership. There is no way a mere man can bring *perfect* deliverance, leadership, and utopia to this earth. The Messiah is not only man, He is the Lord from heaven.

2. Jesus was claiming to be the Son of God Himself. Man's concept has to *go beyond* the mere human and physical. Man's idea has to *stretch upward* into God's very own heart. God loves this earth; therefore, God sent His Son to earth, sacrificing Him in order to save the earth and all those within it (Jn.3:16).

> "For God so loved the world, that he gave his only begotten Son, that whosoever believeth in him should not perish, but have everlasting life" (Jn.3:16).
> "And Simon Peter answered and said, Thou art the Christ, the Son of the living God" (Mt.16:16).
> "The woman saith unto him, I know that Messias cometh, which is called Christ: when he is come, he will tell us all things. Jesus saith unto her, I that speak unto thee am he" (Jn.4:25-26).
> "Then said Jesus unto the twelve, Will ye also go away? Then Simon Peter answered him, Lord, to whom shall we go? thou hast the words of eternal life. And we believe and are sure that thou art that Christ, the Son of the living God" (Jn.6:67-69).
> "I said therefore unto you, that ye shall die in your sins: for if ye believe not that I am he, ye shall die in your sins" (Jn.8:24).
> "Then said Jesus unto them, When ye have lifted up the Son of man, then shall ye know that I am he, and that I do nothing of myself; but as my Father hath taught me, I speak these things" (Jn.8:28).
> "Jesus said unto her, I am the resurrection, and the life: he that believeth in me, though he were dead, yet shall he live: and whosoever liveth and believeth in me shall never die. Believest thou this? She saith unto him, Yea, Lord: I believe that thou art the Christ, the Son of God, which should come into the world" (Jn.11:25-27).
> "And Paul, as his manner was, went in unto them, and three sabbath days reasoned with them out of the scriptures, opening and alleging, that Christ must needs have suffered, and risen again from the dead; and that this Jesus, whom I preach unto you, is Christ" (Ac.17:2-3).
> "Whosoever believeth that Jesus is the Christ is born of God: and every one that loveth him that begat loveth him also that is begotten of him" (1 Jn.5:1).

Thought 1. Christ's emphasis upon the inspiration of Scripture was very important. He was unmistakably declaring the authority of the Old Testament. We should note the attention and reverence Christ gave to Scripture—a striking lesson for us.

Thought 2. The Messiah is the Son of David. He is Man, but He is more: He is both God's Son, the Lord from heaven, as well as man.

MATTHEW 22:41-46

Thought 3. Man's concept of an earthly deliverer or Messiah is foolish. There is no way permanent peace and perfect utopia can be brought to a corruptible world *apart from God*. If permanency of anything is ever to be known, it has to come through Him who is permanent. (See notes—Jn.8:21-22; Ro.10:6-7. These notes discuss the very practical and spiritual needs of man for the Messiah and/or utopia.)

DEEPER STUDY # 1
(22:43) **Old Testament Reference**: see Ps.110:1.

---

5 (22:46) **Jesus Christ, Response to**: Jesus' question silenced His critics. A heart that is truly honest and a mind that is willing to study and think has to confess the truth. If either is missing, the honest heart or the thinking mind, then a man will turn from Christ and be silent. He will be silent in belief and act in unbelief.

MATTHEW 23:1-12

	CHAPTER 23 L. The Warning Against False Religion, 23:1-12 (Mk 12:38-40; Lu 20:45-47)		
1. Jesus spoke to the crowds & to the disciples	Then spake Jesus to the multitude, and to his disciples,	lacteries, and enlarge the borders of their garments,	Dress, clothing
2. False religion is a religion that claims to "sit" in the truth (Moses' seat)	2 Saying, The scribes and the Pharisees sit in Moses' seat:	6 And love the uppermost rooms at feasts, and the chief seats in the synagogues,	b. A religion of position: Positions that honor & exalt men c. A religion of titles: Titles that honor & exalt men

3. False religion is a religion of hypocrisy
  a. It is good to obey the religionists' preaching
  b. It is not good to follow their practice
	3 All therefore whatsoever they bid you observe, *that* observe and do; but do not ye after their works: for they say, and do not.	7 And greetings in the markets, and to be called of men, Rabbi, Rabbi.
		8 But be not ye called Rabbi: for one is your Master, *even* Christ; and all ye are brethren.
		9 And call no *man* your father upon the earth: for one is your Father, which is in heaven.
			6. False religion is a religion to be guarded against
			  a. Because position & relationships are already established
			    1) God is your Father

4. False religion is a religion of heavy burdens
  a. Leaders impose heavy burdens upon others
  b. Leaders do not impose the burdens upon themselves
	4 For they bind heavy burdens and grievous to be borne, and lay *them* on men's shoulders; but they *themselves* will not move them with one of their fingers.	10 Neither be ye called masters: for one is your Master, *even* Christ.
		11 But he that is greatest among you shall be your servant.
			2) Christ is your Teacher
			3) You are brothers
			
			b. Because greatness is measured by service

5. False religion is a religion of show, of display a. A religion of appearance:	5 But all their works they do for to be seen of men: they make broad their phy-	12 And whosoever shall exalt himself shall be abased; and he that shall humble himself shall be exalted.	c. Because judgment is coming

DIVISION XIV

THE MESSIAH'S LAST WEEK: HIS CLAIM CHALLENGED AND REJECTED, 21:1–23:39

L. The Warning Against False Religion, 23:1-12

(23:1-12) **Introduction**: in order to understand what is happening in this passage, it is helpful to recall the events which led up to it. It was still Tuesday of Jesus' last week on earth. On Sunday, just two days before, He had been escorted into the city by teeming thousands proclaiming Him to be the Messiah. On Monday, He had cast out the money changers and those who were doing business within the temple walls. Following these two dramatic events, He had taken upon Himself the right and authority to teach and heal within the temple. Naturally the governing leaders, both religious and civil, were upset and angered by what was happening. More to the point, the leaders felt threatened by Christ, fearing the people might rally around Him as the Messiah and rise up against the Romans. Such action, of course, would cause the Romans to march against Jerusalem and blame the Jewish leadership for not maintaining order. Then after putting the insurrection down, Rome would remove the present Jewish leadership from office. In the minds of the leaders, Christ was a threat to their position, power, wealth, and security (see notes—Mt.12:1-8; note and DEEPER STUDY # 1—12:10; note—15:1-20; DEEPER STUDY # 2—15:6-9; DEEPER STUDY # 3—16:12). They were forced to discredit Jesus before the people.

They sent group after group to challenge Christ, attempting to trip Him up. Each time He answered brilliantly, teaching a much needed lesson not only to those standing around, but to men of all generations. Finally, the leaders were baffled and silenced. But Christ did not give up trying to reach them. He reached out once more, trying to lead them to the truth: the Messiah is not only Man, He is also Lord, the Son of God Himself (see Mt.22:41-46). The result? Again, the leaders refused to open their minds and hearts. They remained closed to the truth, obstinately so. They rejected Christ and turned and walked away. They began the final plot—not to challenge Christ in argument again but to kill Him.

As the present passage is studied, it is helpful to keep in mind the major reason these leaders opposed Jesus so violently: they feared the loss of all they held dear and possessed in this world: position, power, livelihood, wealth, and security. In their minds, as long as Christ was alive, He was a threat to them and to their nation (see notes—Mt.12:1-8; note and DEEPER STUDY # 1—12:10).

The great tragedy was that they were supposed to be the godly teachers and leaders, God's very own representatives and messengers to the people. Yet, they were so far removed from God that they were unable to recognize God's very own Son. Despite appeal after appeal and proof after proof by Christ Himself, they still refused to believe and follow Him. They deliberately chose to be obstinate in their unbelief and chose to follow the way of the world by plotting to kill Him.

This background lies behind the present chapter—the most severe attack Christ ever spoke against a people. The true nature of these religionists, the Scribes and Pharisees, is clearly seen as Christ opened up the hypocrisy of their lives and religion point by point. In this particular passage, Christ warned against their religion—a religion which stands as a symbol of the false religions of the world. (Also see outline, note, and DEEPER STUDY # 1—Ro.2:17-29.)

  1. Jesus spoke to the crowds and to the disciples (v.1).
  2. False religion is a religion that claims to "sit" in the truth (Moses' seat) (v.2).
  3. False religion is a religion of hypocrisy (v.3).
  4. False religion is a religion of heavy burdens (v.4).

MATTHEW 23:1-12

5. False religion is a religion of show, of display (vv.5-7).
6. False religion is a religion to be guarded against (vv.8-12).

1 (23:1) **Religion, False—Scripture**: in this particular passage, Jesus spoke to the multitude and to the disciples, not to the religionists, not to the Pharisees and Scribes. There are at least four reasons why Christ warned the multitude and disciples at this point. These same reasons make this passage extremely applicable to every generation.

a. Everyone needs to know what is true and what is false in religion. Man-made religion always includes some truth and some error. And unfortunately even the true religion, God's revealed religion, is sometimes added to or taken away from by men. This is what had happened to the Pharisees and Scribes, the religionists of Jesus' day. They were staunch followers of God's Word, the Old Testament Scriptures, but they added to the Scripture. Therefore, Christ needed to teach what was true and what was false in the present religion (see v.2-3).

b. Everyone needs to have the hypocrisy and sin of religion exposed. When men add to or take away from God's revealed truth, it creates and causes hypocrisy and sin within religion. When men *add* rules and regulations to Scripture, self-discipline is demanded and super-spirituality results. When men deny or *take away* certain portions of Scripture, it creates and causes the exaltation of man and his rationality, making *gods* out of man and his ability. Again, pride and vain glory result.

c. Everyone needs to be warned against following the error of religion. Just being religious is not enough (see Mt.5:20). A person must follow the truth. If a person follows false religion, he is doomed (v.8-12).

d. Everyone needs to have his false ideas about Christ corrected. The false teaching and attacks of the religionists had influenced the people. Unbelief and false ideas about the Messiah were running rampant. Christ needed to declare the truth (v.7-10).

Thought 1. The warning concerning false religion was directed primarily to the public and the disciples because there is always more hope for them. It is always difficult for a leader who teaches error to repent and change.
(1) He fears embarrassment in admitting that he has held to error and taught error.
(2) He fears the ridicule and rejection of his peers.
(3) He fears the loss of position, power, and security.

2 (23:2) **Religion, False—Minister—Teaching**: false religion is a religion that claims to "sit" in the truth, that is, in Moses' seat. Moses was the great teacher and interpreter of God's law and Word. Christ said that the Scribes and Pharisees "sit in Moses' seat." They were responsible for teaching and interpreting God's Word just as Moses had been. The application is clear: all religions, false and true, "sit in Moses' seat"—all religion is responsible for teaching the truth of God's Word. As shall be seen, all teachers shall be held accountable for how they "sit in Moses' seat," how they *sit* in their position as teachers and interpreters of God's Word.

> "And why call ye me, Lord, Lord, and do not the things which I say?" (Lu.6:46).
> "Therefore thou art inexcusable, O man, whosoever thou art that judgest: for wherein thou judgest another, thou condemnest thyself; for thou that judgest doest the same things" (Ro.2:1).
> "Thou that makest thy boast of the law, through breaking the law dishonourest thou God? For the name of God is blasphemed among the Gentiles through you, as it is written" (Ro.2:23-24).

Thought 1. The place of religion in the world has been *set* and *ordained* by God. Just because bad men may sit in places of leadership does not mean that all religion is bad nor that all religion is to be invalidated or ignored. Hypocrites within the church, even within positions of leadership, do not mean that the church is evil and can be neglected and avoided. We are to *test the spirits*, distinguish between the true and the false, and we are to go on worshipping God and edifying those who follow the truth.

Thought 2. It is a terrible thing for a false teacher to "sit in Moses' seat." The most severe judgment awaits those who teach error (see Mt.23:12; 23:13-36, esp. 14, 15, 33).

> "Ye serpents, ye generation of vipers, how can ye escape the damnation of hell?" (Mt.23:33).

3 (23:3) **Religion, False**: false religion is a religion of hypocrisy (v.3). However, there is a fact that must be noted: not all religion is false, even when it is taught by a false teacher. Christ says, "Observe, obey the truth of what they say, in so far as it is God's Word (v.2); but do not follow after their works." Note several things.

a. Jesus is condemning false religion and teachers, but not the truth. False teachers can and do teach some truth. The truth is to be obeyed, no matter who teaches it. The truth and our duty to obey it are not invalidated just because a hypocrite teaches it.

b. Jesus is saying that teaching the truth does not mean that a person is acceptable to God. Being acceptable to God depends upon one thing and one thing alone: living the truth. A man may teach the truth yet be unacceptable to God. He is unacceptable because he is a hypocrite and does not obey the Lord. He simply does not live the truth. A man is not acceptable just because he proclaims and professes the truth—even if he is a teacher. He is acceptable because he walks in the truth day by day.

> "Thou therefore which teachest another, teachest thou not thyself? thou that preachest a man should not steal, dost thou steal? Thou that sayest a man should not commit adultery, dost thou

MATTHEW 23:1-12

commit adultery? thou that abhorrest idols, dost thou commit sacrilege? Thou that makest thy boast of the law, through breaking the law dishonourest thou God?" (Ro.2:21-23).

c. We must separate the office from the officer, the ministry from the minister, the church from the people, the truth from the teaching, the doctrine from the practice. The spirits must be tried.

"Beloved, believe not every spirit, but try the spirits whether they are of God: because many false prophets are gone out into the world" (1 Jn.4:1).

d. Jesus is saying that the claims of religion and of men must not be allowed to lead us. The doctrine, morality, and discipline of religion and men may be commendable; on the other hand, both religion and men may be false.

"They profess that they know God; but in works they deny him, being abominable, and disobedient, and unto every good work reprobate" (Tit.1:16).
"My little children, let us not love in word, neither in tongue; but in deed and in truth" (1 Jn.3:18).

Thought 1. Preaching and practice must always be separated. There is always some difference. Every man is human, and every man comes short, but God's Word is perfect.

4 (23:4) **Religion, False**: false religion is a religion of heavy burdens. Jesus said that false religion and teachers impose heavy burdens upon men.
There are four ways heavy burdens are laid upon the shoulders of men.
  a. God's Word and law can be imposed upon men in such a strict and severe way that mercy is lacking.
  b. Religion and men can add to God's Word through rules, regulations, rituals, observances, and traditions. Such tends to become more important than the truth.
  c. Religion and men can deny and take away from God's Word, leaving men to stumble around searching for the truth within themselves and other imperfect and frail men.
  d. Religion and men can exercise undue authority, intimidating people, insisting that tradition and ritual and other man-made burdens be kept.

In discussing rules and regulations, many are willing to impose the rules upon others, but not upon themselves. There are two particular failures with such hypocrisy.
1. Some teachers and laymen fail to lift a finger to practice the burden themselves. They are strict in laying the burden upon others but lax in bearing the weight themselves. They will not be bound by such rules themselves, at least not strictly, but they will preach and teach the rules to others and bind them to keep the rules. The shoulders of others are weighed down ever so heavily, yet they will not lift their own fingers to carry the weight of the rule or restriction.
2. Some teachers and laymen fail to lift a finger to ease the burden for the weak and heavy laden. This is another possible interpretation of what Christ is saying. Some just will not show mercy; they will not help those who need help in practicing the burden. Some teachers are so strict and assuming that they know little of the love and mercy of God. They know little about Christian liberty (see Acts 15:28. See outline and notes—Ro.14:1-23.)

"But now, after that ye have known God, or rather are known of God, how turn ye again to the weak and beggarly elements, whereunto ye desire again to be in bondage?" (Ga.4:9).
"Stand fast therefore in the liberty wherewith Christ hath made us free, and be not entangled again with the yoke of bondage" (Ga.5:1).
"Wherefore if ye be dead with Christ from the rudiments of the world, why, as though living in the world, are ye subject to ordinances?" (Col.2:20).

Thought 1. There is the possibility of terrible pride in imposing burdens upon men. The right to impose burdens sets a person up as *lord* over others. Of course, there is a place for authority in proclaiming and exercising God's Word, but not for imposing man-made rules (legalistic conservatism) and human rationalizations (liberalism). Both weigh man down ever so heavily. Both force man to secure the approval of God by keeping rules through a person's own strength. Both know little if any of the mercy and discipline of God's Spirit. God's Word is fully adequate for both faith and practice. God's Word is all man needs to direct and govern his life. We do not have to add to or take away from God's Word.

5 (23:5-7) **Religion, False—Pride**: false religion is a religion of show and ostentation. Christ points out three things these teachers did to be seen by men.
  a. They changed their appearance, dress, and clothing to draw attention to themselves.
    1) They wore phylacteries. These were little leather type boxes which contained a piece of parchment with four passages of Scripture written on it. The Scriptures were Ex.13:1-10; 13:11-16; De.6:4-9; and De.11:13-21.
      The use of the phylacteries seems to have arisen from a literal translation of Ex.13:9 and Pr.7:3. The true meaning of these two passages seems to be that we are to have the word of God in our minds just as clearly as if we had them before our eyes.
      The great fault of the religionists was that they interpreted these passages literally, and they enlarged the little leather boxes to draw attention to themselves as being religious.

MATTHEW 23:1-12

2) They also enlarged the borders of their garments; that is, they wore tassels on their clothing. God had instructed the Jews to make fringes or tassels on the borders of their outer robe. When a person noticed them, he was to be reminded to keep God's commandments. Again, the error was that the religionist changed his appearance from others; he enlarged his tassels, drawing attention to the fact that he was more religious than others.

Thought 1. A person can wear clothes that expose the body, that actually attract attention to certain parts of the body. A person can wear clothes that are too tight, too low cut, too high cut, too thin. A person can wear too little clothing and clothing that fails to cover enough of the body.

Jesus said to beware of dressing to attract attention. The religionists did it to appear righteous. Others do it to appear worldly (appealing).

"Neither yield ye your members [bodily parts] as instruments of unrighteousness unto sin: but yield yourselves unto God, as those that are alive from the dead, and your members as instruments of righteousness unto God" (Ro.6:13).

"In like manner also, that women adorn themselves in modest apparel, with shamefacedness and sobriety; not with broided hair, or gold, or pearls, or costly array; but (which becometh women professing godliness) with good works" (1 Ti.2:9-10).

"[Women] whose adorning let it not be that outward adorning of plaiting the hair, and of wearing of gold, or of putting on of apparel; but let it be the hidden man of the heart, in that which is not corruptible, even the ornament of a meek and quiet spirit, which is in the sight of God of great price" (1 Pe.3:3-5).

b. They loved the positions of honor, special seats, and places of recognition. There are those who love the restricted neighborhoods and clubs and the preferred lists. They love the preeminence (3 Jn.9). Note what is condemned: not being in these positions and places, but the *love* of them. Someone has to hold the upper positions and fill the major places of responsibility. It is the *love* of such, the love and the feeling of pride because of the place and position that is wrong.

"How can ye believe, which receive honour one of another, and seek not the honour that cometh from God only?" (Jn.5:44).

"Nevertheless man being in honour abideth not: he is like the beasts that perish" (Ps.49:12).

c. They loved the titles that honored and exalted them. The title was simply "Rabbi" which meant teacher or master. It carried with it the modern idea of *Doctor* or *My lord*. It was a title that took a man who was supposed to be God's messenger and said, "Here he is; this is he." It honored the man and not the Lord.

"And whosoever shall exalt himself shall be abased; and he that shall humble himself shall be exalted" (Mt.23:12).

"For when he dieth he shall carry nothing away: his glory shall not descend after him" (Ps.49:17).

Thought 1. Too often men change their clothing and seek the upper places, positions, and titles to draw attention to themselves and their abilities. They are honored and not the Lord (see Mt.6:1-7, 16-18).

Thought 2. There is nothing wrong with living holy and godly lives, with being religious. But it is wrong to draw attention to oneself instead of to the Lord. We should not *overdo* or *remake* our outward being (appearance, position, titles) to draw attention to ourselves. We should always walk humbly among men, walk as one of them, walk pointing them to Christ by our lives.

Thought 3. God has no favorites among men. Why should we seek to appear as a favorite? Why should we seek *appearance*, *position*, and *honor* that would point toward us as being special?

Thought 4. If there is anyone who should walk humbly before men and point them toward God, it is the man who professes to serve God. He, of all men, should not love the appearance and positions and titles and honor that point toward him instead of his Lord.

6 (23:8-12) **Religion, False**: false religion is a religion to be guarded against. There are three strong reasons why we are to guard against false religion.

a. All positions and relationships are already set in the Kingdom of God. There is no position and no relationship left to be determined. All have already been determined.

1) God is the Father of our faith, of the true religion. No earthly founder or teacher is *Father*. Therefore no man is to be acknowledged as such. God alone is to be proclaimed *Father*.

"One God and Father of all, who is above all, and through all, and in you all" (Ep.4:6).

"Every good gift and every perfect gift is from above, and cometh down from the Father of lights, with whom is no variableness, neither shadow of turning" (Js.1:17).

2) Christ is our Master. One alone is Master, even Christ. We are not to be called masters (kathegetes, leaders, guides, v.10. See Ro.2:19-20.) We are servants of the Master. Note that Jesus is claiming to be the Messiah.

3) Believers are brothers. One is not above or more exalted than another. Each stands as an equal before God and one another. Each is to serve and help the other.

b. Greatness is measured by service, not by earthly honor. (See outline and notes—Mt.20:20-28. This is a good discussion on "The Price of Greatness.") When religion is conceived by man or influenced by man, that religion focuses upon ritual, ceremony, rules, and regulations and upon honor, recognition, position, and influence.

> "But it shall not be so among you: but whosoever will be great among you, let him be your minister; and whosoever will be chief among you, let him be your servant" (Mt.20:26-27).
>
> "But ye shall not be so: but he that is greatest among you, let him be as the younger; and he that is chief, as he that doth serve" (Lu.22:26).
>
> "For I say, through the grace given unto me, to every man that is among you, not to think of himself more highly than he ought to think; but to think soberly, according as God hath dealt to every man the measure of faith" (Ro.12:3).
>
> "Likewise, ye younger, submit yourselves unto the elder. Yea, all of you be subject one to another, and be clothed with humility: for God resisteth the proud, and giveth grace to the humble" (1 Pe.5:5).

c. Judgment is coming. It is what a person does himself that determines his fate: he exalts himself or humbles himself. Again, someone has to fill positions of leadership; but if a person pushes himself forward for the honor of the position and not for the purpose of serving, he is to be judged by God. The rule is: we are called to serve, not to rule.

> "Whosoever therefore shall break one of these least commandments, and shall teach men so, he shall be called the least in the kingdom of heaven: but whosoever shall do and teach them, the same shall be called great in the kingdom of heaven" (Mt.5:19).
>
> "He hath put down the mighty from their seats, and exalted them of low degree" (Lu.1:52).
>
> "Look on every one that is proud, and bring him low; and tread down the wicked in their place" (Jb. 40:12).
>
> "They that trust in their wealth, and boast themselves in the multitude of their riches; none of them can by any means redeem his brother, nor give to God a ransom for him" (Ps.49:6-7).
>
> "A man's pride shall bring him low: but honour shall uphold the humble in spirit" (Pr.29:23).
>
> "For the day of the Lord of hosts shall be upon every one that is proud and lofty, and upon every one that is lifted up; and he shall be brought low" (Is.2:12).
>
> "For, behold, the day cometh, that shall burn as an oven; and all the proud, yea, and all that do wickedly, shall be stubble: and the day that cometh shall burn them up, saith the Lord of hosts, that it shall leave them neither root nor branch" (Mal.4:1).

Thought 1. One thing that can be said of the Christian faith is this: Christian faith is a faith of *oneness* (Ep.4:1-6, esp. 4-6; 1 Co.12:4-13). There is no room for pride or divisiveness, neither for the love of position, honor, or title.

MATTHEW 23:13-36

M. The Nine Accusations Against False Religionists, 23:13-36

(Lu 11:39-50)

1. **False religionists shut the door of heaven against seekers**[DS1,2,3]
   a. They do not enter themselves
   b. They do not allow seekers to enter

2. **False religionists use the guise of religion for greed, especially to steal from widows**
   a. Their hypocrisy: Use religion & prayer
   b. Their doom: To be a greater damnation

3. **False religionists are missionaries who double the corruption of new followers**[DS4]

4. **False religionists mislead others: They are blind guides in oaths & commitments**[DS5]
   a. Their blindness: They stress the secondary over the primary (two examples)
      1) They stress the temple gold over the temple
      2) They stress the gift over the altar
   b. Their folly: They try to evade commitments & responsibility, vv. 17, 19
   c. The raw facts
      1) All commitments & oaths are heard by God–there is no evasion
      2) All commitments & oaths are binding & are accountable to God

5. **False religionists stress the lighter commandments & neglect the more important ones**[DS6]
   a. They stress the lighter duties & neglect the more important duties

13 But woe unto you, scribes and Pharisees, hypocrites! for ye shut up the kingdom of heaven against men: for ye neither go in *yourselves,* neither suffer ye them that are entering to go in.
14 Woe unto you, scribes and Pharisees, hypocrites! for ye devour widows' houses, and for a pretence make long prayer: therefore ye shall receive the greater damnation.
15 Woe unto you, scribes and Pharisees, hypocrites! for ye compass sea and land to make one proselyte, and when he is made, ye make him twofold more the child of hell than yourselves.
16 Woe unto you, *ye* blind guides, which say, Whosoever shall swear by the temple, it is nothing; but whosoever shall swear by the gold of the temple, he is a debtor!
17 *Ye* fools and blind: for whether is greater, the gold, or the temple that sanctifieth the gold?
18 And, Whosoever shall swear by the altar, it is nothing; but whosoever sweareth by the gift that is upon it, he is guilty.
19 *Ye* fools and blind: for whether *is* greater, the gift, or the altar that sanctifieth the gift?
20 Whoso therefore shall swear by the altar, sweareth by it, and by all things thereon.
21 And whoso shall swear by the temple, sweareth by it, and by him that dwelleth therein.
22 And he that shall swear by heaven, sweareth by the throne of God, and by him that sitteth thereon.
23 Woe unto you, scribes and Pharisees, hypocrites! for ye pay tithe of mint and anise and cummin, and have omitted the weightier *matters* of the law, judgment, mercy, and faith: these ought ye to have done, and not to leave the other undone.
24 *Ye* blind guides, which strain at a gnat, and swallow a camel.
25 Woe unto you, scribes and Pharisees, hypocrites! for ye make clean the outside of the cup and of the platter, but within they are full of extortion and excess.
26 *Thou* blind Pharisee, cleanse first that *which is* within the cup and platter, that the outside of them may be clean also.
27 Woe unto you, scribes and Pharisees, hypocrites! for ye are like unto whited sepulchres, which indeed appear beautiful outward, but are within full of dead *men's* bones, and of all uncleanness.
28 Even so ye also outwardly appear righteous unto men, but within ye are full of hypocrisy and iniquity.
29 Woe unto you, scribes and Pharisees, hypocrites! because ye build the tombs of the prophets, and garnish the sepulchres of the righteous,
30 And say, If we had been in the days of our fathers, we would not have been partakers with them in the blood of the prophets.
31 Wherefore ye be witnesses unto yourselves, that ye are the children of them which killed the prophets.
32 Fill ye up then the measure of your fathers.
33 *Ye* serpents, *ye* generation of vipers, how can ye escape the damnation of hell?
34 Wherefore, behold, I send unto you prophets, and wise men, and scribes: and *some* of them ye shall kill and crucify; and *some* of them shall ye scourge in your synagogues, and persecute *them* from city to city:
35 That upon you may come all the righteous blood shed upon the earth, from the blood of righteous Abel unto the blood of Zacharias son of Barachias, whom ye slew between the temple and the altar.
36 Verily I say unto you, All these things shall come upon this generation.

    b. They avoid the lesser sins & commit the greater sins

6. **False religionists are blind to real cleanness**
   a. Their outside appears clean
   b. Their inside is full of greed & self-indulgence
   c. Their need: First clean the inside; then the outside will be clean

7. **False religionists disguise inner decay**
   a. Illustration: They are like white tombs
      1) Outside: Appear clean & beautiful
      2) Inside: Full of death & uncleanness
   b. Their error, sin
      1) Outside: Appear righteous
      2) Inside: Full of hypocrisy & wickedness

8. **False religionists pride themselves in a godly heritage**
   a. They honor the relics of the past
   b. They denounce the former abuses
   c. They pride themselves in being better: Would not have committed such sins
   d. They testify against themselves (by rejecting Christ)
      1) Show themselves to be descendants of murderers
      2) Take part in their father's pattern of murder
   e. Result: They have become snakes, vipers–doomed to hell

9. **False religionists reject & abuse many of God's present-day messengers**[DS7,8,9]
   a. Their abuse: They persecute & kill
   b. Their judgment
      1) They will have charged to them the sins of all the righteous blood shed throughout history[DS10,11]
      2) All these things will come upon this generation[DS12]

MATTHEW 23:13-36

DIVISION XIV

THE MESSIAH'S LAST WEEK: HIS CLAIM CHALLENGED AND REJECTED, 21:1–23:39

M. The Nine Accusations Against False Religionists, 23:13-36

(23:13-36) **Introduction—Religion, False**: this is probably the most stern and sustained denunciation in all history. It is beyond doubt the most tragic because it involves the souls of men, and it is pronounced by the Judge of all the earth, the Lord Himself. But it was deserved, and it stands as a dramatic warning to all men, in particular religionists of every generation.

Four things need to be seen before studying this passage.
1. The sin of these religionists (Pharisees) was great: it was hypocrisy.
    a. They professed religion, but they did not really follow God. They never entered heaven themselves, and by their lives and teaching, they misled others and kept them out of heaven.
    b. They used religion for their own ends, to advance themselves professionally and materially (see vv.14-15).
2. Christ was angry, but He was also sorrowful. He was harsh and condemning, but He was also broken-hearted and full of pity. Two facts show this.
    a. The Greek word *woe* includes both wrath and pity (see Deeper Study # 1—Mt.23:13).
    b. Jesus expressed great lament over Jerusalem (vv.37-39).
3. Christ was attacking and denouncing the religionists, but He was also warning them. Their sin was a great and terrible sin, but it was not unpardonable. They were shutting the door of heaven against themselves and others, and they were close to never being able to enter themselves. But all was not hopeless, not yet. Those *who will* hear this warning of Christ can respond by fearing and shaking under its denunciation, and they can repent and turn to God with a believing heart.
4. Some Scribes and Pharisees did repent and accept Christ and begin to follow Him (see Lu.13:31; Ac.6:7; 15:5; 18:8, 17).

Christ levelled His denunciation against the religionists of His day. He dealt frankly and openly with them. He exposed the truth of their human hearts: they were full of hypocrisy. Nothing thereafter would be hid; all would be exposed. They had to look at themselves and see the corruption of their hearts; and they had to repent, believe, and follow Christ or else be doomed to "the damnation of hell" (v.33).

Christ, frankly and openly, levelled nine accusations against the religionists.
1. False religionists shut the door of heaven against seekers (v.13).
2. False religionists use the guise of religion for greed, especially to steal from widows (v.14).
3. False religionists are missionaries who double the corruption of new followers (v.15).
4. False religionists mislead others; they are blind guides in oaths and commitments (vv.16-22).
5. False religionists stress the lighter commandments & neglect the more important ones (vv.23-24).
6. False religionists are blind to real cleanness (vv.25-26).
7. False religionists disguise inner decay (vv.27-28).
8. False religionists pride themselves in a godly heritage (vv.29-33).
9. False religionists reject and abuse many of God's present-day messengers (vv.34-36).

1 (23:13) **Religionists—False Teachers**: false religionists shut the door to heaven against seekers. The word *against* (emprosthen) means *in the face of*. The picture is that of men's standing right at the door desperately needing to enter, but the false religionist shuts the door of heaven in their *faces*.

Christ said two things in this point.
a. The false religionists did not enter heaven themselves. There are three reasons why they did not enter. (These reasons are pointed out in the preceding Scriptures.)
   1) They rejected God as Messiah, as being the Lord from heaven, the very Son of God (see Mt.22:41-45; Jn.10:31-39).
   2) They preferred their own ideas of religion rather than God's ideas. They preferred a religion that honored man's ability to do religious things rather than a religion that honored God's mercy for man (see outline and notes—Mt.23:1-12).
   3) They chose the world over God's demand for self-denial. They chose the things of the world such as position, honor, recognition, esteem, wealth, power, authority, and security (see notes—Mt.12:1-8; note and Deeper Study #1—12:10).
b. The false religionists not only did not enter heaven themselves, they did not allow *seekers* to enter. They shut the door by misleading people, and thereby doomed them to an eternity apart from God.
   1) They tried to discredit Jesus Christ, denying that He was the Son of God incarnated in human flesh (Mt.21:23-22:46).
   2) They twisted the Scriptures, falsely interpreting them (see Mt.22:41-46).

> "Jesus answered and said unto them, Ye do err, not knowing the scriptures, nor the power of God" (Mt.22:29).
>
> "For we are not as many, which corrupt the word of God: but as of sincerity, but as of God, in the sight of God speak we in Christ" (2 Co.2:17).
>
> "But [we] have renounced the hidden things of dishonesty, not walking in craftiness, nor handling the word of God deceitfully; but by manifestation of the truth commending ourselves to every man's conscience in the sight of God" (2 Co.4:2).

MATTHEW 23:13-36

"As also in all his [Paul's] epistles, speaking in them of these things; in which are some things hard to be understood, which they that are unlearned and unstable wrest, as they do also the other scriptures, unto their own destruction" (2 Pe.3:16).

3) They ridiculed and threatened anyone who confessed Christ (Jn.9:22, 34).

"Woe unto you, lawyers! for ye have taken away the key of knowledge: ye entered not in yourselves, and them that were entering in ye hindered" (Lu.11:52).
"For the priest's lips should keep knowledge, and they should seek the law at his mouth: for he is the messenger of the LORD of hosts. But ye are departed out of the way; ye have caused many to stumble at the law; ye have corrupted the covenant of Levi, saith the LORD of hosts" (Mal.2:7-8).

Thought 1. The fields are white unto harvest. Many seek to enter heaven, yet the door is often shut in their faces. By whom? By false religionists.

(1) False religionists deny Christ: they do not teach and preach that Jesus is the true Savior of men, the Son of God. Therefore, the seeker never knows the salvation of Christ. He never knows that Christ died for his sins and that he must trust Christ, giving all he is and has to Christ.

"But there were false prophets also among the people, even as there shall be false teachers among you, who privily [secretly] shall bring in damnable heresies, even denying the Lord that bought them, and bring upon themselves swift destruction" (2 Pe.2:1).
"Who is a liar but he that denieth that Jesus is the Christ? He is antichrist, that denieth the Father and the Son" (1 Jn.2:22).

(2) False religionists have their own thoughts about religion and how to be right with God. They teach their own thoughts on religion and righteousness. Therefore, the seeker never knows God's true righteousness and religion.

"For I say unto you, That except your righteousness shall exceed the righteousness of the scribes and Pharisees, ye shall in no case enter into the kingdom of heaven" (Mt.5:20).
"Therefore by the deeds of the law there shall no flesh be justified in his sight: for by the law is the knowledge of sin" (Ro.3:20).
"For they being ignorant of God's righteousness, and going about to establish their own righteousness, have not submitted themselves unto the righteousness of God. For Christ is the end of the law for righteousness to every one that believeth" (Ro.10:3-4).

(3) False religionists often choose the world over the denial of self. They choose place, position, honor, and security over sacrifice and true service.

"Forasmuch as ye know that ye were not redeemed with corruptible things, as silver and gold, from your vain conversation received by tradition from your fathers; but with the precious blood of Christ, as of a lamb without blemish and without spot" (1 Pe.1:18-19).

Thought 2. Many religionists mislead people. They prefer their own ideas of religion rather than God's ideas. They prefer their own ideas that exalt self and honor their own abilities.

Thought 3. A man must guard against his own ideas and prejudices. Personal ideas and prejudice must not replace what God has revealed to be the truth. Personal ideas and prejudices shut the door of heaven to everyone who accepts and believes them.

DEEPER STUDY # 1
(23:13) **Woe** (ouai): means both wrath and sorrow, anger and pity. There is no single English word to express what it means. It is a grieving denunciation; a sorrowful wrath; a pitying anger. It is a godly threat.

DEEPER STUDY # 2
(23:13) **Hypocrites** (hupokrites): one who pretends, puts on a show, acts out something he is not. At first, the word simply meant one who replied or answered. Then it came to mean acting, as actors play-acted the lines of a scene. Finally, the word was used in the worst sense: play-acting; pretending; one who wore a mask to hide his real self; one who acted one way but who was really another way; one who put on an outward show.

The religionists, the Scribes and Pharisees, were hypocrites.
⇒ They acted as though they believed and loved God, yet they did not accept God's Son.
⇒ They pretended to be seeking God; but they were really seeking profession, esteem, recognition, honor, position, power, and security (see notes—Mt.12:1-8; note and DEEPER STUDY # 1—12:10).
⇒ They showed a concern for the things of God, but they were really concerned with the things of this world.
⇒ They acted humble and helpful; but they were really full of pride, envy, possessiveness, selfishness, and covetousness.

> ⇒ They claimed to be ministers of God's religion; but they were really ministers of a man-made religion, a religion that honored man's ability to *be good* and to do enough good to become acceptable to God.
> ⇒ They professed God's Word, but they added to and took away from His Word.
>
> What Christ had to say about hypocrites is very serious. His words are a warning to every pretender and deceiver.
> ⇒ Hypocrites shall receive the greater damnation (v.14).
> ⇒ Hypocrites are children of hell (v.15).
> ⇒ Hypocrites are fools and they are blind (vv.17, 19).
> ⇒ Hypocrites are blind guides (v.24).
> ⇒ Hypocrites are full of extortion and excess (v.25).
> ⇒ Hypocrites are full of all uncleanness (v.27).
> ⇒ Hypocrites are serpents, a generation of vipers (v.33).
> ⇒ Hypocrites shall not escape the damnation of hell (v.33).

DEEPER STUDY # 3
(23:13) **Kingdom of Heaven**: see Deeper Study # 3—Mt.19:23-24.

2 (23:14) **Widows—Religionists**: false religionists use the guise of religion for greed and covetousness, especially to steal from widows. This is a gross sin and it is common. There are some persons—preachers, leaders and professing hypocrites—who court the attention and favor of people, especially widows, for the purpose of securing or getting their money. They seek large donations, endowments, trusts, investments, and gifts *to promote themselves or their institution*. And the great tragedy is this: such false and hypocritical hearts use the guise of religion to promote themselves and their false ideas. Their call to people is to *institutional religion*, not to the honor of God. Of course, vain men are susceptible to such appeals, but widows in particular are exposed to those who seem to be so devoted to God.

Note: Christ said that the damnation of these shall be greater. There are some sins more horrible than others. Using religion for selfish ends is one of them. This sin will receive a greater damnation. Another fact should be noted here: widows hold a special place in God's heart. He has always instructed His people to care for widows in a very special way.

> "He doth execute the judgment of the fatherless and widow, and loveth the stranger, in giving him food and raiment" (De.10:18).
> "Cursed be he that perverteth the judgment of the stranger, fatherless, and widow" (De.27:19).
> "A father of the fatherless, and a judge of the widows, is God in his holy habitation" (Ps.68:5).
> "Learn to do well; seek judgment, relieve the oppressed, judge the fatherless, plead for the widow" (Is.1:17).
> "And there was a widow in that city; and she came unto him, saying, Avenge me of mine adversary. And he would not for a while; but afterward he said within himself, Though I fear not God, nor regard man; yet because this widow troubleth me, I will avenge her, lest by her continual coming she weary me. And the Lord said, Hear what the unjust judge saith. And shall not God avenge his own elect, which cry day and night unto him, though he bear long with them?" (Lu.18:3-7).

Thought 1. Stealing from widows (and widowers) is one of the most serious sins that can be committed. It will receive "the greater damnation," yet it is done every day, even by religious persons. It happens like this: a man covets something—to have his ideas spread through the media, or his institution strengthened and enlarged, or his pockets filled. Therefore, the man begins to court people who have money, especially widows. He seeks either donations and investments or to become trustee of their estates. The sin is twofold.
(1) The money sought is not for the honor of God but for the promotion of oneself or one's institution.
(2) The guise of religion—being a religious person, organization, or institution—is used to secure the money.

Thought 2. There is one question that needs to be asked with an open heart by every man in every generation: Can the *godly concern* for the lost and starving masses of the world and the huge ornate buildings and homes and bank accounts of Christians be from the same God?

The point is this: a man's motives must be pure. He must seek only the honor of God and the salvation and strengthening of people. Two specific things must be done.
(1) Whatever money a man seeks, especially from widows, must be carefully used for God and for people in need, not for oneself nor for institutional religion.
(2) *Every single believer* must deny himself totally. He must give and give, and he must work in order to have enough to give to others (Ep.4:28). He must always be in a state and condition of sacrificing. He must never store up. Storing up can reap only one benefit: to be called *rich* and to feel *materially secure*. The fallacy of this is that true security can come only from God (Mt.6:25-34; 1 Jn.5:11-15).

3 (23:15) **Evangelism—Proselytes**: false religionists are missionaries who double the corruption of new followers. Note that Christ said two significant things.
a. False religionists seek converts.
b. False religionists are very zealous in evangelism; they brave the world to make a single convert.

But there were problems with the zeal of these false religionists, and the problems were serious.

MATTHEW 23:13-36

1. They were missionaries of a false religion. They were not reaching people for God, but for a man-made religion (see Deeper Study # 2—Mt.23:13). They were not bringing people to a personal relationship with God but to their own ideas of religion.

2. They were doubling the damnation of these converts. The primary people they went after were the God-fearing and devout people who had already shown interest in religion (Judaism). Some of these people were so pleased with what Judaism offered them that when one really became a convert, he became extremely zealous for Judaism. He was so indoctrinated that he was made into a fanatic, more devoted than many of the Jews themselves. Thus the false teachers caused these converts to heap damnation upon themselves.

Thought 1. One of the strongest lessons to be learned from the Scribes and Pharisees is zeal in evangelism.

(1) They had a willingness to go. They who held to a false religion were so willing to go. Why are we, who know the truth, so unwilling to go? Where is our zeal to reach people?

(2) They were willing to go anyplace. They travelled worldwide to reach just one convert. Where is our willingness to go as missionaries? As witnesses? Where is our willingness to go even around the corner?

"For the Son of man is come to seek and to save that which was lost" (Lu.19:10).

"Then said Jesus to them again, Peace be unto you: as my Father hath sent me, even so send I you" (Jn.20:21).

"But ye shall receive power, after that the Holy Ghost is come upon you: and ye shall be witnesses unto me both in Jerusalem, and in all Judaea, and in Samaria, and unto the uttermost part of the earth" (Ac.1:8).

"And he said unto them, Go ye into all the world, and preach the gospel to every creature" (Mk.16:15).

Thought 2. The Pharisees should also cause us to search and evaluate our hearts and our religion. Are we teaching the truth? Are we adding to or taking away from God's revelation, that is, from His Word? Are we actually doing just what God has called us to do: to live and work as servants and messengers of God and not as lords of religion and saviors of the world?

DEEPER STUDY # 4

(23:15) **Proselyte** (proselutos): a stranger, a sojourner (Ex.12:48-49; 22:21; 23:9; De.10:19). It is a person who has actually approached and drawn near religion, that is, adopted the beliefs of religion.

There were many proselytes to Judaism. Two things in particular attracted Gentiles.

1. The concept of one God (monotheism). The idea of many gods ran rampant throughout the world. A thinking man often had difficulty with the idea of a multitude of gods (polytheism). The corrupt worship and divisive demands insisted upon by so many religious gods did not make sense. It left the human soul empty.

Judaism worshipped one God alone, and He was proclaimed to be moral in an absolute sense. God's commandments were consistent with that for which the human soul cried; therefore, many turned to Judaism.

2. The concept of morality. The ancient world ran rampant in injustice and immorality, all sorts of sexual perversion. Weak women and men were abused and used as the strong willed to use them. Judaism's idea of purity and justice appealed to many. Women, who were treated as nothing more than pieces of property for the pleasure of men, were especially attracted to Judaism and its doctrine of morality.

Something needs to be noted about these Gentile worshippers, however. Not all were full-fledged converts or proselytes. They did attend the synagogues throughout the world wherever Jews met, but they were not circumcised nor did they participate in all the ceremonies and observances. They were known as *devout* and *God-fearing* converts or proselytes (Ac.10:2; 17:4).

---

4 (23:16-22) **Religionists, False**: false religionists mislead others; they are blind guides in oaths and commitments.

Note: Christ said that they were blind guides; they misled people. How? They stressed the secondary over the primary. They took the least important and made it more meaningful than the essential. Christ gave two examples.

a. They stressed the gold of the temple over the temple itself. Anyone who swore by the temple did not have to keep his commitment nor was he held responsible for his oath. But if he swore by the gold of the temple, he was held responsible and did have to keep his commitment.

b. They stressed the gift over the altar upon which the gift lay. Making a commitment or swearing by the altar was not binding, whereas a commitment or swearing by the gift was binding.

Christ used strong words against the religionists at this point. They were "fools and blind." Christ meant two things by these words.

1. What they were doing and saying was absurd and irrational. Common sense should tell anyone that the temple is greater than what is within it and the altar is greater than the gift that is laid upon it.

2. What they were doing and saying was full of folly and sin. They were merely trying to evade commitments and responsibility for swearing. They wanted the right to make promises and to swear, but they also wanted the right to break their promises if it benefited them later.

Christ pointed out the raw facts about commitments and oaths.

First, all commitments and oaths are heard by God. There is no evading of commitments made or of things sworn to.

⇒ God is the One to whom sacrifices are made upon the altar (implied) (v.20).
⇒ God dwells in the temple (v.21).
⇒ God sits upon His throne in heaven (v.22).

Second, all commitments and oaths are binding and accountable to God.

> "Again, ye have heard that it hath been said by them of old time, Thou shalt not forswear thyself, but shalt perform unto the Lord thine oaths: but I say unto you, Swear not at all; neither by heaven; for it is God's throne: nor by the earth; for it is his footstool: neither by Jerusalem; for it is the city of the great King. Neither shalt thou swear by thy head, because thou canst not make one hair white or black. But let your communication be, Yea, yea; Nay, nay: for whatsoever is more than these cometh of evil" (Mt.5:33-37).

Thought 1. There are at least four sins seen in what the religionists were saying and doing.
(1) The sin of stressing the secondary over the primary.
(2) The sin of evading commitments.
(3) The sin of covetousness. By stressing the gold over the temple, they were centering the people's minds upon the gold, the wealth, and the gifts instead of upon the God who dwelt in the temple.
(4) The sin of self-righteousness. By stressing man's gift over the altar, they were saying in essence that man's gift was more important than God's altar which sanctified the gift. The gift honored the altar instead of the altar's honoring the gift. Such, of course, was ridiculous; for symbolically God stood behind the altar. And no gift is ever greater than God.

Thought 2. The very same sins are committed today.
(1) Ritual, ceremony, programs—commitment to practically every phase of church life is often stressed over God. Commitment to the various phases of church life is even said to be commitment to God.
(2) The gift is stressed more than the altar. A commitment to give and to make sacrifice often takes precedence over the altar (commitment to God). Stewardship of money (the gift and the gold) is even said to be an equal part with the stewardship of life to God.
(3) The motive is often to make the institution stronger instead of making people stronger by centering their lives upon God.

DEEPER STUDY # 5
(23:16-22) **Oath—Swearing—Cursing**: a discussion of oaths can be enlarged to include negative oaths and swearing or what is commonly called *cursing*. It can be broadened on the basis of its definition. An oath is an appeal that something is to be cursed or sworn. (Also see outline and notes—Mt.5:33-37 for more discussion.)
⇒ Sometimes the appeal is for God to do something (damn something); sometimes the appeal (damning) is just declared by the person.
⇒ Sometimes a man swears an oath to God (a commitment); sometimes he swears an oath against something (curses).
⇒ Sometimes a man curses by using words that are distasteful or base; sometimes he chooses words thought to be more socially acceptable such as *rats, doggone it, darn,* etc..

There are at least three things wrong with oaths, swearing, and cursing.
1. Oaths reveal a weak character and lack of trustworthiness. The reason an oath is needed is because a person's word and character are sometimes suspicious and questionable. Therefore, he feels he must enforce his word with an oath. A trustful and trustworthy person only needs to say "yes" or "no." He will stand behind his word (Mt.5:37).
2. All oaths, swearing, and cursing come from the same spirit of emotion and feelings. Just because some words may be more acceptable to society does not mean they are more acceptable to God. It is the heart of emotion and feeling that causes the mouth to speak the words. God judges the heart, not the softness or harshness, tastefulness or distastefulness of the words. It is what is within that God condemns: the untruthfulness, distrustfulness, or willingness to curse because of a self-centered desire to *fit in*.
3. All swearing and cursing makes a person his *own* god. It puts oneself in the place of God. It claims the *right*, the prerogative to act and to curse something. No man has such a right himself. Only God possesses the right and power to speak and act against, to curse and condemn a person.

---

5 (23:23-24) **Religionists, False**: false religionists stress the lighter commandments and omit the weightier ones. Christ said two things.

a. Religionists stress the lighter duties while omitting the greater duties. They pick and choose what they want and are willing to do and omit the rest. They stress *outward* duties such as tithing, observances, rituals, ceremonies, and works; they minimize the change and *inward* duties of the heart. Christ mentions three duties of the human heart that are omitted.
1) There is justice: treating our neighbor as we should; doing and saying nothing that would hurt another person; showing honor and respect to all men; never being guilty of injustice.
2) There is mercy: showing care, concern, kindness, and tenderness to all who are weak, bad, and needy; and not being hard, distant, demanding, or cruel.
3) There is faith: believing God and trusting Him to fulfill His promises.

Christ said that the weightier matters of the law are these: justice and mercy and faith. But the false religionists minimize and omit these matters. They talk about and stress the lighter or outward matters of religion such as tithing. Outward matters such as observances, rituals, and works just do not carry the weight that inward matters of the heart carry. Why? Because, if the heart is right, then outward behavior will follow. All outward behavior will be changed and not just certain areas that have been picked out to show that a person is religious. Note what Christ says: stress the weightier matters and do not leave the other undone. Do the lighter, yes, but major upon the weightier matters.

b. Religionists avoid the lesser sins but commit the greater sins. They strain at a gnat and swallow a camel. This was a humorous proverb in Christ's day. Wine was carefully strained through a piece of linen cloth to catch gnats and other impurities before drinking. This was to avoid violating the law of purity (Le.11:20-23; 17:10-14).

The false religionists strained to keep the lighter matters of religion but failed to keep the weightier matters. They did not sin by straining to keep the lighter matters; they sinned by omitting the weightier matters.

"Thus speaketh the LORD of hosts, saying, Execute true judgment, and show mercy and compassions every man to his brother: and oppress not the widow, nor the fatherless, the stranger, nor the poor; and let none of you imagine evil against his brother in your heart" (Zec.7:9-10).

"Jesus said unto him, If thou wilt be perfect, go and sell that thou hast, and give to the poor, and thou shalt have treasure in heaven: and come and follow me" (Mt.19:21).

"And the second is like unto it, Thou shalt love thy neighbour as thyself" (Mt.22:39).

"Let love be without dissimulation [hypocrisy]. Abhor that which is evil; cleave to that which is good" (Ro.12:9).

"Owe no man any thing, but to love one another: for he that loveth another hath fulfilled the law" (Ro.13:8).

Thought 1. Many have a form of religion, but few pay much attention to the weightier matters of godliness. How many attend church regularly, give of their money, pray, and take part in church affairs; but they...
- do not give an honest day's work to an employer (justice)?
- do not humble themselves, showing mercy toward the weak and less disciplined?
- do not sacrifice, showing mercy toward the needy and less fortunate?
- do not act responsibly and lovingly toward others, even toward their own family (justice and mercy)?

"Having a form of godliness, but denying the power thereof: from such turn away" (2 Ti.3:5).

Thought 2. Think about it. How easy it is to keep up an outward appearance of religion, but how difficult it is to be godly within. Yet inward godliness is what Christ demands. We are to treat all people with pure justice and mercy and to believe God in all things.

Thought 3. One of the great failures of false religionists is this: they emphasize and stress the wrong matters. They stress the lighter matters and omit the weightier matters. What they stress is important and should be done, but they are not the major matters.

Thought 4. The false religionist fails at both points of sin. He sins both by omission and commission. He *omits* the weightier duties, and he *commits* the greater sins.

Thought 5. Christ called false religionists "blind guides." Note three things.
(1) Some are blind to what Christ was saying. They *do not know* they are stressing the lighter matters. The lighter matters are all they have ever known and been taught. Therefore, they are steeped in the lighter matters, knowing very little about the weightier matters of religion.
(2) Some *do know* they are stressing the lighter matters; and they deliberately continue in their error, refusing to change lest they face ridicule, loss of position, security, and all they count dear in this world.
(3) Religionists are guides, teaching the lighter matters of religion and omitting the weightier matters.

DEEPER STUDY # 6
(23:23) **Tithe—Mint—Anise—Cummin**: the tithe was always important to Jewish religion. The tithe was used to keep up the temple and to provide for the priests who served God and the people.

"Thou shalt truly tithe all the increase of thy seed, that the field bringeth forth year by year. And thou shalt eat before the Lord thy God, in the place which he shall choose to place his name there, the tithe of thy corn, of thy wine, and of thine oil, and the firstlings of thy herds and of thy flocks; that thou mayest learn to fear the Lord thy God always" (De.14:22-23).

"And all the tithe of the land, whether of the seed of the land, or of the fruit of the tree, is the Lord's: it is holy unto the Lord" (Le.27:30).

Note that the tithe was to be corn, wine, and oil. The Pharisees expanded the tithe to include all crops, including the smallest potted and garden plants, such as mint, anise, and cummin. Such plants were grown only in small patches for a family's use and never in large quantities. All three were used in cooking. Dill and cummin were also used as medicines. The religionists even included the leaves and stalks of the plants in their tithes. Imagine such strictness that would tithe a certain number of leaves and a small portion of stalk. But note something: Christ says such a spirit of strictness in tithing should be true of our lives. We should never fail to tithe (see note—Mt.23:23-24).

6 (23:25-26) **Religionists, False—Heart—Purity**: false religionists are blind to real cleanness. Christ used an illustration to show just how blind a religionist can be. Religionists are like cups and platters which have been washed on the outside but left dirty on the inside.

Christ made three points about the illustration.

a. The outside of the cup and platter of the religionists appeared clean. It was the outside that concerned them, for it was the outside that was seen. So they washed and cleaned the outside. The point is well taken. They guarded against scandalous sins, sins that would damage their image and reputation among neighbors and the public. Publicly they walked uprightly, just as the public thought they should. Their concern was what people thought, not what God thought.

b. The inside of the cup and platter of the religionists was dirty. The inside was not seen by men, so they paid little or no attention to it. They took what they wanted and lived as they wished. They were full of extortion and excess, that is, greed and selfishness, robbery and indulgence, lusting and consuming, taking and seldom sharing, getting and seldom giving. Such is what is on the inside of the religionists: a selfishness and greed for a following, for security, position, influence, attention, recognition, and acknowledgment. The religionists would never commit a gross visible sin, yet they would hold selfish greed and excessive desires within, living self-centered and indulgent lives.

c. The religionists needed to clean up the inside of their hearts. Once the inside was clean, then the outside would be automatically clean. If their spirits were clean, their outside behavior would be clean. A clean heart will lead to a clean life. Christ teaches that it is the inside of a man that determines his behavior. It is the heart that determines what a man does.

"Keep thy heart with all diligence; for out of it are the issues of life" (Pr.4:23).

"A good man out of the good treasure of the heart bringeth forth good things: and an evil man out of the evil treasure bringeth forth evil things" (Mt.12:35).

"For out of the heart proceed evil thoughts, murders, adulteries, fornication, thefts, false witness, blasphemies: these are the things which defile a man....but to eat with unwashen hands defileth not a man" (Mt.15:19-20).

Note: Christ called the false religionist *blind*. The false religionist does not know that the inside of a man can be cleansed. He does not know that it is a cleansed heart than changes behavior.

Thought 1. The whole approach of man and society is to change the outside of a man in order to change him inside. Change his environment, situation, circumstances, education, housing, nourishment, job, beliefs, philosophy, and self-image, and he will become *good*.

Christ's point is that all of the above are determined by man's heart. A bad environment is due to evil within men. A poor education is due to evil shortcomings within men. A man can have the very best environment and education yet still be evil. It is not the environment and education that changes the evil within men. It is God. Let God change the heart; then a man will be clean on the outside. He will live justly and mercifully toward all men, doing all he can to build the right environment and educational opportunities for all men.

7 (23:27-28) **Religionists, False—Spiritual Death**: false religionists disguise inner decay. Christ again used an illustration to make His point. He said that religionists are like tombs that have been washed white and freshly cleansed. Outwardly they appear clean and white, but within they are full of dead men's bones.

The picture of the freshly cleansed tombs was taken from the countryside of Jesus' day. Tombs dotting the roadways and countryside were a common sight. Jewish law said that anyone who touched a dead body became unclean (Nu.19:16). Therefore, tombs had to be clearly marked and kept up, not only to show respect for the family and deceased but also to prevent travelers from becoming *religiously* unclean.

There was one particular time during the year when the danger of touching a tomb became a serious threat. That was during the Passover season when teeming thousands of pilgrims swarmed over the roads and countryside leading to Jerusalem. One of the preparations made for the feast was the cleansing or washing of the tombs in order to make them clearly visible. It was probably these newly whited tombs, sparkling in the sunlight as they dotted the countryside, that Jesus was picturing.

The great wrong with the false religionist is this: outwardly, he appears righteous; but inwardly, he is full of hypocrisy and iniquity.

The Lord's contrast between outward appearance and inward truth is thought-provoking.

⇒ Outwardly we may attend church regularly, but what is the inward truth during the week?
⇒ Outwardly we may profess religion, but what is the inward truth out in the market place?
⇒ Outwardly we may give thanks as a family at meals, but what is the inward truth toward the hungry of the world?
⇒ Outwardly we may agree with justice and mercy, but what is the inward truth in dealing with money?
⇒ Outwardly we may bow our heads in a prayer of thanksgiving, but what is the inward truth toward other sinners?
⇒ Outwardly we may walk humbly before our peers, but what is the inward truth toward the derelict and those down and out?

Something is often forgotten. Christ preached against the outward sins of passion which society often considers the gross sins, but He condemned much more strongly the inward sins of the spirit such as pride and greed. Sinners and harlots enter heaven much more quickly than *religionists* who do not surrender their lives to Jesus Christ. This is exactly what Jesus Christ said (Mt.21:31-32). The world's concept is that a person is acceptable to God if he does not commit a gross sin. What he is within his heart and what he is behind the scene and closed doors matter little. He is an acceptable member of the community if he is...

- respectable
- successful
- wealthy
- shrewd
- handsome
- well-known
- powerful
- gainfully employed

Note: Christ said the false religionist is "within full of dead men's bones." This is most likely referring to spiritual death. The false religionist goes through life *living acceptably* in the eyes of men, but he is spiritually dead to God. His acts are the acts of a man-made morality and religion, not the acts of true morality and religion as revealed by God in Christ.

> "Even so ye also outwardly appear righteous unto me, but within ye are full of hypocrisy and iniquity" (Mt.23:28).
>
> "Woe unto you, scribes and Pharisees, hypocrites! for ye are as graves which appear not, and the men that walk over them are not aware of them" (Lu.11:44).
>
> "Beware ye of the leaven of the Pharisees, which is hypocrisy. For there is nothing covered, that shall not be revealed; neither hid, that shall not be known" (Lu.12:1-2).
>
> "For it is a shame even to speak of those things which are done of them in secret" (Ep.5:12).
>
> "Now the Spirit speaketh expressly, that in the latter times some shall depart from the faith, giving heed to seducing spirits, and doctrines of devils; speaking lies in hypocrisy; having their conscience seared with a hot iron" (1 Ti.4:1-2).
>
> "They profess that they know God; but in works they deny him, being abominable, and disobedient, and unto every good work reprobate" (Tit.1:16).

Thought 1. False religion is the most beautiful and deadly tomb among men. It leads to the eternal death of man's spirit. It makes him insensitive to the danger of eternal death by instilling a sense...
- of confidence in being religious
- of security in being religious
- of acceptability in being religious
- of pride in being religious
- of righteousness in being religious

Thought 2. Others may not know the truth—the truth of the closed doors and the dark—the sinful secrets of the heart. We may appear respectable to men. The heart can be full of secrets and full of sin; the life can appear free of blame. But God knows all secrets, and God knows what fills the heart.

The point is clear: God shall judge the secrets of men. Then the sinful heart will be in hell, and it will find no comfort in remembering that it appeared respectable to men (Ro.2:16; Lu.16:23).

8 (23:29-33) **Religionists, False—Heritage—Roots**: false religionists pride themselves in a godly heritage. Christ said four significant things about this point.

a. False religionists honor the relics of the past. They show great respect for former prophets. They build, renovate, adorn and look after the tombs of the great men of the past. But note: Christ says they pay honor to their tombs and memory, not to their teaching and godly lives.

b. False religionists denounce former abuses. Their forefathers had rejected, abused, and killed many of the prophets. The false religionists denounced such evil behavior. They preached and taught against murder.

c. False religionists are prideful, claiming that they are better than the religious people of former years. They feel they are beyond such sins and would never have rejected and abused the prophets of God. They believe they would have gladly heard the preachers of the past and done exactly what they said.

d. False religionists witness against themselves. They reverence the prophets of old but reject the prophets who are living. They reverence Abraham, Moses, Jeremiah, and Zechariah; but they reject God's very own Son. In rejecting Him, they prove that they are just as their fathers were: murderers. They are children of their fathers, following in the very steps of their fathers, rejecting the messengers of God. Like father, like son.

Note what Christ said: they were filling up the measure or cup of murder which was begun by their fathers. Christ was probably saying that His death was the last drop. The cup was about to reach the *filled* point; the cup would not be able to take another drop. There would be no chance to turn to God after they killed *the Prophet*, Christ Himself (see outline and notes—Mt.22:1-14).

> "But after thy hardness and impenitent heart treasurest up unto thyself wrath against the day of wrath and revelation of the righteous judgment of God; who will render to every man according to his deeds" (Ro.2:5-6).
>
> "And I saw the dead, small and great, stand before God; and the books were opened: and another book was opened, which is the book of life: and the dead were judged out of those things which were written in the books, according to their works" (Re.20:12; see Re.22:12).
>
> "Also unto thee, O Lord, belongeth mercy: for thou renderest to every man according to his work" (Ps.62:12).
>
> "If thou sayest, Behold, we knew it not; doth not he that pondereth the heart consider it? And he that keepeth thy soul, doth not he know it? And shall not he render to every man according to his works?" (Pr.24:12).
>
> "I the LORD search the heart, I try the reins, even to give every man according to his ways, and according to the fruit of his doings" (Je.17:10).

Thought 1. It is easy to honor great men of the past. They are not present to speak the truth and demand that we follow the truth. A dead man cannot disturb us with his warnings.

Thought 2. Every generation has *this one* great deception: since they are more educated and technologically advanced, they think they are stronger and better off than the former generation. They think...
- if they had been given the opportunities of the past, they would have done more with them
- if they had faced the temptations of the past, they would have withstood them better

9 (23:34-36) **Religionists, False**: false religionists reject and abuse many of God's present-day prophets. Christ said He was going to send forth messengers with the message of God, but false religionists were going to beat (scourge), persecute, and kill them. They were going to be dogged in their persecution, following after God's messenger from city to city.

Note: Christ said something else, something of terrible consequence to false religionists. All the abuse and all the righteous blood shed throughout human history is to be laid to the account of false religionists. Why? Because they of all people had the greatest opportunity.

> "[They had] the adoption, and the glory, and the covenants, and the...law, and the service of God, and the promises" (Ro.9:4).

Thought 1. There is one question that every man needs to face: When I am gone, what will the verdict be? What kind of legacy will I leave behind? Did I hinder or help God?

> "And I saw the dead, small and great, stand before God; and the books were opened: and another book was opened, which is the book of life: and the dead were judged out of those things which were written in the books, according to their works" (Re.20:12).

DEEPER STUDY # 7
(23:34) **Prophets**: see Deeper Study # 1—1 Co.14:3; note—Ep.4:11.

DEEPER STUDY # 8
(23:34) **Wise men**: the wise servants of God who are especially gifted by the Holy Spirit with godly wisdom.

DEEPER STUDY # 9
(23:34) **Scribes**: not the Judaistic Scribe, but men who would be gifted by the Holy Spirit to teach the New Testament, the great Covenant of Christ Himself, of God's very own Son.

DEEPER STUDY # 10
(23:35) **Abel**: see Ge.4:8-10; He.12:24.

DEEPER STUDY # 11
(23:35) **Zacharias**: there is some doubt as to who this is. It is probably not Zacharias the prophet, but the Zachariah who was stoned and killed in the court of the Lord's house (2 Chr.24:20-21). His father, called Jehoiada in the Old Testament and Barachias in the New Testament, was probably known by both names. It was common for Jews to have two names. The main support for this explanation is based upon the Jewish Bible. The books of the Jewish Bible are arranged differently from the Christian Bible. Second Chronicles is the *last book* of the Jewish Bible. Jesus is simply saying (referring to the arrangement of the Jewish Scriptures) that the false religionists are guilty of all the righteous blood throughout history, from the first murder, Abel, to the last murder, Zacharias.

DEEPER STUDY # 12
(23:36) **Generation, This**: *all these things* will come in a terrible judgment upon the generation of Christ's day. They stand especially guilty because they had such a unique opportunity: they had the very presence of God's Son visibly among them (Jn.20:29).

However, does this mean they are to bear a special judgment in eternity because of their special privileges (Ro.9:1-5)? Or is the reference to the destruction of Jerusalem and the nation under Titus in 70 A.D.? Both positions are held by various commentators.

	N. The Great Lament of Jesus: Jesus' Love Rejected, 23:37-39
	(Lu 13:34-35)
1. The past sin of Jerusalem: Persecuted God's messengers	37 O Jerusalem, Jerusalem, *thou* that killest the prophets, and stonest them which are sent unto thee, how often would I have gathered thy children together, even as a hen gathereth her chickens under *her* wings, and ye would not!
2. The great love of Christ for Jerusalem: Longed to *gather* the people under His care^{DS1}	
3. The great sin of Jerusalem: Rejected the Messiah	
4. The terrifying judgment upon Jerusalem	38 Behold, your house is left unto you desolate.
a. To be deserted & desolate^{DS2}	39 For I say unto you, Ye shall not see me henceforth, till ye shall say, Blessed *is* he that cometh in the name of the Lord.
b. To be blinded to the Messiah	
5. The glorious prediction: Jerusalem & Israel will proclaim the Messiah	

DIVISION XIV

THE MESSIAH'S LAST WEEK: HIS CLAIM CHALLENGED AND REJECTED, 21:1-23:39

N. The Great Lament of Jesus: Jesus' Love Rejected, 23:37-39

(23:37-39) **Introduction—Jerusalem—Israel**: God's great love for Jerusalem and for Israel is seen in this passage. This is Christ's great lament for Jerusalem, the city of God, and for Israel, the people of God. God's love, which was demonstrated perfectly by giving His only begotten Son, was rejected. Christ sighed from the depth of His heart and wept. He cried out with intense groanings:

> "O Jerusalem, Jerusalem...how often would I have gathered thy children together, even as a hen gathereth her chickens under her wings" (v.37).

The depth of the Lord's emotion and broken heart can never be known by man. Why? Because Christ knew that God's loving appeal had been in vain. The people who were chosen to be God's witness upon earth, that is, Jerusalem, "[had] grievously sinned" (Lam.1:8). They had rejected the only begotten Son of God, their very own Messiah and Savior.

However, God's great love for Jerusalem is not all that is seen in the Lord's words. God's justice is seen upbraiding Jerusalem.

> "Thou that killest the prophets, and stonest them which are sent unto thee....Behold, your house is left unto you desolate....For I say unto you, Ye shall not see me henceforth" (vv.37-39).

The depth of the city's sin, being stored up over the centuries, could never be known by man (Ro.2:5). The measure of the cup had been filled. The time had now come...

> "[God] will render to every man according to his deeds....Unto them that are contentious, and do not obey the truth, but obey unrighteousness....indignation and wrath....tribulation and anguish....upon every soul of man that doeth evil, of the Jew first, and also of the Gentiles" (Ro.2:6-9).

The place of Jerusalem in God's heart is seen in this great passage, but the terrifying judgment of God's heart is also seen. All those who reject His Son shall be judged and condemned—no matter who they are, both Jew and Gentile. The passage is applicable to all of us (add vs. 10 and 11 to Ro.2:6-9 quoted above and see outline and notes—Ro.11:11-16; 11:17-24 for more discussion).

1. The past sin of Jerusalem: persecuted God's messengers (v.37).
2. The great love of Christ for Jerusalem: longed to *gather* the people under His care (v.37).
3. The great sin of Jerusalem: rejected the Messiah (v.37).
4. The terrifying judgment upon Jerusalem (vv.38-39).
5. The glorious prediction: Jerusalem and Israel will proclaim the Messiah (v.39).

1 (23:37) **Jews, Sins of**: the great sin of Jerusalem is that they persecuted God's messengers. They ridiculed, abused, and killed the messengers of God. Christ, of course, was speaking to all unbelieving Israelites; but He specified Jerusalem because it was the capital, the place where the Sanhedrin (the ruling court of the Jews) sat. Some examples of Israel's rejecting and abusing the messengers of God would be...

MATTHEW 23:37-39

- the reaction against and imprisonment of Hanani (2 Chr.16:7-10, esp. 10).
- the stoning of Zacharias (2 Chr.24:20-21; Mt.23:35).
- the hatred and imprisonment of Micaiah (1 K.22:7-27, esp. 27).
- the casting of Jeremiah into a dungeon (Je.38:6).
- the attempt to silence Amos (Am.7:11-13).

Some examples of persecution by the Sanhedrin after Christ would be...
- the issuing of warrants for the arrest of early believers (Ac.9:2).
- the orders to round up and persecute early believers (Ac.8:1).
- the stoning of Stephen (Ac.7:57-60).

The ridicule and persecution of God's messengers were so common down through the centuries that Christ was led to say on another occasion: "It cannot be that a prophet perish out of Jerusalem" (Lu.13:33).

God holds His messengers very dear to His heart, and He is extremely protective of them. To ridicule and abuse one of His servants is a very serious offense. Jerusalem and the people of Israel were guilty of many sins, but it is this sin that is the *most condemning*. In conjunction with this thought is this fact: it was primarily the grumbling of Israel in the wilderness against God that caused God to judge that generation so severely.

Scripture says:

> "Who art thou that judgest another man's servant? To his own master [the Lord] he standeth or falleth. Yea, he shall be holden up: for God is able to make him stand" (Ro.14:4).

Thought 1. The true messenger of God is often ridiculed, abused and persecuted. Two facts need to be noted about this.
(1) The reason for their persecution: God's concern is the correcting of an unjust world; the changing of a self-righteous heart; the purifying of a lustful mind; the sacrificing of a selfish life. Men oppose God's correction and His demand for change and purity. They oppose the sacrifice of oneself—oppose such restraint by nature. Therefore, men often oppose the messenger who *truly* proclaims God's Word.
(2) The leaders of the persecution are often false religionists who are wrapped up in the world and its institutional religions. They feel threatened by a message that proclaims there is *truth* beyond man himself. Such a positive message endangers their own humanistic beliefs and threatens them with loss of security, livelihood, prestige, and all that this world offers.

2 (23:37) **Jesus Christ, Love**: the great love of Christ is strongly pictured in this passage (see note—Mt.23:37-39)—both His patience and His great desire to care for and protect people.

a. His patience is seen in the words, "How often I would have...." He personally would have saved the people. He would have saved them often. He desired their salvation, not their condemnation (see Jn.3:17). Jerusalem had abused and even killed many of His messengers, yet God had not turned away from them. He continued to send messengers, and finally, He sent His Son. Time and again He reached out to the people through men of God; and each time Jerusalem rejected, abused, and sometimes killed His servants. The patience of God endured and endured with man's sin in the knowledge that some would be saved (see outline—Ro.9:22-24; see 2 Pe.3:8-9).

b. His care and protection are seen in the word *gathered*. The picture of a hen's gathering her chickens under her wings is the picture of care and protection. The very purpose of Christ is to gather and keep a person from wandering around and facing the dangers of the world all alone.

> "He shall cover thee with his feathers, and under his wings shalt thou trust: his truth shall be thy shield and buckler" (Ps.91:4).

Thought 1. Christ longs to gather us to Himself *often*. Every time we hear the gospel and sense a pull within our hearts to draw near Him, He is reaching out to gather us unto Himself.

> "And I, if I be lifted up from the earth, will draw all men unto me" (Jn.12:32).
>
> "But to Israel he saith, All day long I have stretched forth my hands unto a disobedient and gainsaying people" (Ro.10:21).
>
> "Now then we are ambassadors for Christ, as though God did beseech you by us: we pray you in Christ's stead, be ye reconciled to God" (2 Co.5:20).
>
> "Behold, I stand at the door, and knock: if any man hear my voice, and open the door, I will come in to him, and will sup with him, and he with me" (Re.3:20).
>
> "The LORD hath appeared of old unto me, saying, Yea, I have loved thee with an everlasting love: therefore with loving-kindness have I drawn thee" (Je.31:3).

DEEPER STUDY # 1

(23:37) **Jesus Christ, Deity**: the words "How often *would I have gathered* thy children together" point backward to all the history of Israel. Christ was saying He was One with God. He was the One who was overseeing Israel throughout its history, the One who would have gathered Israel under His care and protection.

3 (23:37) **Jews, Sins of:** the *great* sin of Jerusalem was this: the people rejected God's only begotten Son. Note the words "ye would not." He would have saved them, but they would not be saved. They heard Christ; they saw Christ; they were even able to touch Christ (1 Jn.1:1), but they rejected Him. And their rejection was *deliberate*.

⇒ They rejected the love of God which was demonstrated to them in Christ. God demonstrated His love by giving His only begotten Son.

⇒ They rejected the terms of God's demand. God demanded that they live for Him. How? By believing in God's Son and by living holy lives day by day. Then they were to go forth and proclaim the message of salvation in God's Son.

⇒ They rejected God's righteousness (faith in Christ) and trusted their own righteousness (see Deeper Study # 2—Ro.4:22).

Thought 1. Men reject Christ for the very same reasons.
(1) They reject the revelation of God to man.

"For God so loved the world, that he gave his only begotten Son, that whosoever believeth in him should not perish, but have everlasting life" (Jn.3:16).

"But God commendeth his love toward us, in that, while we were yet sinners, Christ died for us" (Ro.5:8).

(2) They reject Christ's claim to be the revelation of God, to be the Son of God.

"Jesus heard that they had cast him out; and when he had found him, he said unto him, Dost thou believe on the Son of God? He answered and said, Who is he, Lord, that I might believe on him? And Jesus said unto him, Thou hast both seen him, and it is he that talketh with thee" (Jn.9:35-37).

"The Jews answered him, saying, For a good work we stone thee not; but for blasphemy; and because that thou, being a man, makest thyself God" (Jn.10:33).

"Say ye of him, whom the Father hath sanctified, and sent into the world, Thou blasphemest; because I said, I am the Son of God?" (Jn.10:36).

"Jesus cried and said, He that believeth on me, believeth not on me, but on him that sent me. And he that seeth me seeth him that sent me" (Jn.12:44-45).

"Jesus saith unto him, Have I been so long time with you, and yet hast thou not known me, Philip? he that hath seen me hath seen the Father; and how sayest thou then, Show us the Father?" (Jn.14:9).

(3) They reject God's righteousness and trust their own righteousness.

"For they being ignorant of God's righteousness, and going about to establish their own righteousness, have not submitted themselves unto the righteousness of God. For Christ is the end of the law for righteousness to every one that believeth" (Ro.10:3-4).

"There is a generation that are pure in their own eyes, and yet is not washed from their filthiness" (Pr.30:12).

4 (23:38-39) **Judgment—Jesus, Judgment of:** the terrifying judgment upon Jerusalem was threefold.

a. Their house was to be deserted by God, "left in their own hands." The word "house" refers to their temple, their nation and their lives. They wanted control of all; to do as they willed with their lives and possessions. Christ said that God would grant their wish. God's presence was going to depart their temple, their nation, and their lives; and He was going to leave all in their hands (see Deeper Study # 2—Mt.23:38).

b. Their house was to be desolated. It was to be destroyed. This would be a reference both to earthly judgment (the lack of God's presence) when Jerusalem was devastated by Titus in 70 A.D. and to eternal judgment (He.9:27). It should be noted, however, that many ancient manuscripts do not have the word "desolate" in their text.

c. They would thereafter be unable to see Christ. This meant two things.
1) They would not be able to see Him soon. He was departing the world, dying, and ascending into God's presence. They would not see Him again until He returned.
2) They would continue to be blind and obstinate in their unbelief. They would not submit to Christ as the Messiah, the very Son of God. Therefore, they would be blinded as part of the judgment of God (Ro.11:7-10, 25).

Thought 1. The same three judgments are applicable to every man and nation who walk in obstinate unbelief.
(1) God shall desert them.

"Wherefore God also gave them up to uncleanness through the lusts of their own hearts, to dishonour their own bodies between themselves" (Ro.1:24).

"For this cause God gave them up unto vile affections: for even their women did change the natural use into that which is against nature: and likewise also the men, leaving the natural use of the woman, burned in their lust one toward another; men with men working that which is unseemly, and receiving in themselves that recompence of their error which was meet. And even as they did not like to retain God in their knowledge, God gave them over to a reprobate mind, to do those things which are not convenient" (Ro.1:26-28).

(2) God shall destroy them.

"And now also the axe is laid unto the root of the trees: every tree therefore which bringeth not forth good fruit is hewn down, and cast into the fire" (Lu.3:9).

"And to you who are troubled rest with us, when the Lord Jesus shall be revealed from heaven with his mighty angels, in flaming fire taking vengeance on them that know not God, and that obey not the gospel of our Lord Jesus Christ: who shall be punished with everlasting destruction from the presence of the Lord, and from the glory of his power" (2 Th.1:7-9).

"The Lord knoweth how to deliver the godly out of temptations, and to reserve the unjust unto the day of judgment to be punished" (2 Pe.2:9).

"But the heavens and the earth, which are now, by the same word are kept in store, reserved unto fire against the day of judgment and perdition of ungodly men" (2 Pe.3:7).

"And Enoch also, the seventh from Adam, prophesied of these, saying, Behold, the Lord cometh with ten thousands of his saints, to execute judgment upon all, and to convince all that are ungodly among them of all their ungodly deeds which they have ungodly committed, and of all their hard speeches which ungodly sinners have spoken against him" (Jude 14-15).

(3) They shall be unable to see Christ.

"Then shall he say also unto them on the left hand, Depart from me, ye cursed, into everlasting fire, prepared for the devil and his angels" (Mt.25:41).

"But he shall say, I tell you, I know you not whence ye are; depart from me, all ye workers of iniquity" (Lu.13:27).

"For the wages of sin is death [separation]; but the gift of God is eternal life through Jesus Christ our Lord" (Ro.6:23).

"And as it is appointed unto men once to die, but after this the judgment [separation from God]" (He.9:27).

DEEPER STUDY # 2

(23:38) **Desolate** (eremos): to lay waste and make into a wilderness; to desert. Without the presence of God a place and person are like a wilderness, deserted and left all alone. They are left to waste away.

---

5 (23:39) **Jews, Restoration**: Jesus shares the glorious prediction that Jerusalem and Israel will proclaim the Messiah. Israel will not be blinded to Jesus as the true Messiah forever; Israel will profess and proclaim Jesus to be the Messiah.

Note two things.

a. The words "till ye shall say" look to the future. Israel will not be blinded forever. Israel will profess Jesus to the Messiah. That day is coming.

b. The words "blessed is He *that cometh*" look to the return of Jesus. Israel is going to proclaim Jesus to be the Messiah when He returns in great glory "in the name of the Lord" (Jehovah) (see Ph.2:9-11). (See outline and notes—Ro.11:25-36. See outline and notes—Ro.9:1-11:36.)

"For I would not, brethren, that ye should be ignorant of this mystery, lest ye should be wise in your own conceits; that blindness in part is happened to Israel, until the fulness of the Gentiles be come in. And so all Israel shall be saved: as it is written, There shall come out of Sion the Deliverer, and shall turn away ungodliness from Jacob: For this is my covenant unto them, when I shall take away their sins" (Ro.11:25-27).

"For the children of Israel shall abide many days without a king, and without a prince, and without a sacrifice, and without an image, and without an ephod, and without teraphim: afterward shall the children of Israel return, and seek the Lord their God, and David their king; and shall fear the Lord and his goodness in the latter days" (Ho.3:4-5).

"And I will pour upon the house of David, and upon the inhabitants of Jerusalem, the spirit of grace and of supplications: and they shall look upon me whom they have pierced, and they shall mourn for him, as one mourneth for his only son, and shall be in bitterness for him, as one that is in bitterness for his first-born" (Zec.12:10).

Thought 1. One of the most glorious moments of life is when a person turns to Christ and proclaims Him to be the Messiah. It is a *turning* that every person should experience. Israel will experience this one day.

MATTHEW 24:1-14

	CHAPTER 24 XV. THE MESSIAH'S PROPHECY OF HIS RETURN & THE END OF THE AGE: THE OLIVET DISCOURSE,^{DS1,2} 24:1–25:46 A. The Signs of the Last Days,^{DS3} 24:1-14 *(Mk 13:1-13; Lu 21:5-11)*		

1. Events that led to the great prophecies
  a. The disciples admired the temple's magnificence
 	
  b. Jesus used the occasion to arouse interest in prophecy: Predicted the temple's utter destruction^{DS4}
 	
  c. The disciples were aroused to ask two questions
    1) When would the temple be destroyed?
    2) What signs would precede Christ's return & the world's end?
  d. Jesus warned: Must guard against deception
 	
2. Sign 1: False messiahs
	And Jesus went out, and departed from the temple: and his disciples came to *him* for to show him the buildings of the temple.
	2 And Jesus said unto them, See ye not all these things? verily I say unto you, There shall not be left here one stone upon another, that shall not be thrown down.
	3 And as he sat upon the mount of Olives, the disciples came unto him privately, saying, Tell us, when shall these things be? and what *shall be* the sign of thy coming, and of the end of the world?
	4 And Jesus answered and said unto them, Take heed that no man deceive you.
	5 For many shall come in my name, saying, I am Christ; and shall deceive many.
		6 And ye shall hear of wars and rumours of wars: see that ye be not troubled: for all *these things* must come to pass, but the end is not yet.
		7 For nation shall rise against nation, and kingdom against kingdom: and there shall be famines, and pestilences, and earthquakes, in divers places.
		8 All these *are* the beginning of sorrows.
		9 Then shall they deliver you up to be afflicted, and shall kill you: and ye shall be hated of all nations for my name's sake.
		10 And then shall many be offended, and shall betray one another, and shall hate one another.
		11 And many false prophets shall rise, and shall deceive many.
		12 And because iniquity shall abound, the love of many shall wax cold.
		13 But he that shall endure unto the end, the same shall be saved.
		14 And this gospel of the kingdom shall be preached in all the world for a witness unto all nations; and then shall the end come.
			3. Sign 2: World violence
			
			4. Sign 3: Natural disasters
			
			(Note: These signs are the beginning of sorrows or birth pains)^{DS5}
			
			5. Sign 4: Severe religious persecution
			
			6. Sign 5: Terrible apostasy–betrayal & division
			
			7. Sign 6: The rise of many false leaders–offering false hope
			8. Sign 7: A great falling away–sin increasing & love growing cold^{DS6,7}
			9. Sign 8: Some enduring & being saved
			
			10. Sign 9: World evangelism

DIVISION XV

THE MESSIAH'S PROPHECY OF HIS RETURN AND THE END OF THE AGE: THE OLIVET DISCOURSE, 24:1–25:46

A. The Signs of the Last Days, 24:1-14

(24:1–25:46) **DIVISION OVERVIEW**—**End Time**: these two chapters, Mt.24-25, deal with three great subjects. All three subjects lay out in the future as Christ discussed them.
  1. The destruction of Jerusalem (v.3; see v.2).
  2. The Lord's return (v.3).
  3. The end of the world (v.3).

A quick glance at the first four verses will show the events that led Jesus to deal with the great prophecies covered by these chapters.
  1. The disciples admire the temple's magnificence and draw Jesus' attention to its beauty (v.1). The temple was magnificent. It sat upon the towering summit of Mount Sion. It was built of white marble plated with gold. The temple was a massive structure that could hold thousands of people (see Acts 4:4 where five thousand men were saved among a crowd which probably numbered many thousands more). The temple had several porches such as Solomon's Porch and the Royal Porch. Each porch was supported with huge towering pillars, each one so large that it took three to four men reaching arm to arm to reach around it. The temple was a striking sight, one of the building wonders of the world. The disciples apparently stood some place where the temple in all its magnificent beauty struck them with awe, and they wanted Christ to see the beautiful sight.
  2. Jesus uses the occasion to arouse the disciples' interest in coming events. He predicts the temple's utter destruction (v.2).
  3. The disciples are aroused to ask two questions of the Lord. When will the temple be destroyed and what will be the sign of His return and of the end of the world (v.3) (see note—Lu.21:5-7).
  4. Jesus warns His disciples. They must guard against being deceived (v.4). This can mean one or two things. A person can be easily deceived when dealing with end-time prophecies, or a person can be easily deceived when facing the

end time events. He can be deceived into thinking that certain cataclysmic events are infallible signs that the end is at hand (vv.6, 14). Such too often results...
- in wild guesses about the end time
- in universal predictions
- in the deceiving of others
- in discouragement of one's faith when the end does not come

DEEPER STUDY # 1
(24:1-31) **End Time**: noting the exact words of Christ will help in understanding this passage.

1. Christ says, "All these are the beginning of sorrows" (v.8). The words "the beginning of sorrows" indicate that Christ is dealing with *the beginning* of a terrible period of trial for the believer ("you," v.9). He is not *just* referring to the normal trials that occur upon earth or the regular persecutions that are launched against believers over the centuries (see DEEPER STUDY # 2—Mt.24:1-31). World trouble and persecutions against God's people have always existed, even from the beginning of time. The great sorrow He now speaks about refers to some terrible period which is so terrible that it can be said to be the "*the beginning* of sorrows" or "woes," a time which is to be distinguished from all other trouble the world and believers have suffered throughout history.

2. Christ says, "When ye therefore shall see the abomination of desolation stand in the holy place...then...flee...for then shall be great tribulation, such as was not since the beginning of the world" (vv.15-16, 21). There is no question about this sign. It launches the worst period of tribulation the world has ever seen. This sign definitely points to a specific period of human history. As to what the period should be called, it is probably best to simply use the words of Scripture and title it *great tribulation* (v.21).

3. Now, note what Christ has said in the above verses.

   "All these are the beginning of sorrows" (v.8).
   "When ye therefore shall see the abomination of desolation...stand in the holy place...then... flee...for then shall be great tribulation such as was not since the beginning of the world" (vv.15-16, 21).

Christ seems to be giving a list of signs, *one of which* is "the abomination of desolation." In verses 5-14 He gives nine signs, the ninth being world evangelism (v.14). He closes this ninth sign with the words, "Then shall the end come" (v.14). But note in verse 15 how He seems to pick up the signs again, giving what seems to be the most visible and terrible sign for which to watch. Note His words, reading verses 14, 15, and 21 together.

   "...Then shall the end come. When ye therefore shall see the abomination of desolation...stand in the holy place...then...flee...for then shall be great tribulation, such as was not since the beginning of the world" (vv.14-16, 21).

Christ is saying there is a difference between the signs that precede "the abomination" and the unparalleled trials that follow. When "the abomination of desolation" stands in the holy place, the trials that follow are much, much worse—unparalleled in human history.

The abomination of desolation is the sign that launches the worst tribulations the world has ever known. Just when this abomination will appear, Christ does not say. But His appearance is one of the ten signs Christ gives; and His appearance will signal the worst devastation ever known by the world.

A chart diagramming Christ's own words will perhaps help in understanding what He says.
1. His words are: "All these (signs) are the beginning of sorrows" (v.8).
2. "When ye therefore *shall see* the abomination of desolation...*then shall be great tribulation*" (vv.15, 21).
3. "Immediately after the tribulation of those days...all...*shall see* the Son of Man coming" (vv.29-31).

THE END OF THE WORLD

Seeing the Sign of the Abomination of Desolation *In the Middle of the Time or Years* (v.15)		Seeing the Son of Man Coming (vv.29-30)
Signs which are "The beginning of sorrows" (v.8).	"Unparalleled trials of "the great tribulation (v.21).	His angels...gather together His elect" (v.31)

Another way to express what Christ is saying in these chapters, which may be of help as we seek to understand His words, is as follows.

1. Christ is asked two questions by the disciples: When shall the temple be destroyed, and what shall be the sign of thy coming and of the end of the world?

2. Christ answers by giving nine signs (vv.5-14). When He gives the ninth sign, world evangelism, He says, "And then shall the end come" (v.14).

3. Christ then says in essence, "But there is a tenth sign, a sign that you should see and for which you should watch. And this tenth sign He discusses at some length. He says: "When ye therefore shall see the abomination of desolation..." (vv.15-28).

   a. It shall launch the worst tribulations the world has ever seen (vv.15-22).
   b. It shall cause a frantic search for the Messiah and false prophets, that is, for a great deliverer (vv.23-26).

c. But know this: the return of Christ will not be in an isolated place or done in secret (v.26). His return will be as lightning: it will be quick, stretching across the sky and visible to all (vv.27-28).
4. Christ then says, "Immediately after the tribulation of those days" He shall return (vv.29-31).

Many Biblical scholars point out great similarities between what Christ says about the end time and sections of Revelation (Mt.24; Mk.13; Lu.21. See notes—Re.6:1-7:1; 7:1; 8:1; 11:15; 16:1-21.)
1. There seems to be a similarity between the structure of what Christ says and the book of Revelation in dealing with the end time (see notes given in paragraph above).

- The beginning of sorrows: preliminary sorrows, trouble and evil in society and nature; yet world evangelism continues (Mt.24:5-14). ....corresponds to ...The Seven Seals (Re.6:1-17)

- "The Great Tribulation": unparalleled...trials (Mt.24:15-28). ....corresponds to ...The Seven Trumpets, the bowls, and the beast (Re.8:1-18:24).

- "The Son of Man coming" ....corresponds to ...The Final Triumph of Christ (Re.19:1-22:21).

2. There seems to be similarity between "the beginning of sorrows" (Mt.24:5-14) and the seals of Revelation (Re.6:1-17). The end of the world *will not come all at once*. The future will be filled with wars, natural disasters, persecutions, and the claims of false deliverers (messiahs). And at the very end, there will be an increase and intensification of the signs. But this is not all. There is to be a terrible sign: the appearance of the rider on the white horse (see note—Re.6:2); "the abomination of desolation" (AV), "the desolating sacrilege" (RSV), "the man of lawlessness" (2 Th.2:3); the "little horn" (Da.7); the Antichrist. This person will afflict the people of God beyond imagination. (See DEEPER STUDY # 1—Re.11:7.)
3. There seems to be a similarity between "the great tribulation" spoken of by Christ and the seven trumpets, the seven bowl judgments, and the beast covered by Revelation.
4. Others point to a great similarity between "the beast" (Antichrist) pictured time and again in Revelation and "the abomination of desolation" spoken of by Christ (see DEEPER STUDY # 2—Mt.24:1-31; DEEPER STUDY # 1—Re.11:7).

DEEPER STUDY # 2
(24:1-31) **End Time**: three other things will help in understanding what Christ is doing in this passage.
1. It will help to remember that Jesus is preparing His disciples for His death and departure from this world and preparing them to carry on after He is gone. His immediate disciples were to face some terrible times, ranging all the way from personal trials brought on by their witness for Christ to national trials involving the utter destruction of their nation. And it would be generations stretching into centuries before He returned to earth. No one knew this at that time—But He did. So He needed to prepare His future disciples as well. They, too, were going to face all kinds of trials; and there was always the danger that His disciples might tire waiting for His return. They were to see and experience so much trouble in the world their faith might falter. They, along with many in the world, might begin to ask:

"Where is the promise of his coming? for since the fathers fell asleep, all things continue as they were from the beginning of the creation" (2 Pe.3:4).

What Christ does is use this occasion to reveal some of the events that are to take place upon the earth during "these last days," the days of the church (Ac.2:16-17; 1 Jn.2:18). By knowing some of the events, His disciples will be better prepared to endure and to keep alive their hope for His return.
⇒ They will know that God is not caught off guard. God is still on the throne and still in control of the events.
⇒ They will not be caught off guard themselves. They will know what to expect in this corruptible and sinful world. When the events happen, they will not be as likely to become discouraged.
⇒ They will be challenged to *keep themselves* ever so close to God in order to be as strong as possible in facing the trials coming upon earth.
⇒ They will be encouraged to place their hope in God and in the new heavens and earth and not in this corruptible world. They will be "looking for that blessed hope, and the glorious appearing of the great God and our Savior Jesus Christ" (Tit.2:13).

2. Remembering that Jesus is dealing with two questions will also help in understanding what is being said. He is answering the questions: When will the temple be destroyed and what shall be the sign of His return and of the end of the world?
Note something. Christ is dealing with the end of the temple and with the end of the world, the destruction of the temple and the destruction of the world. He is covering the signs, the events that both cause the judgment and occur during the judgment of the temple and the world. What is the point? Simply this. The Scripture teaches that the same signs and events cause the judgment of anything. That is, the events (sins) that cause judgment upon one thing are the same events that will bring judgment upon everything else. Thus, the signs that surround the destruction of Jerusalem are much the same as the signs that shall surround the end of the world. Therefore, what Christ is saying has a double meaning and application (see DEEPER STUDY # 3—Mt.24:1-14; 24:15-28. Both notes will help to see the double application.)
The Lord's words apply both to the disciples of His day and to all disciples who were to follow in succeeding generations. As long as the earth stands, the disciples of *the last days* (or ages) will face many of the same signs faced by those

who experienced the destruction of Jerusalem. But there is to be one difference. At the end of the world, the signs will increase and intensify. So terrible a day is coming that it can be called, "the beginning of sorrows" (Mt.24:8) and "the great tribulation" (Mt.24:21). (See Deeper Study #1,2—Mt.24:1-28; note—24:15-28.)

3. A quick overview of the passages dealing with the signs also help in understanding the chapters.
   a. The nine signs of the last days (that is, the last days before both Jerusalem's destruction and the world's end) (Mt.24:1-14).
   b. The tenth and most terrible sign: "the abomination of desolation" and the Great Tribulation (Mt.24:15-28).
   c. The Coming of the Son of Man (Mt.24:29-31).

The rest of what Christ covers deals with the actual time of the Lord's return (Mt.24:32-41) and the believer's duty to watch and be prepared (Mt.24:42-25:46).

DEEPER STUDY # 3

(24:1-14) **End Time:** in Mt.24:1-29 Christ gives at least ten signs of the last days. Several things need to be noted as this passage is studied.

1. Christ is answering two or three very specific questions. When will the temple be destroyed? And what shall be the sign of Christ's return and of the end of the world?

2. The signs given by Christ are to some extent present in every generation. A quick review of world history shows this. In light of this fact, a question has to be asked: why, then, is Christ spelling out every day happenings as signs of the last days? The next point, point three, answers this question.

3. There is to be an intensification of the signs right before the fall of Jerusalem and right before the end of the world. The intensification of the signs is clearly seen by the following.
   a. The emphasis upon the possibility of being deceived.

> "Take heed that no man deceive you" (v.4).
> "Many shall deceive many" (v.5).
> "False prophets...shall deceive many" (v.11).

   b. Christ uses both the word and the idea of "many" time and again, indicating an increase over what had been (the word is used in v.5, 10, 11, 12; and the idea is used in vv.6, 7, 9).
   c. Christ makes three significant statements that definitely point toward an intensification of the signs.

> "All these are the beginning of sorrows" (v.8).
> "But he that shall endure unto the end, the same shall be saved" (v.13).
> "And this gospel of the kingdom shall be preached in all the world for a witness unto all nations; and then shall the end come" (v.14).

   d. Other Scriptures say there is to be an intensification of evil in the last days.

> "This know also, that in the last days perilous times shall come" (2 Ti.3:1).
> "Knowing this first, that there shall come in the last days scoffers, walking after their own lusts" (2 Pe.3:3).
> "How that they told you there should be mockers in the last time, who should walk after their own ungodly lusts" (Jude 18).

4. The present age is considered by God to be "the age of the last days" or "the last time." According to God's timetable, the history of the church, its presence on earth, takes place in "the last days" or during "the last times."

> "But this is that which was spoken by the prophet Joel: And it shall come to pass in the last days, saith God, I will pour out of my Spirit upon all flesh: and your sons and your daughters shall prophesy, and your young men shall see visions, and your old men shall dream dreams" (Ac.2:16-17).
> "Hath in these last days spoken unto us by his son, whom he hath appointed heir of all things, by whom also he made the worlds" (He.1:2).
> "Little children, it is the last time" (1 Jn.2:18).

5. Christ gives these signs for a very specific purpose. He is preparing His disciples to endure and to keep their hope for His return alive. He is strengthening their faith in God and in the world to come, the new heavens and earth (see note, pt. 1—Mt.24:1-31, the three things that help in understanding the passage).

(24:1-14) **Introduction:** in understanding this passage, we have to be very careful not to read into the passage more than Christ was saying, nor to miss what He was saying. Both mistakes were made by religionists concerning Christ's first coming (Mt.2:4-6).

A major fact to keep in mind is this. The disciples did think that all three events (Jerusalem's destruction, the Lord's return, and the world's end) would happen at about the same time. They did think in terms of the Messianic kingdom of God (Ac.1:6 compared with the Jewish concept of the Messiah shows this. See notes—Mt.1:1; Deeper Study # 2—1:18; Deeper Study # 3—3:11; notes—11:1-6; 11:2-3; Deeper Study # 1—11:5; Deeper Study # 2—11:6; Deeper Study # 1—12:16; notes—22:42; Lu.7:21-23). When Christ said that the temple would be destroyed, they assumed it would happen at the same time that He returned and ended the world, thereby restoring the kingdom to Israel.

MATTHEW 24:1-14

Christ, however, gave no timetable. He did not say when the three events would occur. What He did was give signs that will occur before the events, signs that point toward His return, toward the end of Jerusalem, and the end of the world.

It is important to keep in mind that most of the signs happen all through history. But there is this difference: the signs increase and intensify right before the end of Jerusalem and of the world. There will be a period known as "the beginning of sorrows" (v.8), and a period launched by "the abomination of desolation" known as the "great tribulation, such as was not since the beginning of the world" (v.21).

1. Events that lead to the great prophecies (vv.1-4).
2. Sign 1: false messiahs (v.5).
3. Sign 2: world violence (v.6).
4. Sign 3: natural disasters (v.7).
5. Sign 4: severe religious persecution (v.9).
6. Sign 5: terrible apostasy—betrayal and division (v.10).
7. Sign 6: the rising of many false leaders—offering false hope (v.11).
8. Sign 7: a great falling away—sin increasing and love growing cold (v.12).
9. Sign 8: some enduring and being saved (v.13).
10. Sign 9: world evangelism (v.14).

(24:1-14) **Another Outline:** Christ gives at least nine signs of the last days in these fourteen verses. But He divides them into three sections.

1. The beginning signs: the beginning of sorrows (vv.5-8). Verse 8 makes this division. "All these (the signs just given in vv.5-7) are the beginning of sorrows."

2. The succeeding signs: personal threats and sorrows (vv.9-12). Note the word "then" in verse 9. After the beginning of sorrows, "then" these sorrows will happen. At this point, Luke says, "But before all these (the above signs) they shall...persecute you..." (Lu.21:12). The word "before" (pro) should probably be taken in the sense of "more important" than of time. That is, Luke is saying, "But before (more important than) all these...." (see note—Lu.21:12).

3. The promising signs: the result of faithfulness (vv.13-14). The word "but" in verse thirteen points toward two signs that offer all the promise and hope a believer could ever desire. In fact, his salvation and witness are what he lives for. And the fulfillment of both is promised in the last days.

1 (24:1-4) **Prophecy:** The events that lead to the great prophecies (see note above—Mt.24:1-25:46 for discussion).

Thought 1. It is not the outward appearance that makes an object acceptable; it is what is within. The temple showed that this principle is even true with buildings. The glory of a building can be tarnished by what goes on within it. The corruption of the priests within the temple stained its glory, greatly so.

Thought 2. Man's perspective must be kept right. Being honest and remembering two things will help tremendously.
(1) All the glory and magnificence of buildings will lie as dust not too many years hence. If they are not destroyed by war or catastrophe, they shall deteriorate and waste away.
(2) Within a short, short time, the human body itself, even the most beautiful, will decay, becoming nothing more than dirt.

Thought 3. Note the words of Christ: "I say unto you" (v.2). What Christ said happens (see DEEPER STUDY # 3—Mt.24:2). Thus, all nine signs are bound to take place. But, note a critical point. The signs happen not because God destines them but because man sins. They come to pass because of the passion and evil within man.

Thought 4. The world and every single man should know by now what Jesus knew. The way of God is the only way. Every nation who walks its own way without God is doomed (Ps.9:17; Pr.14:34). And every politician and man who walks their own way without God is also doomed (Ro.6:23; He.9:27).

Thought 5. We must be very, very careful when looking into the secret things of God, into the prophecies of the end time. Christ gives us a special warning: "Take heed that *no man* deceive you" (v.4). Note 2 Th.2:3: "Let no man deceive you by any means" (see Mt.24:11).

DEEPER STUDY # 4
(24:2) **Temple:** the prophecy of Jesus was graphically fulfilled. Just a few years after Jesus' words, Rome grew tried of the hard rebellious spirit of the Jews who refused to submit to Roman rule. In 70 A.D., Rome sent Titus to march against the city of Jerusalem. The city and temple were utterly destroyed, so much so that Josephus, the great Jewish historian of that day, said that a passerby would not have known the place was ever inhabited. Not a stone was left upon another.

---

2 (24:5) **Messiah, False:** the first sign of the last days is that of false messiahs. Note what Christ said.

a. "Many shall come." There will not be a few but *many* false messiahs.

b. The false messiahs actually claim, "I am Christ," the Messiah. They will not be the false prophets and teachers mentioned later. They will be persons who claim to be *the Messiah*, the Messenger of God to the world. They will be pseudo-christs or *anti-christs*.

c. The false messiahs *shall deceive many*. Not a few, but many will believe and follow the false messiahs, believing they are the way, the truth, and the life of God (see Jn.14:6).

MATTHEW 24:1-14

Right after Jesus' death, several men arose who claimed to be the Messiah. Josephus, the Jewish historian, said many were led astray by them. Scripture also mentions two who apparently claimed to be the Messiah or at least the deliverer of the Jews: Theudas and Judas of Galilee (Ac.5:36-37). Simon Magus claimed to "the great power of God" (Ac.8:9-10). Every generation has its false messiahs, each one claiming to be the special messenger of God, the deliverer of the human race. Every false religion and sect of every generation has its false messiahs, but there shall be *many* as the last days approach.

Thought 1. Men seek utopia, inward peace and outward security. Unfortunately, too many churches and believers do not demonstrate enough trust in Christ to show that peace and security are found in Him alone. Therefore, they turn to other messiahs.

3 (24:6-7) **World Violence—War:** the second sign of the end time is world violence. Note several things.

a. Believers *shall hear* of so much violence it will sound as though the world is coming apart. Believers can be troubled, extremely troubled over the news.

b. Christ said, *Be not troubled* (me throeithe), disturbed, frightened, confused. Be not put into confusion or commotion. World violence can disturb and frighten. It can lead us into confusion and commotion. But Christ says such is not to be the case of His disciples. Our hearts are to be fixed upon God, trusting His presence, care, and security eternally (Mt.10:28; Lu.12:4).

c. World violence *must come to pass*. Violence does not happen because God wills or destines it to be but because of the passions and evil of men's hearts (Mt.18:7; see Js.4:1-3).

d. World violence can so dominate the news that man is led to believe the end is at hand. But Christ warned, "The end is not yet." He had just said, "Take heed that no man deceive you" (v.4).

Now note something. All the violence mentioned thus far deals with the violence that men hear about. The fact of the violence is given in verse 7: "For nation shall rise against nation, and kingdom against kingdom."

A descriptive picture of the violence that gripped the world during the days immediately following our Lord is given by Tacitus, the Roman historian (55? - after 117). In the opening statements of his *Histories* of the Roman empire, he says:

> *I enter upon a work fertile in vicissitudes, stained with the blood of battles, embroiled with dissensions, horrible even in the intervals of peace. Four princes slain by the sword; three civil wars, more with foreign enemies, and sometimes both at once; prosperity in the East; disasters in the West; Illyricum disturbed; the Gauls ready to revolt; Britain conquered, and again lost; Sarmatians and Suevians conspiring against us; the Dacians renowned for defeats given and sustained; the Parthians almost aroused to arms by a counterfeit Nero. Italy afflicted with calamities unheard of, or recurring only after a long interval; cities overwhelmed or swallowed up in the fertile region of Campania; Rome itself laid waste by fire, the most ancient temples destroyed, the very capital burned by its own citizens: etc. ('Hist.,' 1.2).*

Remember however, despite the bleakness of world events within a particular generation, the words of our Lord stretch over the centuries covering all of history and point toward an intensification of violence toward the end of the world. (See 2 Chr.15:6-7; Lu.21:34; Ph.4:6; 1 Pe.5:7.)

Thought 1. A critical point. God does not cause violence. It is the passion and evil of men that causes violence.

Thought 2. The believer's hope is not in this world; neither is his real citizenship. His hope and his life are in God and in heaven (Ph.3:21). Therefore, we are not to fear men and world events. Men and world events can only take our lives, not our souls. Our lives are in God's hands, even to the end of the world (Mt.28:20; He.13:5).

4 (24:7) **Nature—Famine—Earthquake—Pestilence:** the third sign of the last days is natural disasters. Three disasters of nature are mentioned in particular.

a. Famines. Scripture speaks of a "great famine" throughout all the world "which came to pass in the days of Claudius Caesar" (Ac.11:28-30). Josephus described the famine as being so terrible that when flour "was brought into the temple...not one of the priests was so hardy as to eat one crumb of it...while so great a distress was upon the land" (Josephus, *Ant*. 3. 15:3). He said in another place, "A famine did oppress them (Jerusalem)...and many people died for want of what was necessary to procure food" (*Ibid*. 20. 2:5).

In the very last days before Jerusalem's fall, Josephus spoke of another terrible famine:

> *It was now a miserable case, and a sight that would justly bring tears into our eyes, how men stood to their food, while the more powerful had more than enough, and the weaker were lamenting (for want of it) (Josephus, Wars. 5. 10:3).*
>
> *Then did the famine widen its progress, and devoured the people by whole houses and families; the upper rooms were full of women and children that were dying by famine; and the lanes of the city were full of the dead bodies of the aged; the children also and the young men wandered about the marketplaces like shadows, all swelled with famine, and fell down dead wheresoever their misery seized them (Ibid. 5. 12:3).*

There is evidently to be terrible famine in the last days. The black horse of the four horsemen of the Apocalypse indicates terrible famine (see note—Re.6:5-6). The unbearable pain and terrible evil that hunger can cause is graphically described by Scripture.

MATTHEW 24:1-14

"They that be slain with the sword are better than they that be slain with hunger: for these pine away, stricken through for want of the fruits of the field. The hands of the pitiful women have sodden [boiled] their own children: they were their meat [food] in the destruction of the daughter of my people" (Lam.4:9-10).

b. Pestilence. Whereas the rich can sometimes escape famine by purchasing food at any price, they are helpless against pestilences or plagues. Death by disease and other natural causes shows no partiality.
Josephus' record of a great pestilence that struck during the days of Herod is evidence of the fact.

> *When he [Herod] was in the way, there arose a pestilential disease, and carried off the greatest part of the multitude, and of his best and most esteemed friends [the wealthy] (Josephus, Ant. 15. 7:7).*

Pestilence will also be one of the terrible sufferings at the end time. Part of the suffering caused by the pale horse of the four horsemen of the Apocalypse includes pestilences.

> **"Power was given unto them (Death and Hell) over the fourth part of the earth, to kill with sword [war], and with hunger [famine], and with death [pestilence resulting from war and famine]" (see note—Re.6:8).**

c. Earthquakes. Unbelievable destruction and death are sometimes caused by earthquakes. Again, Josephus recorded the fulfillment of Jesus' prophecy. He even hinted that the natural disasters which happened were a sign of coming destruction.

> *...there broke out a prodigious storm in the night, with the utmost violence, and very strong winds, with the largest showers of rain, and continual lightnings, terrible thunderings, and amazing concussions and bellowings of the earth, that was in an earthquake. These things were a manifest indication that some destruction was coming upon men, when the system of the world was put into this disorder; and any one would guess that these wonders foreshowed some grand calamities that were coming (Josephus, Wars. 4. 4:5).*

Earthquakes will occur in many places during the last days of the earth (Re.6:12; 11:12-13, 19; 16:17-19).

DEEPER STUDY # 5
(24:8) **Sorrows** (odinon): birth pains, labor pains, travailings, intolerable anguish. Quick, sharp, agonizing, continuous pain.

---

5 (24:9) **Persecution:** the fourth sign of the end time is that of severe religious persecution. Christ says two things.
  a. What the persecution will be:
    1) Affliction (Ac.4:3; 8:1; 12:4; 13:50; 14:19; 2 Co.11:23-25).
    2) Killing (Ac.7:59; 12:2).
    3) Hatred by all nations.

> "Concerning this sect, we know that everywhere it is spoken against" (Ac.28:22). (See outline and notes—Mt.10:16-23. See Jn.15:20; 16:2.)

  b. Why believers are persecuted: "For my sake" (see Mt.10:22). "For my sake" means at least three things. Or to say it another way, there are at least three reasons why the world often tries to silence and stamp out the believer.
    1) The world opposes the believer's standard of true godliness. The believer sets before the world a different standard. Neither the world nor its standard are godly. Therefore, any man who lives for the world and does not wish to change his behavior opposes believers. He opposes believers by his very nature (1 Jn.2:14-15).
    2) The world opposes the believer's life of purity and justice. The genuine believer lives such a life. He controls his mind, dresses modestly, converses respectfully, and behaves justly. The world lives to fulfill the lust of the flesh and to have what one wishes. Thus, the believer is opposed by any person who does not wish to live a pure and just life (Ga.5:19-21).
    3) The world opposes the believer's message of repentance and self-denial. The genuine believer proclaims the message of Christ which is repentance and self-denial. Few men are willing to change (repent) to the degree that self is totally denied. Most, even the religious, oppose the idea of giving all one is and has, even if it does mean saving a starving and dying world. (See outline and notes—Mt.19:21-22; 19:23-26.)
Note the words "hated of all nations." This definitely points to persecution all around the world. Christ is again looking well beyond the last days before Jerusalem's fall. He is looking to the persecution that shall be launched against His followers across the centuries and be intensified in the end time. He had even foretold such persecution before.

> "But beware of men: for they will deliver you up to the councils, and they will scourge you in their synagogues; and ye shall be brought before governors and kings for my sake, for a testimony against them and the Gentiles" (Mt.10:17-18).
> "All thy commandments *are* faithful: they persecute me wrongfully; help thou me" (Ps.119:86).
> "For the enemy hath persecuted my soul; he hath smitten my life down to the ground; he hath made me to dwell in darkness, as those that have been long dead" (Ps.143:3).

MATTHEW 24:1-14

6 (24:10) **Apostasy**: The fifth sign is terrible apostasy—betrayal and division. Christ says three things about the apostasy.

a. "Many shall be offended (fall away)." Persecution shall cause droves to turn from professing Christ. They do not know Him: not really, not personally, not inwardly. They have only professed Him with their lips. They have neither trusted Him with their hearts nor denied self, nor lived sacrificially, nor given, nor served to meet the needs of a needy and dying world. They know only the comfort and benefits that rub off from being in the church and associating with genuine believers. They know nothing about the call of God to share in the sufferings of Christ (Ph.1:29; 2 Co.4:11).

Consequently, when the fiery trial comes, they have no idea what denying self and dying daily for Christ is all about. They have no inward desire or strength, actually no real reason, to stand firm. They are offended; therefore, they fall away (see Mt.13:21).

Note something. Every generation has some apostasy. Some who have professed Christ do turn away (2 Ti.4:10; 1 Jn.2:18-19). What Christ is saying is that apostasy is to increase, be intensified in the end time. Many will be offended by the persecution to come, and they will fall away.

b. "(Many) shall betray one another." Again, informing on others, betraying them is to intensify in the end time. Neighbor will turn against neighbor, friend against friend, family against family.

A reading of *The war of the Jews* by Josephus graphically pictures just how inhuman man can become when his survival is threatened. And, of course, the Gospels show rather graphically how greed and power and selfishness can cause men to mistreat, abuse, threaten, plot and kill others (see notes—Mt.12:1-8; note and Deeper Study # 1—12:10).

Both survival and selfishness are seen in the last days of Jerusalem when Titus besieged the city: the wealthy saw to their needs and neglected the poor, and the powerful took what they wanted. As the siege wore on, famine and pestilence struck. The strong took from the weak and the weak informed on his neighbor's hidden supplies, no matter how little, in order to receive a morsel from the strong. Within the city walls, betrayal and murder ran rampant in order to survive. Others just outrightly betrayed their nation and went over to the side of the Romans in order to save their lives.

> *The people, they had a great inclination to desert to the Romans...the main reasons why they were so ready to desert were these: that now they should be freed from those miseries which they had endured in that city...the robbers came running into, and searched men's private houses; and if they found none [food], they tormented them worse, because they supposed they had more carefully concealed it. The indication they made use of whether they had any or not, was taken from the bodies of these miserable wretches; which, if they were in good case, they supposed they were in no want at all of food; but if they were wasted away, they walked off without searching any further...children pulled the very morsels that their fathers were eating, out of their very mouths, and what was still more to be pitied, so did the mothers do as to their infants: and when those that were most dear were perishing under their hands, they were not ashamed to take from them the very last drops that might preserve their lives...the seditious everywhere came upon them immediately, and snatched away from them what they had gotten from others; for when they saw any house shut up, this was to them a signal that the people within had gotten some food; whereupon they broke upon the doors, and ran in, and took pieces of what they were eating, almost up out of their very throats and this by force; the old men, who held their food fast, were beaten; and if the women hid what they had within their hands, their hair was torn for so doing; nor was there any commiseration shown either to the aged or to infants, but they lifted up children from the ground as they hung upon the morsels they had gotten, and shook them down upon the floor; but still were they more barbarously cruel to those that had prevented their coming in, and had actually swallowed down what they were going to seize upon, as if they had been unjustly defrauded of their right. They also invented terrible methods of torment to discover where any food was (Josephus, Wars. 5. 10:1).*

Tacitus, the great Roman historian, summarizes the betrayal of some in the early church.

> *First those were seized who confessed that they were Christians; and then on their information a vast multitude was convicted (Tacitus, Annuals. 15:44).*

Christ had already warned His followers of terrible persecution and even betrayal by one's own family (see outline and Deeper Study # 2—Mt.10:21). The difference in what He is saying now is His stress upon the end time. The persecution and betrayal will increase and intensify in the end time.

> **"This now also, that in the last days, perilous times shall come. For men shall be lovers of their own selves...traitors" (1 Ti.3:1-43).**

Several things cause a person to betray others. All will evidently be involved in the end time, as they were in the last days of Jerusalem.

- ⇒ to escape persecution
- ⇒ to save life
- ⇒ to secure some favor
- ⇒ to get what one wants
- ⇒ to get back at someone (vengeance)
- ⇒ to escape embarrassment
- ⇒ to escape fear
- ⇒ to preserve selfish honor

c. "(Many) shall hate one another." So few will be kind, tender, and loving. Dissension and division will prevail in the last days. Most will begrudge what another has or is doing or is not doing. Such has been the case down through the centuries. Too often the church has experienced one person's disliking and opposing another person. Envy, greed, concern for security and recognition—all the sins of selfishness—have caused too many to stand against another's position, beliefs, abilities, leadership, and on and on. Unfortunately, criticism and judging, dissension and division among believers has been and is one of the most visible traits of the church, both locally and universally. Christ says that such hatred will increase and intensify in the end times.

MATTHEW 24:1-14

Thought 1. Why are professing Christians sometimes "offended" by Christ? Some of the reasons would be...
- fear of ridicule
- fear of abuse
- fear of being ignored
- fear of not fitting in
- fear of persecution
- fear of not having
- fear of losing position, security, wealth, and power

All these, and many other reasons, will be taking their toll in the last days.

Thought 2. The two things that God and Christ desire above all others from the believer are love and unity.

(1) Love is basic.

> "And this is his commandment, That we should believe on the name of his son Jesus Christ, and love one another, as he gave us commandment" (1 Jn.3:23; see Jn.13:34-35; 15:12; 15:17).

(2) Unity is basic.

> "And now I am no more in the world, but these are in the world, and I come to thee. Holy Father, keep through thine own name those whom thou hast given me, that they may be one, as we are" (Jn.17:11).
>
> "Neither pray I for these alone, but for them also which shall believe on me through their word; That they all may be one; as thou, Father, art in me, and I in thee, that they also may be one in us: that the world may believe that thou hast sent me. And the glory which thou gavest me I have given them; that they may be one, even as we are one: I in them, and thou in me, that they may be made perfect in one; and that the world may know that thou hast sent me, and hast loved them, as thou hast loved me" (Jn.17:20-23).

7 **(24:11) Leaders, False—Teachers, False:** The sixth sign is the rise of false leaders offering false hope. Christ makes two points.

a. "Many false prophets shall rise." They will be prophets; that is, they will claim to preach and teach the message of God. Jerusalem, facing the crises of its last days, experienced a great number of false prophets arising; and each had his own message about how the people could be saved.

> *Now, there was then a great number of false prophets suborned by the tyrants to impose upon the people, who denounced this to them, that they should wait for deliverance from God; and this was in order to keep them from deserting, and that they might be buoyed up above fear and care by such hopes. Now, a man that is in adversity does easily comply with such promises; for when such a seducer makes him believe that he shall be delivered from those miseries which oppress him, then it is that the patient is full of hopes of such deliverance (Josephus, Wars. 6. 5:2).*

A false teacher is one who develops his own way, truth, and life for people to follow rather than follow Jesus as the way, the truth, and the life. The church has always had its false teachers: teachers who presented what they wished instead of what Christ said; teachers who taught their own ideas instead of the truth of Christ; teachers who attached people to themselves instead of attaching them to Christ.

b. "Many shall be deceived." There are several reasons why a person is deceived.
⇒ A person's frantic hope for deliverance causes him to search for a savior and to grasp at almost anyone who appears on the scene.
⇒ The humanistic desire to better and strengthen oneself and to impose and control one's destiny causes a person to look to leaders who offer hope and a better world.
⇒ The evidence of signs, wonders, power, reasonableness, logic, knowledge, and help causes a person to follow leaders who demonstrate unusual abilities.

False teachers are both within and without the church, and they shall increase as the last days of the world approach (see 2 Co.11:13; 2 Th.2:1f; 1 Ti.6:3).

> "Little children, it is the last time: and as ye have heard that antichrist shall come, even now are there many antichrists; whereby we know that it is the last time. They went out from us, but they were not of us; for if they had been of us, they would no doubt have continued with us; but they went out, that they might be made manifest that they were not all of us" (1 Jn.2:18-19).
>
> "Beloved, believe not every spirit, but try the spirits whether they are of God: because many false prophets are gone out into the world. Hereby know ye the Spirit of God: Every spirit that confesseth that Jesus Christ is come in the flesh is of God: and every spirit that confesseth not that Jesus Christ is come in the flesh is not of God: and this is that spirit of antichrist, whereof ye have heard that it should come; and even now already is it in the world" (1 Jn.4:1-3).

Thought 1. The genuine believer knows how to pray and commune with God. He knows how to receive strength from God, to conquer and live above the most difficult circumstances (Ph.4:4, 6-7, 11-14, 19. See 1 Co.10:13; Ac.16:25f.)

MATTHEW 24:1-14

Thought 2. Discouragement is a terrible thing. It defeats life. However, there is one sure way to live above discouragement: learn to live and walk in an unbroken communion with God every day. Study His Word and pray without ceasing, learning and claiming His promises (Is.26:3; Ph.4:6-9).

8 (24:12) **Apostasy**: the seventh sign is a great falling away. Sin shall increase and love shall grow cold.

a. "Iniquity shall abound." Lawlessness [sin and wickedness] is always present, but there are times when it seems to multiply and overflow (see note—*Iniquity*—Mt.24:12). It ran rampant in the last days of Jerusalem as the quotations from Josephus clearly show. It shall also run wild in the last days of world history (2 Ti.3:1-5; 2 Th.2:1-12).

b. "The love of many shall grow cold." At least four things can dampen one's love for God. Each of these shall be greatly intensified toward the end of the world.

1) Self-seeking and worldliness. Men will seek what they want and what the world offers instead of sacrificing and serving. They just choose to satisfy their own desires and worldly urges instead of seeking diligently after God.
2) Dissension and division. Both discourage, dishearten, and cause confusion and the desire to flee. Many just cool off and back away, desiring to have no part of anything that is divisive. Even if the truth is under attack, some will withdraw rather than take a stand for the truth.
3) Persecution. Unless a person truly believes and trusts in Christ, whatever affection he has is soon dampened when he is questioned and opposed. Only a *real belief and conviction* will stand up under ridicule and the threat of death.
4) Ignorance and weak faith. Some go through a dampening of spirit and affection simply because they cannot understand why God would let such trials happen. There is no true understanding of man's sin and death, of the world's corruption and destined end, of God's righteousness and promise of life. Therefore, there is little within to stir a fervent love for God when things are going bad and the world seems to be caving in.
5) Lawlessness and immorality. Being around a crowd that lives lawless and immoral lives causes many to lose their love for Christ and turn away.

Christ warns the believer who lets his love grow cold.

"Because thou art lukewarm, and neither cold nor hot, I will spue thee out of my mouth" (Re.3:16).

DEEPER STUDY # 6
(24:12) **Iniquity** (anomia): lawlessness, wickedness, unrighteousness; transgression of the law. It is taking license with the law and righteousness, with morality and discipline.

DEEPER STUDY # 7
(24:12) **Abound** (plethunthenai): to increase, to multiply, to abound.

---

9 (24:13) **Endurance—Salvation**: the eighth sign is that of some enduring and being saved. It must be remembered Christ is talking to His disciples. His promise, "Being saved," is bound to mean the soul's salvation in the last days. It could not mean the safety of human life. He had already said some shall be killed (v.9). Thus, the believer who stands firm through persecution and hatred, betrayal and division, false teaching and deception, lawlessness and immorality, and keeps fervent love shall be saved.

"Fear none of those things which thou shalt suffer: behold, the devil shall cast some of you into prison, that ye may be tried; and ye shall have tribulation ten days: be thou faithful unto death, and I will give thee a crown of life" (Re.2:10).

"To them who by patient continuance in well doing seek for glory and honor and immortality, [they shall receive] eternal life....But unto them that are contentious, and do not obey the truth, but obey unrighteousness, [they shall receive] indignation and wrath, tribulation and anguish" (Ro.2:7-9).

Thought 1. The believer can find great encouragement to endure in such passages as the following. (Scan quickly some of the books that deal heavily with suffering, such as First Peter. See General Subject Index, related subjects.)

"For unto you it is given in the behalf of Christ, not only to believe on him, but also to suffer for his sake" (Ph.1:29).

"For consider him that endured such contradiction of sinners against himself, lest ye be wearied and faint in your minds" (He.12:3).

"If any man speak, let him speak as the oracles of God; if any man minister, let him do it as of the ability which God giveth: that God in all things may be glorified through Jesus Christ, to whom be praise and dominion for ever and ever. Amen. Beloved, think it not strange concerning the fiery trial which is to try you, as though some strange thing happened unto you" (1 Pe.4:11-12).

MATTHEW 24:1-14

10 (24:14) **Evangelism—Witnessing**: the ninth sign is world evangelism. Christ says five very significant things.

a. His gospel is of the Kingdom. What Kingdom? The Kingdom of God that is spiritual and eternal (see Deeper Study #3—Mt.19:23-24; note—Ep.1:3. See 2 Co.5:19.)

b. His gospel is unstoppable: "This gospel of the kingdom *shall* be preached." No amount of trouble and failure can stop it from being preached: neither severe persecution (v.9), nor terrible apostasy (v.10), nor many false teachers (v.11), nor multiplied lawlessness (v.12), nor the love of many growing cold (v.12). God's glorious Word of grace shall force its way over land and sea, no matter the strength of the storms and bodies that oppose it.

c. His gospel shall be triumphant: "This gospel...shall be preached in all the world." Amazingly, in just a brief span of time during the first century, the gospel was evidently carried to all parts of the known world.

> "But I say, Have they not heard? Yes, verily, their sound went into all the earth, and their words unto the ends of the world" (Ro.10:18).
>
> "(The gospel) which is come unto you, as it is in all the world" (Col.1:6).
>
> "The gospel, which ye have heard, and which was preached to every creature which is under heaven" (Col.1:23).

The very tone of Christ's words point to the same sign of world evangelism toward the end of the world. The uttermost part of the earth shall be privileged to hear the gospel before the final appearance of Christ (Ac.1:8; see Mt.28:19-20. See Mt.24:3, 14 with Mt.28:19 noting the word "age." Then see Acts 8:12; 28:23, 28, 30-31 for examples of preaching the Kingdom.)

d. His gospel is a witness: "This gospel...shall be preached...for a *witness* unto all nations." The gospel as a *witness* means at least two things.

1) The gospel is a witness, proclaiming the truth and the will of God for man. It reveals the truth about man and his world. It tells man where he has come from, why he is here, and where he is going. It tells man what he has done, what he is doing, and what he should do. It tells man why he is as he is, why he does what he does, and why he should do as God says.

2) The gospel is a witness, bearing record either for man or against man.

⇒ The gospel is called a "record."

> "And this is the record, that God hath given to us eternal life, and this life is in his Son. He that hath the Son hath life; and he that hath not the Son of God hath not life" (1 Jn.5:11-12).

⇒ The gospel witnesses for a man, that he believes and is saved; or it witnesses against a man, that he does not believe and is damned.

> "He that believeth and is baptized shall be saved; but he that believeth not shall be damned" (Mk.16:16).

e. His gospel shall be preached in all the world before the end comes. The term "the end" refers to both the end of Jerusalem and the end of the world. As Scripture states, the gospel had been preached to all the known world right before the fall of Jerusalem (Ro.10:18; Col.1:6, 23) and shall be preached to the uttermost part of the earth before the end time (Ac.1:8; see Mt.28:19-20).

However, something needs to be noted that is sometimes overlooked. Christ does not say the gospel shall *convert* the world, but rather the gospel shall be *preached* to the world before the end comes. All the world will not respond to the gospel, but all the world shall hear the gospel. Christ does, however, give some indication of the results to expect from preaching the gospel.

> "Many are called, but few are chosen" (Mt.20:16; 22:14).
>
> "Strive to enter in at the strait gate: for many, I say unto you, will seek to enter in, and shall not be able" (Lu.13:24).
>
> "I tell you that he will avenge them speedily. Nevertheless when the Son of man cometh, shall he find faith on the earth" (Lu.18:8)?

MATTHEW 24:15-28

	B. The Most Terrible Sign of the Last Days: The Abomination of Desolation & the Great Tribulation or Distress, 24:15-28 (Mk 13:14-27; Lu 21:20-28)	world to this time, no, nor ever shall be. 22 And except those days should be shortened, there should no flesh be saved: but for the elect's sake those days shall be shortened.	4. There is the promise: The days will be shortened for the elect's sake

1. There is the appearance of the abomination that causes desolation[DS1]
  a. Will be seen
  b. Prophesied by Daniel
  c. Stands in the Holy Place
  d. To be read & understood
	15 When ye therefore shall see the abomination of desolation, spoken of by Daniel the prophet, stand in the holy place, (whoso readeth, let him understand:)	23 Then if any man shall say unto you, Lo, here is Christ, or there; believe it not.
		24 For there shall arise false christs, and false prophets, and shall show great signs and wonders; insomuch that, if it were possible, they shall deceive the very elect.
			5. There is the frantic search for a deliverer, for an earthly messiah
			  a. They will arise
			  b. They will show great signs & miracles
			  c. They will be convincing, deceiving even the elect

2. There is the warning to flee immediately
  a. To forget all comfort of home[DS2]
  b. To forget all personal possessions
  c. To grieve for those who cannot flee rapidly
  d. To pray for good conditions in fleeing
	16 Then let them which be in Judaea flee into the mountains:
	17 Let him which is on the housetop not come down to take any thing out of his house:
	18 Neither let him which is in the field return back to take his clothes.
	19 And woe unto them that are with child, and to them that give suck in those days!
	20 But pray ye that your flight be not in the winter, neither on the sabbath day:
		25 Behold, I have told you before.
		26 Wherefore if they shall say unto you, Behold, he is in the desert; go not forth: behold, he is in the secret chambers; believe it not.
		27 For as the lightning cometh out of the east, and shineth even unto the west; so shall also the coming of the Son of man be.
			6. There is the truth about deliverance, about Messiah's coming
			  a. Comes not from the desert: An unknown or remote spot
			  b. Comes not in secret: Unseen, quietly
			  c. Comes as lightning
			    1) From heaven
			    2) Suddenly–surprising
			    3) Visibly–seen east to west

3. There is the great tribulation or distress: Unparalleled in history	21 For then shall be great tribulation, such as was not since the beginning of the	28 For wheresoever the carcase is, there will the eagles be gathered together.	d. Comes to execute judgment

DIVISION XV

THE MESSIAH'S PROPHECY OF HIS RETURN AND THE END OF THE AGE: THE OLIVET DISCOURSE, 24:1–25:46

B. The Most Terrible Sign of the Last Days: The Abomination of Desolation and the Great Tribulation or Distress, 24:15-28

(24:15-28) **Introduction—End Time—The Great Tribulation**: the disciples had asked two questions. First, when was Jerusalem to be destroyed; and second, what was to be the sign of His coming and of the end of the world (Mt.24:3). This passage evidently has a double meaning. It refers both to the destruction of Jerusalem by Titus in 70 A.D. and to the end time when Christ will return. The passage has to be severely strained to make it refer to only one of these events. It should be remembered that Christ was experiencing the most severe emotions during these days. Death was only hours away, and He was the only One aware of it. He had just gone through the triumphal entry (Mt.21), the cleansing of the temple (Mt.21), the savage attacks by the religionists (Mt.21-22), His severe denunciation of the religionists (Mt.23), and His lament over Jerusalem (Mt.23). No ordinary man could possibly bear so many pressuring and diverse emotions in so short a time. Jesus loved Jerusalem; He had just wept and wept bitterly over the city. They had been a people of sin and were to commit the most heinous sin of human history—killing the Messiah, the Son of God Himself. They were to experience two judgments for their sinful rejection. They were to be immediately judged in 70 A.D. Then at the end of the world, they, along with the rest of the world, were to be finally judged.

Simply stated the situation was this: Jesus, filled with so wide a range of emotions, began to answer the two questions the disciples had asked. He gave the signs of the coming destruction of Jerusalem and of the end of the world. He said, in essence, that the fall of Jerusalem was judgment upon sin, and the fall of the world would be judgment upon sin. The questions asked refer to similar conditions that bring about judgment. Thus, the signs of both the fall of Jerusalem and of the end of the world are similar. (See notes and DEEPER STUDY # 3—Mt.24:1-14; note and DEEPER STUDY # 1—Mk.13:14; note—Lu.21:5-38.)

As a person studies this passage, two things need to be kept in mind.
1. The overall outline of *Christ's answer*, His actual words (see DEEPER STUDY # 1,2—Mt.24:1-31).
2. The fact that Christ *was answering* two questions dealing with the end of Jerusalem and with the end of the world, and that the end of both is due to judgment upon sin. Thus, the signs that point to the end of both Jerusalem and of the world are bound to be similar, for both are *ending* and being judged because of sin. The only difference is that in the end of the world there is to be an increase and intensification of the signs. (See DEEPER STUDY # 1,2—Mt.24:1-31.)

MATTHEW 24:15-28

A quick glance at the overall outline of Matthew 24-25 will show the following:
1. The Nine Signs of the Last Days, Mt.24:1-14.
2. The Tenth and Most Terrible Sign: The Abomination of Desolation and The Great Tribulation, Mt.24:15-28.
3. The Coming of Messiah, the Son of Man, Mt.24:29-31.
4. The Time of the Lord's Return, Mt.24:32-41.
5. The Lord's Return and The Believer's Duty: Watch—Be Ready—Be Faithful, Mt.24:42-51.
6. The Warning to Watch and Be Wise, Not Foolish, Mt.25:1-13.
7. The Believer's Duty to Work Anticipating the Lord's Return, Mt.25:14-30.
8. The Final Judgment of the Nations, Mt.25:31-46.

Note the Lord's words: "the *abomination of desolation*" and "*great tribulation*, such as was not since the beginning of the world." It is for this reason that the title given to this tenth sign is, "The Most Terrible Sign: The Abomination of Desolation and The Great Tribulation."
1. There is the appearance of the abomination that causes desolation (v.15).
2. There is the warning to flee immediately (vv.16-20).
3. There is the great tribulation or distress: unparalleled in history (v.21).
4. There is the promise: the days will be shortened for the elect's sake (v.22).
5. There is the frantic search for a deliverer, for an earthly Messiah (vv.23-24).
6. There is the truth about deliverance, about Messiah's coming (vv.25-28).

1 (24:15) **Abomination of Desolation—Antichrist—End Times**: there is the appearance of the abomination of desolation. Christ said four things about this sign.

a. It (He) will be seen. Believers can see it take place and prepare for the terrible trials which will follow it (see DEEPER STUDY # 2—Mt.24:1-31).

b. It (He) was also prophesied by Daniel (see DEEPER STUDY # 1—Mt. 24:15).

c. It (He) will stand in the Holy Place. The sign will take place and be seen in the temple. Some hold that the sign will be repeated in the end time and literally fulfilled within the temple, just as it was literally fulfilled twice in the past when Antiochus and Titus stood within the temple. Others hold the words "the temple" to be representative of all religion. They believe the abomination will be the desolation of all religion, in particular genuine Christianity.

d. Whosoever reads about the sign, as revealed by Christ, is to understand it. Daniel had said, "Know therefore and understand" (Da.9:25; see Da.12:10). Believers are to study the sign and gain an understanding of it, so that they can be better prepared to "endure to the end... [and] be saved" (Mt.24:13). There is the idea that a person is to know and understand the *times*, to watch and observe the happenings of the times in which he lives.

Thought 1. The terrible desolation that took place upon Jerusalem and that is to take place at the end of the world is due to sin. Jerusalem *cut off the Messiah*, that is, killed Him. They committed the most heinous of sins: they rejected God for centuries and eventually killed God's very own Son. Therefore, Jerusalem was desolated. There is a critical warning here for believers: sin results in desolation.

Thought 2. Note two significant facts.
(1) Christ predicted the terrible desolation of Jerusalem. His words were spoken somewhere around 30 A.D. The desolation occurred just forty years later in 70 A.D.
(2) Christ has predicted the "abomination of desolation" at the end of the world (see the questions of the disciples, v.3 and v.15). The sign *will occur* at the appointed time.

Thought 3. Something is of critical importance.
(1) If we interpret "the abomination of desolation" only as historical and Christ meant it to be future as well as historical, we are more likely to miss the sign.
(2) If we interpret the sign only as future and Christ meant it to be historical as well as future, we will have already missed a significant part of the sign and will not be looking at the past to help us understand the future.
   Making sure we are accurate in our understanding of the sign is important. It involves the Lord's words and the Lord's people and their testimony. There may be different interpretations, but each one must humbly secure his understanding bowed in prayer before the Lord.

Thought 4. God's Word is not a secret; it is a revelation. It is to be searched out and understood.

DEEPER STUDY # 1
(24:15) **End Times—Antichrist—Abomination of Desolation** (To Bdelugma Tes eremoseos): the abomination that makes desolate. Note Christ's words, "the abomination of desolation, *spoken of by Daniel the prophet.*" There are three passages in Daniel that speak of "the abomination of desolation."

> "Seventy weeks are determined upon thy people and upon thy holy city...Know therefore and understand, that from the going forth of the commandment to restore and to build Jerusalem unto the Messiah the Prince shall be seven weeks, and threescore and two weeks: the street shall be built again, and the wall, even in troublous times. And after threescore and two weeks shall Messiah be cut off, but not for himself: and the people of the prince that shall come shall destroy the city and the sanctuary; and the end thereof shall be with a flood, and unto the end of the war desolations

are determined. And he shall confirm the covenant with many for one week: and in the midst of the week he shall cause the sacrifice and the oblation to cease, and for the overspreading of abominations he shall make it desolate, even until the consummation, and that determined shall be poured upon the desolate" (Da.9:24-27).

"And arms shall stand on his part, and they shall pollute the sanctuary of strength, and shall take away the daily sacrifice, and they shall place the abomination that maketh desolate" (Da. 11:31).

"And from the time that the daily sacrifice shall be taken away, and the abomination that maketh desolate set up, there shall be a thousand two hundred and ninety days" (Da.12:11).

In Daniel 9:27, the term is *Bdelugma ton eremoseon*. The Hebrew says, "Upon the wing [or pinnacle] of abominations [shall come] the desolater" or "upon wings as a desolater [shall come] abomination."

In Daniel 11:31 the Hebrew says, "they shall put [place] the abomination that desolates."

In Daniel 12:11 the Hebrew says, "and from the time the daily [sacrifice] shall be taken away, and the abomination that makes desolate set up, [shall be]...."

Several matters need to be discussed about the "abomination of desolation" spoken of by Christ and Daniel.

1. When was Daniel's prophecy fulfilled?
   a. There was a past fulfillment; that is, there was a fulfillment before the time of Christ about 170 B.C. This is clear. Antiochus Epiphanes, the king of Syria, conquered Jerusalem and tried to force Grecian society upon the Jews. He wanted the Jews to become full-fledged Greeks both in custom and religion. He knew that to be successful he had to destroy the Jewish religion. He therefore did three of the most horrible things that could ever be done in the mind of the Jewish people. He desecrated the temple (1) by taking the great altar of the burnt offering and turning it into an altar for the Greek Olympian god Zeus, (2) by sacrificing swine's' flesh upon it, and (3) by setting up a trade of prostitution in the temple chambers (see 1 Maccabees 1:20-62; see also Josephus, *Ant*. 12. 5:3-4; *Wars*. 1. 1:2).
   b. Christ said there is a future fulfillment: "When ye therefore *shall see* the abomination of desolation, spoken of by Daniel the prophet...." There are primarily four views of the future fulfillment of Daniel's prophecy.
      ⇒ One view says there is no future fulfillment; all the signs were fulfilled in the destruction of Jerusalem in 70 A.D. by Titus.
      ⇒ Others see Christ's referring to the church age and to the trials which the church has to go through before Christ returns.
      ⇒ Still others view the prophecy as referring exclusively to the end time, having nothing to do with the destruction of Jerusalem in 70 A.D.
      ⇒ Others believe Christ is answering the very questions the disciples asked. He predicts both the destruction of Jerusalem and the end of the world.

In looking at what Christ was saying, it is best to let Him speak for Himself without *adding to* or *taking away* from His words. An attempt to let Him speak for Himself has been made in the former notes (see all notes—Mt.24:1-25:46; DEEPER STUDY # 1,2—24:1-31; 24:1-14; 24:15-28). The conclusion of the notes is that the prophecy is *fulfilled* in both Jerusalem's destruction and the end of the world. The Lord is answering the disciples' questions.

Christ was saying this: the same thing that happened under Antiochus Epiphanes will happen again to the Holy Place. In fact, Christ was saying that the temple would be so destroyed that not one stone would be left upon another. This destruction did happen: what Christ said took place in a most literal sense under Titus in 70 A.D. (See outline and notes—Mt. 24:1-14, especially the notes that quote Josephus, the Jewish historian. Reading Josephus' record of Jerusalem's desolation reveals just how terrible the temple, the city, and the people were devastated.)

However, as discussed in the former notes, Christ was not only answering the disciples' question about when the destruction of Jerusalem would take place, He was *also answering* their question about His return and the end of the world. Daniel's prophecy and the Lord's elaboration on Daniel's prophecy are to have a double fulfillment. The signs that point toward one who had sinned so terribly (Jerusalem) are much the same as the signs that point toward another who is guilty of terrible sin (the world in the end time). The sin of Jerusalem was the most heinous sin that could be committed: the killing of God's own Son. And the sin of the world at the end of time will be just as terrible by following "the abomination of desolation." Therefore, the world will witness an increase, an intensification of the signs at the end of time. As a result, there will be *great trial* such as the world has never seen (v.21). (Again, see the outline and notes—Mt. 24:1f.)

2. A second matter that needs to be discussed about "the abomination of desolation" is the division of time that Christ and Daniel both seem to give. Christ says that the abomination of desolation launches the worst tribulation the world has ever known (Mt. 24:15, 21). In His own words, the signs that occur up until the abomination of desolation are called "the beginning of sorrows" (Mt. 24:8); and the trials that take place after the abomination of desolation are called "great tribulations," tribulations so great that they are unparalleled in history (Mt.24:21). Daniel also gives a division of time just as Christ does.

"And he [the prince] shall confirm the covenant with many for one week: and in the midst of the week he shall cause...the overspreading of abominations" (Da.9:27).

"In the midst of the week" (Daniel's seventieth week) definitely points to a period of time (one week) that is divided into two parts. Now note these factors.
   a. Daniel was dealing with the "seventieth week," the *end* of his prophecy. Two facts tell us that Daniel was also dealing with the *end time* just as Christ was: (1) the fact that Christ was dealing with the end of Jerusalem and the end of the world and, (2) the fact that Christ said He was elaborating on Daniel's prophecy.

b. Daniel said that what begins the second half of his seventieth week is "the abomination of desolation" or the prince who causes "abominable idols" (H.C. Leupold. *Exposition of Daniel*. Grand Rapids, MI: Baker, 1969, p.434).

The words of Christ should be carefully noted: "When ye therefore shall see the abomination of desolation, spoken of by Daniel the prophet...." (Mt.24:15). Christ was about to explain in more detail what Daniel had prophesied. Thus Christ explained that the first half of Daniel's week would consist of signs which were "the beginning of sorrows" (Mt.24:8; see Mt.24:5-14), and the last half of Daniel's week would consist of unparalleled trials of "great tribulations." The second half of the week would be launched by "the abomination of desolation standing in the holy place" (Mt. 24:15, 21).

3. A third matter that needs to be looked at is the time frame of the end time (the seventieth week) as predicted by Christ and Daniel.

Scripture does refer to the length in these words (see notes—Re.11:2; 12:6).

"Time, times, and half a time" (Da.7:25; 12:7).
"1260 days" (Re.12:6).
"42 months" (Re.11:2; 13:5-6).

Based upon the days and months given in the *Book of Revelation*, if Daniel's time equals one year, then his words, "Time [1 year], times [2 years], and half a time [1/2 year]" are equal to 3 1/2 years. Daniel stated that the abomination of desolation shall be executed "in the midst of the week," that is, after three and one-half years. It is assumed that Christ's words "the beginning of sorrows" (that is, the first half of the week) are also three and one-half years. Thus in combining the two periods of time (3 1/2 years each), the length of the last days or end time is said to be a literal seven years. Based upon the words of Revelation the prophecy of Christ can be charted as follows.

THE END OF THE WORLD

Seeing the Sign of the Abomination of Desolation *In the Middle of the Time or Years* (v.15)		Seeing the *Son of Man Coming* (vv.29-30)
3 1/2 years Signs which are "The beginning of sorrows" (v.8).	3 1/2 years "Unparalleled trials of "the great tribulation (v.21)	His angels...gather together His elect" (v.31)

However, it should be noted that many Biblical scholars say that the words *times* in Daniel and "days" and "months" in Revelation (in fact, throughout all Scripture) are often used to refer to blocks of time, that is, to longer periods or indefinite periods of time.

4. A fourth matter that needs to be looked at is this: What or who is meant by *the abomination of desolation*? As has already been discussed, many excellent commentators hold that the prophecy refers to the destruction of Jerusalem under both Antiochus Epiphenes (170 B.C.) and under Titus (70 A.D.). There is strong historical evidence, as well as the fact that Christ was answering a specific question of the disciples (Mt. 24:3), to support a past fulfillment of the prophecy. But, what about the future fulfillment? What or who is meant by *the abomination of desolation* at the end of the world? (See DEEPER STUDY # 1—Re.11:7; see 2 Th.2:3-4; Re.13:1; 13:3 13:5-6. See Master Subject Index.)

   a. Some indication is perhaps given by the phrase itself. In the Old Testament the word *abomination* is connected with idolatry or sacrilege. *Of desolation* means the same as *causes desolation*. In this case, it is *the abomination that causes desolation*. That is, the abomination acts upon the Holy Place and personally causes the desolation. This, of course, points toward a person's fulfilling the prophecy in the future just as there were two literal persons who fulfilled it in the past, Antiochus and Titus.
   b. Mark 13:14 actually uses the *masculine* participle which indicates strongly that the abomination of desolation is a person.
   c. Daniel 9:27 speaks of a prince who causes the desolation. Leupold, the great Lutheran theologian, translates the prince as *the destroyer*. (Leupold. *Exposition of Daniel*, p.433. Because of his extraordinary scholarship and simplicity of writing, Leupold should be referred to in studying Daniel.)
   d. Second Thessalonians and Revelation identify an *antichrist* who is to arise in the last days and cause unparalleled havoc upon the world and God's people.

   "That man of sin [shall] be revealed, the son of perdition; who opposeth and exalteth himself above all that is called God, or that is worshipped; so that he as God sitteth in the temple of God, showing himself that he is God. Remember ye not, that, when I was yet with you, I told you these things?" (2 Th.2:3-5). (See notes and DEEPER STUDY # 1—Mk.13:14; notes—2 Th.2:4-9; Re.6:2-7; DEEPER STUDY # 1—11:7; notes—13:1-10; 13:11-18; 17:7-14. See Da.9:20-27; 11:31; 12:11.)

2 (24:16-20) **Antichrist—Abomination of Desolation**: there is the warning to flee "the abomination of desolation"—immediately. No believer will be able to stand up against the abomination, not even the strongest. The imminent danger and urgency is stressed by Christ in four statements.

a. A person is to forget all comfort of home: pictured by arising from his roof and immediately fleeing (see DEEPER STUDY # 2—Mt.24:17).

MATTHEW 24:15-28

b. A person is to forget all personal possessions: pictured by not returning from his work to get his clothes (or possessions).

c. A person is to grieve for those who cannot flee rapidly: pictured by pregnant women who are responsible for small children.

d. A person is to pray for good conditions in fleeing: pictured by both winter and the sabbath day. The sabbath day represented certain religious rules that would forbid fleeing (travel) for the religiously strong.

> "But when he saw many of the Pharisees and Sadducees come to his baptism, he said unto them, O generation of vipers, who hath warned you to flee from the wrath to come? Bring forth therefore fruits meet for repentance" (Mt.3:7-8).

Thought 1. The danger is so imminent that Christ said, "Remember Lot's wife" (Lu.17:32).

Thought 2. There is a great stress here: when life is threatened, our minds need to be focused upon doing what we can to save our lives. As we walk day by day, what we should really be thankful for is our lives and not things.

Thought 3. Note to whom Christ speaks, who are the ones to forget worldly possessions and comforts of home: His disciples, His followers. Was He thinking of the materialistic comforts that characterize so many of His followers?

DEEPER STUDY # 2
(24:17) **House—Rooftop**: in ancient days, the rooftops of houses were flat; they were used for rest, meditation, and neighborly visits. Most houses had steps both inside and outside that led up to the roof. When the abomination is seen, the danger is so imminent that a person should flee from his roof immediately, using the outside stairs.

---

3 (24:21) **Great Tribulation**: there is the great tribulation that will be unparalleled in history.

a. In 66-70 A.D., Jerusalem experienced one of the most terrible sieges in all of history. In 66 A.D. the Jews revolted, and the Roman army was swift to attack. However, the city was difficult to take, primarily for two reasons. It sat upon a hill, well protected by the terrain, and the leaders of the revolt were religious fanatics. Well over a million people had fled into the city behind its protective walls.

As the siege wore on, the predictions of Christ were literally fulfilled. Outside the walls was the Roman army and all the maiming and killing of war. Inside the walls, neighbor after neighbor faced famine, pestilence, false deliverers (messiahs), betrayal, murder, revolt, rebellion, and hatred. And all took their toll. Josephus says over 1,000,000 people died and 97,000 were taken captive. The horrors of the siege are well described by him (see notes—Mt.24:7; 24:10; 24:11. See Josephus, *Wars*. 5. 12:3; 6. 3:4; 6. 8:5.)

> *It appears to me that the misfortunes of all men, from the beginning of the world, if they be compared to these of the Jews, are not so considerable as they were* (Josephus, *Wars*. Preface 4).

b. In the end time, the world will experience great tribulations unparalleled in history. Note that Christ does not describe the great trials beyond what He has already said in vv.5-12. A quick glance at the great tribulation period covered in Revelation will give some idea of the trials (see outlines and notes—all of the following. See Da.12:1-2.)
⇒ Thunderings, lightnings, and an earthquake (Re.8:5; see Re.8:1-5).
⇒ Natural catastrophes (Re.8:6-12).
⇒ Demonic-like locusts or plagues (Re.8:13-9:11).
⇒ Demonic-like army (Re.9:12-21).
⇒ Angry nations who destroy the earth (Re.11:18; see Re.11:14-19).
⇒ An evil political ruler (Re.13:1-10).
⇒ A false and evil religious ruler (Re.13:11-18).
⇒ Terrible destruction and suffering, both upon nature and men (Re.16:1-21).
⇒ An evil, deceptive world power (Re.17:1-18:24).

4 (24:22) **End Time—Great Tribulation**: there is the promise that the days shall be shortened for the elect's sake. Note that Christ said two things.

a. The days of "the great tribulation" shall be shortened. What is meant by shortened?
⇒ Shorter than what God would usually allow for such great sinfulness.
⇒ Shorter than what the enemy expected.
⇒ Shorter than what others would expect of a ruling government against such revolting fanatics.

In dealing with Jerusalem, God in His providence used His power to shorten the days for Israel's sake. In the midst of judgment, He was merciful—Israel was not totally annihilated. The siege was shorter than expected. Many have listed *the natural causes* that led to the shorter siege.
⇒ Division and factions. The Jewish leaders were divided from the first. They never could form a cohesive policy.
⇒ A disastrous fire. The fire destroyed too many weapons and provisions for the city to continue fighting.
⇒ Rampaging gangs. These were set on self-preservation by any means: stealing, assaulting and killing. They are well documented by Josephus.

⇒ Treason and betrayal. Some even surrendered their fortifications without a fight.
⇒ The quick attack by Rome. Rome sent the armed force under Titus much quicker than expected.
⇒ Weak fortifications. Herod Agrippa had intended to strengthen the walls of Jerusalem, but he never did.

The believer, of course, sees God's hand in these natural causes. God *worked all things out for good* in order to shorten the days and to fulfill His Word. Despite *the terrible tribulation*, some lives were saved—saved because God was compassionate (2 Pe.3:9).

In dealing with the end time, the tribulations upon the earth and its inhabitants will also be shortened.

"Woe to the inhabiters of the earth and of the sea! for the devil is come down unto you, having great wrath...[but note]... because he knoweth that he hath but a short time" (Re. 12:12).

"When he [antichrist] cometh, he must continue [but note] a short time" (Re.17:10).

"And then shall that Wicked be revealed, whom the Lord shall consume with the spirit of his mouth, and shall destroy with the brightness of his coming" (2 Th.2:8).

b. God will shorten the days of the great tribulation for the elect's sake. From the historical perspective, some of the Christians remembered the Lord's warning and fled Jerusalem before the attack, sometime around 66 A.D. They fled to a smaller town called Pella in the district of Decapolis. These believers prayed for their neighbors and their beloved city, and God heard their intercessions. He shortened the days of terrible trials—shortened them because of the prayers of the elect.

God's mercy toward the lost—even toward civilizations and cities—and His willingness to save the lost in answer to the believers' intercessory prayer are clearly illustrated in Scripture. Abraham's prayer for Sodom and Gomorrah is an example. If just ten righteous people could have been found, the cities would have been spared despite their terrible sin (Ge.18:23f). Lot's prayer for Zoar is another example (Ge.19:20-22).

"Confess your faults one to another, and pray one for another, that ye may be healed. The effectual fervent prayer of a righteous man availeth much" (Js.5:16).

"Run ye to and fro through the streets of Jerusalem, and see now, and know, and seek in the broad places thereof, if ye can find a man, if there be any that executeth judgment, that seeketh the truth; and I will pardon it" (Je.5:1).

"For there stood by me this night the angel of God, whose I am, and whom I serve, saying, Fear not, Paul; thou must be brought before Caesar: and, lo, God hath given thee all them that sail with thee....And we were in all in the ship two hundred threescore and sixteen souls....But the centurion, willing to save Paul, kept them from their purpose; and commanded that they which could swim should cast themselves first into the sea, and get to land: and the rest, some on boards, and some on broken pieces of the ship. And so it came to pass, that they escaped all safe to land" (Ac.27:23-24, 37, 43-44).

Thought 1. God will honor the prayers of His *true followers*, even to the point of overriding natural disasters. How much change could occur in the evil of the world, both natural and human, if God's people really believed in intercessory prayer and became real intercessors for this corruptible world?

Thought 2. Too many of us are complainers, not intercessors. Too many of us complain over our affliction or else the length of our affliction. It is beyond us how God could ever allow such suffering. Three things are needed.
(1) We must realize that God does not cause evil and suffering. God does not afflict; He delivers.
(2) We must realize that we never suffer as much as we deserve. We are ever so sinful and have so polluted the earth with evil that we deserve the worst.
(3) We must realize that God is merciful. What is needed is not complaining, but prayer—intercessory prayer. We need to pray, thanking God that the evil is not worse. Then in unceasing prayer, we need to ask Him to correct and shorten the evil.

5 (24:23-24) **False Messiahs—End Times**: there is the frantic search for a deliverer, for an earthly Messiah. Christ says three things.

a. False messiahs and prophets will arise. When men are oppressed and oppressed, witnessing scene after scene of death by hunger, pestilence, murder, and war, they cry for deliverance. They are ever so open to *a deliverer's* arising on the scene, and some are always ready to assume the power and leadership for which men cry. In the siege of Jerusalem, such men (deliverers) arose who promised deliverance from both the Romans and the natural disasters. Apparently there had been the constant belief and rumors that the Messiah had returned, and He was either out in the desert or in some secret room within the city. He was just awaiting the hour to strike. The scene in Jerusalem was somewhat like Jeremiah's day.

"Then said I, Ah, Lord God! behold, the prophets say unto them, Ye shall not see the sword, neither shall ye have famine; but I will give you assured peace in this place. Then the Lord said unto me, The prophets prophesy lies in my name: I sent them not, neither have I commanded them, neither spake unto them: they prophesy unto you a false vision and divination, and a thing of nought, and the deceit of their heart" (Je.14:13-14).

MATTHEW 24:15-28

The same kind of scene will repeat itself in the last days. The antichrist, the false deliverer of the earth, shall arise to deceive the whole earth (see outlines and note—Re.13:1-18 and related passages). Note that Christ simply says, "Believe it not"—believe neither the rumors nor the false deliverer.

b. False deliverers will show great signs and wonders. Deliverers, local and national, always claim to be destined. They point to signs and wonders. This has always been true—and always will be true—through all times. The end time will witness an increase and intensification of signs and wonders that will stretch across the whole world.

> "Then shall that Wicked (one) be revealed, whom the Lord shall consume with the spirit of his mouth, and shall destroy with the brightness of his coming: even him....and with all deceivableness" (2 Th.2:8-10).

> "And he doeth great wonders, so that he maketh fire come down from heaven on the earth in the sight of men, and deceiveth them that dwell on the earth by the means of those miracles which he had power to do in the sight of the beast; saying to them that dwell on the earth, that they should make an image to the beast, which had the wound by a sword, and did live" (Re.13:13-14).

c. False deliverers will be so convincing they will even threaten the elect. The elect, of course, are genuine believers who stick with Christ regardless of the temptation, trials, threat and danger. An excellent passage that describes much of the same picture is seen in 2 Th.2:1-17. The way the elect are able to stand is clearly stated.

> "Therefore, brethren, stand fast, and hold the traditions which ye have been taught, whether by word, or our epistle. Now our Lord Jesus Christ himself, and God, even our Father, which hath loved us, and hath given us everlasting consolation and good hope through grace, comfort your hearts, and stablish you in every good word and work" (2 Th.15-17).

6 (24:25-28) **Jesus Christ, Return**: there is the truth about deliverance and about the Messiah's coming. Christ said four things about His return.

a. He shall not come from the desert, that is, from some unknown and remote spot. When people proclaim that the great deliverer has appeared in a certain place, the message or rumor is not to be believed: "go not forth."

b. He shall not come from a secret chamber, that is, in secret, unseen, quietly. Again, when such a message or rumor is proclaimed, "believe it not."

c. He shall come "as lightning."
  1) His coming shall be out of heaven (out of the spiritual world and dimension)—just as lightning.
  2) His coming shall be sudden and surprising—just as lightning.
  3) His coming shall be visible to all, seen from east to west—just as lightning (see Re.1:7).

> "And then shall appear the sign of the Son of man in heaven: and then shall *all the tribes* of the earth mourn, and they shall see the Son of man coming in the clouds of heaven with power and great glory" (Mt.24:30).

> "And when he had spoken these things, while they beheld, he was taken up; and a cloud received him out of their sight. And while they looked stedfastly toward heaven as he went up, behold, two men stood by them in white apparel; which also said, Ye men of Galilee, why stand ye gazing up into heaven? this same Jesus, which is taken up from you into heaven, shall so come in like manner as ye have seen him go into heaven" (Ac.1:9-11).

> "For the Lord himself shall descend from heaven with a shout, with the voice of the archangel, and with the trump of God: and the dead in Christ shall rise first: then we which are alive and remain shall be caught up together with them in the clouds, to meet the Lord in the air: and so shall we ever be with the Lord. Wherefore comfort one another with these words" (1 Th.4:16-18).

> "Behold, he cometh with clouds; and every eye shall see him, and they also which pierced him: and all kindreds of the earth shall wail because of him. Even so, Amen" (Re.1:7; see Re.19:11-19).

d. He shall come to execute judgment (v.28. See Is.30:30; Re.19:20-21.) The eagles, birds of prey, always gather where the carcase is. There are at least two meanings to this verse.
  1) The carcase is the Jewish people, and the eagles are the Roman armies under Titus who gathered around Jerusalem to consume the prey.
  2) The carcase is the world, the spiritually dead, and the eagles are Christ and His holy angels and saints. They come to gather around the dead world, executing judgment.

The point of this passage is that the coming of Christ shall be to execute universal judgment. He shall come for the carcase, for all the spiritually dead in order to execute judgment upon them. Christ shall execute judgment upon the whole world.

> "And I saw an angel standing in the sun; and he cried with a loud voice, saying to all the fowls that fly in the midst of heaven, Come and gather yourselves together unto the supper of the great God; that ye may eat the flesh of kings, and the flesh of captains, and the flesh of mighty men, and the flesh of horses, and of them that sit on them, and the flesh of all men, both free and bond, both small and great" (Re.19:17-18).

> "When the Son of man shall come in his glory, and all the holy angels with him, then shall he sit upon the throne of his glory: and before him shall be gathered all nations: and he shall separate them one from another, as a shepherd divideth his sheep from the goats" (Mt.25:31-32).

"And as it is appointed unto men once to die, but after this the judgment" (He.9:27).

"The Lord knoweth how to deliver the godly out of temptations, and to reserve the unjust unto the day of judgment to be punished" (2 Pe.2:9).

"But the heavens and the earth, which are now, by the same word are kept in store, reserved unto fire against the day of judgment and perdition of ungodly men" (2 Pe.3:7).

"And Enoch also, the seventh from Adam, prophesied of these, saying, Behold, the Lord cometh with ten thousands of his saints, to execute judgment upon all, and to convince all that are ungodly among them of all their ungodly deeds which they have ungodly committed, and of all their hard speeches which ungodly sinners have spoken against him" (Jude 14-15).

MATTHEW 24:29-31

	C. The Coming of the Son of Man: Five Events, 24:29-31	sign of the Son of man in heaven: and then shall all the tribes of the earth mourn, and they shall see the Son of man coming in the clouds of heaven with power and great glory. 31 And he shall send his angels with a great sound of a trumpet, and they shall gather together his elect from the four winds, from one end of heaven to the other.	will appear
1. He comes immediately after the tribulation or distress 2. Event 1: There will be astronomical happenings 3. Event 2: The sign of Christ	29 Immediately after the tribulation of those days shall the sun be darkened, and the moon shall not give her light, and the stars shall fall from heaven, and the powers of the heavens shall be shaken: 30 And then shall appear the		4. Event 3: All the nations will see Christ coming in the clouds 5. Event 4: All the nations of the earth will mourn 6. Event 5: The angels will be sent forth to gather the elect

DIVISION XV

THE MESSIAH'S PROPHECY OF HIS RETURN AND THE END OF THE AGE: THE OLIVET DISCOURSE, 24:1–25:46

C. The Coming of the Son of Man: Five Events, 24:29-31

(24:29-31) **Jesus Christ, Return—Tribulation—Israel**: Christ revealed exactly when He was to return—"immediately after the tribulation of those days." The great tribulation occurs, then our Lord returns—"immediately." (See outline and notes—Mt.24:1-28 for background to this passage.)

1. Now note: Christ did not return immediately after the downfall of Jerusalem; therefore, what did He mean? Luke explains:

> "But woe unto them that are with child, and to them that give suck, in those days! for there shall be great distress in the land, and wrath upon this people. And they shall fall by the edge of the sword, and shall be led away captive into all nations: and Jerusalem shall be trodden down of the Gentiles, until the times of the Gentiles be fulfilled" (Lu.21:23-24).

Very simply, Christ said that the fall of Jerusalem was only the beginning of the tribulation of the Jews. Their tribulation continues until "the times of the Gentiles be fulfilled." The accuracy of the Lord's words is clearly seen by simply breaking down the verses of Luke and thinking through world history since Christ.
⇒ There is still "great distress in the land" of Israel.
⇒ There is still "great wrath upon this people."
⇒ Many Jews still "fall by the sword."
⇒ Many are still "captive [dispersed] in all nations."
⇒ Jerusalem is still "trodden down of the Gentiles."

No people have ever gone through such great tribulation as the Jews. They are still suffering at the hands of the Gentiles (for example, World War II, where over 5,000,000 were slaughtered in less than eight years); and they shall suffer great tribulation "until the times of the Gentiles be fulfilled." It is *immediately after the great tribulation of the Jews* and after *the great tribulation* coming at the end of the world that the coming of Christ shall take place.

Note a very significant fact: Luke's prophecy definitely points toward the double meaning of Christ's words. Since the *great tribulation* of the Jews in 70 A.D. (see v.20), they have continued to suffer *great tribulation* through the present age, and they shall suffer right on through the great tribulation that is to occur at the end of the world.

2. Also note it is immediately after the *"great tribulation"* of the world (v.21) that Christ returns (see DEEPER STUDY #1,2—Mt. 24:1-31; notes—24:1-14; 24:15-28).

1. He comes immediately after the tribulation or distress (v.29).
2. Event 1: there will be astronomical happenings (v.29).
3. Event 2: the sign of Christ will appear (v.30).
4. Event 3: all the nations will see Christ coming in the clouds (v.30).
5. Event 4: all the nations of the earth will mourn (v.30).
6. Event 5: the angels will be sent forth to gather the elect (v.31).

1 (24:29) **Jesus Christ, Return—Tribulation**: the scene is immediately after the tribulation (see note—Mt.24:29-31 for discussion).

Thought 1. There are several lessons in the words "after the tribulation"—lessons for us as well as for those who will follow Christ through the tribulation.
(1) God is in control. He can, does, and will end the trials. Note the word "*after* the tribulation." There *shall* be an end to all the trials of the tribulation.
(2) God's people are to look to Him and hope in Him. The end of all trials is coming.
(3) God's people are always to be waiting and watching for the Lord's return.

MATTHEW 24:29-31

2 (24:29) **Jesus Christ, Return—End Times—Astronomical Bodies—Outer Space**: the very first event to occur when Christ returns in glory will be astronomical happenings. The heavenly bodies—the sun, moon, stars, and *the powers of the heavens*—will be affected.

Note the exact words of the astronomical happenings.

⇒ "The sun shall be darkened."
⇒ "The moon shall not give its light."
⇒ "The stars shall fall from heaven."
⇒ "The powers of the heavens shall be shaken."

Very practically, such astronomical happenings occur now. The earth is sometimes darkened by dust from earthly catastrophes such as volcanic eruptions, wind storms, and smoke from huge fires. Of course, whatever darkens the sun hides the light of the moon from earth. Stars or meteorites of varying sizes fall throughout space often. "The powers of the heavens" being shaken could be the heavenly bodies outside our solar system that are called by the Bible "the host of heaven" (De.4:19).

Is this what Christ meant? There is no way to know for sure; however, it is likely that this is the meaning. *But note*: His coming is going to trigger astronomical happenings worldwide and universally. The whole universe is going to be affected, or to word it in a much more meaningful way: the whole universe is going to open up and receive Him, including the astronomical bodies; and every man is going to know beyond any doubt that He is coming in all the power and the glory of God Himself. Christ says He is coming "with power and great glory." He is coming that "every knee should bow, of things in heaven, and things in earth, and things under the earth; and that every tongue should confess that Jesus Christ is Lord, to the glory of God the Father" (Ph.2:10-11).

He is coming, and "all the tribes of the earth shall [know it] and mourn [for] they shall see the Son of Man coming in the clouds of heaven with power and great glory." The words "power and great glory" convey the idea that He is coming to subject all men, to rule and reign over all the tribes or nations of the earth.

Scripture definitely reveals that astronomical happenings will precede and accompany the coming of the Lord.

"For the stars of heaven and the constellations thereof shall not give their light: the sun shall be darkened in his going forth, and the moon shall not cause her light to shine. And I will punish the world for their evil, and the wicked for their iniquity; and I will cause the arrogancy of the proud to cease, and will lay low the haughtiness of the terrible. I will make a man more precious than fine gold; even a man than the golden wedge of Ophir. Therefore I will shake the heavens, and the earth shall remove out of her place, in the wrath of the Lord of hosts, and in the day of his fierce anger" (Is.13:10-13).

"Fear, and the pit, and the snare, are upon thee, O inhabitant of the earth. And it shall come to pass, that he who fleeth from the noise of the fear shall fall into the pit; and he that cometh up out of the midst of the pit shall be taken in the snare: for the windows from on high are open, and the foundations of the earth do shake. The earth is utterly broken down, the earth is clean dissolved, the earth is moved exceedingly. The earth shall reel to and fro like a drunkard, and shall be removed like a cottage; and the transgression thereof shall be heavy upon it; and it shall fall, and not rise again. And it shall come to pass in that day, that the Lord shall punish the host of the high ones that are on high, and the kings of the earth upon the earth. And they shall be gathered together, as prisoners are gathered in the pit, and shall be shut up in the prison...." (Is.24:17-22).

"And I will show wonders in the heavens and in the earth, blood, and fire, and pillars of smoke. The sun shall be turned into darkness, and the moon into blood, before the great and the terrible day of the Lord come" (Joel 2:30-31).

"The sun and the moon shall be darkened, and the stars shall withdraw their shining. The Lord also shall roar out of Zion, and utter his voice from Jerusalem; and the heavens and the earth shall shake: but the Lord will be the hope of his people, and the strength of the children of Israel" (Joel 3:15-16).

"But in those days, after that tribulation, the sun shall be darkened, and the moon shall not give her light, And the stars of heaven shall fall, and the powers that are in heaven shall be shaken" (Mk.13:24-25).

"But the same day that Lot went out of Sodom it rained fire and brimstone from heaven, and destroyed them all. Even thus shall it be in the day when the Son of man is revealed" (Lu.17:29-30).

"And there shall be signs in the sun, and in the moon, and in the stars; and upon the earth distress of nations, with perplexity; the sea and the waves roaring; men's hearts failing them for fear, and for looking after those things which are coming on the earth: for the powers of heaven shall be shaken" (Lu.21:25-26).

"And I will show wonders in heaven above, and signs in the earth beneath; blood, and fire, and capor of smoke: the sun shall be turned into darkness, and the moon into blood, before that great and notable day of the Lord come" (Ac.2:19-20).

"And I beheld when he had opened the sixth seal, and, lo, there was a great earthquake; and the sun became black as sackcloth of hair, and the moon became as blood; and the stars of heaven fell unto the earth, even as a fig tree casteth her untimely figs, when she is shaken of a mighty wind. And the heaven departed as a scroll when it is rolled together; and every mountain and island were moved out of their places. And the kings of the earth, and the great men, and the rich men, and the chief captains, and the mighty men, and every bondman, and every free man, hid themselves in the dens and in the rocks of the mountains; and said to the mountains and rocks, Fall on us, and hide us from the face of him that sitteth on the throne, and from the wrath of the Lamb: for the great day of his wrath is come; and who shall be able to stand?" (Re.6:12-17). (See outline and notes—Re.6:12-17.)

MATTHEW 24:29-31

Note the exact words of the verses in Revelation above, for they are referring to the same event as Christ (v.30; see Re.6:17). Christ triggers a great earthquake on earth and astronomical happenings in the heavens above (vv.12-14). Men, great and small, are terrified and hide themselves (v.15) and cry for immediate death instead of having to face Christ (v.16). Why? Because they know something: "The great day of God's wrath is come; and who shall be able to stand?" (v.17).

The disciples had asked, "What shall be the sign of thy coming, and of the end of the world?" And Christ is answering them. Terrifying astronomical happenings will be a sign.

> **Thought 1.** Happenings in nature should cause us to turn our attention toward God. They are reminders of the *stressful* events that are to occur in the end time. As Christ said: "Look up, and lift up your heads; for your redemption draweth nigh" (Lu.21:28). If we look up and trust Him *now*, catastrophes and circumstances can be borne much better. His presence with us assures us of strength and endurance and victory (He.12:3; see 1 Co.10:13; Mt.28:20; see He.13:5-6).

3 (24:30) **Jesus Christ, Return—End Times**: when Christ returns, there will be a second event to occur—there will be *the* sign of Christ's appearing in the heavens. What is the sign? Christ does not specifically say. There are four different thoughts.

⇒ Some say the sign will be a star, just like the star that proclaimed His birth.
⇒ Others say it will be the Shekinah glory, His glory shining forth in all the splendor and brightness of God Himself. His glory will, of course, shine forth as described; but again, Christ does not say specifically that this is the sign.
⇒ Some, including many of the early church fathers, believe the sign will be the cross of Christ. There is no question that seeing the cross appear in the sky universally would attract attention and signal that something is about to happen. The cross is the symbol of Christianity and points toward the purpose of God in the world more than any other single thing.
⇒ Many believe the sign to be simply the appearance of the Son of Man Himself (Mt.26:64; Da.7:13-14).

Note four points.
a. When the sign appears, "all the tribes of the earth mourn." They know exactly what the sign is and what it means: the judgment and rule and reign of Christ. The tribes (people) do not have to guess and interpret what it means.
b. When the sign appears, "all the tribes of the earth mourn...and see the Son of Man coming in the clouds of heaven."
c. The Lord says that His coming will be as lightning, quick and sudden (v.27). Will there be time for a sign other than His personal appearance?
d. The disciples had asked about the *sign*: "What shall be the sign of thy coming...?" (v.3). Christ gives them a number of signs. Perhaps He is simply saying, "Then shall appear the sign of the Son of Man [Himself]...." This would, of course, be a fulfillment of Daniel's well-known sign of the Son of Man and His coming (Da.7:13-14).

Whatever the sign, there is one important thing to note: everyone knows exactly what it means. God's Son is coming to judge and to rule and reign over all the earth.

> "When the Son of man shall come in his glory, and all the holy angels with him, then shall he sit upon the throne of his glory: and before him shall be gathered all nations: and he shall separate them one from another, as a shepherd divideth his sheep from the goats" (Mt.25:31-32).
>
> "The Lord knoweth how to deliver the godly out of temptations, and to reserve the unjust unto the day of judgment to be punished" (2 Pe.2:9).
>
> "But the heavens and the earth, which are now, by the same word are kept in store, reserved unto fire against the day of judgment and perdition of ungodly men" (2 Pe.3:7).
>
> "And Enoch also, the seventh from Adam, prophesied of these, saying, Behold, the Lord cometh with ten thousands of his saints, to execute judgment upon all, and to convince all that are ungodly among them of all their ungodly deeds which they have ungodly committed, and of all their hard speeches which ungodly sinners have spoken against him" (Jude 14-15).
>
> "And I saw a great white throne, and him that sat on it, from whose face the earth and the heaven fled away; and there was found no place for them. And I saw the dead, small and great, stand before God; and the books were opened: and another book was opened, which is the book of life: and the dead were judged out of those things which were written in the books, according to their works. And the sea gave up the dead which were in it; and death and hell delivered up the dead which were in them: and they were judged every man according to their works. And death and hell were cast into the lake of fire. This is the second death. And whosoever was not found written in the book of life was cast into the lake of fire" (Re.20:11-15).

> **Thought 1.** There shall be a sign that triggers the coming of the Son of Man. Whatever the sign is, four things are certain.
> (1) *Now* the stars point toward the eternal power and Godhead and love of God in a beautiful creation. *Then* the stars shall point toward the wrath of God.
> (2) *Now* the Shekinah glory, the glory of God, shines before men calling them to righteousness. *Then* the Shekinah glory shall shine before men consuming them for their unrighteousness.
> (3) *Now* the cross stands before the world attracting the world to God. *Then* the cross shall stand before the world condemning the world.
> (4) *Now* Christ stands before the world as its Savior. *Then* Christ shall stand before the world as its Judge.

Thought 2. There are sign(s) of Christ's presence *now*. There are also signs that His return is ever so near. How much better to *mourn* and repent now than to be left with nothing but *mourning* then. The day is coming when it will be too late to turn to Christ.

Thought 3. Today, every man is without excuse. There are sign(s) and evidence(s) that He is the Savior of the world, God's very own Son. Much better to have the Son of Man appear now, in a person's heart and life by faith, than to have Him appear in the skies as a person's Judge (He.9:27; see Jn.3:18).

4 (24:30) **Jesus Christ, Return**: the third event of the Lord's return is that it will be visible to all—all the tribes of the earth will see Christ's coming in the clouds with power and great glory. There are four things said in this brief prophecy.

a. It is the Son of Man who shall come. Christ claims He is the Son of Man, God's very own Son, the Ideal Man, the Perfect Man, the Son of God incarnate in human flesh (see DEEPER STUDY # 3—Mt.8:20). In that day, there will be no doubt about who He is (see Mk.14:61-62). Right now He is recognized only by believers, but then He will be recognized by all men. It will be unmistakable: He is the Son of Man.

b. All the tribes of the earth will see His coming—visibly. How will everyone on earth, a round planet, see Him all at once? It is useless to speculate how God's power *works* (effects) any miracle. The point Christ is making is that His return will be visible and that every man on earth will see Him and acknowledge Him to be the Son of Man (see Re.1:7). (Note: the light—the great splendor and brightness—of the Lord's glory can easily be manifested throughout the universe and surround the earth when He returns.)

c. Christ will come in the clouds of heaven. In Scripture, clouds are often associated with God.

> "And he rode upon a cherub, and did fly: yea, he did fly upon the wings of the wind. He made darkness his secret place; his pavilion round about him were dark waters and thick clouds of the skies. At the brightness that was before him his thick clouds passed, hail stones and coals of fire" (Ps.18:10-12).
> "Who maketh the clouds His chariot" (Ps.104:3).
> "Behold, the Lord rideth upon a swift cloud" (Is.19:1).
> "I saw in the night visions, and behold, one like the Son of man came with the clouds of heaven, and came to the Ancient of days, and they brought him near before him" (Da.7:13).

When Jesus departed this earth after His resurrection, He departed in a cloud, and it was foretold that He would return in a cloud (Ac.1:9-11). Christ clearly says that He is going to return in a cloud and every eye will see Him come in the clouds of heaven. There is a strong claim here, a claim to be the God of the clouds.

d. Christ will come with power and great glory. There are at least two points being stressed in this fact.
1) Christ will come in the full dignity of His person. He will not come as a babe in a manger who lives through the stages of life to secure salvation for man. He will come with power and great glory. He will come in all the omnipotence and glory of God, revealing just who He is.
2) Christ will come as a Judge to execute justice upon the earth. He will come to rule and reign in His rightful position as Sovereign Lord over the earth.

Thought 1. Every man will acknowledge Christ to be the Son of Man. There will not be a single exception.
⇒ Now, there is *voluntary* acknowledgement; then, there will be *involuntary* acknowledgement.
⇒ Now, there is *wilful* confession; then, there will be *enforced* confession.
⇒ Now, there is a *loving* appeal; then, there will be the *condemning* judgment.

> "Because he hath appointed a day, in the which he will judge the world in righteousness by that man whom he hath ordained; whereof he hath given assurance unto all men, in that he hath raised him from the dead" (Ac.17:31).
> "In the day when God shall judge the secrets of men by Jesus Christ according to my gospel" (Ro.2:16).
> "Wherefore God also hath highly exalted him, and given him a name which is above every name: that at the name of Jesus every knee should bow, of things in heaven, and things in earth, and things under the earth; and that every tongue should confess that Jesus Christ is Lord, to the glory of God the Father" (Ph.2:9-11).
> "And if ye call on the Father, who without respect of persons judgeth according to every man's work, pass the time of your sojourning here in fear" (1 Pe.1:17).

5 (24:30) **Jesus Christ, Return**: the fourth event is that all the tribes of the earth will mourn when Christ returns in power and great glory. Why? Because they will see beyond any question that Christ is the Son of Man. They will realize that they ignored, neglected, rejected, abused, and cursed Him. They will know that they have missed His salvation and that they are now to be judged. There is a picture of this great mourning in Revelation where "all the kindreds of the earth...wail because of Him" (Re.1:7). They wail and mourn because of the terrible judgment which is to be inflicted upon them.

Very simply, Christ is going to return and every eye will see Him and know beyond any question that He is the Son of Man. The worldly will mourn because He comes as Judge; the elect will rejoice because they are to be gathered together with Him.

MATTHEW 24:29-31

Thought 1. Every man has a choice. He mourns now, or he shall mourn when Christ returns. A man experiences a godly sorrow that leads to repentance *now*, or he shall experience a worldly sorrow that leads to eternal sorrow when Christ returns (see Deeper Study #1—2 Co.7:10).

"Then Peter said unto them, Repent, and be baptized every one of you in the name of Jesus Christ for the remission of sins, and ye shall receive the gift of the Holy Ghost" (Ac.2:38).

"Repent ye therefore, and be converted, that your sins may be blotted out, when the times of refreshing shall come from the presence of the Lord" (Ac.3:19).

"Repent therefore of this thy wickedness, and pray God, if perhaps the thought of thine heart may be forgiven thee" (Ac.8:22).

"For godly sorrow worketh repentance to salvation not to be repented of: but the sorrow of the world worketh death" (2 Co.7:10).

"Cast away from you all your transgressions, whereby ye have transgressed; and make you a new heart and a new spirit: for why will ye die?" (Eze.18:31).

6 (24:31) **Jesus Christ, Return**: the fifth event of the Lord's coming is that the angels will be sent forth to gather the elect. There are four points made in this verse.

a. Christ will send forth *His* angels. He is God, the Lord of the angels. They are His; He is over them. They are at His beck and call to carry out His sovereign will. This again is a claim to deity.

b. Christ will send forth His angels with the "great sound of a trumpet." The trumpet was used to call an assembly of the people together. This is probably the meaning here. (See 1 Co.15:52; 1 Th.4:16.)

c. The angels will gather together the Lord's elect. Only the elect will be gathered at this point. The elect may be but a few when compared to the mass of humanity. But there will be a remnant of genuine believers scattered all over the earth, a remnant who will have endured to the end. They will be saved (v.13. See Mt.20:16; 22:14.)

As Christ said:

"I tell you, in that night there shall be two men in one bed; the one shall be taken, and the other shall be left. Two women shall be grinding together; the one shall be taken, and the other left. Two men shall be in the field; and one shall be taken, and the other left" (Lu.17:34-36; see Mt.24:40-41).

d. The elect will be gathered from the four winds, from one end of heaven to the other. The meaning is this: the elect will be scattered all over the world; they will be everywhere, in all nations of the world (see De.4:32; Re.7:9). As Christ had just said:

"And this gospel of the kingdom shall be preached in all the world for a witness unto all nations; and then shall the end come" (Mt.24:14).

Thought 1. There is one glorious hope for every believer, whatever his generation and the trials of it:

"Looking for that blessed hope, and the glorious appearing of the great God and our Savior Jesus Christ; who gave himself for us, that he might redeem us from all iniquity, and purify unto himself a peculiar people, zealous of good works" (Tit.2:13-14).

Thought 2. The angels are subject to Christ; we, too, should be subject to Him. The angels do His sovereign will; we, too, should do His sovereign will. If we administer His will now, we shall be in that select company in that glorious day.

Thought 3. Not a single believer will be missed when Jesus returns. No matter where we are or how isolated and lonely and forgotten we may feel, He is coming for us.

MATTHEW 24:32-41

	D. The Time of the Lord's Return, 24:32-41 (Mk 13:28-34; Lu 21:29-35)	angels of heaven, but my Father only. 37 But as the days of Noe *were*, so shall also the coming of the Son of man be.	
1. The time can be generally discerned	32 Now learn a parable of the fig tree; When his branch is yet tender, and putteth forth leaves, ye know that summer is nigh:	38 For as in the days that were before the flood they were eating and drinking, marrying and giving in marriage, until the day that Noe entered into the ark,	3. The day will come suddenly—unexpectedly—shattering to the world of unbelievers^{DS2} a. Its counterpart is Noah's day: A day of worldliness, of sensuality, & of refusing to heed the message of coming judgment^{DS3,4}
a. Its events are compared to a fig tree b. Its events will be witnessed & experienced by only one generation^{DS1}	33 So likewise ye, when ye shall see all these things, know that it is near, *even* at the doors. 34 Verily I say unto you, This generation shall not pass, till all these things be fulfilled.	39 And knew not until the flood came, and took them all away; so shall also the coming of the Son of man be. 40 Then shall two be in the field; the one shall be taken, and the other left.	b. Its shock: "Knew nothing"—were unbelieving, closed-minded, ignorant c. Its certainty: "How it will be" 4. The day will be a time of & judgment
c. Its events are certain 2. The actual day & hour are known only by God	35 Heaven and earth shall pass away, but my words shall not pass away. 36 But of that day and hour knoweth no *man*, no, not the	41 Two *women* shall be grinding at the mill; the one shall be taken, and the other left.	

DIVISION XV

THE MESSIAH'S PROPHECY OF HIS RETURN AND THE END OF THE AGE: THE OLIVET DISCOURSE, 24:1–25:46

D. The Time of the Lord's Return, 24:32-41

(24:32-41) **Introduction—End Time**: the disciples had asked, "When shall these things be?" At this point of His discussion, Christ said, "*Now* learn a parable of the fig tree, *when*...." Note the word *when*. He was beginning to discuss the end time and His return. It should be noted that the first part of His discussion can apply to the fall of Jerusalem in 70 A.D. as well as to the end time (vv.4-35). However, Christ definitely said this passage had to do with the end time only, with the coming of the Son of Man (vv.37, 39). When will Christ return? He revealed four significant points.

1. The time can be generally discerned (vv.32-35).
2. The actual day and hour are known only by God (v.36).
3. The day will come suddenly—unexpectedly—shattering to the world of unbelievers (vv.37-39).
4 The day will be a time of separation and judgment (vv.40-41).

1 (24:32-35) **Jesus Christ, Return**: Christ said that the time of His return can be generally discerned.

a. The events (signs) that point to His return are compared to a fig tree. When the fig tree begins to put forth its leaves, it is known that summer is near. So when we see "all these things," the signs He has been sharing, "know that it [His coming] is near, *even* at the doors." His coming is at the very threshold; He is about to enter into the world again (see Js.5:9).
Note what Christ said:
   1) When the leaves on a fig tree are seen, summer is not yet. But we *know* summer is near, at hand.
   2) "So likewise ye, when *ye shall see* all these things, *know* that it [His coming, His kingdom] is near." He definitely says we can "know that it is near."
b. The events (signs) will be witnessed by one generation. The disciples had asked two questions—one about Jerusalem's destruction and one about the end of the world. In answering their questions, Christ nowhere drew a definite line between the two questions. The signs and events that precede one shall precede the other. The implication is clear: just as the signs and destruction of Jerusalem took place within a generation, the signs and destruction of the world will also occur within a generation. (See DEEPER STUDY # 2, pt.2—Mt.24:1-31.)
c. The events (signs) are certain. Christ was definite about what He had said. "Heaven and earth *shall* pass away, but my words shall not pass away."
Note two things.
   1). Heaven and earth will pass away. Christ was saying they are actually going to be done away with (2 Pe.3:10-11).
   2) All that He had said about the great tribulation and His return will happen. The great tribulation and His return are more sure than heaven and earth.

Thought 1. *Expectation* is a key word when dealing with the Lord's return. When we see a fig tree's putting forth its leaves, we *expect* summer to be near. "So likewise" we should expect two things.
(1) We should expect the signs, "all these things" that Christ has been mentioning (v.33a).
(2) We should expect and "know that it [His coming] is near" (v.33b).

Thought 2. In the eyes of men, it has been a long time since Christ spoke these words, and an innumerable list of events have happened. Therefore, men assume that the second coming is a fable, the figment of hopeful imagination. God knew this would happen.

> "Knowing this first, that there shall come in the last days scoffers, walking after their own lusts, and saying, Where is the promise of his coming? for since the fathers fell asleep, all things continue as they were from the beginning of the creation....But, beloved, be not ignorant of this one thing, that one day is with the Lord as a thousand years, and a thousand years as one day. The Lord is not slack concerning his promise, as some men count slackness; but is longsuffering to us-ward, not willing that any should perish, but that all should come to repentance. But the day of the Lord will come as a thief in the night; in the which the heavens shall pass away with a great noise, and the elements shall melt with fervent heat, the earth also and the works that are therein shall be burned up. Seeing then that all these things shall be dissolved, what manner of persons ought ye to be in all holy conversation and godliness, looking for and hasting unto the coming of the day of God, wherein the heavens being on fire shall be dissolved, and the elements shall melt with fervent heat? Nevertheless we, according to this promise, look for new earth, wherein dwelleth righteousness" (2 Pe.3:3-4, 8-13).

Thought 3. Three things are certain to happen in human history: "the beginning of sorrows" (v.8); "the great tribulation, such as was not since the beginning of the world" (v.21); and "the Son of Man coming in the clouds of heaven with power and great glory" (v.30). Heaven and earth shall pass away, but not the words He spoke, not what He said would happen. What He said would happen will happen. These three events are certain.

DEEPER STUDY # 1
(24:33-34) **Jesus Christ, Return**: note the time involved in these two verses—they agree. "When ye shall see all these things...it is near" (v.33). All will happen in one generation, whether dealing with the fall of Jerusalem in 70 AD or the return of Christ (v.34).

---

2 (24:36) **End Time**: the actual day and hour that Christ will return are known only by God. Note two things.

a. The return of Christ is a real event that is yet to happen. There is "that day and hour." There is *a fixed day and a fixed hour* when Christ will return. It is an actual event.

b. The return of Christ is secret. "No man knoweth...my Father only." Some have thought they knew, but Christ is explicit: "No man knoweth, not the angels of heaven, but my Father *only*." (See note—2 Th.2:1-2.)

> "And no man in heaven, nor in earth, neither under the earth, was able to open the book, neither to look thereon" (Re.5:3).
> "The secret things belong unto the LORD our God: but those things which are revealed belong unto us and to our children for ever, that we may do all the words of this law" (De.29:29).

Thought 1. Some things are to be left entirely in God's hands. The exact day and hour of the Lord's return is one of these things. *Watchful* believers will be sensitive to the season (fig tree, v.32-33) and know the generation (v.34), but the exact hour and day are hid from men, even from the wisest and most spiritual men. *Only* God Himself knows when Christ shall return. If a man claims to know the hour and day, he is the man from which we should flee. That man's word conflicts with the Lord's Word.

3 (24:37-39) **Jesus Christ, Return**: the coming of the Lord will be sudden—unexpected—shattering to the world of unbelievers. Christ says three things.

a. When will Christ return? His coming finds its counterpart in Noah's day. He will come when the world is living just as it was living in Noah's day:

⇒ Living sensual lives, eating, drinking, marrying, divorcing, and remarrying time after time (see *Deeper Study* 3,4—Mt.24:38; see Lu.17:26-30).
⇒ Refusing to heed Noah's message of righteousness and coming judgment (2 Pe.2:5).

1) Note that eating, drinking (water), and marriage are all necessary to maintain life. It is the excessiveness, the lust for more and more, the extravagance that is sinful. It is setting one's mind upon the pleasure of the flesh and of the world and lusting for more and more. (See note—Js.4:1; DEEPER STUDY # 1—4:1-3; note—4:2. See Ro.1:24.)

2) Note another point: What is it that Christ says will characterize the age? Not stealing and murder and immorality, but eating and drinking and marrying time after time. When the earth was destroyed the first time, it was because "the earth was corrupt...and...filled with violence" (Ge.6:11). However, the sins that bring the second destruction of the earth seem to be eating and drinking and marrying time after time. These are the sins stressed by Christ.

3) Note the words "*until the day* that Noah entered into the ark." While Noah was building the ark, he preached the righteousness of God and the coming judgment. The people had the testimony of Noah's life and his belief in God's Word as a warning, a warning that man was responsible to live righteously and that judgment was coming. They saw Noah's building the ark. They saw the ark sitting there, yet they rejected Noah's message and testimony. They went on living in worldliness, in their eating and drinking and in pursuing their own lustful desires, and

they did so right up until the very day that "Noah entered into the ark." Then suddenly, unexpectedly, their world was shattered.

b. When will Christ come? He will come just as He came in Noah's day: at a shocking time. Just as they "knew not" that the end was coming, so He will come again when the world *knows not*.

1) They *knew not* means this: they did not expect the coming judgment. They *did not believe* the fact, the word, the message. They *were close-minded*; they did not bother too much about listening and studying the matter. Therefore, they *were ignorant* about the truth. They did not know the Word of God.
2) "They knew not" means this: they felt secure in themselves and in their world. As Scripture says in another place:

> "For when they shall say, Peace and safety; then sudden destruction cometh upon them, as travail upon a woman with child; and they shall not escape" (1 Th.5:3).

3) They "knew not" means this: they were living worldly and materialistic lives, eating and drinking when they should have been sensible and clear-minded, listening and turning to God.
4) They "knew not" means this: their concern was "Let us eat and drink: for tomorrow we shall die" (Is.22:13); whereas their concern should have been *righteousness* (2 Co.5:21).

c. When will Christ come? He will come when people are living just as they were living in the days of Noah: "As the days of Noah were, so shall also the coming of the Son of Man be" (v.37, 39). His coming is certain and assured.

> "For as in the days that were before the flood they were eating and drinking, marrying and giving in marriage, until the day that Noe entered into the ark, and knew not until the flood came, and took them all away; so shall also the coming of the Son of man be" (Mt.24:38-39).
> "And take heed to yourselves, lest at any time your hearts be overcharged with surfeiting, and drunkenness, and cares of this life, and so that day come upon you unawares" (Lu.21:34).
> "Teaching us that, denying ungodliness and worldly lusts, we should live soberly, righteously, and godly, in this present world; looking for that blessed hope, and the glorious appearing of the great God and our Saviour Jesus Christ" (Tit.2:12-13).
> "Ye adulterers and adulteresses, know ye not that the friendship of the world is enmity with God? whosoever therefore will be a friend of the world is the enemy of God" (Js.4:4).
> "Love not the world, neither the things that are in the world, If any man love the world, the love of the Father is not in him. For all that is in the world, the lust of the flesh, and the lust of the eyes, and the pride of life, is not of the Father, but is of the world" (1 Jn.2:15-16).

Thought 1. Note the words "knew not." They *knew not* because they were steeped in sensual living. A person can eat, drink, and be immoral until he is gripped and enslaved (see notes—Ro.1:24; Js.4:1-6).
⇒ *Conscience* becomes dull, hardened, and insensitive to right.
⇒ *Will* becomes more craving.
⇒ *Spirit* becomes more selfish.
⇒ *Life* becomes more worldly.
⇒ *Hope* becomes more materialistic.
⇒ *Death* becomes more final.

Thought 2. Christ's return will shatter the world of the person...
- who eats and eats
- who drinks and drinks
- who marries and marries
- who "knows not"
- who does not believe
- who is close-minded
- who is ignorant

Thought 3. There are many genuine believers in the world. The testimony of righteousness should be right before the face of most people just as it was before the face of the people in Noah's day. We are without excuse. We should be prepared for His coming. His *sudden* coming should not catch us unexpectedly; it should not shock or shatter our world.

Thought 4. A man must not allow himself to be so immersed in worldliness that he forgets eternity (1 Jn.2:15-16; Ro.12:1-2; 2 Co.6:17-18).

DEEPER STUDY # 2

(24:37) **Jesus Christ, Return**: it must be remembered that the righteous, that is, the only believers of Noah's day, were Noah himself and his family. They were not caught unaware. It was to the unbelieving world that the day came unexpectedly and with shattering suddenness. This is understandable: the true believer is ever "looking for that blessed hope and the glorious appearing of the great God and our Savior, Jesus Christ" (Tit.2:13). When that day begins to approach, believers will see and discern the times through the power of the Holy Spirit. The Holy Spirit will be preparing the believer's

MATTHEW 24:32-41

heart for that day. But the unbelieving world will be mocking what it considers foolish belief. It will be going about its merry way and wantonness, paying no attention whatever to an event that it considers foolish. (See Da.12:10.)

DEEPER STUDY # 3
(24:38) **Eating** (trogontes): to gnaw; to chew. It has the idea of grabbing and gnawing greedily like a hungry dog. Here it means the habitual practice of eating with a gluttonous appetite, eating excessively.

DEEPER STUDY # 4
(24:38) **Drinking** (pinontes): to drink; to participate in the partying spirit of drink; to participate in the abomination of drinking. The idea is a habitual practice, drinking to excess (see Gal.5:21; see Ep.5:18).

"And take heed to yourselves, lest at any time your hearts be overcharged with surfeiting, and drunkenness, and cares of this life, and so that day come upon you unawares" (Lu.21:34).
"Nor thieves, nor covetous, nor drunkards, nor revilers, nor extortioners, shall inherit the kingdom of God" (1 Co.6:10).
"Woe unto him that giveth his neighbor drink, that puttest thy bottle to him, and makest him drunken also, that thou mayest look on their nakedness!" (Hab.2:15).

4 (24:40-41) **Jesus Christ, Return**: the coming of the Lord will be a time of separation and judgment. Several things are seen in these two verses.

a. On the day when Jesus comes, no one knows He is coming, not even believers. All go about their affairs, their occupations as usual.

b. On the day when Jesus comes, while people are going about their affairs, all of a sudden one shall be taken and the other left.

c. On the day when Jesus comes, there will be separation from those nearest us—from those right by our side. The believer will be caught up to be with the Lord; the unbeliever will be left behind to face judgment (vv.30-31, 50-51; see 2 Th.1:7-10).

"Let both grow together until the harvest: and in the time of harvest I will say to the reapers, Gather ye together first the tares, and bind them in bundles to burn them: but gather the wheat into my barn" (Mt.13:30).
"So shall it be at the end of the world: the angels shall come forth, and sever the wicked from among the just" (Mt.13:49).
"And before him shall be gathered all nations: and he shall separate them one from another, as a shepherd divideth his sheep from the goats" (Mt.25:32).
"And these shall go away into everlasting punishment: but the righteous into life eternal" (Mt.25:46).
"And beside all this, between us and you there is a great gulf fixed: so that they which would pass from hence to you cannot; neither can they pass to us, that would come from thence" (Lu.16:26).
"I tell you, in that night there shall be two men in one bed; the one shall be taken, and the other shall be left" (Lu.17:34).

Thought 1. The basis of separation and judgment is belief. In Noah's day no one believed the message of righteousness. Only the man who believes the message of righteousness and adheres to it will be taken (2 Co.5:21 see Jn.3:16; Mt.24:13).

MATTHEW 24:42-51

	E. The Lord's Return & the Believer's Duty: Watch—Be Ready—Be Faithful & Wise, 24:42-51 *(Mk 13:35-37; Lu 21:36)*	household, to give them meat in due season? 46 Blessed *is* that servant, whom his lord when he cometh shall find so doing. 47 Verily I say unto you, That he shall make him ruler over all his goods.	a. His responsibility: To oversee & feed the household b. His accountability: He proves faithful c. His reward: He will be put in charge of the Lord's property
1. The believer's duty: Watch a. The Lord does return b. The exact time is unknown	42 Watch therefore: for ye know not what hour your Lord doth come.	48 But and if that evil servant shall say in his heart, My lord delayeth his coming;	**4. Parable 3: A wicked servant** a. His attitude: He has plenty of time
2. Parable 1: The owner of the house (a professing believer) a. He had a house to look after b. He lived without watchfulness c. He suffered disaster d. The point: Readiness is essential, for Christ comes unexpectedly	43 But know this, that if the goodman of the house had known in what watch the thief would come, he would have watched, and would not have suffered his house to be broken up. 44 Therefore be ye also ready: for in such an hour as ye think not the Son of man cometh.	49 And shall begin to smite *his* fellowservants, and to eat and drink with the drunken; 50 The lord of that servant shall come in a day when he looketh not for *him,* and in an hour that he is not aware of, 51 And shall cut him asunder, and appoint *him* his portion with the hypocrites: there shall be weeping and gnashing of teeth.	b. His behavior: He acts unjustly & worldly c. His judgment: He is doomed 1) The Lord catches him unexpectedly 2) The Lord condemns him to death—with the hypocrites
3. Parable 2: A faithful & wise servant (a genuine believer)	45 Who then is a faithful and wise servant, whom his lord hath made ruler over his		

DIVISION XV

THE MESSIAH'S PROPHECY OF HIS RETURN AND THE END OF THE AGE: THE OLIVET DISCOURSE, 24:1–25:46

E. The Lord's Return and the Believer's Duty: Watch—Be Ready—Be Faithful and Wise, 24:42-51

(24:42-51) **Introduction**: it is most important to remember that this was Christ's last week on earth. This was His last chance to teach the disciples. All that He said was of critical importance and, out of necessity, must be clear and pointed. He had led the disciples to ask two intriguing questions: "When shall the temple [or Jerusalem] be destroyed? and what shall be the sign of thy coming and of the end of the world?" (v.3). (See note—Mt.24:1-25:46.)

Christ had just answered the disciples' questions. Now He came to the all important point of application. Since He would be returning to earth and God wanted the hour to be kept secret, what was the believer to do? How was the believer to live? What was the believer's duty? Christ answered these questions in one forceful word: "Watch!" Then He shared three parables to explain what He meant by the strong exhortation, "Watch."

1. The believer's duty: watch (v.42).
2. Parable 1: the owner of the house (a professing believer) (vv.43-44).
3. Parable 2: a faithful and wise servant (a genuine believer) (vv.45-47).
4. Parable 3: a wicked servant (vv.48-51).

1 (24:42) **Watch** (gregoreo): to keep awake; to stay alert; to be watchful and sleepless; to be vigilant. It also includes the idea of being motivated, of keeping one's attention (mind) upon a thing. Watching also has the idea of being alert at the *right time*. It is at night that a person really needs to stay awake to watch for the thief (see 1 Th.5:4-9).

The Lord said, "Watch." What does it mean for a believer to *watch*? (Mt.26:41; Mk.13:33, 34, 36; 14:38; see 1 Co.16:13; 1 Th.5:6; 2 Ti.4:5; 1 Pe.4:7).

a. The believer *watches* and stays *ready* for the Lord's return. He does not know the exact hour of the Lord's return; therefore, he is to watch and stay ready at all times (vv.42-44). He should be so ready that his eyes are open and watching for the signs of Christ's return.

b. The believer *watches* his ministry and his duty to God. He sees to it that he serves faithfully and wisely (v.45).

c. The believer *watches* his *attitude and behavior* (vv.48-49). He stays his mind upon the Lord's return and walks soberly and godly among others.

> "For though we walk in the flesh, we do not war after the flesh: (For the weapons of our warfare are not carnal, but mighty through God to the pulling down of strong holds;) casting down imaginations, and every high thing that exalteth itself against the knowledge of God, and bringing into captivity every thought to the obedience of Christ" (2 Co.10:3-5).
>
> "Teaching us that, denying ungodliness and worldly lusts, we should live soberly, righteously, and godly, in this present world; Looking for that blessed hope, and the glorious appearing of the great God and our Savior Jesus Christ" (Tit.2:12-13).

d. The believer *watches* by being ready to die and to meet the Lord through death (He.9:27). Christ does not mention this point, but its truth is ever so clear to the maturing believer.

MATTHEW 24:42-51

2 (24:43-44) **Jesus Christ, Return**: the first parable Christ shared concerned the owner of a house. He represents the professing believer. Christ shared four things.

a. The owner had a house to look after. He was blessed, for he owned a house, and it was full of possessions. The belongings were valuable enough to attract a thief.

b. The owner lived without watchfulness.

1) The owner knew the thief was coming, and he knew he was coming that night. He just did not know in what watch he was coming. (Every watch was divided into three hours, for example, 12-3 a.m., 3-6 a.m.)

2) The owner began to watch. He had tried to protect his house; he had bolted the doors and closed the windows. He was staying up listening to every noise and was ready to try to protect his house.

3) The owner failed to protect his house, and he failed in an area least expected. He simply did not watch *long enough*. As the hours wore on and on, he grew more and more drowsy and nodded more and more. The owner simply failed...

- to stay awake long enough
- to keep his mind alert long enough
- to look and listen to the noises (signs) long enough
- to keep active long enough
- to stand guard long enough

c. The owner suffered disaster. The thief came while the owner was asleep. The owner ceased watching, and the thief broke into his home, taking his most prized valuables.

d. Christ's point made is clear: readiness is essential. By *readiness*, Christ meant diligence. We are to be diligently living a life of righteousness, looking for His return.

> "Seeing then that all these things shall be dissolved, what manner of persons ought ye to be in all holy conversation and godliness....Nevertheless we, according to his promise, look for new heavens and a new earth, wherein dwelleth righteousness" (2 Pe.3:11, 13).

Christ gave two reasons why we are to be ready: (a) He is definitely coming, and (b) He is coming in an hour when the unprepared will not expect Him (v.44, 50).

> "And this know, that if the goodman of the house had known what hour the thief would come, he would have watched, and not have suffered his house to be broken through" (Lu.12:39).
>
> "In my Father's house are many mansions: if it were not so, I would have told you. I go to prepare a place for you. And if I go and prepare a place for you, I will come again, and receive you unto myself; that where I am, there ye may be also" (Jn.14:2-3).
>
> "For yourselves know perfectly that the day of the Lord so cometh as a thief in the night....But ye, brethren, are not in darkness, that that day should overtake you as a thief" (1 Th.5:2, 4).
>
> "But the day of the Lord will come as a thief in the night; in the which the heavens shall pass away with a great noise, and the elements shall melt with fervent heat, the earth also and the works that are therein shall be burned up" (2 Pe.3:10).
>
> "Remember therefore how thou hast received and heard, and hold fast, and repent. If therefore thou shalt not watch, I will come on thee as a thief, and thou shalt not know what hour I will come upon thee" (Re.3:3).
>
> "And I heard the angel of the waters say, Thou art righteous, O Lord, which art, and wast, and shalt be, because thou hast judged thus" (Re.16:5).

Thought 1. The Lord's return is imminent. This is the point. We must stay alert and be diligent in looking for His return—today!

Thought 2. The owner's house can represent a man's life. Every man is responsible for taking care of his life. Christ says we keep our house (life) by "watching" and being ready for His return, for He may return at any moment.

3 (24:45-47) **Jesus Christ, Return**: the second parable Christ shared concerned the faithful and wise servant. He represents a genuine believer, a person who not only professes Christ but lives for Christ. The genuine believer may be a minister, a teacher, or a young learner in Christ. But note: the point is not the believer's position but his being faithful and wise. The simplest believer is to be faithful and wise, no matter who he is or what his calling is.

Christ put this parable in the form of a question: "Who then is a faithful and wise servant?" He does this to stir more thought about the issue at hand and to force a much more personal application. Christ covers three points about the faithful and wise servant.

a. His responsibility is twofold. He is *to oversee* the Master's household and he is *to feed* the Master's family.

1) He is to oversee the Master's household. Note: it is the Master who sets him over His household. The servant does not appoint himself, nor is he appointed by other servants (or churches) of the household. The Master alone sets him over His family.

He is given the responsibility to rule, to oversee, to look after the household and family of the Master. But he is under his Lord and he is to oversee primarily by example.

MATTHEW 24:42-51

"Feed the flock of God which is among you, taking the oversight thereof, not by constraint, but willingly; nor for filthy lucre, but of a ready mind; Neither as being lords over God's heritage, but being examples to the flock" (1 Pe.5:2-3).

"Obey them that have the rule [ownership] over you, and submit yourselves: for they watch for your souls, as they that must give account, that they may do it with joy, and not with grief: for that is unprofitable for you" (He.13:17).

2) He is to provide food for the Master's family, and he is to do it in due season. His family has to be fed. It is the servant's duty to provide food for them. Note that he gives; it is his duty to give, not to take (see Eze.34:8; Ac.20:35). He gives food for their nourishment, and He gives the food "in due season," at the right time.

"Feed the flock of God which is among you" (1 Pe.5:2).
"Feed my lambs...my sheep" (Jn.21:15-17).

b. His accountability is clearly stated. The Lord is coming, and when He comes, He will judge what the faithful servant is doing. The servant will be looked at and observed to see if he is managing the household and feeding the family *faithfully and wisely*.

"Blessed is that servant [who is] so doing" (Mt.24:46).
"Moreover it is required in stewards, that a man be found faithful" (1 Co.4:2).
"As every man hath received the gift, even so minister the same one to another, as good stewards of the manifold grace of God" (1 Pe.4:10).
"Therefore, my beloved brethren, be ye stedfast, unmoveable, always abounding in the work of the Lord, forasmuch as ye know that your labour is not in vain in the Lord" (1 Co.15:58).
"Take heed unto thyself, and unto the doctrine; continue in them: for in doing this thou shalt both save thyself, and them that hear thee" (1 Ti.4:16).

c. His reward will be unbelievable. The Master will make the faithful servant ruler over all His goods. The idea is that he will be placed first: looked upon, loved, and considered first, as though he were the only one. He had been managing, looking after only a small portion for the Master. Now he will be given a much greater responsibility to oversee for his Lord.

"He that is faithful in that which is least is faithful also in much: and he that is unjust in the least is unjust also in much" (Lu.16:10).
"He that spared not his own Son, but delivered him up for us all, how shall he not with him also freely give us all things?" (Ro.8:32).
"As it is written, Eye hath not seen, nor ear heard, neither have entered into the heart of man, the things which God hath prepared for them that love him" (1 Co.2:9; see Rev.2:26; 3:21).

Thought 1. Who is faithful and wise? The believer who is found "so doing." This means he is enduring (v.13) and watching over the task the Lord has given him (v.42). (See note—Mt.24:42.)

Thought 2. This is a precious thought: to picture Christ's renting the skies above and returning, and to know that His first sight of us will be that of our laboring for Him. May the Lord grant just this: when He returns, may His first sight be to see us working for Him. Blessed is that servant "whom his Lord...shall find so *doing*." Note the word "doing" is continuous action.

This is a frightful thought: to picture Christ's appearing and His first sight of us is that of...
- sleeping late
- working half-heartedly
- mistreating someone
- arguing
- being engaged in an immoral act
- overeating

4 (24:48-51) **Servant, Unfaithful; Evil; Untrustworthy**: the third parable Christ shared concerns the evil servant. He represents a professing believer. Some say he is even a professing minister. If so, he is not a genuine believer, despite his profession and ministerial position. He is *unfaithful* and *untrustworthy* (1 Ti.1:12). His life is tragic. Christ covers his attitude, his behavior, and his end or judgment.

a. His attitude. Note the word *heart*. The attitude of his heart is, "My Lord delayeth His coming; there is plenty of time." Several things can cause such an attitude.
⇒ Doubting the Lord's Word, that He is ever coming.
⇒ Misinterpreting the Lord's coming as being only symbolic, instead of accepting it as literal; symbolizing it to mean some spiritual truth such as the Lord's meeting a person when the person dies.
⇒ Ignoring the Lord's coming in order to allow the person to live as he wishes.
⇒ Thinking the Lord's coming is so far away that it has little meaning for today.

MATTHEW 24:42-51

    b. His behavior. Note that it is after the evil servant says there is plenty of time that he begins to live as he wishes. *His attitude* (his heart) *determines his behavior*.
       1) He acts unjustly. He begins to "smite his fellowservants." He seeks more and more materially, both power and things. He strikes and mistreats anyone who stands in his way. He seeks "filthy lucre" (acceptance, esteem, gain, property, money), and he seeks to *lord it over people* (1 Pe.5:2-3).
       2) He lives carnally. He begins "to eat and drink with the worldly [drunken]." He walks with them, sits with them, lies with them. He is their companion in sin. He is indulgent, living to please the flesh.
    c. His end and his judgment are certain. There is no escape.
       1) The Lord will catch the evil servant unexpectedly. Some deny that the Lord is coming to judge them; others ignore His coming; and still others put the thought out of their minds. But nothing will keep the Lord from coming: "the Lord of that [evil] servant shall come." And He will come when the evil man is not looking for Him. To the evil person, the Lord's coming will be the most frightful experience of human history (see vv.21-22; Re.6:15-17).
          In talking about meeting the Lord, it must be remembered that every man meets the Lord at death: "It is appointed unto men once to die, but after this the judgment" (He.9:27). The point Christ makes is that the evil man will face eternal doom at the end of the world. As other Scriptures point out, the Great White Throne of judgment is to take place at the end of the world.
       2) The Lord will condemn the evil servant to death—with the hypocrites. He will be "cut asunder," cut off from among the living and from among believers; and most tragic, he will be "cut asunder" from God's presence. His position and place will be with hypocrites. Where are the hypocrites? Christ says "[Where] there shall be weeping and gnashing of teeth" (see note—Mt.8:12).

The sin of the evil servant, of a person who makes a false profession, does several terrible things.
1. He deceives himself and others. He deceives people into thinking that they will not have to face the judgment of the Lord's return, or if they do, it will be minimal.
2. He minimizes the truth of eternity, of heaven, of life with God, and of the judgment which every man must face.
3. He takes away from the message and effectiveness of the gospel.
4. He keeps people from the truth. He keeps them from watching and preparing, from protecting and guarding, from living and walking with their eyes upon the Lord's coming.

> "And when these things begin to come to pass, then look up, and lift up your heads; for your redemption draweth nigh" (Lu.21:28).
>
> "In my Father's house are many mansions: if it were not so, I would have told you. I go to prepare a place for you. And if I go and prepare a place for you, I will come again, and receive you unto myself; that where I am, there ye may be also" (Jn.14:2-3).

Thought 1. Note that Christ still speaks of a servant. The difference is onefold: this is an evil servant. He may be a minister, a teacher, or a layman. Christ says that he is an evil servant and spells out what it is that makes him evil.

Thought 2. The worst of all men is the man who professes, and while he professes, he is living in sin. As Christ says, "his portion [is] with the *hypocrite*" (v.51). His only hope is to confess his evil and repent, turning back to God, ever trusting His wonderful mercy and grace.

> "If we confess our sins, he is faithful and just to forgive us our sins, and to cleanse us from all unrighteousness" (1 Jn.1:9).

Thought 3. The man who walks ignoring, twisting, misinterpreting, or denying the Lord's return is walking by his *senses*—what he knows about the physical universe. He is walking as he *senses* things to be, not as God has revealed them to be.

MATTHEW 25:1-13

Outline	Scripture	Outline
	CHAPTER 25 **F. The Parable of the Ten Virgins: The Warning to Watch,**DS1,2 **25:1-13** *(See Lu 12:35-37)*	c. The awakening: To prepare their lampsDS5 d. The foolish discover their lamps are out: Frantic–beg for oil e. The wise scarcely have enough for themselves

1. The Kingdom of Heaven is compared to ten virgins
2. The wise & foolish virgins (believers) attend the wedding
  a. Five are wise; five are foolish
  b. The foolish take no oil for their lamps: Do not prepare
  c. The wise take oil for their lamps: Do prepare
3. The bridegroom delays: All are drowsy & fall sleepDS3,4
4. A great summons is made when the bridegroom comes
  a. A surprise: Midnight
  b. A cry: "Come–meet Him"
	Then shall the kingdom of heaven be likened unto ten virgins, which took their lamps, and went forth to meet the bridegroom.
	2 And five of them were wise, and five *were* foolish.
	3 They that *were* foolish took their lamps, and took no oil with them:
	4 But the wise took oil in their vessels with their lamps.
	5 While the bridegroom tarried, they all slumbered and slept.
	6 And at midnight there was a cry made, Behold, the bridegroom cometh; go ye out to meet him.
	7 Then all those virgins arose, and trimmed their lamps.
	8 And the foolish said unto the wise, Give us of your oil; for our lamps are gone out.
	9 But the wise answered, saying, *Not so;* lest there be not enough for us and you: but go ye rather to them that sell, and buy for yourselves.
	10 And while they went to buy, the bridegroom came; and they that were ready went in with him to the marriage: and the door was shut.
	11 Afterward came also the other virgins, saying, Lord, Lord, open to us.
	12 But he answered and said, Verily I say unto you, I know you not.
	13 Watch therefore, for ye know neither the day nor the hour wherein the Son of man cometh.
		5. The bridegroom returns & the gathers the wise, the prepared
		6. The door is shut to the foolish, the unprepared
		  a. The foolish cry for entry
		
		  b. The foolish will be rejected
		
		7. The point: We must watch & expect the Lord's return at any moment

DIVISION XV

THE MESSIAH'S PROPHECY OF HIS RETURN AND THE END OF THE AGE: THE OLIVET DISCOURSE, 24:1–25:46

F. The Parable of the Ten Virgins: The Warning to Watch, 25:1-13

(25:1-13) **Introduction**: the believer must *watch* for the Lord's return, and he must be wise and not foolish in watching (see note—Mt.24:42). This is the point of Jesus' parable in this passage (v.13): the parable of the ten virgins, five foolish and five wise.

⇒ The *bridegroom*, of course, is Christ Himself.
⇒ The *virgins* are believers, all professors of religion. The *five wise virgins* are genuine believers; the *five foolish virgins* are false believers, those who have a false profession.
⇒ The *lamps* represent the lives, that is, the testimony, the witness, the heart, and the profession of the virgins (professing believers).
⇒ The *oil* is the provision of righteousness, the supply of the Holy Spirit that is to fill the lamps (lives) of the professing believers.

The parable is a dramatic picture of just what will happen to all professing believers, both the wise and the foolish, when the Lord returns.
1. The Kingdom of Heaven is compared to ten virgins (v.1).
2. The wise and foolish virgins (believers) attend the wedding (vv.1-4).
3. The bridegroom delays: All are drowsy and fall sleep (v.5).
4. A great summons is made when the bridegroom comes (vv.6-9).
5. The bridegroom returns and the gathers the wise, the prepared (v.10).
6. The door is shut to the foolish, the unprepared (vv.10-12).
7. The point: We must watch and expect the Lord's return at any moment (v.13).

DEEPER STUDY # 1
(25:1-13) **Wedding, Jewish**: this event, so unlike what occurs in most countries, was a common custom among Jews. The wedding festivities, which lasted for a whole week, were centered in the home where the couple was to live. The bridegroom was allowed to show up at any moment and enter the house; but when he chose to come, he always sent a man ahead crying out, "Behold, the bridegroom comes." This enabled everyone to prepare for his arrival. The bride had ten young ladies (virgins) who were always to be prepared to rush out and meet the bridegroom. In the event that he came at night, they were to have lamps ready so they could go out to light his path along the streets. This is the picture Christ was painting of His return.

> **DEEPER STUDY # 2**
> (25:1-13) **Jesus Christ, Bridegroom—Great Marriage Feast**: throughout Scripture the symbolism lying behind this parable involves three pictures.
>   1. Christ is pictured as the bridegroom.
>
>   "For as a young man marrieth a virgin, so shall thy sons marry thee: and as the bridegroom rejoiceth over the bride, so shall thy God rejoice over thee" (Is.62:5).
>   "And Jesus said unto them, Can the children of the bridechamber mourn, as long as the bridegroom is with them? but the days will come, when the bridegroom shall be taken from them, and then shall they fast" (Mt.9:15).
>   "He that hath the bride is the bridegroom: but the friend of the bridegroom, which standeth and heareth him, rejoiceth greatly because of the bridegroom's voice: this my joy therefore is fulfilled" (Jn.3:29).
>   "But in the days of the voice of the seventh angel, when he shall begin to sound, the mystery of God should be finished, as he hath declared to his servants the prophets....And I went unto the angel, and said unto him, Give me the little book. And he said unto me, Take it, and eat it up: and it shall make thy belly bitter, but it shall be in thy mouth sweet as honey" (Re.10:7, 9).
>   "And I John saw the holy city, new Jerusalem, coming down from God out of heaven, prepared as a bride adorned for her husband" (Re.21:2).
>
>   2. Believers and the church are pictured as the bride of Christ.
>
>   "For as a young man marrieth a virgin, so shall thy sons marry thee: and as the bridegroom rejoiceth over the bride, so shall thy God rejoice over thee" (Is.62:5).
>   "And I will betroth thee unto me for ever; yea, I will betroth thee unto me in righteousness, and in judgment, and in lovingkindness, and in mercies" (Ho.2:19).
>   "Wherefore, my brethren, ye also are become dead to the law by the body of Christ; that ye should be married to another, even to him who is raised from the dead, that we should bring forth fruit unto God" (Ro.7:4).
>   "For we are members of his body, of his flesh, and of his bones" (Ep.5:30).
>   "For I am jealous over you with godly jealousy: for I have espoused you to one husband, that I may present you as a chaste virgin to Christ" (2 Co.11:2).
>   "Let us be glad and rejoice, and give honour to him: for the marriage of the Lamb is come, and his wife hath made herself ready" (Re.19:7).
>   "And I John saw the holy city, new Jerusalem, coming down from God out of heaven, prepared as a bride adorned for her husband" (Re.21:2).
>   "And the Spirit and the bride say, Come. And let him that heareth say, Come. And let him that is athirst come. And whosoever will, let him take the water of life freely" (Re.22:17).
>
>   3. The return of the Lord is pictured as a great marriage feast.
>
>   "Let us be glad and rejoice, and give honour to him: for the marriage of the Lamb is come, and his wife hath made herself ready....And he saith unto me, Write, Blessed are they which are called unto the marriage supper of the Lamb. And he saith unto me, These are the true sayings of God" (Re.19:7, 9).
>   "And there came unto me one of the seven angels which had the seven vials full of the seven last plagues, and talked with me, saying, Come hither, I will show thee the bride, the Lamb's wife" (Re.21:9; see outline and notes—Mt.22:1-14).

1 (25:1) **Kingdom of Heaven—Jesus Christ, Return**: the word *then* refers back to the Lord's return discussed in Chapter 24. He was saying, "Then [when the Lord returns] the kingdom of heaven shall be like ten virgins [believers]." Five are foolish and five are wise, and there is going to be a separation of the wise from the foolish. Note *the kingdom of heaven* does not refer only to the perfect state of being in the future; it also refers to the present imperfect state of religion in the church (see DEEPER STUDY #3—Mt.19:23-24; see Mt.13:1-58).

When Christ returns, something will be clearly seen—the foolish within the kingdom, those who have a false profession within the church and religion, shall be separated from the wise, "Watch therefore" (v.13).

2 (25:1-4) **Parable**: there are wise and foolish virgins or believers who attend a wedding. Christ says three things about them.

a. The ten virgins (all professing believers) take their lamps (lives or testimonies) and go forth to meet the bridegroom. All believers take their lives and go forth, professing a testimony that they live for Christ and look to Christ. All professing believers (whether genuine or just religionists and church people) go forth to meet the Lord. However, as they *go forth* some (five) are wise and some (five) are foolish.

b. The *foolish* virgins (believers) take no oil *except what they already have in their lamps (lives)*. They have *no provision of righteousness* beyond themselves, beyond their own righteousness. They have no supply of the Holy Spirit.

MATTHEW 25:1-13

"He answered and said unto them, Well hath Esaias prophesied of you hypocrites, as it is written, This people honoureth me with their lips, but their heart is far from me" (Mk.7:6).

"For from within, out of the heart of men, proceed evil thoughts, adulteries, fornications, murders" (Mk.7:21).

"As it is written, There is none righteous, no, not one" (Ro.3:10).

c. The *wise* virgins (believers) take oil; they do not depend upon what they have in their lamps (lives). As they go forth through life to meet the bridegroom (Christ), they lay hold of additional oil, the provision of righteousness, the supply of God's Spirit.

"For he hath made him to be sin for us, who knew no sin; that we might be made the righteousness of God in him" (2 Co.5:21).

"For I am jealous over you with godly jealousy: for I have espoused you to one husband, that I may present you as a chaste virgin to Christ" (2 Co.11:2).

"These are they which were not defiled with women; for they are virgins. These are they which follow the Lamb whithersoever he goeth. These were redeemed from among men, being the firstfruits unto God and to the Lamb" (Re.14:4).

Thought 1. The main duty of the virgins (believers) is to meet and light the path for the bridegroom.

Thought 2. Note: there was no visible difference between the virgins. They all had lamps, and they were all called to participate in the marriage feast. The lack of provision by the foolish could not be seen until the Bridegroom actually came.

Thought 3. How foolish! To depend only on the oil in one's lamp or life. No one has enough oil, enough righteousness, to make himself perfect, that is, to make himself acceptable to God.

Thought 4. When Christ comes, He must find righteousness in a person if that person is to be allowed in God's presence. A man must be a "partaker of the Divine nature" by faith (2 Pe.1:4). (See DEEPER STUDY # 2, *Justification*—Ro.4:22; 5:1.)

[3] (25:5) **Jesus Christ, Return**: Christ said an interesting thing. There is a long delay before the bridegroom came and *all* the virgins slumbered and slept—not just the foolish virgins, but *all* the virgins slumbered and slept.

a. The idea is that this bridegroom waited much longer than was expected. The virgins had lit their lamps expecting him any moment, but he never came. As they waited and waited, the night wore on and on.

In the eyes of many, the Lord's return *has* lingered and lingered, well beyond what many have thought and taught (see 2 Pe.3:3-4, 9-10).

b. All the virgins slumbered and slept. Not just the foolish slept, but the wise slept as well (see DEEPER STUDY # 3,4—Mt.25:5). This is true throughout life. Even the wise grow weary and find it difficult to stay awake and alert, to stay at peak performance all the time. No believer, whoever he is, walks anywhere as close as he should. The world is too dark and the darkness too heavy for the believer to see enough light so that he can always be victorious over the pull of heavy eyelids.

⇒ His body is too weak to be *always laboring*.
⇒ His mind is too undeveloped to be *always concentrating*.
⇒ His energy is too limited to be *always driving*.
⇒ His spirit is too young to be *always sacrificing*.
⇒ His motives are too self-centered to be *always walking unselfishly*.

"Watch ye therefore: for ye know not when the master of the house cometh, at even, or at midnight, or at the cockcrowing, or in the morning: lest coming suddenly he find you sleeping. And what I say unto you I say unto all, Watch" (Mk.13:35-37).

"Say not ye, There are yet four months, and then cometh harvest? behold, I say unto you, Lift up your eyes, and look on the fields; for they are white already to harvest" (Jn.4:35).

"And that, knowing the time, that now it is high time to awake out of sleep: for now is our salvation nearer than when we believed" (Ro.13:11).

"Therefore, my beloved brethren, be ye stedfast, unmoveable, always abounding in the work of the Lord, forasmuch as ye know that your labour is not in vain in the Lord" (1 Co.15:58).

"And whatsoever ye do, do it heartily, as to the Lord, and not unto men" (Col.3:23).

"Therefore let us not sleep, as do others; but let us watch and be sober" (1 Th.5:6).

"Wherefore I put thee in remembrance that thou stir up the gift of God, which is in thee by the putting on of my hands" (2 Ti.1:6).

"Whatsoever thy hand findeth to do, do it with thy might; for there is no work, nor device, nor knowledge, nor wisdom, in the grave, whither thou goest" (Ec.9:10).

Thought 1. Christ has delayed His coming longer than many thought He would. Why? Only God really knows, but Scripture does give some indication.
(1) God's purposes have to be completely fulfilled.
(2) "The time of the Gentiles" has to be completely fulfilled.

(3) God's love must be fully demonstrated, apparently to a certain number of people. A certain number of people apparently have to be saved before Christ returns.
(4) The gospel must first be preached "in *all* the world for a witness to *all* nations" (Mt.24:14).
(5) The harvest must *be ripened* and then *fully gathered*.
(6) The sufferings of Christ must be completely filled up (see note—Col.1:24).
(7) God is longsuffering, not willing that any should perish (2 Pe.3:9).

Thought 2. A pointed question needs to be answered. Remember the fervent zeal we had when we were first saved? Why does it die out as time passes by?
⇒ We have not lost all love for Christ, but we have left our first love (Re.2:4).
⇒ We have not stopped all worship of God, but we have lost our first duty to worship.
⇒ We have not ceased all witness for Christ, but we have cooled our first passion.
⇒ We have not turned from all righteousness, but we have been diverted from our first attention.

Thought 3. Note that the virgins allowed themselves to slumber, then the slumber led to sleep. We must guard against slumbering, against cooling off. A little slumber and a little cooling of fervor for just a little while may not seem too serious; but the first step, as small as it may seem, leads to heavy eyelids.

DEEPER STUDY # 3
(25:5) **Slumbered** (enustazan): to nod; to nap.

DEEPER STUDY # 4
(25:5) **Slept - Sleep** (katheudo): to be in a state of rest where the powers of the body are restored and consciousness is temporarily suspended. This is the natural sleep of a person at night.

---

4 (25:6-9) **Jesus Christ, Return**: there is to be a great summons. Christ said several things.

a. The summons will be a great surprise, totally unexpected. It will come at a surprising hour: at midnight, the most surprising hour, the hour when sleep is most desired and unlikely to be disturbed. It is an hour when all are asleep. Christ is coming as a thief in the night.

b. The summons will be a cry, a shout: "Go ye out to meet Him: (see Mt.24:31; 1 Th.4:16). The word *cometh* is not in the oldest and best Greek manuscripts. The cry is simply, "Behold, the bridegroom!" which makes the shout much more forceful. Note two things.
 1) What the shout is: "Go out to meet Him."
 2) What the shout does: it awakens; it shocks; it disturbs. It is totally unexpected. The shout awakens the sleeping and demands, "Go out to meet Him."

c. All arise and prepare their lamps. All the virgins (professing believers) arise, for the shout pierces the air and shocks the virgins, demanding immediate arousal. *Not one remains asleep*. Each leaps up. The voice demands obedience, for the bridegroom comes. And all begin immediately to prepare their lamps (see DEEPER STUDY # 5—Mt. 25:7).

d. All the foolish discover a shocking fact: their lamps are burned out. The bridegroom had not come while their lamps were burning, and now their lamps had used up all the oil they had. They became frantic, for they saw that they were not prepared. They did not have the oil (righteousness) necessary to burn their lamps (lives) for the bridegroom's coming.

> "And take heed to yourselves, lest at any time your hearts be overcharged with surfeiting, and drunkenness, and cares of this life, and so that day come upon you unawares. For as a snare shall it come on all them that dwell on the face of the whole earth" (Lu.21:34-35).
>
> "For they being ignorant of God's righteousness, and going about to establish their own righteousness, have not submitted themselves unto the righteousness of God" (Ro.10:3).
>
> "Having the understanding darkened, being alienated from the life of God through the ignorance that is in them, because of the blindness of their heart" (Ep.4:18).
>
> "But they know not the thoughts of the LORD, neither understand they his counsel: for he shall gather them as the sheaves into the floor" (Mi.4:12).

e. All the wise scarcely have enough for themselves. Note two things.
⇒ They had prepared. They had the oil (righteousness) necessary to burn the lamps (lives) for the bridegroom's coming
⇒ They had only enough, and barely enough, for their own lamps. They were not able to give any of their own oil to those who had none.

> "Let your loins be girded about, and your lights burning; and ye yourselves like unto men that wait for their lord, when he will return from the wedding; that when he cometh and knocketh, they may open unto him immediately" (Lu.12:35-36).
>
> "Awake to righteousness, and sin not; for some have not the knowledge of God: I speak this to your shame" (1 Co.15:34).
>
> "Wherefore he saith, Awake thou that sleepest, and arise from the dead, and Christ shall give thee light" (Ep.5:14).
>
> "Ye are all the children of light, and the children of the day: we are not of the night, nor of darkness. Therefore let us not sleep, as do others; but let us watch and be sober" (1 Th.5:5-6).

MATTHEW 25:1-13

"Behold, I come as a thief. Blessed is he that watcheth, and keepeth his garments, lest he walk naked, and they see his shame" (Re.16:15).

"Let us be glad and rejoice, and give honour to him: for the marriage of the Lamb is come, and his wife hath made herself ready" (Re.19:7).

Thought 1. Death is usually a surprise, yet it comes to every one of us. The same fact is true with the Lord's return. His return is as certain as death, and it will be as surprising as most deaths are.

Thought 2. When the summons comes, all will arise. Not a person—whether in the grave, in the sea, or scattered all over the world—shall remain. Shockingly, surprisingly, all will arise when the shout comes. Both the dead and the living will arise to meet the Lord in the air (1 Th.4:14f).

Thought 3. When Christ first came to earth, no announcement to the world was made. Only a few knew when He came as a babe in Bethlehem. But when He returns, the world—all men—will know. A universal shout, the voice of the archangel, will summon all to arise and to prepare for the coming of the Bridegroom.

Thought 4. *The righteousness of Christ* is the only oil that lights the lamp of life. *The righteousness of Christ* is the only oil that is acceptable to God. A person who depends only upon the oil in his lamp or life, who does not secure additional oil, is foolish—as foolish as the foolish virgins—for the bridegroom shall come. It will be at midnight, yes, but midnight is coming. In fact, our watches tell us it is almost midnight now.

Thought 5. *Wise* is the correct word to call the man who secures additional oil (righteousness), for he does prepare for the inevitable.

Thought 6. Some things cannot be borrowed. Righteousness is one of those things (2 Co.5:21; Ep.4:24).

DEEPER STUDY # 5
(25:7) **Lamps**: trimming a lamp simply means that the burned top of the wick, the charred top, had to be trimmed or cleaned. Of course, the lamp had to be refilled with oil from the additional supply.

---

[5] (25:10) **Jesus Christ, Return**: the Lord will return and gather the wise. Christ shared two major points.

a. *The bridegroom came*: three simple but powerful words. So Christ shall come. The day will come when it will be said, "The bridegroom, Christ Himself, came."

"When the Son of man shall come in his glory, and all the holy angels with him, then shall he sit upon the throne of his glory" (Mt.25:31).

"For the Lord himself shall descend from heaven with a shout, with the voice of the archangel, and with the trump of God: and the dead in Christ shall rise first" (1 Th.4:16).

b. Only they who were *ready* went in with the bridegroom to the marriage. This was their purpose, the reason they were ready. They had looked for His coming; therefore, they were ready. When the summons came, they were able to join in the processional of the Bridegroom and to enter the great marriage feast. The joy of the marriage was theirs (Jn.17:24. See DEEPER STUDY # 2 *Great Marriage Feast*—Mt.25:1-13.)

"And he shall send his angels with a great sound of a trumpet, and they shall gather together his elect from the four winds, from one end of heaven to the other" (Mt.24:31).

Thought 1. "The fulness of time" is to come again: the time for the great marriage feast of the Lamb and His church.

Thought 2. The *ready* shall enter the marriage feast. Only those who are *ready* will be allowed to enter. It is God who makes us ready (2 Co.5:5).

[6] (25:10-12) **Jesus Christ, Return**: the door is to be shut to the foolish.

a. The door was shut. This was a custom in the East. When all the guests had arrived, the doors were closed. They were closed in order to *secure* the marriage party and to *exclude* intruders. Only the guests belonged; others were to be kept out. When Christ comes, the door to heaven will be closed. Only the *ready*, the genuine guests will be *secured* in the joys of the great marriage feast. The unprepared will find the door shut *in order to exclude them*.

b. The foolish cry for entrance. Very simply, the foolish were *too late*. They were too late to join in the procession and too late to enter the door. Note the Lord's emphasis upon their desperation: they cry out, "*Lord, Lord.*" They now know something they had not paid much attention to before: *preparation was essential*. The door has now been closed, and they are excluded. They are shut out from the Bridegroom's great wedding feast. It is too late for them.

c. The foolish will be rejected. The reason is simple: the Bridegroom does not know them. They were not ready when He arrived nor were they in the processional; therefore, He does not recognize them. He has to say, "I know you not." He can say nothing else, for...

- they had not *prepared* themselves: they were not ready when He came
- they had not *participated* in His journey to the marriage feast: He did not recognize them; He did not know them

Christ taught time and again that the day is coming when the door will be shut (see Jn.10:9).

"Not every one that saith unto me, Lord, Lord, shall enter into the kingdom of heaven; but he that doeth the will of my Father which is in heaven. Many will say to me in that day, Lord, Lord, have we not prophesied in thy name? and in they name have cast out devils? and in thy name done many wonderful works? And then will I profess unto them, I never knew you: depart from me, ye that work iniquity" (Mt.7:21-23).

"When once the master of the house is risen up, and hath shut to the door, and ye begin to stand without, and to knock at the door, saying, Lord, Lord, open unto us; and he shall answer and say unto you, I know you not whence ye are: then shall ye begin to say, We have eaten and drunk in thy presence, and thou hast taught in our streets. But he shall say, I tell you, I know you not whence ye are; depart from me, all ye workers of iniquity" (Lu.13:25-27).

Note the words, "I know you not." The importance of Christ's *knowing us* is also stressed time and again in Scripture. Of course, the way Christ gets to know us is by our participating in His journey, simply walking with Him day by day.

"I never knew you: depart from me" (Mt.7:23).
"I am the good Shepherd, and know my sheep" (Jn.10:14).
"But now, after that ye have known God, or rather are known of God" (Ga.4:9).
"I know Him" (Ge.18:19. God said this of Abraham.)
"I know thee by name" (Ex.33:12. God said this of Moses.)
"I have redeemed thee, I have called thee by thy name: thou art mine" (Is.43:1).

Thought 1. The idea of the shut door is twofold.
(1) To *secure* the wise (believer). The wise person is brought and welcomed into the great marriage feast of the Lord, and he participates in all the joy of the festive occasion. Whatever goes on within the great banqueting hall is his to enjoy. Other Scriptures point out that love, joy, and peace will be perfected and will be the unbroken experience of the believer. He will never again have to go out into an unjoyful, unhappy, corruptible, or painful world.

"Him that overcometh will I make a pillar...of my God, and he shall go no more out" (Re.3:12).

(2) To *exclude* the foolish (who profess only). There has been plenty of time and plenty of signs and warnings to prepare, but the foolish have refused to prepare for the Lord's return (see outline—Ro.1:18-23; 2:11-15).

Thought 2. The foolish believer is a person who fails at two points.
(1) Preparation: he does not provide any oil (righteousness) for his lamp *except* what oil is already there. He sees no need for additional oil or righteousness. Therefore, he does not prepare.
(2) Participation: he is unable to join the Bridegroom on His journey to the great marriage feast. He has no additional oil (righteousness), so his lamp (life) is no good to the bridegroom. His lamp (life) is not able to provide light for the bridegroom.

7 (25:13) **Watch—Jesus Christ, Return**: the point is that we must *watch* and expect the Lord's return at any moment.

a. The exhortation is strong: "Watch therefore." The believer must prepare and participate in the journey to the great marriage feast. He must walk with the Lord, the bridegroom. (See note, *Watch*—Mt.24:42.)

b. The reason for watching is strong: "Ye know neither the day nor the hour when the Son of man cometh." Unbroken preparation is essential, for He can come at any moment.

"Watch therefore, for ye know neither the day nor the hour wherein the Son of man cometh" (Mt.25:13).
"Blessed are those servants, whom the lord when he cometh shall find watching: verily I say unto you, that he shall gird himself, and make them to sit down to meat, and will come forth and serve them" (Lu.12:37).
"Ye are all the children of light, and the children of the day: we are not of the night, nor of darkness. Therefore let us not sleep, as do others; but let us watch and be sober" (1 Th.5:5-6).
"Behold, I come quickly; hold that fast which thou hast, that no man take thy crown" (Re.3:11).
"Behold, I come as a thief. Blessed is he that watcheth, and keepeth his garments, lest he walk naked, and they see his shame" (Re.16:15).

MATTHEW 25:14-30

1. The Lord went on a journey
2. The Lord entrusted His property to His servants^{DS2}
  a. Called His servants
  b. Gave each servant a different portion
  c. Gave each servant according to his ability
 	
3. The servants treated the Lord's goods differently
  a. Two were responsible: Immediately worked
    1) Were faithful & diligent
    2) Were successful
 	
  b. One was irresponsible: Did not try
 	
4. The day of settling accounts came much later
  a. The Lord returned
  b. The Lord judged them
5. The reward for work well done: More work to do
  a. The first servant
    1) Acknowledged God's gifts & grace
    2) Labored 100 percent for the Lord
    3) Was commended & given a great reward: Rulership & joy
 	
  b. The second servant
    1) Acknowledged God's
	G. The Parable of the Talents: The Believer's Duty to Work,^{DS1} 25:14-30
	
	14 For *the kingdom of heaven is* as a man travelling into a far country, *who* called his own servants, and delivered unto them his goods.
	15 And unto one he gave five talents, to another two, and to another one; to every man according to his several ability; and straightway took his journey.
	16 Then he that had received the five talents went and traded with the same, and made *them* other five talents.
	17 And likewise he that *had received* two, he also gained other two.
	18 But he that had received one went and digged in the earth, and hid his lord's money.
	19 After a long time the lord of those servants cometh, and reckoneth with them.
	20 And so he that had received five talents came and brought other five talents, saying, Lord, thou deliveredst unto me five talents: behold, I have gained beside them five talents more.
	21 His lord said unto him, Well done, *thou* good and faithful servant: thou hast been faithful over a few things, I will make thee ruler over many things: enter thou into the joy of thy lord.
	22 He also that had received two talents came and said,
		Lord, thou deliveredst unto me two talents: behold, I have gained two other talents beside them.
		23 His lord said unto him, Well done, good and faithful servant; thou hast been faithful over a few things, I will make thee ruler over many things: enter thou into the joy of thy lord.
		24 Then he which had received the one talent came and said, Lord, I knew thee that thou art an hard man, reaping where thou hast not sown, and gathering where thou hast not strawed:
		25 And I was afraid, and went and hid thy talent in the earth: lo, *there* thou hast *that is* thine.
		26 His lord answered and said unto him, *Thou* wicked and slothful servant, thou knewest that I reap where I sowed not, and gather where I have not strawed:
		27 Thou oughtest therefore to have put my money to the exchangers, and *then* at my coming I should have received mine own with usury.
		28 Take therefore the talent from him, and give *it* unto him which hath ten talents.
		29 For unto every one that hath shall be given, and he shall have abundance: but from him that hath not shall be taken away even that which he hath.
		30 And cast ye the unprofitable servant into outer darkness: there shall be weeping and gnashing of teeth.
			gifts & grace
			    2) Labored 100 percent for the Lord
			
			    3) Was commended & given a great reward: Rulership & joy
			
			6. The punishment for work not done: Stripping & separation
			  a. The servant's reasons for not working
			    1) He misunderstood God: Thought God was too demanding
			    2) He feared loss while on earth
			
			  b. God's reasons for condemning the servant
			    1) He was wicked & lazy
			    2) He was inconsistent
			
			    3) He failed to use his gift
			
			  c. The judgment
			    1) He was stripped of what he had^{DS3}
			
			    2) He was thrown into outer darkness^{DS4}

DIVISION XV

THE MESSIAH'S PROPHECY OF HIS RETURN AND THE END OF THE AGE: THE OLIVET DISCOURSE, 24:1–25:46

G. The Parable of the Talents: The Believer's Duty to Work, 25:14-30

(25:14-30) **Introduction**: Jesus said that the point of this parable was twofold.
    First, while Jesus is away, the believer is to do something: work—work faithfully and diligently.
    Second, while Jesus is away, the believer is to know something: his work will be greatly rewarded or severely judged.

    Again, Christ was dealing with His return. He went "into a far country" (v.14), and "after a long time, the Lord" returned (v.19). Christ was teaching a much needed lesson: we must be faithful and diligent, for if we are not, when He returns there will be severe judgment. (See outline and notes—Ep.4:7-16; 1 Co.12:1-14:40.)
    1. The Lord went on a journey (v.14).
    2. The Lord entrusted His property to His servants (vv.14-15).
    3. The servants treated the Lord's goods differently (vv.16-18).
    4. The day of settling accounts came much later (v.19).
    5. The reward for work well done: More work to do (vv.20-23).
    6. The punishment for work not done: Stripping and separation (vv.24-30).

> **DEEPER STUDY # 1**
> (25:14-30) **Talents—Gifts**: the talent spoken of is a weight not a coin. The value of a talent varied as to whether it was gold, silver, or copper. Christ is probably using money to describe what He is talking about because money is one of the most understood commodities anywhere on earth.
> Christ was teaching that His followers are to be faithful and diligent in whatever He gives them, whether a gift, ability, responsibility, or blessing.

1 (25:14) **Jesus Christ, Ascension—Exaltation**: Christ foretold that He was like a man who was travelling to a far country, and what He foretold happened. He travelled away from the earth and ascended into heaven for a specific purpose: to sit at the right hand of God. He is to sit there until His servants complete the work He has given them to do. When He returns, it will be the time for reward and for judgment.

> "In my Father's house are many mansions: if it were not so, I would have told you. I go to prepare a place for you. And if I go and prepare a place for you, I will come again, and receive you unto myself; that where I am, there ye may be also" (Jn.14:2-3).
>
> "Therefore being by the right hand of God exalted....The LORD said unto my Lord, Sit thou on my right hand, until I make thy foes thy footstool" (Ac.2:33-35).
>
> "Him hath God exalted with his right hand to be a Prince and a Savior, for to give repentance to Israel, and forgiveness of sins" (Ac.5:31).
>
> "Wherefore God also hath highly exalted him, and given him a name which is above every name: that at the name of Jesus every knee should bow, of things in heaven, and things in earth, and things under the earth; and that every tongue should confess that Jesus Christ is Lord, to the glory of God the Father" (Ph.2:9-11).

2 (25:14-15) **Gifts**: the Lord has entrusted His *goods* (gifts, abilities, responsibilities) to His servants. There is a verse that says it all: "Wherefore He saith, When He ascended up on high, He led captivity captive [a host of vanquished foes], and gave gifts unto men" (Ep.4:8).

In this particular point Christ says three things.

a. The Lord called His *own* servants. The word for *servant* is bond-slave. He called those who were supposedly His own (a precious thought) and who were *supposedly* faithful and responsible to His service. He had bought them. They were to be His own and to serve Him (see note—Ro.1:1). Note why He called them: to put His *goods* (gifts) into their hands while He was away. His property had to be looked after and increased and bettered while He was away. The property of the Lord means the world and the souls of men. The servants are given the very same mission and work that Christ had: to minister to the souls of men and to the desperate of the world.

b. The Lord gave each servant a different portion of His goods to look after. The point is that each person was given a special talent (gift or responsibility). No one was left out (Ep.4:7). Each servant was therefore expected to work and serve.

c. The Lord gave to each servant according to his ability. Four factors are important here.

1) No two servants have the same ability: environment, opportunity, genes, heritage, training, mind, heart, discipline, initiative. Each is different.

> "And unto one he gave five talents, to another two, and to another one; to every man according to his several ability; and straightway took his journey" (Mt.25:15).
>
> "For who maketh thee to differ from another? and what hast thou that thou didst not receive? now if thou didst receive it, why dost thou glory, as if thou hadst not received it?" (1 Co.4:7).

2) God endows His *goods* (gifts) as He wills, knowing each servant perfectly.

> "But all these worketh that one and the selfsame Spirit, dividing to every man severally [exactly] as he will" (1 Co.12:11).

3) Each servant receives all the gifts he needs and can use.

> "For as we have many members in one body, and all members have not the same office: so we, being many, are one body in Christ, and every one members one of another. Having then gifts differing according to the grace that is given to us, whether prophecy, let us prophesy according to the proportion of faith; or ministry, let us wait on our ministering: or he that teacheth, on teaching; or he that exhorteth, on exhortation: he that giveth, let him do it with simplicity; he that ruleth, with diligence; he that showeth mercy, with cheerfulness (Ro.12:4-8).
>
> "Now there are diversities of gifts, but the same Spirit. And there are differences of administrations, but the same Lord. And there are diversities of operations, but it is the same God which worketh all in all. But the manifestation of the Spirit is given to every man to profit withal" (1 Co.12:4-7).

MATTHEW 25:14-30

4) Each servant has equal opportunity to be faithful in using what God has given him. We are to be judged on our faithfulness, not on the number of gifts or the size of the work we are assigned (see v.21 and v.23).

"For the Son of man shall come in the glory of his Father with his angels; and then he shall reward every man according to his works" (Mt.16:27).

"And if ye call on the Father, who without respect of persons judgeth according to every man's work, pass the time of your sojourning here in fear" (1 Pe.1:17).

Thought 1. There are three precious and wonderful facts here.

(1) We are "His own." We are God's, His possession (Ep.1:14). Note: God also says, "I am their possession."

"And it shall be unto them for an inheritance: I am their inheritance: and ye shall give them no possession in Israel: I am their possession" (Eze.44:28).

"I have redeemed thee. I have called thee by thy name: thou art mine" (Is.43:1).

(2) We are taken care of by Christ. Each one is given "His goods," very special gifts, abilities, and responsibilities to look after for God. God gives us exactly what we need to fulfill our lives and to give us purpose, meaning, and significance in life—to conform us to the very image of Christ Himself.

"But seek ye first the kingdom of God, and his righteousness; and all these things shall be added unto you" (Mt.6:33).

"If ye then, being evil, know how to give good gifts unto your children: how much more shall your heavenly Father give the Holy Spirit to them that ask him?" (Lu.11:13).

"The thief cometh not, but for to steal, and to kill, and to destroy: I am come that they might have life, and that they might have it more abundantly" (Jn.10:10).

"And I give unto them eternal life; and they shall never perish, neither shall any man pluck them out of my hand" (Jn.10:28).

"And I will give them a heart to know me, that I am the LORD: and they shall be my people, and I will be their God: for they shall return unto me with their whole heart" (Je.24:7).

(3) The church is taken care of by Christ. During His absence, He has provided all that is necessary to care for and to advance the church.

"And he gave some, apostles; and some, prophets; and some, evangelists; and some, pastors and teachers; for the perfecting of the saints, for the work of the ministry, for the edifying of the body of Christ: till we all come in the unity of the faith, and of the knowledge of the Son of God, unto a perfect man, unto the measure of the stature of the fulness of Christ" (Ep.4:11-13).

Thought 2. Note: every believer has at least one gift.

DEEPER STUDY # 2

(25:14-15) **Gifts**: the Lord's *goods* are the gifts, talents, and responsibilities He gives to men. The Lord endows His gifts as He pleases (1 Co.12:11). Each servant receives all the gifts he needs and can use (Ro.12:4-9; 1 Co.12:4-30). Note the gifts are the Lord's; they are merely entrusted to His servants. Different men have different capacities for different ministries (v.15).

---

3 (25:16-18) **Gifts—Faithfulness—Unfaithfulness**: the servants treated the Lord's *goods* differently.

a. Two servants were responsible, very responsible. They went to work *immediately*. They *lost no time* and began to serve *quickly*.
  1) They were faithful and diligent. They used their abilities and energy immediately. They exerted themselves, expended their energy and effort to use what the Lord had given them.
     Note: the less gifted servant worked and labored as much as the more gifted servant. He did not have as many gifts, but he exerted the same initiative, energy, and effort (see Lu.12:48).
     Again, the picture is that of a business transaction, but the point is that the two servants used what the Lord had given them; and they used their gifts faithfully and diligently.
  2) They were successful. Each one gained and doubled what the Lord had given him. Each servant's gifts bore fruit *in proportion* to his gifts. The one given more (five talents) bore more (ten talents). The one given less (two talents) bore less (four talents). But both were *equally successful*, doubling what the Lord had given them.

"Not slothful in business; fervent in spirit; serving the Lord" (Ro.12:11).

"Moreover it is required in stewards, that a man be found faithful" (1 Co.4:2).

"Therefore, my beloved brethren, be ye stedfast, unmoveable, always abounding in the work of the Lord, forasmuch as ye know that your labour is not in vain in the Lord" (1 Co.15:58).

"As every man hath received the gift, even so minister the same one to another, as good stewards of the manifold grace of God" (1 Pe.4:10).

MATTHEW 25:14-30

"Wherefore, beloved, seeing that ye look for such things, be diligent that ye may be found of him in peace, without spot, and blameless" (2 Pe.3:14).

b. One servant was irresponsible. He simply did not use the Lord's gift. But note: he was somewhat active. He spent time and energy to go out and bury the Lord's gift—he hid it. His days, his time, and his energy were to be the Lord's; but he took his life and days into his own hands. What was he doing? We are not told, but his efforts were not spent in the Lord's cause. He served only himself. He was worldly, lusting after the flesh and possessions of this world. He was out to serve himself instead of God

"And every one that heareth these sayings of mine, and doeth them not, shall be likened unto a foolish man, which built his house upon the sand: and the rain descended, and the floods came, and the winds blew, and beat upon that house; and it fell: and great was the fall of it" (Mt.7:26-27).

"And that which fell among thorns are they, which, when they have heard, go forth, and are choked with cares and riches and pleasures of this life, and bring no fruit to perfection" (Lu.8:14).

"He spake also this parable; A certain man had a fig tree planted in his vineyard; and he came and sought fruit thereon, and found none" (Lu.13:6).

"And take heed to yourselves, lest at any time your hearts be overcharged with surfeiting, and drunkenness, and cares of this life, and so that day come upon you unawares. For as a snare shall it come on all them that dwell on the face of the whole earth" (Lu.21:34-35).

"Therefore to him that knoweth to do good, and doeth it not, to him it is sin" (Js.4:17).

"Ye have lived in pleasure on the earth, and been wanton; ye have nourished your hearts, as in a day of slaughter" (Js.5:5).

"And shall receive the reward of unrighteousness, as they that count it pleasure to riot in the day time. Spots they are and blemishes, sporting themselves with their own deceivings while they feast with you" (2 Pe.2:13).

"Ye have plowed wickedness, ye have reaped iniquity; ye have eaten the fruit of lies: because thou didst trust in thy way, in the multitude of thy mighty men" (Ho.10:13).

Thought 1. Note four lessons.
(1) Immediate work—immediate action—immediate use of God's gifts are expected. Each hesitation—each hour—each day where maximum energy and effort are not given is a lost opportunity. Each lost opportunity equals unfaithfulness and slothfulness. What a strong example the two faithful servants were!
(2) The efforts of the faithful and diligent will bear interest (fruit). The servant who uses his gifts faithfully and diligently will witness a manifold increase in the *goods* of his Lord.
(3) A striking point: the person with one talent is as responsible to use his gift as the person with many talents.
(4) Too often, a person who is gifted with little feels his service matters little, that it is not really worth the time and effort it takes. This attitude forgets something: the gift is not ours; the gift is the Lord's. It is to be used, and full energy and effort are to be exerted in its use. The use of a single gift is to occupy what days and hours we have on earth. We are to be faithful, even in the single gifts—always faithful and always using what we have for the Lord, even if it is a single gift.

4 (25:19) **Jesus Christ, Return**: the day of reckoning came, but it was only "after a long time." By the time Christ returns, it will have been a long time in the eyes of men. However, it will have been only a short time to Christ: "Lo, I come quickly" (Re.3:11; see 2 Pe.3:3-4, 8-11).

Note a second fact: Christ says the Lord did return, and He returned to reckon with His servants, not with the world. Christ is talking about His servants in this passage—professing believers and church members, some genuine believers and some only professing believers, who are making a false profession (v.30).

"Therefore is the kingdom of heaven likened unto a certain king, which would take account of his servants" (Mt.18:23).

"And when the time of the fruit drew near, he sent his servants to the husbandmen, that they might receive the fruits of it" (Mt.21:34).

"After a long time the lord of those servants cometh, and reckoneth with them" (Mt.25:19).

"And it came to pass, that when he was returned, having received the kingdom, then he commanded these servants to be called unto him, to whom he had given the money, that he might know how much every man had gained by trading" (Lu.19:15).

"So then every one of us shall give account of himself to God" (Ro.14:12).

"And as it is appointed unto men once to die, but after this the judgment" (He.9:27).

"Wherein they think it strange that ye run not with them to the same excess of riot, speaking evil of you" (1 Pe.4:4).

Thought 1. We must always remember this: the Lord is not slack concerning His promise to return. He is *ready* to judge the living and the dead (1 Pe.4:5). He is ready now, but He is *longsuffering*, wanting more and more to come to repentance (2 Pe.3:9).

5 (25:20-23) **Reward**: the reward for work well done will be more work to do. Note that the experience was the same for the first and second servants.

a. They both acknowledged God's gifts and graces: "Lord, thou delivered unto me." All that the servant had was given to him by Christ. There is *appreciation, thankfulness, privilege,* and a sense of responsibility expressed. The two servants had counted it a privilege to serve their Lord. He had given them purpose and meaning in life and the greatest privilege in all the world: the privilege of serving the Lord Himself. They were appreciative and thankful.

b. Therefore, they were bold in approaching the Lord: "Behold, I have gained." Their boldness was not in a boastful spirit, but in a spirit that knew it had been faithful in what the Lord had said to do.

"Herein is our love made perfect, that we may have boldness in the day of judgment" (1 Jn.4:17).

c. The Lord commended the two servants and gave them great rewards: rulership and joy, the joy of the Lord. The Lord commended them for being *good* men (kind, gracious, moral, disciplined) and faithful in the trust (gifts) He had given them. They had worked and worked hard. They had been the kind of men He had wanted them to be and they had done the work He had wanted them to do. They were both *good and faithful* servants. The point is this: the first two servants worked at full capacity, exerting 100 percent energy and effort. Both increased the Lord's goods 100 percent. Note the reward: both received responsibility over many things in the Kingdom of Heaven.

The Lord rewarded both servants greatly. He gave them a twofold reward.

First, they were given rulership: the responsibility and rule over many things in the Kingdom of Heaven *after the Lord returned* (see notes and DEEPER STUDY # 1—Mt.19:28; 19:29; Lu.19:15-23).

Second, they were given entrance into the joy of the Lord. The servants were to be ushered into the everlasting kingdom of our Lord and Savior Jesus Christ, where there is nothing but joy. The joy is the joy "of the Lord" Himself—a joy which He Himself possesses within His very being. Joy is the state of the Lord's being because He is perfect; His perfection gives rise to a *fulness of joy*. Believers also experience this joy because of heaven, for heaven is perfect; and where perfection is, there are no tears, pain, or sorrow. There is only joy.

"His lord said unto him, Well done, good and faithful servant; thou hast been faithful over a few things, I will make thee ruler over many things: enter thou into the joy of thy lord" (Mt.25:23).

"Then shall the King say unto them on his right hand, Come, ye blessed of my Father, inherit the kingdom prepared for you from the foundation of the world" (Mt.25:34).

"But love ye your enemies, and do good, and lend, hoping for nothing again; and your reward shall be great, and ye shall be the children of the Highest: for he is kind unto the unthankful and to the evil" (Lu.6:35).

"Ye are they which have continued with me in my temptations. And I appoint unto you a kingdom, as my Father hath appointed unto me" (Lu.22:28-29).

"For if by one man's offence death reigned by one; much more they which receive abundance of grace and of the gift of righteousness shall reign in life by one, Jesus Christ" (Ro.5:17).

"Do ye not know that the saints shall judge [reign over, hold authority over] the world? and if the world shall be judged by you, are ye unworthy to judge the smallest matters? Know ye not that we shall judge angels? how much more things that pertain to this life?" (1 Co.6:2-3).

"If we suffer, we shall also reign with him: if we deny him, he also will deny us" (2 Ti.2:12).

"And from Jesus Christ, who is the faithful witness, and the first begotten of the dead, and the prince of the kings of the earth. Unto him that loved us, and washed us from our sins in his own blood, and hath made us kings and priests unto God and his Father; to him be glory and dominion for ever and ever" (Re.1:5-6).

"And he that overcometh, and keepeth my works unto the end, to him will I give power over the nations" (Re.2:26).

"To him that overcometh will I grant to sit with me in my throne, even as I also overcame, and am set down with my Father in his throne" (Re.3:21).

"And there shall be no night there; and they need no candle, neither light of the sun; for the Lord God giveth them light: and they shall reign for ever and ever" (Re.22:5).

Thought 1. Two things are highly commendable among God's servants:
(1) To acknowledge that their gifts are of God.
(2) To be so faithful and diligent that they can be bold in the day of judgment.

Thought 2. Just how *wise* we are is shown by how much work we do for God and how well we use our gifts.

"Who is a wise man and endued with knowledge among you? let him show out of a good conversation [behavior] his works with meekness of wisdom" (Js.3:13).

Our *works* will follow us.

"And I heard a voice from heaven saying unto me, Write, Blessed are the dead which die in the Lord from henceforth: Yea, saith the Spirit, that they may rest from their labors; and their works do follow them" (Re.14:13).

Thought 3. A precious, precious truth: God will be accepting both our person ("thou *good*...servant") and our labor ("thou...*faithful* servant"). Amen!

MATTHEW 25:14-30

6 (25:24-30) **Minister—Servant**: the punishment for work not done will be stripping and separation. Christ covers three points in discussing this unprofitable servant. Remember: Christ is speaking of a person who professes and is in the church (see note, *Kingdom of Heaven*—Mt.25:1).
  a. Note the servant's reasons for not using the gifts the Lord had entrusted into his care.
   1) He misunderstood God. The unprofitable servant said that the Lord was too demanding, exacting, stern, and unsympathetic. He was a Lord who demanded too much and was too strict. He did not allow man the right to enjoy this world and its pleasures enough. The servant felt that if he spent his time in the service of the Lord, he would miss out on life. The demands of the Lord upon his time and affairs were just too burdensome. The servant was too involved in the world and its affairs to give that much time and effort to labor for the Lord and to concentrate upon His demands.
   2) He added that he feared—feared using and putting his talent to work for the Lord. Therefore, he hid the Lord's talent and did not use it to increase the Lord's kingdom.
  b. Note God's reasons for condemning the servant; note the vast difference between what the Lord said and what the servant had to say.
   1) The unprofitable servant was wicked and slothful. He was *wicked* because he went about doing exactly what he wished to do, spending his time and energy on his own thing. He transgressed God's command and will. He was *slothful* because he did nothing with God's gift. He buried and hid it.
   2) The unprofitable servant was inconsistent, or perhaps a better description would be deceptive, double-minded, and self-contradictory. If he really believed the Lord was harsh and stern, he would have labored and worked his fingers to the bone. The servant was either lying or terribly deceived and self-contradictory—all in an attempt to justify his behavior.
   3) The unprofitable servant failed to use his gift. Christ was direct: the servant should have used the gift and served (v.27). He was without excuse.
  c. Note the judgment of the unprofitable servant (vv.28-30). Christ pronounced a twofold judgment upon him.
   1) The unprofitable servant was stripped of what he had. All that he had was taken from him. The servant's responsibility—*the glorious privilege of* working for and serving the Lord—was not to be his any more. *He was to have nothing else to do with the Lord. His responsibility* was taken from him and given to the one who proven most faithful.
   2) The unprofitable servant was cast into outer darkness. He was cast out of the Lord's presence and banished forever. And there was no joy there, nothing but outer darkness and weeping and gnashing of teeth (see notes—Mt.8:12 and DEEPER STUDY # 4—25:30 for discussion and verses).

Thought 1. There are two gross errors in the thinking of the world.
(1) Many persons think God is hard, stern, demanding, and unsympathetic. They are unwilling to follow such a hard, narrow way. So they bury, hide their God-given gifts and travel along the easy, broad way.
(2) Others think that what they have is their own, and they can use it to live as they please. They think that what they do is no one's affair except their own, not even God's.

Thought 2. Few persons feel any responsibility to God for what they have, and even fewer feel the necessity to serve God faithfully and diligently.

Thought 3. Slothfulness, doing nothing for God, is one of the great sins of professing Christians (Ro.12:11; 2 Th.3:11; Heb.6:12; Pr.18:9; see 1 Co.15:58).

Thought 4. Sins of omission are as serious as sins of commission. Being idle and slothful, being complacent and doing nothing, being lethargic and self-satisfied—all are condemning sins: sins that condemn a person to outer darkness where there shall be weeping and gnashing of teeth.

Thought 5. Men deceive themselves. They rationalize their comfort, ease, and slothfulness by minimizing their gift. They think that they will be excused by *downing* or denying their gift.
⇒ Inactive righteousness is as condemning as active wickedness.
⇒ Idle service is as condemning as a busy sin.
⇒ Sleepy concern is as condemning as stimulating flesh.
⇒ Indulging comfort is as condemning as assault and robbery.
⇒ Being *unprofitable* is as condemning as being evil (see Mt.25:42-46).

DEEPER STUDY # 3
(25:28-29) **Judgment**: see note—Lu.8:18 for discussion.

DEEPER STUDY # 4
(25:30) **Outer Darkness**: a darkness outside some realm or space of light. The rewards have to do with the assignment of responsibility. Therefore, it is probably accurate to say that the judgment is a darkness outside the joy (light) of the Lord's presence and outside the joy of responsibility. What a darkness! To be cast into outer darkness away from the Lord's presence and to be stripped of responsibility—to be responsible for nothing throughout all eternity.

"But the children of the kingdom shall be cast out into outer darkness: there shall be weeping and gnashing of teeth" (Mt.8:12).

MATTHEW 25:14-30

"And shall cast them into a furnace of fire: there shall be wailing and gnashing of teeth" (Mt.13:42).

"Then said the king to the servants, Bind him hand and foot, and take him away, and cast him into outer darkness; there shall be weeping and gnashing of teeth" (Mt.22:13).

"And shall cut him asunder, and appoint him his portion with the hypocrites: there shall be weeping and gnashing of teeth" (Mt.24:51).

"And cast ye the unprofitable servant into outer darkness: there shall be weeping and gnashing of teeth" (Mt.25:30).

"These are wells without water, clouds that are carried with a tempest; to whom the mist of darkness is reserved for ever" (2 Pe.2:17).

"And the angels which kept not their first estate, but left their own habitation, he hath reserved in everlasting chains under darkness unto the judgment of the great day" (Jude 6).

"Yea, the light of the wicked shall be put out, and the spark of his fire shall not shine" (Jb.18:5).

"The wicked shall see it, and be grieved; he shall gnash with his teeth, and melt away: the desire of the wicked shall perish" (Ps.112:10).

"Whoso curseth his father or his mother, his lamp shall be put out in obscure darkness" (Pr.20:20).

MATTHEW 25:31-46

H. The Parable of the Sheep & Goats: The Final Judgment of Nations, 25:31-46

1. **The Son of Man is coming to judge**
   a. Coming in glory
   b. Coming with angels^{DS1}
   c. Coming to be enthroned
   d. Coming to gather all nations
   e. Coming to separate the nations, both sheep & goats

   1) Sheep–favored seat
   2) Goats–unfavored seat

2. **The judgment of sheep will occur**
   a. The Judge: The King
   b. The invitation: Come
   c. The reward: The kingdom

   d. The basis of judgment: Ministering for Christ

   e. The ministry defined
   1) A humble, instinctive ministry: No thought of reward, only of helping people in need

31 When the Son of man shall come in his glory, and all the holy angels with him, then shall he sit upon the throne of his glory:
32 And before him shall be gathered all nations: and he shall separate them one from another, as a shepherd divideth *his* sheep from the goats:
33 And he shall set the sheep on his right hand, but the goats on the left.
34 Then shall the King say unto them on his right hand, Come, ye blessed of my Father, inherit the kingdom prepared for you from the foundation of the world:
35 For I was an hungred, and ye gave me meat: I was thirsty, and ye gave me drink: I was a stranger, and ye took me in:
36 Naked, and ye clothed me: I was sick, and ye visited me: I was in prison, and ye came unto me.
37 Then shall the righteous answer him, saying, Lord, when saw we thee an hungred, and fed *thee*? or thirsty, and gave *thee* drink?
38 When saw we thee a stranger, and took *thee* in? or naked, and clothed *thee*?
39 Or when saw we thee sick, or in prison, and came unto thee?
40 And the King shall answer and say unto them, Verily I say unto you, Inasmuch as ye have done *it* unto one of the least of these my brethren, ye have done *it* unto me.
41 Then shall he say also unto them on the left hand, Depart from me, ye cursed, into everlasting fire, prepared for the devil and his angels:
42 For I was an hungred, and ye gave me no meat: I was thirsty, and ye gave me no drink:
43 I was a stranger, and ye took me not in: naked, and ye clothed me not: sick, and in prison, and ye visited me not.
44 Then shall they also answer him, saying, Lord, when saw we thee an hungred, or athirst, or a stranger, or naked, or sick, or in prison, and did not minister unto thee?
45 Then shall he answer them, saying, Verily I say unto you, Inasmuch as ye did *it* not to one of the least of these, ye did *it* not to me.
46 And these shall go away into everlasting punishment: but the righteous into life eternal.

   2) A ministry to the Lord's "brothers"^{DS2}

3. **The judgment of goats will occur**
   a. The judgment
   1) Cut off from God
   2) Eternal fire^{DS3}
   b. The basis of judgment
   1) A failure to minister

   2) A selfish life

   3) A spiritual blindness

4. **The judgment is for eternity**

DIVISION XV

THE MESSIAH'S PROPHECY OF HIS RETURN AND THE END OF THE AGE: THE OLIVET DISCOURSE, 24:1–25:46

H. The Parable of the Sheep and Goats: The Final Judgment of Nations, 25:31-46

(25:31-46) **Introduction—The Final Judgment**: a person must guard against confusing the judgment of a nation's works with the judgment of individuals (sheep and goats). Judging nations is really judging individuals within them. Christ was painting a picture of the final judgment of all men. The final judgment will include *all nations* of men; it shall be the judgment of the *whole world*.

It is important to see that Jesus was judging two types of beings, sheep and goats, not the same type of being of whom some behaved in one way and some another. Note the sheep (truly born again believers) serve with Christ's heart of love *because they are sheep*. The ministry they rendered came from within. It was a natural ministry performed by sheep. It arose from a selfless, God-centered nature. Goats do not serve with Christ's heart of love *because they are goats*. The acts of kindness identified the sheep as sheep. The neglect of the goats identified them as goats. The sheep acted like sheep; that is, they served because they were sheep. And the goats acted like goats because they were goats. This is the very point of the picture. When Christ sets them at His hand, they are already sheep and goats. Judgment is passed upon the goats because they did not serve Christ, and blessing is bestowed upon the sheep because they served Christ. Scripture says, "Show me thy faith without thy works, and I will show thee my faith with my works" (Js.2:18). The only faith that God knows and accepts is the faith that serves Christ by ministering to people. A man who says he has faith and does not minister to people is *only professing* faith in Christ. The true believer is "God's workmanship [creation], created in Christ Jesus unto [to do] good works" (Ep.2:10). God knows no faith apart from good works, that is, apart from ministering to the needs of people.

1. The Son of Man is coming to judge (vv.31-33).
2. The judgment of sheep will occur (vv.34-40).
3. The judgment of goats will occur (vv.41-45).
4. The judgment is for eternity (v.46).

MATTHEW 25:31-46

1 (25:31-33) **Jesus Christ, Return**: the Son of Man is coming to judge. Christ said five things about His coming in these three verses.

   a. When He comes, He is coming in glory. This means at least two things. First, He is coming in His glorified body, that is, His transfigured body (Mt.17:2); in a body full of light and splendor; in a body shining as the sun in all the brilliance of God's glory. Second, He is not coming in the humiliation which He suffered as a man, but He is coming as the Son of Man and as the King of the universe.

   b. When He comes, He is coming with His holy angels. An innumerable number of glorious beings will accompany Him, demonstrating the glory and honor of His person as God. The holy angels will be the attendants and ministers of His justice.

   c. When He comes, He is coming to be enthroned. When He sits upon "the throne of His glory," He sits in judgment. He will become the One before whom every knee shall bow (Ph.2:9-11). He will become the Judge of the whole universe, the Judge who is exalted above all (Re.20:11f).

   d. When He comes, He is coming to gather all nations. All men will be gathered by the angels and brought before Him. The word *nations* stresses that every single country, place, nationality, race, creed, color, language—every living citizen will be gathered before Him in judgment.

   e. When He comes, He is coming to separate the nations.
   1) Throughout history, there has been a mixture of sheep and goats, of good and evil. The tares and the wheat have grown together. The sinner and the godly have lived together...
      - in the same world
      - in the same nations
      - in the same cities
      - in the same employments
      - in the same churches
      - in the same families

   When Christ comes, however, there is going to be a separation—a separation of the good from the bad, of the sheep from the goats (see Mt.13:49; Eze. 34:17).

   2) The sheep will be placed on His right hand and the goats on His left hand. The sheep represent genuine believers. They are...
      - the ones who believe in God's "only begotten Son" (Jn.3:16).
      - the ones who are truly "born again" (Jn.3:3, 7).
      - the "good and faithful" servants (Mt.25:21, 23).
      - the "righteous" (Mt.25:37).
      - the ones who are "patient" and "continue in well doing" (Ro.2:7).
      - the ones who "seek for glory and honor and immortality" (Ro.2:7).
      - the ones who "work good" (Ro.2:10).

   Note that God sets the sheep at His right hand, the position of honor, glory, acceptance, and favor.

   The goats represent *all* unbelievers, those who never professed Christ and those who professed Christ but were not genuine believers. They are...
      - the "unprofitable servants" (Mt.25:30).
      - the "wicked and slothful servants" (Mt.25:26).
      - the "cursed" (Mt.25:41).
      - the ones who "are contentious" (Ro.2:8).
      - the ones who "do not obey the truth" (Ro.2:8).
      - the ones who "obey unrighteousness" (Ro.2:8).
      - the ones who "do evil" (Ro.2:9).

   Thought 1. Judgment is coming. It is inevitable; it cannot be avoided nor evaded. No person can escape the coming judgment of God. God is going to judge the world by His Son, the Lord Jesus Christ.

   "For the Father judgeth no man, but hath committed all judgment unto the Son" (Jn.5:22).
   "And he commanded us to preach unto the people, and to testify that it is he which was ordained of God to be the Judge of quick [the living] and dead" (Ac.10:42).
   "Because he hath appointed a day, in the which he will judge the world in righteousness by that man whom he hath ordained; whereof he hath given assurance unto all men, in that he hath raised him from the dead" (Ac.17:31).
   "In the day when God shall judge the secrets of men by Jesus Christ according to my gospel" (Ro.2:16).
   "So then every one of us shall give account of himself to God" (Ro.14:12).
   "I charge thee therefore before God, and the Lord Jesus Christ, who shall judge the quick and the dead at his appearing and his kingdom" (2 Ti.4:1).
   "And I saw the dead, small and great, stand before God; and the books were opened: and another book was opened, which is the book of life: and the dead were judged out of those things which were written in the books, according to their works" (Re.20:12).

   Thought 2. Very simply put, the day is coming when every citizen of every nation and tribe on earth will stand before Christ—stand either in His *favor* or in His *disfavor*.

   Thought 3. Note the two claims to deity that Christ makes.
   (1) He calls Himself "the Son of Man": He is the Ideal Man. As the Ideal Man, He is to judge the sons of men.
   (2) He says that "the Son of Man shall sit upon the throne of His glory." He said this three days before He was killed.

MATTHEW 25:31-46

Thought 4. Note a significant fact: Christ is *now* sitting on the throne at the right hand of God. There is a difference between the throne of grace and the throne of judgment pictured in this passage. We can now come to the throne of grace for help (He.4:16). But when Christ returns in glory, it will be too late to receive help. His throne will be a *throne of judgment* to which there will be no approach apart from judgment.

DEEPER STUDY # 1
(25:31) **Angels—Jesus Christ, Return**: when Christ returns, He will be accompanied by angels who will serve as His ministers throughout the judgment.
- ⇒ They shall gather the tares, the children of the wicked one (Mt.13:38-40).
- ⇒ They shall gather the elect (Mt.24:31).
- ⇒ They shall witness the believers' glory (Lu.12:8).
- ⇒ They shall call believers together to meet the Lord in the air (Mt.24:31; 1 Th.4:16).
- ⇒ They shall witness the torment of the wicked (Re.14:10).

---

2 (25:34-40) **Judgment**: the judgment of sheep will occur.

    a. The Judge is the King. Christ sits upon His *throne of glory* and reigns as "King of Kings, and Lord of Lords" (Re.19:16).

    b. The invitation is "come, ye blessed of my Father." The sheep are the blessed, the beloved of God (see note—Ep.1:3). The word *come* is the picture of entering the very presence of God Himself and being privileged to remain there forever.

    c. The reward is an inheritance—the inheritance of the Kingdom of God.
      1) *An inheritance* is a gift. It is given because the giver cares enough to give it, and it becomes one's own possession as much as it was the former owner's.
      2) The inheritance is a *kingdom*. It is a place of responsibility and duty, of ruling and reigning, of honor and joy, of wealth and glory.
      3) The inheritance or the kingdom had been *prepared* for the sheep (see Jn.14:2-3). It was built to suit them and designed for their habitation. "All things are [prepared] for their sakes" (2 Co.4:15).
      4) The kingdom had been prepared from *the foundation of the world*. It was in the eternal plan and will of God (Ep.1:4-5, 11-12).

    d. The basis of judgment—the reason the sheep are given the kingdom—is because they ministered to Christ. Several important facts need to be noted.
      1) The sheep ministered *to Christ*; that is, what they did was done "for Christ's sake." They ministered "as believers" in Him.
      2) The sheep ministered because they loved their brothers (see DEEPER STUDY # 2—Mt. 25:40; see 1 Jn.4:7-8, 12, 20-21).
      3) Christ is not disregarding or minimizing the part of faith in salvation. We shall be judged for both our confession of faith and our works (Mt.10:32; Lu.12:8; Ro.10:9-10; 2 Co.5:10).
      4) Note that the works are simple works, some of which anyone can do. They are expressions of care and love that *can* serve as the basis of judgment, as the basis for judging anyone.

    e. The ministry is defined by Christ; He shares just what He means by ministering. Note it is the righteous who ask Him what He means.
      1) The ministry is a humble, instinctive ministry. It has no thought of reward, only of helping people in need. The true believer serves Christ because Christ has done so much for him. It is "the love of Christ" which constrains him (2 Co.5:14). *Even while he is serving, a humble servant knows something...*
- He is not even worthy to be serving
- He has done, is doing, and will do so little
- He deserves nothing

      He is serving simply because he loves Jesus and the people of the earth. All he knows and wishes to know is Jesus. To serve Jesus and to help all those for whom Jesus died is within him instinctively.
      2) The ministry is a ministry to the Lord's brothers (see DEEPER STUDY # 2—Mt.25:40). The thought here is of critical importance. It determines a man's destiny.

    Christ has so *identified* Himself with men in their pain and suffering that He counts men as one with Himself. Christ clearly said that if we minister to men, we are ministering to Him personally. He is identified as one with His people (Mt.8:17; see Is.53:4). He accused Saul of actually persecuting Him when Saul was threatening and slaughtering Christians (Ac.9:4).

> "And whosoever shall give to drink unto one of these little ones a cup of cold water only in the name of a disciple, verily I say unto you, he shall in no wise lose his reward" (Mt.10:42).
>
> "But so shall it not be among you: but whosoever will be great among you, shall be your minister: and whosoever of you will be the chiefest, shall be servant of all" (Mk.10:43-44).
>
> "Which now of these three, thinkest thou, was neighbour unto him that fell among the thieves? And he said, He that showed mercy on him. Then said Jesus unto him, Go, and do thou likewise" (Lu.10:36-37).
>
> "If I then, your Lord and Master, have washed your feet; ye also ought to wash one another's feet" (Jn.13:14).
>
> "He saith to him again the second time, Simon, son of Jonas, lovest thou me? He saith unto him, Yea, Lord; thou knowest that I love thee. He saith unto him, Feed my sheep" (Jn.21:16).

MATTHEW 25:31-46

"Bear ye one another's burdens, and so fulfil the law of Christ....As we have therefore opportunity, let us do good unto all men, especially unto them who are of the household of faith" (Ga.6:2, 10).

"With good will doing service, as to the Lord, and not to men" (Ep.6:7).

Thought 1. Several points are clearly pictured in these verses.
(1) The rightful position of Christ before the world: He is the King.
(2) The glorious inheritance of the believer.
(3) The initial importance of ministry.

Thought 2. Think how many *lonely* of this world become His. How many of the hungry, the thirsty, the strangers, the naked, the sick, the prisoners become His? (See Mt.1:26-27.)

Thought 3. No ministry and no amount of suffering on this earth are so lowly that the ministry and suffering will not be worth the glory which shall be revealed in us (Ro.8:18).

Thought 4. There are those who will give huge sums of money and help enormously if they can be recognized. But such is rooted in selfishness; it is pandering to our egos and desires for recognition and esteem.

DEEPER STUDY # 2
(25:40) **Brethren**: without exception, Christ is consistent in His use of the word brothers. His brothers are His disciples (see Mt.23:8; 12:46-50; 28:10; Mk.3:31-35; Lu.8:21; Jn.20:17-18). Jesus is saying that the nations (the leaders and citizens of the nations) are to be judged for their actions toward His followers and their message. If they have received His people and their message with open arms and with righteous and brotherly behavior, then they will show that they have definitely received Him.

---

3 (25:41-45) **Judgment**: the judgment of goats will occur.
a. The judgment will be twofold.
1) The goats will be cut off and separated from God. Christ will say, "Depart from me"—words that mean a world of misery, a world of outer darkness, a world of weeping and gnashing of teeth, a world of everlasting punishment, a world without God and hope (see Mt.25:30, 46). The goats rejected Christ and refused to be identified with Him while on earth. When they stand before Him, they will never have been associated with Him. Therefore, they will not be allowed to associate with Him.
   Note what Christ calls the goats: "Ye cursed." They did not choose to be called "brothers" (v.40), nor did they choose to inherit the kingdom. They will, therefore, be called "cursed;" and they will inherit the curse (Ga.3:10). As Scripture says "It is a fearful thing to fall into the hands of the living God" (He.10:31).
2) The goats will be placed into "everlasting fire" (see Deeper Study # 2—Mt.5:22; Deeper Study # 4—Lu.16:24; note—Re.9:2. See Re.20:2.) Note three things. It is a place of anguish, torment, and punishment (see Mt.25:30, 46 with notes listed above). It is everlasting, having no end. It is prepared for the devil and his angels, not for man.
b. The basis of judgment and the reasons why the goats will be separated from God are revealing.
1) The goats failed to minister. Very simply, the goats are persons who fail to help the hungry, the thirsty, the stranger, the naked, the sick, and the prisoner. They are persons who do not become *involved* in meeting the needs of people. They are persons who do not dedicate themselves to meeting the desperate needs of a corruptible world (see Mt.20:28. See Jn.20:21; Lu.9:23.)
2) The goats lived a selfish life. The goats are people who live a life of comfort and ease, a life of no concern and care, a life of materialism and things, a life of pleasure and indulgence, a life of money and plenty. They live selfishly while the world around them is suffering with hunger and sickness and death.
3) The goats were spiritually blind. The goats are people who refuse to see the truth about Christ, that He *identifies Himself* with the suffering masses, with the pain and need of individuals. The goats refuse to open their eyes to see those lying all around, those desperately in need: the hungry, the thirsty, the stranger, the naked, the sick, the prisoner. They refuse to see the *stamp* of God, His glorious love for every man. They refuse to see that they are failing to help Christ when they fail to help the needy.

"Jesus said unto him, If thou wilt be perfect, go and sell that thou hast, and give to the poor, and thou shalt have treasure in heaven: and come and follow me" (Mt.19:21).

"I was a stranger, and ye took me not in: naked, and ye clothed me not: sick, and in prison, and ye visited me not" (Mt.25:43).

"And the cares of this world, and the deceitfulness of riches, and the lusts of other things entering in, choke the word, and it becometh unfruitful" (Mk.4:19).

"And there was a certain beggar named Lazarus, which was laid at his gate, full of sores, and desiring to be fed with the crumbs which fell from the rich man's table: moreover the dogs came and licked his sores" (Lu.16:20-21).

"But they that will be rich fall into temptation and a snare, and into many foolish and hurtful lusts, which drown men in destruction and perdition" (1 Ti.6:9).

"Pure religion and undefiled before God and the Father is this, To visit the fatherless and widows in their affliction, and to keep himself unspotted from the world" (Js.1:27).

"Therefore to him that knoweth to do good, and doeth it not, to him it is sin" (Js.4:17).

MATTHEW 25:31-46

"But whoso hath this world's good, and seeth his brother have need, and shutteth up his bowels of compassion from him, how dwelleth the love of God in him?" (1 Jn.3:17).

"If there be among you a poor man of one of thy brethren within any of thy gates in thy land which the LORD thy God giveth thee, thou shalt not harden thine heart, nor shut thine heart, nor shut thine hand from thy poor brother" (De.15:7).

"[Woe to them] that lie upon beds of ivory, and stretch themselves upon their couches, and eat the lambs out of the flock, and the calves out of the midst of the stall" (Am. 6:4).

Thought 1. Christ says to the goats, "Depart from me." Where are the goats sent?
⇒ It is not a place of comfort and pleasure. It is a place of weeping and gnashing of teeth.

"And cast ye the unprofitable servant into outer darkness: there shall be weeping and gnashing of teeth" (Mt.25:30).

⇒ It is not a place of light and justice. It is outer darkness.

"Then said the king to the servants, Bind him hand and foot, and take him away, and cast him into outer darkness; there shall be weeping and gnashing of teeth" (Mt.22:13; see Mt.25:30).

⇒ It is not a place of short duration. It is everlasting.

"Then shall he say also unto them on the left hand, Depart from me, ye cursed, into everlasting fire, prepared for the devil and his angels" (Mt.25:41).

⇒ It is not a place of good friends and fellowship. It is the company of the devil.

"And the devil that deceived them was cast into the lake of fire and brimstone, where the beast and the false prophet are, and shall be tormented day and night for ever and ever. And I saw the dead, small and great, stand before God; and the books were opened: and another book was opened, which is the book of life: and the dead were judged out of those things which were written in the books, according to their works. And the sea gave up the dead which were in it; and death and hell delivered up the dead which were in them: and they were judged every man according to their works. And death and hell were cast into the lake of fire. This is the second death. And whosoever was not found written in the book of life was cast into the lake of fire" (Re.20:10-15; see Mt.25:41).

Thought 2. Note the *striking* difference between the sheep and the goats.
⇒ The sheep heard "come"; the goats heard "depart."
⇒ The sheep are called "blessed"; the goats are called "cursed."
⇒ The sheep are invited to "inherit"; the goats are "cursed."
⇒ The sheep receive a kingdom; the goats receive "everlasting fire."
⇒ The sheep dwell in a place *prepared* for God's people; the goats dwell in a place prepared for the devil and his angels.
⇒ The sheep spend eternity with God and their Christian brothers; the goats spend eternity with the devil and his angels.

Thought 3. Note a critical point. Goats are not condemned for what they did, but for what they did not do. Their sin was the sin of omission, not commission. But note how terrible the sin is, how many destitute people were left suffering all through life because a goat did not help them.

Thought 4. Selfishness, indulgence, extravagance, hoarding—all that leads to and indicates the neglect of others—will visibly condemn a man when he stands before Christ. (For a clear study of this point see outline and notes—Mt.19:16-22; 19:23-26; 19:27-30.)

Thought 5. Note that the unprofitable servant's sin is the same as the goats: the sin of neglect and omission. Each neglected to do what they should have done. (See outline and notes—Mt.25:14-30.)

DEEPER STUDY # 3

(25:41) **Everlasting fire** (to pur to aionion): this literally reads, *fire which is everlasting*. It is a fire that lasts forever, burns on and on. Note the fire is not prepared for men, but for the devil and his angels. God never intended men to spend eternity in everlasting fire. Men who choose to follow the devil in his evil ways are choosing to be with the devil wherever he is. (See DEEPER STUDY # 2, *Hell*—Mt.5:22 for more discussion.)

---

4 (25:46) **Judgment**: it is critical to note the words of Christ: "These shall go away into *everlasting* punishment." The judgment is for eternity. There is no second chance; judgment is unchangeable.

"The righteous [shall go] into life *eternal*." Life eternal is also permanent and unchangeable. Note: it is *life* that is eternal, not some dreamy, unconscious, or semiconscious state of being. The sheep will live, and their life will be eternal, never ending.

MATTHEW 26:1-5

	CHAPTER 26 XVI. THE MESSIAH'S ARREST, TRIAL, & CRUCIFIXION, 26:1–27:66 A. The Messiah's Death Explained & Plotted, 26:1-5 (Mk 14:1-2; Lu 22:1-2)	2 Ye know that after two days is *the feast of* the passover, and the Son of man is betrayed to be crucified. 3 Then assembled together the chief priests, and the scribes, and the elders of the people, unto the palace of the high priest, who was called Caiaphas, 4 And consulted that they might take Jesus by subtilty, and kill *him*. 5 But they said, Not on the feast *day*, lest there be an uproar among the people.	a. Was tied to the Passover^{DS1} b. Was the Son of Man dying c. Was caused by betrayal d. Was to be by crucifixion **2. Jesus' death was plotted by the religionists**^{DS2} a. Was planned by all the leaders b. Was to be by deception 1) To arrest on false charges & kill 2) To arrest quietly, after the pilgrims had left the feast^{DS3}
1. Jesus' death was explained to His disciples	And it came to pass, when Jesus had finished all these sayings, he said unto his disciples,		

DIVISION XVI

THE MESSIAH'S ARREST, TRIAL AND CRUCIFIXION, 26:1–27:66

A. The Messiah's Death Explained and Plotted, 26:1-5

(26:1-5) **Introduction**: it was apparently Wednesday of Jesus' last week (see notes—Mt.21:1-11; 21:12-16; 21:17-22; 21:23-27). He was to be killed on Friday, just two days away. In these few verses, Matthew gives a glimpse into the drama that was rapidly building. Two scenes are pictured: Jesus was intensely preparing His disciples for His death, and the religionists were behind closed doors demonically plotting His death.

What Jesus explained about His death is explicit: He was to be betrayed and crucified. What the religionists plotted was explicit: they were going to kill Jesus.

1. Jesus' death was explained to His disciples (vv.1-2).
   a. Was tied to the Passover.
   b. Was the Son of Man dying.
   c. Was caused by betrayal.
   d. Was to be by crucifixion.
2. Jesus' death was plotted by the religionists (vv.3-5).
   a. Was planned by all the leaders.
   b. Was to be by deception
      1) To arrest on false charges and kill.
      2) To be arrest quietly, after the pilgrims had left the feast.

1 (26:1-2) **Jesus Christ, Death**: Jesus' death was explained to His disciples. In just two days, He was to be crucified. The disciples had to be strengthened for the hour of trial lest their dreams become dashed upon the rocks of despair and they loose faith. Remember, their thoughts were focused on the Messiah's restoring the kingdom of David to Israel. They were thinking that He, the Messiah, was going to deliver Israel from Roman bondage. The Messiah would free the nation and establish it as the greatest nation on earth under the rule of God Himself (see notes—Mt.1:1; DEEPER STUDY # 2—1:18; DEEPER STUDY # 3—3:11; notes—11:1-6; 11:2-3; DEEPER STUDY # 1—11:5; DEEPER STUDY # 2—11:6; DEEPER STUDY # 1—12:16; notes—22:42; Lu.7:21-23). There was the very live possibility that the apostles could lose faith when they saw His being put to death by the hands of mere men. It could appear as though He were being forsaken by God! Christ had to do everything He could to prepare them. There were four basic facts about His death that would help and help tremendously.

a. Christ's death was tied to the Passover (see DEEPER STUDY # 1—Mt.26:2; DEEPER STUDY # 1—Lu.22:7; DEEPER STUDY # 2—22:19-20). He was foretelling the disciples the exact day He was to be killed, and it was to be the very same day the Passover lamb was to be sacrificed. And note, He was tying His death to the sacrifice of the lamb. As John the Baptist had proclaimed earlier, "Behold the Lamb of God, which taketh away the sin of the world" (Jn.1:29, 36).

> "Whoso eateth my flesh, and drinketh my blood, hath eternal life; and I will raise him up at the last day. For my flesh is meat indeed, and my blood is drink indeed. He that eateth my flesh, and drinketh my blood, dwelleth in me, and I in him. As the living Father hath sent me, and I live by the Father: so he that eateth me, even he shall live by me. This is that bread which came down from heaven: not as your fathers did eat manna, and are dead: he that eateth of this bread shall live for ever" (Jn.6:54-58).
>
> "In whom we have redemption through his blood, the forgiveness of sins, according to the riches of his grace" (Ep.1:7).
>
> "But with the precious blood of Christ, as of a lamb without blemish and without spot" (1 Pe.1:19).
>
> "But if we walk in the light, as he is in the light, we have fellowship one with another, and the blood of Jesus Christ his Son cleanseth us from all sin" (1 Jn.1:7).

> "My little children, these things write I unto you, that ye sin not. And if any man sin, we have an advocate with the Father, Jesus Christ the righteous: and he is the propitiation for our sins: and not for ours only, but also for the sins of the whole world" (1 Jn.2:1-2).

b. Christ's death was the Son of Man Himself dying (see Deeper Study #3—Mt.8:20). "Son of Man" means that He perfectly identified with man in human flesh. But it means more, much more: it means that He is the Ideal Man, the Man who lived a perfect and sinless life. By living without sin, He has become the Ideal and Perfect Man, the Pattern Man for all men. It is the Son of Man who knows our trials and hurts, pain and suffering. It was the Son of Man who lived a perfect life and who secured a perfect righteousness—the Son of Man who died for us. And because He died, His Ideal righteousness and Ideal death can *stand* for our righteousness and death.

> "I am the good shepherd: the good shepherd giveth his life for the sheep" (Jn.10:11).
> "For when we were yet without strength, in due time Christ died for the ungodly" (Ro.5:6).
> "For I delivered unto you first of all that which I also received, how that Christ died for our sins according to the Scriptures" (1 Co.15:3).
> "Who gave himself for our sins, that he might deliver us from this present evil world, according to the will of God and our Father" (Ga.1:4).
> "And walk in love, as Christ also hath loved us, and hath given himself for us an offering and a sacrifice to God for a sweetsmelling savour" (Ep.5:2).
> "Who gave himself for us, that he might redeem us from all iniquity, and purify unto himself a peculiar people, zealous of good works" (Tit.2:14).
> "So Christ was once offered to bear the sins of many; and unto them that look for him shall he appear the second time without sin unto salvation" (He.9:28).
> "And ye know that he was manifested to take away our sins; and in him is no sin" (1 Jn.3:5).
> "Hereby perceive we the love of God, because he laid down his life for us: and we ought to lay down our lives for the brethren" (1 Jn.3:16).
> "And they sung a new song, saying, Thou art worthy to take the book, and to open the seals thereof: for thou wast slain, and hast redeemed us to God by thy blood out of every kindred, and tongue, and people, and nation" (Re.5:9).

He is our Ideal righteousness and life. When we seek for a Savior, it is He for whom we must seek. It was the Son of Man Himself who was to die, the only Man who could die as the Ideal Man; and because He was the Ideal Man, His death can cover all men. His death is the Ideal death, the Pattern death which covers any man who calls upon Him.

> "But God commendeth his love toward us, in that while we were yet sinners, Christ died for us" (Ro.5:8).
> "Who his own self bare our sins in his own body on the tree, that we, being dead to sins, should live unto righteousness: by whose stripes ye were healed" (1 Pe.2:24).
> "For Christ also hath once suffered for sins, the just for the unjust, that he might bring us to God, being put to death in the flesh, but quickened by the Spirit" (1 Pe.3:18).

c. Christ's death was caused by betrayal. One of the disciples was going to betray Him (see notes—Mt.26:20-25; 27:3-5; Mk.14:10-11; Lu.22:4-6; note and Deeper Study #1—Jn.13:18; note—13:21-26). Note that Christ used the present tense, "is betrayed." The betrayal was certain, immediate, staring Him right in the face.

d. Christ's death was to be by crucifixion. (Death by crucifixion is graphically described in the outline, notes, and Deeper Study #1—Mt.27:26-44; notes—Mk.15:16-41; Lu.23:26-49; Jn.19:16-37.)

> "Who his own self bare our sins in his own body on the tree, that we, being dead to sins, should live unto righteousness: by whose stripes ye were healed" (1 Pe.2:24).
> "Christ hath redeemed us from the curse of the law, being made a curse for us: for it is written, Cursed is every one that hangeth on a tree" (Ga.3:13).
> "But God commendeth his love toward us, in that, while we were yet sinners, Christ died for us. Much more then, being now justified by his blood, we shall be saved from wrath through him. For if, when we were enemies, we were reconciled to God by the death of his Son, much more, being reconciled, we shall be saved by his life" (Ro.5:8-10).

Thought 1. The Passover clearly shows *the glorious preparation* of God for salvation, for taking away the sins of the world. The Paschal lamb was given by God as a picture of the giving of His Son for the sins of the world.

Thought 2. Jesus died for us. He has taken away the sins of the world.

> "Who his own self bare our sins in his own body on the tree, that we, being dead to sins, should live unto righteousness: by whose stripes ye were healed" (1 Pe.2:24).
> "For Christ also hath once suffered for sins, the just for the unjust, that he might bring us to God, being put to death in the flesh, but quickened by the Spirit" (1 Pe.3:18. See note—Mt.17:22-23; note and Deeper Study #1—20:18.)

MATTHEW 26:1-5

Thought 3. Jesus did all He could to prepare His disciples for the great trial they were to face in witnessing His death. He does all He can to prepare us for whatever lies ahead. Just think of the things He has told us that lie out in the future. How well He has prepared us—lest we be caught off guard (see outlines and notes—Mt.24:1-25:46).

Thought 4. Jesus' death not only saves us, but it encourages us to bear the trials of life.

"For consider Him that endured such contradiction (hostility) of sinners against Himself, lest ye be wearied and faint in your minds" (He.12:3).

DEEPER STUDY # 1

(26:2) **Passover—Jesus Christ, Death**: note Jesus' words "ye know." The disciples did know both facts. The Passover was only two days away, and Jesus had been telling them for months that He was to be killed. Why, then, was He pointing out facts that the disciples already knew? What Jesus was doing was *revealing* to the disciples that His death was tied to the Passover (see outline and notes—Mt.26:17-19). The Passover throughout history had pictured His death. Christ was fulfilling the Passover with the shedding of His own blood upon the cross.

1. Historically, the Passover refers back to the time when God delivered Israel from Egyptian bondage (Ex.11:1f). God had pronounced judgment, the taking of the firstborn, upon the people of Egypt for their injustices. As God prepared to execute the final judgment, those who believed God were instructed to slay a pure lamb and sprinkle its blood over the door posts of their homes. The blood of the innocent lamb would then serve as a sign that the coming judgment had already been carried out. When seeing the blood, God would *pass over* that house.
2. Symbolically, the passover pictured the coming of Jesus Christ as the Savior. The "lamb without blemish" pictured His sinless life (see Jn.1:29), and the "blood sprinkled on the door posts" pictured His blood shed for the believer. It was a sign that the life and blood of the innocent lamb had been substituted for the firstborn. The "eating of the lamb" pictured the need for spiritual nourishment gained by feeding on Christ, the Bread of Life. The unleavened bread (bread without yeast) pictured the need for putting evil out of one's life and household (see Deeper Study # 1, *Feast of Unleavened Bread*—Mt.26:17).

---

2 (26:3-5) **Religionists, Plot Jesus' Death**: Jesus' death was plotted by the religionists. Matthew painted a dramatic picture. While Christ was on one side of town preparing His disciples for His death, the religionists were on the other side of town plotting His death. And note: they were in the house of the high priest behind closed doors.

  a. Christ's death was plotted by all the leaders: the chief priests, the Scribes, and the elders (see Deeper Study # 1—Mt.16:21; Deeper Study # 2—26:3).
    1) Note where they met, how deceptive it was. They met in the home (palace) of the high priest, not in the official court. It was a secret plot, to be kept quiet until the right moment for the arrest and murder.
    2) Note who it was that took the lead in the plot: Caiaphas, the high priest himself, the very person who was supposed to be the spiritual leader of the people.
  b. Christ's death was to be wrought by deception and lies.
    1) He was to be arrested on false charges and killed (see outline and notes—Mt.26:60-66).
    2) He was to be arrested quietly, after all the pilgrims had left the feast to return home. The *feast day* refers to all eight days of the feast. The danger of an uprising would not have passed until they had all left the city. Of course, the threat of an uprising was removed by the willingness of Judas' to betray Christ. In the crowded masses of about two million bodies within the city, Judas was able to show them where Christ was and to quietly identify Him. He was able to show them how Christ could be quietly taken in the dark of the night (see Mt.26:47-50).

> "Their throat is an open sepulchre; with their tongues they have used deceit; the poison of asps is under their lips" (Ro.3:13).
>
> "Know ye not that the unrighteous shall not inherit the kingdom of God? Be not deceived" (1 Co.6:9).
>
> "Be not deceived; God is not mocked: for whatsoever a man soweth, that shall he also reap" (Ga.6:7).
>
> "Let no man deceive you with vain words: for because of these things cometh the wrath of God upon the children of disobedience" (Ep.5:6).
>
> "Little children, let no man deceive you: he that doeth righteousness is righteous, even as he is righteous. He that committeth sin is of the devil; for the devil sinneth from the beginning. For this purpose the Son of God was manifested, that he might destroy the works of the devil" (1 Jn.3:7-8).
>
> "But be ye doers of the word, and not hearers only, deceiving your own selves" (Js.1:22).
>
> "For he flattereth himself in his own eyes, until his iniquity be found to be hateful" (Ps.36:2).
>
> "There is a generation that are pure in their own eyes, and yet is not washed from their filthiness" (Pr.30:12).
>
> "Most men will proclaim every one his own goodness: but a faithful man who can find?" (Pr.20:6).
>
> "And they will deceive every one his neighbor, and will not speak the truth: they have taught their tongue to speak lies, and weary themselves to commit iniquity" (Je.9:5).
>
> "The heart is deceitful above all things, and desperately wicked: who can know it?" (Je.17:9).

MATTHEW 26:1-5

Thought 1. Note how even the most religious can be gripped by the fear of losing position, power, recognition, esteem, and security (see notes—Mt.12:1-8; note and Deeper Study #1—12:10; note—15:1-20; Deeper Study #2—15:6-9; Deeper Study #3—16:12). How worldly, how attached to the things of the world even the most religious become!

DEEPER STUDY # 2
(26:3) **High Priest—Chief Priests—Caiaphas**: the office of High Priest began with Aaron and his sons (Ex.28:1). The office was hereditary and was for life, but when the Romans conquered Palestine, they made the office political. They chose their own man, a man who would cooperate with the Roman government. Finding such a man was often difficult. For example, between 37 B.C. and 67 A.D. there were at least twenty-eight High Priests. These men were greatly respected and highly honored throughout life, and even when they were removed from power by the Romans, they were still consulted by other Jewish leaders. The ex-high Priest, Annas, was a prime example. He still wielded unusual power (see Jn.18:13; Acts 4:6). He and the others who had served as High Priests or else held the top positions of leadership were also called *chief priests*.

The term of office for a High Priest was determined solely by the Romans. The Romans let a High Priest reign so long as he pleased them. The reign of the twenty-eight averaged only about three years, except for Caiaphas. Caiaphas was High Priest for about eighteen years (18 A.D. to 36 A.D.). Apparently he was a master at intrigue and compromise. This throws great light on his fearing an uproar and wishing to wait until the feast was over to arrest Jesus (Mt.26:5). There was the danger that the people might rally to support Jesus if they saw Him arrested; so many believed Him to be a great prophet that a serious uprising was a real possibility. Caiaphas knew the Romans would hold him responsible and remove him from office. He would lose everything he had. The shrewdness of the man was seen in the strategy he laid. They were to arrest Jesus quietly after the masses had left the feast.

DEEPER STUDY # 3
(26:5) **Passover**: the atmosphere of Jerusalem at the Passover Feast was always explosive. The city was overly packed with pilgrims. Josephus, the notable Jewish historian, says that by law each sacrifice had to represent at least ten persons. He reports over a quarter million sacrificial lambs were slain; therefore, he estimates that two million or more pilgrims were celebrating at this particular feast (Josephus, *Wars*. 6. 9:3). (See notes—Mt.26:3-5.)

	B. The Messiah Anointed for Death: A Picture of Sacrificial Love & Faith, 26:6-13 *(Mk 14:3-9; Jn 12:1-8)*	given to the poor. 10 When Jesus understood *it*, he said unto them, Why trouble ye the woman? for she hath wrought a good work upon me.	**4. The anointing was a grasping of opportunity**
1. The anointing of Jesus by a woman in Bethany: In Simon the Leper's house^{DS1}	6 Now when Jesus was in Bethany, in the house of Simon the leper,	11 For ye have the poor always with you; but me ye have not always.	
2. The anointing was an act of love & faith in the Lord Jesus^{DS2}	7 There came unto him a woman having an alabaster box of very precious ointment, and poured it on his head, as he sat *at meat*.	12 For in that she hath poured this ointment on my body, she did *it* for my burial.	**5. The anointing pointed to the burial of Jesus, to His death**
3. The anointing was a sacrificial gift, a commitment beyond common sense	8 But when his disciples saw *it*, they had indignation, saying, To what purpose *is* this waste? 9 For this ointment might have been sold for much, and	13 Verily I say unto you, Wheresoever this gospel shall be preached in the whole world, *there* shall also this, that this woman hath done, be told for a memorial of her.	**6. The anointing was an eternal memorial**

DIVISION XVI

THE MESSIAH'S ARREST, TRIAL AND CRUCIFIXION, 26:1–27:66

B. The Messiah Anointed for Death: A Picture of Sacrificial Love and Faith, 26:6-13

(26:6-13) **Introduction—Jesus Christ, Anointed—Jesus Christ, Death—Love—Worship**: Mark and John also record this anointing of Jesus. John says it actually took place six days before the Passover (Jn.12:1). Matthew, as pointed out before, arranges events by subjects. He is discussing the death of Christ, so He places it here. John also identifies the woman as Mary, the sister of Lazarus and Martha. Matthew says that they were in the house of Simon the leper, and John says Martha served (Jn.12:2). Apparently Simon the leper was the husband of Martha (although others feel that he could be her father or father-in-law) (Mt.26:6; see Jn.12:2).

What happened was this: the multitudes were flowing into the city for the Passover, and the excitement of the Passover was filling the air. There was a sense that something significant was about to happen. Of course, Mary had no idea of the events that were to take place in the last week of Jesus' life, events which were to begin the very next morning with the triumphal entry. But Mary, along with everyone else, sensed that the time for the kingdom to be established was at hand. Mary, who was always sitting at Jesus' feet, sat there again, gazing into His eyes. As she gazed, she sensed two things. She sensed the need to repent of her recent criticism of Jesus (see Jn.12:3; see note—Jn.12:3), and she sensed a foreboding of trouble surrounding Him. She saw within His eyes a weight so heavy that she was *drawn* to express the most profound faith and appreciation in Him possible. She took the most precious thing she had, an invaluable bottle of perfume, and anointed Him as the Messiah, the anointed One of her life.

Mary's act was one of the most loving and precious acts ever shown to Jesus, if not *the* most loving and precious act. It was an act of supreme love and adoration. What Jesus had to say about it shows this (vv.10-13). Just how loving an act it was can be seen by picturing all that was going on throughout the city at this time and all that was yet to happen: the plotting, the intrigue, the hostility, the attacks, the planned murder, the crowds streaming into the city by the teeming thousands—crowds who created a worldly, carnival atmosphere. Even Simon's own household had an enormous crowd in it with all the disciples present. Just imagine the noise from the conversation alone. Yet there sat Mary at Jesus' feet, once again soaking up all He said, loving and adoring Him. He had done so much for their family. Simon the leper was apparently her brother-in-law (husband to Martha). He had probably been healed by her Lord. Her brother, Lazarus, had been raised from the dead. They had all been saved by Him. How she loved Him! How she wished to express her love and faith in Him! He seemed so tired, so weary, so foreboding; there was something in His eyes that expressed His concern and preoccupation as she gazed into them. She wanted to help and encourage Him, to show Him that she cared for and loved Him, so she arose and went to get the most precious thing she had to give Him. And she gave it in the most precious way she knew: she anointed her Lord, even as David and all the kings of Israel had been anointed in the past. She anointed Him, not from any official position, but from her heart. It is for this reason that she lives in the memory of all as a memorial. In the behalf of all, she anointed the Lord to be the One who was to experience death for all. In behalf of all, she anointed Him as the Lord and Savior, the true Messiah of all hearts and lives who worship and serve Him as the anointed One of God.

1. The anointing of Jesus by a woman in Bethany: In Simon the Leper's house (v.6).
2. The anointing was an act of love and faith in the Lord Jesus (v.7).
3. The anointing was a sacrificial gift, a commitment beyond common sense (vv.8-9).
4. The anointing was a grasping of opportunity (vv.10-11).
5. The anointing pointed to the burial of Jesus, to His death (v.12).
6. The anointing was an eternal memorial (v.13).

MATTHEW 26:6-13

1 (26:6) **Bethany**: see note—Mt.21:17.

> **DEEPER STUDY # 1**
> (26:6) **Simon the Leper**: Jesus was in the house of Simon the leper. Little is known about Simon. He was probably a leper who had been healed by Jesus. Tradition says he was the husband of Martha. Scripture also seems to indicate this. Matthew says Jesus was dining in the house of Simon the leper, and John says Martha was serving. This would seem to indicate a close relationship. Martha was probably his wife or older daughter. If she were Simon's wife, then her brother and sister, Lazarus and Mary, seemed to be living with her and Simon. Note that Simon's house was large enough to entertain Jesus and His disciples all at once. On such occasions, he would probably have had servants serving under the direction of his wife and not an older daughter. However, if Martha were Simon's oldest daughter, then Simon was the father of Mary and Lazarus as well. It was while Jesus was in Simon the leper's home that Mary came up to Jesus and anointed Him.

Thought 1. Note a striking point: the man who welcomes the Lord into his home will learn much about the Lord. Just imagine the experience Simon the leper had by inviting Jesus to dinner! The important thing to know about Simon the leper is this: he welcomed Jesus into his home.

Thought 2. Note the closeness of the family. Throughout Scripture they are mentioned together, in particular Mary, Martha, and Lazarus. When Christ is a constant guest in a family's home, there is usually a close bond that does not exist otherwise.

Thought 3. Mary's love for Jesus was a most unusual love. Its depth is clearly seen in this most wonderful act (see note—Mt.26:6-13).

2 (26:7) **Faith—Love**: the anointing was an act of love and faith in the Lord Jesus. Very simply put, Mary anointed Jesus to show Him how deeply she loved Him and believed Him to be the true Messiah, "the anointed One of God" (see notes—Mt.26:6-13; see Mt.1:18). He was her Savior, Lord, and King. He had done so much for her and her family. She wanted Him to know how much she appreciated, loved, and believed Him.

Something else needs to be noted as well. Mary sensed something within Jesus: a foreboding, a preoccupation of mind, a heaviness of heart, a weight of tremendous pressure. Her heart reached out to Him and wanted to encourage and help Him. Being a young woman in the presence of so many men, she was not allowed to vocally express herself that much. Such a privilege was not allowed women of that day, so she did all that she could: she acted. She arose and went for the most precious gift she could think of—a most costly bottle of perfume. And she gave it to Him in such a way that He would know that at least one person truly loved Him and believed Him to be the Messiah. Her hope was that such faith and love would boost His spirit.

Thought 1. How do we show our love and faith in Christ? Imagine how difficult it was for Mary to do what she did in the presence of so many. She set aside pride and shyness in order to demonstrate her love and faith in Him. How far are we willing to go in order to show our love and faith for Christ?

Thought 2. Note how Mary demonstrated her love and faith.
(1) Mary gave the most precious thing she had to the Lord.

> "But lay up for yourselves treasures in heaven, where neither moth nor rust doth corrupt, and where thieves do not break through nor steal" (Mt.6:20).
> "Sell that ye have, and give alms; provide yourselves bags which wax not old, a treasure in the heavens that faileth not, where no thief approacheth, neither moth corrupteth" (Lu.12:33).
> "So likewise, whosoever he be of you that forsaketh not all that he hath, he cannot be my disciple" (Lu.14:33).
> "Yea doubtless, and I count all things but loss for the excellency of the knowledge of Christ Jesus my Lord: for whom I have suffered the loss of all things, and do count them but dung, that I may win Christ" (Ph.3:8).
> "Laying up in store for themselves a good foundation against the time to come, that they may lay hold on eternal life" (1 Ti.6:19).

(2) Mary bore the witness of her love and faith in Christ publicly. Her love and faith in Christ was demonstrated for all to witness.

> **DEEPER STUDY # 2**
> (26:7) **Anointing**: see DEEPER STUDY # 1—Acts 10:38.

3 (26:8-9) **Commitment—Sacrifice**: the anointing was a sacrificial gift, a commitment beyond common sense.

a. The anointing was sacrificial. It was worth 300 denarii. A denarius was a small silver coin worth a laborer's daily wage (Mt.20:2), so the perfume was costly, valued at approximately a year's wage (based on a six-day working week).

There is another fact to note about the sacrificial gift. Perfume was a precious item to Eastern women. Mary was taking a most precious possession and giving it to her Lord.

MATTHEW 26:6-13

b. The anointing was a commitment beyond common sense. Imagine the scene: a bottle of perfume worth a whole year's wage being broken and poured upon the head of Christ. Common sense would say to the genuine Christian, "Sell it. Use the money for the poor, the hungry, and the homeless." This is just what the disciples did; in fact, they were indignant and vexed about it. They questioned the act; they considered it a waste. After all, if she wished to anoint Christ, she could have used a less expensive perfume. But the disciples failed to see two points.

1) Mary was driven to express her faith in her Lord and her love for Him *personally*. The most meaningful way she could do this was to anoint Him as her Lord with the most expensive perfume she possessed.
2) The most significant person in Mary's life was the Lord. He was the Messiah, the Savior and Lord of her life and family. She wished to show Him that He was deserving of all she was and had.

The point is this: the disciples questioned what Mary did, just as most people would. In the eyes of the world, they would be right. A cheaper perfume could have been used, and not just a few, but a multitude of poor could have been helped with so much money. But what they and the world fail to see is that true love has to be expressed in a personal way. Love is never known unless it is experienced and shared by the believer.

"And why beholdest thou the mote that is in thy brother's eye, but considerest not the beam that is in thine own eye?" (Mt.7:3; see vv.1-5).

"Who art thou that judgest another man's servant? to his own master he standeth or falleth. Yea, he shall be holden up: for God is able to make him stand" (Ro.14:4).

"Let us not therefore judge one another any more: but judge this rather, that no man put a stumblingblock or an occasion to fall in his brother's way" (Ro.14:13).

"Therefore judge nothing before the time, until the Lord come, who both will bring to light the hidden things of darkness, and will make manifest the counsels of the hearts: and then shall every man have praise of God" (1 Co.4:5).

"Ye lust, and have not: ye kill, and desire to have, and cannot obtain: ye fight and war, yet ye have not, because ye ask not" (Js.4:2).

Thought 1. True love sacrifices self, gives of itself—all that one is and has. Love is not really shown when we give only what we can afford. It is when we sacrifice, dig deep into our lives and money, giving of ourselves all we are and have, that we really show love. The more we sacrifice, the more we demonstrate our love.

Thought 2. There is a strong message in Mary's act—a strong message on giving much and giving sacrificially. But note: the gift and sacrifice were made out of a heart of genuine love and faith in Christ. This is the most important thing to keep in mind about Mary's gift: her heart and life were wholly focused upon Christ.

Thought 3. Sacrifice is sometimes more important than common sense. Sometimes sacrifice should take precedence over common sense. Sometimes common sense must be stretched into sacrifice. Sacrifice is what brings about enlarged horizons, growth, development, advancement, more and more of whatever we are doing. In fact, the more we sacrifice under God's care, the more growth, development, and advancement we see. Name the field, name the area, name the work—the principle holds truth. The more we (or society) sacrifice under God's care, the more advancement we witness. There is a place for common sense, but there is a greater place for sacrifice.

However, there is one area that we often shrink from and ignore and do not allow the principle to take effect: the area of giving money or of tithing. We do not want our *easy living* and wealth to be touched. Because of evil hearts, men have allowed money and the power to purchase to become the object and judge of life. Too often a man's image, esteem, power, influence, and rights are determined by how much he has.

4 (26:10-11) **Love—Works—Service**: the anointing was a grasping of opportunity. The disciples censored Mary and condemned her act, but Christ defended her. He gave two reasons why Mary's act was justified.

a. Mary's anointing was a *good work*, a work poured out upon Him *personally*; that is, it was a *personal* gift. Yes, it was an extravagant gift, but it was a gift to Christ Himself. It was not a gift to an idea or program of His. This fact, that it was done to Him personally, makes the difference.

b. Mary's opportunity to show her love for Christ would not always be present. Christ was soon to be gone and ascended to the Father. Bodily, He would not be present for Mary to show her love. The poor would always be present to whom Mary could minister, but not Jesus. He would be gone. If she were ever going to demonstrate her love and faith, she had to do it now. The opportunity had to be grasped now; it would soon be gone.

"Jesus saith unto them, My meat is to do the will of him that sent me, and to finish his work" (Jn.4:34).

"I must work the works of him that sent me, while it is day: the night cometh, when no man can work" (Jn.9:4).

"Redeeming the time, because the days are evil" (Ep.5:16).

"Brethren, I count not myself to have apprehended: but this one thing I do, forgetting those things which are behind, and reaching forth unto those things which are before, I press toward the mark for the prize of the high calling of God in Christ Jesus" (Ph.3:13-14).

"Walk in wisdom toward them that are without, redeeming the time" (Col.4:5).

Thought 1. Note four lessons.
  (1) Opportunities do pass. In fact, they pass ever so rapidly. If we do not act and act immediately, we miss the chance forever. The privilege of witnessing, helping, growing, advancing, improving, and discovering—on and on the opportunities arise. If we fail to act, the opportunities pass on never to return, and we lose the chance to ever reach out and help and improve.
  (2) The great tragedy of most lives can be summed up in two simple words: missed opportunity.
  (3) What others think, even their condemnation and censorship, should never keep us from showing our love and faith in the Lord Jesus. Our witness should always be strong for Christ, just as strong as Mary's was: strong in grace and kindness, in courage and unashamedness.
  (4) Our works and gifts should first of all be given to Christ personally. Our thoughts should be upon Him, concentrating and not wandering as we serve and give. They should be performed and given as though they were being laid at His feet.

5 (26:12) **Jesus Christ, Death**: the anointing pointed toward the burial of Jesus, that is, His death. This is exactly what Christ said: "She did it for my burial." Some commentators think that Mary knew what she was doing, that she understood what Christ had been predicting, that He was to die soon. They feel Mary grasped the fact when others did not, but this is unlikely. The atmosphere surrounding the Lord's followers was that the kingdom was about to be set up. However, whether she knew what she was doing or not, Christ took her act and *applied it* to His death. He said that her love and faith and the anointing of His body pointed toward His death. In simple terms, Mary's love and faith, gift and anointing was *a witness of anticipation*. She was witnessing to the Lord's death by looking ahead to it.

Today, the believer's love and faith, gift and anointing *are a witness of fact*. The believer is to witness to the Lord's death by looking back to it. It is a fact: He did die for the sins of the world (see 1 Jn.2:1-2).

> "But God commendeth his love toward us, in that, while we were yet sinners, Christ died for us" (Ro.5:8).
>
> "For I delivered unto you first of all that which I also received, how that Christ died for our sins according to the scriptures; and that he was buried, and that he rose again the third day according to the scriptures" (1 Co.15:3-4).
>
> "Who his own self bare our sins in his own body on the tree, that we, being dead to sins, should live unto righteousness: by whose stripes ye were healed" (1 Pe.2:24).
>
> "For Christ also hath once suffered for sins, the just for the unjust, that he might bring us to God, being put to death in the flesh, but quickened by the Spirit" (1 Pe.3:18).
>
> "My little children, these things write I unto you, that ye sin not. And if any man sin, we have an advocate with the Father, Jesus Christ the righteous: and he is the propitiation for our sins: and not for ours only, but also for the sins of the whole world" (1 Jn.2:1-2).

Thought 1. Every act of love and faith for Christ is a witness to Christ's death, and the more we sacrifice in giving money and in working, the stronger our witness is to His death. The depth and strength of our belief in His death can be measured by the depth and strength of our sacrifice. The death of Christ would be seen much clearer if we demonstrated stronger love and faith in Him, or to put it another way, if we sacrificed more for Him.

Thought 2. Mary witnessed and pointed to the Lord's death by honoring and anointing His body publicly. We witness and point to the Lord's death by honoring and anointing (proclaiming) the fact of His death.

6 (26:13) **Devotion**: the anointing was an eternal memorial. Christ honored Mary because she had so greatly honored Him.

Several things about Mary stand as an ideal for all: her deep love and faith in Christ, her sacrificial gift, her courage in proclaiming her strong love and faith by anointing Jesus before a room full of men. Such devotion and love could not be allowed to fade from history. Christ memorialized it. He will memorialize the faith and love of any believer who so sacrifices for Him—throughout all of eternity.

> "Verily I say unto you, Wheresoever this gospel shall be preached in the whole world, there shall also this, that this woman hath done, be told for a memorial of her" (Mt.26:13).
>
> "When I call to remembrance the unfeigned faith that is in thee, which dwelt first in thy grandmother Lois, and thy mother Eunice; and I am persuaded that in thee also" (2 Ti.1:5).
>
> "Surely he shall not be moved for ever: the righteous shall be in everlasting remembrance" (Ps.112:6).
>
> "The memory of the just is blessed: but the name of the wicked shall rot" (Pr.10:7).

Thought 1. Mary proclaimed the gospel, the death of Christ from a heart of love and faith. This is what Christ wants: hearts that love and believe Him and will proclaim His death. Thus, He has seen to it that Mary's act lives on eternally.

MATTHEW 26:14-16

	C. The Messiah Betrayed by Judas: The Picture of a Ruined Life, 26:14-16 (Mk 14:10-11; Lu 22:3-6)
1. Picture 1: A great call rejected	14 Then one of the twelve, called Judas Iscariot, went unto the chief priests,
2. Picture 2: The gnawing sin of greed & the love of money	15 And said *unto them,* What will ye give me, and I will deliver him unto you? And they covenanted with him for thirty pieces of silver.
3. Picture 3: Deceit & intrigue	16 And from that time he sought opportunity to betray him.

DIVISION XVI

THE MESSIAH'S ARREST, TRIAL, AND CRUCIFIXION, 26:1–27:66

C. The Messiah Betrayed by Judas: The Picture of a Ruined Life, 26:14-16

(26:14-16) **Introduction**: Judas stands as a great warning to every man including the strongest believer. Judas was one of the original twelve apostles chosen by Christ. He was a man with so much potential that he was chosen to serve with God's very own Son during His earthly journey, but he failed and came ever so short. Just why he failed needs to be closely studied and heeded by all.
1. Picture 1: a great call rejected (v.14).
2. Picture 2: the gnawing sin of greed and the love of money (v.15).
3. Picture 3: deceit and intrigue (v.16).

1 (26:14) **Judas**: the first picture is that of Judas' great call. Judas' great tragedy was his failure as one of the twelve apostles. Just think about the fact. Judas had been personally chosen by Christ. He had some great potential, some unique qualities that attracted the Lord. Therefore, the Lord gave Judas the most honored opportunity in all the world to develop his abilities—the privilege of walking with Him personally.
⇒ Judas knew Christ face to face.
⇒ Judas walked with Christ day after day.
⇒ Judas heard most, if not all, that Christ taught.
⇒ Judas saw most, if not all, that Christ did.
⇒ Judas was trained to be an apostle by Christ Himself.
⇒ Judas served as an apostle, even on witnessing tours, under Christ's personal command (Mk.6:7f).
⇒ Judas was warned of sin's consequences by Christ Himself.

Nevertheless, despite all the opportunities, Judas' life was a terrible tragedy. He was so gifted and had so much opportunity, yet he lost it all. Why? Simply because he turned his back on the Lord Jesus Christ. He went to "the chief priests" of this earth and put his fate into their hands instead of placing his life into the hands of Christ. He had allowed his craving for more and more to blind him to the truth about Christ—that He was truly the Son of God who demanded loyalty, even when man could not understand the events and happenings that surrounded Him (see note—Mt.26:15. This note will explain what is behind this statement.) Judas simply did not believe that Christ was truly God's Son. Therefore, he did not give his heart and life to Christ—not really. He was a follower of Christ; he was even one of the first twelve apostles, but he was not a genuine believer who entrusted his life to Christ.

"But it shall not be so among you: but whosoever will be great among you, let him be your minister; and whosoever will be chief among you, let him be your servant: even as the Son of man came not to be ministered unto, but to minister, and to give his life a ransom for many" (Mt.20:26-28).

"And whosoever shall exalt himself shall be abased; and he that shall humble himself shall be exalted" (Mt.23:12).

"And he said to them all, If any man will come after me, let him deny himself, and take up his cross daily, and follow me" (Lu.9:23).

"How can ye believe, which receive honour one of another, and seek not the honour that cometh from God only?" (Jn.5:44).

Thought 1. Judas' great potential and terrible tragedy teaches so much.
(1) It is not ability, but availability that counts.
(2) Gifts do not assure permanent success; Christ alone assures permanent (eternal) success.

(3) Walking among godly people does not assure salvation; allowing Christ to enter one's heart and life is the only assurance of salvation.
(4) Christ sees the potential of every man's gifts. What is lacking is man's seeing the necessity of Christ in the use of his gifts.

Thought 2. Think of the people who have heard the truth of Christ time after time, yet they still have not trusted Him as the Son of God. They are traitors, having turned their backs upon God; therefore, they are guilty of high treason against God.

2 (26:15) **Judas Iscariot**: the second picture is Judas' gnawing sin of greed and love of money. Various commentators give different reasons why Judas betrayed Christ, but Scripture clearly says that the reason was greed: "What will ye give me, and I will give [betray] Him to you."

Judas' gnawing greed was a *growing* sin. This is seen by looking at what is said about him in the Scripture.

a. Judas was chosen by Christ to be an apostle (Mt.10:4); therefore, we know he was sincere in the beginning. There was something within Judas—qualities that attracted Christ, qualities that Christ knew could mean a lot to the Kingdom of God.

b. Judas was a man gifted in financial affairs, apparently even more so than Matthew, the wealthy tax collector, and the businessmen among the apostles such as Peter, James, and John (see Master Subject Index under each name for discussions on their business backgrounds). Among all these, Judas was placed in charge of the Lord's funds and the purchasing of whatever was needed (Jn.12:6; 13:29; see Lu.8:2-3 for some who supported Jesus' ministry). His appointment from among so many was bound to be due to unusual spiritual qualities as well as to unusual ability in financial management.

c. Judas, at some unknown point, began to embezzle from the Lord's funds. John says unmistakably that Judas was a thief (Jn.12:6). John relates this fact when he says that Judas was greatly disturbed with Mary, the sister of Martha. Mary used some very expensive perfume to anoint Christ instead of selling it to secure money for the Lord's treasury. John says the reason for Judas' disturbance was because Judas was a thief and could have embezzled some of the money (Jn.12:5-6).

d. Judas refused to repent, and he hardened his heart more and more in his sin. Christ knew of Judas' embezzlement and hinted at it, giving Judas opportunity after opportunity to repent.

> "But there are some of you that believe not. For Jesus knew from the beginning who they were that believed not, and who should betray him...Jesus answered them, have not I chosen you twelve, and one of you is a devil? He spake of Judas Iscariot the son of Simon: for he it was that should betray him, being one of the twelve" (Jn.6:64, 70-71).

Judas was bound to feel the pangs of guilt at such times, yet he continued to deceive himself that Christ did not really know and had no real proof. Judas kept right on taking what he felt he could safely embezzle, hardening his heart more and more.

e. Judas apparently followed Christ out of a heart of greed and worldly ambition, and not out of a heart of love and faith in Him as the Son of God. This seems to be indicated by two facts.

  1) He felt that wealth, power, and position would be his when Christ set up his kingdom. The other apostles thought the same, but there was a vast difference. They mistook the Messiah's method of saving the world, not His person; whereas Judas mistook both the Lord's method and person. He did not believe and trust the Lord to be the Son of God. The others did.

  2) He apparently was disillusioned with Christ after the triumphal entry. Christ did not immediately set up His kingdom, and as the days passed, the fact that He was not going to set up His kingdom became more and more apparent. The authorities were mobilizing against Christ to kill Him, and it seemed as though they were going to be successful. Jesus had even been teaching that they were to be successful. He was to be killed by their hands (see Mt.26:1-2).

  Judas became convinced that he was mistaken about Christ. Christ was not the real Messiah. He was just another mistaken self-proclaimed messiah. He was doomed, and there was no way out. Judas experienced his dreams of wealth, power, and position with Christ being shattered. Thus what he was trying to do was to get what he could out of the situation. He wanted to be in good standing with what he perceived to be the winning side.

f. Judas filled his heart with the lust for more and more instead of filling it with Christ. He went too long without repenting and letting Christ in his life, and the devil was able to fill his being. The devil blinded and took control of his thoughts (Lu.22:3). Hence Judas was able to justify his betrayal in his own mind. He was, after all, helping the leading religionists of his day as well as himself. Thus he betrayed Jesus of Nazareth, who apparently in Judas' mind was just another mistaken self-proclaimed messiah.

In looking at the bargain to which Judas agreed in betraying Christ, thirty pieces of silver seems to be a small price for betraying someone of the Lord's stature. It amounted to only about four to five months' wages. However, two things need to be kept in mind.

1. Judas probably expected to get much more. But he did not dictate the terms, the chief priests did. They were going to arrest Christ in just a few days anyway, just as soon as the pilgrims left the city (Mt.26:5). All Judas did was move their schedule up a few days.

2. Judas felt Christ was doomed, without any hope of escape. Again, he had become convinced that Christ was not the true Messiah, but just another mistaken self-proclaimed messiah. There is a possibility that Judas betrayed Christ because he was angry for having been deceived as well as for having been disillusioned. He was willing to get what he could, no matter how small the amount.

MATTHEW 26:14-16

"And he said unto them, Take heed, and beware of covetousness: for a man's life consisteth not in the abundance of the things which he possesseth" (Lu.12:15).

"For the love of money is the root of all evil: which while some coveted after, they have erred from the faith, and pierced themselves through with many sorrows" (1 Ti.6:10).

"Your gold and silver is cankered; and the rust of them shall be a witness against you, and shall eat your flesh as it were fire. Ye have heaped treasure together for the last days" (Js.5:3).

"He that is greedy of gain troubleth his own house; but he that hateth gifts shall live" (Pr.15:27).

"Yea, they are greedy dogs which can never have enough, and they are shepherds that cannot understand: they all look to their own way, every one for his gain, from his quarter" (Is.56:11).

Thought 1. Greed is a growing sin. It has to be fed to grow. Desire for things is normal and natural. It is when we feed the desire time and again, indulging and hoarding more and more, that our desire becomes sin and grows and grows (see notes—Js.4:1-6. These notes will stir additional thoughts for application in dealing with desires and lust.)

Thought 2. Greed is very dangerous. It is one of the most dangerous sins.
⇒ Greed enslaves quickly.
⇒ Greed can lead to all other sins.
⇒ Greed can make a person sell his country, body, or friends—anything and anyone—all for greed.

Thought 3. Covetousness, the desire for more and more, will eat at us just like a cancer. Judas had what he needed: food, clothing, housing, purpose, meaning, and significance. He did not go without. What was he after? The sin of lust—lusting for more and more—ate away at him, causing him to put his hand into the till.

Thought 4. It is not money that is sinful. It is the love of money (1 Ti.6:10). Money is a *thing*; it is inanimate, lifeless. It has no feelings, no desires, no will to act. Man is the culprit. Man is the one who lusts for more and more; thus man is the one who sins, not a piece of paper or metal.

Thought 5. Many follow Christ not out of a deep conviction and belief but out of the desire to get what they can out of Him. They are religious in order to *fit in* with a so-called Christian society. They want to promote themselves or their business within the community. To profess Christ and to belong to a church is the thing to do. But their profession in Christ does not hamper their human lusts at all. They live just as all other men live, paying little if any attention to true morality and just relationships, pure behavior and honest dealing, clean living and fair treatment.

Thought 6. Judas allowed his strength to become his weakness. This is often true with us.
⇒ Gifts of administration can lead to being overbearing.
⇒ Gifts of speaking can lead to being super-spiritual.
⇒ Gifts of leadership can lead to being self-seeking.
⇒ Gifts of loveliness can lead to being sensual.
⇒ Gifts of humility can lead to no service.

3 (26:16) **Judas**: the third picture is that of Judas's carrying out a deceitful intrigue against Christ. Note the words "He sought opportunity to betray Him." The picture is that of being on the prowl, searching and seeking, looking here and there for the right moment. Judas' heart was set, full of intrigue, plotting evil and planning its strategy. He did not believe Jesus was the Son of God, but he did not stop at unbelief. He willed to do evil against Christ, to hurt Him and to destroy Him, and he sought opportunity to do so. Just how deceitful Judas was can be seen by noticing that immediately after bargaining with the authorities, he sat down to eat with Jesus. He sat at the very table where the Lord's Supper was being instituted.

Thought 1. Judas not only rejected but also sought to destroy Jesus. Many reject Christ, but they do not all seek to harm and destroy Him. Some do, but not all.
⇒ Some curse Him, consciously and unconsciously dishonoring His name.
⇒ Some talk and teach against His divine nature, that He is the Son of God.
⇒ Some talk and teach against the written revelation of Christ Himself and the truth, that is, the Word.
⇒ Some talk and teach against His active presence in the life of the genuine believer.

"Beware of false prophets, which come to you in sheep's clothing, but inwardly they are ravening wolves" (Mt.7:15).

"Now the Spirit speaketh expressly, that in the latter times some shall depart from the faith, giving heed to seducing spirits, and doctrines of devils; speaking lies in hypocrisy; having their conscience seared with a hot iron" (1 Ti.4:1-2).

"This know also, that in the last days perilous times shall come. For men shall be lovers of their own selves, covetous, boasters, proud, blasphemers, disobedient to parents, unthankful, unholy, without natural affection, trucebreakers, false accusers, incontinent, fierce, despisers of those that are good, traitors, heady, highminded, lovers of pleasures more than lovers of God; having a form of godliness, but denying the power thereof: from such turn away" (2 Ti.3:1-5).

Thought 2. Note something: even after Judas' bargain to betray Christ, Christ gave him opportunity to repent.

MATTHEW 26:17-30

	D. The Messiah's Last Supper: The Lord's Supper Instituted, 26:17-30 (Mk 14:12-26; Lu 22:7-23; Jn 13:1-30)	with me in the dish, the same shall betray me. 24 The Son of man goeth as it is written of him: but woe unto that man by whom the Son of man is betrayed! it had been good for that man if he had not been born.	b. He warned the sinner of terrible judgment
1. The Lord's Supper was based upon the Passover^{DS1} a. Christ tied the Lord's Supper to the Feast of Unleavened Bread	17 Now the first *day* of the *feast of* unleavened bread the disciples came to Jesus, saying unto him, Where wilt thou that we prepare for thee to eat the passover?	25 Then Judas, which betrayed him, answered and said, Master, is it I? He said unto him, Thou hast said.	c. He identified the sinner
b. Christ tied the Lord's Supper to His death: His "appointed time was near"	18 And he said, Go into the city to such a man, and say unto him, The Master saith, My time is at hand; I will keep the passover at thy house with my disciples.	26 And as they were eating, Jesus took bread, and blessed *it,* and brake *it,* and gave *it* to the disciples, and said, Take, eat; this is my body.	3. The Lords' Supper was given as a permanent ordinance a. Christ took the bread, gave thanks, broke it, & distributed it: His body^{DS2}
c. Christ tied the Lord's Supper to religious obedience: "I am going to celebrate the passover"	19 And the disciples did as Jesus had appointed them; and they made ready the passover.	27 And he took the cup, and gave thanks, and gave *it* to them, saying, Drink ye all of it;	b. Christ took the cup, gave thanks, & distributed it: His blood^{DS3}

2. The Lord's Supper was used as an appeal to a sinner
  a. He revealed the treachery
    1) The sinner was a disciple
	20 Now when the even was come, he sat down with the twelve.
	21 And as they did eat, he said, Verily I say unto you, that one of you shall betray me.
		28 For this is my blood of the new testament, which is shed for many for the remission of sins.
		29 But I say unto you, I will not drink henceforth of this fruit of the vine, until that day when I drink it new with you in my Father's kingdom.
			c. Christ instituted a new covenant: Forgiveness^{DS4}
			
			  d. Christ promised to celebrate the supper with His followers in the future

2) The revelation caused a stir 3) The sinner committed a monstrous deception	22 And they were exceeding sorrowful, and began every one of them to say unto him, Lord, is it I? 23 And he answered and said, He that dippeth *his* hand	30 And when they had sung an hymn, they went out into the mount of Olives.	e. Christ & His disciples sang a hymn & departed

DIVISION XVI

THE MESSIAH'S ARREST, TRIAL, AND CRUCIFIXION, 26:1–27:66

D. The Messiah's Last Supper: The Lord's Supper Instituted, 26:17-30

(26:17-30) **Introduction—The Lord's Supper—The Passover**: this is the passage where Christ instituted the Lord's Supper, one of the ordinances which He charged His followers to practice on a regular basis (Mt.26:2). He instituted the Supper in verses 26-30. Note that the preparations made in verses 17-25 are the preparations for the Passover. The disciples knew nothing about the Lord's intentions to institute a new ordinance in His name. They thought Christ was preparing to celebrate the Jewish Passover. This is significant, for it shows that Christ tied both His death and the Lord's Supper to the Passover. By so doing, Christ was saying two things.

1. Jewish tradition held that the Messiah was going to redeem Israel during the Passover. In fact, they believed He would redeem them on the very day that God delivered Israel out of Egyptian bondage. By tying His supper to the Passover, Christ was proclaiming Himself to be the Messiah whom Israel anticipated.

2. The sacrificial lamb used in the Passover was a picture of Christ, the Lamb of God, sacrificing Himself for man. By instituting the Lord's Supper on this day, Christ was not only tying His death to the Passover, He was proclaiming two new things:

  a. He was proclaiming Himself to be the Lamb of God who was to be slain for the sins of men.

  b. He was proclaiming the Lord's Supper to be the new celebration which was to be observed by His followers. The Lord's Supper was to replace the Passover, a man's celebration of God's deliverance from bondage.

1. The Lord's Supper was based upon the Passover (vv.17-19).
2. The Lord's Supper was used as an appeal to a sinner (vv.20-25).
3. The Lord's Supper was given as a permanent ordinance (vv.26-30).

[1] (26:17-19) **Lord's Supper—Passover**: the Lord's Supper is based upon and tied to the Passover.

a. The Lord's Supper is tied to the *Feast of Unleavened Bread*, to the first day of the Feast, the day of preparation and the sacrifice of the lamb (see DEEPER STUDY # 1—Mt.26:17).

  1) It was on the first day of the Feast that the disciples came to Christ. Again, they knew nothing about Christ's plans to institute a new celebration. They just assumed He was going to celebrate the Passover as always. But by

instituting the Lord's Supper on this day, Christ definitely tied the Supper to the Passover (see Deeper Study # 1—Mt.26:17).

2) It was the disciples who came to Christ. Christ did not have to approach them. They knew that it was His practice to observe the celebration.

3) Christ faced *great difficulty* in observing the celebration. He had no home, no place of His own for the observance. But there was a much greater obstacle confronting Him at this particular celebration: enemies within the city were seeking to kill Him. Note His faithfulness in observing the celebration despite this fact.

b. The Lord's Supper is tied to *Christ's death*. Christ said "My time is at hand." "My time" or "My hour" is a term which Christ constantly used to refer to His death (see note, pt.2—Jn.2:3-5). He tied His death to the Passover with the words, "My time [death] is at hand; I will keep the Passover." And, of course, His death is what the Lord's Supper celebrates (vv.26-28).

c. The Lord's Supper is tied to *religious obedience*. Christ said, "I will keep the Passover." Jewish tradition held that the Messiah was going to redeem Israel during the Passover. In fact, the Jews believed the Messiah would redeem them on the very day God delivered Israel out of bondage to Egypt. By obeying this religious celebration, the Passover, Christ was doing three significant things.

1) He was proclaiming Himself to be the Messiah whom Israel had always anticipated.
2) He was, again, definitely tying the Lord's Supper to the Passover.
3) He was stressing the importance of *religious obedience*, that is, being obedient in celebrating the Lord's Supper.

Thought 1. Christ kept the Passover. *Religious obedience* is important to God; therefore, we are to be obedient and faithful to religious observances. Note how Christ was faithful in His observance, even in the face of death. What a rebuke to us—we who allow the comfort of our homes, the enjoyment of our recreation, the pleasing of our flesh to keep us away from the Lord's Supper and other religious observances!

"He that hath my commandments, and keepeth them, he it is that loveth me: and he that loveth me shall be loved of my Father, and I will love him, and will manifest myself to him" (Jn.14:21).

"Jesus answered and said unto him, If a man love me, he will keep my words: and my Father will love him, and we will come unto him, and make our abode with him" (Jn.14:23).

"If ye keep my commandments, ye shall abide in my love; even as I have kept my Father's commandments, and abide in his love" (Jn.15:10).

"Ye are my freinds, if ye do whatsoever I command you" (Jn.15:14).

"For as often as ye eat this bread, and drink this cup, ye do show the Lord's death till he come" (1 Co.11:26).

"Though he were a Son, yet learned he obedience by the things which he suffered" (He.5:8).

Thought 2. The Lord's "time was at hand." He had to grasp the opportunity while it was at hand. So must we. But the day is coming when it will be too late to celebrate the Lord's Supper. We must celebrate it while we can.

DEEPER STUDY # 1
(26:17) Feast of Unleavened Bread: this feast is another name for the Passover Feast (see Le.23:5-8; Lu.22:1). However, on the first day of the Passover week, the Feast of Unleavened Bread had special significance. It was the day that all preparations were made to celebrate the Passover. (See Deeper Study # 1—Mt.26:2; see Ex.12:1-51, esp. 11-28 for the background of the Passover.) Preparations included securing the lamb and taking it to the temple to be sacrificed. Preparations also included securing the food and drink items necessary for the Passover and arranging the room for the Feast. But there were two preparations for which the Feast of Unleavened Bread received its name.

1. There was the baking of unleavened bread. On the very night of the Passover, God had told Israel to make final preparations for being delivered from Egyptian bondage. But the Israelites did not have time to bake leavened bread. They had to bake bread without leaven because of the time it takes for leavened bread to rise. The Feast of Unleavened Bread was simply one of the Passover ceremonies by which Israel remembered God's glorious deliverance of their forefathers from Egyptian bondage. (See Deeper Study # 1—Mt.26:2.)

2. There was a ceremony by which all leaven within the house had to be removed. It must be remembered that leaven was a symbol of evil to the Jews. Therefore, in removing all leaven, they were picturing the need for putting evil out of their lives and households. There was an actual search made throughout the rooms of the house looking for any crumb of leaven that might have fallen upon the floor or between some furniture. Whatever leaven was found, no matter how small a crumb, it was removed from the house. By removing all leaven from their households, the Jews were saying they wanted to be included among the faithful of their forefathers, the faithful who had cleansed their lives and households for the journey of deliverance from bondage.

---

2 **(26:20-25) Judas—Lord's Supper**: the Lord's Supper was used as an appeal to a sinner. Christ used the occasion of the Supper to appeal to Judas. He gave Judas a last chance to repent of his sin. Christ took three steps with Judas.

a. Christ revealed the sin and the treachery of Judas. It was a shock, for the Lord said the betrayer was a disciple: "One of you shall betray me" (v.21). It was treachery and deception. Judas had tried to hide his sin, and he had done a good job. No one knew about his plot, not even the disciples, his closest associates. But Jesus knew.

The apostles were, of course, stirred: "exceeding sorrowful" (v.22). They became so heavily burdened over the news that they began to question their own loyalty. "Is it I?" each began to ask.

The sinner committed a monstrous deception (v.23). It was the one who "dippeth his hand with me in the dish." Imagine the deception: the sinner sat with Christ, partook of the Lord's Last Supper, plotted and was guilty of the most terrible sin.

MATTHEW 26:17-30

"Yea, mine own familiar friend, in whom I trusted, which did eat of my bread, hath lifted up his heel against me" (Ps.41:9).

b. Christ warned the sinner of terrible judgment (v.24). Jesus knew the destiny of the sinner, the terrible fate that awaited him. It would have been better had the sinner never been born.

c. Christ identified the sinner (v.25). He answered Judas, letting him know that his sin was not hid. Christ knew. Note what Judas called Christ: "Rabbi," teacher. The other disciples had called Him, "Lord" (v.22).

"I tell you, Nay: but, except ye repent, ye shall all likewise perish" (Lu.13:3, 5).

"Repent ye therefore, and be converted, that your sins may be blotted out, when the times of refreshing shall come from the presence of the Lord" (Ac.3:19).

"Repent therefore of this thy wickedness, and pray God, if perhaps the thought of thine heart may be forgiven thee" (Ac.8:22).

Thought 1. The Lord's Supper is an occasion that speaks to sinners. It can be used to point out sin for which Christ died and to warn about the consequences of sin if a person does not repent.

Thought 2. Judas sat at Jesus' Last Supper, and he deceptively partook of it with sin in his life. Too many believers do the same. Their close associates and fellow believers may be deceived, but not God. He knows all about the sin.

Thought 3. Judas deceived the apostles. People can deceive others, even family and friends, and never be discovered, but God knows the heart and the sin.

Thought 4. The disciples examined themselves. They looked at themselves to see if they were the sinner. Believers are exhorted to examine themselves before partaking of the Supper (1 Co.11:27-28). Examining oneself is necessary. No believer is sinless nor beyond sin. The exhortation is clear: "Be not highminded, but fear" (Ro.11:20).

Thought 5. Christ revealed that He was to be betrayed in order to strengthen the faith of the disciples (Jn.13:19). He revealed His omniscience, that He was truly God (see Jn.14:29).

Thought 6. Note how Judas tried to continue His deception. Even after the Lord had revealed that a sinner sat among them, Judas turned to the Lord and asked, "Is it I?" How like so many! They continue to deceive and deceive, ever seeking to satisfy the lust of their sin.

Thought 7. Judas illustrated a significant point: the reason for continuous sin. The reason was unbelief in Jesus. Jesus was not *Lord* to Judas. To Judas Jesus was only a man, a misguided and self-proclaimed messiah (see outline and notes—Mt.26:14-16).

3 (26:26-30) **Lord's Supper**: the Lord's Supper was given as a permanent ordinance.

a. It was while *they were eating* the Passover meal that Christ instituted the Lord's Supper. He was replacing the Passover with the Lord's Supper. The Lord's Supper is the new ordinance of God to celebrate His deliverance of man from bondage and slavery (see DEEPER STUDY # 1—Mt.26:2).

b. In God's eternal plan, the sacrificial lamb used in the Passover had always been a picture of Christ, the real Lamb of God who was to be sacrificed for man. By instituting the Lord's Supper during the Passover meal, Christ was not only tying His Supper to the Passover, He was proclaiming Himself to be the Lamb of God who was to be slain for the sins of men (vv.27-28; see 1 Co.5:7; Re.13:8).

c. Christ instituted the Lord's Supper before He died, not after His resurrection. This is very significant. It means that His death was voluntary. He had not yet died; He did not have to die. He could have slipped out of town and escaped, but He chose to willingly lay down His life for the sins of men. Therefore, the Lord's Supper is the great celebration of *the voluntary* sacrifice of God's Son for man. The broken bread and poured wine picture the *willingness* of God's Son to lay down His life for man's sins.

Christ instituted the Lord's Supper by doing five things.

1. Christ took the bread, His body, and He gave thanks, broke it, and gave it to the disciples (v.26).
    a. By taking the bread into His hands, Christ was indicating that His death was a voluntary act. His destiny was in His hands.

"As the Father knoweth me, even so know I the Father: and I lay down my life for the sheep" (Jn.10:15).

"Therefore doth my Father love me, because I lay down my life, that I might take it again. No man taketh it from me, but I lay it down of myself. I have power to lay it down, and I have power to take it again. This commandment have I received of my Father" (Jn.10:17-18).

b. By giving thanks, Christ was offering praise for deliverance and for a life full of provision, a provision that came from God Himself.

c. By breaking the bread, Christ was saying that His body was to be broken and sacrificed as a victim for man's deliverance (Is.53:5). This act was so significant that the early church sometimes called the Lord's Supper simply

MATTHEW 26:17-30

"the breaking of bread" (Ac.2:42, 46; 1 Co.10:16). Under the Old Testament, the broken bread pictured the sufferings of the Israelites. Now, under the New Testament, the bread is to picture the broken body of Christ (1 Co.11:24).

"But he was wounded for our transgressions, he was bruised for our iniquities: the chastisement of our peace was upon him; and with his stripes we are healed" (Is.53:5).

d. By giving the bread and saying, "Take, eat, this is my body," Christ was saying that He is to be received into a man's life. And that moment of redemption is to be remembered in this ordinance (see note—Mt.26:26).

"This is the bread which cometh down from heaven, that a man may eat thereof, and not die. I am the living bread which came down from heaven: if any man eat of this bread, he shall live for ever: and the bread that I will give is my flesh, which I will give for the life of the world" (Jn.6:50-51).

2. Christ took the cup, gave thanks, and gave it to the disciples (v.27).
   a. By taking the cup into His own hands, Christ was again teaching that His death was voluntary (see Jn.10:11, 17-18).
   b. By giving thanks, Christ was again expressing praise and appreciation for deliverance promised through sacrifice.
   c. By giving the cup and saying, "Drink ye all of it," Christ was again saying that He must become a part of man's very being if man wished deliverance. Note: the word "gave" (edoken) is in the Greek aorist tense which means that Christ gave the cup *once for all*. He died once and only once, and man partakes of His death once and only once.

"Knowing this, that our old man is crucified with him, that the body of sin might be destroyed, that henceforth we should not serve sin" (Ro.6:6).
"For in that he died, he died unto sin once: but in that he liveth, he liveth unto God" (Ro.6:10).

3. Christ instituted a new covenant: forgiveness (v.28). Note the Lord's exact words.
   a. "This is my blood." His blood was to become the sign and symbol of the new covenant. His blood was to take the place of the sacrificial lamb of the Passover.
   b. "The new testament." His blood, the sacrifice of His life, established a New Testament, a new covenant between God and man (see He.9:11-15). Faith in His blood and sacrifice is the way man is to approach God. Before, under the Old Testament, a man who wanted a right relationship with God approached God through the sacrifice of an animal's blood. The Old Testament believer believed that God accepted him because of the sacrifice of the animal. Now, under the New Testament, the believer believes that God accepts him because of the sacrifice of Christ. This is what Christ said: "This is my blood of the New Testament, which is shed for many for the remission of sins" (see Deeper Study # 4—Mt.26:28; see Ep.1:7; 1 Jn.2:1-2; He.9:22). A man's sins are forgiven and he becomes acceptable to God by believing that Christ's blood was shed for him (1 Jn.1:7. See Deeper Study # 2, *Justification*—Ro.4:22; 5:1.)

"In whom we have redemption through his blood, the forgiveness of sins, according to the riches of his grace" (Ep.1:7).
"But if we walk in the light, as he is in the light, we have fellowship one with another, and the blood of Jesus Christ his Son cleanseth us from all sin" (1 Jn.1:7).
"My little children, these things write I unto you, that ye sin not. And if any man sin, we have an advocate with the Father, Jesus Christ the righteous: and he is the propitiation for our sins: and not for ours only, but also for the sins of the whole world" (1 Jn.2:1-2).
"Whoso eateth my flesh, and drinketh my blood, hath eternal life; and I will raise him up at the last day. For my flesh is meat indeed, and my blood is drink indeed. He that eateth my flesh, and drinketh my blood, dwelleth in me, and I in him. As the living Father hath sent me, and I live by the Father: so he that eateth me, even he shall live by me. This is the bread which came down from heaven: not as your fathers did eat manna, and are dead: he that eateth of this bread shall live for ever" (Jn.6:54-58).

   c. Now note the words, *Drink ye all of it*. A man must receive what Christ has done for him. He must drink, partake, absorb, assimilate Christ's blood into his life. That is, a man must believe and trust the death of Christ to forgive his sins. He must allow Christ's death to become the very nourishment, the innermost part and energy and flow of his life (see Deeper Study # 3—Mt.26:27-28).
4. Christ promised to celebrate the Supper with His followers in the future (v.29). This is the glorious promise to all genuine believers: they shall sit down with Christ at the great marriage Feast of the Lamb (see outline and notes—Mt.22:1-14). It is the promise of perfection and of being a part of the new heavens and earth, of sitting with Christ in the Kingdom of God which is to be established in the future (see Deeper Study # 3—Mt.19:23-24). Note that Christ again predicted His death.

"The Spirit itself beareth witness with our spirit, that we are the children of God: and if children, then heirs; heirs of God, and joint-heirs with Christ; is so be that we suffer with him, that we may be also glorified together" (Ro.8:16-17).
"When Christ, who is our life, shall appear, then shall ye also appear with him in glory" (Col.3:4).

"For our light affliction, which is but for a moment, worketh for us a far more exceeding and eternal weight of glory" (2 Co.4:17).

"The elders which are among you I exhort, who am also an elder, and a witness of the sufferings of Christ, and also a partaker of the glory that shall be revealed" (1 Pe.5:1).

"For so an entrance shall be ministered unto you abundantly into the everlasting kingdom of our Lord and Saviour Jesus Christ" (2 Pe.1:11).

5. Christ and His disciples sang a hymn and departed. Christ closed the Lord's Supper with a hymn. In the midst of great sorrow and perplexity, of a heavy and burdening atmosphere, Christ led His people in a hymn. It was probably the Hallel (Ps.115-118).

"These things have I spoken unto you, that my joy might remain in you, and that your joy might be full" (Jn.15:11).

"As sorrowful, yet alway rejoicing; as poor, yet making many rich; as having nothing, and yet possessing all things" (2 Co.6:10).

"Rejoice in the Lord alway: and again I say, Rejoice" (Ph.4:4).

"Let the word of Christ dwell in you richly in all wisdom; teaching and admonishing one another in psalms and hymns and spiritual songs, singing with grace in your hearts to the Lord" (Col.3:16).

Thought 1. How do we become sons or children of God and receive eternal life? Christ said (1) by receiving Him (Jn.1:12), and (2) by feeding upon Him (Jn.6:53-54, 57-58).

Thought 2. Under the Old Testament, the blood of Christ was symbolized in the blood of animals. Under the New Testament, the blood of Christ is symbolized in the wine of the Lord's Supper.

Thought 3. Note the glorious confidence and surety of Christ. In the face of being murdered, He promised that He would sit down with his followers in the coming kingdom. The death of Christ was not the end; it was the beginning of eternal life for the person who really believed in the death of Christ.

DEEPER STUDY # 2

(26:26) **Lord's Supper**: the words *Take, eat; this is my body* are not cannibalism (see outline and notes—Jn.6:52-58). The words simply mean that a man is to receive Christ into his life. A man's deliverance from the bondage of sin and death is by *taking or eating* of Christ's body. That is, the man must receive, partake, consume, absorb, and assimilate Christ into His life. He must allow Christ to become the very nourishment, the innermost part and energy, the very consumption of his being.

DEEPER STUDY # 3

(26:27-28) **Lord's Supper**: the words *Drink ye all of it* (the blood of Christ) mean to receive the death of Christ in place of one's own death. A man's deliverance from sin and death comes by receiving Christ's death as his own. The man must identify with Christ's death. He must drink, partake, absorb, and assimilate the Lord's death. The death of Christ must become the very nourishment, the innermost part and energy, the very flow of his life. (See 1 Co.2:2.)

DEEPER STUDY # 4

(26:28) **Forgiveness** (aphesin): to send off, to send away. The wrong is cut out, sent off, and sent away from the wrongdoer. The sin is separated from the sinner.

There are four main ideas in the Biblical concept of forgiveness.

1. There is the idea of why forgiveness is needed. Forgiveness is needed because of wrongdoing and guilt and the penalty arising from both (see Ro.3:23; 6:23; 8:1).

2. There is the idea of a *once-for-all* forgiveness, a total forgiveness. A man is *once-for-all* forgiven when he receives Jesus Christ as his Savior. Belief in Jesus Christ is the only condition for being forgiven *once-for-all* (Ep.1:7; Ro.4:5-8).

3. There is the idea of forgiveness that maintains fellowship. Fellowship exists between God as Father and the believer as His child. When the child does wrong, the fellowship is disturbed and broken. The condition for restoring the fellowship is confessing and forsaking the sin (Ps.66:18; Pr.28:13; 1 Jn.1:7).

4. There is the idea of a *releasing from guilt*. This is one of the differences between man's forgiving a man and God's forgiving a man. A man may forgive a person for wronging him, but he can never remove the guilt that his friend feels. And often he cannot remove the resentment he feels within his own heart. Only God can remove the guilt and assure the removal of resentment, and God does both. God forgives and erases the guilt and resentment (Ps.51:2, 7-12; 103:12; 1 Jn.1:9).

MATTHEW 26:31-35

	E. The Messiah Foretells the Disciples' Failure: Stumbling & Falling Away in Life, 26:31-35 (Mk 14:27-31; Lu 22:31-34; Jn 13:36-38)	Galilee. 33 Peter answered and said unto him, Though all *men* shall be offended because of thee, *yet* will I never be offended.	2. There is the claim of over-confidence
1. There is the prediction: All will fall away a. Fall away^{DS1} because of Christ b. Fall away because Christ is rejected c. The remedy: The Lord's resurrection^{DS2}	31 Then saith Jesus unto them, All ye shall be offended because of me this night: for it is written, I will smite the shepherd, and the sheep of the flock shall be scattered abroad. 32 But after I am risen again, I will go before you into	34 Jesus said unto him, Verily I say unto thee, That this night, before the cock crow, thou shalt deny me thrice. 35 Peter said unto him, Though I should die with thee, yet will I not deny thee. Likewise also said all the disciples.	a. Caused by comparing oneself with others b. Caused by being blind to the cross c. Caused by not knowing oneself, one's weak flesh d. Caused by contradicting Christ

DIVISION XVI

THE MESSIAH'S ARREST, TRIAL, AND CRUCIFIXION, 26:1–27:66

E. The Messiah Foretells the Disciples' Failure: Stumbling and Falling Away in Life, 26:31-35

(26:31-35) **Introduction**: one of the great convictions of believers is that they must warn the world of sin and its consequences. Yet in the midst of this warning and its fervor, something is often missed: believers, too, must be warned of sin and its consequences. Believers are not above sin; they are not removed from human flesh. However, there is something that makes them different: they have been given a spiritual nature. They now live *in the spirit* as well as *in the flesh*. The flesh is still with every believer. Therefore, every believer must be warned: here and there he will stumble and fall. But Christ is ever waiting to receive and forgive him if he will do but one thing: genuinely confess and repent. Such is the warning that Christ gives to His disciples in this most meaningful passage.

1. There is the prediction: all will fall away (vv.31-32).
2. There is the claim of over-confidence (vv.33-35).

(26:31-35) **Another Outline**: The Warning about Falling Away (Mt.26:31-35).
1. Some fall because they are offended *in* Christ (v.31).
2. Some fall because Christ is rejected by the crowd (v.31).
3. Some fall because they fail to see and believe the resurrection of Christ, (v.32).
4. Some fall because of over-confidence (v.33).
5. Some fall because they are blind to the cross (v.34).
6. Some fall because they do not know self, that is, the flesh (v.35).

1 (26:31-32) **Backsliding**: there is the prediction—*all* shall fall away. "All ye" is emphasized; not a single one will stand fast. Every disciple will fall away.

Christ shared two reasons why the disciples would fall away, two reasons that are common to every man.

a. "All shall be offended *because of me*" (en emoi, *in me*). Men question who Christ is, wondering about Him and sometimes being turned off by Him. The word offend means to stumble, to fall (see DEEPER STUDY # 1—Mt.26:31). When facing Christ, men stumble over three things. (For a thorough discussion see DEEPER STUDY # 9,10—Mt.21:44; see note—Lu.20:17-18.)
   1) Men stumble over the identity of Christ (Jn.6:54-58, 60, 66).
   2) Men stumble over the cross of Christ (1 Co.1:21-23, esp.23).
   3) Men stumble over the cross God calls them to bear (see note and DEEPER STUDY # 1—Lu.9:23).

Very simply, when men look at Jesus Christ and His cross, many react. They...

- doubt
- deny
- ignore
- reject
- close their hearts
- spiritualize
- consider Him and His cross to be irrational in the modern, scientific world

When Christ was arrested, the apostles questioned and wondered if Christ were really the Messiah. He did not resist arrest, and He did not use His mighty power. He was not leading the people in an uprising against the Romans, nor was He freeing Israel and setting up the nation as the center of God's kingdom. The apostles were disillusioned and perplexed; they simply could not understand. Their hopes were hanging upon a cross of despair. In this passage, Christ was foretelling them of their falling away. He knew that after His resurrection, they would remember His words and be able to return more easily and understand more fully. Remembering that He had foretold them would help them to return and to become stronger (see Jn.14:29; 13:19).

b. The disciples would be offended because Christ was rejected. Visibly, He was rejected by the crowd. But behind the scenes, in the invisible world, it was God who smote the Shepherd; that is, God put Christ to death (see Zec.13:7). It was in "the determinate counsel and foreknowledge of God" that Christ was to die (Ac.2:23). Christ had to give His life for man if man were to be saved.

"For David speaketh concerning him, I foresaw the Lord always before my face, for he is on my right hand, that I should not be moved" (Ac.2:25).

"But God commendeth his love toward us, in that, while we were yet sinners, Christ died for us" (Ro.5:8).

"Who his own self bare our sins in his own body on the tree, that we, being dead to sins, should live unto righteousness: by whose stripes ye were healed" (1 Pe.2:24).

"For Christ also hath once suffered for sins, the just for the unjust, that he might bring us to God, being put to death in the flesh, but quickened by the Spirit" (1 Pe.3:18).

c. When the crowd rejected Christ, the disciples felt threatened. They feared the crowd and lacked the courage to take a stand with Him. They turned away, fled, and deserted. Peter even denied Him vocally (Mt.26:69-75).

There is a remedy for *falling away*: the resurrection. Note the Lord's words, "I will go *before you.*" Christ was telling the apostles two things:
1) They were to come to Him after His resurrection (see DEEPER STUDY # 2—Mt.26:32). Despite their fall, He would still accept them. In fact, He would be waiting for them.
2) They would be *forgiven* for having denied Him.

"Repent therefore of this thy wickedness, and pray God, if perhaps the thought of thine heart may be forgiven thee" (Ac.8:22).

"If we confess our sins, he is faithful and just to forgive us our sins, and to cleanse us from all unrighteousness" (1 Jn.1:9).

"He that covereth his sins shall not prosper: but whoso confesseth and forsaketh them shall have mercy" (Pr.28:13).

Thought 1. How quickly a *fall* can come. Picture the disciples' sitting in the Upper Room with Christ as He shared with them. It was this very night that they would fall—not the next week, not the next month, but this night—the very night that He and they were sharing so much, so intimately (v.34). (See Jn.14-16 to see just how much Jesus shared and how precious and intimate the occasion was.)

Thought 2. Christ knew His disciples would stumble and fall. He knew they would be extremely discouraged. Knowing this, note what He did.
(1) He did not upbraid, scold, reproach, or condemn them.
(2) He planned to meet them, forgiving and receiving them—all in the power of His love and resurrection.

Thought 3. Christ knows nothing but love for the believer who stumbles and falls, even if the believer commits the most terrible sin, that of denying Christ with his lips. However, one thing is essential for forgiveness: repentance.

DEEPER STUDY # 1
(26:31) **Offend** (skandalizo): to stumble, to cause to stumble, to fall.

DEEPER STUDY # 2
(26:32) **Resurrection—Galilee**: Galilee was not to be the first place where Christ was to appear after His resurrection. He made a number of appearances over several days to different groups of the disciples. Galilee was to be the official meeting place, a meeting place where all the disciples were to be present and receive the renewing of their commission (Mt.28:16-20).

---

2 (26:33-35) **Self-Confidence—Flesh, Weakness of**: there was the claim of over-confidence by Peter. Peter's over-confidence was caused by four things.

a. His over-confidence was caused by comparing himself with others. Peter could not believe what he was hearing. Christ said, "All shall stumble," including him. Others may, Peter thought, but not him. There was not a chance, and he wanted Christ to know it. Note that Peter compared himself with others, in fact, with "all others": "Though all men shall be offended...yet will I never be." Peter saw the weaknesses and the flaws of others. Perhaps they could fail, but not him; he could never fall away from Christ. Others may be weak, but not him. Peter committed the terrible sin of humanity: pride (1 Co.10:12). Peter thought himself stronger than others, above and beyond them spiritually.

b. Peter's over-confidence was caused by being blind to the cross (v.34). Peter just did not see the cross. It was Christ's hanging upon the cross that was going to cause Peter to deny Christ. Christ had told him all about the cross, but he had refused to believe it (see notes—Mt.17:22; 18:1-2). The fact that human flesh was so sinful, so depraved that God would have to crucify it was just too much to grasp (see outline, notes, and DEEPER STUDY # 1—Lu.9:23; Ro.6:1-10; 6:10-13; Gal.2:19-21; 5:24; 6:14-17. See Ro.6:2; Col.3:3.)

c. Peter's over-confidence was caused by not knowing himself, his own personal weaknesses, the weaknesses of his human flesh. Peter's self-image was strong. He saw himself above *serious* sin and failure. He asserted with all the confidence in the world that he would die for Christ before denying Him.

Note several things:
1) Peter was a strong believer, one of the strongest.
2) Peter really failed to understand himself and his flesh. The one sin that a believer should not commit is to deny Christ. To die for Christ rather than to deny Him is the one thing a genuine believer would be expected to do.
3) Peter believed and believed strongly that he, his flesh, was above serious sin (see Ro.3:9f; 7:8, 14-18; Gal.5:19f).
4) Peter failed not once, but three times, and all three times were in the same night when Christ was right off to his side being tried for His life (Lu.22:61).

d. Peter's over-confidence was caused by contradicting Christ instead of listening to Him. Christ was warning the disciples about the deceitfulness and weakness of the human heart. Peter and the rest just refused to accept the fact. They denied personal weaknesses.

Thought 1. The fact that others fail is not reason for confidence in oneself but a reason for guarding oneself even more.

Thought 2. All men come short, stumble, and fall. Falling and stumbling are the way of human flesh. One falls in a particular area; another falls in another area. The difference between men is that one confesses and repents in his heart and the other does not. In fact, many do not even acknowledge the need to repent.

Thought 3. Over-confidence is a dangerous sin.

"Pride goeth before destruction, and a haughty spirit before a fall" (Pr.16:18).

"Let another man praise thee, and not thine own mouth; a stranger, and not thine own lips" (Pr.27:2).

"He that trusteth in his own heart is a fool: but whoso walketh wisely, he shall be delivered" (Pr.28:26).

"Woe unto them that are wise in their own eyes, and prudent in their own sight!" (Is.5:21).

"Therefore hear now this, thou that art given to pleasures, that dwellest carelessly, that sayest in thine heart, I am, and none else beside me: I shall not sit as a widow, neither shall I know the loss of children: But these two things shall come to thee in a moment in one day, the loss of children, and widowhood" (Is.47:8-9).

"And he spake this parable unto certain which trusted in themselves that they were righteous, and despised others" (Lu.18:9).

"And if any man think that he knoweth any thing, he knoweth nothing yet as he ought to know" (1 Co.8:2).

"Wherefore let him that thinketh he standeth take heed lest he fall" (1 Co.10:12).

"For if a man think himself to be something, when he is nothing, he deceiveth himself" (Ga.6:3).

Thought 4. We are not to compare ourselves with others. We are to "bear ye one another's burdens" (Ga.6:2).

"Be of the same mind one toward another. Mind not high things, but condescend to men of low estate. Be not wise in your own conceits" (Ro.12:16).

"Brethren, if a man be overtaken in a fault, ye which are spiritual, restore such an one in the spirit of meekness; considering thyself, lest thou also be tempted. Bear ye one another's burdens, and so fulfil the law of Christ. For if a man think himself to be something, when he is nothing, he deceiveth himself" (Ga.6:1-3).

Thought 5. Peter really felt he was above serious sin. How like human nature! How common to us all, how self-righteous!

Thought 6. No believer is above serious sin, and all sin is serious. In particular, the very thought that one is above serious sin *is* serious sin.

MATTHEW 26:36-46

	F. The Messiah's Agony in Gethsemane: Confronting Death & the Terrifying Trials of Life, 26:36-46 (Mk 14:32-42; Lu 22:39-46; Jn 18:1; He 5:7-8; 12:3-4)	asleep, and saith unto Peter, What, could ye not watch with me one hour? 41 Watch and pray, that ye enter not into temptation: the spirit indeed *is* willing, but the flesh *is* weak.	a. He found them asleep b. He warned them of temptation c. He warned them of the body & its weakness, vv. 43, 45
1. Christ entered the garden of Gethsemane^{DS1} a. With all the disciples b. For the purpose of praying	36 Then cometh Jesus with them unto a place called Gethsemane, and saith unto the disciples, Sit ye here, while I go and pray yonder.	42 He went away again the second time, and prayed, saying, O my Father, if this cup may not pass away from me, except I drink it, thy will be done.	5. Christ continued to pray, agonizing for release a. He asked His Father to remove the cup a second time
c. With just three disciples 2. Christ suffered agonizing grief & pain^{DS2,3}	37 And he took with him Peter and the two sons of Zebedee, and began to be sorrowful and very heavy.	43 And he came and found them asleep again: for their eyes were heavy.	b. He found the disciples asleep a second time
a. Felt pain to the point of death b. Requested companionship c. Warned: Watch & pray for yourselves as well	38 Then saith he unto them, My soul is exceeding sorrowful, even unto death: tarry ye here, and watch with me.	44 And he left them, and went away again, and prayed the third time, saying the same words.	c. He prayed a third time—the same words
3. Christ turned to God, crying a. Prostrated Himself b. Prayed: "My Father" c. Asked God to remove the cup from Him^{DS4}	39 And he went a little farther, and fell on his face, and prayed, saying, O my Father, if it be possible, let this cup pass from me: nevertheless not as I will, but as thou *wilt*.	45 Then cometh he to his disciples, and saith unto them, Sleep on now, and take *your* rest: behold, the hour is at hand, and the Son of man is betrayed into the hands of sinners.	6. Christ received release—great peace & courage a. The words of great release
4. Christ stood alone, neglected by His closest friends	40 And he cometh unto the disciples, and findeth them	46 Rise, let us be going: behold, he is at hand that doth betray me.	b. The words of great courage

DIVISION XVI

THE MESSIAH'S ARREST, TRIAL, AND CRUCIFIXION, 26:1–27:66

F. The Messiah's Agony in Gethsemane: Confronting Death and the Terrifying Trials of Life, 26:36-46

(26:36-46) **Introduction—Death—Jesus Christ, Sacrifice and Death**: death for Jesus Christ was different than death for all other men. In death, Jesus took all the sins of the world upon Himself and stood before God the Judge and...
- accepted the verdict of *guilty* for every man
- accepted the penalty and punishment of death for every man

It is in the word *death* that the difference lies. *Death* is not what some people conceive it to be: some dreamy state of being or euphoric existence in another world, or the end (disfunctioning) of the body with only the spirit of one's life left behind in others' memories, or simply annihilation. Death means separation from God (see Deeper Study # 1—He.9:27), and it is this that makes Christ's death different from the deaths of other men. In confronting death, Christ experienced unbelievable agony and pain because He was to be separated from His Father; and the one thing Christ did not want to face was having to be cut off from His Father. In addition, He did not experience death just for *one man's sins*; He experienced death for *every man's sins*. If there were any other way to save man, He, in His human nature, wanted it.

This is the terrifying struggle Christ was suffering in the Garden of Gethsemane—a struggle so terrible that it would have killed Him if God had not sent an angel to strengthen Him (Lu.22:43). In His great struggle and persevering prayer, Christ shows us how to confront death and the terrifying trials of life.
1. Christ entered the Garden of Gethsemane (vv.36-37).
2. Christ suffered agonizing grief and pain (vv.37-38).
3. Christ turned to God, crying (v.39).
4. Christ stood alone, neglected by His closest friends (vv.40-41).
5. Christ continued to pray, agonizing for release (vv.42-44).
6. Christ received release—great peace and courage (vv.45-46).

1 (26:36-37) **Jesus Christ, Prayer Life—Prayer**: Christ entered the Garden of Gethsemane.

a. He entered with all the disciples except Judas who had already begun his terrible betrayal. The disciples were all still with Him. Knowing the dark hour and terrible tragedy He was about to endure, He was doing all He could to keep them close to Himself. He wanted them to remember His great dependence upon God. By having the experience of Gethsemane fresh in their minds, they would be better able to face their disillusionment, blindness, unbelief, and desertion.

MATTHEW 26:36-46

They would be better able to overcome their weaknesses when He arose and confronted them. Thus He was holding them together as closely as possible as long as He could.

b. Christ entered the garden to pray. His words suggested that they, too, should begin seeking God in prayer: "Sit ye here, while I go and pray." Luke actually says that He told them all to pray: "Pray that ye enter not into temptation" (Lu.22:39-40).

c. Christ withdrew some distance farther into the garden, taking Peter, James, and John with Him. Why these three? The reason seemed clear. Christ had a double need: a need to be alone with God and a need for close companionship and prayer from those closest to Him. This becomes clearer in the discussion of v.38.

> "Seek the LORD and his strength, seek his face continually" (1 Chr.16:11).
>
> "Ask, and it shall be given you; seek, and ye shall find; knock, and it shall be opened unto you" (Mt.7:7).
>
> "And he spake a parable unto them to this end, that men ought always to pray, and not to faint" (Lu.18:1).
>
> "Is any among you afflicted? let him pray. Is any merry? let him sing psalms" (Js.5:13).

Thought 1. A man needs a garden, a private spot where he can get all alone with God in times of great trial.

Thought 2. Two things are essential when we face a desperate hour of need.
(1) Withdrawing, getting all alone in some private spot.
(2) Praying and sharing our need with God.

Thought 3. Note something of paramount importance: How does our desperate hour affect our loved ones? Christ was thinking as much of His disciples as He was of His own need. He was holding them together and encouraging them to pray for themselves as well as for Him.

DEEPER STUDY # 1

(26:36) **Gethsemane**: the word *Gethsemane* means *oil press* or *olive press*. Gethsemane was a garden sitting on the Mount of Olives. It was probably a garden of olive trees, beautifully situated on the slopes of the mountain overlooking all the surrounding area including the city of Jerusalem. Private and public gardens on the surrounding mountains were common because of the beauty of the mountains and because of the lack of space within the city. It was to such a garden that Christ withdrew in His desperate hour of need.

---

2 (26:37-38) **Jesus Christ, Death**: in confronting death, Christ suffered agonizing grief and pain (see DEEPER STUDY # 3—Mt.26:37). Note three things.

a. Christ felt so much sorrow and heaviness, so much inner pain, that it almost killed Him. Note His words: "My soul is exceeding sorrowful, even unto death." The pain and agony were so intense that He sweated great drops of blood. God the Father had to send an angel to strengthen Him (Lu.22:43-44. See the reference to this experience in He.12:3-4, esp. 4.) Apparently, all that Christ had been through and was about to go through was opened up to His mind. His whole being was now focusing upon the suffering He had to experience as the sin-bearer for the world. The mental vision literally compressed His physical body, almost to the point of crushing Him. (See DEEPER STUDY # 2—Mt.26:37-38.)

b. Christ was suffering so much agonizing grief and pain that He requested the presence of close friends. He needed them to *pray* for Him and be a *comfort* to Him. This is seen in His words, "Watch *with me*." Christ needed to be alone with God, but He also needed friends close by who were also praying for Him. Just knowing that they were close by praying and feeling for Him would be a strong encouragement.

c. Christ warned: watch and pray for yourselves as well. The greatest trial the disciples were to ever know was at hand, and they did not know it. In just a few hours, they were going to fall away. They desperately needed to pray that they "enter not into temptation" (v.41); that the depth of sin would not discourage them to the point that they would feel too unworthy to repent.

Thought 1. The greatest lesson to be learned from Gethsemane is probably this: we are to strive against sin at any cost. The Scripture clearly proclaims this lesson:

> "For consider him that endured such contradiction [hostility] of sinners against himself, lest ye be wearied and faint in your minds. Ye have not yet resisted unto blood, striving against sin" (He.12:3-4).

Christ strove against sin, against the temptation to save the world by some other way than the cross (being separated from God the Father). He strove and strove against the temptation, experiencing so much pressure that His sweat was as "*great* drops of blood" (Lu.22:44). Just imagine striving against sin to such a point! (See note—Mt.27:26-44.)

Thought 2. Something needs to be meditated upon time and again: the great agony that Christ bore for us. Nothing pictures His great agony any more than the Garden of Gethsemane.

Thought 3. Think of the Lord's enormous love for us. He foresaw all that He was to bear for us. All was opened up to His mind, yet He willingly surrendered Himself to bear it all (to get a quick picture of all that He was to bear, glance quickly at note, pt. 1—Mt.26:37-38).

MATTHEW 26:36-46

Thought 4. The presence, prayer, and comfort of close friends can be a tremendous source of help when we face desperate needs.

DEEPER STUDY # 2
(26:37-38) **Jesus Christ, Suffering—Death**: words could never express what Christ experienced. Words are just inadequate, totally inadequate. Using all the descriptive words in the world would be as inadequate in describing the sufferings of Christ as using a syringe to drain an ocean.

1. There was the *mental and emotional agony*: the weight, pressure, anguish, sorrow, and excessive strain such as no man has ever experienced. He was the Son of God, Maker of heaven and earth, yet images and thoughts were pressing ever so heavily in upon His spirit, the images and thoughts of...
   - the *unbelief* of all men everywhere
   - the *rejection* of His own people, the Jews
   - the *malice* of the world's leaders, both Jew and Gentile, religious and civil
   - the *betrayal* of one of His own, Judas
   - the *desertion* of all His men
   - the *denial* by the leader of His own men, Peter
   - the *injustice and condemnation* of His trial
   - the *ridicule and pain* of being scourged, spit upon, slugged, cursed, mocked, crowned with thorns, and nailed to the cross and killed

2. There was the *physical experience of death* while being the Son of God. What is it like for the Son of God to die just as all men die? If just the physical aspect of Christ's death is considered, His death is still different from all other men.
   a. Christ as the Son of God possessed the very seed, quality, ingredient, and energy of life within His being (see DEEPER STUDY # 1—Jn.17:2-3).
   b. Christ as the Son of God possessed no seed, quality, or ingredient of death (Jn.14:6; 1 Ti.6:16; 1 Jn.1:1-2; see Jn.1:4); but man does. Man possesses the seed of corruption and death. Man's sinful nature knows nothing and expects nothing but death, but the sinless nature of Christ knows nothing of sin and death. His sinless nature and the agony and pain of death were bound to be as different from man's death as white is different from black.

   There is another point to note as well. Man suffers humiliation in death. No matter how much man struggles to live, he wastes and wastes away until he is carried into the grave to become dust of the ground. But not Christ; He was sinless and perfect even in His human nature. His sinless nature knew nothing of death. Imagine the humiliation: the Son of God—the Perfect Man, the Perfect God—having to die upon this earth! No wonder He "began to be sorrowful and *very heavy*!" No wonder He could say, "My soul is exceeding sorrowful, *even unto death.*" In some mysterious way, God made Christ to become sin for us (2 Co.5:21).

3. There was *the spiritual experience of death* while being the Son of Man (see note—Mt.5:17-18; DEEPER STUDY #3—8:20; note—Ro.8:2-4). There is so much here, yet so little can ever be known.
   a. First, what is it like to be without sin? Christ, made in the image of man and being fully man, was sinless. He lived as all men live facing all the trials and temptations that men face, yet He never sinned. He was without sin. He became the Perfect and Ideal Man—all that God wants man to be. He became the Pattern for all men.

   > **"For we have not an high priest which cannot be touched with the feeling of our infirmities; but was in all points tempted like as we are, yet without sin" (He.4:15; see 2 Co.5:21; 1 Pe.2:22; 1 Jn.3:5).**

   > **"Though he were a Son, yet learned he obedience by the things which he suffered; and being made perfect, he became the author of eternal salvation unto all them that obey him" (He.5:8-9).**

   b. Second, what is it like to bear all the sins of the world? What is it like to be perfect and sinless and then, all of a sudden, to have all the sins of the world laid upon Oneself? In some mysterious way, God took all the sins of the world and laid the whole *body of sin* upon Christ. In some mysterious way, God made Christ to become sin for us (2 Co.5:21). Christ, as the Ideal Man, became the Ideal Sin-Bearer. He bore all the sins and all that sin causes—all the...

darkness	weight	worry	strife	poison
pollution	pressure	guilt	war	corruption
filthiness	anxiety	savagery	torture	consumption
dirt	turmoil	conflict	enmity	disturbance

   > **"All we like sheep have gone astray; we have turned every one to his own way; and the Lord hath laid on him the iniquity of us all" (Is.53:6).**

   > **"In due time Christ died for the ungodly" (Ro.5:6).**

   > **"Christ died for our sins according to the Scriptures" (1 Co.15:3).**

   > **"For he hath made him to be sin for us, who knew no sin; that we might be made the righteousness of God in him" (2 Co.5:21).**

   > **"So Christ was once offered to bear the sins of many; and unto them that look for him shall he appear the second time without sin unto salvation" (He.9:28).**

   > **"Who his own self bare our sins in his own body on the tree, that we, being dead to sins, should live unto righteousness: by whose stripes ye were healed" (1 Pe.2:24).**

c. Third, what is it like to bear all the judgment and condemnation of sin for all men? Christ suffered for the sins of the whole world, suffered *separation* from God. The terrifying mystery of this hellish experience is seen in His cry upon the cross, "My God, My God, why hast thou forsaken me?" (see note and Deeper Study # 1—Mt.27:26-44; note—27:46-49; note and Deeper Study # 1—1 Pe.2:21-25).

> "But he was wounded for our transgressions, he was bruised for our iniquities: the chastisement of our peace was upon him; and with his stripes we are healed" (Is.53:5).
>
> "Christ hath redeemed us from the curse of the law, being made a curse for us: for it is written, Cursed is every one that hangeth on a tree" (Ga.3:13).
>
> "But we see Jesus, who was made a little lower than the angels for the suffering of death, crowned with glory and honor; that he by the grace of God should taste death for every man" (He.2:9).
>
> "For Christ also hath once suffered for sins, the just for the unjust, that he might bring us to God, being put to death in the flesh, but quickened by the Spirit" (1 Pe.3:18).

DEEPER STUDY # 3
(26:37) **Sorrowful (lupeisthai)—Very Heavy (ademonein)**: *sorrowful* means to be distressed, grieved, pained. It means to be *consumed* with intense sorrow of heart. *Very heavy* means to be troubled, dismayed, disturbed. It means to be *gripped* with intense heaviness of soul. *Very heavy* pictures the trouble and dismay that is caused by an *unexpected calamity*. It is consternation, a heaviness that drives a man to be alone, for he is unfit for company. He desperately needs quiet, and he needs a few companions to understand and help him bear the trouble.

3 (26:39) **Jesus Christ, Death**: in confronting death Christ turned to God, crying with strong cries and tears (see He.5:7). Four things are seen in this verse.

a. Christ got all alone and prostrated Himself before God. Luke says He withdrew *about a stone's cast* from the three apostles. Note two significant points: (a) He needed to be alone with God—He was desperate. (b) He fell on His face—the pressure and weight were unbearable.

b. Christ prayed, "O my Father [pater mou]." Note that Christ called God "My Father." This is what a small child calls his father day by day. It is the address of a child's love, of dependency and trust. The child knows that His father will hear and turn to him when he calls *Father*. But note also the words, "O my Father." Christ was broken, weighed down, fallen, prostrate on the ground. In desperation He cried out "*O my* Father." Just like a child, He cried out to His Father in childlike brokenness and dependency; He knew that His Father would hear and turn to help Him.

c. Christ asked God to remove the cup from Him. (See Deeper Study # 4, *Cup*—Mt.26:39. Also see Deeper Study # 1—Mt.27:26-44; see Mt.20:19.) The human nature and will of Christ are clearly seen here. He was as much man as any man is. Thus He begged God to choose another way other than the cup (cross), if possible. The experience of being separated from God upon the cross was too much to bear.

d. The Divine nature and will of Christ were also clearly seen. Note the Lord's words: "Let this cup pass from me: nevertheless...." The first act and impulse, the first struggle and movement of His will had come from His flesh: to escape the cup of separation from God. But the second act and impulse, the second struggle and movement of His will came from His Divine nature: to do not as He willed, but as God willed.

Christ's surrender to do God's perfect will was critical.
⇒ It was through His surrender that He was made perfect and stood before God as the Ideal and Perfect Man.
⇒ It was through His surrender to be the Ideal and Perfect Man that His righteousness is still able to stand for every man.
⇒ It was through His surrender to be the Ideal and Perfect Man that He was able to bear the cup of God's wrath against sin *for every man*.
⇒ It was through His surrender to be the Ideal and Perfect Man that His sacrifice and sufferings are still able to stand for every man.

> "But we see Jesus, who was made a little lower than the angels for the suffering of death, crowned with glory and honor; that he by the grace of God should taste death for every man. For it became him, for whom are all things, and by whom are all things, in bringing many sons unto glory, to make the captain of their salvation perfect through sufferings" (He.2:9-10).
>
> "Though he were a Son, yet learned he obedience by the things which he suffered; and being made perfect, he became the author of eternal salvation unto all them that obey him" (He.5:8-9).
>
> "For he hath made him to be sin for us, who knew no sin; that we might be made the righteousness of God in him" (2 Co.5:21).

Thought 1. There are three vivid pictures in this point that should speak to our hearts.
(1) The picture of Christ's child-like dependency and trust in His Father.
(2) The picture of Christ's bearing the awful cup of God's wrath *for us*.
(3) The picture of our enormous obligation to Christ: the obligation to be appreciative and to express our appreciation in love, adoration, worship, and service.

Thought 2. Note both the human will and the Divine will of Christ. The first impulse of the human will is to get and possess what one desires, but the second impulse of the Divine will is to do as God wills. Genuine believers are "partakers of the divine nature" (2 Pe.1:4). Therefore, they too possess both wills. Note that this is a good way to describe temptation. The first impulse to do as one wishes comes from the human will, but the second impulse to do as God wills comes from the divine will. What we must do is learn to surrender to the divine will, to the godly impulse, just as Christ did.

> "But we see Jesus, who was made a little lower than the angels for the suffering of death, crowned with glory and honor; that he by the grace of God should taste death for every man. For it became him, for whom are all things, and by whom are all things, in bringing many sons unto glory, to make the captain of their salvation perfect through sufferings" (He.2:9-10).
> "Though he were a Son, yet learned he obedience by the things which he suffered; and being made perfect, he became the author of eternal salvation unto all them that obey him" (He.5:8-9).
> "For he hath made him to be sin for us, who knew no sin; that we might be made the righteousness of God in him" (2 Co.5:21).

DEEPER STUDY # 4

(26:39) **Cup**: Jesus Christ was not fearing nor shrinking from death itself. This is clearly seen in Jn.10:17-18. Death for a cause is not such a great price to pay. Many men have so died—fearlessly and willingly, some perhaps more cruelly than Christ Himself. Shrinking from betrayal, beatings, humiliation and death, increased by foreknowledge is not what was happening to Christ. As stated, some men have faced such persecution courageously, even inviting martyrdom for a cause. The Lord knew He was to die from the very beginning, and He had been preparing His disciples for His death (see Mt.26:1-2). It was not just human or physical suffering that Christ was shrinking from. Such an explanation is totally inadequate in explaining Gethsemane. The great cup or trial that Jesus was facing was separation from God (see DEEPER STUDY # 2—Mt.26:37-38). He was to be the sacrificial "Lamb of God" who takes away the sins of the world (Jn.1:29). He was to bear the judgment and wrath of God for the sins of the world (see note—Mt.27:46-49; see Is. 53:10). Jesus Himself had already spoken of the *cup* when referring to His sacrificial death (see DEEPER STUDY # 2—Mt.20:22-23; note—Mk.14:35-36; DEEPER STUDY # 2—Jn.18:11).

Scripture speaks of the cup in several ways.

1. The cup is called "the cup of the Lord's fury."

> "Awake, awake, stand up, O Jerusalem, which hast drunk at the hand of the LORD the cup of his fury; thou hast drunken the dregs of the cup of trembling, and wrung them out" (Is.51:17).

2. The cup is associated with suffering and God's wrath.

> "Upon the wicked he shall rain snares, fire and brimstone, and an horrible tempest: this shall be the portion of their cup" (Ps.11:6).
> "Saying, Father, if thou be willing, remove this cup from me: nevertheless not my will, but thine, be done" (Lu.22:42).

3. The cup is also associated with salvation. Because Jesus drank the cup of suffering and wrath for us, we can "take the cup of salvation and call upon the name of the Lord" (Ps.116:13). He bears the judgment of God for the sins of the world.

> "Yet it pleased the LORD to bruise him; he hath put him to grief: when thou shalt make his soul an offering for sin, he shall see his seed, he shall prolong his days, and the pleasure of the LORD shall prosper in his hand" (Is.53:10).

---

4 (26:40-41) **Jesus Christ, Death**: in confronting death Christ stood alone, neglected by His closest friends.

a. He arose from prayer and went to the three who were supposed to be praying with Him. They were asleep. The companionship, the spirit of prayer and comfort He had sought, was not there. All were asleep. He had been left alone to wrestle with God by Himself.

b. Christ warned of temptation. The disciples had failed to pray for Him, but they must not fail to pray for themselves. Christ said, "Watch and pray." Both were important. *Watchfulness* sees and *praying* prepares. They were to watch in order to see temptation coming, and they were to pray in order to be prepared when temptation struck.

c. Christ warned of the flesh and its weakness. They were sleeping because of the emotional strain and distress of the evening. As Luke says, they slept because of *sorrow*, that is, sadness (Lu.22:45). The evening had been shocking and taxing. They were weary, fatigued, and preoccupied. Concentration in prayer was difficult. They probably fought to stay awake and to pray for their Lord. But the importance of prayer and spiritual dependency upon God in facing trials had not yet been learned. They were making two mistakes common among believers.

1) The disciples were depending upon their own wisdom and strength instead of God's Spirit to fight whatever battles lay ahead.
2) The disciples were taking God's deliverance for granted instead of assuring His deliverance through the testimony of prayer. They believed Christ to be the Messiah; therefore, they believed God was going to deliver them against the Romans no matter what. As carnal, fleshly men are apt to do, the disciples no doubt thought prayer mattered little. They were just presuming upon God, taking His deliverance for granted. What Christ said was, "Watch and pray; for only as you watch and pray can you keep from falling when the trial comes." Watchfulness and prayer bear *testimony* to God.

This point needs to be noted: watchfulness and prayer bear *testimony* to God. When men watch and pray, they demonstrate that dependency and trust in God are well founded. When God answers the prayers of men, He demonstrates that

He loves and cares and delivers those who truly look up to Him. Without watching and praying, God allows men to fall in order to teach that dependency and trust in Him are absolutely essential.

d. They were failing to stay awake to pray, to watch and to be watchful in prayer. Their spirits were not alive and alert enough to overcome the flesh. The drowsiness and slumber of the flesh were stronger than the spirit (see note 5, pt.2—Mt.26:42-44; see Ep.6:18).

> "Blessed are those servants, whom the lord when he cometh shall find watching: verily I say unto you, that he shall gird himself, and make them to sit down to meat, and will come forth and serve them" (Lu.12:37).
>
> "Ye are all the children of light, and the children of the day: we are not of the night, nor of darkness. Therefore let us not sleep, as do others; but let us watch and be sober" (1 Th.5:5-6).
>
> "Be sober, be vigilant; because your adversary the devil, as a roaring lion, walketh about, seeking whom he may devour" (1 Pe.5:8).
>
> "O LORD, I know that the way of man is not in himself: it is not in man that walketh to direct his steps" (Je.10:23).

Thought 1. No believer is ever alone. Even if his closest friends neglect the spirit of prayer and comfort, God is with him.

Thought 2. Many trials arise immediately and unexpectedly. They jump right up in front of us. Only persistent, sleepless prayer will prepare us for such crises (see Ep.6:18).

Thought 3. The flesh struggles against the spirit (Ga.5:17).

5 (26:42-44) **Jesus Christ, Death**: in confronting death, Christ continued to pray—agonizing for release.

a. He asked His Father to remove the cup a second time. Matthew is the only writer to give the words of Christ in this second prayer. Mark simply says that He "spoke the same words" (Mk.14:39). There are two views about what Jesus was saying.
  1) Some commentators say that He was accepting the cup and consenting to the fact that He must drink it: "If [since] this cup may not pass away from me, except I drink it, thy will be done." When reading the verse this way, the battle does seem to be already won. Christ seems to have already accepted the fact that there just was no other way than to bear the cup. His human nature already seems to be subjected to the Divine nature.
  2) Other commentators understand the verse to say what Mark seems to be saying: "And again He went away; and prayed, and *spoke the same words*" (Mk.14:39). Christ was continuing to pray and to agonize for release from the cup. He, of course, was willing to bear it, but His soul was crying out with "strong tears" for another way. Two facts always need to be remembered.
  First, Christ was not shrinking from death; He was shrinking from drinking the cup of separation from God.
  Second, the pressure of bearing all the suffering of the world as the Son of Man was unbearable. He felt as though He would die, and Scripture seems to indicate this by mentioning that an angel had to be sent to strengthen Him against the pressure.

b. Christ found the disciples asleep again. Note "their eyes were heavy." This indicates they fought against drowsiness but lost the fight. They could not shake off their...
  • physical drowsiness
  • spiritual blindness (not accepting Christ's former prophecies of death)
  • carnal security (taking God for granted)

c. Christ prayed a third time, praying the same words (v.44). The pressure was unbearable. He must have release. Note: this was the third time Christ prayed, and note the statement *the same words* (ton auton logon). This seems to be saying that He was struggling in the *same agonizing spirit*, struggling *to be released* from the life-threatening pressure. *Three times* He came before God pouring out His soul, with "strong tears," begging for *release*. In so doing, He has demonstrated forever the necessity of persevering in prayer in order to secure release from agonizing pressure. God answers persevering prayer.

> "Ask, and it shall be given you; seek, and ye shall find; knock, and it shall be opened unto you" (Mt.7:7).
>
> "Continue in prayer, and watch in the same with thanksgiving" (Col.4:2).
>
> "Submit yourselves therefore to God. Resist the devil, and he will flee from you. Draw nigh to God, and he will draw nigh to you" (Js.4:7-8).

Thought 1. Persevering prayer is the great lesson of Gethsemane, and our Lord Himself gives us the greatest example of persevering prayer. When facing the pressuring and terrifying trials of life, Christ teaches us by example to seek release by coming before God in prayer. And He teaches us to stay before God—asking and asking, praying and praying—continuing and persevering in prayer until God answers. (See outlines and notes—Mt.7:7-11. See Ep.6:18; Lu.18:1-8.)

Thought 2. There are three enemies that constantly fight against persevering prayer, that must be struggled and struggled against (see note, pt.2—Mt.26:42-44).

MATTHEW 26:36-46

(1) Physical drowsiness.
(2) Spiritual blindness: not believing the Lord's words, wanting to understand and interpret Him as we wish instead of letting Him speak for Himself.
(3) Carnal security: presuming upon and taking God for granted.

6 (26:45-46) **Jesus Christ, Death**: in confronting death, Christ received great release, great peace and courage.

a. There were His words, the evidence of great release: "Sleep on now, and take your *rest*." Christ's agony, His desperate need for friends to "watch" with Him was now gone. God had given Him great relief of soul. The very tone of His words to His disciples revealed a calmness of spirit, a peace of mind, a relief of the physical and emotional strain that was about to kill Him. God had met His need in a most wonderful way.

> "In the day when I cried thou answeredst me, and strengthenedst me with strength in my soul" (Ps.138:3).
> "And there appeared an angel unto him from heaven, strengthening him" (Lu.22:43).
> "Who in the days of his flesh, when he had offered up prayers and supplications with strong crying and tears unto him that was able to save him from death, and was heard in that he feared" (He.5:7; see 5:7-9).

b. There were His words, the evidence of great courage: "Behold, the hour is at hand, and the Son of Man is betrayed into the hands of sinners."

Note two things:

1) There was no shrinking now, no agony, no desperation. Christ was relieved and strengthened, ready to face the sufferings necessary to secure the salvation of man.
2) Christ said He was being "betrayed into the hands of sinners." All those taking part in His death were *sinners*. His death was the most heinous crime of history. He, the Son of Man, the Ideal and Perfect Man, was killed by men. But there is more here: He died for the sins of the world. It was every man's sin that caused Him to be crucified. Every sin is an act of rebellion, of simply saying "No!" to God (Ro.3:23). Therefore, every man is guilty of putting Christ to death. There is a sense in which every sin and every act of rebellion crucifies "the Son of God afresh, and put[s] Him to an open shame" (He.6:6).

Thought 1. Note a critical point: God did not give Christ what He asked; that is, God did not remove the cup. Christ had to drink the cup, but God did answer His prayer. God relieved the agony and strengthened Him to bear the cup. God kept Him from failing. The lesson is clear: God sometimes answers our prayers with "No." But He strengthens us and gives us something much better.

> "I delight to do thy will, O my God: yea, thy law is within my heart" (Ps.40:8).
> "I can of mine own self do nothing: as I hear, I judge: and my judgment is just; because I seek not mine own will, but the will of the Father which hath sent me" (Jn.5:30).
> "Who gave himself for our sins, that he might deliver us from this present evil world, according to the will of God and our Father" (Ga.1:4).
> "And walk in love, as Christ also hath loved us, and hath given himself for us an offering and a sacrifice to God for a sweetsmelling savour" (Ep.5:2).
> "Then said, I, Lo, I come (in the volume of the book it is written of me,) to do thy will, O God. Above when he said, Sacrifice and offering and burnt offerings and offering for sin thou wouldest not, neither hadst pleasure therein; which are offered by the law; then said he, Lo, I come to do thy will, O God. He taketh away the first, that he may establish the second. By the which will we are sanctified through the offering of the body of Jesus Christ once for all....But this man, after he had offered one sacrifice for sins for ever, sat down on the right hand of God" (He.10:7-10, 12).

MATTHEW 26:47-56

	G. The Messiah Betrayed, Arrested, & Deserted: Four Pictures of Commitment, 26:47-56 (Mk 14:43-52; Lu 22:47-53; Jn 18:3-11)	drew his sword, and struck a servant of the high priest's, and smote off his ear. 52 Then said Jesus unto him, Put up again thy sword into his place: for all they that take the sword shall perish with the sword.	a. He misunderstood Jesus' kingdom & fought in the flesh b. Jesus rebuked carnal commitment: Rebuked warring in the flesh
1. Picture 1: A commitment of betrayal–by Judas a. He was an apostle b. He led a large crowd c. He had them armed d. He was sent by the religionists	47 And while he yet spake, lo, Judas, one of the twelve, came, and with him a great multitude with swords and staves, from the chief priests and elders of the people.	53 Thinkest thou that I cannot now pray to my Father, and he shall presently give me more than twelve legions of angels?	4. Picture 4: A commitment of purpose–Jesus' willingness to die for man a. He could save Himself
2. Picture 2: A commitment of deception–by Judas a. The deceiver laid his plans b. The deceiver carried out his plan c. The deceiver was given a clear-cut charge: Told to do what he came for	48 Now he that betrayed him gave them a sign, saying, Whomsoever I shall kiss, that same is he: hold him fast. 49 And forthwith he came to Jesus, and said, Hail, master; and kissed him. 50 And Jesus said unto him, Friend, wherefore art thou come? Then came they, and laid hands on Jesus, and took him.	54 But how then shall the scriptures be fulfilled, that thus it must be? 55 In that same hour said Jesus to the multitudes, Are ye come out as against a thief with swords and staves for to take me? I sat daily with you teaching in the temple, and ye laid no hold on me.	b. He was determined to fulfill Scripture & die, v. 56 5. Picture 5: A commitment of opposition–the world's treatment
3. Picture 3: A commitment of carnality–Peter's carnal militancy	51 And, behold, one of them which were with Jesus stretched out *his* hand, and	56 But all this was done, that the scriptures of the prophets might be fulfilled. Then all the disciples forsook him, and fled.	6. Picture 6: A commitment of desertion–the disciples' fleeing & forsaking Christ

DIVISION XVI

THE MESSIAH'S ARREST, TRIAL, AND CRUCIFIXION, 26:1–27:66

G. The Messiah Betrayed, Arrested, and Deserted: Four Pictures of Commitment, 26:47-56

(26:47-56) **Introduction**: humanly speaking, this is a tragic scene. Jesus was betrayed, arrested, and deserted within a few minutes. Just imagine facing all three events within so short a time: being betrayed by one of His own disciples; being falsely arrested by a mob determined to kill Him; and being deserted by all His closest friends, the apostles themselves. Jesus stood alone. He did not *have* to; not a single hand or abusive word or indignity *had* to be borne. But He chose to stand there. He willingly suffered all the abuse and indignity that He might save the world.

Much can be learned from what happens in this event. There are four separate events or pictures seen.
1. Picture 1: A commitment of betrayal–by Judas (v.47).
2. Picture 2: A commitment of deception–by Judas (vv.48-50).
3. Picture 3: A commitment of carnality–Peter's carnal militancy (vv.51-52).
4. Picture 4: A commitment of purpose–Jesus' willingness to die for man (vv.53-54).
5. Picture 5: A commitment of opposition–the world's treatment (v.55).
6. Picture 6: A commitment of desertion–the disciples' fleeing and forsaking Christ (v.56).

1 (26:47) **Judas—Jesus Christ, Betrayed**: Judas betrayed Jesus. Judas is seen leading a large crowd to arrest Jesus. Note the four facts stated.

a. Judas was one of the twelve apostles, a disciple, a professing follower of the Lord. Just a few hours before, that very evening, he had been sitting at the table of the Lord eating bread with Him. Now, ever so quickly, he had turned away and had actually taken the lead in betraying the Lord (see Ac.1:16).

> **Thought 1.** There are too many within the church just like Judas. They profess Christ, yet ever so quickly they turn away. Some even give leadership to others in opposing Christ (or righteousness).

b. Judas led a large crowd to arrest Jesus (see note—Lu.22:47-48).

c. Judas made sure they were armed. He feared Jesus ("hold Him fast," he had said, v.48). Judas had witnessed Jesus' power and His escaping from crowds before (see Lu.4:30; Jn.8:59).

d. Judas was officially sent by the religionists: the chief priests and leaders (Mt.26:3-5, 14-16). The very people who should have received Him rejected Him. His severest enemies were those who professed to believe in God and who gave religious leadership to the people.

MATTHEW 26:47-56

Thought 1. If Jesus returned to earth today, how many religionists would reject and oppose Him? In fact, how many religionists are already rejecting Him? How many reject Him as He is revealed by those who follow Him? How many go about formulating an image of Christ as they wish, after their own lusts?

2 (26:48-50) **Commitment—Deception—Judas**: the first picture of commitment is a deceptive commitment—that of Judas' betrayal.

a. The deceiver Judas laid his plans. It would be dark. How would the temple guard be able to recognize Jesus in the dark and keep Him from slipping away? Judas thought and thought and came up with a plan. He would identify Jesus for them by walking up and greeting Jesus with a kiss. A kiss was a sign of friendship and commitment among people in the East, in particular among friends. Judas felt he could deceive the disciples; they would never suspect his sin.

Thought 1. The point here is the planning and plotting of evil while professing Christ. How many profess Christ and yet lay plans to steal, lie, cheat, sin? How many profess loyalty to Christ and yet plan to give their allegiance to someone else? How many of us profess Christ and yet, just like Judas, plan to serve our own self-interest?

Thought 2. When we plan and plot to sin, we play the deceiver.

b. The deceiver Judas carried out his plan. What he planned he did: "He came to Jesus, and said, 'Hail Master,' and kissed Him." The word for *kissed Him* (katephilesen) is strong. It means to kiss strongly, forcefully, passionately, fervently, repeatedly. Either Judas had planned to really put on a show to hide his sin or else his nervousness caused him to act passionately. The sin was bad enough, but the deception was worse.

Thought 1. What we plan, we often do, both good and evil.

Thought 2. Professing Christ and living in sin makes two things out of us: a betrayer and a deceiver. We betray Christ and deceive others.

c. Jesus asked a searching question: "Friend, why have you come?" Note that Jesus did not rebuke or reproach Judas. He asked Judas a question, a question that forced Judas to search his deceptive heart. Christ still wanted to reach Judas, if possible. He asked, "Why have you come, Judas? You have greeted me as a loyal companion. Have you come committed and loyal to me?" The question was bound to pierce and arouse a searching conviction within the deceptive heart. The deception and sin were completed. Christ was arrested (v.50).

> "And they will deceive every one his neighbour, and will not speak the truth: they have taught their tongue to speak lies, and weary themselves to commit iniquity" (Je.9:5).
> "The heart is deceitful above all things, and desperately wicked: who can know it?" (Je.17:9).
> "That we henceforth be no more children, tossed to and fro, and carried about with every wind of doctrine, by the sleight of men, and cunning craftiness, whereby they lie in wait to deceive" (Ep.4:14).
> "But evil men and seducers shall wax worse and worse, deceiving, and being deceived" (2 Ti.3:13).
> "For there are many unruly and vain talkers and deceivers" (Tit.1:10).
> "Take heed, brethren, lest there be in any of you an evil heart of unbelief, in departing from the living God" (He.3:12).
> "[These] shall receive the reward of unrighteousness, as they that count it pleasure to riot [party] in the day time. Spots they are and blemishes, sporting themselves with their own deceivings while they feast with you [the church]; having eyes full of adultery, and that cannot cease from sin; beguiling unstable souls: an heart they have exercised with covetous practices; cursed children" (2 Pe.2:13-14).
> "For many deceivers are entered into the world, who confess not that Jesus Christ is come in the flesh. This is a deceiver and an antichrist" (2 Jn.7).

Thought 1. Note that God's glorious long-suffering toward us was demonstrated by Christ (see 2 Pe.3:9).
(1) Christ submitted to the hypocritical profession of Judas and the mistreatment of the barbarous crowd.
(2) Christ tried to reach Judas again, just as He had tried and tried before.

Thought 2. Christ asks every one of us: "Friend, why have you come? Why have you come to me? To the church?"
(1) Because you are really committed and loyal?
(2) Because you want gain: social standing, business, livelihood, security, influence, position, religious recognition?
(3) Because you want acceptability within the community?
(4) Because you want to satisfy conscience: to have just enough religion to keep you from feeling guilty?
(5) Because you want to please family or friends?
(6) Because you were taught to come?
(7) Because all your friends come?

Thought 3. The question of Christ should pierce every one of our hearts and arouse a searching conviction.

3 (26:51-52) **Carnal—Peter**: the second picture of commitment is a carnal commitment—that of Peter's carnal militancy.

a. Peter misunderstood Jesus' kingdom and he "warred in the flesh." The disciple was Peter and the servant whose ear was cut off was Malchus (Jn.18:10). Jesus restored the ear; He miraculously healed it (Lu.22:51).

MATTHEW 26:47-56

Peter thought the Messiah's hour had come. Christ was now ready to free Israel and establish the throne of David as the dominant nation in the world (see notes—Mt.1:1; Deeper Study # 2—1:18; Deeper Study # 3—3:11; notes—11:1-6; 11:2-3; Deeper Study # 1—11:5; Deeper Study # 2—11:6; Deeper Study # 1—12:16; notes— 22:42; Lu.7:21-23). Peter drew his sword (note that he had one) and struck, slashing off the ear of Malchus.

  b. Christ rebuked Peter and his carnal commitment, his warring in the flesh.
    1) He told Peter to put his sword back into its sheath where it belonged.
    2). He healed Malchus' ear (Lu.22:51).
    3) He told Peter that "they that take the sword shall perish with the sword."

The picture painted by Peter's behavior is carnal commitment, acting and struggling in the flesh. Peter took his stand for Christ *in the flesh*; therefore, he failed. Eventually, he deserted Christ. Acting in the flesh will always result in failing and deserting Christ. Peter's carnal commitment is seen in four mistakes. Each mistake is too often seen in the lives of believers.

1. Peter misunderstood the Lord's Word. First, Peter thought Christ was to establish an earthly kingdom. He thought in terms of the earthly, the physical, the material. Therefore, he failed to grasp the spiritual and eternal kingdom (the spiritual world, the spiritual dimension of being) proclaimed by Christ. Second, Peter never accepted the Lord's word. Christ had predicted His death and forewarned the apostles, giving them extensive training for months (see notes—Mt.16:13-20; 16:21-28; 17:1-13; 17:22; 17:24-27). Yet Peter refused to give up his preconceived ideas and accept what Christ was saying. Therefore, he did not see the eternal world of the Spirit nor the eternal salvation which Christ was securing.

2. Peter did not wait for instructions from Christ. He acted on his own; he took matters into his own hands. The disciples had asked, "Lord, shall we smite with the sword?" But Jesus had not yet answered. However, this did not stop Peter. He acted on his own. How like so many of us! Too often, we act without waiting on the Lord.

3. Peter did not ask Christ what to do, not again and again. He did not persist until Christ answered.

> "Watch and pray, that ye enter not into temptation: the spirit indeed is willing, but the flesh is weak" (Mt.26:41).
> "Watch ye therefore, and pray always, that ye may be accounted worthy to escape all these things that shall come to pass, and to stand before the Son of man" (Lu.21:36).
> "Seek the LORD and his strength, seek his face continually" (1 Chr.16:11).

4. Peter did not think clearly nor use discretion nor act wisely. His action could have led to the failure of God's will. It could have led to the death of many. That is what Christ said: "Violence leads to violence. If you draw the sword, the soldiers will cut you down." Among God's people, the place of the sword is in the sheath, not drawn and slashing at people. God's people are to proclaim love and peace, not war and violence, not carnal and fleshly behavior.

> "Not by might, nor by power, but by my spirit, saith the LORD of hosts" (Zec.4:6).
> "As many as I love, I rebuke and chasten: be zealous therefore, and repent" (Re.3:19).
> "But sanctify the Lord God in your hearts: and be ready always to give an answer to every man that asketh you a reason of the hope that is in you with meekness and fear" (1 Pe.3:15).

Thought 1. The weapons of the believers warfare are spiritual, not physical or carnal (see 2 Co.10:3-5; see Ro.8:5-8; Ga.5:17).

4 (26:53-54) **Jesus Christ, Love—Obedience**: the third picture of commitment is a purposeful commitment—that of Jesus' willingness to die for man.
  a. Jesus could have saved Himself. He could have prayed to His Father and seventy-two thousand angels would have rallied to His defense and blasted His enemies away. He does not need the weak efforts of men to defend Him. He is God's Son, God's only Son, and God will defend His Son as He wills.
  b. However, Jesus was determined to fulfill Scripture: He had to die, and He was willing to die for man. His life was not being taken from Him by men. He was laying it down willingly as God had purposed.

> "But he was wounded for our transgressions, he was bruised for our iniquities: the chastisement of our peace was upon him; and with his stripes we are healed. All we like sheep have gone astray; we have turned every one to his own way; and the Lord hath laid on him the iniquity of us all. He was oppressed, and he was afflicted, yet he opened not his mouth: he is brought as a lamb to the slaughter, and as a sheep before her shearers is dumb, so he openeth not his mouth" (Is.53:5-7).
> "Therefore doth my Father love me, because I lay down my life, that I might take it again. No man taketh it from me, but I lay it down of myself. I have power to lay it down, and I have power to take it again. This commandment have I received of my Father" (Jn.10:17-18).
> "Him, being delivered by the determinate counsel and foreknowledge of God, ye have taken, and by wicked hands have crucified and slain" (Ac.2:23).

Thought 1. Christ is the perfect example of purposeful commitment. The commitment God wants from us is a purposeful commitment: a commitment to die daily for Christ and His cause (see note and Deeper Study # 1—Lu.9:23).

Thought 2. Purpose, meaning, and significance are what every man desires and needs. Such is found in Christ alone. He and His cause alone fill the heart of man with purpose, meaning, and significance.

MATTHEW 26:47-56

5 (26:55-56) **Commitment**: the fourth picture of commitment is that of two tragic commitments.
   a. A commitment to oppose Jesus: the world's treatment of Jesus.
      1) Note how the world treated Jesus: they treated Him as (1) a thief, as though He were going to steal from them, (2) as a dangerous man who must be opposed with weapons, and (3) as a man who must be opposed in the dark and in secret.
      2) Note how the world opposed Jesus and cut His heart. The words of Jesus are spoken with feeling, hurt, and intense sorrow.

   > "Are ye come out as against a thief with swords and staves for to take me? I sat daily with you teaching in the temple, and ye laid no hold on me" (v.55).

   Jesus allowed such indignities and shameful behavior, but it hurt and broke His heart. He was, after all, the Son of God.

   > "He was in the world, and the world was made by him, and the world knew him not. He came unto his own, and his own received him not" (Jn.1:10-11).
   > "Father, glorify thy name. Then came there a voice from heaven, saying, I have both glorified it, and will glorify it again" (Jn.12:28).
   > "For they that dwell at Jerusalem, and their rulers, because they knew him not, nor yet the voices of the prophets which are read every sabbath day, they have fulfilled them in condemning him" (Ac.13:27).

   b. A commitment that forsakes Jesus: the disciples' fleeing. They fled for at least two reasons.
      1) They feared for their own lives. Jesus was not using His power to free Himself. They could not understand. They fled to save themselves.
      2) They were disillusioned; they could not understand Jesus' behavior and why He would not blast His enemies away to free Himself. A point needs to be noted about their disillusionment: it was their own fault.
      First, they were closed-minded; therefore, they were weak in faith. They had closed their minds to His full mission and purpose. They had *refused* to literally accept His word about dying and rising again. They had failed to grasp the spiritual and eternal nature of His kingdom. They symbolized what He was saying. Now that it was happening, they were not prepared for it. Their faith was too weak.
      Second, they were worldly and materialistic-minded. They had hung on to their earthly concept of the Messiah: the Messiah who was coming to bring utopia to this material and physical world. They were, therefore, not prepared to deal with their earthly Messiah's being bound and taken prisoner by men of this earth. Their faith lacked the strength to bear such a trial.

   > "Ye therefore, beloved, seeing ye know these things before, beware lest ye also, being led away with the error of the wicked, fall from your own stedfastness. But grow in grace, and in the knowledge of our Lord and Saviour Jesus Christ. To him be glory both now and for ever" (2 Pe.3:17-18).
   > "And Jesus said unto him, No man, having put his hand to the plough, and looking back, is fit for the kingdom of God" (Lu.9:62).
   > "A double minded man is unstable in all his ways" (Js.1:8).
   > "Blessed is the man that endureth temptation: for when he is tried, he shall receive the crown of life, which the Lord hath promised to them that love him" (Js.1:12).
   > "Draw nigh to God, and he will draw nigh to you. Cleanse your hands, ye sinners; and purify your hearts, ye double minded" (Js.4:8).

   Thought 1. The world opposes Christ.
   (1) Many treat Him as a thief. They believe He withholds pleasure and prevents (cheats) people from really living. They believe that His commandments cause people to miss out on life.
   (2) Others oppose Him as though He is dangerous. They actually curse and try to stamp out His name and church. They oppose Him and His church with every weapon they can find.
   (3) Still others oppose Him by plotting and sinning in the dark and in secret.

   Thought 2. All opposition and shameful behavior—all sin cuts the heart of Jesus. It was because of sin that He died (2 Pe.2:24).

   Thought 3. Too many disciples forsake Jesus for the same reason: disillusionment. And too often our disillusionment is caused by the same two reasons: either being closed-minded or being worldly and materialistic-minded.

	H. The Messiah's Trial Before Caiaphas & the Sanhedrin: Facing the Great Trials of Life, 26:57-68 (Mk 14:53-65; Lu 22:54, 63-71; Jn 18:12-14, 19-24)	thou nothing? what *is it* which these witness against thee? 63 But Jesus held his peace. And the high priest answered and said unto him, I adjure thee by the living God, that thou tell us whether	6. The claim of Jesus: He is the Messiah, the Son of God a. He was questioned: Put under oath to answer
1. The picture of Jesus being led to trial	57 And they that had laid hold on Jesus led *him* away to Caiaphas the high priest, where the scribes and the elders were assembled.	thou be the Christ, the Son of God. 64 Jesus saith unto him, Thou hast said: nevertheless I say unto you, Hereafter shall	b. He claimed to be the Messiah[DS2] c. He gave two proofs
2. The confused faith & loyalty of Peter a. He could not understand b. But he loved: He came back to see the end	58 But Peter followed him afar off unto the high priest's palace, and went in, and sat with the servants, to see the end.	ye see the Son of man sitting on the right hand of power, and coming in the clouds of heaven. 65 Then the high priest	1) His resurrection & exaltation[DS3] 2) His second coming 7. The tragic verdict
3. The stacked court: Predetermined rejection & opposition[DS1]	59 Now the chief priests, and elders, and all the council, sought false witness against Jesus, to put him to death;	rent his clothes, saying, He hath spoken blasphemy; what further need have we of witnesses? behold, now ye have heard his blas-	a. The crime: Blasphemy b. The evidence: His claim
4. The false charge: A revolutionary a. Many false witnesses came: But their charges were unconvincing b. Two convincing false witnesses finally came: Charged Him with being a revolutionary	60 But found none: yea, though many false witnesses came, *yet* found they none. At the last came two false witnesses, 61 And said, This *fellow* said, I am able to destroy the temple of God, and to build it in three days.	phemy. 66 What think ye? They answered and said, He is guilty of death. 67 Then did they spit in his face, and buffeted him; and others smote *him* with the palms of their hands, 68 Saying, Prophesy unto us,	c. The sentence: Death 8. The physical abuse inflicted a. Bitter hatred & behavior b. Ridicule of His claim to be the Messiah
5. The calm assurance of Jesus	62 And the high priest arose, and said unto him, Answerest	thou Christ, Who is he that smote thee?	

DIVISION XVI

THE MESSIAH'S ARREST, TRIAL, AND CRUCIFIXION, 26:1–27:66

H. The Messiah's Trial Before Caiaphas and the Sanhedrin: Facing the Great Trials of Life, 26:57-68

(26:57-68) **Introduction**: Christ had been rejected and opposed throughout all His ministry. Now He was being officially condemned to die by the high court of the Jews, the Sanhedrin. Christ was standing before the court, and all the negative feelings of humanity against God were beginning to seep through: confusion, disloyalty, unbelief, rejection, disregard, opposition, bitterness, enmity, hatred.

A glance at the major points of the passage gives some insight into what really lies within the heart of man toward God. Because Christ stood so magnificently before the court, the believer can look and learn lesson after lesson that helps him to stand before the great trials of his own life.

1. The picture of Jesus being led to trial (v.57).
2. The confused faith and loyalty of Peter (v.58).
3. The stacked court: Predetermined rejection and opposition (v.59).
4. The false charge: a revolutionary (vv.60-61).
5. The calm assurance of Jesus (v.62).
6. The claim of Jesus: He is the Messiah, the Son of God (vv.63-64).
7. The tragic verdict (vv.65-66).
8. The physical abuse inflicted (vv.67-68).

1 (26:57) **Jesus Christ, Trials**: Jesus was led to trial. He had been arrested and now He was being put on trial for His life. In the span of just a few hours, He was to be tried at least six times (see DEEPER STUDY # 1—Lu.22:66-71). The first trial was an informal trial before Annas, the retired High Priest who was highly respected by the Jewish leaders (Jn.18:13, 19-24). The trial before Caiaphas, in the present passage, was the second trial. The court (Sanhedrin) was already assembled. These were the very men who had Jesus arrested (Mt.26:3-5). They were the High Priest, the Scribes and the elders, that is, the Sanhedrin, the council who ruled the Jewish people for the Romans (v.59). In a hastily called meeting, the council was sitting there waiting for the guards to bring Jesus to them. Several facts reveal the evil of their

MATTHEW 26:57-68

hearts (see note and Deeper Study # 1—Mt.12:10; note—15:1-20; Deeper Study # 2—15:6-9; note—16:1-12; Deeper Study # 3—16:12).

    a. They had hastily assembled the court *at night*. It was illegal to try cases at night. All criminals had to be tried in the day.

    b. They were meeting in Caiaphas' palace (home), not in the official court. This, too, was illegal. All cases had to be tried in court.

    c. Jesus was being tried during the Passover week. No cases could be tried during the Passover week.

    d. They had not met to try Jesus but to secretly devise charges that would condemn Him to death.

Thought 1. A heart that wants to do evil will twist the rules. These religionists had to twist the law if they were going to condemn Christ.

Thought 2. A person often finds it easier to oppose Christ within a group than when alone. Not all among these religionists felt malice toward Christ, but most went along with those who did. They did not stand against the malicious and unjust treatment of our Lord. (It is doubtful if Nicodemus and Joseph of Arimathaea had been summoned to the hastily called illegal meeting. Their favorable feelings toward Christ were probably well known to the council. However, this is disputable, see Mt.27:57; Jn.3:1f.)

Thought 3. The house of Caiaphas, the religious leader, should have been an ideal home, a home that stood forth as a strong testimony for God. Yet, here it is seen as a center for evil.

Thought 4. Two things need to be observed and searched out in our lives.
(1) How far institutional religion twisted the minds of these men. Has it twisted our minds?
(2) How much these men were concerned for personal security, position, and influence (power). How far away these men were from God, and they were religionists (see note and Deeper Study # 1—Mt.12:10; note—15:1-20; Deeper Study # 2—15:6-9). How far have we allowed security, position, and influence to lead us away from God?

2 (26:58) **Peter**: there was the confused faith and loyalty of Peter. Peter was confused. He just could not understand why Jesus was not blasting His enemies and setting up His earthly kingdom (see note—Mt.26:51-52). When it was clear that Jesus was not going to act, Peter fled for his life, but he had not gone far. His love for Christ had stopped him, and now his love was turning him around to follow Christ along the trail to Caiaphas' palace. He wanted to see the end, just what would happen to His Lord.

> "Wherefore I put thee in remembrance that thou stir up the gift of God, which is in thee by the putting on of my hands. For God hath not given us the spirit of fear; but of power, and of love, and of a sound mind" (2 Ti.1:6-7).
>
> "There is no fear in love; but perfect love casteth out fear: because fear hath torment. He that feareth is not made perfect in love" (1 Jn.4:18).

Thought 1. Peter was caught between two forces: loyalty to Christ and fear for self. We are often caught between the same two forces. If we stand for Christ, we often find that we suffer ridicule or abuse or being passed over for some position, or a host of other possible acts of persecution.

Thought 2. Peter's failure was due to misunderstanding the truth about Christ (see note—Mt.26:51-52). Failure to understand Christ will lead to failure now and doom us to eternal failure.

3 (26:59) **Religionists**: there was the stacked court against Christ—predetermined rejection and opposition. The court was not convening to see if Jesus were guilty. The court was meeting to seek false witnesses against Christ (see Ps.35:11). They wanted to sentence Him to death. They had already determined in their hearts to reject and oppose Him. He was a threat to both their nation and their personal security and position. They feared the loss of both, so they were set on killing Him. (For a discussion of the reasons for their opposition, see note—Mt.12:1-8; note and Deeper Study # 1—12:10; note—15:1-20; Deeper Study # 2—15:6-9; Deeper Study # 3—16:12.)

Thought 1. The religionists rejected and opposed Christ for two primary reasons, the same two reasons that men reject and oppose Him today.
(1) They were unwilling to deny self, to surrender all they were and had to Christ. They feared loss, the loss of some security, money, position, pleasure. They loved the world and self more than they loved God.

> "Wherefore come out from among them, and be ye separate, saith the Lord, and touch not the unclean thing; and I will receive you, and will be a Father unto you, and ye shall be my sons and daughters, saith the Lord Almighty" (2 Co.6:17-18).

(2) They were unwilling to deny their institutional religion, their rituals and ceremonies and their religious practices that were *man-made, man-conceived,* and *man-honoring*.

> "Therefore to him that knoweth to do good, and doeth it not, to him it is sin" (Js.4:17).

"Beloved, follow not that which is evil, but that which is good. He that doeth good is of God: but he that doeth evil hath not seen God" (3 Jn.11).

> **DEEPER STUDY # 1**
> (26:59) **Sanhedrin**: the ruling body of the nation of Israel, both the governing council and supreme court of the Jews. It had seventy-one members and was presided over by the High Priest. Its membership was made up of the Pharisees, Sadducees, Scribes or lawyers, and the elders who were leaders from among the people. A quorum was twenty-three. The legal power of the Sanhedrin to pass the death sentence was restricted about twenty some years before the trial of Jesus. However, they did retain the right of excommunication (see Jn.9:22). To secure Jesus' death, they were forced by law to appeal to the Romans for the death sentence.

4 (26:60-61) **Jesus Christ, Charges Against**: there was the false charge—a revolutionary. Note the words "found none" are repeated twice. The religionists sought false witnesses but found none whose charges were strong enough. The law required two witnesses who had no contact with each other and who agreed on the same evidence. The court was to examine each separately. Apparently, the religionists ran into several problems...
- The evidence of the false charges was just too weak to convince the Roman authorities of Jesus' guilt.
- A strong case could not be formulated from the charges made.
- Two witnesses who agreed on a single charge could not be found.

Finally, two witnesses did come forth with a charge that seemed to be strong enough. Note the words "at last." The case almost broke down and failed. Imagine! Even in seeking false witnesses, the case against our Lord could not be established.

Note the following facts.
  a. The two witnesses with adequate testimony were false witnesses.
  b. The two were crude and base. This is shown by their contemptuous attitude and public animosity: "this fellow" (autos)—a disrespectful, contemptuous address.
  c. The two distorted Jesus' words. Jesus had said, "Destroy *ye* this temple, and in three days I will raise it up" (Jn.2:19). Jesus had actually said the Jews were to be the destroyers. But the false witnesses said, "*This fellow said*, I am able to destroy the temple of God." They distorted His words, making Him the destroyer.

The false witnesses also misunderstood Jesus' words. Jesus was referring to His body, to the temple of His body and to the resurrection of His body. The Jews apparently thought He meant He would destroy and rebuild the Jerusalem temple in three days. It was this charge, the charge of being a revolutionary, that the religionists believed they could use to convince the Romans to execute Jesus.

> "But his citizens hated him, and sent a message after him, saying, We will not have this man to reign over us" (Lu.19:14).
>
> "The world cannot hate you; but me it hateth, because I testify of it, that the works thereof are evil" (Jn.7:7).
>
> "If the world hate you, ye know that it hated me before it hated you....But this cometh to pass, that the word might be fulfilled that is written in their law, They hated me without a cause" (Jn.15:18, 25).

Thought 1. When men are bent on doing something, they often go ahead and do it—regardless of the method.
(1) When a man is bent on rejecting Christ, he rationalizes and justifies himself and rejects Christ.
(2) When a man is bent on doing something wrong, he rationalizes and justifies himself and does it.

Thought 2. One of the greatest mistakes we make is to distort the Word of Christ. The two false witnesses distorted and twisted His Word. When we distort and twist what He said, we condemn ourselves to destruction.

> "And account that the longsuffering of our Lord is salvation; even as our beloved brother Paul also according to the wisdom given unto him hath written unto you; as also in all his epistles, speaking in them of these things; in which are some things hard to be understood, which they that are unlearned and unstable wrest, as they do also the other scriptures, unto their own destruction" (2 Pe.3:15-16).

5 (26:62-63) **Jesus Christ, Trials**: there was the calm assurance of Jesus. Note these facts.
  a. The two witnesses who charged Jesus with being a revolutionary could not agree (Mk.14:59).
  b. The High Priest and court become disturbed and perhaps confused by Jesus' silence. They needed Him to begin speaking, hoping He would add evidence to the charge, thereby incriminating Himself. The High priest turned and attempted to pressure or browbeat Jesus: "Answerest thou nothing?" (v.62).
  c. Jesus *held His peace* (v.63). He said nothing to defend Himself against the false charges. Why did He say nothing? He was calm, assured, peaceful, and confident in the midst of turmoil.
   1) He stood in the will of God. He had been and was obedient to God. In the *determinate counsel of God,* it was God's will for Him to die (Ac.2:23; see Is. 53:7; Ps.38:13-14). Therefore, He would surrender to the false charge and murderous intention of the council.
   2) He said nothing because He would not become entangled in a useless argument. To answer would be useless, for He would be defending Himself against a false charge and against a group of men who were set on opposing and destroying Him.

3) He would answer only when an opportunity arose to proclaim the truth of the gospel: that He is the Messiah and that God does love the world (Mt.26:63-64; see Jn.3:16).

> "For he that will love life, and see good days, let him refrain his tongue from evil, and his lips that they speak no guile" (1 Pe.3:10).
> "He that keepeth his mouth keepeth his life: but he that openeth wide his lips shall have destruction" (Pr.13:3).
> "Whoso keepeth his mouth and his tongue, keepeth his soul from troubles" (Pr.21:23).

Thought 1. Christ taught that there are times when silence is the best policy.
(1) When words would entangle us in *useless argument*.
(2) When men are *set on opposing and destroying* us.
(3) When men *persecute* us (see note—Mt.10:23).
(4) When men *reject* our message (Mt.10:12-14).

Thought 2. God will give us an inner peace and calm assurance in great trial (see Jn.14:27; 16:33).

> "There hath no temptation taken you but such as is common to man: but God is faithful, who will not suffer you to be tempted above that ye are able; but will with the temptation also make a way to escape, that ye may be able to bear it" (1 Co.10:13).
> "[You] are kept by the power of God through faith unto salvation ready to be revealed in the last time. Wherein ye greatly rejoice, though now for a season, if need be, ye are in heaviness through manifold temptations: that the trial of your faith, being much more precious than of gold that perisheth, though it be tried with fire, might be found unto praise and honor and glory at the appearing of Jesus Christ" (1 Pe.1:5-7).
> "Beloved, think it not strange concerning the fiery trial which is to try you, as though some strange thing happened unto you: but rejoice, inasmuch as ye are partakers of Christ's sufferings; that, when his glory shall be revealed, ye may be glad also with exceeding joy" (1 Pe.4:12-13).

Thought 3. Jesus Christ willingly submitted to such false charges so that no man could "lay anything to the charge of God's elect" (Ro.8:33). Jesus Christ was falsely accused that we might not be condemned (Ro.8:34).

6 (26:63-64) **Jesus Christ, Deity**: there was the claim of Jesus: He is the Messiah, the Son of God. Four things happened here.

a. The High Priest questioned Jesus and put Him under oath to answer. The words "I adjure thee by the living God" was an official oath which demanded an answer. The High Priest used his office as God's representative to demand an answer: "*By the living God*, answer. Are you claiming to be the Messiah, the Son of God?" he asked Jesus.

b. Jesus claimed to be the Messiah, the Son of God (see note—Mt.1:18). Jesus answered, "Thou hast said." It was a strong assertion. All that Caiaphas had said was true. Mark added the striking words of deity, *I am* (ego eimi) (Mk.14:62; see Deeper Study # 1—Jn.6:20; note—18:6).

Note that Christ also called Himself "the Son of Man" (see Deeper Study # 3—Mt.26:64).

Thought 1. Jesus claimed beyond question to be the promised Messiah, the Son of God. He was claiming to be God of gods, Lord of lords, One with the Father in every respect (see Deeper Study # 1—Jn.6:20; note—18:4-6. See outline and notes—Ph.2:5-11.)

Thought 2. What if Jesus had said, "No. I am not the Messiah. I am not the Son of God." Where would we be today? Honestly and objectively, where would the world be today? Just imagine a world without the cross of Christ!

c. Jesus gave two proofs for His claim. His resurrection and exaltation and His second coming prove both His person and authority.

Thought 1. The believer hopes in the resurrection and exaltation and in the second coming of Christ, but the emphasis of Christ to these unbelievers is judgment.

⇒ His resurrection declares Him to be the Son of God (Ro.1:4).

> "And declared to be the Son of God with power, according to the spirit of holiness, by the resurrection from the dead" (Ro.1:4).

⇒ His exaltation declares His position and authority to rule and reign over all men (Ph.2:9-11).

> "Wherefore God also hath highly exalted him, and given him a name which is above every name: that at the name of Jesus every knee should bow, of things in heaven, and earth, and things under the earth; and that every tongue should confess that Jesus Christ is Lord, to the glory of God the Father" (Ph.2:9-11).

⇒ His return will declare His execution of justice and judgment (Mt.24:30; Jn.5:28).

MATTHEW 26:57-68

"And then shall appear the sign of the Son of man in heaven: and then shall all the tribes of the earth mourn, and they shall see the Son of man coming in the clouds of heaven with power and great glory" (Mt.24:30).

"Marvel not at this: for the hour is coming, in the which all that are in the graves shall hear his voice" (Jn.5:28).

DEEPER STUDY # 2
(26:64) **Christ**: see Deeper Study # 2—Mt.1:18.

DEEPER STUDY # 3
(26:64) **Son of Man**: see Deeper Study # 3—Mt.8:20.

---

[7] (26:65-66) **Jesus Christ, Condemned**: there was the tragic verdict. Note that Caiaphas tore his clothes. Mark even says he tore his under garments (tunic). This was a custom among Jews when they heard or saw God's name dishonored or disgraced (2 K.18:37; 19:1 see Is.36:22; 27:1; Ac.14:14). Caiaphas had gotten what he wanted. Christ had committed blasphemy which was punishable by death among the Jews (Le.24:16; see Ac.7:58). No other witnesses were needed. *A vote by acclamation* was quickly called for: "What think ye? They answered and said, He is guilty of death."

[8] (26:67-68) **Jesus Christ, Death**: there was the physical abuse inflicted. The bitter enmity and hatred of the Jews broke through. The rights and expectation of justice was completely forgotten. The abuse took two forms.

a. Bitter hatred and behavior. Spitting in the face was a sign of monstrous disrespect. Beating with the fists and palms (erra pisan, rods) was an outburst of the inner bitterness within the hearts of the religionists against Christ.

"I gave my back to the smiters, and my cheeks to them that plucked off the hair: I hid not my face from shame and spitting" (Is.50:6; see Is.52:14).

"They shall smite the judge of Israel with a rod upon the cheek" (Mi.5:1).

b. Ridicule of His claim, mocking His supernatural power and sarcastically calling Him "thou Christ."

Thought 1. Rejecting and opposing can cause bitterness. Too many harbor an inner bitterness against God and Christ. Too many have allowed their rejection and opposition and the events which happened to them to grow into bitterness. Thus when opportunity arises, they vent their feelings and hostility. Too many believers, in rejecting or opposing Christ, allow bitterness to seep into their hearts. Too many vent their feelings and bitterness when they have a chance to attack some movement of God or some true believer who faithfully follows Christ day by day.

MATTHEW 26:69-75

	I. The Messiah Denied by Peter: A Look at Denying Christ, 26:69-75
	(Mk 14:66-72; Lu 22:54-62; Jn 18:15-18, 25-27)
		Nazareth.
		72 And again he denied with an oath, I do not know the man.
		73 And after a while came unto *him* they that stood by, and said to Peter, Surely thou also art *one* of them; for thy speech bewrayeth thee.
		74 Then began he to curse and to swear, *saying,* I know not the man. And immediately the cock crew.
		75 And Peter remembered the word of Jesus, which said unto him, Before the cock crow, thou shalt deny me thrice. And he went out, and wept bitterly.
			b. Denial by oath: Called Jesus *the man*–downgraded Him
			4. The denial by cursing & swearing
			a. Charge: Peter was a disciple
			  1) A crowd came
			  2) Speech betrayed
			b. Denial by cursing & swearing
			5. The answer to denial: Repentance^{DS2}
			a. Remembering the Lord's Word
			b. Getting alone
			c. Repenting: Godly sorrow

1. The cause of denial: Sitting with the crowd^{DS1}
2. The denial by pretension
a. Charge: Peter had been with Jesus
b. Denial: Peter pretended he did not know Jesus
3. The denial by oath
a. Charge: Peter had been with Jesus
  1) Made by a girl
  2) Made before a crowd
	69 Now Peter sat without in the palace: and a damsel came unto him, saying, Thou also wast with Jesus of Galilee.
	70 But he denied before *them* all, saying, I know not what thou sayest.
	71 And when he was gone out into the porch, another *maid* saw him, and said unto them that were there, This *fellow* was also with Jesus of		

DIVISION XVI

THE MESSIAH'S ARREST, TRIAL, AND CRUCIFIXION, 26:1-27:66

I. The Messiah Denied by Peter: A Look at Denying Christ, 26:69-75

(26:69-75) **Introduction—Apostasy—Jesus Christ, Denied**: denying Christ is serious, very serious. It is a tragic and terrible sin, yet Christ forgives even a man who denies Him. He forgave Peter; and in forgiving Peter, He has demonstrated forever God's unbelievable love for man, no matter how terrible man's sin. Just think for a moment. Christ forgave a man who professed an undying loyalty to Him yet who ended up denying Him three times when the man felt pressured and threatened by a crowd. No greater picture of God's great love and marvelous grace can be found.

Note another point as well: Peter wanted the world to know about the Lord's great love. The story of His denying Christ originates with him. No other disciple was there to witness it. He shared the terrible experience and God's wondrous grace in forgiving him. Mark was Peter's disciple, and Mark is the gospel writer who shares the most detail about Peter's denials.

Peter's tragic experience in denying Christ says much to believers of all generations.
1. The cause of denial: sitting with the crowd (v.69).
2. The denial by pretension (vv.69-70).
3. The denial by oath (vv.71-72).
4. The denial by cursing and swearing (vv.73-74).
5. The answer to denial: repentance (v.75).

1 (26:69) **Apostasy—Denial**: the cause of Peter's denial was that he *sat without in the palace*. He sat down with the crowd, the crowd which represented the world of rejecters. Very frankly, Peter was failing Christ and failing Him miserably. Sitting down among the crowd was the last place he should have been. Of course, He should have never forsaken Christ. But having fled, he should have been off alone with God in prayer, seeking answers and understanding from God (see notes—Mt.26:51-52; 26:55-56). Or he should have been with the other apostles, leading them to seek the face of God for understanding and direction.

There are at least three causes for denial—three things that can lead a person to deny Christ. All three are seen in Peter's experience (also see notes—Jn.18:12-27).

a. Deserting Christ: turning away from Him and fleeing from Him (see Mt.26:56).
b. *Following Christ afar off*: not walking close to Him, not standing and being identified with Him (see Mt.26:58).

> "For God hath not given us the spirit of fear; but of power, and of love, and of a sound mind. Be not thou therefore ashamed of the testimony of our Lord, nor of me his prisoner: but be thou partaker of the afflictions of the gospel according to the power of God" (2 Ti.1:7-8).

c. *Sitting without* or sitting with the crowd: not being where one should be, with the disciples of the Lord.

> "Wherefore come out from among them, and be ye separate, saith the Lord, and touch not the unclean thing; and I will receive you, and will be a Father unto you, and ye shall be my sons and daughters, saith the Lord Almighty" (2 Co.6:17-18).

> "Now we command you, brethren, in the name of our Lord Jesus Christ, that ye withdraw yourselves from every brother that walketh disorderly, and not after the tradition which he received of us" (2 Th.3:6).

MATTHEW 26:69-75

> **DEEPER STUDY # 1**
> (26:69) **Palace**: Peter was not actually in the palace proper. He was in the courtyard. The first denial took place in the courtyard, the second on the porch of the palace.

2 (26:69-70) **Apostasy—Denial**: there was the denial by pretension. This is always a denial that pretends to have nothing to do with Christ.

The guard at the gate (a woman) knew John and allowed him to enter (Jn.18:15). Apparently John requested her to let Peter enter. Note the words, "thou *also* wast with Jesus." She seemed to be making a simple statement to Peter, perhaps for identification purposes. There seemed to be no threat or danger to Peter, yet Peter pretended to know nothing about Jesus. Again, note his exact words: "I know not what thou sayest"; that is, he pretended to know nothing about what she was saying or to know nothing about this Jesus of Nazareth. In either case, Peter denied and pretended to have nothing to do with Jesus.

> "Whosoever therefore shall be ashamed of me and of my words in this adulterous and sinful generation; of him also shall the Son of man be ashamed, when he cometh in the glory of his Father with the holy angels" (Mk.8:38).
>
> "The fear of man bringeth a snare: but whoso putteth his trust in the LORD shall be safe" (Pr.29:25).
>
> "But sanctify the Lord God in your hearts: and be ready always to give an answer to every man that asketh you a reason of the hope that is in you with meekness and fear" (1 Pe.3:15).

Thought 1. Pretending is one of the constant sins of men.
⇒ We are asked if we think something. We do, yet we deny it.
⇒ We are asked if we feel something. We do, yet we deny it.
⇒ We are asked if we fear something. We do, yet we deny it.
⇒ We are asked if we did something. We did, yet we deny it.

Thought 2. Too many believers deny Christ by pretension. Very simply, they pretend not to know Christ when out in the world...

- at their employment
- at their school
- at their social functions
- among their neighbors
- among their friends
- among strangers

Thought 3. Pretension is two things.
(1) Pretension is hypocrisy. It is pretending to be something we are not.
(2) Pretension is denial of Christ. It is shying away from or lying about one's confession of Christ.

3 (26:71-72) **Apostasy—Denial**: there was the denial by oath. This is a denial that is strong and emphatic, "I swear by God, I do not know the man. I know nothing about Him."

a. This charge was made by another maid or servant girl, and it was made before a crowd of people. By being made before a crowd, Peter felt more threatened. The charge is the same, "This fellow was also with Jesus." Note the charge was true.
⇒ Peter had been with Jesus. He was an apostle; in fact, he was supposedly the leader of the apostles.
⇒ Peter was the disciple who had professed that Jesus was the Christ, the Son of God (Mt.16:16).
⇒ Peter was the disciple who had sworn loyalty to Christ even if it meant death (Mt.26:33-35).

b. The denial which uses an oath downgrades Christ. Note that Peter called Christ, "the man!" He, of course, was the Man; but Peter did not mean the Man in this sense. Peter ignored who Jesus really was, pushing his responsibility to profess Christ out of his mind. Embarrassment, ridicule, abuse, persecution, and the threat of arrest and death intimidated him; so he denied any knowledge of Christ with an emphatic oath: "I swear to God, I do not know the man."

> "But whosoever shall deny me before men, him will I also deny before my Father which is in heaven" (Mt.10:33).
>
> "Be not thou therefore ashamed of the testimony of our Lord, nor of me his prisoner: but be thou partaker of the afflictions of the gospel according to the power of God" (2 Ti.1:8).
>
> "Be strong and of a good courage, fear not, nor be afraid of them: for the LORD thy God, he it is that doth go with thee; he will not fail thee, nor forsake thee" (De.31:6).

Thought 1. Note something important. In the first denial, Peter was charged by only one person. His denial was a simple denial by pretension, of simply ending the issue: "I know not what thou sayest." But in this second denial, Peter was charged before a crowd. He felt more threatened; therefore, his denial was stronger and more emphatic: he used an oath. The lesson for us is clear. The more we are among the crowds of the world, the more we are threatened with ridicule, embarrassment, abuse, and persecution for our profession in Christ. And the more we are threatened, the more likely we are to deny Christ (see Ro.12:1-2; 2 Co.6:17-18; 1 Jn.2:15-16).

MATTHEW 26:69-75

Thought 2. There is a strong warning for us in Peter's denials.
⇒ Peter was a strong disciple.
⇒ Peter knew and had trusted Christ as the Messiah, the Son of God.
⇒ Peter had a strong profession of loyalty to Christ.
⇒ Peter had just partaken of the Lord's Supper; in fact, he had just been privileged to partake of the very first Supper.
⇒ Peter had left all to follow Christ.
⇒ Peter had been taught about God, taught by Christ Himself.
⇒ Peter had even been forewarned that the flesh was weak and that he would fail.

Thought 3. Every denial (in fact, every neglect) of Christ downgrades the Lord. Denial (and neglect) ignores just who Christ is, the Son of God who possesses all power and majesty and dominion. Denial shows that we fear men more than we fear and reverence God. Neglect of Christ shows how little we fear and reverence Him. The Biblical exhortation always needs to be kept in mind: "The Lord shall judge His people. It is a fearful thing to fall into the hands of the living God" (He.10:30-31).

Thought 4. Peter had forgotten Christ's exhortation: "Swear not at all...." (Mt.5:34-37).

Thought 5. Too many believers fear, and because they fear, they lose their testimony for Christ and the opportunity to witness and win others to Christ. Too many fear...
- embarrassment
- ridicule
- abuse
- loss of position
- worldly friends
- worldly neighbors
- business management
- loss of promotion

4 (26:73-74) **Apostasy—Denial**: there was the strongest and most terrible denial of all, the denial by cursing and swearing.

a. The charge was made by a crowd this time, a crowd who actually came up to Peter to charge him. Luke says it happened about one hour after the second charge (Lu.22:59). And John says that one of the persons in the crowd was a kinsman of Malchus, whose ear Peter had cut off in the garden of Gethsemane (Jn.18:26). Note that the third charge differed from the other two: Peter was no longer charged with having been with Jesus; he was now charged with being "one of them," one of the disciples. Note also that it was his speech, his accent that gave him away. Peter was from the north, from Galilee, and his northern accent differed significantly from the speech of Judaea and Jerusalem.

b. The denial by cursing and swearing is a terrible sin. A man who is put under pressure to prove himself often resorts to cursing and swearing. Note three things.
1) Peter *began* to curse. His cursing was a continuous thing.
2) Peter's failure was a deteriorating failure. His first denial was simply pretending not to know Christ, simply evading the issue. His second denial was stronger, using a socially acceptable oath (although it was wrong and a sin). His third denial declines into depraved cursing, totally unacceptable to righteous hearts and pure minds and clean lips.
3) As soon as Peter had cursed and swore for a while, "immediately the cock crew."

Thought 1. A crowd of unbelievers can put pressure upon any of us. Peter was where he did not belong. He was hanging around in the midst of a worldly crowd. He belonged in one of three places: by the side of Christ, or alone with God seeking answers and understanding, or with the other apostles, rallying them in prayer for understanding and direction.

> "And have no fellowship with the unfruitful works of darkness, but rather reprove them" (Ep.5:11).
> "They profess that they know God; but in works they deny him, being abominable, and disobedient, and unto every good work reprobate" (Tit.1:16).
> "Ye therefore, beloved, seeing ye know these things before, beware lest ye also, being led away with the error of the wicked, fall from your own stedfastness" (2 Pe.3:17).
> "Enter not into the path of the wicked, and go not in the way of evil men" (Pr.4:14).

Thought 2. Our speech should give us away. Our speech should be kind, gentle, yet strong—strong for the Lord. A person should be able to tell we are believers by our speech. Note that Peter used his speech, his cursing to try to deceive the crowd into thinking that he was anything but a disciple. The Lord's disciples are not to curse and swear. Cursing and swearing are terrible sins in the eyes of the Lord (see outline and notes—Mt.5:33-37).

Thought 3. Sin causes man to deteriorate: it causes him to deteriorate more and more, to wax worse and worse. Note what happened to Peter.
(1) Peter's first denial: he pretended ignorance, simply sinned.
(2) Peter's second denial: he committed apostasy, infidelity.
(3) Peter's third denial: he committed perjury, blasphemy.

MATTHEW 26:69-75

5 (26:75) **Denial**: there was the answer to denial—repentance. Three steps were involved in Peter's repentance.

a. Remembering the Lord's words: apparently while the rooster was crowing, the Lord, standing in the chamber of the palace, turned around and caught Peter's eye (Lu.22:61). And Peter, eye to eye with the Lord, remembered the words the Lord had spoken to him:

> "And the Lord said, Simon, Simon, behold, Satan hath desired to have you, that he may sift you as wheat: but I have prayed for thee, that thy faith fail not: and when thou art converted, strengthen thy brethren" (Lu.22:31-32).

In the midst of all His own pain and suffering, the Lord took time to look at Peter. His look told Peter that His Lord had not forgotten him. The Lord still loved and cared for Him and wanted his loyalty and service. Christ had prayed for Peter, and the power of that prayer was now moving in Peter's heart and life. Peter now remembered His Lord's word and that word began to take effect.

b. Getting alone: Peter left the porch or courtyard as fast as he safely could. He rushed out through the gate into the night to get alone with God. He was broken and full of anguish and pain for having failed his Lord: he "wept bitterly."

c. Repenting and experiencing godly sorrow. Peter repented and expressed godly sorrow (see DEEPER STUDY # 1—2 Co.7:10).

> "If we confess our sins, he is faithful and just to forgive us our sins, and to cleanse us from all unrighteousness" (1 Jn.1:9).
>
> "Repent therefore of this thy wickedness, and pray God, if perhaps the thought of thine heart may be forgiven thee" (Ac.8:22).
>
> "Now therefore make confession unto the LORD God of your fathers, and do his pleasure: and separate yourselves from the people of the land" (Ezr. 10:11).
>
> "He that covereth his sins shall not prosper: but whoso confesseth and forsaketh them shall have mercy" (Pr.28:13).
>
> "Only acknowledge thine iniquity, that thou hast transgressed against the LORD thy God, and hast scattered thy ways to the strangers under every green tree, and ye have not obeyed my voice, saith the LORD" (Je.3:13).

Thought 1. The same steps Peter took are the steps we need to take in repenting of sin.

DEEPER STUDY # 2
(27:75) **Repentance**: see note and DEEPER STUDY # 1—Ac.17:29-30.

MATTHEW 27:1-10

	CHAPTER 27
	
	J. The Messiah's Traitor, Judas, & His End: A Picture of Wrong Repentance & Human Religion, 27:1-10
	(Ac. 1:16-19)
		What *is that* to us? see thou *to that*.
		5 And he cast down the pieces of silver in the temple, and departed, and went and hanged himself.
		6 And the chief priests took the silver pieces, and said, It is not lawful for to put them into the treasury, because it is the price of blood.
		7 And they took counsel, and bought with them the potter's field, to bury strangers in.
		8 Wherefore that field was called, The field of blood, unto this day.
		9 Then was fulfilled that which was spoken by Jeremy the prophet, saying, And they took the thirty pieces of silver, the price of him that was valued, whom they of the children of Israel did value;
		10 And gave them for the potter's field, as the Lord appointed me.
			e. He was not helped; he was left to himself
			f. He cast the money at the priests
			g. He fell into utter despair & hanged himself
			3. The religionists' human religion
			  a. They were inconsistent: In behavior & religious rules
			  b. They were deceptive: They tried to hide their evil by public service–bought a cemetery
			    1) It became known as the *Field of Blood*
			    2) It was a fulfillment of Scripture, Zec.11:12-13[DS1]

1. Jesus' tragic punishment: By the Sanhedrin
  a. They met to finalize the charge to convince the Romans
  b. They bound Jesus
  c. They led Jesus away–to Pilate
2. Judas' wrong repentance
  a. He saw his sin: Jesus was condemned
  b. He felt remorse, but to the priests not to God
  c. He made restitution, but too late
  d. He confessed, but to the priests not to God
	When the morning was come, all the chief priests and elders of the people took counsel against Jesus to put him to death:
	2 And when they had bound him, they led *him* away, and delivered him to Pontius Pilate the governor.
	3 Then Judas, which had betrayeth him, when he saw that he was condemned, repented himself, and brought again the thirty pieces of silver to the chief priests and elders,
	4 Saying, I have sinned in that I have betrayed the innocent blood. And they said,		

DIVISION XVI

THE MESSIAH'S ARREST, TRIAL, AND CRUCIFIXION, 26:1–27:66

J. The Messiah's Traitor, Judas, and His End: A Picture of Wrong Repentance and Human Religion, 27:1-10

(27:1-10) **Introduction—Judas**: there were two misguided culprits involved in the death of Christ—Judas Iscariot and the Sanhedrin, the ruling body of the Jews. Judas was the culprit who betrayed Christ; the body of the Sanhedrin was the culprit who condemned Christ in a stacked and unjust trial.

There is recorded in this passage something often overlooked: Judas did repent (v.3). He turned away from his terrible sin and tried to make restitution. However, his repentance was a wrong repentance. What he did fell far short of what he needed to do. Nevertheless, he did try to right his wrong. It is this picture, the picture of wrong repentance, that is discussed in the first part of this passage.

The second part of the passage pictures the humanistic religion of the priests. It discusses how they treated Judas' repentance and blood money, that is, the money they themselves had paid him for betraying Christ. The incident shows just how much man uses and twists religion to suit his own desires and lusts.

1. Jesus' tragic punishment: By the Sanhedrin (vv.1-2).
2. Judas' wrong repentance (vv.3-5).
   a. He saw his sin: Jesus was condemned.
   b. He felt remorse, but to the priests not to God.
   c. He made restitution, but too late.
   d. He confessed, but to the priests not to God.
   e. He was not helped; he was left to himself.
   f. He cast the money at the priests.
   g. He fell into utter despair and hanged himself.
3. The religionists' human religion (vv.6-10).
   a. They were inconsistent: in behavior and religious rules.
   b. They were deceptive: they tried to hide their evil by public service—bought a cemetery.

1 (27:1-2) **Jesus Christ, Trial—Sanhedrin**: Jesus was condemned by the Sanhedrin (see notes—Mt.26:57-68). They had met the evening before in a hastily called meeting to put Christ on trial for His life. They had secured the false witnesses and charges they sought. Now, in these verses, they are seen meeting to formulate the charges in such a way that the Romans would be forced to condemn Christ as a revolutionary. As soon as the charge was worded, they bound and led Christ away in an atmosphere of triumph.

The fact to note is that Judas apparently witnessed these unjust proceedings against Christ. "He saw that Christ was condemned" (v.3), and it was his witnessing the unjust condemnation of Christ that led to the two events of the present passage.

2 (27:3-5) **Judas—Repentance**: Judas' wrong repentance. Judas did repent, but his repentance was a worldly repentance, not a godly repentance. Seven things are said about Judas.

a. Judas saw his sin; he saw Jesus condemned. Note the words, "When he saw that he [Christ] was condemned." It was seeing Jesus so unjustly condemned that caused Judas to do what he now did. He knew Christ, how good Christ was. He did not believe Jesus to be the Messiah, but he knew that Jesus was a tremendously good man, and he knew that it was because of his sin that Jesus was being condemned to death in a most unjust and savage way (see notes—Mt.26:57-68). This fact—plus the fact that Jesus was definitely God's Son and that God was causing a sharp pang of guilt in the chest of Judas—drove Judas to seek relief. He felt boiling up within him an intense remorse and grief, the sense of being all alone, even without God, and a sense of not knowing what to do. It was too much, more than he could bear. He felt he would explode if he did not get relief of soul and some deliverance.

Note: Judas knew the religionists were seeking to kill Jesus. Apparently many knew of the plot (Jn.5:18; 7:1, 19-20). This was the very reason Judas went to the authorities and betrayed Christ into their hands. Some say there is a possibility that he thought sufficient charges could never be formulated against Christ. However, this is not likely, and Scripture gives no hint of this possibility. Jesus was a revolutionary. The religionists feared for their religion (Judaism), position, and security (see notes—Mt.12:1-8; note and DEEPER STUDY # 1—12:10; note—15:1-20; DEEPER STUDY # 2—15:6-9). Judas knew Christ was making changes, and when the authorities began to make their move, Judas set out to get what he could out of a bad situation. He wanted to assure his own safety and security (see outline and notes—Mt.26:14-16). The guilt and remorse boiling up within him seems to be the explanation for his deep conviction of sin and repentance.

> "Now when they heard this, they were pricked in their heart, and said unto Peter and to the rest of the apostles, Men and brethren, what shall we do?" (Ac.2:37).
>
> "And as he reasoned of righteousness, temperance, and judgment to come, Felix trembled, and answered, Go thy way for this time; when I have a convenient season, I will call for thee" (Ac.24:25).
>
> "For mine iniquities are gone over mine head: as an heavy burden they are too heavy for me" (Ps.38:4).
>
> "For I acknowledge my transgressions: and my sin is ever before me" (Ps.51:3).

Thought 1. Believers see Christ condemned practically every day, that is, cursed, ridiculed, and abused by various people standing around talking. Such condemnation should convict us. Our silence should stir turmoil within our hearts. We need to speak up and take a position by the side of our Lord. Too many betray our Lord in such moments. Jesus is God's Son, and He deserves the utmost respect from every man.

b. Judas repented. However, he repented to the priests, not to God. Note the words "Judas...repented himself...to the chief priests and elders." There is no mention of God at all. This was his mistake. Repentance means to change and to turn away from sin to God (see note and DEEPER STUDY # 1—Acts 17:29-30). Judas needed to change, to turn from his terrible sin. But he needed to turn to God, not to other men.

> "Repent therefore of this thy wickedness, and pray God, if perhaps the thought of thine heart may be forgiven thee" (Ac.8:22).
>
> "Let the wicked forsake his way, and the unrighteous man his thoughts: and let him return unto the LORD, and he will have mercy upon him; and to our God, for he will abundantly pardon" (Is.55:7).
>
> "But if the wicked will turn from all his sins that he hath committed, and keep all my statutes, and do that which is lawful and right, he shall surely live, he shall not die" (Eze.18:21).
>
> "Therefore also now, saith the LORD, turn ye even to me with all your heart, and with fasting, and with weeping, and with mourning" (Joel 2:12).

Thought 1. Sin should lead to repentance. When we sense *guilt* for real sin, we should repent and turn from the sin. *But to whom we turn* is the critical factor: we are to turn to God. Turning away from sin is not enough. Changing and turning our backs and walking away from sin is not enough. We must turn our faces toward God and walk with Him.

c. Judas made restitution. Judas did what God wants every man to do: make restitution for his sin. But he was too late. He should have made restitution while events could be changed. He should have shown a repentance to God and returned the money *before Christ was condemned*. It was too late now. Christ was already condemned and his life was doomed.

Note that this was the second mistake Judas made. He repented to the priests, not to God; and here he made restitution, but too late.

Thought 1. We should make restitution for our sins, but we must act soon enough to make amends and to change events. We must act soon enough to save the situation. The first step, of course, is to repent before God; and then we can make restitution. But note, there is a right way and a wrong way to do both. Judas repented, but he repented in a wrong way. He turned in remorse to men instead of turning to God. He made restitution, but he made restitution too late. We must *turn to God and make restitution*, being sure to correct the situation soon enough.

MATTHEW 27:1-10

Thought 2. Money and other things which are secured through evil ways will eat away at a person's mind and heart.

> "Your gold and silver is cankered; and the rust of them shall be a witness against you, and shall eat your flesh as it were fire. Ye have heaped treasure together for the last days" (Js.5:3).

d. Judas confessed, but he confessed to the priests not to God. Note Judas' words, "I have sinned." But he was speaking to the chief priests and elders, not to God. Note something important: Judas accepted personal responsibility for his sin; he blamed no one else. He said, "I have sinned." His problem was that he went to men instead of going to God. He should have confessed his sin to God; instead, he carried his burden to men. He should have gone to God for relief and confession, for only God could have saved and relieved him.

Note: Judas was gripped with a worldly sorrow, not a godly sorrow (see DEEPER STUDY # 1—2 Co.7:10).

> "If we confess our sins, he is faithful and just to forgive us our sins, and to cleanse us from all unrighteousness" (1 Jn.1:9).
> "Now therefore make confession unto the Lord God of your fathers, and do his pleasure: and separate yourselves from the people of the land, and from the strange wives" (Ezr. 10:11).
> "Only acknowledge thine iniquity, that thou hast transgressed against the Lord thy God, and hast scattered thy ways to the strangers under every green tree, and ye have not obeyed my voice, saith the Lord" (Je.3:13).

Thought 1. Confession is essential if we wish forgiveness, but confession is to be made to God not to men.

Thought 2. We sin and are personally responsible for our own sin. No one else is responsible for our sin. Blame cannot be laid at anyone else's feet.

Thought 3. There is a wrong confession, a worldly sorrow, as well as a right confession, a godly sorrow (see DEEPER STUDY #1—2 Co.7:10).

e. Judas was not helped, and he was left to himself. Judas felt guilt, for he had betrayed Christ. The religionists did not feel guilt for they saw Christ as a threat to their religion and nation (Mt.12:1-8; 12:10; 15:1-20; 15:6-9). Therefore, in their minds, they were serving their religion (God) and their nation (God's chosen people). If Judas were bothered with a guilty conscience, he was a fool. They had no time, especially right now in the *busyness* of the moment. They did not have time to be concerned with a guilt stricken fool who could not see *the good* he had done in helping his nation and religion. Note the words of the religionists to Judas, and keep in mind that Judas was a man who was desperately crying out for help: "What is that to us? See thou to it [that is your concern]."

Four terrible things are seen in the action and words of the religionists.

1) Hardness of heart: a hardness that keeps a man from helping those in need, even those who are desperate for help.
2) Misunderstanding the ministry: not understanding the true ministry and call of God which is to help people at any cost. (The religionists were the priests of God; yet instead of helping, they just left Judas to himself.)
3) Extreme blindness: a blindness of mind caused by rationalizing and twisting the truth. They were able to justify their behavior in their minds, so they were able to turn from Judas and to continue on in their sin of putting Christ to death.
4) Obstinate unbelief: unbelief that persists, that just marches on in its own will and way, rejecting and rejecting the truth (see DEEPER STUDY #4—Mt.12:24; note—12:31-32).

> "But after thy hardness and impenitent heart treasurest up unto thyself wrath against the day of wrath and revelation of the righteous judgment of God" (Ro.2:5).
> "But exhort one another daily, while it is called To day; lest any of you be hardened through the deceitfulness of sin" (He.3:13).
> "Happy is the man that feareth always: but he that hardeneth his heart shall fall into mischief" (Pr.28:14).
> "He, that being often reproved hardeneth his neck, shall suddenly be destroyed, and that without remedy" (Pr.29:1).

Thought 1. The mind can easily twist the truth and rationalize. It can easily take misbehavior and justify it. If we lust to do something, the mind can usually find a way to do it, a way that allows us to justify ourselves. But, just as the priests were guilty of terrible sin, so are we. No matter how much we rationalize and justify our behavior, the truth condemns us. The truth of righteousness cannot be changed.

Thought 2. *Busyness* to some degree kept the religionists from helping Judas. The claim is too often made that we are too busy to help. The first priority of ministry is to help those in need.

Thought 3. Note the four terrible things seen in the action of the religionists. They are applicable to many.

Thought 4. What would have happened if Judas had run up to Christ, begging forgiveness? If he had run to the disciples for help?

f. Judas threw the money at the feet of the priests. This was an act of frustration and anger, of hopelessness and helplessness. What could he do? The religionists were not going to change their verdict against Christ. Neither were they going to help him in his desperate need. In his mind, there was no one to help. He was stricken with guilt, standing all alone with no hand to help. Hopelessness and helplessness set in. In anger against the priests, he threw the blood money into the court at the feet of the priests and raced out of the temple into the streets of the city. He passed through the city gate into the country, seeking to escape his gnawing conscience, the glare of human eyes, and the haunting face of Him whom he had betrayed.

"O my God, my soul is cast down within me...." (Ps.42:6).
"But as for me, my feet were almost gone; my steps had well nigh slipped" (Ps.73:2).
"Withhold thy foot from being unshod, and thy throat from thirst: but thou saidst, There is no hope: no; for I have loved strangers, and after them will I go" (Je.2:25).

Thought 1. There is a fact that always needs to be remembered. When facing spiritual need, God is the One to whom we should turn, not man. The help of man in providing spiritual deliverance is empty. The end result of man's deliverance is always frustration, helplessness, and hopelessness. Man cannot erase guilt and liberate the anguished soul of man.

g. Judas fell into utter despair and hung himself. He was gripped by guilt, grief, despair, and helplessness. He was haunted and saw no hope. Left alone with his thoughts, he felt his sin was too terrible to be forgiven. He felt God could never forgive him for so great a sin. So he took his belt, and as Peter seems to indicate, tied it to an overhanging rock on a mountain precipice and hung himself. The belt broke and Judas fell headlong, bursting his body asunder (Ac.1:18).

Note a significant fact: Judas' sin was not unpardonable. He could have been forgiven. Throughout history many murderers have been forgiven, but Judas make a common mistake, a mistake that is more clearly seen by being stated in several ways.

⇒ He felt his sin was too great to be forgiven.
⇒ He thought the mercy of God was limited, too small to forgive his sin.
⇒ He thought his sin was greater than the mercy of God.
⇒ He allowed his sin to overshadow and blot out the mercy of God.

"My soul is weary of my life; I will leave my complaint upon myself; I will speak in the bitterness of my soul" (Jb.10:1).
"I sink in deep mire, where there is no standing: I am come into deep waters, where the floods overflow me" (Ps.69:2).
"When I thought to know this, it was too painful for me" (Ps.73:16).
"But Zion said, The LORD hath forsaken me, and my Lord hath forgotten me" (Is.49:14).
"Christ...having no hope, and without God in the world" (Ep.2:12).

Thought 1. We should never abandon ourselves to despair nor become suffocated with grief. We should never be haunted with helplessness and hopelessness. Christ Jesus delivers and helps meet our need perfectly.

Thought 2. God's mercy is so great and so sufficient it will cover any sin. We just need to come to Him, confess and repent, then He will forgive and deliver us unto eternal life.

Thought 3. Note the difference between Judas and Peter. Both sinned against the Lord and regretted their sinful acts, but only Peter repented. He repented and was received by the Lord and recommissioned for service (Jn.21:15-17). But Judas gave up in utter despair and destroyed himself. Regret can lead to repentance or to remorse and destruction.

3 (27:6-10) **Religionists**: the religionists' human religion. These verses show just how the chief priests took their religion and twisted it to suit their own desires. The corruption of their lives and religion is clearly seen.

a. Their corruption is seen in their inconsistency. They were inconsistent in both their behavior and their religious rules. They held the position of serving God, yet they sought false witnesses against an innocent man and condemned Him to death (Mt.26:57-68). They claimed to be the servants of God, yet they turned away from ministering to a man (Judas) in desperate need. Neither their behavior nor their religion matched their profession.

They were also inconsistent in their religious rules. They took the money out of the temple treasury to pay a bribe, but they would not put the same money back into the treasury. They were careful to keep the religious rules that suited them, but they were loose in true justice and mercy.

The law said that money gained or used in an evil way was not acceptable for God's service (De.23:18). It was this rule that they haggled over, this rule that shows how inconsistent they had become in behavior and religion. They had taken the religion given by God and twisted it to suit their own wills and desires. They had developed a man-made religion that allowed them to do as they wished.

b. Their corruption is also seen in their deception. They tried to hide their evil by public service. They took the blood-money of Judas and purchased land for a public cemetery. The purpose of the religionists seems clear. They had hoped that such a service to the public would help in quieting any grumbling over the death of Christ. But note: their scheme failed. The public, discovering through talk and rumor that the field had been purchased with the blood-money of Jesus' betrayer, began to call the cemetery "the field of blood."

"Even so ye also outwardly appear righteous unto men, but within ye are full of hypocrisy and iniquity" (Mt.23:28).

"And God looked upon the earth, and, behold, it was corrupt; for all flesh had corrupted his way upon the earth" (Ge.6:12).

"But they also have erred through wine, and through strong drink are out of the way; the priest and the prophet have erred through strong drink, they are swallowed up of wine, they are out of the way through strong drink; they err in vision, they stumble in judgment. For all tables are full of vomit and filthiness, so that there is no place clean" (Is.28:7-8).

"They are waxen fat, they shine: yea, they overpass the deeds of the wicked: they judge not the cause, the cause of the fatherless, yet they prosper; and the right of the needy do they not judge" (Je.5:28).

DEEPER STUDY # 1
(27:9-10) **Old Testament Quotation**: this quotation is from Zec.11:12-13, not from Jeremiah. There are several explanations for Jeremiah's being credited with the statement. Two of the more reasonable explanations are as follows.

1. Some later writer added the word *Jeremiah* to the Scripture while making a copy. The word is omitted in the Syriac, Persic, and other Latin copies.

2. Many Hebrew manuscripts list Jeremiah as the first prophetic book. Matthew, unable to remember exactly where the prophecy was found, uses the first prophetic book, Jeremiah, to stand for the roll of the prophets. Jeremiah, by being the first prophet, represented the prophets.

MATTHEW 27:11-25

	K. The Messiah's Tragic Trial Before Pilate: The Tragedy of an Indecisive Man, DS1 27:11-25 (Mk 15:1-15; Lu 23:1-25; Jn 18:28-40)		

1. The governor rejected the Lord's strong confession
  a. Jesus' strong & straightforward claim: He is King
 	
  b. Jesus' strong & controlled behavior: Under severe accusation, He was silent & purposed
  c. Jesus' strong & enduring purpose: Under repeated questioning, He endured
 	
  d. Jesus' impact: Pilate was impressed but still indecisive
 	
2. He compromised clear evidence
  a. Pilate's custom: To release a notorious prisoner at the Passover Feast
 	
  b. Pilate's planned compromise: Offering Barabbas for Jesus
 	
  c. Pilate's great injustice: He
	11 And Jesus stood before the governor: and the governor asked him, saying, Art thou the King of the Jews? And Jesus said unto him, Thou sayest.
	12 And when he was accused of the chief priests and elders, he answered nothing.
	13 Then said Pilate unto him, Hearest thou not how many things they witness against thee?
	14 And he answered him to never a word; insomuch that the governor marvelled greatly.
	15 Now at *that* feast the governor was wont to release unto the people a prisoner, whom they would.
	16 And they had then a notable prisoner, called Barabbas.
	17 Therefore when they were gathered together, Pilate said unto them, Whom will ye that I release unto you? Barabbas, or Jesus which is called Christ?
	18 For he knew that for envy
		they had delivered him.
		19 When he was set down on the judgment seat, his wife sent unto him, saying, Have thou nothing to do with that just man: for I have suffered many things this day in a dream because of him.
		20 But the chief priests and elders persuaded the multitude that they should ask Barabbas, and destroy Jesus.
		21 The governor answered and said unto them, Whether of the twain will ye that I release unto you? They said, Barabbas.
		22 Pilate saith unto them, What shall I do then with Jesus which is called Christ? *They* all say unto him, Let him be crucified.
		23 And the governor said, Why, what evil hath he done? But they cried out the more, saying, Let him be crucified.
		24 When Pilate saw that he could prevail nothing, but *that* rather a tumult was made, he took water, and washed *his* hands before the multitude, saying, I am innocent of the blood of this just person: see ye *to it*.
		25 Then answered all the people, and said, His blood *be* on us, and on our children.
			knew Jesus was innocent
			3. He failed to listen to a strong warning
			
			4. He ignored the influence of evil men upon people
			
			5. He gave in to worldly pressure
			
			6. He tried to escape responsibility for evil
			
			7. The conclusion: The responsibility for Jesus' blood is cried out for by the Jews

DIVISION XVI

THE MESSIAH'S ARREST, TRIAL, AND CRUCIFIXION, 26:1–27:66

K. The Messiah's Tragic Trial Before Pilate: The Tragedy of an Indecisive Man, 27:11-25

(27:11-25) **Introduction**: Pilate's treatment of Jesus is better understood by referring to note three, which discusses Pilate himself (see DEEPER STUDY # 1—Mt.27:11-25). Despite his enormous and proven ability as a leader, he was indecisive as he stood before Christ. He knew Christ was innocent, for he saw no evil in Him (see Lu.23:22). Yet he had to tread carefully with the Jewish authorities lest he fall into their disfavor. If they reported him to Rome, he could lose his position and wealth.

In the behavior of Pilate is seen the picture and tragedy of an indecisive man. (Also see outline, notes, and DEEPER STUDY # 1—Mk.15:1-15; outline and notes Lu.23:1-25; Jn.18:28-19:15.)

1. He rejected the Lord's strong confession (vv.11-14).
2. He compromised clear evidence (vv.15-18).
3. He failed to listen to a strong warning (v.19).
4. He ignored the influence of evil men upon people (v.20).
5. He gave in to worldly pressure (vv.21-23).
6. He tried to escape responsibility for evil (v.24).
7. Conclusion: the responsibility for Jesus' blood is cried out for by the Jews (v.25).

(27:11-25) **Another Outline**: The Tragedy of an Indecisive Man (27:11-25).
1. Pilate marvelled, was impressed with Jesus (vv.11-14).
2. Pilate sought an escape for Jesus (vv.15-18).
3. Pilate received a warning from his disturbed wife (vv.19-21).
4. Pilate sought the counsel of a frenzied mob (vv.20-23).
5. Pilate sought to unshoulder the responsibility (vv.24-25).

MATTHEW 27:11-25

> **DEEPER STUDY # 1**
> (27:11-25) **Pilate**: the procurator of Judaea. He was directly responsible to the Emperor for the administrative and financial management of the country. A man had to work himself up through the political and military ranks to become a procurator. Pilate was, therefore, an able man, experienced in the affairs of politics and government as well as the military. He had held office for ten years, which shows that he was deeply trusted by the Roman government. However, the Jews despised Pilate, and Pilate despised the Jews; in particular, he despised their intense practice of religion. When Pilate became procurator of Judaea, he did two things that aroused the people's bitter hatred against him forever. First, on his state visits to Jerusalem, he rode into the city with the Roman standard, an eagle sitting atop a pole. All previous governors had removed the standard because of the Jews' opposition to idols. Second, Pilate launched the construction of a new water supply for Jerusalem. To finance the project, he took the money out of the temple treasury. The Jews never forgot nor forgave this act. They bitterly opposed Pilate all through his reign, and he treated them with equal contempt (see note—Mk.15:9). On several occasions, Jewish leaders threatened to exercise their right to report Pilate to the emperor. This, of course, disturbed Pilate greatly, causing him to become even more bitter and contemptuous toward the Jews.

1 (27:11-14) **Jesus Christ, Trials**: Pilate (the indecisive man) rejected the Lord's clear confession. Paul refers to the Lord's strong confession before Pilate: "Christ Jesus, who before Pontius Pilate witnessed a good confession" (1 Ti.6:13). Note the strength of that confession.

a. Jesus' strong, straightforward claim: He is King. This is one of the charges brought against Christ, that He claimed to be a King (Lu.23:2). Pilate, somewhat surprised, reacted scornfully, asking Christ: "Art thou the King of the Jews?" Christ strongly claimed He was King: "Thou hast said" (see Mt.26:25, 64. See esp. Jn.18:36-37.)

b. Jesus' strong, controlled behavior: under severe accusation, Jesus was silent and purposed (see Is.53:7). The religionists, fitfully aroused, accused and accused Jesus, yet He remained silent. Note His control and nobility. (a) He knew there was no need to argue with a closed-minded person. He would not dignify their behavior by being drawn into argument with them. (b) He was purposed to do God's will by dying for the sins of the world. His hour to die had come. There was no need to argue, no need to try to escape death by argument. The depth of man's depravity was to be demonstrated for now. He would be noble: silent, purposed in His behavior.

c. Jesus' strong, enduring purpose: under repeated questioning He endured. Apparently Pilate wished to release Jesus (see v.18). He knew Jesus was innocent and to release Him would be a way to get at these contemptible religionists. Thus Pilate tried to get Jesus to answer the charges. He did not understand why Jesus would not answer, what Jesus was doing. All Jesus did was stand there, silent, portraying an image of strength, of some enduring purpose. But Pilate was unable to grasp its meaning.

d. Jesus' impact: Pilate was impressed, but still indecisive. He marvelled at Jesus' claim to be King and at His silence. Yet he still lacked the courage to make the right decision. He still wavered under the pressure of the accusers and failed to release Jesus.

> "No man can serve two masters: for either he will hate the one, and love the other; or else he will hold to the one, and despise the other. Ye cannot serve God and mammon" (Mt.6:24).
> "Ye cannot drink the cup of the Lord, and the cup of devils: ye cannot be partakers of the Lord's table, and of the table of devils" (1 Co.10:21).
> "A double minded man is unstable in all his ways" (Js.1:8).
> "How long halt ye between two opinions? if the LORD be God, follow him" (1 K.18:21).

Thought 1. Christ has given man a strong confession.
(1) A strong claim: He is King (Jn.18:36-37).
(2) A strong, controlled behavior: perfection (He.5:8-9; see 2 Co.5:21).
(3) A strong, enduring purpose: to die for the sins of the world (1 Pe.2:24; 3:18).

Thought 2. An indecisive man is just like Pilate: he rejects the clear confession of our Lord.

Thought 3. Christ teaches a lesson here about arguing. It is futile to argue with a closed-minded or fitfully aroused person. To argue only dignifies their behavior.

Thought 4. Christ endured in His great purpose, even unto death. We must be just as enduring.

2 (27:15-18) **Indecision—Compromise—Pilate—Jesus Christ, Trials**: Pilate (the indecisive man) compromised clear evidence. Pilate saw the evidence. Jesus was innocent; the religionists were envious of Christ and His threat to their security (v.18). He wanted to declare Christ innocent, but he felt he had to satisfy the cries of these religious worldlings as well. Thus, he conceived a compromise. It was a long-time custom for Rome to release a prisoner to the Jews at the Passover Feast. By such, Rome sought to humor and secure more cooperation from the Jews. Within the prison was a notorious criminal, Barabbas. Pilate had him brought before the people along with Christ and shouted out that the people could choose which one was to be released. At this point Pilate walked back into the Judgment Hall giving the crowd time to decide (v.19).

Note two things.

a. Pilate was seeking a compromise. He was trying to declare Christ innocent and to please the worldlings who were accusing Christ. Despite the clear evidence that Christ was innocent, he still lacked the courage and decisiveness to take a stand for Christ.

b. Pilate fully expected the people to choose to release Christ. He thought his compromise had worked, for who would not choose a great teacher over a notorious criminal?

> "He that is not with me is against me: and he that gathereth not with me scattereth" (Lu.11:23).
>
> "All men should honour the Son, even as they honour the Father. He that honoureth not the Son honoureth not the Father which hath sent him. Verily, verily, I say unto you, He that heareth my word, and believeth on him that sent me, hath everlasting life, and shall not come into condemnation; but is passed from death unto life" (Jn.5:23-24).
>
> "And this is the record, that God hath given to us eternal life, and this life is in his Son. He that hath the Son hath life; and he that hath not the Son of God hath not life" (1 Jn.5:11-12).
>
> "Submit yourselves therefore to God. Resist the devil, and he will flee from you. Draw nigh to God, and he will draw nigh to you. Cleanse your hands, ye sinners; and purify your hearts, ye double minded. Be afflicted, and mourn, and weep: let your laughter be turned to mourning, and your joy to heaviness. Humble yourselves in the sight of the Lord, and he shall lift you up" (Js.4:7-10).

Thought 1. Two facts about the nature of man need to be noted.
(1) Compromising with a man set on doing evil will not work. He will go on with his evil no matter the compromise. It is the way of nature.
(2) Compromising when the evidence is clear will not work. It weakens character and principle and position.

Thought 2. We need to declare Christ innocent, declare loudly and clearly that He is the Son of God. This is not a day for indecision and compromise of the truth. Christ is King, perfectly innocent of sin and evil. We need to be decisive, to take a stand for Christ.

3 (27:19) **Warning—Pilate**: Pilate (the indecisive man) failed to listen to strong warning. While Pilate was sitting on his judgment seat waiting on the people's decision, his wife came to him. She had had a dream about Christ. Note three things.

a. She declared Jesus to be just, righteous. She was declaring that Christ was not only an innocent man, but a righteous and good man.

b. She warned there was something very unusual about Jesus, something that could cause suffering and sorrow. She warned Pilate that he must declare Jesus to be innocent or hereafter be sorry.

c. Pilate listened to the warning but still chose to seek a compromise, still lacked the courage to declare Christ innocent.

Thought 1. The indecisive man is warned: suffering and sorrow lie ahead. Judgment is coming upon any man who does not take his stand for Christ (Mt.10:32; Lu.12:8).

Thought 2. God uses many ways in His attempt to reach men. He used the dream of a wife to warn Pilate. He also warns us: we must be courageous, not indecisive. Today is the day of salvation.

> "For he saith, I have heard thee in a time accepted, and in the day of salvation have I succoured thee: behold, now is the accepted time; behold, now is the day of salvation" (2 Co.6:2).
>
> "But exhort one another daily, while it is called To day; lest any of you be hardened through the deceitfuless of sin" (He.3:13).
>
> "Go to now, ye that say, To day or to morrow we will go into such a city, and continue there a year, and buy and sell, and get gain" (Js.4:13).

4 (27:20) **Evil, Ignoring—Pilate**: Pilate (the indecisive man) ignored the influence of evil men upon people. The picture is tragic. Religious leaders were either moving or sending their emissaries among the people to influence them to do this evil deed—the deed of murdering Christ. All the while Pilate sat indecisively upon his throne, ignoring the reality of the situation.

> "For the name of God is blasphemed among the Gentiles through you, as it is written" (Ro.2:24).
>
> "But evil men and seducers shall wax worse and worse, deceiving, and being deceived" (2 Ti.3:13).
>
> "Who is a liar but he that denieth that Jesus is the Christ? He is antichrist, that denieth the Father and the Son. Whosoever denieth the Son, the same hath not the Father....These things have I written unto you concerning them that seduce you" (1 Jn.2:22-23, 26).

Thought 1. Evil men will try to influence others in order to get their way. To ignore the fact is to hide one's head as an ostrich in the sand.

Thought 2. Indecision and compromise are not the way to stop the influence of evil men. Evil men will continue to influence people as long as we are indecisive and compromising.

MATTHEW 27:11-25

Thought 3. The perfect innocence and righteousness of Christ must be proclaimed. Proclaiming His righteousness is the only way to stop the influence of evil men in the world. We cannot ignore the fact.

5 (27:21-23) **Pilate**: Pilate (the indecisive man) gave in to worldly pressure. The scene is again tragic. Pilate walked back out to the people for their decision. They shocked him, crying for the release of Barabbas and the crucifixion of Jesus.

Pilate had cornered himself, creating the most terrible dilemma imaginable. Stunned, somewhat in a state of shock, he cried back to the people, "Why, what evil hath He done?" But it was too late. The people, aroused by the worldly religionists, fitfully and repeatedly shouted back, "Let Him be crucified." Note several things.

a. The people preferred an evil man to the Holy Man, preferred a man who *took* life to the Prince who *gave* life (see Ac.3:14-15).

b. Pilate was weak, indecisive, non-courageous throughout the whole episode. He would not act decisively; he would not courageously declare Christ to be what he knew: innocent.

c. The people asked for Jesus to be executed in the most horrible and painful way—by crucifixion. This was just as Christ had foretold (Mt.20:19).

> "Love not the world, neither the things that are in the world. If any man love the world, the love of the Father is not in him. For all that is in the world, the lust of the flesh, and the lust of the eyes, and the pride of life, is not of the Father, but is of the world" (1 Jn.2:15-16).
>
> "And be not conformed to this world: but be ye transformed by the renewing of your mind, that ye may prove what is that good, and acceptable, and perfect, will of God" (Ro.12:2).
>
> "By faith Moses, when he was come to years, refused to be called the son of Pharaoh's daughter; choosing rather to suffer affliction with the people of God, than to enjoy the pleasures of sin for a season" (He.11:24-25).

Thought 1. The pressure of the world to do evil is great. Indecision and compromise are not the way to face the world: decisive dedication and separation are (Ro.12:1-2; 2 Co.6:17-18; 1 Jn.2:15-16).

Thought 2. Most do prefer the company of evil, sinful men to that of the Prince of life. Note: even worldly religionists choose the worldly over the Prince of life.

Thought 3. Note a critical point. It is when we are indecisive or willing to compromise that the pressure of the world to do evil gets to us. Hesitating and being indecisive will cause us to give in to pressure and sin. We usually choose to go along with sin when we are indecisive.

6 (27:24) **Man, Weakness—Pilate**: Pilate (the indecisive man) tried to escape responsibility for evil. The picture is dramatic. Pilate was overruled by the people's choice. His own opinion availed nothing, had no influence whatsoever over Jesus' death. Thus he took a bowl of water and lifted it high; he washed his hands and dried them off. By such an act, Pilate was symbolizing two things.

a. He was declaring the innocence of Jesus.

b. He was washing his hands of the whole affair, declaring the people to be the guilty party in the death of Jesus.

But Pilate was not free of guilt. He was the governor, and he knew Christ was innocent of the charge. The responsibility to declare Jesus innocent was his, even if he had to override the accusers. Pilate had the authority and responsibility to do right, to see that justice was done.

> "I call heaven and earth to record this day against you, that I have set before you life and death, blessing and cursing: therefore choose life, that both thou and thy seed may live" (De.30:19).
>
> "And Elijah came unto all the people, and said, How long halt ye between two opinions? if the LORD be God follow him: but if Baal, then follow him. And the people answered him not a word" (1 K.18:21).

Thought 1. We cannot wash our hands from guilt. If we act irresponsibly, we stand guilty. We stand guilty...
- for rejecting the Lord's strong confession.
- for compromising.
- for failing to listen to strong warning.
- for ignoring the influence of evil men.
- for giving in to worldly pressure.
- for trying to escape the responsibility for evil.

Thought 2. Everyone is responsible for his actions. Decisive action is what God calls for, decisive action that declares Christ to be innocent and righteous (2 Co.5:21).

7 (27:25) **Jews—Israel**: the crowd cried out for the responsibility of Jesus' blood to be laid to their charge. This is a tragic and unbelievable scene. The mob cried out for God to hold them responsible for the death of Christ. The people did not know what they were saying, yet they were still killing Christ and still acting in an unjust, sinful, savage spirit. Because of their evil spirit against God's Son, all the evidence of history points toward their request's being granted.

⇒ Their nation and its capital, Jerusalem, were destroyed and taken from them.
⇒ Their people have been exiled and scattered for centuries.
⇒ Their very name is often the object of prejudice and hatred.
⇒ Annihilation of their race has been attempted time and again.

Amazingly, the Jewish people remain a nationality, yet the evoked vengeance has fallen upon them for centuries. Despite their terrible sin, the Jews hold a very special place in God's heart and plan. He will continue to hold them together as a race until the fulness of the Gentiles is completed (see Ro.11:25f).

"**Therefore say I unto you, The kingdom of God shall be taken from you, and given to a nation bringing forth the fruits thereof**" (Mt.21:43).

"**I say unto you, That none of those men which were bidden shall taste of my supper**" (Lu.14:24).

"**He shall come and destroy these husbandmen, and shall give the vineyard to others. And when they heard it, they said, God forbid**" (Lu.20:16).

"**And if some of the branches be broken off, and thou, being a wild olive tree, wert graffed in among them, and with them partakest of the root and fatness of the olive tree**" (Ro.11:17).

"**My God will cast them away, because they did not hearken unto him: and they shall be wanderers among the nations**" (Ho.9:17).

MATTHEW 27:26-44

	L. The Messiah's Suffering & Crucifixion: A Picture of the World's Treatment of God's Son,^{DS1} 27:26-44 (Mk 15:16-32;Lu 23:43; Jn 19:16-24)	drink mingled with gall: and when he had tasted *thereof*, he would not drink.	with gall, a bitter drink
1. The rulers passed judgment upon Christ	26 Then released he Barabbas unto them: and when he had scourged Jesus, he delivered *him* to be crucified.	35 And they crucified him, and parted his garments, casting lots: that it might be fulfilled which was spoken by the prophet, They parted my garments among them, and upon my vesture did they cast lots.	m. They crucified Him n. They gambled away His clothes
2. The soldiers mocked & tortured Christ			
a. They flogged Him	27 Then the soldiers of the governor took Jesus into the common hall, and gathered unto him the whole band *of soldiers*.	36 And sitting down they watched him there;	o. They sat down & stared at Him
b. They humiliated Him before a company, a hundred or more soldiers		37 And set up over his head his accusation written, THIS IS JESUS THE KING OF THE JEWS.	p. They ridiculed His claim again
c. They stripped Him & put a scarlet robe on Him	28 And they stripped him, and put on him a scarlet robe.	38 Then were there two thieves crucified with him, one on the right hand, and another on the left.	q. They crucified Him between two thieves
d. They put a crown of thorns on His head & a staff in His hand	29 And when they had platted a crown of thorns, they put *it* upon his head, and a reed in his right hand: and they bowed the knee before him, and mocked him, saying, Hail, King of the Jews!	39 And they that passed by reviled him, wagging their heads,	**3. The average persons, the passers-by, mocked & abused Christ**
e. They bowed & ridiculed His claim to be King		40 And saying, Thou that destroyest the temple, and buildest *it* in three days, save thyself. If thou be the Son of God, come down from the cross.	a. Mocked His power to destroy & rebuild the temple b. Mocked His claim to be God's Son
f. They spat upon Him	30 And they spit upon him, and took the reed, and smote him on the head.		
g. They beat Him on the head with a staff			
h. They ridiculed Him & aggravated the wounds	31 And after that they had mocked him, they took the robe off from him, and put his own raiment on him, and led him away to crucify *him*.	41 Likewise also the chief priests mocking *him*, with the scribes and elders, said,	**4. The religionists & government leaders mocked & taunted Christ**
i. They forced Him to carry the cross until He was exhausted		42 He saved others; himself he cannot save. If he be the King of Israel, let him now come down from the cross, and we will believe him.	a. Mocked His claim to be the Savior, to save others b. Mocked His claim to be the King of Israel
j. They enlisted a Gentile to help carry His cross	32 And as they came out, they found a man of Cyrene, Simon by name: him they compelled to bear his cross.	43 He trusted in God; let him deliver him now, if he will have him: for he said, I am the Son of God.	c. Mocked His claim to trust God perfectly d. Mocked His claim to be the Son of God
k. They escorted Him to Golgotha, a terrible place for execution	33 And when they were come unto a place called Golgotha, that is to say, a place of a skull,		
l. They gave Him wine mixed	34 They gave him vinegar to	44 The thieves also, which were crucified with him, cast the same in his teeth.	**5. The criminals mocked Christ**

DIVISION XVI

THE MESSIAH'S ARREST, TRIAL, AND CRUCIFIXION, 26:1–27:66

L. The Messiah's Suffering and Crucifixion: A Picture of the World's Treatment of God's Son, 27:26-44

(27:26-44) **Introduction—Jesus Christ, Death**: this Scripture covers the sufferings and crucifixion of our Lord. Matthew, in his organized way, presented a picture of the world's treatment of God's Son. He saw various classes of people, symbolizing the world, stand before Christ. Their treatment of Him was unbelievable and horrible. The people of *God's world* were not only rejecting God's Son, they were torturing and destroying Him.

1. The rulers passed judgment upon Christ (v.26).
2. The soldiers mocked and tortured Christ (vv.26-38).
3. The average persons, the passers-by, mocked and abused Christ (vv.39-40).
4. The religionists and government leaders mocked and taunted Christ (vv.41-43).
5. The criminals mocked Christ (v.44).

(27:26-44) **Another Outline**: The Crucifixion.
1. The scourging of Jesus (v.26).
2. The soldiers' horseplay and torture (vv.27-31).
3. The journey to Golgotha—Simon of Cyrene (vv.32-33).

4. The drugging (v.34).
5. The crucifixion (v.35).
6. The gambling for His clothes (v.35).
7. The title of accusation on the cross (vv.36-37).
8. The two thieves (v.38).
9. The passers-by who taunted and mocked (vv.39-43).
10. The thieves who taunted and mocked (v.44).

DEEPER STUDY # 1
(27:26-44) **Jesus Christ, Death**: the Lord's sufferings and torture were marked by Divine pain and human cruelty.
  1. The divine pain of the Lord Jesus came from being fully conscious of the judgment He was to bear for man—separation from God (see note—Mt.27:46-49). The pressure of this hellish experience is seen in Gethsemane. Under great emotional stress, the tiny capillaries right under His skin which lined the sweat glands apparently gave way and burst. Jesus sweated great drops of blood. Such an experience causes marked weakness and sometimes a state of shock. The terrifying mystery of this hellish experience is seen in His cry upon the cross, "My God, my God, why hast thou forsaken me?" This was the point at which the great separation from God began (see notes—Mt.27:46-49; Ep.4:8-10; Deeper Study # 1— 1 Pe.3:19-20).
  2. The physical torture He bore at the hands of men was abhorrent. Before the High Priest, an officer struck Jesus across the face (Jn.18:22). The palace guards blindfolded, mocked, spat upon, and slapped Him in the face; and they kept Him up all night (Lu.22:63-66).
  Before Pilate, the Roman trial: His hands were tied to a post above His head and He was scourged (Jn.19:1). The prisoner was lashed until He was judged near death by the presiding centurion (Jewish trials allowed only forty lashes).
  Still before Pilate: the guards called the whole band of soldiers together and began to mock His claim to be King of the Jews (Mk.15:16). They threw a robe around Him and continued to strike Him across the face. They took the scepter from His hand and used it to whip Him and to drive the thorns even deeper. Finally, they ceased this sadistic treatment and ripped the robe from His back. This tore open the dried blood caked to its lining. Excruciating pain followed (see Mt.27:28-31; Mk.15:16-20; Jn.10:1-5).
  Bearing the cross itself: it was heavy, very heavy. He had to carry it up and down the streets of the city, taking a meandering route. The Romans did this as a living lesson to all that crime does not pay. Christ just broke down under the load; and Simon, the Cyrene, was forced to carry the cross for Him (Mt.27:32; Mk.15:21; Lu.23:26).

---

1 (27:26) **Sanhedrin—Pilate**: the rulers passed judgment. Christ was a threat; He must be destroyed. The Sanhedrin, both its religious and civil (elders) leaders, and Pilate passed judgment upon Christ. In their minds, Christ was a threat to them. Even Pilate gave in, despite his doubts, to the execution of Christ in order to preserve the peace of his rule and the security of his position (see outline, notes, and Deeper Study # 1—Mt.27:11-25).

> **Thought 1.** Position, power, wealth, security, envy, and much more—all cause the powerful of this earth to seek to destroy Christ and His influence.

2 (27:26-38) **Jesus Christ, Suffering**: the soldiers mocked and tortured Christ. Their treatment included at least seventeen abuses.
  a. They *scourged* Christ (v.26). He was stripped and beaten with a whip. This was a savage, excruciating punishment. The whip (phagellow) was made of leather straps with two small balls attached to the end of each strap. The balls were made of rough lead or sharp bones or spikes, so that they would cut deeply into the flesh. His hands were tied to a post above His head and He was scourged (Jn.19:1). It was the custom for the prisoner to be lashed until He was judged near death by the presiding centurion (Jewish trials allowed only forty lashes.) The criminal's back was, of course, nothing more than an unrecognizable mass of torn flesh (see Is.50:6).

> **Thought 1.** Two important facts.
> (1) Christ was being punished and chastised for our sins:
>
> **"The chastisement of our peace was upon Him; and with His stripes we are healed" (Is.53:5).**
>
> (2) Christ suffered the chastisement for our sins *willingly*:
>
> **"I gave my back to the smiters" (Is.50:6).**

  b. They humiliated Christ before a hundred or more soldiers (v.27). Note the words, *the whole band* (speiran). A *band* of soldiers usually meant a *cohort* which was made up of six hundred soldiers. However, *band* (speiran) sometimes meant maniple. Every cohort consisted of three maniples, about two hundred soldiers. Which is meant here is not known. Most believe the number of soldiers was large, certainly close to the two hundred serving in a maniple.

> **Thought 1.** Christ was humiliated and made a spectacle in order to save us. We are to become spectacles for Christ in order to reach some for Him.

MATTHEW 27:26-44

"For I think that God hath set forth us the apostles last, as it were appointed to death: for we are made a spectacle unto the world, and to angels, and to men" (1 Co.4:9).

"Ye endured a great fight of afflictions; partly, whilst ye were made a gazingstock both by reproaches and afflictions; and partly, whilst ye became companions of them that were so used" (He.10:32-33).

c. They stripped Christ and put a scarlet robe on Him (v.28). Christ was stripped *naked and shamed* and made to appear *ridiculous* by being clad with a royal robe.

Thought 1. Sin made man naked and shamed him (Ge.3:7). We are naked before Him who is to judge the world. Christ was stripped naked and shamed that He might secure clothing that is white and pure for us (that is, righteousness).

"I counsel thee to buy of me gold tried in the fire, that thou mayest be rich; and white raiment, that thou mayest be clothed, and that the shame of thy nakedness do not appear" (Re.3:18; see Ep.4:23-24).

Thought 2. Christ *wore* (*bore*) the scarlet robe for us. The scarlet robe symbolized that He was to bear our sins.
(1) Because He wore the scarlet robe of our sins, our sins can be as white as snow.

"Come now, and let us reason together, saith the Lord: though your sins be as scarlet, they shall be as white as snow; though they be red like crimson, they shall be as wool" (Is.1:18).

(2) Because He wore the scarlet robe of our sins, we can wash our robes in the blood of the lamb.

"These are they which came out of great tribulation, and have washed their robes, and made them white in the blood of the Lamb" (Re.7:14).

d. They put a crown of thorns on the head of Christ and a reed in His hands (v.29). A mock crown was made out of some limbs from a thorn bush and jammed upon His head. The thorns pierced through the skin of His brow and under His hair. Blood streamed down his head and face. A mock scepter was made out of the weak, limber reed and thrust into His hand.

Thought 1. Thorns are a symbol of God's *curse* upon the earth, a result of sin (Ge.3:18). Christ was bearing the sin that brought about the curse. He was made a curse for us.

"Christ hath redeemed us from the curse of the law, being made a curse for us: for it is written, Cursed is every one that hangeth on a tree" (Ga.3:13).

Thought 2. Christ held the limber, weak reed, the reed that is so easily shaken with the wind (Mt.11:7), that wavers and withers and wastes away. He held the reed that symbolizes the weak kingdoms of the world, kingdoms that are so easily shaken and withered and wasted away. He held it as part of His sufferings so that He might secure an eternal scepter, an eternal throne and kingdom.

"But unto the Son he saith, Thy throne, O God, is for ever and ever: a sceptre of thy kingdom" (He.1:8).

e. They bowed and ridiculed the claim of Christ to be king (v.29). They ridiculed His claim to be king by *jokingly* bowing the knee before Him and mockingly shouting, "Hail, King of the Jews." They scorned Him as a sham king.

Thought 1. The day is coming when bowing the knee and confessing Christ to be Lord will be no joke. There will be no mocking and no scorning in that day.

"Wherefore God also hath highly exalted him, and given him a name which is above every name: that at the name of Jesus every knee should bow, of things in heaven, and things in earth, and things under the earth; and that every tongue should confess that Jesus Christ is Lord, to the glory of God the Father" (Ph.2:9-11).

f. They spat upon Christ (v.30). (See Is.50:6.) It was the custom for subjects to kiss their rulers as a sign of homage and allegiance. The soldiers gave the Lord a mock allegiance by spitefully spitting in His face.

Thought 1. Christ bore the spite, spitting, and mocking homage in order to deliver men from perishing. But the day has now come when the Lord is not to be spit upon, but kissed. He is to be given a genuine, not a mocking, allegiance.

"Kiss the Son, lest he be angry, and ye perish from the way, when his wrath is kindled but a little. Blessed are all they that put their trust in him" (Ps.2:12).

MATTHEW 27:26-44

   g. They beat Christ on the head with the reed (v.30). The Greek word for *smote Him* (etupton, imperfect tense) means they *kept on beating Him*. They took the reed, the mock scepter, and used it as a weapon, beating Him on the head continuously. They probably passed the reed from one soldier to another, giving many an opportunity to vent their folly and spite. He was bruised and bleeding, a horrible sight.

     Thought 1. Two important facts.
     (1) "He was wounded for our transgressions, He was bruised for our iniquities" (Is.53:5).
     (2) "It pleased the Lord to bruise Him" (Is.53:10).

   h. They stripped Christ of the kingly robe and put His own robe back on Him, aggravating the wounds. They were now ready to get to the matter at hand, His crucifixion. As they stripped the kingly robe off, two things happened.
     1) The dried blood clinging to the robe ripped away from the wounds. As Christ suffered excruciating pain, His blood began to flow from the wounds again.
     2) In removing the kingly robe, the soldiers were stripping Him of the authority they had given Him. It was just a mock authority and homage, but it had symbolized the attitude of the world toward paying homage to God's Son.

     Thought 1. No man determines the authority of God's Son. He possesses authority because He is God's Son, not because man gives Him authority. God has given Him all authority and rule because He has borne the sufferings and death of the cross for man.

         "And Jesus came and spake unto them, saying, All power is given unto me in heaven and in earth" (Mt.28:18).
         "For the Father judgeth no man, but hath committed all judgment unto the Son: that all men should honor the Son, even as they honor the Father. He that honoreth not the Son honoreth not the Father which hath sent him" (Jn.5:22-23).

     Thought 2. "The blood of Jesus Christ His (God's) Son cleanseth us from all sin" (1 Jn.1:7).

   i. They forced Christ to carry the cross until He was exhausted (v.32). The condemned criminal's carrying his own cross was the common practice. A centurion riding upon his stallion led the way. A herald followed, shouting out the criminal charges against the condemned. Immediately behind the herald was the condemned man bearing his cross and a small detachment of soldiers. The criminal had to carry his cross up and down through the streets of the city, taking a meandering route. The Romans did this as a living lesson to the citizens of a city that crime did not pay.

     Thought 1. Note two important facts.
     (1) Man forced Christ to carry the cross to Golgotha. There is a spiritual symbol here. Spiritually, it is man's sin that forced Christ to bear the cross for man.

         "Who his own self bare our sins in his own body on the tree, that we, being dead to sins, should live unto righteousness: by whose stripes ye were healed" (1 Pe.2:24).

     (2) God forced Christ to bear the cross for man.

         "Him, being delivered by the determinate counsel and foreknowledge of God, ye have taken, and by wicked hands have crucified and slain" (Ac.2:23).

   j. They enlisted a Gentile to help with the cross of Christ (v.32). Christ broke under the weight of the cross. This is not surprising, for He had just suffered so much...
- suffered the agony of the Garden.
- suffered the tension and excitement of the trials.
- suffered the ridicule and torture of the soldiers.

He had lost too much blood from the savage torture, and He had gone without food and sleep for hours. The soldiers had the legal authority to tap a bystander upon the shoulder and enlist the citizen to help with whatever load needed carrying. In this case, of course, they needed someone to carry the cross for Christ. They tapped Simon of Cyrene, and he bore the cross for Christ. It is an event used by God to change the life of Simon forever (see note—Mk.15:21).

     Thought 1. Christ bore the cross for us that He might enlist us in the service of God. Even as He bore the cross, we are now to bear the cross for Him. Simon literally bore the cross, symbolizing that we are to bear the cross for Christ spiritually (see note—Lu.9:23).

         "And he said to them all, If any man will come after me, let him deny himself, and take up his cross daily, and follow me" (Lu.9:23).

   k. They escorted Christ to a terrible place for execution (v.33). The place was called Golgotha, the place of a skull. Why it was given this name is not known. But note that it was known as a place of death, of dead men's bones. It was a rugged place which stirred thoughts of death, of corruptible and decaying flesh. It was a terrible place to die.

MATTHEW 27:26-44

Thought 1. Even the very place where Christ was crucified symbolized death itself. Every act seemed to point to His dying for the deliverance of man. Here upon Golgotha was the picture or thought of death, and here upon Golgotha He was to die to deliver all men from the bondage of death.

> "Forasmuch then as the children are partakers of flesh and blood, he also himself likewise took part of the same; that through death he might destroy him that had the power of death, that is, the devil; and deliver them who through fear of death were all their lifetime subject to bondage" (He.2:14-15).

Thought 2. Christ was judged unworthy to live among the people of the world, so He was led out of the city and sent out of the world through execution. He was cast out of the vineyard (Mt.21:39). In the Old Testament, the sacrifice of animals took place outside the camp, and the blood was brought into the congregation. The Lamb of God was led outside the gate as a sheep is led to the slaughter.

> "For the bodies of those beasts, whose blood is brought into the sanctuary by the high priest for sin, are burned without the camp. Wherefore Jesus also, that he might sanctify the people with his own blood, suffered without the gate" (He.13:11-12).

Thought 3. He bore the reproach of sin for us. We should, therefore, bear the reproach of righteousness for Him.

> "Let us go forth therefore unto him without the camp, bearing his reproach" (He.13:13).

l. They gave Christ vinegar mixed with gall (v.34). It was the custom to give the criminal spiked wine right before he was raised on the cross. The spiked wine was a strong, stupefying liquor used as a narcotic drink. Scripture foretold this event (Ps.69:21).

Thought 1. Christ came to do the will of God, to die as a sacrifice for man. He refused to do God's will unthoughtfully, with deadened senses and a semi-conscious mind. He had work to do in sacrificing His life for man: He was to taste death for all men, and He would taste it in full consciousness and by being as mentally alert as possible.

> "But we see Jesus, who was made a little lower than the angels for the suffering of death, crowned with glory and honor; that he by the grace of God should taste death for every man" (He.2:9).
>
> "In burnt offerings and sacrifices for sin thou hast had no pleasure. Then said I, Lo, I come (in the volume of the book it is written of me,) to do thy will, O God....By the which will we are sacrificed through the offering of the body of Jesus Christ once for all" (He.10:6-7, 10).

m. They crucified Christ (v.35). The crucifixion itself was the most horrible of deaths. The ancient writer, Tacitus, called it "a despicable death." Cicero called it "the most cruel and horrifying death." He simply said it was "incapable of description." There was the pain of the driven spikes forced through the flesh of Jesus' hands and feet or ankles. There was the weight of His body jolting and pulling against the spikes as the cross was lifted and rocked into place. There was the scorching sun and the unquenchable thirst gnawing away at His dry mouth and throat. There was the blood oozing from His scourged back, His thorn crowned brow, His feet, and His stick-beaten head. In addition, just imagine the aggravation of flies, gnats, and other insects. There was also the piercing of the spear thrust into His side. On and on the sufferings could be described. There has never been a more cruel form of execution than crucifixion upon a cross.

Thought 1. In the simplest of terms, Christ was crucified for our sins in order to bring us to God.

> "Who his own self bare our sins in his own body on the tree, that we, being dead to sins, should live unto righteousness: by whose stripes ye were healed" (1 Pe.2:24).
>
> "For Christ also hath once suffered for sins, the just for the unjust, that he might bring us to God, being put to death in the flesh, but quickened by the Spirit" (1 Pe.3:18).

n. They gambled for the clothes of Christ (v.35). Apparently, it was a custom for the executing soldiers to claim whatever they wished of the clothes of the crucified criminal. The soldiers stripped Christ and divided His clothes among themselves. His coat was valuable. It was seamless, one piece of cloth, woven from top to bottom just as the high Priest's coat or cloak was. The soldiers, therefore, decided to gamble by casting lots for it (Jn.19:23-24). This event was foretold in Ps.22:18.

Thought 1. Note two things.
(1) Christ was stripped by the soldiers. But He stripped Himself of His glory in order to become man and die for us.

> "Forasmuch then as the children are partakers of flesh and blood, he also himself likewise took part of the same; that through death he might destroy him that had the power of death, that is, the devil; and deliver them who through fear of death were all their lifetime subject to bondage" (He.2:14-15).

(2) The coat was a symbol of Christ, *the Mediator*, the Pontifex, which means in Latin, *the bridge-builder* between God and man.

> "For there is one God, and one mediator between God and men, the man Christ Jesus; who gave himself a ransom for all, to be testified in due time" (1 Ti.2:5-6).

o. They sat down and stared at Christ (v.36). Death by crucifixion was usually slow, very slow. It sometimes took days for the sufferer to die from his agony. Hence, soldiers had to be posted to guard the sufferer to keep any friends from trying to save him from death. In dealing with Christ, the soldiers' horseplay and work in crucifying Him was now done. They had only to wait. They sat down and watched His hanging there. We can imagine what they saw by picturing what He looked like after all the torture and by reviewing the seven sayings of the cross. Jesus hung there naked, being stared at; the whole scene was a shameful sight. The embarrassment of the shame must have cut the heart of Christ to the core. The stare of the soldiers was prophesied (Ps.22:17).

Thought 1. Sin is the nakedness, the shame, of man. Sin strips man and makes him naked before God. The cross is the shame of Christ, yet He bore the shame of the cross for us.

"I counsel thee to buy of me...white raiment, that thou mayest be clothed, and that the shame of thy nakedness do not appear" (Re.3:18).

"Looking unto Jesus the author and finisher of our faith; who for the joy that was set before him endured the cross, despising the shame, and is set down at the right hand of the throne of God" (He.12:2).

Thought 2. God, in His providence, saw that guards were posted around the cross. Why? So that there could never be any legitimate question about His Son's really dying.

Thought 3. What the honest and thinking soldier saw was a noble, righteous man being unjustly put to death.

"And when the centurion, which stood over against Him, saw that he so cried out, and gave up the ghost, he said, Truly this man was the Son of God" (Mk.15:39).

p. They shamed Christ and reproached His claim again (v.37). It was the custom for the charges against a crucified criminal to be written out on a board and nailed to the cross above his head. This served both as information and as a warning to the public. It, of course, added shame and reproach to the crucified sufferer. In Christ's case, the charges were written in three different languages (Jn.19:20). Note the exact words, "This is Jesus the King of the Jews." This inscription disturbed the religious leaders. They went to Pilate and said, "Write not, the King of the Jews; but that He said, I am King of the Jews." Pilate simply answered, "What I have written, I have written" (Jn.19:21-22).

Thought 1. God overruled the shame and reproach of our Lord. God saw to it that the very charges against Him proclaimed His deity and honor. He was proclaimed King in three languages, languages which symbolized the world: the Aramaic (Jews), the Latin (the Gentiles), and the Greek (the intellectual Jew and Gentile).

"He humbled himself, and became obedient unto death, even the death of the cross. Wherefore God also hath highly exalted him, and given him a name which is above every name: that at the name of Jesus every knee should bow, of things in heaven, and things in earth, and things under the earth; and that every tongue should confess that Jesus Christ is Lord, to the glory of God the Father" (Ph.2:8-11).

"Our Lord Jesus Christ: Which in his times he shall show, who is the blessed and only Potentate, the King of kings, and Lord of lords; Who only hath immortality, dwelling in the light which no man can approach unto; whom no man hath seen, nor can see: to whom be honour and power everlasting. Amen" (1 Ti.6:14-16).

q. They added shame and reproach by crucifying Christ between two thieves (v.38). Perhaps this was a day set aside for execution. Or perhaps the Jewish leaders pressed Pilate to execute Jesus with other criminals. Such would add weight to their position that He was no more than a mere man, an imposter who deserved to die just as other criminals. Whatever the reason, the fact that the Son of God was executed right along with other criminals added to the shame and reproach He bore. Again, this event had been prophesied (Is.53:12).

Thought 1. Christ was counted as a sinner that He might bear the sin of many.

"He was numbered with the transgressors; and he bare the sin of many, and made intercession for the transgressors" (Is.53:12).

"This is a faithful saying, and worthy of all acceptation, that Christ Jesus came into the world to save sinners; of whom I am chief" (1 Ti.1:15).

3 (27:39-40) **Jesus Christ, Mocked**: the average persons and the passers-by mocked and abused Christ. There were a large number of passers-by (Jn.19:20). Golgotha was close to the city, sitting on a hill that was probably close to a main road and a large gate leading into the city.

First, only Christ was mocked and abused; the two criminals were not. No abuse was heaped upon them. The murderers of the Lord were not satisfied with His death; they were filled with enmity and a bitterness that sought revenge and humiliation. Therefore, they sowed the seeds of enmity and mockery among those who passed by, and they too were caught up in the excitement of the sin and shame of the evil crowd.

MATTHEW 27:26-44

Second, the passers-by saw Christ's hanging there, believing He had claimed to be a King. Being spurred on by His accusers, they reviled Him. The word for revile (blasphemoun) is strong, meaning to blaspheme, profane, rail at. They also wagged their heads at Him. This was a gesture of that day which showed insult, contempt, and mockery.

The passers-by mocked Christ for two things: His claim to have the power to destroy and rebuild the temple (see note—Mt.26:60-61), and His claim to be the Son of God (Mt.26:64). Note that the crowd used the very same words that the devil had tempted Jesus with at the beginning of His ministry: "If thou be the Son of God" (Mt.4:6).

Thought 1. Too many curse and profane Christ when they hear about the claim that He makes upon their lives as the Messiah, the Son of God. The reaction of most men was predicted generations ago.

> "All they that see me laugh me to scorn: they shoot out the lip, they shake the head" (Ps.22:7).
> "I became also a reproach unto them: when they looked upon me they shaked their heads" (Ps.109:25).

Thought 2. Christ possessed the deity and all the dignity, power, and riches of God. Yet for our sake, He became weak and poor for us. He surrendered to the mockery and abuse of men in order to die.

> "For though he was crucified through weakness, yet he liveth by the power of God. For we also are weak in him, but we shall live with him by the power of God toward you" (2 Co.13:4).
> "For ye know the grace of our Lord Jesus Christ, that, though he was rich, yet for your sakes he became poor, that ye through his poverty might be rich" (2 Co.8:9).

Thought 3. The average person, the passer-by, often mocks and abuses Christ. How?
⇒ By ridiculing Christ's claim to be the Son of God.
⇒ By cursing and profaning the name of Christ.
⇒ By challenging Christ to prove His power by meeting his needs when he has not lived for Christ.
⇒ By acting worse toward Christ and His followers than toward the rest of society, even criminals.

4 (27:41-43) **Jesus Christ, Mocked**: the religionists and government leaders (elders) mocked and taunted Christ. Men of religion and government should be above this kind of behavior. However, being part of a sinful unbelieving crowd, men filled with enmity and bitterness are led to do shameful things. These leaders ridiculed the four major claims of Christ:
⇒ that He was the Savior
⇒ that He was the King
⇒ that He was the Son of Man who trusted God perfectly
⇒ that He was the Son of God

Their purpose was to vent their enmity and humiliate Christ, hoping to reinforce in the minds of the crowd that He was an imposter and deceiver. The religionists completely misunderstood God's Messiah, even the Lord Jesus Christ.

> "This is a faithful saying, and worthy of all acceptation, that Christ Jesus came into the world to save sinners; of whom I am chief" (1 Ti.1:15).
> "For there is one God, and one mediator between God and men, the man Christ Jesus; who gave himself a ransom for all, to be testified in due time" (1 Ti.2:5-6).

Thought 1. Christ was all that He claimed to be.
(1) The Savior.

> "For the Son of man is come to seek and to save that which was lost" (Lu.19:10. See note—Mt.8:20.)

(2) The King.

> "And Jesus stood before the governor: and the governor asked him, saying, Art thou the King of the Jews? And Jesus said unto him, Thou sayest" (Mt.27:11).
> "Pilate therefore said unto him, Art thou a king then? Jesus answered, Thou sayest that I am a king. To this end was I born, and for this cause came I into the world, that I should bear witness unto the truth. Every one that is of the truth heareth my voice" (Jn.18:37).

(3) The Son of Man who trusted God perfectly.

> "Jesus saith unto them, My meat is to do the will of him that sent me, and to finish his work" (Jn.4:34).
> "I can of mine own self do nothing: as I hear, I judge: and my judgment is just; because I seek not mine own will, but the will of the Father which hath sent me" (Jn.5:30).
> "If the Son therefore shall make you free, ye shall be free indeed" (Jn.8:36).

MATTHEW 27:26-44

(4) The Son of God.

"For God so loved the world, that he gave his only begotten Son, that whosoever believeth in him should not perish, but have everlasting life. For God sent not his Son into the world to condemn the world; but that the world through him might be saved. He that believeth on him is not condemned: but he that believeth not is condemned already, because he hath not believed in the name of the only begotten Son of God" (Jn.3:16-18).

"Say ye of him, whom the Father hath sanctified, and sent into the world. Thou blasphemest; because I said, I am the Son of God" (Jn.10:36).

Thought 2. Leaders, civil and religious, are still men. It is not the position or profession that makes a man, but the heart. A heart of unbelief and enmity, a heart willing to become a participant with the sinful crowd will stoop to do shameful things, no matter the position or profession.

Thought 3. If Christ had used His power to save Himself, what would have happened to our salvation?

5 (27:44) **Jesus Christ, Mocked**: the criminals mocked Christ. The picture of the thieves joining in the mockery of Christ shows...
- the intensity of the ridicule and abuse.
- the bitterness and enmity against Christ within hearts.
- the depraved heart of a man who lets loose in a crowd, even when he is facing, or is going to face, punishment.
- the depth of shame to which men will stoop.

"Who, when he was reviled, reviled not again; when he suffered, he threatened not; but committed himself to him that judgeth righteously: who his own self bare our sins in his own body on the tree, that we, being dead to sins, should live unto righteousness: by whose stripes ye were healed" (1 Pe.2:23-24).

MATTHEW 27:45-56

		M. The Messiah's Great Triumph: The Miraculous Events Surrounding the Cross, 27:45-56
		(Mk 15:33-41; Lu 23:44-49; Jn 19:30-37)
			yielded up the ghost.
			51 And, behold, the veil of the temple was rent in twain from the top to the bottom; and the earth did quake, and the rocks rent;
			52 And the graves were opened; and many bodies of the saints which slept arose,
			53 And came out of the graves after his resurrection, and went into the holy city, and appeared unto many.
			54 Now when the centurion, and they that were with him, watching Jesus, saw the earthquake, and those things that were done, they feared greatly, saying, Truly this was the Son of God.
			55 And many women were there beholding afar off, which followed Jesus from Galilee, ministering unto him:
			56 Among which was Mary Magdalene, and Mary the mother of James and Joses, and the mother of Zebedee's children.
				4. The great curtain, or veil, of the temple torn: From top to bottom
				5. The terrifying earthquake
				6. The resurrection of many godly believers
				
				7. The confession of the centurion & others
				
				8. The courage & love of the women
				  a. Many women were at the crucifixion
				
				  b. Some identified

1. **The terrifying darkness**
  a. For three hours
  b. Over all the land
2. **The mysterious loud cry**
  a. The great separation: God forsook Him
 	
  b. The cry misunderstood
 	
    1) One showed compassion
 	
    2) Others superstitiously mocked
 	
3. **The great shout of triumph & the yielding up of Jesus' spirit**
			45 Now from the sixth hour there was darkness over all the land unto the ninth hour.
			46 And about the ninth hour Jesus cried with a loud voice, saying, Eli, Eli, lama sabachthani? that is to say, My God, my God, why hast thou forsaken me?
			47 Some of them that stood there, when they heard that, said, This man calleth for Elias.
			48 And straightway one of them ran, and took a spunge, and filled it with vinegar, and put it on a reed, and gave him to drink.
			49 The rest said, Let be, let us see whether Elias will come to save him.
			50 Jesus, when he had cried again with a loud voice,	

DIVISION XVI

THE MESSIAH'S ARREST, TRIAL, AND CRUCIFIXION, 26:1–27:66

M. The Messiah's Great Triumph: The Miraculous Events Surrounding the Cross, 27:45-56

(27:45-56) **Introduction**: while Christ hung on the cross, some miraculous events happened—events which demonstrated perfectly that the cross was a triumph, not a tragedy. The cross was the Messiah's great triumph. Eight events show this clearly.

1. The terrifying darkness (v.45).
2. The mysterious, loud cry (vv.46-49).
3. The great shout of triumph and the yielding up of Jesus' spirit (v.50).
4. The great curtain, or veil, of the temple torn: from top to bottom (v.51).
5. The terrifying earthquake (v.51).
6. The resurrection of many godly believers (vv.52-53).
7. The confession of the centurion and others (v.54).
8. The courage and love of the women (vv.55-56).

1 (27:45) **Jesus Christ, Death—Earth, Darkness**: the terrifying darkness. A supernatural darkness hung over the land from the sixth to the ninth hour, or according to our time from noon to 3 p.m.
   Think for a moment. Just imagine...
     Who it was hanging on the cross...
- God's only Son, the Sovereign Lord of all beings, both visible and invisible (see Col.1:16).
- The great architect and creator of the whole universe, of all nature.

What He was doing there on the cross...
- Bearing the sins of all men.
- Bearing the judgment and wrath of God against sin *for all men*.
- Dying the death of man for all men.
- Doing all that was necessary to free men from sin, death, and judgment so that they might live forever.

What the depth of God's plan is...

> "O the depth of the riches both of the wisdom and knowledge of God! how unsearchable are his judgments, and his ways past finding out! For who hath known the mind of the Lord? or who hath

MATTHEW 27:45-56

been his counsellor? Or who hath first given to him, and it shall be recompensed unto him again? For of him, and through him, and to him, are all things: to whom be glory for ever. Amen" (Ro.11:33-36).

When one really meditates upon the facts, is there any wonder that all things, including nature itself, were drastically affected by the death of God's Son? The darkness demonstrated and symbolized several things.

a. The darkness demonstrated that Christ was definitely God's Son. Before Him, all mouths are to be stopped in fear and reverence. There is no doubt that fear and wonder stopped the mocking mouths of the crowd standing around the cross. There is no mention of jeering taking place during these hours. The crowd was stricken with a sense of terror, wondering just what was happening (v.54).

"And he taketh with him Peter and James and John, and began to be sore amazed, and to be very heavy" (Mk.14:33).

"For God so loved the world, that he gave his only begotten Son, that whosoever believeth in him should not perish, but have everlasting life. For God sent not his Son into the world to condemn the world; but that the world through him might be saved. He that believeth on him is not condemned: but he that believeth not is condemned already, because he hath not believed in the name of the only begotten Son of God" (Jn.3:16-18).

"And being found in fashion as a man, he humbled himself, and became obedient unto death, even the death of the cross. Wherefore God also hath highly exalted him, and given him a name which is above every name: that at the name of Jesus every knee should bow, of things in heaven, and things in earth, and things under the earth; and that every tongue should confess that Jesus Christ is Lord, to the glory of God the Father" (Ph.2:8-11).

b. The darkness symbolized the darkest day of human history. This was the day when the Son of God Himself was being put to death for the sins of men.

"Who his own self bare our sins in his own body on the tree, that we, being dead to sins, should live unto righteousness: by whose stripes ye were healed" (1 Pe.2:24).

"For Christ also hath once suffered for sins, the just for the unjust, that he might bring us to God, being put to death in the flesh, but quickened by the Spirit" (1 Pe.3:18).

c. The darkness symbolized the darkness of sin:
⇒ sin which demands darkness to carry on its acts.

"And this is the condemnation, that light is come into the world, and men loved darkness rather than light, because their deeds were evil. For every one that doeth evil hateth the light, neither cometh to the light, lest his deeds should be reproved. But he that doeth truth cometh to the light, that his deeds may be made manifest, that they are wrought in God" (Jn.3:19-21).

⇒ sin which leads to the most terrible darkness of all—death.

"For the wages of sin is death; but the gift of God is eternal life through Jesus Christ our Lord" (Ro.6:23).

d. The darkness symbolized the darkness of the human soul and its works. The darkness of the human soul was now being borne by the Son of God—all for man.

"So Christ was once offered to bear the sins of many; and unto them that look for him shall he appear the second time without sin unto salvation" (He.9:28).

"And you hath he quickened, who were dead in trespasses and sins; wherein in time past ye walked according to the course of this world, according to the prince of the power of the air, the spirit that now worketh in the children of disobedience: among whom also we all had our conversation in times past in the lusts of our flesh, fulfilling the desires of the flesh and of the mind; and were by nature the children of wrath, even as others. But God, who is rich in mercy, for his great love wherewith he loved us, even when we were dead in sins, hath quickened us together with Christ, (by grace ye are saved)....But now in Christ Jesus ye who sometimes were far off are made nigh by the blood of Christ" (Ep.2:1-5, 13).

"But I am a worm, and no man; a reproach of men, and despised of the people" (Ps.22:6).

e. The darkness symbolized the withdrawal of the light of God's presence from the sinner. Christ hung upon the cross as the sinner—all for us—the sinner who was becoming sin for us.

"And about the ninth hour Jesus cried with a loud voice, saying, Eli, Eli, lama sabachthani? that is to say, My God, my God, why hast thou forsaken me?" (Mt.27:46).

"For he hath made him to be sin for us, who knew no sin; that we might be made the righteousness of God in him" (2 Co.5:21).

f. The darkness symbolized the anger of God at sin. Sin and the sinner deserve nothing but the judgment of darkness. Sin deserves no light from God's presence, none whatsoever.

"Christ hath redeemed us from the curse of the law, being made a curse for us: for it is written, Cursed is every one that hangeth on a tree" (Ga.3:13).

"My little children, these things write I unto you, that ye sin not. And if any man sin, we have an advocate with the Father, Jesus Christ the righteous: and he is the propitiation for our sins: and not for ours only, but also for the sins of the whole world" (1 Jn.2:1-2).

"Surely he hath borne our griefs, and carried our sorrows: yet we did esteem him stricken, smitten of God, and afflicted. But he was wounded for our transgressions, he was bruised for our iniquities: the chastisement of our peace was upon him; and with his stripes we are healed. All we like sheep have gone astray; we have turned every one to his own way; and the LORD hath laid on him the iniquity of us all" (Is.53:4-6).

2 (27:46-49) **Jesus Christ, Separated from God**: the mysterious, loud cry: "My God, my God, why hast thou forsaken me." This was the great separation, the moment when God forsook Christ, His only Son. What is the meaning of this shocking statement? The very idea that God could and would "forsake" His only Son staggers the human mind. Yet Christ shouted out: "My God, my God, why hast thou forsaken me?" The meaning cannot be ventured into lightly. The meaning requires reverence and much prayerful thought. But even then, even after an eternity of prayerful thought, the depth of the meaning remains fathomless and unreachable to man. (See note—Mt.20:19.)

Scripture indicates at least the following meanings.

a. "Why hast thou forsaken me?" Jesus sensed that God had withdrawn His presence from Him. He sensed that God was no longer with Him.

b. "Why hast thou forsaken me?" Jesus sensed that God had withdrawn His deliverance. Always in the past when Jesus was troubled, God had met His need. For example, God had sent a voice from heaven to assure Him (Jn.12:27-28); and when He was facing the cup in the garden of Gethsemane, God had even sent an angel to strengthen Him. But now, hanging upon the cross, God had forsaken Him. There was no deliverance from God. He was left all alone.

c. "Why hast thou forsaken me?" Jesus sensed that He was bearing the *curse* of God, the curse of separation from God, the curse of the judgment and condemnation of God against sin (see Ga.3:13. See DEEPER STUDY # 1—Heb.9:27.)

d. "Why hast thou forsaken me?" Jesus sensed that God's life and holiness had left Him, that He had been delivered into the hands of the enemies of life and holiness, that is, into the hands of sin and death. He was being made sin and having to die. And both sin and death were foreign to God, alien to God's nature which is life and holiness. Both sin and death stood as enemies of God and enemies to all that belonged to God.

⇒ In becoming sin and in dying, Christ experienced all that was contrary to the nature of God—all that was involved in God's separating Himself from sin and death. (See DEEPER STUDY # 1—Jn.10:10; DEEPER STUDY # 1—17:2-3. See 2 Co.5:21; He.2:14-15. See Col.2:15 with Ep.6:12 and note—Ep.4:8-10; DEEPER STUDY # 1—1 Pe.3:19-20.)

Jesus' cry was prophesied in Ps.22:1. The reason God had to forsake Jesus is given in Ps.22:3: "Thou art holy." Jesus had "become sin" for many (2 Co.5:21).

⇒ Christ bore sin for man; therefore, He had to bear the penalty due man—the penalty of separation from a perfectly holy God (see note and DEEPER STUDY # 2—Mt.26:37-38; DEEPER STUDY # 4—26:39). In all the mystery of His death, Scripture proclaims: "[Jesus] His own self *bore our sins in His own body* on the tree...." (1 Pe.2:24).

Note that some of the crowd misunderstood the words of Jesus' cry. One had compassion and sought to help Him by giving Him a drink. But others stopped the man and superstitiously mocked by demanding that He be left alone to see if Elijah would come to save Him.

"For he hath made him to be sin for us, who knew no sin; that we might be made the righteousness of God in him" (2 Co.5:21).

"Christ hath redeemed us from the curse of the law, being made a curse for us: for it is written, Cursed is every one that hangeth on a tree" (Ga.3:13).

"But we see Jesus, who was made a little lower than the angels for the suffering of death, crowned with glory and honour; that he by the grace of God should taste death for every man" (He.2:9).

"So Christ was once offered to bear the sins of many; and unto them that look for him shall he appear the second time without sin unto salvation" (He.9:28).

"The reproaches of them that reproached thee are fallen upon me" (Ps.69:9).

"But he was wounded for our transgressions, he was bruised for our iniquities: the chastisement of our peace was upon him; and with his stripes we are healed" (Is.53:5).

"Therefore will I divide him a portion with the great, and he shall divide the spoil with the strong; because he hath poured out his soul unto death: and he was numbered with the transgressors; and he bare the sin of many, and made intercession for the transgressors" (Is.53:12).

3 (27:50) **"It is finished"**: the great shout of triumph and the yielding up of Jesus' spirit. There are three important points here.

a. Jesus cried, "It is finished" (Jn.19:30). The Greek word *tetelestai* is the shout of victorious purpose. Christ had completed His work, mission, and task. He was not crying the cry of a defeated martyr; He was crying the cry of a victorious conqueror.

b. *Yielded up the ghost* (apheken to pneuma) means that He willingly yielded and gave up His spirit. It must always be remembered that Jesus *willingly* died. He willingly came to this moment of yielding and giving up His spirit unto death. Both Paul and Peter cover the Lord's work during the three days immediately following His death until the resurrection.

MATTHEW 27:45-56

1) On the cross:

"[He] spoiled principalities and powers, He made a show of them openly, triumphing over them in it [the cross]" (Col.2:15. See Ep.6:12.)

2) On the cross and after death:

"For Christ also hath once suffered for sins, the just for the unjust, that he might bring us to God, being put to death in the flesh, but quickened by the Spirit: by which also he went and preached unto the spirits in prison; which sometime were disobedient, when once the longsuffering of God waited in the days of Noah" (1 Pe.3:18-20. See note—1 Pe.3:19-20.)

3) After death:

"Wherefore he saith, When he ascended up on high, he led captivity captive, and gave gifts unto men. (Now that he ascended, what is it but that he also descended first into the lower parts of the earth? He that descended is the same also that ascended up far above all heavens, that he might fill all things.)" (Ep.4:8-10. See note—Ep.4:8-10.)

c. Christ died at the ninth hour, that is, 3:00 p.m. (vv.45, 50). This was the very hour when the priests began to make the evening offering of the Passover Lamb. While the priests were going about sacrificing the symbolic lamb for the people, the true Lamb of God was being sacrificed for the people's sins outside the city walls (1 Co.5:7; Heb.13:12).

4 (27:51) **Veil Torn**: the great veil of the temple was torn from top to bottom. In the minds of the Jews, the veil was one of the most important things in the temple. Why? Because it surrounded the ark of the covenant which symbolized the very presence of God Himself. It was huge and beautiful, made of the very finest materials. It was sixty or more feet high. To get some idea of the magnificence of the veil, imagine one of the other temple veils described by Josephus:

...before these doors there was a veil of equal largeness with the doors. It was embroidered with blue and fine linen, and scarlet, and purple, and of a contexture that was truly wonderful. This mixture of colors [had] its mystical interpretation, but [it] was a kind of image of the universe; for by the scarlet, there seemed to be signified fire, by the fine flax the earth, by the blue the air and by the purple the sea....This curtain had also embroidered upon it all that was mystical in the heavens (Josephus, Wars. 5. 5:4).

The significant point to note is that the veil was torn from top to bottom. This symbolizes that it was torn by an act of God himself. It symbolizes direct access to God (He.6:19; 9:3-12, 24; 10:19-23). It was the veil that separated the Holy of Holies from the Holy Place. Up until this time, only the High Priest could enter the Holy of Holies; and He could enter only one day a year, the Day of Atonement (Ex.26:33). Now through the body of Christ, any man can enter the presence of God. He can enter God's presence and pray any time, any place.

"For he is our peace, who hath made both one, and hath broken down the middle wall of partition between us; having abolished in his flesh the enmity, even the law of commandments contained in ordinances; for to make in himself of twain one new man, so making peace" (Ep.2:14-15).
"Which hope we have as an anchor of the soul, both sure and stedfast, and which entereth into that within the veil; whither the forerunner is for us entered, even Jesus, made an high priest for ever after the order of Melchisedec" (He.6:19-20).
"For Christ is not entered into the holy places made with hands, which are the figures of the true; but into heaven itself, now to appear in the presence of God for us" (He.9:24).
"By the which will we are sanctified through the offering of the body of Jesus Christ once for all" (He.10:10).
"Having therefore, brethren, boldness to enter into the holiest by the blood of Jesus, by a new and living way, which he hath consecrated for us, through the veil, that is to say, his flesh; and having an high priest over the house of God; let us draw near with a true heart in full assurance of faith, having our hearts sprinkled from an evil conscience, and our bodies washed with pure water" (He.10:19-23).

5 (27:51) **Earthquake**: the terrifying earthquake. The symbolism could be threefold.

a. The earth could have quaked under the weight of the sin placed upon its Architect and Creator.

"Who his own self bare our sins in his own body on the tree, that we, being dead to sins, should live unto righteousness: by whose stripes ye were healed" (1 Pe.2:24).
"But he was wounded for our transgressions, he was bruised for our iniquities: the chastisement of our peace was upon him; and with his stripes we are healed" (Is.53:5).

b. The earth could have quaked and torn at its rocks to symbolize the fatal blow to Satan's domain.

"Now is the judgment of this world: now shall the prince of this world be cast out. And I, if I be lifted up from the earth, will draw all men unto me" (Jn.12:31-32).

"And having spoiled principalities and powers [upon the cross], he made a show of them openly, triumphing over them in it" (Col.2:15).

"Forasmuch then as the children are partakers of flesh and blood, he also himself likewise took part of the same; that through death he might destroy him that had the power of death, that is, the devil; and deliver them who through fear of death were all their lifetime subject to bondage" (He.2:14-15).

c. The earth could have quaked to symbolize that it, too, is stirred to await the glorious day of redemption.

"Because the creation itself also shall be delivered from the bondage of corruption into the glorious liberty of the children of God" (Ro.8:21).

"But the day of the Lord will come as a thief in the night; in the which the heavens shall pass away with a great noise, and the elements shall melt with fervent heat, the earth also and the works that are therein shall be burned up. Seeing then that all these things shall be dissolved, what manner of persons ought ye to be in all holy conversation and godliness, looking for and hasting unto the coming of the day of God, wherein the heavens being on fire shall be dissolved, and the elements shall melt with fervent heat? Nevertheless we, according to his promise, look for new heavens and a new earth, wherein dwelleth righteousness" (2 Pe.3:10-13.)

6 (27:52-53) **Believers, Resurrected**: the resurrection of many saints. Just who these saints were is not known, not for certain. But several facts mentioned in Scripture need to be noted.

a. The graves were opened during the terrifying earthquake (v.51), but the bodies did not arise until after Jesus' resurrection (v.53). Christ had to be the first to arise from the dead—the first who was never to die again (1 Co.15:20; Col.1:18; Re.1:5).

b. Between these two events, the cross and the resurrection, was evidently the time that Jesus bore the full punishment of death and hell for man's sins. He tasted death for every man—both physical and spiritual death (He.2:9, 14).

c. Peter adds, "He went and preached unto the spirits in prison" (1 Pe.3:19). This probably means that He confronted the lost in hell and proclaimed that the way of the righteous is now vindicated. John quotes Christ in Re.1:18, "[I] was dead; and behold, I am alive for evermore, Amen: and have the keys of hell and death."

Many believe that before the resurrection of Christ all dead people went to a place known in Scripture as Hades (see Deeper Study # 2—Lu.16:23). Hades was divided into two areas, paradise and hell. The spirits of believers went to paradise; the spirits of unbelievers went to hell. Some commentators believe that when Christ arose He took the saints of paradise with Him to live in the presence of God forever. Now, since Christ's resurrection, all believers go immediately into the presence of God.

d. Paul adds "When He ascended up on high, He led captivity captive...but He also descended first into the lower parts of the earth...." (Ep.4:8-10; see the graves' opening in Mt.27:51 and the bodies' being raised in Mt.27:52). The idea is that Christ led captivity—sin, death and hell—captive. He conquered all the enemies of man, setting man free to arise and live forever in the presence of God.

The resurrection of these saints symbolized at least two things.

1. It symbolized the conquest of death by Christ. The sting is now taken from death; the power of death is now broken.

"For he must reign, till he hath put all enemies under his feet. The last enemy that shall be destroyed is death" (1 Co.15:25-26).

"Behold, I show you a mystery; We shall not all sleep, but we shall all be changed, in a moment, in the twinkling of an eye, at the last trump: for the trumpet shall sound, and the dead shall be raised incorruptible, and we shall be changed. For this corruptible must put on incorruption, and this mortal must put on immortality. So when this corruptible shall have put on incorruption, and this mortal shall have put on immortality, then shall be brought to pass the saying that is written, Death is swallowed up in victory. O death where is thy sting? O grave, where is thy victory? The sting of death is sin; and the strength of sin is the law. But thanks be to God, which giveth us the victory through our Lord Jesus Christ" (1 Co.15:51-57).

"Forasmuch then as the children are partakers of flesh and blood, he also himself likewise took part of the same; that through death he might destroy him that had the power of death, that is, the devil" (He.2:14).

2. It symbolized the resurrection of believers. Believers shall arise and be recognized and know one another (Mt.27:53).

"Marvel not at this: for the hour is coming, in the which all that are in the graves shall hear his voice, and shall come forth; they that have done good, unto the resurrection of life; and they that have done evil, unto the resurrection of damnation" (Jn.5:28-29).

"And this is the will of him that sent me, that every one which seeth the Son, and believeth on him, may have everlasting life: and I will raise him up at the last day" (Jn.6:40).

"Knowing that he which raised up the Lord Jesus shall raise up us also by Jesus, and shall present us with you" (2 Co.4:14).

"For the Lord himself shall descend from heaven with a shout, with the voice of the archangel, and with the trump of God: and the dead in Christ shall rise first: then we which are alive and remain shall be caught up together with them in the clouds, to meet the Lord in the air: and so shall we ever be with the Lord" (1 Th.4:16-17).

7 (27:54) **Centurion**: the confession of the centurion and others. A magnificent thing happened to some of those standing at the foot of the cross. When the earth quaked upon the heels of the darkness, the centurion and his soldiers feared and exclaimed: "Truly this was the Son of God." The confession was probably genuine, much more than just feeling that Christ was innocent and a special person to His God. Of course, the soldiers could not fully understand what *Son of God* meant; but they knew Christ claimed to be the Son of God. And in witnessing Christ's words and purposeful behavior on the cross, they more than likely believed His claim to be true.

"That if thou shalt confess with thy mouth the Lord Jesus, and shalt believe in thine heart that God hath raised him from the dead, thou shalt be saved. For with the heart man believeth unto righteousness; and with the mouth confession is made unto salvation" (Ro.10:9-10).

Thought 1. The magnetic power of the cross begins its work with the centurion and his soldiers.

"And I, if I be lifted up from the earth, will draw all men unto me" (Jn.12:32).

Thought 2. Truly believing the claim of Christ to be the Son of God is what it takes to be saved.

8 (27:55-56) **Women**: the courage and love of the women. Note the following phrases.
⇒ *Many women*: many were there. When the men fled, many women demonstrated courage.
⇒ *Afar off*: some did stand far off, but some stood at the very foot of the cross (Jn.19:25). Their love ran deep and their devotion and courage clear. They triumphed over fear. They did not fear the enemies of Christ: they triumphed simply because they loved (1 Jn.4:18).

"For whosoever will save his life shall lose it; but whosoever shall lose his life for my sake and the gospel's, the same shall save it" (Mk.8:35).
"There is no fear in love; but perfect love casteth out fear: because fear hath torment. He that feareth is not made perfect in love" (1 Jn.4:18).

MATTHEW 27:57-66

	N. The Messiah's Burial: Reactions to His Death, 27:57-66 (Mk 15:42-47; Lu 23:50-56; Jn 19:38-42)		
1. **A secret disciple: Was stirred to step forward for Christ** a. He was a disciple, but a secret follower b. He was stirred to step forward for Christ: He requested the body c. He embalmed the body d. He buried the body 1) In his own tomb 2) Closed the entrance with a great stone 2. **Two believing women: Showed loyalty & affection**	57 When the even was come, there came a rich man of Arimathaea, named Joseph, who also himself was Jesus' disciple: 58 He went to Pilate, and begged the body of Jesus. Then Pilate commanded the body to be delivered. 59 And when Joseph had taken the body, he wrapped it in a clean linen cloth, 60 And laid it in his own new tomb, which he had hewn out in the rock: and he rolled a great stone to the door of the sepulchre, and departed. 61 And there was Mary Magdalene, and the other	Mary, sitting over against the sepulchre. 62 Now the next day, that followed the day of the preparation, the chief priests and Pharisees came together unto Pilate, 63 Saying, Sir, we remember that that deceiver said, while he was yet alive, After three days I will rise again. 64 Command therefore that the sepulchre be made sure until the third day, lest his disciples come by night, and steal him away, and say unto the people, He is risen from the dead: so the last error shall be worse than the first. 65 Pilate said unto them, Ye have a watch: go your way, make *it* as sure as ye can. 66 So they went, and made the sepulchre sure, sealing the stone, and setting a watch.	3. **Unbelievers & worldly religionists: Faced a serious problem** a. Their twofold problem 1) The Lord's claim: He would arise 2) The message of a risen Messiah, Savior b. Their request: Secure the tomb c. Their error: Believing Jesus' claims were false d. Their extensive security of the tomb^{DS1} 1) Sealed the tomb 2) Posted a military guard

DIVISION XVI

THE MESSIAH'S ARREST, TRIAL, AND CRUCIFIXION, 26:1–27:66

N. The Messiah's Burial: Reactions to His Death, 27:57-66

(27:57-66) **Introduction**: Jesus was now dead. In this passage, there are three reactions to His death, reactions that reveal how we should and should not react to His death.
1. A secret disciple: was stirred to step forward for Christ (vv.57-60).
2. Two believing women: showed loyalty and affection (v.61).
3. Unbelievers and worldly religionists: faced a serious problem (vv.62-66).

1 (27:57-60) **Joseph of Arimathaea**: there was the reaction of a secret disciple. He was stirred to step forward for Christ. Several things are said about Joseph of Arimathaea that show the kind of man he was.
⇒ He was an honorable counsellor, that is, a member of the Sanhedrin (Mk.15:43).
⇒ He was a good and just man (Lu.23:50).
⇒ He waited for the Kingdom of God (Mk.15:43).
⇒ He was rich (Mt.27:57).
⇒ He did not vote for Jesus' death when the Sanhedrin voted (Lu.23:51).
⇒ He was a disciple, but a secret disciple, fearing his fellow Jews (Jn.19:38).

It is this last fact that reveals a marked change in Joseph. Up until the death of Jesus, He had been a secret disciple. He had probably had several meetings with Christ when the Lord visited Jerusalem. But after the Lord's death, he was no longer secret. He became bold.
Four acts show a remarkable boldness, a boldness that reveals the strength of Joseph's discipleship.
1. Joseph actually marched in "boldly to Pilate" and requested the body of Jesus (Mk.15:43). This was a tremendous act of courage. The Romans either dumped the bodies of crucified criminals in the trash heaps or left the bodies hanging upon the cross for the vultures and animals to consume. The latter served as an example of criminal punishment to the public. Joseph also braved the threat of Pilate's reaction, for Pilate was fed up with the *Jesus matter*. Jesus had proven to be very bothersome to Pilate. Pilate could have reacted severely against Joseph.
2. Joseph risked the disfavor and discipline of the Sanhedrin. They were the ruling body who had instigated and condemned Christ, and Joseph was a member of the council. Unquestionably, he would face harsh reaction from some of his fellow Sanhedrin members and from certain of his closest friends.
3. Joseph demonstrated a care, even an affection, for Jesus by giving his own tomb for the burial of Jesus. This act alone would leave no question about his stand with Christ.
4. Joseph also eliminated himself from taking part in the great Passover Feast. This was just never done, even for the most serious reasons. Joseph, by handling Jesus' body, was considered defiled for seven days for having come in contact with a corpse. Once defiled, Jewish law forbade a person from taking part in Jewish ceremonies.

MATTHEW 27:57-66

The thing that turned Joseph from being a secret disciple to a bold disciple seems to be the phenomenal events surrounding the cross (the behavior and words of Christ, the darkness, the earthquake, and the torn veil). When Joseph witnessed all this, his mind connected the claims of Christ with the Old Testament prophecies of the Messiah. Joseph saw the prophecies fulfilled in Jesus. He stepped forward and braved all risks: he took his stand with Christ. A remarkable courage! A courage stirred by the death of Christ.

Note that Joseph embalmed the body and laid it in *his own tomb*, and he closed the tomb's entrance with a huge stone (see DEEPER STUDY #1—Mt.27:65-66). (See Is.53:9.)

Thought 1. Every secret believer needs to study the cross of Christ. Really seeing the cross will turn any secret believer into a bold witness for Christ.

"For God so loved the world, that he gave his only begotten Son, that whosoever believeth in him should not perish, but have everlasting life" (Jn.3:16).

"But God commendeth his love toward us, in that, while we were yet sinners, Christ died for us" (Ro.5:8).

"Who his own self bare our sins in his own body on the tree, that we, being dead to sins, should live unto righteousness: by whose stripes ye were healed" (1 Pe.2:24).

"For Christ also hath once suffered for sins, the just for the unjust, that he might bring us to God, being put to death in the flesh, but quickened by the Spirit" (1 Pe.3:18).

Thought 2. Position, power, wealth, and fame—none of these make us bold for Christ. Only true affection for Christ will make us bold, and only as we see the cross of Christ will affection for Christ be aroused.

Thought 3. Christ identified with men perfectly.
⇒ He lived as a man, but perfectly.
⇒ He died as a man, but perfectly (as the Ideal Man).
⇒ He was buried as a man, but perfectly.

"And he made his grave with the wicked, and with the rich in his death; because he had done no violence, neither was any deceit in his mouth" (Is.53:9).

"Wherefore in all things it behooved him to be made like unto his brethren, that he might be a merciful and faithful high priest in things pertaining to God, to make reconciliation for the sins of the people" (He.2:17).

Thought 4. God's own Son had nothing when He was on earth. This means two things.
⇒ Christ is the Savior of the poorest. He was born in a stable. He had no place of His own to lay His head (Mt.8:20; Lu.9:58). His tomb was a borrowed tomb.
⇒ Yet the rich can serve Him just as Joseph of Arimathaea did.

2 (27:61) **Women Believers**: there was the reaction of two believing women. They showed affection and loyalty. There are three facts to note about these women.

a. The women were loyal to Christ despite all danger. The men forsook Christ, but not the women (Mt.26:56, 69-75; see 27:55-56, 61).

b. The women had a deep affection for Christ. They took what they had, money to buy spices and ointments, and used it for Christ. This they did because they loved Him (Mt.27:61; see Mk.16:1; Lu.23:56).

c. The women had not yet understood the resurrection of Christ. They were preparing His body to lie, and eventually to decay, in the tomb. The true meaning of living forever, the human body's being remade, recreated, and becoming incorruptible, had not yet been grasped by them (Jn.5:24-29; see 1 Co.15:42f. See 1 Co.15:1-58.)

Thought 1. The two women were great examples for all men. All men believers...
• should be loyal to Christ no matter how furious the danger.
• should love Christ to such an extent that they give all they are and have to Christ.
• should seek to understand and grasp the full meaning of the resurrection of Christ.

"For I am not ashamed of the gospel of Christ: for it is the power of God unto salvation to every one that believeth; to the Jew first, and also to the Greek" (Ro.1:16).

"Be not thou therefore ashamed of the testimony of our Lord, nor of me his prisoner: but be thou partaker of the afflictions of the gospel according to the power of God" (2 Ti.1:8).

3 (27:62-66) **Jesus Christ, Response to**: there was the reaction of unbelievers and worldly religionists. They faced a serious problem. They were so uneasy and fearful that they went to Pilate in an attempt to prevent the disciples from stealing the body.

a. The unbelievers had a twofold problem.
1) The unbeliever had the problem of the Lord's claim. He had said He would arise from the dead. These worldly religionists did not believe He would, but they knew He had predicted some kind of resurrection (Mt.12:40; Jn.2:19; 10:17-18). Some of them had heard Him personally talk about rising from the dead. The disciples had shared with their families and closest associates the words of Christ about His death and resurrection; and, as

with all matters shared with another, the families and closest associates shared with their closest friends and the prediction had spread. Moreover, during the last months Christ had intensified His prediction in order to drill the truth into the disciples to prepare them for what lay ahead (see notes—Mt.15:21-22; 15:29; 16:21-28; 17:22).

It should be remembered that the disciples did not take Jesus' words literally. They spiritualized the prediction of His death, resurrection, and return. They probably thought Jesus was referring to some events dealing with the upcoming struggle to free Israel from Roman domination and establishing the Messiah's kingdom in glory.

"Say ye of him, whom the Father hath sanctified, and sent into the world, Thou blasphemest; because I said, I am the Son of God?" (Jn.10:36).

"She saith unto him, Yea, Lord: I believe that thou art the Christ, the Son of God, which should come into the world" (Jn.11:27).

"Whosoever shall confess that Jesus is the Son of God, God dwelleth in him, and he in God" (1 Jn.4:15).

Thought 1. Unbelievers of all generations have to deal with the problem of the Lord's claim to be the Messiah, the Son of God.

Thought 2. Many spiritualize Jesus' words even today.

2) The unbeliever had the problem of the message about the risen Messiah. What they feared was that the disciples would come during the night to steal the body and begin to preach that Jesus had arisen from the dead. Note: there was no chance of this.
   ⇒ The disciples were *emotionally destitute*, utterly hopeless and depressed. In addition, they were *terrorized*, thinking they were being hunted down like a pack of wolves.
   ⇒ The disciples, if they lied about the resurrection, would have been deceiving themselves; and above all men, they would have lost the most. They had left everything for Christ: their families, homes, and businesses. They had left all because of their faith in Christ and their hope in the next world. If there were no other world, they would be the most miserable men of all. And remember: at that particular time, they were the most miserable.
   ⇒ The disciples, if they lied about the resurrection, would have been deceiving others. They would have been lying and deceiving people with the very opposite of everything Christ had taught them. There was no chance the disciples could ever pull off so mammoth a deception on the world.

Thought 1. The unbeliever has to deal with the message of the risen Lord. He actually arose.

"But for us also, to whom it shall be imputed, if we believe on him that raised up Jesus our Lord from the dead" (Ro.4:24).

"That if thou shalt confess with thy mouth the Lord Jesus, and shalt believe in thine heart that God hath raised him from the dead, thou shalt be saved" (Ro.10:9).

"For I delivered unto you first of all that which I also received, how that Christ died for our sins according to the scriptures; and that he was buried, and that he rose again the third day according to the scriptures" (1 Co.15:3-4).

"Blessed be the God and Father of our Lord Jesus Christ, which according to his abundant mercy hath begotten us again unto a lively hope by the resurrection of Jesus Christ from the dead" (1 Pe.1:3).

b. The unbelievers requested Pilate to secure the tomb, making it as secure as was humanly possible (see DEEPER STUDY # 1—Mt.27:65-66).

c. The unbelievers made one drastic mistake: they believed that Jesus' claims were false (v.64). Note the wording of what they said. They feared the last error (Jesus' claim to be the Messiah, the Son of God), and they feared the possibility of a new error, the message of a risen messiah. Note: they felt the message of a risen Lord might be more powerful than the claims to deity—and it is.

d. The unbelievers planned extensive security of the tomb. Pilate gave permission to post a guard and to seal the tomb. Both measures were taken (see DEEPER STUDY # 1—Mt.27:65-66).

DEEPER STUDY # 1

(27:65-66) **Jesus' Tomb**: cave tombs were closed by rolling a huge cartwheel-like stone in front of the entrance. They were almost impossible to remove. A deep slanting groove was hewn out of the rock at the base of the entrance for the circular stone to rest in. The stone usually weighed several tons. Such precautions were essential because there were so many tombs ransacked in those days of poverty.

The tomb was further secured by being sealed. When it was necessary to seal a tomb, the huge stone was cemented to the entrance walls or else some type of rope or binding was wrapped around the entrance stone and fastened to both sides of the tomb. Then the binding was cemented with a hardening clay or wax-like substance. In the case of some burials, usually political figures, the seal of the Emperor was also attached to the walls of the entrance. This was to strike fear of Roman retaliation against any intruder.

In the case of Jesus' tomb, further precautions were taken by placing a patrol to guard against any foul play. This guard consisted of a large number of men (Mt.28:4, 11f).

MATTHEW 28:1-15

	CHAPTER 28 XVII. THE MESSIAH'S TRIUMPHANT RESURRECTION, 28:1-20 A. The Messiah's Resurrection: Surrounding Events, 28:1-15 (Mk 16:1-13; Lu 24:1-49; Jn 20:1-23)		

1. The time of the resurrection
2. The first witnesses of the resurrection
  a. Mary Magdalene
  b. The other Mary
3. The miraculous events of the resurrection
  a. The great earthquake
  b. The great stone rolled back
  c. The radiant figure
    1) Appearance: Dazzling
    2) Clothing: White as snow
  d. The terrified guards
    1) Shook
    2) Acted as dead men
4. The appeals of the resurrection
  a. Do not fear: Your seeking for the Messiah is known to God
    1) He was crucified
    2) He is risen[DS1]
  b. Come, see: Believe & live
 	
  c. Go quickly & tell the glorious news
	In the end of the sabbath, as it began to dawn toward the first *day* of the week, came Mary Magdalene and the other Mary to see the sepulchre.
	2 And, behold, there was a great earthquake: for the angel of the Lord descended from heaven, and came and rolled back the stone from the door, and sat upon it.
	3 His countenance was like lightning, and his raiment white as snow:
	4 And for fear of him the keepers did shake, and became as dead *men*.
	5 And the angel answered and said unto the women, Fear not ye: for I know that ye seek Jesus, which was crucified.
	6 He is not here: for he is risen, as he said. Come, see the place where the Lord lay.
	7 And go quickly, and tell his disciples that he is risen from the dead; and, behold,
		he goeth before you into Galilee; there shall ye see him: lo, I have told you.
		8 And they departed quickly from the sepulchre with fear and great joy; and did run to bring his disciples word.
		9 And as they went to tell his disciples, behold, Jesus met them, saying, All hail. And they came and held him by the feet, and worshipped him.
		10 Then said Jesus unto them, Be not afraid: go tell my brethren that they go into Galilee, and there shall they see me.
		11 Now when they were going, behold, some of the watch came into the city, and showed unto the chief priests all the things that were done.
		12 And when they were assembled with the elders, and had taken counsel, they gave large money unto the soldiers,
		13 Saying, Say ye, His disciples came by night, and stole him *away* while we slept.
		14 And if this come to the governor's ears, we will persuade him, and secure you.
		15 So they took the money, and did as they were taught: and this saying is commonly reported among the Jews until this day.
			1) He will meet you
			2) You will see Him
			
			3) The women obeyed: With fear & great joy
			
			5. The glorious encounter[DS2] with the Lord of the resurrection
			
			6. The attempt to discredit the resurrection[DS3]
			  a. The guards reported the resurrection
			
			  b. The authorities were baffled: Devised a plan
			  c. The authorities bribed & assured the soldiers of protection from Pilate
			  d. The soldiers were to claim that Jesus' body had been stolen by His disciples
			
			  e. The lie was found out: The truth marched on (indicated by the witness of Matthew & the other disciples of Christ)

DIVISION XVII

THE MESSIAH'S TRIUMPHANT RESURRECTION, 28:1-20

A. The Messiah's Resurrection: Surrounding Events, 28:1-15

(28:1-15) **Introduction**: Matthew reports five significant events surrounding the resurrection—events that stir interest and challenge action.
1. The time of the resurrection (v.1).
2. The first witnesses of the resurrection (v.1).
3. The miraculous events of the resurrection (vv.2-4).
4. The appeals of the resurrection (vv.5-8).
5. The glorious encounter with the Lord of the resurrection (vv.9-10).
6. The attempt to discredit the resurrection (vv.11-15).

1 (28:1) **Jesus Christ, Resurrection**: the time of the resurrection. Jesus arose after the Sabbath was over, that is, on Sunday, the first day of the week. There are four facts to note about this.
  a. Matthew said, "In the end of the Sabbath" which means late on the Sabbath. Matthew was not speaking of strict Jewish time. This would mean the Sabbath had ended at 6 p.m. the preceding evening of Saturday (see DEEPER STUDY # 1—Mk.6:48). He was using the common day-to-day idea of time. He was simply adding the night time to the preceding day (see Mk.16:1).
  b. Jesus arose before dawn, before the sun arose on Sunday morning. This was significant to the early Christian believers, so significant that they broke away from the practice of worshipping on the Sabbath or Saturday. They began to worship on Sunday, the day of the resurrection of their Lord.

MATTHEW 28:1-15

"And upon the first day of the week, when the disciples came together to break bread, Paul preached unto them, ready to depart on the morrow; and continued his speech until midnight" (Ac.20:7).

"Upon the first day of the week let every one of you lay by him in store, as God hath prospered him, that there be no gatherings when I come" (1 Co.16:2).

c. Jesus arose on the first day of the week, on Sunday morning. This means that He arose on the third day just as He had said (Mt.12:40; 16:21; 17:23; 20:19; Mk.9:31; 10:34; Lu.9:22; 18:33; 24:7, 46). His arising from the dead is a triumph, a conquest over death. Death reigns no more. Its rule has been broken. (See note—Ro.8:2-4.)

"But we had the sentence of death in ourselves, that we should not trust in ourselves, but in God which raiseth the dead: who delivered us from so great a death, and doth deliver: in whom we trust that he will yet deliver us" (2 Co.1:9-10).

"But is now made manifest by the appearing of our Saviour Jesus Christ, who hath abolished death, and hath brought life and immortality to light through the gospel" (2 Ti.1:10).

"But we see Jesus, who was made a little lower than the angels for the suffering of death, crowned with glory and honour; that he by the grace of God should taste death for every man....Forasmuch then as the children are partakers of flesh and blood, he also himself likewise took part of the same; that through death he might destroy him that had the power of death, that is, the devil; and deliver them who through fear of death were all their lifetime subject to bondage" (He.2:9, 14-15).

d. Again, Jesus arose on the first day of the week, Sunday morning. He was in the grave on the Sabbath, unable to observe the laws governing the great season of the Passover and the Sabbath. He was dead; therefore, the law and its observances had no authority over Him. This is symbolic of the identification believers gain in Christ. When a man believes in Jesus Christ, God identifies the man with Christ, in particular with the death of Christ. God counts the man as having died with Christ. Therefore, in Christ's death believers become dead to the law (see note—Ro.7:4; DEEPER STUDY # 2—8:3; note—Mt.5:17-18 for more discussion).

"Knowing this, that our old man is crucified with him, that the body of sin might be destroyed, that henceforth we should not serve sin" (Ro.6:6).

"I am crucified with Christ: nevertheless I live; yet not I, but Christ liveth in me: and the life which I now live in the flesh I live by the faith of the Son of God, who loved me, and gave himself for me" (Ga.2:20).

"Wherefore if ye be dead with Christ from the rudiments [elements, things] of the world, why, as though living in the world, are ye subject to ordinances" (Col.2:20).

2 (28:1) **Jesus Christ, Resurrection**: the first witnesses of the resurrection. Note several things.

a. The first witnesses were women, not men, not even his own disciples. The women took the lead in love and care for the Lord Jesus.

b. Two reasons are given for the women's coming to the tomb of Jesus.
1) Matthew says the women "came...*to see* the sepulchre." The Greek word *to see* (theoresai) means to contemplate, to gaze, to observe in order to grasp. They came to be close to their Lord, the One who meant so much to them, to mourn over Him, to think through all that had happened. This is an important point, for it perhaps explains why the women were more prepared to believe the miracle of the resurrection.

"Now when Jesus was risen early the first day of the week, he appeared first to Mary Magdalene, out of whom he had cast seven devils. And she went and told them that had been with him, as they mourned and wept. And they, when they had heard that he was alive, and had been seen of her, believed not" (Mk.16:9-11).

"It was Mary Magdalene, and Joanna, and Mary the mother of James, and other women that were with them, which told these things unto the apostles. And their words seemed to them as idle tales, and they believed them not" (Lu.24:10-11).

Thought 1. Thinking and meditating upon the Lord will help us to understand the Lord and prepare us to receive the great truth of His resurrection.

"Come now, and let us reason together, saith the LORD: though your sins be as scarlet, they shall be as white as snow; though they be red like crimson, they shall be as wool" (Is.1:18).

2) Mark says the women came to "anoint Him" (Mk.16:1). They cared, so they wanted to take care of His body as loved ones do.

Thought 1. The women are an example to us in taking care of the bodies of our loved ones.

c. Mary Magdalene stands out as the most prominent of the women who witnessed the resurrection of the Lord. Her love and devotion must have been deep, very deep. Mary had a very special quality about her, possessing a deeper love and devotion than most (see Mk.16:1, 9; Lu.24:10; Jn.20:11-18).

d. The other Mary was the mother of James and Joses. She just could not tear herself away from the body of Jesus which indicates a very special love and devotion for Him (Mt.27:56, 61; 28:1; Mk.15:40; Lu.24:10). She was probably the mother of Cleopas as well (see Jn.19:25).

3 (28:2-4) **Jesus Christ, Resurrection**: the miraculous events of the resurrection.

a. There was the "great earthquake." Nothing more is said, only that it was *great*. The earthquake symbolized that a *historical convulsion* was taking place, an event that never before had happened: a man was rising from the dead, the man Christ Jesus, the Son of God Himself. Tragically, He had been put to death by the hands of men, but gloriously He was being raised from the dead by the power of God (Ro.1:4; Ep.1:19-20). The historical event was a picture of the unbelievable convulsion that God was planning for the end time: the resurrection of all the dead. The resurrection of God's dear Son paved the way and prefigured the resurrection of all men. History was witnessing the most convulsive event of all time; the quaking of the earth was bound to happen.

b. There was the great stone rolled back (see Deeper Study #1—Mt.27:65-66). The stone was not rolled back for the benefit of Christ, but for the witnesses to the resurrection. When Christ arose, He was in His resurrection body, the body of the spiritual dimension of being which has no physical bounds. But the witnesses needed to enter the tomb to see the truth (see outline and notes—Jn.20:1-10).

c. There was the radiant figure, the angel of the Lord. Note two facts about the angel.
1) He rolled back the stone for the sake of the witnesses. He was a ministering spirit of God's, serving by helping God's people (see Deeper Study #1—Heb.1:4-14).
2) His appearance was dazzling:
   ⇒ just like lightning—visible, quick, startling, striking, frightening, brilliant.
   ⇒ just like snow—white, pure, glistening.

d. There were the guards and their terror. Matthew seems to indicate that the guards witnessed the flashing appearance of the angel and the rolling back of the stone. The suddenness of the event, the brilliant appearance and the enormous strength of the angel were like a volcanic eruption to them. They quaked, shook, and fell as dead men to the ground. They were either stricken unconscious or were so terrified they pretended to be unconscious.

Thought 1. The power of God is awesome and terrifying. The guards had been told they were to guard a dead body against thieving men. They were totally unprepared and unable to stand against the power of God and His messenger (angel). There is a strong lesson here for every unbeliever.

"For with God nothing shall be impossible" (Lu.1:37).
"And Jesus came and spake unto them, saying, All power is given unto me in heaven and in earth" (Mt.28:18).
"No man taketh it from me, but I lay it down of myself. I have power to lay it down, and I have power to take it again. This commandment have I received of my Father" (Jn.10:18).
"And declared to be the Son of God with power, according to the spirit of holiness, by the resurrection from the dead" (Ro.1:4).
"[God's power] which he wrought in Christ, when he raised him from the dead, and set him at his own right hand in the heavenly places" (Ep.1:20).
"He divideth the sea with his power, and by his understanding he smiteth through the proud" (Jb.26:12).
"Which by his strength setteth fast the mountains; being girded with power" (Ps.65:6).
"But our God is in the heavens: he hath done whatsoever he hath pleased" (Ps.115:3).
"Yea, before the day was I am he; and there is none that can deliver out of my hand: I will work, and who shall let [hinder] it?" (Is.43:13).

4 (28:5-8) **Jesus Christ, Resurrection**: the appeals of the resurrection. When the women arrived at the tomb, they saw the dazzling angel sitting on the stone. Mark says they saw "a young man sitting on the right side, clothed in a long white garment" (Mk.16:5). Luke says "two men stood by them in shining garments" (Lu.24:4). Apparently, many angels were all about the tomb and the surrounding area attending Christ, joying and rejoicing over what God had done. At the right time, one angel appeared to the women, then two. Note that they appeared as men, that is, as messengers of God.

The appeals of the resurrection are a message within themselves.

a. Fear not. There are three reasons why the person who seeks after Christ should not fear.
1) God knows the person who is seeking after the Messiah. He knows the movement of every heart. The person who seeks diligently shall find (Mt.7:7).

"Ask, and it shall be given you; seek, and ye shall find; knock, and it shall be opened unto you: for every one that asketh receiveth; and he that seeketh findeth; and to him that knocketh it shall be opened" (Mt.7:7-8).
"But if from thence [idolatry] thou shalt seek the LORD thy God thou shalt find him, if thou seek him with all thy heart and with all thy soul" (De.4:29).
"For I know the thoughts that I think toward you, saith the LORD, thoughts of peace, and not of evil, to give you an expected end. Then shall ye call upon me, and ye shall go and pray unto me,

MATTHEW 28:1-15

and I will hearken unto you. And ye shall seek me, and find me, when ye shall search for me with all your heart" (Je.29:11-13).

2) Christ has been crucified to save every man.

"Jesus answered them, Many good works have I showed you from my Father; for which of those works do ye stone me? The Jews answered him, saying, For a good work we stone thee not; but for blasphemy; and because that thou, being a man, makest thyself God" (Jn.10:32-33).
"For when we were yet without strength, in due time Christ died for the ungodly" (Ro.5:6).
"And that he died for all, that they which live should not henceforth live unto themselves, but unto him which died for them, and rose again" (2 Co.5:15).
"Who his own self bare our sins in his own body on the tree, that we, being dead to sins, should live unto righteousness: by whose stripes ye were healed" (1 Pe.2:24).
"And they sung a new song, saying, Thou art worthy to take the book, and to open the seals thereof: for thou wast slain, and hast redeemed us to God by thy blood out of every kindred, and tongue, and people, and nation" (Re.5:9).

3) Christ has now risen from the dead and conquered death.

"But for us also, to whom it [righteousness] shall be imputed, if we believe on him that raised up Jesus our Lord from the dead; who was delivered for our offences, and was raised again for our justification" (Ro.4:24-25).
"[God's] power, which he wrought in Christ, when he raised him from the dead, and set him at his own right hand in the heavenly places" (Ep.1:19-20).

b. Come, see: believe and live. Note that the angel reminded the women of the Lord's words: "He is risen, as He said" (see Mt.16:21; 17:23; 20:19; 26:32). Note also that the women were told to "come, see the place." They were eyewitnesses of His resurrection.

Thought 1. Believers of every generation can become clear witnesses of the Lord's death and resurrection. They can see as though they were eyewitnesses—all by God's Spirit.

"O foolish Galatians, who hath bewitched you, that ye should not obey the truth, before whose eyes Jesus Christ hath been evidently set forth, crucified among you?" (Ga.3:1).
"But the Comforter, which is the Holy Ghost, whom the Father will send in my name, he shall teach you all things, and bring all things to your remembrance, whatsoever I have said unto you" (Jn.14:26).

c. Go quickly and tell the glorious news. Sharing the glorious news is essential. It is the greatest news of all history: Christ is risen. Notice the encouraging words the angel spoke, "He will meet you and you will see Him."
Note several things:
⇒ The women obeyed. They became the very first witnesses for the risen Lord.
⇒ The discouraged believers (disciples) were the first ones the women were to tell. The discouraged were to be encouraged and stirred to join the great force of witnesses.
⇒ The witnessing was to be done quickly.

5 (28:9-10) **Jesus Christ, Resurrection**: the glorious encounter with Jesus Himself. Note what happened when the women personally encountered Christ.
a. He said, "All hail"; that is, rejoice.

"Verily, verily, I say unto you, That ye shall weep and lament, but the world shall rejoice: and ye shall be sorrowful, but your sorrow shall be turned into joy" (Jn.16:20).
"Rejoice in the Lord alway: and again I say, Rejoice" (Ph.4:4).

b. The women worshipped Him in amazement, adoration, and awe.
c. Jesus said, "Be not afraid."

"For God hath not given us the spirit of fear; but of power, and of love, and of a sound mind" (2 Ti.1:7).

d. He then said, "Go and tell my brothers." The commission was repeated because of the extreme importance of bearing the glorious news.

"Go ye therefore, and teach all nations, baptizing them in the name of the Father, and of the Son, and of the Holy Ghost: teaching them to observe all things whatsoever I have commanded you: and, lo, I am with you alway, even unto the end of the world" (Mt.28:19-20).
"And he said unto them, Go ye into all the world, and preach the gospel to every creature" (Mk.16:15).

"And the things that thou hast heard of me among many witnesses, the same commit thou to faithful men, who shall be able to teach others also" (2 Ti.2:2).

"...Christ in you, the hope of glory: whom we preach, warning every man, and teaching every man in all wisdom; that we may present every man perfect in Christ Jesus: whereunto I also labor, striving according to his working, which worketh in me mightily" (Co.1:27-29).

DEEPER STUDY # 1

(28:6-7) **Resurrection Predicted**: Christ predicted His resurrection time and again.

"From that time forth began Jesus to show unto his disciples, how that he must go unto Jerusalem, and suffer many things of the elders and chief priests and scribes, and be killed, and be raised again the third day" (Mt.16:21).

"And they shall kill him, and the third day he shall be raised again. And they were exceeding sorry" (Mt.17:23).

"And shall deliver him to the Gentiles to mock, and to scourge, and to crucify him: and the third day he shall rise again" (Mt.20:19).

"But after I am risen again, I will go before you into Galilee" (Mt.26:32).

"And as they came down from the mountain, he charged them that they should tell no man what things they had seen, till the Son of man were risen from the dead" (Mk.9:9).

"But after that I am risen, I will go before you into Galilee" (Mk.14:28).

"Jesus answered and said unto them, Destroy this temple, and in three days I will raise it up" (Jn.2:19).

"Having therefore obtained help of God, I continue unto this day, witnessing both to small and great, saying none other things than those which the prophets and Moses did say should come: that Christ should suffer, and that he should be the first that should rise from the dead, and should show light unto the people, and to the Gentiles" (Ac.26:22-23).

DEEPER STUDY # 2

(28:9) **Hail** (chairete): rejoice. The word means more than just a simple greeting or welcome. Jesus was telling the women to be glad, to celebrate. He wanted them to rejoice because He was with them. He had risen from the dead just as He had predicted.

---

6 (28:11-15) **Jesus Christ, Resurrection**: the attempt to discredit the resurrection. The outline above is adequate to see the event being described. (See outline and note—Mt.27:62-66 for more discussion.)
  a. The guards reported the resurrection.
  b. The authorities were baffled, and they took counsel to decide what to do.
  c. The authorities bribed and assured the soldiers of protection from Pilate.
  d. The soldiers were to claim that Jesus' body had been stolen by His disciples.
  e. The lie was found out; the truth marched on (indicated by the witness of Matthew and the other disciples of Christ).

Thought 1. If the guards were asleep, how would they know what happened? Deception and lying are always contradicted by the truth.

Thought 2. Truth will always prevail (v.15). It may take some time, but its triumph is assured.

"And ye shall know the truth, and the truth shall make you free" (Jn.8:32).

"Stand therefore, having your loins girt about with truth, and having on the breastplate of righteousness" (Ep.6:14).

"The lip of truth shall be established for ever: but a lying tongue is but for a moment" (Pr.12:19).

DEEPER STUDY # 3

(28:11-15) **Jesus—Plots Against**: note the plots against Jesus. The authorities had used treachery to arrest Him; an illegal court to try Him (Mt.26:59); false charges to accuse Him before Pilate (Mt.27:1, 2, 11f); and now they were using bribery to discredit His resurrection.

MATTHEW 28:16-20

	B. The Messiah's Final Commission to His Disciples, 28:16-20 (Mk 16:15-18; Lu 24:46-49; Jn 17:18; 20:21; Ac 1:8)	spake unto them, saying, All power is given unto me in heaven and in earth. 19 Go ye therefore, and teach all nations, baptizing them in the name of the Father, and of the Son, and of the Holy Ghost: 20 Teaching them to observe all things whatsoever I have commanded you: and, lo, I am with you alway, *even* unto the end of the world. Amen.	His power a. Is a given power b. Is in heaven & earth 3. He commissioned His disciples a. To make disciples of all nations b. To baptize c. To teach all that He had commanded 4. He promised to be with His disciples
1. He met the disciples in Galilee a. They met on a preappointed mountain b. They worshipped Him c. Some doubted **2. He assured the disciples of**	16 Then the eleven disciples went away into Galilee, into a mountain where Jesus had appointed them. 17 And when they saw him, they worshipped him: but some doubted. 18 And Jesus came and		

DIVISION XVII

THE MESSIAH'S TRIUMPHANT RESURRECTION, 28:1-20

B. The Messiah's Final Commission to His Disciples, 28:16-20

(28:16-20) **Introduction**: Matthew began his gospel by proclaiming that the baby Jesus was the Son of David, the promised King of Israel (Mt.1:1-2). He now closes his gospel by proclaiming that the Lord Jesus possesses all power and authority in heaven and earth. The Lord Jesus had risen from the dead, and in the power of His resurrection His followers are to go forth proclaiming His glorious kingdom.

In this great passage, Matthew covers the great commission of the resurrected Lord, the King to whom all power and authority belong.

1. He met the disciples in Galilee (vv.16-17).
2. He assured the disciples of His power (v.18).
3. He commissioned His disciples (vv.19-20).
4. He promised to be with His followers (v.20).

1 (28:16-17) **Disciples**: the disciples met Jesus in Galilee. Note several background facts.

a. Matthew says the eleven disciples met Christ. The eleven were the prominent ones, but apparently there were over five hundred believers present, all seeing Him at once (1 Co.15:6). The reference to "they" and "some doubted" (v.17) seems to indicate that this was the great appearance to the mass of believers mentioned by Paul. Christ had already appeared to the eleven on several occasions. They already knew the reality of His resurrection. It is unlikely that they were the ones who were questioning at this time (Mk.16:12-14; Lu.24:13-48; Jn.20:19-25; 20:26-31; 21:1-25).

b. The disciples met the Lord in Galilee on a pre-appointed mountain (see Mt.26:32; 28:7, 10). The Lord had apparently instructed the apostles to pass the word along and to gather all His disciples to meet Him in a mass meeting in Galilee. A particular mountain was designated as the meeting place. Note that Galilee was where the Lord had conducted most of His ministry and where most of His disciples lived. It was also some distance from Jerusalem, a place somewhat safe from the immediate enemies of Christ.

Thought 1. There are appointed places where we are to meet the Lord: in prayer, devotions, worship, and Bible study. When we meet the Lord as He says, He meets us. We must meet the Lord as He instructs if we are to know the reality of His resurrection.

c. This is significant. They worshipped Him, but some doubted. They just were not sure. Note what Jesus did: He "came and spake to them" (v.18). Apparently, His *coming and speaking to them* erased their doubt and questioning.

Thought 1. When we meet Christ as He instructs, He meets us. When He meets us, all fear and doubt vanish. The person who truly seeks after Christ, who truly seeks to meet Him, will have his doubts erased. Christ will *come and speak to him*.

2 (28:18) **Power**: Jesus assured His followers of His power.

a. Jesus' power or authority is a given power. It is given by God, and it is given for one reason: to exalt Christ above and over all.

> "And being found in fashion as a man, he humbled himself, and became obedient unto death, even the death of the cross. Wherefore God also hath highly exalted him, and given him a name which is above every name" (Ph.2:8-9).

MATTHEW 28:16-20

    b. Jesus' power is above and over all that is in heaven and in earth. His authority is over all the universe. His authority includes at least three areas.
      1) The Lord's authority includes the power to rule and reign...
- to receive the worship and subjection of all men who willingly surrender to His dominion.

> "I beseech you therefore, brethren, by the mercies of God, that ye present your bodies a living sacrifice, holy, acceptable unto God, which is your reasonable service. And be not conformed to this world: but be ye transformed by the renewing of your mind, that ye may prove what is that good, and acceptable, and perfect, will of God" (Ro.12:1-2).
>
> "For ye are bought with a price: therefore glorify God in your body, and in your spirit, which are God's" (1 Co.6:20).
>
> "That if thou shalt confess with thy mouth the Lord Jesus, and shalt believe in thine heart that God hath raised him from the dead, thou shalt be saved. For with the heart man believeth unto righteousness; and with the mouth confession is made unto salvation" (Ro.10:9-10).
>
> "Saying with a loud voice, Worthy is the Lamb that was slain to receive power, and riches, and wisdom, and strength, and honour, and glory, and blessing" (Re.5:12).

- to bow the knee of all men and to receive their acknowledgement of His Lordship.

> "Wherefore God also hath highly exalted him, and given him a name which is above every name: that at the name of Jesus every knee should bow, of things in heaven, and things in earth, and things under the earth; and that every tongue should confess that Jesus Christ is Lord, to the glory of God the Father" (Ph.2:9-11).

      2) The Lord's authority includes the power to govern and direct...
- the affairs of men without violating man's freedom.

> "So then after the Lord had spoken unto them, he was received up into heaven, and sat on the right hand of God" (Mk.16:19).
>
> "Hereafter shall the Son of man sit on the right hand of the power of God" (Lu.22:69).
>
> "Let every soul be subject unto the higher powers. For there is no power but of God: the powers that be are ordained of God" (Ro.13:1).
>
> "Who is gone into heaven, and is on the right hand of God; angels and authorities and powers being made subject unto him" (1 Pe.3:22).

- the affairs of nature and the world without violating the laws of nature.

> "But the men marvelled, saying, What manner of man is this, that even the winds and sea obey him!" (Mt.8:27).
>
> "And hath put all things under his feet, and gave him to be the head over all things to the church" (Ep.1:22).

      3) The Lord's authority includes the power to forgive sins, to judge, receive and reject men, and to save and deliver men through life and death. (See outline and notes—Ro.8:28-39.)

> "But that ye may know that the Son of man hath power on earth to forgive sins, (then saith he to the sick of the palsy,) Arise, take up thy bed, and go unto thine house" (Mt.9:6).
>
> "And when he saw their faith, he said unto him, Man, thy sins are forgiven thee. And the scribes and the Pharisees began to reason, saying, Who is this which speaketh blasphemies? Who can forgive sins, but God alone?" (Lu.5:20-21).
>
> "For the Father judgeth no man, but hath committed all judgment unto the Son" (Jn.5:22).
>
> "And hath given him authority to execute judgment also, because he is the Son of man" (Jn.5:27).

    c. Jesus' power assures the believer of deliverance. Note *when* Jesus "came and spake" of His power: immediately upon the heels of some doubting and immediately before charging His disciples to go into a hostile world. He proclaimed His power in order to erase doubt and to strengthen His disciples in going forth. His power was the disciples' assurance of victory.

    Now, in dealing with the supreme power and authority of Jesus Christ, there are two points that must always be remembered.

    1. The Lord's supreme reign is not yet fully seen. God has not yet revealed His Son's supremacy in an absolute sense. However, there is *a striking reason* for God's delaying the visible enthronement of His Son. God wants His Son to still be seen as the Savior of the world. He wants more and more persons to be saved before He ends the world and begins the sovereign reign of His Son upon earth.

> "Knowing this first, that there shall come in the last days scoffers, walking after their own lusts, and saying, Where is the promise of his coming? for since the fathers fell asleep, all things continue as they were from the beginning of the creation....But beloved, be not ignorant of this one thing, that one day is with the Lord as a thousand years, and a thousand years as one day. The Lord is not slack

concerning his promise, as some men count slackness; but is longsuffering to us-ward, not willing that any should perish, but that all should come to repentance" (2 Pe.3-4, 8-9).

2. The Lord's supreme reign over all the universe is assured.

"But the day of the Lord will come as a thief in the night; in the which the heavens shall pass away with a great noise, and the elements shall melt with fervent heat, the earth also and the works that are therein shall be burned up. Seeing then that all these things shall be dissolved, what manner of persons ought ye to be in all holy conversation and godliness, looking for and hasting unto the coming of the day of God, wherein the heavens being on fire shall be dissolved, and the elements shall melt with fervent heat? Nevertheless we, according to his promise, look for new heavens and a new earth, wherein dwelleth righteousness" (2 Pe.3:10-13).

"Thou hast put all things in subjection under his feet. For in that he put all in subjection under him, he left nothing that is not put under him. But now we see not yet all things put under him. But we see Jesus, who was made a little lower than the angels for the suffering of death, crowned with glory and honor; that he by the grace of God should taste death for every man. For it became him, for whom are all things, and by whom are all things, in bringing many sons unto glory, to make the captain of their salvation perfect through sufferings" (He.2:8-10).

"Then cometh the end, when he [Christ] shall have delivered up the kingdom to God, even the Father; when he shall have put down all rule and all authority and power. For he must reign, till he hath put all enemies under his feet. The last enemy that shall be destroyed is death. For he hath put all things under his feet. But when he saith all things are put under him, it is manifest that he is excepted, which did put all things under him. And when all things shall be subdued unto him, then shall the Son also himself be subject unto him that put all things under him, that God may be all in all" (1 Co.15:24-28).

3 (28:19-20) **Commission, Great—Disciples, Making**: Jesus commissioned His followers. He commissioned not only the eleven apostles, but all who were present, more than five hundred disciples. However, note something of crucial importance: it was impossible for that generation to reach the whole world in its lifetime. Therefore, the commission given to the first generation of believers extends beyond to all generations of believers. The very same charge given to them is given to us. Our Lord charges us with the very same words, "Go ye therefore, and make disciples of all nations...."

The Lord's commission was threefold.

a. He commissions us to "go ye...and make disciples of all nations." This is one of the crucial verses in the Bible. No verse is more important for genuine believers.

Teaching and baptizing are not enough to reach the world for Christ. Both are important, and Christ commissions both; but He says something else must precede both: discipleship. "Go ye therefore and 'metheteusate' all nations" (Mt.28:19). *Metheteusate* means to make disciples. Thus the verse accurately reads, "Go ye therefore and 'make disciples' of all nations...." Most messages that are preached on this passage stress the objective of our Lord, the reaching of all nations, as though this is what our Lord had in mind. There is no question, the great commission is what Christ had in mind. He has instructed us to go to all nations and evangelize them. But there is the strong conviction that He had more than that objective in mind, more than just an overriding purpose—much more.

Our Lord was not only telling us "to go and evangelize," He was telling us *how* to go and *how* to evangelize. He was not only giving His ultimate *objective* and overriding purpose, He was giving *the method* to use in evangelizing the world.

Think about the word *metheteusate* (make disciples). What does our Lord mean by *make disciples*? Does it not mean that we are to do what He did: make disciples and do things with them as He did. Is He not telling us to do exactly as He did?

What *did* He do? Christ "came to seek and save that which was lost" (Lu.19:10). He sought the lost, those who were willing to commit their lives to Him. And when He found such a person, He saved that person. When Christ found a person who was willing to commit his life, Christ attached Himself to that person. Christ began to mold and make that person into His image. The word *attach* is the key word. It is probably the word that best describes discipleship. Christ made disciples of men by attaching Himself to them; and through that personal attachment, they were able to observe His life and conversation; and in seeing and hearing, they began to absorb and assimilate His very character and behavior. They began to follow Him and to serve Him more closely. In simple terms, this is what our Lord did. This is the way He made disciples. This was His mission and His method, His obsession: to attach Himself to willing believers.

There is another way to describe what Christ did. Christ envisioned something beyond Himself and beyond His day and time. He envisioned an *extension* of Himself, an *extension* of His very being, and an *extension* of His mission and method. The way He chose to extend Himself was discipleship, attaching Himself to committed persons; and through attachment, the persons absorbed and assimilated the Lord's very character and mission. They in turn attached themselves to others and discipled them. They, too, expected their disciples to make disciples of others who were willing to commit their lives to Christ. Thus was the glorious message of Christ to march down through the centuries (2 Ti.2:2).

There is no question what our Lord's commission is: we are to go; but more than that, we are to make disciples, to attach ourselves to those persons who will follow our Lord until they in turn can make disciples (2 Ti.2:2).

"And as ye go, preach, saying, The kingdom of heaven is at hand" (Mt.10:7).

"Go ye therefore, and teach all nations, baptizing them in the name of the Father, and of the Son, and of the Holy Ghost: teaching them to observe all things whatsoever I have commanded you: and, lo, I am with you alway, even unto the end of the world" (Mt.28:19-20).

"And he said unto them, Go ye into all the world, and preach the gospel to every creature" (Mk.16:15).

"But these are written, that ye might believe that Jesus is the Christ, the Son of God; and that believing ye might have life through his name" (Jn.20:31).

"But ye shall receive power, after that the Holy Ghost is come upon you: and ye shall be witnesses unto me both in Jerusalem, and in all Judaea, and in Samaria, and unto the uttermost part of the earth" (Ac.1:8).

"Go, stand and speak in the temple to the people all the words of this life" (Ac.5:20).

"Preach the word; be instant in season, out of season; reprove, rebuke, exhort with all longsuffering and doctrine" (2 Ti.4:2).

"But sanctify the Lord God in your hearts: and be ready always to give an answer to every man that asketh you a reason of the hope that is in you with meekness and fear" (1 Pe.3:15).

b. He commissioned us to baptize all nations (see Deeper Study # 1—Mk.16:16; note—Lu.3:21; Deeper Study # 1—Ac.2:38). Two things need to be noted here.
  1) Baptism is of crucial importance. Christ says that it is as essential as teaching, despite the fact that it is a one-time act. It is as much a part of the commission of Christ as discipling and teaching. Christ is definitely teaching that baptism is to be the immediate sign and the identifying sign that a person is now stepping out of the heathen (unbelieving) ranks and taking his stand with Christ.
  2) Baptism "in the name of the Father, and of the Son, and of the Holy Ghost" means more than just saying a formula as one is baptized, much more. It means...
     - a statement of faith: of belief in God as the true Father of Jesus Christ; of belief in Christ as the true Son of God, the Savior of the world; of belief in the Holy Spirit as the Comforter of the believer.
     - a commitment to follow God: to follow Him as revealed in the Father, the Son, and the Holy Spirit (see Christ's constant references to God as His Father, to Himself as the Son, and to the Holy Spirit throughout the Gospel of John. Also see Mt.11:27; 24:36. Also see outlines and notes, *Holy Spirit*—Jn.14:15-26; 16:7-15; Ro.8:1-17.)

"He that believeth and is baptized shall be saved; but he that believeth not shall be damned" (Mk.16:16).

"Repent, and be baptized every one of you in the name of Jesus Christ for the remission of sins, and ye shall receive the gift of the Holy Ghost" (Ac.2:38).

"And he commanded them to be baptized in the name of the Lord. Then prayed they him to tarry certain days" (Ac.10:48).

"And now why tarriest thou? arise, and be baptized, and wash away thy sins, calling on the name of the Lord" (Ac.22:16).

c. He commissioned us to teach all that Christ had commanded. Teaching is just as essential as making disciples and baptizing. One is not to be emphasized over the other. All are part of the commission of our Lord. Note what is to be taught: "all things whatsoever I have commanded you."

"Go ye therefore, and teach all nations, baptizing them in the name of the Father, and of the Son, and of the Holy Ghost: teaching them to observe all things whatsoever I have commanded you: and, lo, I am with you alway, even unto the end of the world" (Mt.28:19-20).

"It is written in the prophets, And they shall be all taught of God. Every man therefore that hath heard, and hath learned of the Father, cometh unto me" (Jn.6:45).

"Let the word of Christ dwell in you richly in all wisdom; teaching and admonishing one another in psalms and hymns and spiritual songs, singing with grace in your hearts to the Lord" (Col.3:16).

"If thou put the brethren in remembrance of these things, thou shalt be a good minister of Jesus Christ, nourished up in the words of faith and of good doctrine, whereunto thou hast attained" (1 Ti.4:6).

"These things command and teach" (1 Ti.4:11).

"And the servant of the Lord must not strive; but be gentle unto all men, apt to teach, patient" (2 Ti.2:24).

"And these words, which I command thee this day, shall be in thine heart: and thou shalt teach them diligently unto thy children, and shalt talk of them when thou sittest in thine house, and when thou walkest by the way, and when thou liest down, and when thou risest up" (De.6:6-7).

"And they shall teach my people the difference between the holy and profane, and cause them to discern between the unclean and the clean" (Eze.44:23).

Thought 1. What Christ taught and commanded must be studied and studied, to the point of learning and knowing and practicing. The commandments of Christ will be the first things taught. They should be the rule of society.

Thought 2. Society deteriorates and crumbles when it neglects the teaching and commandments of Christ.

MATTHEW 28:16-20

4 (28:20) **Jesus Christ, Presence**: Jesus promised to be with His followers—always.

a. Note the word *lo,* or behold. Christ used this striking word to get the attention of His followers, to startle them to wake up and listen. He was about to encourage them in the great task He had charged to their care.

b. Note the great promise: "I am with you." He gave emphatic assurance: not "I will be with you," but "I am with you." Christ is with the believer as the believer goes forth to make disciples of all nations. Christ is with us...

- every step
- every decision
- every trial
- every joy
- every day
- every hour
- every sorrow
- when without
- when poor
- when having nothing
- when having plenty
- when abused
- when sick
- when facing death

c. Note the boundless promise: "alway, even unto the end of the world." There is not a moment when Christ is not with the believer to help him in his witness, even if his witness means abuse, persecution, and martyrdom.

"For where two or three are gathered together in my name, there am I in the midst of them" (Mt.18:20).

"Teaching them to observe all things whatsoever I have commanded you: and, lo, I am with you alway, even unto the end of the world" (Mt.28:20).

"Let your conversation be without covetousness; and be content with such things as ye have: for he hath said, I will never leave thee, nor forsake thee. So that we may boldly say, The Lord is my helper, and I will not fear what man shall do unto me" (He.13:5-6).

"And, behold, I am with thee, and will keep thee in all places whither thou goest, and will bring thee again into this land; for I will not leave thee, until I have done that which I have spoken to thee of" (Ge.28:15).

"Fear thou not; For I am with thee: be not dismayed; for I am thy God: I will strengthen thee; yea, I will help thee; yea, I will uphold thee with the right hand of my righteousness" (Is.41:10).

"When thou passest through the waters, I will be with thee; and through the rivers, they shall not overflow thee: when thou walkest through the fire, thou shalt not be burned; neither shall the flame kindle upon thee" (Is.43:2).

THE
OUTLINE & SUBJECT INDEX

REMEMBER: When you look up a subject and turn to the Scripture reference, you have not only the Scripture, but also an outline and a discussion (commentary) of the Scripture and subject.

This is one of the GREAT VALUES of *The Preacher's Outline & Sermon Bible®*. Once you have all the volumes, you will not only have what all other Bible indexes give you, that is, a list of all the subjects and their Scripture references, BUT in addition you will have...
- An outline of every Scripture and subject in the Bible
- A discussion (commentary) on every Scripture and subject
- Every subject supported by other Scriptures or cross references

DISCOVER THE GREAT VALUE for yourself. Quickly glance below to the very first subject of the Index of *Matthew*. It is:

ABILITIES (See **TALENTS—GIFTS**)
Duty. To surrender to Christ. 14:18-21

Turn to the reference. Glance at the Scripture and outline of the Scripture, then read the commentary. You will immediately see the GREAT VALUE of the INDEX of *The Preacher's Outline & Sermon Bible®*.

OUTLINE & SUBJECT INDEX

ABILITIES (See **TALENTS—GIFTS**)
Duty. To surrender to Christ. 14:18-21

ABOMINATION OF DESOLATION
(See **ANTICHRIST**)

ABUSE
Physical. (See **INJURY**)

ACCEPTANCE - ACCEPTABLE
Discussed. Receiving and rejecting men. 8:5-13

ACCOUNTABLE - ACCOUNTABILITY
Described as.
    A king's day of **a**. 18:21-35
    A lord's day of **a**. 25:14-30
    A property owner's **a**. 21:33-46
Meaning. 18:24
Who is **a**.
    A king's subjects. 18:21-35
    A servant. 25:14-30
    A tenant. 21:33-46
Why men are **a**.
    Acting wickedly. 24:48-51
    Lack of compassion. 18:21-35
    Not expecting Jesus' return. 24:48-51
    Rejecting God's message. 21:33-46

ADULTERY
Acts of: four. 5:28
Commandment against. Reasons for. 5:27
Culprits. Hands and eyes. 5:28
Discussed. 5:28
Duty of the **a**. To pluck out, cut off. 5:27-30
Grounds for divorce. 5:31-32; 19:9
Is committed.
    By looking and desiring. 5:27-30
    By marrying a divorced person. 5:31-32
Kinds of **a**.
    Mental **a**. Desiring and lusting. 5:27-30
    Spiritual **a**. Apostasy toward God. 12:39
Meaning. 5:28; 19:9
Misconceptions. **A**. is excusable & acceptable. 5:27-30
Penalty. Death by stoning. 1:19

Results. Breaks the union of marriage. 5:32; 19:1-2

ADULTERY, SPIRITUAL
Meaning 12:39

AGE
New **a**. Ushered in by Christ. 9:14-17

AGNOSTIC
Described. 6:14-15

ALCOHOL
Results. Drinking, partying. 14:6-8; 24:38

ALMS
Meaning. 6:1

AMBITION
Discussed. 18:1-4; 20:20-28
Duty.
    Not to seek position for self-glory. 20:20-28
    To seek to become as a child. 20:20-28
Evil **a**. Causes. An air of superiority. 18:1-4
False **a**. vs. true **a**. 20:20-21

AMEN
Meaning. 6:13

ANDREW, THE APOSTLE
A fisherman. 4:18-19
One of the first disciples called by Jesus. 4:18-22
One of the twelve disciples. 10:1-4

ANGELS
Appearances.
    To Joseph. 1:18-25
    To women at resurrection. 28:1-10
Fallen **a**. (See **SATAN**)
    Under the devil. 25:41
Function toward believers. To deliver. 24:30-31
Function toward Christ.
    To announce His conception. 1:20-21
    To return with Him. 13:40-42; 13:49-50

Function toward unbelievers.
    To execute God's judgment. 13:40-42
    To harvest in the end time. 13:40-43; 13:49-50
Guardian. Children have **g**. angels. 18:10
Nature.
    Holy. 25:31
    Not omniscient. 24:36
    Unmarried. 22:30
Work of. In the end time. Five works. 24:31; 25:31

ANGER
Danger of. 5:25
Demonstrated by Jesus. Over the abuse of the temple. 21:12-13
Discussed. 5:21-26
Judgment of. 5:25
Justified **a**. 5:21-22
Kinds. 5:22
Meaning. 5:21-26; 5:21-22
Results of. 5:22; 5:25
View of. World's view of. 5:21-26

ANIMALS
Less important than man. 12:11

ANISE
Described. 23:23
Pharisees tithe **a**. but omit money. 23:23

ANTICHRIST
Described. Abomination of Desolation. 24:15
Discussed. 24:15-28; 24:15; 24:16-20
Prophesied.
    By Daniel. 24:15
    Past & future fulfillment. 24:15

ANXIETY - ANXIOUS
Caused by.
    Worrying about things and life. 6:25-34
    Worrying over appearance. 6:27
Discussed. 6:25-34
How to conquer.
    Considering God's provision. 6:28-34
    Living one day at a time. 6:34
    Looking at nature. 6:26-30
    Seeking God first. 6:33

INDEX

APOSTASY (See **BACKSLIDING; DENIAL**)
  Caused by—Sources of. 26:69
  Described as. A time existing now. 13:20-21
  Discussed. A look at denying Christ. Peter's d. 26:69-75
  Examples.
    Judas. 26:14-16
    Religious leaders. 12:38-45
  Kinds of. 26:69-75
  Marks - Characteristics of.
    Forsaking when tried or persecuted. 13:20-21
    Seek signs - physical evidence. 12:38-45

APOSTLE - APOSTLES (See **DISCIPLES**)
  Brothers. Three sets named. 10:2
  Call of.
    Andrew and Peter, James and John. 4:18-22
    Commissioning and commitment. 10:1-4
  Meaning. 10:2
  Mission of. 28:19-20
  Rewards of. 19:27-28
  Training of. Intensive t. on the death of Christ. 16:13-20; 16:21-28; 17:1-13; 17:22; 17:24-27; 20:17; 20:20-28
  Twelve. Why twelve. 10:2
  Weakness - Failure of.
    Seeking greatness in Christ's kingdom. 18:1
    Spiritualize death & resurrection of Christ. 17:22; 18:1

APPEARANCE, OUTWARD
  Warning. Against changing a. to appear religious. 23:5

APPOINT - APPOINTED
  What is a. Man's place - destiny. 24:51

ARCHELAUS
  Discussed. 2:22

ASS—COLT—DONKEY
  Used in Triumphal Entry. 21:2-5

ASSURANCE
  Needed. When questioning who Christ is. 11:1-6

ASTRONOMICAL SIGNS—HAPPENINGS
  Predicted. In end time. 24:29-31

AUTHORITY (See Power)
  Of Christ. A. of His teaching. 7:28-29
  Of Scribes. 7:29
  Of the church. Instituted. 16:13-20, esp. 18
  Purpose. To equip and give assurance. 10:1
  Source. Of God. Given to disciples. 10:1

AVAILABLE - AVAILABILITY
  Essential. Must be a. to people.
    Discussed. 15:30-31
    Steps. 15:30-31

BABES
  Described. Teachable. Sees the truth. 11:25

BABYLON
  Captivity. God preserved Jews through Babylon c. 1:11

BACKSLIDING (See **APOSTASY; DENIAL**)
  Caused by.
    Forsaking Jesus. 26:55-56
    Overconfidence. 26:31-35; 26:33-35
  Described as. 13:5-6, 20-21
    Being offended by Christ. 26:31-35; 26:69-75
    Denying Christ. 26:31-34, 54-62
  Examples.
    Disciples. Stumbling & falling away. 26:31-35, 56
    Judas. Picture of a ruined life. 26:14-16
  Reasons. 13:5-7, 20-22; 18:12

BAPTISM
  Essential. 3:11; 3:14; 3:15
  Meaning. 3:11; 3:14
    Discussed. 3:11
    In Holy Spirit & fire. 3:11; 3:14
    Jesus' b. 3:11
    John the Baptist b. 3:11
  Meaning. B. of suffering. 20:22-23
  Why a person must be b. 3:11; 3:14; 3:15

BARABBAS
  Prisoner freed instead of Christ. 27:15-25

BARRIERS (See **DIVISION—PREJUDICE**)
  Described. Physical, ideological, spiritual. 8:5-13
  Receiving & rejecting men. 8:5-13

BASKET
  Described. 15:37

BATHSHEBA
  Saved by God. 1:6

BEATITUDES
  Identifies disciples. 5:1-12

BEELZEBUB
  Christ is charged with being possessed with **B.**, the devil. 12:24

BEHAVIOR
  Loose vs. strict. 14:6-8

BELIEVE - BELIEVING - BELIEFS (See **FAITH**)
  Essential - Importance of. What one must b. to enter God's kingdom. 21:32
  Kinds. Little b. "O ye of little faith." Meaning. 6:30
  Vs. signs. God works by b. not signs. 12:38-40

BELIEVER - BELIEVERS (See **APOSTLES; DISCIPLES; LABORERS; MINISTERS**)
  Call - called.
    Kind of person c. 4:18-22
    To be "God's own possession." 25:14-15
    To fish for men. 4:18-20
    To know Christ first. 4:18-20
    To personal attachment. 4:18-20
  Care of. (See **CARE - CARING**)
  Character. (See **BELIEVER**, Life - Walk)
    Believer and his mission. 5:13; 5:14-16
  Commission of. (See **COMMISSION**)
  Described.
    As a hypocrite. 24:48-51
    As evil servant. 24:48-51
    As faithful & wise servant. 24:45-47
    As great in the Kingdom of Heaven. 11:11
    As light. 5:14-16
    As owner of a house. 24:43-44
    As salt. 5:13
    As sheep. 25:33
    As wise & foolish. 25:1-4
  Devotion. (See **DEVOTION**)
  Discipline. (See **CHURCH DISCIPLINE**)
  Divisiveness between. (See **DIVISION**)
  Duty - Work.
    Responsible for the keys to the kingdom. 16:19
    Three great d. 6:1-8
    To be like God. 5:45; 5:48
    To be loyal. 5:10-12; 10:32-33
    To be wise as serpents, harmless as doves. 10:16
    To bear the cup and baptism of Christ. 20:22-23
    To bind and loose. 16:19
    To care for the church & the world. 21:33
    To labor for reward. 10:1-16
    To labor one hundred percent. 13:8, 23
    To live by the golden rule 7:12
    To loose and bind. 16:19
    To love one's enemies. 5:43-48
    To guard against offending others. 18:5-10; 18:15-17; 18:15-20
    To receive one another. 18:5
    To watch & be ready for the Lord's return. 24:42-51
    To watch & work for judgment is coming. 25:14-30
    To witness & preach. 16:19
  Facts.
    Hairs. Are numbered. 10:29-31
    Offended by Christ. Reasons. 26:31-32
  Heirs. (See **INHERITANCE**)
  Life - Walk - Behavior.
    Faithful vs. unfaithful. 24:42-51; 25:14-30
    Feel scattered abroad. 1:2
    Following Christ is not enough. 26:14-16
    "In Egypt" but not "of Egypt" (the world). 2:13-18
    Led step by step. 2:19-23
    Sermon on the Mount given for believer's behavior. 5:1-2
    Strengthened to bear the cross. 17:1-13
    Toward others. 6:12
    Traits. Essentials. 4:18-20; 4:21-22
    Wise and foolish. Prepared and unprepared. 25:1-13
  Mission. (See **COMMISSION—MISSION**)
  Names—Titles.
    Babes. 11:25
    Building stones of the church. 16:18
    Light of the earth. 5:14-16
    Salt of the earth. 5:13

INDEX

Severalfold. 21:43
Steward. 16:19
True disciples. 5:1-16
Nature.
  "In Egypt" but not "of Egypt" (world). 2:13-18
  Light. 5:14-16
  New creation. Discussed. 21:43
  Not above sin. 26:31-35
  Not a "lifeless rock" but a "living stone." 7:24-25
  Salt. 5:13
Position.
  Discussed. 11:11
  Greater than Old Testament believers. Great privileges. 13:16-17
Purpose. (See **PURPOSE**)
Questioning. (See **QUESTION - QUESTIONING**)
Relation - Relationships. To God as Father. 6:9
Types of **b**. 4:18-22
Value of.
  A great treasure. 13:44, 45-46
  Of more value than sparrows. 10:29-31
Warning. About offending others. 18:5-10; 18:15-17; 18:15-20

BELOVED SON
Two precious thoughts. 12:17-18

BETHANY
Discussed. 21:17

BETHSAIDA
Discussed. 11:20-22

BETRAYAL (See **APOSTASY; BACKSLIDING; DENIAL**)
Of Christ. By Judas. Picture of a ruined life. 26:14-16

BETROTHED
Steps in marriage. 1:18

BEWARE
Meaning. 7:15

BIRDS
Symbolized. Unbelievers lodging in Christianity. 13:31-32

BLASPHEMY
Against the Holy Spirit. 12:31-32
Meaning. 9:3

BLESSED
Meaning. 5:3

BLESSINGS
Misconceptions. Wealth is a sign of God's **b**. 19:25

BLIND - BLINDNESS (See **SPIRITUAL BLINDNESS**)
Healed. Two **b**. men. 9:27-31

BOASTING (See **PRIDE; SELF-IMPORTANCE**)
Described. Favoritism. 8:4

BODY, HUMAN
Duty. Not to worry about. 6:25
Facts. Means more than things. 6:25
God cares for. Five things show. 6:11
Sins of. Immoral looks, dress. 5:27-30

BORROWING
Attitude. 5:42

BREAD
Meaning. 6:11
Necessity of life. 4:2-4; 6:11

BREAKING THE LAW (See **LAW**, Breaking)

BRIDEGROOM
Parable of. 9:14-16
Symbolizes. Jesus Christ. 9:15

BROAD WAY, THE
Those who follow. 7:13

BROTHER - BROTHERHOOD (See **UNITY**)
Duties - Essential.
  Not to offend. 18:5-10
  To be giving. 19:16-22, esp. 20-21
  To correct offending **b**. 18:15-20
  To have a forgiving spirit. 18:22
  To love one's neighbor. 22:39
  To practice the golden rule. 7:11
Meaning. 25:40
  What true **b**. is. 12:46-50
Nature. Called **b**. by Christ. Tender word. 25:40
Purpose of **b**. The second great commandment. 22:34-40
Steps to correcting offending **b**. 18:15-20

BUILD - BUILDERS - BUILDING (See **FOUNDATION**)
Carpentry. Christ was a **c**. 7:24-27
How to **b**. 7:24-27
Instructions for **b**. Critical. 7:24-27
Wise & foolish **b**. 7:24-27

BURDEN - BURDENED
Answer to **b**. To rest in Christ. 11:28-30
Discussed. 11:28-30

CAESAR
And God. Question about state & God. 22:15-22

CAIAPHAS
High Priest. Discussed. 26:3-5
Judges Christ. 26:57-68

CALL - CALLED (See **DISCIPLES**)
Accepted - Acceptance of.
  Last minute **c**. 20:9-10
  Then rejected. Judas. 26:14-16
  Vs. rejected. 21:28-32
God's great invitation. 22:1-14
Kinds of **c**.
  Discussed. 4:18-22
  Fourfold. 20:1-7
  Severalfold. 22:4
Of minister. To leave all. 4:21-22
Warning. The Spirit does not always strive with man. 12:14-16; 20:5

CALVARY - GOLGOTHA
Place where Christ was crucified. 27:33

CAMEL
Cp. to a rich man. Going through the eye of a needle. 19:24

CANAANITES
Enemies of Jews. 15:22.

CAPERNAUM
Discussed. 4:12; 4:12-13; 11:23
Headquarters of Jesus. 4:12
Is to be judged. 11:23-24

CARE - CARING (See **ANXIETY; WORRY**)
Duty to **c**.
  For one's needs. 6:25-34; 15:29-30
  For the spiritual. 6:25-34
  To be touched over suffering. 18:31
Examples of. Supreme **e**. 18:11-14
For whom - examples of.
  For disabled. 9:1-8
  For families. Jesus' purpose. 8:14-17
  For individuals. Jesus' purpose. 8:14-17
  For multitudes. Jesus' purpose. 8:14-17
  For rejected, hopeless, helpless. 9:18-34
  For sinful friends. 9:10-11
Of God.
  Discussed. 10:29-31
  Provision—all **p**. made. 6:25-34

CARNAL - CARNALITY
Caused by. A commitment to the world & its things. 26:51-52
Described as.
  Immaturity. 17:14-21
  Unbelief. 17:19-21

CARPENTER (See **BUILDING**)

CAST AWAY
The unprofitable will be. 25:14-30, esp. 30

CAST OUT
Reason for judgment. 5:13

CAUSE
A man needs a **c**. 9:9-13
Dying for a **c**. Not rare. 10:23

CENTURION
At the cross. Confessed Christ to be the Son of God. 27:54
Faith of. Great. 8:5-13

CHEEK, TURNING OTHER
Discussed. 5:39

CHILDISH
Message to. Discussed. 11:16-19

CHILDREN - CHILDLIKENESS
Acceptance of. 19:13-15
Attitudes toward. Not important & indulged. 19:13
Described. Contrary, playful, mindless. 11:16-19
Discussed. 19:13-15
Duties of. To praise Christ. Proclaim His Messiahship. 21:15-16; 10:13-15
Duties toward.
  Not to lead astray. 18:5-10
  To bring **c**. to Christ.
    Benefits of. 19:13
    For dedication. 19:13-15
    Why parents do not bring **c**. 19:13
  To receive **c**. 18:1-4; 18:5; 19:13-15

INDEX

Example.
   Caring for others. 18:5
Herod slaughters. 2:13-18
Jesus and c.
   Discussed. 18:1-4; 19:13-15
   J. treatment of. 18:2
   Received by J. 18:1-4
Nature. Discussed. 18:1-4
Reactions toward.
   Offending - leading astray. 18:5-10
   Slaughtered by Herod. 2:13-18
Symbolize - Illustrated.
   Followers of wisdom. 11:19
   God's Kingdom. 10:14-15
   Greatness. 18:1-4
   Heaven. 18:1-4; 19:13-15
   New Christians. 18:5-6
   Worshipping God. 21:15-16
Traits.
   Humility. 18:1-4
   Playful. 11:16-19

CHILDREN OF GOD (See **BELIEVERS**)

CHRISTIAN - CHRISTIANS (See **BE-LIEVER; SPIRITUAL STRUGGLE**)

CHRISTIANITY
Good and bad within. 13:24-30; 13:31-32; 13:33;13:36-43; 13:47-50
Growth of. Growth & greatness of. 13:31-32
Modern day. Described. 13:1-58
Nature. Of mercy, not sacrifice. 12:7

CHURCH
Authority over. God. 21:12-16
Basis - Foundation.
   Discussed. 16:18
   Is Christ, not Satan or man. 16:18
Chosen. By God after Israel's failure. 21:33-46; 21:43
Cleansed - cleansing.
   Christ casts out money changers. 21:12-16
   Of commercialism. 21:12-16
Discussed. 16:13-20; 21:12-16
Duty.
   Not to exploit people. 21:12-16
Meaning. 16:18
Ministry to.
   To care, provide for the c. 21:33
   To support the c. 17:25
   To witness, reach the c. 16:19
Mission.
   To bind and loose. 16:19
   To disciple & teach faithful men. 28:16-20
   To seek the lost. 22:1-14
Names - Titles.
   Building stones. 16:18
   House of God.
      For prayer, ministry, and praise. 21:12-16
      For receiving the Word. 13:1-9
   Severalfold. 21:43
Nature.
   For prayer, ministry, and praise. 21:12-16
   For receiving the Word. 13:1-9
   God, the authority over. 21:12-16
   Good and bad within. 13:24-30; 13:31-32; 13:33; 13:36-43; 13:47-50
   Head of. God. 21:12-16
   House of prayer. 21:13
   Impregnable - unconquerable. 16:18
   Set apart. Hallowed ground. 21:13
Problems.
   Bad within. 13:24-30; 13:31-32; 13:33; 13:36-43; 13:47-50
   Commercialism. Within c often. 21:12-16
   Exploiting people. 21:12-16
   Misplaces Christ. 23:14
   Rejects poor & less privileged. 20:31-32
Purpose.
   Discussed. 21: 12-16
Revelation of.
   By Jesus. (See **REVELATION**) 16:13-20
   Peter's great confession. 16:13-20
Security. (See **ASSURANCE**)
   Basis of. 16:13-20
Why unbelievers want to belong to the c. 13:47-48

CHURCH DISCIPLINE
Discussed. 18:15-20
Question of d. discussed. 13:27-30

CITIZENSHIP (See **GOVERNMENT; STATE**)
Discussed. 17:24-27; 22:15-22;
Duty toward the government.
   Good c. 17:24-27
   To pay taxes. 17:24-27; 22:15-22
False concepts of.
   Sins common to. 22:16-17
   Vs. true concepts. 22:15-22
Of believer.
   Has two c. 22:15-22
   Of heavenly kingdom. 17:25
   Often misunderstood. 22:15-22
Two c. God and Caesar. 22:15-22
Views of. Pharisees and Herodians. 22:15-16
Why Christ paid taxes. Six reasons. 17:27

CLEAN - CLEANLINESS - CLEANSING
Heart determines. 23:25-26
Inward c. essential. 23:25-28

CLEAVE - CLEAVING
In marriage. 19:1-12; 19:5
Meaning. 19:5

CLOSED-MINDEDNESS
Sin common to false citizenship. 22:16-17

CLOTH & WINE BOTTLES
New & old c. 9:14-17

CLOTHING
Attitude about. Right vs. wrong. 6:25-34
Purpose for. Three p. 6:28-30
Religious c. Problem with. 23:5

CLOUD
Descriptive of - symbolic of. Jesus returns in. 24:30

COLT - ASS
Jesus uses in Triumphal Entry. 21:2-5

COMFORT - COMFORTED
Present & eternal c. 5:4
Sin of. Answer to. 11:8
Source. Christ. 9:18-34, esp. 22, 25, 30, 33

COMMANDMENT – COMMANDMENTS
God's c.
   Are explained by Christ. 5:17-48
   Are the c.'s of Christ. 5:17-20
   Obeying assures greatness in heaven. 5:17-20
Greatest c. Love God & neighbor. 22:34-40
Subjects.
   Adultery. Reasons for c. 5:27; 5:27-30
   Anger. 5:21-26
   Divorce. Reasons for c. 5:31
   Injury. 5:38-42
   Lighter vs. weightier. 23:23-24
   Love. 5:43
   Murder. 5:21
   Resistance. 5:38-42
   Retaliation. 5:38-42
   Revenge. 5:38-42
   Swearing—Cursing. Law against. Reasons. 5:33-37
   Vengeance 5:38-42
The great or first c. 22:34-40

COMMISSION
Duty. To teach & make disciples. 28:19-20
Given to. Disciples. Discussed. 10:5-15; 28:16-20
Great c. Messiah's final c. to disciples. 28:16-20

COMMIT - COMMITMENT (See **DEDICATION—DEVOTION**)
Call to.
   Argument for. 16:21-28
   Give up all for Christ. 13:44
   Go beyond common sense. 26:8-9
   Total c. Demanded by Jesus' death. 16:21-28
Degrees of. 13:8, 23
Kinds of. Self c. vs. Christ's c. 8:18-22
Law of. 13:12; 13:13-15
Misuse of. 23:16-22
Pictures of. Fourfold pictures. 26:47-56
Reward. Receives, understands more & more. 13:11-12

COMMON SENSE
To be set aside sometimes for sacrifice. 26:8

COMMUNION (See **DEVOTION**)
Essential to conquer temptation. 4:1

COMPASSION (See **JESUS CHRIST, Compassion of**)
Duty. To have mercy, not sacrifice. Discussed. 9:13; 12:7
Essential - Necessary.
   Because of world's condition. 9:36
   For ministry. 14:15; 15:32
Meaning. 9:36
Of Jesus.
   For Jerusalem. 23:37-39
   For physical needs. 15:29-39, esp. 32
   For the desperate. 20:34
   For the scattered and shepherdless. 9:35-38
   Led Christ to teach. 5:1
Stirred by. Seeing the world as it really is. 9:36

INDEX

COMPLACENT - COMPLACENCY
Caused by. 26:40-41
Described. As slumber. 25:1-13
Discussed. 20:3-4
Law of. 13:12; 13:13-15
Results. To be judged. 25:24-30

COMPROMISE
Illust. by Pilate. 27:11-25
Temptation to. Discussed. 4:8; 4:8-10

CONFESS - CONFESSION
Discussed. 16:15-16
Essential.
  Confessing vs. denying. 10:32-33
  Jesus is the Christ. 16:13-20
Fact. Words either c. or deny. 12:33
Of Christ.
  Causes Christ to confess bel. 10:32-33
  Demanded by His presence. 14:33
  Must be a personal discovery. 16:13-20
  The foundation of the church. 16:13-20
Of Judas. But to religionists, not to God. 26:1-5
Of Peter. Great c. Jesus is the Christ. 16:13-20

CONFORM - CONFORMED - CONFORMITY
To God's image. Discussed. 5:45; 5:48

CONSCIENCE
Described. 6:14-15
Function - Purpose - Work.
  To condemn. 14:1-14
  To disturb, stir quietly. 14:1-14

CONSERVATIVE
School of thought. 19:1-12

CONTEMPT
Caused by. Threefold. 13:53-58

CONTRARY
Message to the c. Discussed. 11:16-19

CONVERSION
Dramatic. But does not last. 13:5-6, 20-21
Essential. For greatness. 18:3
Meaning. 18:3
  Becoming as a little child. 18:1-4
Of Matthew. Dramatic. 9:9; 9:9-13

CONVICTION
Source of. Holy Spirit vs. natural man. 16:17

CORNERSTONE
Christ is. Discussed. 21:42; 21:44

CORRUPTION
Cause. Ultimate c. 8:17
Meaning. 6:19-20
  Decaying, aging, deteriorating. 6:19

COURAGE
In standing with Christ. 26:56, cp. 47-56

COVET - COVETOUSNESS (See **GREED**)
Meaning. Preferring property over Christ. 8:28-34
Results. Reject Christ. Reasons. 8:33-34
Sin of. Desiring, lusting for more & more. 26:15

CRITICISM - CRITICIZER (See **JUDGMENT**)
Discussed. 7:1-6
Judgment of. Described. 7:2
Nature. Blinds one to own faults. 7:1-6
Reasons for. Sixfold. 7:1
Sins committed by. 7:1-6
Unworthy of the gospel. 7:1-6; 7:6
Warning against. Usurps God's authority. Makes one as a god. 7:1
Why should not c. 7:1

CROSS—SELF-DENIAL (See **JESUS CHRIST, CROSS; DEATH; SELF-DENIAL**)
Discussion. 10:38
Essential. Must bear the c. 10:34-39; 16:21-28
Meaning.
  Death to self. 10:34-39
  Discipleship - cost of. 10:34-39
  Dying daily. 16:21-28
Power of. Illust. 27:54
Reactions to.
  Man accepts or is repulsed by. 16:22
  Man rebels against. 16:22

CROWDS
Why the c. followed Christ. Five reasons. 20:29

CRUCIFIXION
Described. 27:26

CUMMIN
Described. 23:23

CUP, THE
Of Christ's death & suffering. Gethsemane. 26:39; 26:42-44
Of suffering. Meaning. 20:22-23

CURSING (See **SWEARING**)
Discussed. 5:33-37; 23:16-22
Five types. 5:33-37
Shows man's depravity. 5:37

DANCING
Results. 14:6-8

DANIEL
Seventieth week. 24:15

DARKNESS
Swept the earth at Jesus' crucifixion. 27:45

DARKNESS, OUTER (See **OUTER DARKNESS**)
Discussed. 8:12
Meaning. 8:12, cp. 22:13; 25:30

DAVID
Eating showbread in the tabernacle. 12:3-4
Illustrates. Need has precedence over tradition. 12:3-4

DEATH - DYING
Dead raised. Jairus' daughter. 9:18-19, 23-26
Deliverance from. Confronting d. & terrible trials. 26:36-46
Described.
  As a day of accounting. 18:32-34
  As dead men's bones. 23:27-28
Fact.
  D. for a cause is not rare. 10:23
  Difference between Christ d. & man's **d**. 26:36-45
  Need to think about. Reasons. 20:18
Of believers. Shall never taste d. 16:28
To self. (See **CROSS—SELF-DENIAL**)

DEBTS
Meaning. 6:12

DECEIVE - DECEPTION
Of Judas. Intrigue against Christ. 26:16; 26:20-25
Sin of. Betrays Christ. 26:48-50
Sin of. Common to false citizenship. 22:16-17

DECISION
Discussed. 7:13-14
Last minute **d**. 20:6-7
Of life. Twofold. 7:13-14
Duty - Essential. Moment of **d**. must be grasped. 8:21-22
Facts.
  Christ will not force. 9:1
  Neutrality impossible. 12:30; 12:33
  Spirit does not always strive with man. 12:14-16; 20:5
  Rejected. Deliberate, wilful **r**. 13:10-17; 13:13-15; 21:27

DEDICATION (See **COMMITMENT; MINISTRY; SERVICE; SURRENDER**)
Discussed. 13:1-9
Duty.
  To **d**. self. To three things. 6:9
  To give all one is & has. 19:21-22; 19:23-26; 19:27-30
Meaning
  Sacrificial giving. 26:6-13
  Surrender. 6:9
Why a person should be **d**.
  Degrees of. 13:8, 23
  Is demanded by Christ's death. 16:21-28

DEFILE - DEFILEMENT
Meaning. 15:17-20
What **d**. a man. 15:1-20

DELIVERANCE
How. By prayer. 6:13

DEMONS (See **EVIL SPIRITS**)

DENY - DENIAL
By whom.
  Peter. A look at the **d**. of Christ. 26:69-75
  The disciples. Foretold. Stumbling, falling away. 26:31-35
Causes of. Discussed. 26:69
Discussed. 10:32-33
Kinds of. Three **k**. 26:69-75
Meaning. 16:24
Warning against. Illogical & inconsistent. 12:22-30; 12:27-28

DENYING SELF (See **CROSS—SELF DENIAL**)

DEPART
Meaning. 7:23

INDEX

DEPRAVITY
    Fact. Shown by cursing. 5:37
    Of heart. What defiles the **h**. 15:17-20

DEPRESSION
    Example of. Judas. 27:1-10; 3-5

DESERTION (See **APOSTASY—DENIAL**)

DESOLATE
    Meaning. 23:38

DESPAIR
    Of Judas. Hopeless & helpless. 26:1-5

DESPERATE - DESPERATION
    Examples. Answer to. 9:18-34
    How the **d**. can be saved. 20:29-34

DESPISE - DESPISING
    Warning against. Ways **d**. 18:10

DESTINY
    Determined by.
        Decision for Christ. Neutrality impossible. 12:30; 12:33
        Man's words determine his **d**. 12:31-37

DESTROY
    Meaning. 10:28

DEVOTION - DEVOTIONS (See **COMMISSION; COMMITMENT; QUIET TIME**)
    Duty. Three areas. 13:51-52
    Need - Essential.
        Concentrating on Christ's death. 20:17
        Failure. Reasons. 6:6
        Not to stay on mountain top. 17:14
        Sacrificial love & faith. 26:6-13
        To be with Jesus. 10:1
        To guard against inconsistency. 6:6
    Glory of. Purpose is to minister. 17:14
    Purpose of. To minister. 17:14

DIFFICULTIES
    Handled by faith. 17:20

DISCIPLE - DISCIPLES (See **APOSTLES; BELIEVERS; LABORERS; MINISTERS**)
    Behavior. Rules for. 5:1-7
    Call. (See **CALL**)
        Commitment & commissioning **c**. 10:1-4
        Of Matthew. 9:9-13
        Of the twelve. 4:18-22; 10:1-4
        Three different calls. 10:1-4
        To be with Jesus. 10:1
    Character.
        Discussed. 5:13-16
        Kind of men they were. 4:18-22; 5:13
        Light of the world. 5:13
        Salt of the earth. 5:13
    Discussed. 5:1-2
    Essential.
        Compassion & reproduction. 5:1-2
        Discussed. 8:19-20; 8:20; 8:21
        Personal attachment. 4:18-20
        To be as a little child. 18:1-4
        To be with Jesus. 10:1
    Failure of.
        Spiritualized Jesus' death & resurrection. 17:22; 18:1
        Worldly ambition. Seek worldly greatness & position. 18:1

    False. (See **APOSTASY; DENIAL; PROFESSION ONLY**)
    Kinds of. Average **d**. Attracted to Jesus. 8:21-22
    Method.
        Number needs to be limited. 10:2
        Two by two. 10:3-4
    Mission - Commission. Discussed. 5:13-16
    Preparation.
        For death of Christ. 26:1-2
        Sermon on the Mount given for **p**. 5:1-2
    Training of. Intensive. Death of Christ. 16:13-20; 16:21-28; 17:1-13; 17:22; 17:24-27; 20:17; 20:20-28

DISCIPLESHIP (See **CROSS**)
    Cost - demands of. 8:18-22; 10:34-42
    Essential.
        Compassion & reproduction. 5:1-2
        Personal attachment. 4:18-20
        To be with Jesus. 10:1
    False **d**. (See **APOSTASY; DENIAL; PROFESSION ONLY**)
    Illust. Profession. 8:21
    Method.
        Number needs to be limited. 10:2
        Two by two. 10:3-4
    Rules for. 5:1-7:29

DISCIPLINE
    In church. (See **CHURCH**, Discipline)
    Of offending brothers. Discussed. 18:15-20

DISCRIMINATION
    Example. Woman with a hemorrhage. 9:20

DISEASE
    Cause of.
        Jesus bore our **d**. 8:17
        Ultimate cause. 8:17

DISOBEDIENCE
    Influence of. 5:19
    Judgment for. 5:19
    Who is **d**. 5:19

DIVISION—DISSENSION
    Answer to.
        Primary **a**. is prayer. 18:19
        Steps to correction. 18:15-20
    Caused by.
        Bad feelings. Proves four things. 6:15
        Barriers. 8:5-13
        Christ's sending sword to earth. 10:34-37
    Of families. Caused by Christ. 10:34-37
    Results.
        Divided allegiance. 12:25-26
        Split & ruin. 12:25-26
    Vs. peacemakers. 5:9

DIVORCE
    Allowance for. 5:32; 19:7-8
    Discussed. 5:31-32; 19:1-12
    Real meaning of. 5:31-32

DOCTRINE
    False. 16:5-12

DOVE
    Described. 10:16

DOXOLOGY
    Meaning. 6:13

DRAGNET
    Described. 13:47
    Parable of. Separating the bad from the good. 13:47-50

DRESS (See **CLOTHING**)
    Can cause problems.
        Anxiety. 6:28-34
        Identifies one with the world & the heathen. 6:32
    Proper **d**. is to seek God first. 6:31-34
    Warning against. Worrying, thinking too much about. 6:28-34

DRINKING - DRUNKENNESS
    Described. Partying. 14:6-8; 24:38

DROWNING
    Form of capital punishment. 18:6

EAGLES
    Symbol of judgment. 24:25-28

EARTH
    Heart of. Meaning. 12:40
    Not approved by Christ. 10:34-37

EARTHQUAKE
    At Jesus' death. 27:51
    At Jesus' resurrection. 28:2
    Predicted in last days. 24:7

EASY
    Meaning 11:29-30

EAT - EATING (See **FOOD**)
    Described. As partying, drinking, carousing. 24:38

EDUCATION
    Can hurt & damage 4:18-22

EGYPT
    Jesus led to **E**. for 6 years 2:13-18
    Jews often fled to **E**. 2:13
    Type. Of World. 2:13-18

ELIJAH
    Appeared at transfiguration. Reason. 17:3

EMBARRASSED
    Needs of **e**. men met. 9:1-8

EMPLOYMENT (See **LABOR; PROFESSION; SERVICE**)
    Failure in. Can know four things. 6:33

END TIME
    Attitude toward. To look for signs. 24:1-14; 24:15-28; 24:29-31
    Believer's duty.
        To watch. 24:42-51; 25:1-13
        To work. 25:14-30
    Great Tribulation. (See **TRIBULATION, GREAT**)
    Signs of - Events.
        Abomination of Desolation. (See **ANTICHRIST**)
        Discussed. 24:1-14
        World's end. 24:15-28
        Worldly state. As Noah's day. Carousing. 24:37-39

INDEX

ENDURANCE (See **PERSEVERANCE; STEADFASTNESS**)
Essential. For salvation. 24:43-44

ENEMIES
Discussed 5:43; 5:44; 5:44-48; 5:48
Duty toward. Love. 5:43; 5:44; 5:44-48; 5:48

ENTANGLE
Meaning. 22:15

EQUALITY (See **ONENESS; UNITY**)

ESPOUSED
Steps in marriage. 1:18

ESTEEM
Fails. Several ways. 6:5

ETERNAL LIFE
Described. 19:16
How to secure. Four steps. 19:16-22
Man's idea of. Discussed. 19:17
Nature.
Perfected. 19:28
Spiritual dimension. 22:29
Reality. Discussed. 22:29
Results of rejecting.
Losing one's life. 16:25
Reward. For self-denial. 19:28; 19:29
Vs. existence. 19:16

EUNUCH
Choice to be. 19:12

EVANGELISM
Zeal for. By Pharisees. Were strong in. 23:15

EVERLASTING FIRE (See **FIRE**)
Meaning. 25:41

EVIL (See **LOST; SIN**)
Duty. To cast out of life. Discussed. 12:43-45
In the church. (See **KINGDOM OF HEAVEN**)
In the Kingdom of Heaven (See **KINGDOM OF HEAVEN**)
In the world. Questioned. Why is e. in the church & in the world? 13:27
Results. Causes swearing. 5:37

EVIL SPIRITS
Discussed. 8:28-34; 9:32-34; 17:15-16
Conquered. By the cross. 8:28-34
Deliverance from forces of evil. 8:28-34
Denied. Discussed. 8:28-34
Said to be mental illness. 8:28-34
Duty. To wrestle against. 8:28-34
Enslave - Enslaved by. 8:28-34; 17:15-16
Nature. Forces of evil. 8:28-34
Type of. Evil force. 8:28-34; 8:28-31; 17:15

EXHAUSTION (See **TIRED; BURDENED; PRESSURE; YOKE**)

EXISTENCE - EXISTING
Of man. E. forever with or without God. 19:16

EXORCISTS (See **EVIL SPIRITS**)
Jewish e. In Jesus' day. 12:27-28

EYES
Culprit in immorality. 5:28; 5:29
Gate to the Mind. 6:21-23

FAINT - FAINTING
Meaning. 9:36

FAITH
Described as.
A mustard seed. Discussed. 17:20
Great. 8:8-10
Discussed. 9:18-34
Essential.
Must be in Christ. Meaning. 8:8-10
Must not doubt at all. 21:20-21
Vs. proof. 4:3-11; 12:38-40
Vs. signs. 4:3-11; 12:38-40
What it takes to enter God's Kingdom. 21:28-32
Example.
Of friends. Saves a friend. 9:2
Of others. Saves another. 9:18-34
Picture of sacrificial love & f. 26:6-13
Great f.
Described. 15:28
Jesus acknowledged great f. Two times. 8:10; 15:28
Meaning. 9:2
Meaning. 21:20-21
Object of. Discussed. 9:18-34
Power of.
Great power of. 17:14-21
To remove mountains. Meaning. 17:20
Results. Power. 21:22
Source of.
Established by Christ. 4:3-11
God. God works by f. not signs. 4:3-11; 12:38-40
Stages - Kinds of.
A faltering f. 14:28-31
Great f. (See **FAITH**, Great)
Little f. Meaning. 6:30
Persistent f. Jesus answers p. faith. 9:1-8

FAITHFUL - FAITHFULNESS
Duty. To watch & work. Because judgment is coming. 25:14-30
Vs. unfaithfulness. 25:14-30

FAITHLESSNESS
Discussed. 17:14-21; 17:17-18

FALLING AWAY (See **APOSTASY; BACKSLIDING; DENIAL**)

FALSE PROFESSION (See **PROFESSION**, False)

FALSE PROPHETS (See **TEACHERS, FALSE**)

FAME - FAMOUS (See **HONOR; PRIDE; RECOGNITION**)
Duty. Not to seek after. 6:1-5
Facts about. Fourfold. 14:5
Rejected. By Christ. 4:5-10
Seeking. Discussed. 18:1-4

FAMILY - FAMILIES (See **PARENTS; FATHERS**)
Basis of a f. Discussed. 19:1-12; 19:5
Division of.
Caused by Christ. 10:34-37
Reasons. 10:34-37
Duty.
Not to be affected by a f. member's sin. 18:25
To achieve potential. Cannot without Christ. 10:35-37
To be godly. Essential for service. 4:18-20
To be loyal. To Christ first. 10:34-37
To be reached first. 10:5-6
To be the strongest of relationships. 10:35-37
To esteem highly. Example of. Christ. 12:46-47
To go & reach first. 9:4-7
Failures - Weaknesses of.
Doubts & questions Christ & His claims. 12:46-50
Opposes & persecutes.
Believing member of one's family. 10:34-37; 10:35-37; 12:46-50
Other f. members. Reasons. 10:21
Needs of. Jesus cares & meets. 8:14-17
Of apostles. Greatly influenced them. 10:2
Of Jesus. (See **JESUS CHRIST**, Family)
Protected. By law on divorce. 5:32

FAMILY OF GOD
Of God.
Discussed. 12:48-50
Father-child relationship. 7:11

FASTING
Dangers. Fourfold. 6:16
Duty. Discussed. 6:16-18; 6:16
Essential. For preparation & temptation. 4:1
Jesus' disciples questioned about. 9:14-17
Motive. Right vs. wrong. 6:16-18
Result. Power. Great power for ministry. 17:21
When.
Discussed. 6:16-18
Vs. when not. 9:15

FATE
Man's words determine his f. 12:31-37

FATHER, GOD AS (See **GOD, NAMES - TITLES OF**)

FATHERS
Mistakes of. Threefold. 7:11

FAULT-FINDERS
Described. 11:16-19

FAVORITISM
In grace. But for the grace of God, there go I. 8:4

FEAR
Caused by.
Unexplainable events. 27:54; 28:4
Causes one to.
Act as dead, asleep, or unnoticed. 28:4
Confess Christ. 27:11-14
Fails to confess Christ. 26:69-74
Kinds. Godly f. vs. bad f. 8:26

INDEX

Meaning. 10:28
Overcome by. Christ's power. 8:23-27
What to fear.
   Not men. 10:28
   Not persecution. 10:28

FEAST
Of unleavened bread. 26:17

FEEDING FIVE THOUSAND
Essentials for ministry. 14:15-21

FIG TREE
Cursed. Why Jesus destroyed. 21:17-22
Symbolized.
   Israel. 21:19
   Lord's return. 24:32-35

FINANCIAL SUPPORT
Of temple. By Christ. Reasons. 17:25
Support of ministers. Discussed. 10:9-10

FIRE, EVERLASTING (See **HELL**)
Described. As hell. A furnace of **f**. 13:30, 42
Meaning. 25:41

FLESH
Reaction of **f**. To being offended. 18:15-17

FOLLOW
Meaning. 16:24

FOLLOW THROUGH
Essential for God's leadership. 2:12

FOOD
Attitude about. Right vs. wrong. 6:25; 6:31-32
What defiles a man. 15:17-20

FOOLISH VS. WISE BUILDER
Discussed. 7:24-27

FORERUNNER (See **JOHN THE BAPTIST**, Forerunner)

FORGIVENESS, HUMAN
Attitudes toward. 6:14-15
Described. 18:22
Discussed. 6:12; 6:14-15; 26:28
How often **f**. 18:21-35
How one receives. through forgiving others. 6:14-15
Importance.
   Basic principle of prayer. 6:14-15
   Most important thing in life. 6:14
   Relationships are impossible without **f**. 18:22
Of others. Essential time after time. 18:21-22
Pre-requisites. Discussed. 6:14-15
Reason God does not **f**. 6:14-15
Results. Assures prayers being answered. 6:14-15
Spirit of. 18:21-35

FORGIVENESS, SPIRITUAL
Attitudes toward. 6:14-15
Described. 18:22
Discussed. 6:12; 6:14-15; 26:28
How often **f**. 18:21-35
How one receives. Through forgiving others. 6:14-15
Importance.
   Basic principle of prayer. 6:14-15
   Most important thing in life. 6:14
Pre-requisites. Discussed. 6:14-15
Reason God does not **f**. 6:14-15
Source. Christ. 9:2
Spirit of. 18:21-35

FORNICATION
Meaning. 19:9

FOUNDATION
Wise vs. foolish. 7:24-27

FREE WILL
God trusts man. Gave him free will. 21:33

FRIENDS - FRIENDSHIP (See **BROTHERHOOD**)

FRUGAL - FRUGALITY
Duty. To be industrious, **f**., & saving. 4:21-22

FRUIT BEARING (See **BELIEVER**, Life - Walk; **DEDICATION**)
Degrees of. 13:8, 23
Discussed. 13:8, 23
Duty. To bear fruit. 13:26
Expected. Two times expected. 21:19

FUNERALS
Atmosphere needed. 9:23-26

FUTURE
Attitudes toward. Three **a**. 6:34

GALILEE
Discussed. 4:12

GALL
Mixed with vinegar. An intoxicating drink. Offered Christ on the cross. 27:26-38

GATE
Broad vs. narrow. Two **g**. in life. 7:13-14

GEHENNA (See **HELL**) 5:22

GENEALOGY
Honoring, relying upon. 23:29-33
Of Jesus Christ. 1:1-17; 1:1

GENERATION
Discussed.
   Answer to an evil generation. 12:38-45
   Described. Childish, playful, mindless. 11:16-19
   Jesus' great invitation to. 11:28-30
   Message to a childish **g**. 11:16-27

GENNESARET
Discussed. 14:34

GENTILES
Accepted. By God.
   God's great invitation to. 9:10; 22:1-14; 22:7
   Turned to by God. 21:43; 22:1-14
Prophecy of.
   Conversion of. 8:11
   Trusting Christ. 12:21
Sins of. Executed Jesus. 17:22

GENTILES, COURT OF
Temple. Discussed. 21:12-16

GETHSEMANE
Confronting death & terrible trial. 26:36-46
Meaning. 26:36

GIFTED, THE
How the **g**. enter heaven. 19:16-22

GIFTS, SPIRITUAL
Discussed. 25:14-15
Duty.
   To guard against misuse. Strong **g**. can become weakness. 26:15
   To work & use gifts. 25:14-30

GIVE - GIVING (See **HELP - HELPING; STEWARDSHIP; WORKS**)
Described. As the great Christian ethic. 5:42
Discussed. 5:40; 5:41; 5:42
Duty. To **g**. to all who ask or take. 5:40; 5:41; 5:42
How to **g**. Two descriptive ways. 6:3
Meaning. 6:1
Motive.
   Discussed. 6:1-4
   Wrong **m**. 6:2

GLORY - GLORIFIED
How God is **g**. 6:9-10
Of Christ. Described. 17:2
Shekinah **g**. 17:5-8

GNASHING
Meaning. 8:12

GOATS
Type. Of unbeliever. 25:33

GOD
Duty. To seek first. 6:33
Existence of.
   God of the living, not of the dead. 22:31-32
   Proves the resurrection. 22:31-32
Family of. (See **FAMILY OF GOD**)
Father. Discussed. 6:9
Glory of.
   Described. 17:2
   Discussed. 6:9
   Duty. To be honored & glorified. 6:9
   How **G**. is glorified. 6:9-10
God of Israel. 15:31
Image of. Man's false image. 13:57
Long-suffering. Discussed. 22:1-14; 22:4
Mercy (See **MERCY**)
   Invites people to accept Him. 22:1-14; 22:4
Names - Titles.
   Father. Discussed. 6:9
   God of Israel. 15:31
Nature. Not unjust because He chooses to reward some persons. 20:11-14
Omniscient. Knows a man's thoughts & plans. 2:13-18
Power. Seen in two events. 1:11-16
Presence of. Effect. 9:15
Providence. Overruling the affairs of men. 2:7-8
Trinity.
   First mention in the N.T. 3:16
   Identity and function. 28:19-20
Vs. Satan. 13:27-30
Will of. Discussed. 6:10

INDEX

GOD, FALSE (See **IDOLS - IDOLATRY**)

GODLY
Vs. ungodly man. 14:1-14

GOLDEN RULE
Discussed. 7:12

GOLGOTHA
Hill on which Christ was crucified. 27:26-38

GOMORRHA
Discussed. 10:15

GOOD
Meaning. 7:11

GOOD WORKS (See **WORKS**)

GOODMAN OF HOUSE
Discussed. 24:43-44
Parable of. 24:43-44

GOSPEL
Described.
  Additive only. Some add gospel to life. 13:7, 22
  As a treasure. 13:44
Discussed. How men receive the **g**. 13:1-9
Duty. To spread by peaceful means. 5:9
Facts. Critical, judgmental person undeserving. 7:16
Message of.
  Kingdom of Lord. 3:2; 4:23
  Points. 3:1-12; 4:17
  Proclaimed by John. 3:1-12
Power of. Transforming **p**. 13:33
Response to.
  Hardened to. Reasons. 13:4, 19
  Two encouragements. 13:47-48
Value of. Discussed. 13:44; 13:45-46

GOVERNMENT (See **CITIZENSHIP**)

GRACE
Danger.
  Feeling one is a favorite of God. 8:4
  Pride. But for the **g**. of God, there go I. 8:4
God's glorious grace. 20:1-16

GREATNESS
Conditions for. 18:1-4
Price of. Discussed. 20:20-28
Seeking. Discussed. 18:1-4

GREED
Discussed. 26:15
Example of. Judas. 26:15

GROWTH (See **SPIRITUAL GROWTH**)

GUIDANCE
Assurance of **g**. In God's purpose & will. 4:12

GUILT
Described. 6:14-15; 14:1-14

HAIL - REJOICE
Meaning. 28:9

HALLOWED
Meaning. 6:9

HANDS
Duty. To guard against using in immorality. 5:27-30
Fact. Is culprit in immorality. 5:27-30

HARD - HARDENED - HARDNESS OF HEART
Discussed.
  In & out of marriage. 19:8
  Reasons become **h**. 13:4, 19

HARDLY
Meaning. 19:23

HARVEST
Of souls. Discussed. 9:37-38

HATE - HATRED
Ct. with love thy neighbor. 5:43-44
Discussed. 5:43-48
Meaning. Discussed. 5:21-26
Of whom. Of one's enemies. 5:43-48; cp. 21-26

HEALS - HEALING
By Jesus Christ. Examples of.
  All diseases & sicknesses. 4:24; 8:16-17; 9:35; 11:5;15:29-31
  Blind & dumb man. 12:22-24
  Blind men. 9:27-31; 20:20-34
  Canaanite woman's daughter. 15:21-28
  Centurion's servant. 8:5-13
  Demon possessed.
    Daughter of Canaanite woman. 15:21-28
    Dumb man possessed. 9:32-33
    Many possessed. 4:24
    Two possessed. 8:28-34
  Dumb man. 9:32-34; 12:22
  Hemorrhaging woman. 9:20-22
  Leper. Proves deity. 8:1-4
  Paralyzed man. 9:1-8
  Peter's mother-in-law. 8:14-15
  Raised the dead. Ruler's daughter. 9:18-19, 23-26
  Whole man. 4:24
  Withered hand. 12:9-13
Errors of. Mentioned. 9:35
Kinds. Spiritual, physical, mental. 4:24
Meaning. Through & through. Soul & body. 14:36
Power to **h**. 4:24
Request for. 9:20; 14:36
Steps to. Being made whole. 14: 34-36
Why God does not always heal. 8:1-4

HEAR - HEARING
Gospel. Deliberate closing of ears. 13:13-15

HEART
Defilement of. What **d**. 15:17-20
Described.
  Fruit bearing. 13:8, 23
  Hard. By wayside. 13:4, 19
  Thorny. Worldly. 13:7, 22
  Hard - Hardened. Judas hardened his heart time & again. 26:15
Meaning. 22:37
Set on.
  Earthly or heavenly treasure. 6:21-23

Exposed by words. 12:34-35
Treasure is where the **h**. is. 6:21-23
State - Kinds of.
  Corrupt **h**. 15:15-20
  Pure **h**. 5:8
What the heart does.
  Defiles a man. 15:10-20
  Determines outside. 23:25-26
  Loves. 22:37

HEART OF THE EARTH
Meaning. 12:40

HEAVEN (See **KINGDOM OF HEAVEN**)
Believers.
  Are to be rewarded. 5:11-12
  Position in **h**. 11:11
Characteristics - Nature.
  Another dimension of being. 19:16
  Dimension of being. Christ proclaimed. 9:35
  Spiritual dimension. Discussed. 22:29
  Three **h**'s. 6:9
Entrance.
  Difficult for a rich man to enter. 19:24
  How a rich man enters **h**. 19:16-22
  What it takes to enter **h**. 21:28-32
Experience of. (See **GLORY**)
  Foretaste of. Described. 17:2; 17:3; 17:4; 17:5-8; 17:5
  Mysteries of. Meaning. 13:1-58
How to enter.
  By being poor in spirit. 5:3
  How a rich man enters. 19:16-22
  Requires more righteousness than a religionist has. 5:20
Least in **h**. 11:11

HEAVEN, KINGDOM OF
Described. As narrow gate. Meaning. 6:9; 7:13-14
Entrance into.
  Need more righteousness than a religionist. 5:20
  Not by profession only. 7:21-23

HEIRS (See **INHERITANCE**)

HELL
And Jesus.
  Jesus bore **h**. for man. 27:52
  Jesus descended into. 26:52-53
Described. 18:9;
  Everlasting fire. 25:41; 25:46
  Everlasting punishment. 25:46
  Furnace of fire. 13:30, 42
  Gnashing of teeth. 8:12
  Outer darkness. 8:12; 13:42
  Weeping. 8:12; 13:42
  What **h**. is not. 25:41-45
Discussed. 5:22
Prepared for. Devil & his angels. 25:41
Who is to be in **h**.
  Goats. People who do not minister or help others in life. 25:41
  Sinners. Offenders. 18:8
  Tares. All who offend & do iniquity. 13:41-42, 50
  Unfruitful. 3:10; 7:19
  Unrighteous. 25:41-46

HELP - HELPING (See **GIVE - GIVING**; **WORKS**)
Duty. Discussed. 5:40; 5:41; 5:42

INDEX

HERITAGE
    Family cannot save. 3:7-10
    Inadequate to save. 1:7-8; 3:7-10

HEROD THE GREAT, RULER OF JUDEA (37 BC)
    Discussed. 2:3-4
    Reacts to Jesus' birth. 2:1-11
    Slaughters children. 2:13-18

HEROD ANTIPAS (4 BC - AD 39)
    Discussed. 14:1-14
    Murdered John the Baptist. A godly vs. an ungodly man. 14:1-14

HERODIANS
    Discussed. 22:16

HERODIAS
    Discussed. 14:6-11

HIDDEN TREASURE
    Parable of. 13:44

HIGH PRIEST
    A political office in Jesus' day. 26:3
    And Jesus. Stood against Jesus. 26:3-5
    Discussed. 26:3

HIGHEST
    Meaning. 21:9

HILLEL SCHOOL
    Liberal school of thought. 19:1-12

HISTORY (See **END TIMES**)
    Christ and **h**. Ushers in a new age. 9:14-17
    Daniel's seventieth week. 24:15
    Perspective of. God's **p**. 21:33-46
    Pivotal points of.
        Discussed. 5:17-18
        Measure years, calendar by Christ. 8:18-22
        Symbolized. 1:1-17
    Spiritual **h**. Discussed. 1:17

HISTORY, SPIRITUAL
    Periods of. 1:17

HOLY PLACE - HOLY OF HOLIES
    Veil torn at Christ's death: access to God. 27:50-51

HOLY SPIRIT
    Came upon—indwelt Christ fully. 3:16; 12:18
    Rejected.
        Does not always strive with man. 12:14-16; 20:5
        Rejected. Turns away. 12:14-16
    Sins against. Blasphemy. Unpardonable sin. 12:31-32
    Work of. Conviction vs. natural man. 16:17

HOMAGE
    Demonstrated by obedience. 21:6-7

HONOR
    Seeking. Loving to receive **h**. is wrong. 23:5

HOPELESSNESS
    Christ's power to meet. 9:18-34

HOSANNA
    Meaning. 21:9

HOSPITALITY
    How ministers are to be received. 10:40-42

HOUSE
    Rooftops. Discussed. 24:17

HOUSEHOLDER
    Parable of. Devotion, study, sharing. 13:51-52

HOUSING
    Attitude about. Right vs. wrong. 6:26

HUMANISM - HUMANIST
    Warning to. Inadequate to meet man's needs. 14:15-21

HUMILITY
    Attitude. Required. 3:14
    Condition for greatness. 18:1-4
    Essential.
        Discussed. 8:5-9
        For greatness. 18:4
    Example.
        Canaanite woman. 15:26-27
        Centurion. Great **h**. 8:5-9
        Christ. 12:19; 18:4
        John the Baptist. 3:14
        Matthew. 10:3-4
    Men fear. Reasons. 18:4
    Results. Greatness. 18:1-4
    Source - comes by.
        How to become humble. 18:4
        Ideal humility. Jesus Christ. 12:19
    Steps involved. 18:4

HUNGER & THIRST
    Meaning. 5:6

HYPOCRISY - HYPOCRITE - HYPOCRITICAL
    Described.
        As criticizing. 7:5
        As false religion. 23:1-36
        As fasting for recognition. 6:16
        As giving for recognition. 6:2
        As judging. 7:5
        As praying for recognition. 6:5
    Discussed. 23:13
    Examples.
        Pharisees - religionists. 15:1-9; 23:1-33
    Meaning. 23:13
    Results. Hopeless. 7:26-27
    Traits of.
        Claims & teaches, but does not live. 23:3
        Committed by false teachers. 23:3; 23:13-36

IDLE - IDLENESS
    A symbol of lostness. 20:3-4
    Meaning. 12:36

IDOLATRY
    Described. Mental image of God. 13:57

ILLOGICAL
    What is **i**.
        Denial. 12:27-28
        Rejection. 13:13-15

IMMORALITY (See **ADULTERY; LUST**)
    Cause - causes. Threefold. 5:27-30
    Concept of. Acceptable, excusable. 5:27-30
    Prevention - cure. Discussed. 5:28; 5:30

INCORRUPTION
    Meaning. 6:19-20

INDECISION - INDECISIVENESS
    Example of. Pilate. 27:11-25

INDULGE - INDULGENCE
    Judgment of. Why God does not forgive a person who indulges time & again. 6:14-15

INFERIORITY
    Caused by. Discussed. 13:53-54

INFIRMITIES
    Borne by Jesus. 8:16-17

INHERITANCE (See **REWARD; SPIRITUAL INHERITANCE**)

INIQUITY
    Meaning. 7:23

INJURY
    Law governing. Discussed. 5:38; 5:39-41; 5:405:41; 5:42
    Personal **i**. Discussed. 5:39-41; 5:41
    Property **i**. Discussed. 5:40

INTELLECTUAL PRIDE
    Result. Blinds to the truth. 11:25-27

INTERCESSION
    Example. Canaanite woman for daughter. 15:22
    For what. Loved ones. 15:22

INTRIGUE
    Of Judas. Described as on the prowl after Christ. 26:16

INVITATION
    Kinds of. Severalfold. 22:4
    Rejected. God's great invitation. 22:1-14
    Source.
        Extended by Christ.
            Christ. Seeks to gather as a mother hen. 23:37
            Come unto me. 11:28-30
            To this generation. Rest. 11:28-30
        Extended by God.
            God sends message after message. 22:1-10
            God sets a great feast before. 22:1-10

ISRAEL (See **JERUSALEM; JEWS**)
    Discussed. 10:12; 21:33-46; 21:43; 22:1-14
    Duty toward.
        To be reached first. Reasons. 10:5-6
        Why **I**. was to be evangelized. 10:5-6
    Failures - Errors - Mistakes of.
        Persecuted God's messengers. 23:37
        Rejected the Messiah & His love. 23:37
    History.
        God's great invitation to **I**. 22:1-14
        God's perspective, dealings with. 21:33-46 21:43; 22:1-14
        Symbolizes spiritual journey. 1:17

INDEX

Nation of. "Binding force" held together. 12:10
Parables describing.
   P. of the Marriage Feast. 22:1-14
   P. of the Wicked Husbandman. 21:33-46
Rejection of.
   By God. 21:17-22; 21:33-46
   Christ. Parable of Wicked Husbandman. 21:33-46; 22:1-14
   God's great invitation. 22:1-14
   Jesus, the Messiah. 21:33-46
Restoration of. (See **JEWS**, Restoration)

JAIRUS
Ruler of synagogue. Discussed. 9:18-19

JAMES, THE APOSTLE, THE SON OF ALPHAEUS
Had a believing mother. 27:56

JAMES, THE APOSTLE, THE SON OF ZEBEDEE
Discussed. 10:2
Martyred by Herod. 20:23
One of Jesus' inner circle. 17:1

JAMES THE BROTHER OF JESUS
Discussed. 13:55-56

JEALOUSY (See **ENVY**)
Caused by. Another's pay and labor. 20:12

JERUSALEM (See **ISRAEL**)
Discussed. 24:15-28; 24:29-31
Fall. Predicted. Signs of. 24:15-28
Rejected Christ. His love. Great lament over J. 23:37-39

JESUS CHRIST (See **MESSIAH - MESSIAHSHIP**)
Abused. Physically beaten, ridiculed at trial. 26:67-68
Accused - Accusation against. (See **JESUS CHRIST**, Challenged; Questioned; Opposed)
   Of Beelzebub. Of David. 9:34; 12:24
   Of being revolutionary. 26:60-61
   Of blasphemy. 9:3; 26:65-66
   Of breaking the ceremonial law. 12:1-8
   Of breaking the Sabbath law. 12:1-8
   Of claiming false authority. 21:23-27
And the law. Fulfilled the law. 5:17
Anger of.
   Caused. By a great hypocrisy. Religionists. 23:13-36
   Included sorrow & brokenness. 22:41-46; 23:13-36
   Over the abuse of God's temple. 21:12-16
Anointed.
   Mary's a. Sacrificial love & faith. 26:6-13
   Pointed toward His burial & death. 26:12
Approved by God. Audible voice. 3:17
Arrest - Arrested.
   Betrayed & deserted. 26:47-56
   Plotted by three groups. 16:21; 26:3-5
Attracts - Attraction.
   Power to a. Reasons. 8:18-22
Authority. (See **JESUS CHRIST**, Power)
   Over God's House, the Temple. 21:12-16
   Questioned. The problem with unbelief. 21:23-27

Baptism.
   By fire & the Holy Spirit. 3:11; 3:14
   Discussed. 3:15
   Reasons for **b**. 3:13; 3:15
Betrayed.
   Arrested. Deserted. 26:47-56
   By Judas.
      Picture of a ruined life. 26:14-16
      Picture of wrong repentance. 27:1-10
   How men **b**. 26:16
Birth. (See **VIRGIN BIRTH**)
   Convulsive & disturbing. Seven reasons. 1:18-25
   Created a serious predicament. 1:18-19
   Divine. Of Holy Spirit. 1:16; 1:20-21
   Star that guided the Wise Men. Discussed. 2:2
   Three quick facts. 2:1
   Unusual events. 1:18-25
   Virgin **b**. Discussed. 1:16; 1:23
   World did not know. 2:2
Blood of.
   Denied. Thought repulsive. 16:21-23
   Drinking & eating of Christ's body. Not cannibalism. 26:26; 26:27-28
Burial. Reactions to Jesus' death. 27:57-66
Care - Caring. (See **CARE - CARING**)
Carpenter. Knew building. 7:24-27
Challenged about.
   Forgiving sins. 9:3
   God & Caesar. Two citizenships. 22:15-22
   Greatest commandment. 22:34-40
   His authority. 21:23-27
   Reasons. Threefold. 13:53-58
   Resurrection in the last day. 22:23-33
   The great commandment. 22:34-40
   The state and religion. 22:15-22
Charges against. (See **JESUS CHRIST**, Accused; Trials, Legal)
Childhood.
   Discussed. 13:53-58
   Education. 13:53-58
   Facing danger after danger. 2:12-23
   Lived in Egypt for 6-7 years. 2:13-18
   Three threats against. 2:12-23
Claims.
   Authority is of God. 21:23
   Bridegroom of disciples. 9:15; 25:1-13
   God's Son. (See Son of God) 21:37-39
   Head cornerstone. Discussed. 21:42; 21:44
   I AM. 14:27
   King. 27:11-14
   Messiah, Son of God. 26:63-64
   Not just a man, but God. 19:17
   Protector of Israel. 23:37
   Son of God. 1:16; 1:23; 14:33
   Son of Man. 8:20; 26:1-2
   Stone, The. 21:42; 21:44
   The Christ, Son of the Living God. 16:15-16
   Threefold claim. 17:25-26
Cleanses the temple. 21:12-16
Composure. Calm assurance. 26:62-63
Condemned. (See **JESUS CHRIST**, Trials, Legal)
Cross. (See **JESUS CHRIST**, Death)
   Miraculous events surrounding the cross. 27:45-56
Crucifixion. (See **JESUS CHRIST**, Death)
   Discussed. 27:26-44

Cursed the fig tree. 21:17-22
Daily activities. 4:23-25
Death.
   Blood denied. (See **JESUS CHRIST**, Blood of) 16:22
   Destined - Determined. By God. Delivered up by God. 17:22; 17:23; 20:18
   Discussed. 16:21-23; 27:26-44; 27:45-56
   Reasons could not reveal to multitudes. 20:17
   Events of. 27:26-44; 27:45-56
      Average persons, passers-by, mock & abuse. 27:39-40
      Miraculous **e**. surrounding. 27:45-56
      Religionists & civil leaders mock & taunt. 27:41-43
      Rulers pass judgment. 27:26
      Soldiers mock & torture. 27:26-38
   Meaning. Died as the Son of Man, as the substitute for man. 26:1-2
   Necessity.
      Dear to the heart of Christ. Reasons. 20:18
      Misunderstood & spiritualized. By disciples. 20:20-21
   Plotted. 20:17-19; 26:3-5; 26:57-68
      Culprits involved in death. 16:21; 27:1-10
      Groups involved in **d**. 16:21; 27:26-44
   Predicted - Foretold. 9:15; 17:12; 17:22-23 20:17-19
      Demands total commitment. 16:21-28
      Predictions intensified. Launches new stage. 16:21-28; 17:1-13; 17:22; 17:24-27
   Prepared for.
      All verses in N.T. given. 17:23
      Anointed for **d**. Sacrificed love & faith. 26:6-13
      By the transfiguration. 17:1-13
      Confronting death & terrible trials. Gethsemane. 26:36-46
   Prosecutors of. Discussed. 20:19
   Purpose.
      To descend into hell for man & to conquer death. 27:52-53
      Twofold **p**. 17:23
   Rebelled against. Man rebels at idea of cross. Considered repulsive. 16:21-23
   Results - Effects.
      History revolves around **d**. 17:22-23
      Several results. 9:15
      Should cause fasting. 9:15
   Spiritualized. By disciples. Misunderstood. 17:22; 18:1
   Sufferings of.
      At death. 27:26-38
      Different from man's **d**. Several ways. 26:37-38
      Discussed. 26:37-38
      Felt in Gethsemane. 26:37-38
      Mental, physical, spiritual experience of. 26:37-38
      Picture of world's treatment of God's Son. 27:26-44
      Separation from God. 27:46-49
      Strengthened to bear the cross. 17:1-13
      Tortured, physically beaten, ridiculed. 26:67-68
      Ultimate degree of pain. 20:19

INDEX

Symbolized. Conquest of death. 27:52-53
Triumphant. 27:50
Deceiver if not the Christ. Hoax. 16:15-16
Deity. (See **JESUS CHRIST,** Claims; Names - Titles; **MESSIAH - MESSIAHSHIP**)
    Acknowledged as Lord. Meaning. 8:5-9
    Chosen Servant, The. 12:18
    Citizenship. Origin. Of heaven, God's kingdom. 17:25-26
    Discussed. 11:25-27; 22:41-46
    God's beloved Son. 12:18
    Greater than religion. 12:1-8
    Is wrapped in the glory of God. 16:27; 17:2
    Not just a man, but God. 19:17
    Person. 12:17-18
    Questioned by John the Baptist. 11:1-6
    Seen as the special representative of God. 15:31
    Son of God. 1:16; 1:23; 3:16-17
    Spirit endowed fully. 12:18
    Three proofs at baptism. 3:16-17
    Unacceptable confessions. 16:13-14
    Works. 12:19-21
Denial. (See **DENY - DENIAL**)
Descendant. Of Abraham & of David. 1:1-2
Descent into hell. 27:50; 27:52
Devotion to. (See **COMMITMENT - DEDICATION; DEVOTION**)
Early life. (See **JESUS CHRIST,** Childhood)
Education. (See **JESUS CHRIST,** Childhood)
Fame of. Discussed. 4:23-25
Family.
    Answer to doubting **f.** 12:46-50
    Brothers & sisters. 13:53-58; 13:55
    Doubted & misunderstood Him. 12:46-47
    Father died. 13:53-58
    Humble. 13:53-58
    Poor. 2:19-23
Fulfilled prophecy. 1:22-23; 2:15; 2:23; 4:14-16
Fulfilled the law. 5:17-48; 5:17-20; 5:17-18
Genealogy. 1:1-17; 1:1
Gethsemane. (See **GETHSEMANE**)
Glory - glorified. Wrapped in the glory of God. 16:27
Healing (See **HEALS - HEALING**)
Humanity of.
    Compassion. (See **JESUS CHRIST,** Compassion) 15:32
    Personal poverty. 8:20
    Preoccupation, pressure, etc., just as all men. 26:6-13; 26:7
    Pressured. By being challenged time & again. 22:23-33
    Tired, yet ministered. 8:16
Humility of. Ideal humility. 12:19
Ideal, Perfect Man. (See Son of Man)
    Pattern. 5:17-18
Impact. Upon history. Calendar & years. 8:18-22
Incarnation. (See **JESUS CHRIST,** Deity; Origin & Nature; Virgin Birth)
    Discussed. 1:16; 1:23
    Pivotal point of history. 5:17-18

Last week.
    Atmosphere in Jerusalem during last **w.** 26:6-13
    Discussed. 21:23-27:22; 22:23-33; 22:41-46
Life of. Pivotal point of history. 5:17-18
Love.
    For Jerusalem. Rejected. 23:37-39
    Great lament for Jerusalem. 23:37-39
Marriage of the Lamb.
    Discussed. 25:1-13
    Feast of. God's great invitation. 22:1-14
Message of.
    Kingdom of heaven. 9:35
    Repent. 4:17
Method. To go everywhere. 9:35
Ministry.
    Power & tenderness of. 9:18-19, 23-26
    Successful. 4:23-25
    To Gentiles. Discussed. 15:29
Misconceptions of.
    Death & resurrection. 17:22; 18:1; 20:20-28; 20:21
    Is a man only. 19:17
Mission. (See **JESUS CHRIST,** Works of)
    Discussed. 9:35-38
    Onefold: people 4:15-16
    Threefold. 4:15-16; 9:35-38
    To preach. 4:17; 4:23
    To save from sins. 1:21
    To usher in a new age & life & covenant. 9:14-17
    Work. Discussed. 12:18-21
Names - Titles.
    Beloved Son. 3:17
    Bridegroom. 9:15; 25:1-13
    Chosen Servant of God. 12:18
    Christ - Messiah. Meaning. 1:18; 16:13-16, 20
    Christ, the Son of the Living God. 16:15-16
    Emmanuel. God with us. Meaning. 1:23
    God Himself. 22:41-46
    God's Beloved. 12:18
    God's servant. 12:17-21
    Head cornerstone. Discussed. 21:42; 21:44
    I AM. 14:27
    Jesus. Meaning. 1:21
    Lamb of God. 26:17-30
    Master. 8:19
    Son of David. Meaning. 1:1; 1:18; 3:11; 11:1-6; 15:22
    Son of God. 1:16; 1:23; 3:17; 14:33
    Son of Man. Meaning. 8:20; 26:1-2
    Stone. Fourfold picture. 21:44
    Who men said He was. 16:14
Nature - Origin.
    All knowing (omniscient). (See **JESUS CHRIST,** Knowledge of)
    All powerful (omnipotent). (See **JESUS CHRIST,** Power of.)
    Approachable. 18:2; 18:3
    Ever present (omnipresent). 18:20
    Innocent. 27:4
    Meek. 11:29
    Miraculous - of the Holy Spirit. 1:18; cp. 1:16; 1:23
    Not a lifeless rock, but a "living stone." 7:24-25
Neighbors of. Discussed. 13:53-58
Obedience. 26:39

Omniscient. Knows thoughts & rejection. 9:4-7
Opposed - Opposition. (See **RELIGIONISTS,** Opposed Christ)
    By obstinate unbelief. 21:23-27
    By religionists. 21:23-27
    By Sanhedrin. 21:23
    Easy to **o.** in a group. 26:57
    Enemies try to discredit. Feel threatened. Reasons. 12:1-8; 12:10; 15:1-20; 15:6-9; 16:1-12; 21:23; 22:15-22; 22:23-33; 22:34-40; 23:1-12
    Executioners of. 20:19
    Death explained & plotted. 26:1-5
    How men oppose. 26:16
    Pharisees & Sadducees cooperate. Request sign. 16:1-12
    Three groups who opposed. 16:21; 17:22
Origin. (See **JESUS CHRIST,** Nature - Origin)
Persecuted. (See **PERSECUTION**)
Person.
    Discussed. 11:25-27
    Greater than Jonah. 12:41
    Greater than Solomon. 12:42
Plot against. (See **JESUS CHRIST,** Death; Opposition)
Poverty. No place to lay head. 8:20; 21:1
Power.
    Over nature, a storm.
        Conquering fear. 8:23-27
        Power of His presence. 14:22-33
    Over physical universe.
        Fig tree destroyed. 21:17-22
        Storm calmed. 14:22-33
    Over the whole man. 4:24
    Promised to disciples. 28:19-20
    Revealed in word and work. 8:1-9:34
    Scorned. 9:23-26
    Sought & trusted. Steps to being made whole. 14:34-36
    To attract people. 8:18-22
    To cleanse the most defiled. 8:1-4
    To destroy Satan's house. 12:28-29
    To feed the multitude. Essentials for ministry. 14:15-21
    To forgive sins. 9:1-8
    To heal. (See **HEALS - HEALING**)
    To meet man's desperate needs. 9:18-34
    To receive and reject men. 8:5-13
    To receive sinners. 9:9-13
    To save men. 8:28-34
    To usher in a new age, life, covenant. 9:14-17
Praise of. By children. Proclaimed Messiahship. 21:15-16
Prayer life.
    Model prayer. 6:9-13
    Perseveres in. Gethsemane. 26:36-46
Presence.
    Instilled sense of God's **p.** 9:15
    Power of. 14:22-33
Priestly office. Transferred to Christ. 17:3
Prophetic office. Transferred to Christ. 17:3
Purpose. (See Related Subjects)
    Not to sanction world & its sin. 10:34-37
    To bear our infirmities & sicknesses & sins. Meaning. 8:16-17
    To cause division. 10:34-37
    To destroy Satan. 12:25-26; 12:29
    To die. Willingness. 26:53-54

INDEX

To heal the bruised, not to condemn them. 12:20
To seek & save the lost. 18:11-14
To send a sword, not peace on earth. 10:34-37
Twofold. 11:4-6
Questioned (See **JESUS CHRIST**, Accused; Challenged)
Response to.
  By people & religionists. 12:22-24
  By sinners. Felt comfortable with. 9:10-11
  By the crowd.
    Amazed - astonished - glorified God. 7:28-29; 9:8, 33
    Follow and crowd Him. 4:25
  Rejected - rejection. 8:34; 13:53-58
    By Nazareth, hometown. 13:53-58
    Lordship rejected. 12:14-16
    Obstinate unbelief. 12:24; 12:31-32; 13:13-15
  Why J. disturbs people. 2:3
Resurrection.
  All verses in N.T. given. 17:23
  Appearances to.
    Disciples. 28:16-20
    Official **a**. was to be in Galilee. 26:32
    Some women. 28:9
  Discussed with His death. Does three things. 20:19
  Events. Discussed. 28:1-15
  Evidence of. Witnesses to. Disciples. 28:16-20
  Misunderstood. Spiritualized by disciples. 17:22; 18:1; 20:21
  Predicted. 28:6-7
    All verses in N.T. 17:23
    Some understood better than others. 16:21-23; 17:12; 17:22-23
  Results.
    Four **r**. 17:23
    Proves two things. 17:9-13
  Sign of. Jonah predicted. 12:38-40
Return.
  Described.
    Five things. 26:31-33
    Marriage of the Lamb. 22:1-14; 25:1-13
  Discussed. 24:29-31
  Duty.
    Not to slumber, sleep. 25:5
    To watch & work for judgment is coming. 25:14-30
    To watch. Be ready. 24:42-51; 25:1-13
  Four things about. 24:25-28
  Events. Fivefold. 24:29-31
  How coming. Four facts. Sudden, unexpected, shattering. 24:37-39
  Purpose.
    To reward & punish. 25:14
    To separate & judge. 24:40-41; 25:31-46
  Response. Of world. 24:30
  Sign of. Discussed. 24:30
  State of the world. When Jesus returns. As Noah's day. 24:37-39
  When.
    Believers will know. Not caught off guard. 24:37
    Can be discerned. Within one generation. 24:32-35
    Discussed. 24:32-41
    Known only to God. Hour & day. 24:36
  Why Christ delays return. Six reasons. 25:5

Satan's attempt to destroy. 2:12-23
Savior. Seeks and saves the lost. 18:11-14
Seek - seeking. (See **SEEK - SEEKING**)
Suffering of. (See **JESUS CHRIST**, Death, Sufferings of)
  In Gethsemane. Discussed. 26:37-38
  Tortured, physically beaten, ridiculed. 26:67-68
  Ultimate degree of pain. 20:17; 20:18; 20:19
Teaching.
  Authority of. Meaning. 7:29
  Effect.
    Astonished, amazed. 7:28-29
    Astonished vs. discipleship. 7:28-29
  Method. 9:35
Temptation of. Discussed. 4:1-11
Tomb of. Discussed. 27:65-66
Training of disciples. (See **DISCIPLES**, Training of)
Transfiguration. Approved for the cross. 17:1-13
Trials, Legal.
  Accusers. False witnesses. 26:60-61
  Before Caiaphas. 26:57-68
  Before Pilate. Tragedy of an indecisive man. 27:11-25
  Before Sanhedrin. A picture of wrong repentance & human religion. Condemned to die by Sanhedrin. Lessons under trial. 26:57-68; 27:1-10
  Behavior.
    Composure. Calm assurance. 26:62-63
    Strong, controlled, impressive. 27:11-14
  Charges against.
    Blasphemy. 26:65-66
    Revolutionary. 26:60-61
  Life threatened time after time. 2:12-23
Triumphal Entry. Demonstrates Jesus' Messiahship. 21:1-11; 21:12-16 21:17-22
Value of. Most valuable Treasure. 13:44; 13:45-46
Virgin Birth. Discussed. 1:16; 1:23
Vision. Discussed. 9:37-38
Why crowds followed. Five reasons. 20:29
Work - Work of. (See **JESUS CHRIST**, Mission)
  Busy, very busy. 4:23
  Described. 4:23-25
  Discussed. 4:16-17; 9:35-38; 12:18-21
  Preaching, teaching, & healing. 9:35
  Proves Messiahship. 12:25-26; 12:29
  Revealed. The church. 16:13-20
  To fulfill Scripture. 4:12-17
  To fulfill the law. 5:17
  To save the sinner. Threefold. 9:12-13
  To secure righteousness. 5:17
  To seek man. 13:44; 13:45
Worship of. As king by the wise men. 2:1-11

JEWISH LEADERS (See **RELIGIONISTS; PHARISEES; SADDUCEES; SCRIBES; HERODIANS; ELDERS**)

JEWS (See **ISRAEL; JERUSALEM**)
Errors - Mistakes of.
  Counting some laws weightier, others lighter. 22:36
  Cry for Jesus' blood to be upon them. 27:25
  Discussed. 12:10
  Persecuted God's messengers. 23:37
  Rejected the Messiah. 23:37-39; 23:37
  Required a sign. 12:38-45
History.
  Binding force of nation. 12:10
  Descendants of Jacob. 1:2
  Fled to Egypt often. 2:13-18
  Refugees. Preserved by God. 1:11
Hope. Christ. 1:2
Judgment of.
  Because of sins. 23:37-39; 23:38-39
  Threefold. 23:38-39
Laws of. Sabbath. 12:1-9
Love for.
  Messiah's great lament for Jerusalem. 23:37-39
  Messiah's patience & care & protecting. 23:37
Opposed Christ. (See **JESUS CHRIST**, Opposition)
  Reasons. 12:1-8; 12:9-13; 12:10
  Ways opposed. 12:10
Plotted & killed Jesus. Accused of. 17:22-23
Religion of.
  Rules & regulations. 15:1-20
  Stressed outside, external appearance. 15:1-20
  Stressed tradition. 15:1-20; 15:6-9
Restoration. Predicted. Will proclaim Messiah. 23:39
Vs. Gentile. Example. 15:23-28

JOHN THE APOSTLE
Death of. 20:23

JOHN THE BAPTIST
Baptism of. Meaning. 3:11-12
Death.
  A godly vs. an ungodly man. 14:1-14
  Imprisoned & martyred. 14:1-14
Ended age of Old Testament prophecy. 11:14
Forerunner. Discussed. 11:10
Greatest among men. 11:11
In prison. Discussed. 11:2-3
Message of. 3:1-12; 3:2-6; 3:7-10; 3:11-12
Ministry. Discussed. 11:7-15
Needed assurance. Questioned Jesus' Messiahship. 11:1-6
Vindicated.
  By Christ. 11:7-15
  Reminder to fickle people. 11:7-15
Vs. Herod. 14:1-14
Who he was & was not. 11:7-15

JONAH
Compared with Christ. 12:41
Symbolized the resurrection of Christ. 12:38-40

JOSEPH OF ARIMATHAEA
Buried Jesus. Discussed. 27:57-60

JOSEPH, THE FATHER OF JESUS
Father of Jesus. Discussed. 1:18-19; 1:20-21

INDEX

JOY
    Described. 25:21
    Experience of. Involves three **e**. 13:44
    Source. Leading a person to Christ. Great **j**. over one lost person saved. 18:14

JUDAISM
    Converts to. Many Gentiles. Reasons. 23:15

JUDAS ISCARIOT, THE APOSTLE
    Betrayed Christ. Picture of a ruined life. 26:14-16; 26:47-56
    Given a last chance. Called to repent. 26:20-25
    Repentance of. Wrong **r**. & human religion. 26:1-10
    Suicide of. Despair. Hopelessness. 27:1-5

JUDEA
    Wilderness of. Discussed. 3:1

JUDGE - JUDGING OTHERS (See **CRITICISM**)
    Discussed. 7:1-6
    How we judge others. 13:54-56; 19:30
        Separating bad from good. 13:47-50
    Illust. Unmerciful servant. 18:28-31; 18:28; 18:30
    Judgment of. Described. 7:2
    Meaning. 7:1
    Overcoming. Example of. Joseph. 1:18-19
    Reasons for. Sixfold. 7:1
    Sins of. Discussed. 7:1-6
    Why one should not **j**. 7:1
        Makes one unworthy of the gospel. 7:1-6; 7:6
        Often inaccurate. 19:30
        Usurps God's authority. Makes one as a god. 7:1

JUDGING - RULING
    Meaning. 19:28

JUDGMENT
    Basis of - why God **j**.
        Failure to minister. 25:41-45
        Man's words. 12:31-37
        Ministering, serving, helping. 25:31-46
        Slothfulness. 25:24-30
        Three factors. 11:20-24
    Degrees of. Reason. 11:20-24
    Deliverance from. Hope for **d**. A day of victory is coming. 12:20
    Described. 22:11-14
        As appointed time for receiving wages. 20:8-15
        Cast out. 5:13
        Day of accounting. 18:28; 18:30; 18:32-34
        Day of reckoning, accountability. 25:19
        Deserted, desolated, blinded. 23:38-39
        Final **j**. Of nations, of sheep & goats. 25:31-46
        Gnashing. 8:12
        God's great confrontation with man. 22:11-14
        Hell. 5:22
        Judicial blindness. 13:13-15
        Messianic fire of **j**. 1:1; 3:11; 11:1-6; 11:2-3; 11:6; 11:4-6
        Separated & cast into everlasting fire, punishment. 25:41, 25:46
        Stripping & separation. 25:24-30
        Weeping. 8:12
    How God **j**. In justice. Straightens things out. 19:30
    Of believers.
        Cast out. 5:13
        False profession. Threefold. 7:21; 13:30
        Reason. 5:13
    Of unbelievers. Professions only. Threefold. 7:21
    Surety.
        To be straightened out. 19:30
        Will vindicate, reveal truth someday. 10:26
    When will God **j**. At the Lord's return. A separation. 25:1-13
    Who is to be **j**.
        False professors. Threefold. 7:21
        Foolish. Door shut to **f**. 25:10-12
        Jews. Described. Deserted, blinded. 23:38-39
        Last. To be first & first to be last. 19:30
        Nations. Meaning. 25:31-46; 25:32
        Some in kingdom. Who they are. 13:41
        This generation. Ninevah to testify against. 12:41
        Two men doomed. 21:44
        Unprepared & evil. 24:51
        World. In end time. 24:15-28; 24:25-28

JUDICIAL BLINDNESS
    Discussed. 13:13-15

JUSTICE (See **RIGHTEOUSNESS**)
    Hope of. Day of victory coming. 12:20
    Meaning. 12:18
    Surety. To be straightened out. 19:30
    Weakness of. Lacks love, compassion, & mercy. 18:28; 18:30

KINGDOM OF GOD
    Stages of. 19:23-24
    What it takes to enter. 21:28-32

KINGDOM OF HEAVEN (See **ETERNAL LIFE; HEAVEN**)
    Attitudes toward. Six **a**. 5:1-2
    Concept of. Discussed. 18:1
    Discussed.
        As a priceless treasure. 13:44
        As fisherman's net. 13:47
        As leaven. Cp. evil. 13:33
    Growth. Greatness of. 13:31-32
    Inherited. Now & eternally. 5:3
    Judgment within. Who are to be judged. 13:41
    Meaning. 19:23-24
    Message of.
        Proclaimed by Jesus. 4:17
        Proclaimed by John. 3:2-6
    Mysteries of. Discussed. 13:1-58
    Nature.
        Comes violently. Meaning. 11:12
        Greatness of believers in. 11:11
        Misunderstood. By disciples. 18:1
        Mixture of good & bad, presently. 13:1-58; 13:1-9; 13:24-30; 13:31-32; 13:33; 13:47-50
        Surpasses world in two ways. 4:23
    Position in. Least in. Greater than John the Baptist. 11:11
    Value of.
        Giving up all for Christ. 13:44
        Parable of Hidden Treasure. 13:44

KNOW - KNOWING - KNOWLEDGE
    Christ. Must **k**. about Christ before one can seek. 18:1

LABOR - LABORERS (See **BELIEVERS; DISCIPLES; MINISTERS**)
    Demanded by God. Imperative! Today! 21:28
    Discussed. 20:1-16
    Duty.
        To care for the world & the church. 21:33
        To pray for. 9:37-38
        To watch & work for judgment is coming. 25:14-30
    Enforced. Discussed. 5:41
    Failure in. Believer can know four things. 6:33
    Kinds of. Six kinds. 20:3-4
    Need for. Discussed. 9:37-38
    Why there are not more **l**. 9:37-38
    Work for all to do. 20:1

LAMB
    Sacrificial. Type of Christ. 26:17-30

LAMP
    Described. 25:7

LAW (See **SCRIBAL LAW; COMMANDMENT**)
    Breaking.
        Criteria for **b**. 12:3-4
        Teaching others. 5:19
        Voiding. 5:19
    Defined. Greatest **l**. Is **l**. of love. 22:34-40
    Discussed. 5:17-20
    Duty.
        To be controlled by love. 22:40
        To obey. Seriousness of. 5:19
    Fulfilled by Christ. 5:17; 5:17-48; 5:17-20
    Importance. To Scribes & Pharisees. 5:17-18
    Jews view of. Fourfold. 5:17
    Principles. Discussed. 5:17-48
    Scribal. (See **SCRIBAL LAW**)
    Vs. Christ. Before Christ vs. after Christ. 5:17-18
    Vs. love & forgiveness. 5:17-20
    Weakness & powerlessness of. Lacks love, compassion, & mercy. 18:28; 18:30
    Weightier vs. lighter matters. 22:34-36; 23:23-24

LAWYER
    Described. 22:35
    Questioned Christ. About great law. Heart touched. 22:34-40

LAZY
    Law of. 13:12; 13:13-15
    Reward. Receive less & less. 13:12; 13:13-15

INDEX

LEAVEN
Meaning. 13:33
Power of. What it does. Transforming p. of gospel. 13:33

LEADING ASTRAY
Warning against. 18:5-10

LEARN OF ME
Meaning. 11:29

LEGALISM - LEGALIST
Described. As heavy burdens. Laid upon men. 23:4
Strict vs. loose. 5:17-18
Error - Problem with. Lacks love, compassion, mercy. 18:28; 18:30

LENDING
Discussed. 5:42

LEPER - LEPROSY
Discussed. 8:1-4
Healed by Jesus. One l. 8:1-4
Legal requirements for a healed l. 8:1-4; 8:4
Type of sin. 8:1-4

LICENSE
God does not give l. 6:14-15
God does not pamper l. 6:25-34

LIFE
Attitude about.
 Living one day at a time. 6:34
 Right vs. wrong. 6:25-34
Concepts of. What men call life. 10:39
Described.
 As narrow gate. 7:13-14
 As two gates, roads. Five d. 7:13-14
 As wise & foolish builder. 7:24-27
 Two choices in l. 7:13-14
Discussed. More than things. 6:25
Essential - Duty.
 Losing vs. gaining l. 10:39; 16:25-28
 Not to worry about. 6:25
 To build wisely, not foolishly. 7:24-27
 To deny self. 10:39
 To love l. in order to gain l. 10:39
Foundation of - Privileges of. Wise vs. foolish. 7:24-27
Golden rule of. 7:12
How to secure. Building l. 7:24-27
Invitation to. 11:28-30
Kinds of. Wise vs. foolish. 7:24-27
Meaning. 10:39
Mystery to man. 1:23
Nature. Existing forever in some state. 19:16
New. (See **NEW LIFE**)
Picture of a ruined l. Judas. 26:6-13; 26:14-16
Righteousness of. 7:12
Storms of. Calmed by Christ. 7:24-25; 7:26-27

LIGHT
Discussed. 5:14
Essential - Duty. To shine for God. 5:14-16
Symbolized. As believers. 5:14-16
What l. does. 5:14

LONG-SUFFERING (See **GOD**, Long-suffering)

LORD'S SUPPER
Discussed. 26:17-30
Symbolized. In Passover. 26:17-30; 26:17-19
Words, "Take, eat...drink." Meaning. 26:26; 26:27-28

LOST, THE
Described. Sheep without shepherd. 9:36
Reasons. 18:12
State of.
 Being found is not assured. 18:13
 Blind. 9:27-31
Why men are lost. 19:22

LOVE (See **BROTHERHOOD**)
Described.
 Love is not doing religious things, but people. 22:39
 Love is not inactive, but active. 22:39
Discussed. 5:44; 22:37-40
 Greek words for l. Four words. 5:44
 Picture of sacrificial l. & faith. 26:6-13
 What l. involves. 22:37-38
Essential - Duty.
 Chief d. To love God first. 22:37-38
 To love Christ before family. 10:35-37
 To love enemies. 5:44
 To love neighbor second. 22:39
 To love self. 22:39
Example. Of mother's great love for child. 15:22
Importance of. Embraces all commandments. 22:40
Kinds. Four k. 5:44
Of self. Legitimate. Are to love self. How. 22:39
Study of. 22:34-40
Views of l. In Old Testament. 5:43
Why l.
 Is Jesus' commandment. 22:34-40
 Is the greatest commandment. 22:37-39

LOYALTY
Essential. To follow Christ. 8:21-22

LUST
Caused by.
 Dancing & passion. 14:6-8
 Foolish behavior & promises. 14:6-8
Concept of. Viewed as acceptable & natural. 5:27-30
Enslaves.
 Craves more & more. 24:37-39
 Example. Judas' greed. 26:15
 Grows & grows. 5:27-30; 26:15
 Immoral looking, dressing. 5:27-30
Prevention - cure. Discussed. 5:28; 5:30
Vs. need. 12:3-4

MAN (See **JUDGMENT; LUST; SIN;** Related Subjects)
Concept of God. (See **GOD**, Concepts of)
Decision. (See **DECISION**)
 Chooses between two lives. 7:13-14
Depravity.
 Debt of sin is huge. 18:24
 Exposed by words. 12:34-35
 Reasons. Fourfold. 8:28-31
 Shown by cursing. 5:33-37
 What defiles a m. 15:1-20

Described.
 As childish: contrary, playful, mindless. 11:16-18
 As sheep without a shepherd. 9:36
 As wise & foolish. 25:1-4
 Evil generation. Answer to. 12:38-45
Duty - Behavior. To be wise as serpents; harmless as doves. 10:16
Errors of - Misconceptions of.
 Allows division within & without. 10:34-36
 Blinds self to Messiah. 11:25-27
 Creates gods, mental gods. 13:57
 Idle. Slothful. 20:3
 Inconsistent. 11:16-19; 11:19
 Loose vs. strict. 11:16-19; 11:19
 Misconceptions of.
  Christ is just a man. 19:17
  Man is good & can achieve goodness. 19:17
  Of eternal life. 19:17
  Self-righteousness. 19:17
 Seeks recognition. How. Failure of. 6:5
 Setting priorities. Basic priorities. 6:25
 Shrinks Christ to mere man. 13:57
 Wrapped up in this world. Reasons. 6:31-32
Free will. (See **FREE WILL**)
Natural m. Cannot save self. 16:17
Nature.
 Adversary to God. 16:21-23
 Esteem. Fails. Several ways. 6:5
 Fickle & forgetful. 11:7-15
 Fierce, wild, mean. Reasons. 8:28-31
 Some like wolves. 10:16
 Stature. Cannot be changed. 6:27
 Tastes are different from God's taste. Natural vs. spiritual. 16:21-23
 Three things. 5:3
Needs of. (See **NEEDS**)
Reformation. (See **REFORMATION**)
Response to Christ.
 Betrays Christ. How men b. 26:16
 Disturbed. Reasons. 2:3
 Evil. Some men extremely evil. 2:13-18
 Fourfold. 13:4-7
 Offended by Christ. Reasons. 26:31-32
 Oppose Christ. How men oppose Christ. 26:16
 Rebels. Wants to rule own life & world. 21:34-35
 Rejects.
  God's great invitation. 22:1-14
  Reasons. Threefold. 23:37
Seeking after Jesus. (See **SEEK - SEEKING**)
State of - Present. (See **MAN**, Depravity; Nature; Origin)
 Fainting; scattered; no shepherd. 9:36
 Fivefold s. 4:16
 Lost. (See **LOST, THE**)
 Often rejected because of condition. 9:20-22
 Spiritual blindness. 16:1-4
 Wandering in wilderness. 18:11
 Weighed down by. Several things. 9:36
Value - worth.
 More important than animals. 12:11
 More important than birds. Three reasons. 6:26
 More important than religion. 12:9-13

317

INDEX

More valuable than sparrows. 10:29-31
Sacred to God. 12:13
Vs. religion. 12:1-8; 12:9-13; 12:10
Will. (See **FREE WILL; WILL**)

MARK, JOHN
Disciple of Peter. Records Peter's denial. 26:69-75

MARRIAGE - MARRIED
Attitudes toward. Loose attitudes. 5:32
Basis. Only one **b**. 5:32
Ceremony. Jewish. 25:1-13
Discussed. 19:1-12
Duty - Essentials. Discussed. 19:11
Ideal. Highest ideal. Concentration upon God. 19:12
Jewish. Steps involved. Three. 1:18
Kinds of. Fourfold. 5:32
Ordained. By God. 19:5-6; 19:5
Sanctity of. 19:1-12
Special power is needed. 19:10-11; 19:11
Union of. Weakened & broken by adultery. 5:32

MARRIAGE SUPPER OF THE LAMB
Marriage of the Lamb. 25:1-13
Parable of. Rejection of God's great invitation. 22:1-14

MARTHA
Home opened to Jesus. 21:17
Sister of Mary. Discussed. 26:6-13

MARTYR - MARTYRDOM
In the end time. 24:9

MARY MAGDALENE
Witnessed the cross, burial, & resurrection of Christ. 27:55-56; 27:61; 28:1

MARY, SISTER OF MARTHA
Anointed Jesus. Sacrificed love & faith. 26:6-13
Discussed. 26:6-13

MASTER
Kinds of **m**. God & world. 6:24
Meaning. 8:19

MATERIALISM
Answer to. Self-denial, discipline. 11:8
Dangers of. 19:23-26
Denial of. Essential to follow Christ. 8:19-20
Described.
  As a master. 6:24
  As evil. Reasons. 6:21-23
  As necessary & niceties or extravagant. 6:25
Discussed. 6:19-24
Duty.
  Not to be wrapped up in. 6:31-32
  To set mind on God, not on materialism. 6:19-24
Error of. Four **e**. 6:26
Meaning. 6:19-20
Problems with - Dangers of.
  Are evil. Reasons. 6:21-23
  Are insecure. 6:19-20
  Passes away. 6:25-34
Results.
  Can enslave. 6:25
  Loss of life. Meaning, purpose. 6:19-20
Vs. God. 6:19-24
Warning against. 6:19-24

MATTHEW
Conversion. Discussed. 9:9-13; 9:9
Humility. Discussed. 10:3-4

MATURITY (See **SPIRITUAL GROWTH**)

MEANING (See **PURPOSE**)

MEDITATE - MEDITATION
Essential. 3:1
  For preparation & temptation. 4:1

MEEK - MEEKNESS
Meaning. 5:5
Reward. Three **r**. 5:5

MERCHANT MAN
Parable of. 13:45-46

MERCY - MERCIFUL (See **GOD**, Mercy)
Cry for. Saves the desperate. 20:30-32
Described. As supreme law. 12:7
God desires **m**, not sacrifice. Discussed. 12:7
Meaning. 5:7
Of Christ. Purpose. To have **m**., not sacrifice. 9:12-13
Of God. Symbolized. 1:3-6
Parable of. Unmerciful servant. 18:21-35
Results. Seven **r**. 5:7
Women (four) who received **m**. 1:3

MESSAGE (See **PREACHING**)
Content. Summary of Jesus' **m**. 4:17

MESSIAH - MESSIAHSHIP
Belief in. Essential for salvation. 21:32
Blind to. World is. 11:25-27
Claimed. By Jesus. Confronting death. 26:63-64
Concept of. 1:18
  Jewish **c**. 1:1
Deity. Lord of man. 22:43-45
Demonstrated. Triumphal Entry. 21:1-11
Described. 22:42; 22:41-46
Discussed. 1:1; 1:18; 11:1-6; 22:41-46
False concept - Misunderstood.
  Human, earthly deliverer. 22:42
  Position & power. 18:1; 21:8-9
  Questioned by John the Baptist. 11:1-6
  Son of David, a mere man. 22:42
Greater than religion. 12:1-8
Names - Titles.
  Prophet, The. 21:11
  Son of Abraham. 1:1
  Son of David. 1:1; 1:18; 3:11; 11:1-6; 15:22; 22:42
Origin. 22:42
Proclaimed.
  By children. 21:15-16
  By John. 3:2-6, 11-12
  By people at the Triumphal Entry. 21:8-11
Proof. (See **JESUS CHRIST**, Heals; Power; Works; Related Subjects)
  Four logical arguments. 12:22-30
  Work of. Discussed. 11:4-6
Search for. People pant for. 1:18

MESSIAH, FALSE
Sign of end time. 24:23-24

MILLENNIUM
Description. New order of things. 19:28

MIND
Fact. Set on earth or God. 6:19-24
Meaning. 22:37

MINDLESS
Message to. 11:16-19

MINISTER (See **BELIEVERS; DISCIPLES; MINISTRY**)
Call - called.
  Accepted vs. rejected. 21:28-32
  Commitment & commissioning **c**. 10:1-4
  Discussed. 10:1-4
  Kind of person **c**. 4:18-22
  Many are called, but few are chosen. 22:14
  Three different **c**. 10:1-4; 10:1
  To a different profession. 4:18-20; 4:21-22
  To fish for men. 4:18-20; 4:21-22
Commission - Mission.
  Discussed. 10:5-15; 28:16-20
  Onefold: People. 4:15-16
  Threefold. 4:15-16
  To heal the bruised, not to condemn. 12:20
  To leave & forsake all, including employment. 4:21-22
  To light the world. 5:14-16
  To minister & to serve. 20:23-28
  To preach. 4:17
  To salt the earth. 5:13
  To seek & save the lost. 18:11-14
Duty - Work.
  Activities of. 4:23
  Demanding, busy. 4:23
  Failure in. 6:2
  Faithful vs. unfaithful. 24:42-51; 25:14-30
  Not to compete with others. 4:12
  Not to neglect the world. Not to be cloistered in the church. 5:13
  To families. Jesus' purpose. 8:14-17
  To have a realistic view of the world. 6:3-4
  To meet hopeless & desperate needs. 9:18-34
  To open the door of salvation. 16:19
  To step aside for others. 4:12
  To the multitude. Jesus' purpose. 8:16-17
  To watch & work for judgment is coming. 25:14-30
  When to begin. 4:12
Equipped - Resources.
  Discussed. 12:18
  Power. 4:24
False. (See **TEACHERS, FALSE**)
Ideal. Christ, Chosen Servant of God. 12:14-21
Message. Discussed. 10:27
Motive.
  Discussed. 6:1-4
  Wrong vs. right. 6:1-4
Place.
  Where to minister. 4:23
  Where to serve strategically. 4:12-13
Preparation. Sermon on Mount given for **p**. 5:1-2
Successful. Discussed. 4:23-25
Support of. Financial. Discussed. 10:9-10

INDEX

Traits. Essential. 4:18-20; 4:21-22
Treatment. Persecuted. Rejected by world. (See **PERSECUTION**) 21:34-35
Work. (See **MINISTERS**, Duty)

MINISTRY - MINISTERING (See **BE-LIEVERS; DISCIPLES; MINISTERS**)
Basis. To be instinctive - from within. 25:37
Call.
  God entrusts world to man. 21:33
  Lay and professional witness. 10:5
Discussed. 11:4-6; 21:28-32
  Rules governing. 10:5-15
Duty - Work.
  Activities of. 4:23
  Demanded. Imperative! Today! 21:28-32
  Demanding, busy. 4:23
  Excuses for not m. 15:33-34
  How to minister. Two ways. 6:3
  Is same as m. to Christ Himself. 25:40-42
  Learning how to minister. 15:29-39
  More important than religion. 12:1-8; 12:9-13
  To be done to the Lord **personally**. 26:10-11
  To give. Great ethic of believer. 5:42
  To grasp opportunity while one can. 26:10-11
  To meet hopeless & desperate needs. 9:18-34
  To open the door to heaven by preaching. 16:19
  Two areas. Preaching & ministering. 10:7
Equipped - Resources. 14:15-21
  Christ uses one's r. 14:18-21
  Fivefold. 15:29-39
  Power. By prayer & fasting. 17:20-21
  Power. To heal. 4:24
  Prayer & fasting. 17:20-21
Meaning. 25:34-40
Methods.
  Discussed. 10:5-15
  Two by two. 10:3-4
Place.
  Earth. 5:13; 5:14; 5:14-15
  Where to minister. 4:23
  Where to serve strategically. 4:12-13
Reward. Discussed. 25:40-42
Training. Precedes service. 10:1

MINT
Described. 23:23

MIRACLES
Power to heal. 4:24
Purpose. Major p. 10:1

MISSION
Duty.
  To light the world. 5:14-18
  To preach. 4:17
  To reach people. 4:15-16
  To salt the earth. 5:13

MOCKERY (See **JESUS CHRIST**, Response; Rejected)
Of Christ. At crucifixion. 27:26-44

MONEY
Love of. Discussed. 26:15

MONEYCHANGERS
Cast out of the Temple. 21:12-16

MOSES
Appeared with Jesus at Transfiguration. Reason. 17:3

MOTIVE
For giving & doing good. 6:1-4
For prayer. Discussed. 6:5-6
For works. 6:1-4
Pure m. vs. impure. 5:8
Wrong m. vs. right m. 6:1-4; 6:5-6

MOUNTAINS
Power to remove m. Meaning. 17:20
Symbolized. Difficulties. Discussed. 17:20

MOURN
Meaning. 5:4

MULTITUDE
Why m. followed Christ. 20:29

MURDER
Meaning. 5:21-26; 5:21-22

MUSTARD SEED
Described. 17:20
Discussed. 13:31-32
Parable of. Greatness of Christianity. 13:31-32

MYSTERY
Meaning. 13:1-58

NARROW GATE
Vs. wide gate. 7:13-14

NATURAL SENSES
Vs. spiritual senses. 16:2-3

NATURE
Power over. Christ's p. over. (See **JESUS CHRIST**, Power)

NAZARETH
Discussed. Hometown of Jesus. 2:23
Rejected Christ. Reasons. 13:53-58

NEEDLE
Camel's passing through. 19:24

NEEDS - NECESSITIES
Attitude toward. 6:25-34
Met - Provided.
  By Jesus Christ. Jesus' purpose & power to meet. 8:14-17
  By necessary work. Discussed. 12:5
  Each n. a foretaste of cross. 8:16
  How to meet. Persevering prayer. 7:7-11
Of life.
  Discussed. 6:25-34
  God provides for. 6:25-34
  Meaning. 6:11
Of men.
  Great n. 4:23
  How desperate can be saved. 9:18-34; 20:29-34
  Needs have precedence over tradition & ritual. 12:3-4; 12:9-13
  Steps to meeting n. 15:29-39
  What it takes to have n. met. 15:21-28
Temptation. To secure n. illegally. 4:2-4
Vs. lust. 12:3-4

NEIGHBOR (See **LOVE**)
Law governing. Old Testament view. 5:43

NET
Parable of the fisherman's n. 13:47-50

NEUTRALITY
Fact. Is impossible to be n. 12:30; 12:33

NEW AGE (See **AGE**, New)
Ushered in by Christ. 9:14-17

NEW COVENANT
Described. As forgiveness. 26:26-30
Established. Ushered in by Christ. 9:14-17
Old vs. new. Described. 17:8

NEW CREATION
Discussed. 21:43

NEW LIFE
Ushered in by Christ. 9:14-17

NEW TESTAMENT
Believers. Difference between O.T. and N.T. believers. 11:11
Fulfills the O.T. 13:52

NINEVEH
Illustration. Of rejection. To condemn this generation. 12:41

NOAH
Illustrates. End of the world. Will be like N. day. 24:37-39

OATHS
Discussed. 5:33-37; 23:16-22
Law governing. 5:33-37
Misuse of. 23:16-22
Types. Fivefold. 5:33-37

OBEY - OBEDIENCE
Described. Wise & foolish builders. 7:24-27
Duty. To o. because God expects obedience. 2:13-18
Example. Joseph, father of Jesus. 1:24-25
Reward for. Made great in the Kingdom of Heaven. 5:19

OBJECTIONS
To ministering. 15:33-34

OBSTINATE (See **UNBELIEF**, Obstinate)

OFFEND - OFFENDING
Meaning. 5:29; 17:27
Steps to correcting. 18:15-20
Warning against. 18:5-10
Ways one offends others. 18:15

OIL
Symbol of the Holy Spirit & righteousness. 25:1-4

OLD TESTAMENT
Believers. Difference between O.T. and N.T. bel. 11:11
Duty. To be shared right along with the N.T. 13:52
Fulfilled by the N.T. 13:52

ONENESS (See **UNITY**)

INDEX

OPPORTUNITY
  Duty. Must grasp while there is still time. 26:10-11

ORAL LAW (See **SCRIBAL LAW**)

ORDINANCE
  Of the Lord's Supper. 26:17-30

OSTRACIZED
  Who was o.
    A woman with a hemorrhage. 9:20
    Tax collectors. 9:9-13

OUTCASTS
  Who was o. Gentiles. 15:30-31; 15:32

OUTER DARKNESS
  Meaning. 8:12; 25:30
  Unprofitable cast into. 25:30

OVER-CONFIDENCE
  Discussed. 26:33-34

OXEN
  Yoke of. Meaning. 11:29

PAMPER
  God does not p. 6:25-23

PARABLE
  Listed.
    Bridegroom. A new life & a new age. 9:15
    Dragnet. Separating the bad from the good. 13:47-50
    Evil servant. 24:48-51
    Faithful & wise servant. 24:45-47
    Goodman of house. 24:43-44
    Hidden Treasure. Giving up all for Christ. 13:44
    Householder. Devotion, study, sharing. 13:51-52
    Laborers in the Vineyard. God's grace. 20:1-16
    Leaven. Transforming power of gospel. 13:33
    Light of the world. Shining for God. 5:14-16
    Lost Sheep. Supreme example of caring. 18:11-14
    Marriage Feast. Rejection of God's invitation. 22:1-14
    Merchant Man. 13:45-46
    Mustard Seed. Growth of Christianity. 13:31-32
    New and old cloth. New vs. old life. 9:16
    New wine and old bottles. New vs. old life. 9:17
    Pearl of Great Price. Giving up all. 13:45-46
    Salt. Serving God. 5:13
    Sheep and goats. Final judgment of nations. 25:31-46
    Sower. How wise men receive the gospel. 13:1-9
    Talents. Work for judgment is coming. 25:14-30
    Ten virgins. Watch for the Lord's return. 25:1-13
    Two sons. What it takes to enter heaven. 21:34-35
    Unmerciful Servant. Spirit of forgiveness. 18:21-35
    Wheat & Tares. The question of evil. 13:24-30; 13:36-43
    Wicked Husbandman. Israel's rejection of Christ. 21:33-46
    Wise and foolish builders. Life. 7:24-27
  Reasons for. Speaking in p. 13:10-17; 13:34-35

PARADISE, EARTHLY
  Inadequate. 14:34

PARALYZED MAN
  Healed by Jesus. Forgiving sin. 9:1-8

PARENTS
  Discussed. 19:13-15
  Duty of. Influence on children. 2:19-23
  Duty toward. Care for. Example. 8:8
  Why p. do not bring children to Christ. 19:13

PARTIALITY (See **FAVORITISM**)

PARTYING
  Described. As drinking & carousing. 24:38
  Results. 14:6-8

PASSIONS
  Indulgence of. God does not indulge passions. 6:14-15

PASSOVER
  Atmosphere at P. 26:5
  Basis for the Lord's Supper. 26:17-30; 26:17-19
  Discussed. 26:17-30
  Symbolized - Pictured. Death of Christ. 26:2

PEACE
  Answer to. Christ. 6:15
  Source. Prayer, agonizing prayer. 26:45

PEACEMAKERS
  Meaning. 5:9
  Vs. Troublemakers. 5:9

PEARL
  Parable of great price. 13:45-46

PEOPLE (See **MAN**)

PERFECT - PERFECTION
  Discussed. 6:5-6

PERSECUTION - PERSECUTORS
  By whom.
    Family. Reasons. 10:21
    Three groups. 10:17-18
    World. 21:34-35
  Described. Doing evil against. 6:12
  Duty.
    To endure. 10:22
    To flee. 10:23
  Fear of.
    Causes several things. 10:28
    Reasons for not f. 10:28
  How to overcome in p.
    What to fear and not fear. 10:24-33
    Worry not. Reasons. 10:19-20
  Judgment of. Great. Discussed. 10:26-27; 23:34-36
  Kinds. 5:10-12
  Meaning. 5:10-12; 7:7
  Methods of. Various m. 10:24-33
  Privilege of. Discussed. 10:24-25
  Purpose of. Discussed. 10:16
  Response to.
    Encouragement not to fear. 10:24-33
    Fear not. Three reasons. 10:24-33; 10:28
    Four things believers must do. 6:12
  Results.
    Reveals evil nature of the world. 5:10-12
    Share in the sufferings of Christ. 10:24-25
  Warning of. 10:16-23
  Who is to be p.
    God's messengers. 21:34-35
    Prophets. Present day p. 23:34-36
  Why believers are p. Four reasons. 5:10-12

PERSEVERANCE - PERSISTENCE (See **ENDURANCE; STEDFASTNESS**)
  Duty to p. In prayer. Meaning. 7:7
  Example of. Two blind men. The cry for sight. 9:27-31
  Meaning. 7:7
  Results.
    Healing & sins forgiven. 9:1-8
    Saves the desperate. 9:29-34; 20:29-34

PERVERSE
  Meaning. 17:17
  Generations of men are p. 11:16-19

PETER, SIMON, THE APOSTLE
  Commitment. Carnal. 26:51-52; 26:58
  Death of. Dies with wife. 8:14
  Denial of Christ.
    A look at d. Jesus. 26:69-75
    Foretold. Falling away. 26:31-35
  Discussed. 8:14
  Family life of. 8:14
  Great confession of. Jesus is Messiah. 16:13-20

PHARISEES (See **RELIGIONISTS**)
  Accusations against. Nine a. 23:13-36
  Belief - teaching.
    Teaching was false. 16:1-12
    Tradition. 15:1-9
  Charges against. Discussed. 23:13-36
  Discussed. 12:10
  Error - fault of.
    Put tradition before God's commandment. 15:1-9
    Separated selves from sinners. 9:10-11
    Spiritual blindness. 15:12-14
    Teaching was false. (See Belief - Teaching) 16:1-12
    Worship was empty & hypocritical. 15:7-9
  Vs. Jesus. Opposed Jesus. (See **RELIGIONISTS**, Opposed Christ)
  Some did accept Christ. 23:13-36

PHYLACTERIES
  Described. 23:5

PILATE
  Discussed. 27:11-25

PLAN - PLANNING
  Of ministry. Discussed. 10:5-15; 10:12-15

INDEX

POLLUTION
What defiles a man. 15:1-20

POOR - POVERTY (See **NEED - NECESSITIES**)
Essential. To follow Christ. 8:19-20
Facts.
    Jesus was **p**. 2:19-23
    Not a disgrace. 2:19-23
Special objects of the Messiah's ministry. 11:4-6

POOR IN SPIRIT
Meaning. 5:3

POSITION
Seeking.
    Discussed. 18:1-4
    Love of position is wrong. 23:5

POSSESSIONS (See **MATERIALISM; WEALTH; WORLDLINESS**)
Surrendered. Essential to meet the world's needs. 14:18-21

POWER - POWERFUL (See **JESUS CHRIST**, Power)
Facts about. Fourfold. 14:5
Lack of - Problems. Tempted to seek. 4:3
Of faith. Great power of **f**. 17:14-21
Purpose.
    Discussed. 11:4-6; 21:17-22
    To carry the gospel to the whole world. 28:18-20
    To control fear & nature. 8:23-27
    To direct **p**. against evil. Threefold. 10:1
    To equip & give assurance. 10:1
    To exercise **p**. over the whole man. 4:24
    To heal. 4:24
    To receive & reject men. 8:5-13
    To remove mountains. Meaning. 17:20
    Twofold. 10:8
Source. A given power. 10:8

POWERLESSNESS
Caused by. Unbelief. 17:14-21; 17:19-20
Discussed. 17:14-21
Results. Discussed. 17:15-16
Warning against. Christ warns. 17:17-18

PRAY - PRAYER - PRAYING
Answers - Answered.
    Assured. 7:7-11
    Clearly seen. 6:6
    Two ways. 7:8
Discussed. 6:5-6; 6:7-8
Duty. Commanded. Several verses. 6:5-6
Essentials.
    Forgiveness. 6:14-15
    For personal preparation. 14:22-33
    Three **e**. 6:6
    What it takes to receive things of God. 15:21-28
For what. Discussed. 6:9-13
For laborers. 9:37-38
Hindrances to.
    Empty repetition. 6:7-8
    Failure to **p**. 26:40-41
    Hypocritical **p**. 6:5
    Long **p**. 6:7
    Today's problem twofold. 6:7
    Unforgiving spirit. 6:14-15
    Wrong motive. 6:5-6
How to pray.
    Agreeing. Discussed. 18:19
    Approach God as our Father. 7:11
    Basic principle of. Forgiveness. 6:14-15
    Discussed. 6:9-13
    In secret, in one's closet. 6:6
    Three great rules. 6:7-8
    Persevering. 7:8-11
Kinds. Chance **p**. vs. persistent **p**.. 15:23-24
Meaning. Talking & sharing with God. 6:5-6
Model **p**. of Jesus. 6:9-13
Perseverance in.
    Meaning. 7:7
    Saves the desperate. 20:21-34; 20:31-32
Purpose.
    To have one's needs met. 6:8
    To minister. 17:14
Results - Assurance.
    Peace & release. 26:45
    Power—great power for ministry. 17:20; 21:21-22
When to **p**. At meals. Listed. 14:19
Where to **p**. - Places.
    Churches & streets. 6:5
    Discussed. 6:5-6
    Mountain top. 14:22-33
    Public. 6:5
    Temple. 21:12-16

PREACH - PREACHING
Described. As sowing seed. 13:3
Errors of. Mentioned. 9:35
How men receive the gospel. 13:1-9
Meaning. 9:35
Mission.
    Of believers. 4:17
    Of Christ. 4:17; 11:4-6
Responses to. Discussed. 13:1-9

PREJUDICE (See **BARRIERS**)
Broken down - Abolished. By Christ's ministry. 15:21-28; 15:29; 15:30-31
Discussed. Receiving & rejecting men. 8:5-9
Jew vs. Gentile. Example. 15:23-28

PREPARATION
Discussed. 10:1
Essential. Before service. 10:1
Personal **p**. Power of Lords' presence. 14:22-33

PRESENCE (See **INDWELLING PRESENCE**)

PRESSURE
Discussed. 11:28-30

PRETEND - PRETENDING - PRETENSION (See **PROFESSION ONLY**)
Denial of **p**. Do not know Christ. 26:69-70

PRIDE (See **BOASTING; SELF-IMPORTANCE**)
Caused by.
    Roots. Heritage. 23:29-33
    Spiritual superiority. "But for the grace of God, there go I." 8:4
    Wealth. Creates "big I." 19:23
Overcome by. Serving others. 20:26-28
Warning against. Religious **p**. 23:1-12
Vs. humility. 18:1-4

PRIESTLY OFFICE (Of Christ; See **JESUS CHRIST**, Priestly Office)

PRIVILEGE
Degrees of. Determines judgment. 11:20-24

PROBLEMS (See **TRIALS**)
Answer to. Faith. 17:20

PROCURATOR
Discussed. 27:11-25

PROFANITY (See **CURSING**)

PROFESSION, FALSE - PROFESSION ONLY
Danger of religionists. 3:7-10
Described as.
    Big "I." 7:21
    Birds lodging in Christianity. 13:31-33
    By the wayside. 13:4
    Rocky soil. 13:5-6, 20-21
    Tares. Unregenerate. 13:31-32
    Thorns. 13:7, 22
    Wayside, hard soil. 13:4, 19
Discussed. 7:21-23
    Dramatic conversion, but false. 13:5-6, 20-21
    Four **f**. professions. 16:13-14
    Two kinds of people. 7:21-23
Evidence of. Inadequate. 9:4-7
Identified.
    As false religion. 21:28-32
    As tares - growing with wheat. 13:24-30
Judgment of.
    Discussed. 7:23
    Intellectual pride. 11:25-27
    Threefold plea in the day of judgment. 7:22
Meaning. 7:21
Misconceptions of false **p**.
    Error. Does not do God's will. 7:21
    Fails to see Christ. 7:21
    Self-righteousness vs. Christ's righteousness. 7:22
    Spectator is enough. 3:7-10
Results in.
    Being denounced. 21:28-32
    False religion. 21:28-32
    Honoring self. 7:21
    Hypocrisy. 23:25-28
    Misjudging. 11:16-19
Vs. action. 9:4-7
What it takes to enter God's kingdom. 21:28-32

PROOF - PROOFS
Discussed. 4:3-11

PROPERTY
Damage to. Discussed. 5:39-41

PROPHECY
Fulfilled by Christ.
    Deliberately **f**. Triumphal Entry. 21:1-11; 21:2-5
    F. in Jesus' childhood. 2:15
    F. in Jesus' ministry. 11:5
Elements of. 1:22

PROPHET
Discussed. 11:9
Meaning. 11:9

INDEX

PROPHETIC OFFICE (See **JESUS CHRIST**, Prophetic Office)
Transferred to Christ. 17:3

PROPHETS, FALSE (See **FALSE TEACHERS**)

PROSELYTE
To Judaism. Discussed. 23:15

PUBLICITY
Reasons for not seeking. Christ's reasons. 12:16

PURE - PURITY
Meaning. 5:8
Perfect p. impossible. 5:8
Source. Heart. 23:25-26

PURPOSE
Earthly p. vs. spiritual p. 6:19-20
God's. Blind to. 11:25-27
Of believer.
  To do good works & to glorify God. 5:14-16
  To glorify God. 6:9
  To heal the bruised, not condemn. 12:20
  To light the world. 5:14-16
Unknown. By many. 4:12-17

QUEEN OF THE SOUTH
Example. Of great wisdom. 12:42

QUESTION - QUESTIONING
A q. disciple. Assurances given. 11:1-6
Answer to. Discussed. 11:7
Discussed. Questioning, yet still believing. 11:2-3

QUIET TIME (See **DEVOTIONS**)
Inconsistent. Reasons. 6:6

QUIETNESS
Essential. 3:1
  To conquer temptation. 4:1

RAHAB
Saved by God. 1:5

RANSOM
Meaning. 20:28

RATIONALISM
Arguments that corrupt. 23:13-36

REBELLION
Against the Lordship of Christ. 12:14-16

RECKON
Meaning. 18:24

RECOGNITION
Discussed. 6:1-4
Human. Fails. Ways f. 6:5

RECONCILIATION
Reasons for. 5:23-24
Steps to. Correcting divisiveness. 18:15-20

REDEEM - REDEMPTION
Meaning. 20:28

REFORMATION
Discussed. 12:43-45

REGENERATION (See **BORN AGAIN; NEW BIRTH**)
Meaning. 19:28
Vs. reformation. 12:43-45

REJECT - REJECTED - REJECTION (See **UNBELIEF**)
Answer to. 9:20-22
Call. Being r. vs. being accepted. 21:28-32
Care for the r. 9:20-22; 9:20
Jesus leaves - never returns. 9:1
Of Jesus Christ. (See **JESUS CHRIST**, Response to; Unbelief)
Of what.
  God's great invitation. Time & again. 22:1-14
  Gospel. Hardened to. 13:4, 19
  Men. Often r. because of condition. 9:20-22; 9:20
  Word. Various persons. 13:4-7
Results.
  Causes Christ to turn away. 9:1
  Judicial blindness & r. by God. 13:13-15
  Turns Spirit away. 12:14-16
Who r. Several described. 22:5-6
Why men reject. Many reasons. 19:22; 22:3-4

RELATIONSHIP (See **BROTHERHOOD**)

RELIGION (See **RITUAL**)
Conflict with Jesus. Reasons. 12:1-8; 12:9-13; 12:10
Jewish. (See **JUDAISM**)
Laws of. Jewish l. 12:1-8
Need.
  To know that Christ is greater than r. 12:1-8
  To know that man is greater than r. 12:9-13
  To know that mechanisms of r. are torn by Christ. 9:16-17; 9:16
  To know that need has precedence over. 12:5
Old vs. new religion. 9:16-17
Problem with.
  Accusation against. Nine a. 23:13-36
  Attachment to. Many. 9:16-17
  Deceives. 15:1-9
  Defiles. 15:1-9
  Discussed. 23:1-12
  Fourfold. 12:10
  Four terrible things. 27:1-5
  Humanistic. 13:33
  Imposed rules & regulations upon men. 23:4
  Inconsistent & deceptive. 27:6-10
  Misconceptions of man. R. is righteousness. 21:31
  Profession only. 21:28-32
  Put religion before man. 12:1-8; 12:9-13; 12:10
  Reformation. 12:43-45
  Rejects men because of their condition. 9:20-22
True r.
  Christ is greater than r. 12:1-8
  Inside, the inner side is stressed. 15:1-20
  Man is greater than r. 12:9-13
  Need supersedes r. 12:5
  Outside vs. inside stressed. 15:1-20
  Regeneration is stressed. 12:43-45
  Takes more than r. to enter heaven. 21:31; 21:32
Vs. Christ. 12:1-8; 12:9-13; 12:10
Vs. man. 12:1-8; 12:9-13; 12:10
Vs. regeneration. 12:43-45
Warning against. 23:1-12

RELIGIONISTS (See **PHARISEES; SCRIBES; SADDUCEES; HERODIANS; ELDERS**)
Accusations against. Nine a. 23:13-36
Beliefs of. Strong, steeped in. 12:10
Dangers confronting. 3:7-10
Described. "Vipers." Meaning. 3:7
Opposed Christ.
  Arrested Christ. Four pictures of commitment. 26:47-56
  Because they feared the loss of position, esteem, & livelihood. 12:1-8; 12:10; 16:12;21:23; 22:15-22; 22:23-33;22:34-40; 23:1-12
  Broke tradition. Scribal law. 12:1-8; 12:9-13; 12:10; 15:1-20;15:6-9; 16:1-12
  Discussed. 12:10; 16:21; 17:22
  Mocked Jesus upon the cross. 27:42-43
  Plotted the death of Jesus. 16:21; 26:3-5
  Response of Christ to r. opposition. 22:41-46; 23:13-36
Problem with.
  Change appearance, seek position, etc. 23:5
  Corrupted God's Word. 12:1-2
  Fourfold. 12:10
  Ignorant of Christ's coming. 2:3-6
  In the church, but not planted by God. 15:12-14
  Mistakes of. 5:20
  Not of God. 15:12-14
  Social r. Described. 6:14-15
  Some righteousness, but not enough for heaven. 5:20
  Strict vs. loose. 5:17-18
Teaching of. Errors of. 16:12
Vs. Jesus. (See Opposed Christ, above)

RELIGIOUS LIFE
Activities of. 7:21

REMISSION (See **FORGIVENESS**)
Discussed. 26:28

REMORSE
Illust. Judas. 27:3-5

REPENT - REPENTANCE (See **SALVATION**; Related Subjects)
Answer to denial. 26:75
Discussed. 4:17
Essential. What it takes to enter God's kingdom. 21:28-32
False.
  Of Judas. Wrong r. 27:1-5
  Verbal only. 3:7-10
  Wrong r. & human religion. Picture of. 27:1-10
Illustrated.
  By Nineveh. 12:41
  Finding a great treasure. 13:44
Message.
  Of Jesus Christ. 4:17
  Of John the Baptist. 3:2-6

INDEX

REPETITION
In prayer. Problem with. 6:7

RESIST NOT EVIL
Meaning. 5:38-42

RESISTANCE
Discussed. 5:38; 5:39-41; 5:42

RESOURCES
Duty. To surrender to Christ. 14:18-21

RESPONSIBILITY
Determines destiny - reward. 13:8; 25:19-30
Duty. To be r. for the world & the church. 21:33

REST, SPIRITUAL
Meaning. 11:28-30
Vs. pressure & burdens. 11:28-30

RESTITUTION
Made by Judas, but too late. 27:1-5

RESURRECTION
Denied. Scoffed at. Discussed. 22:23-33
Discussed. 22:23-33; 22:31-32
How the dead are raised. By a great summons. 24:29-31
Nature of. 22:30
Stages. Past. Some believers r. at Christ's death. 27:52
Surety of. Discussed. 22:31-32
Verses. List of. 22:31-32

RETALIATION - RESISTANCE
Discussed. 5:38; 5:39; 5:40; 5:41; 5:42

REVEALED - REVELATION
Is given. Only to true disciples. 13:10-17
The r. of the church. 16:13-20

REVENGE
Discussed. 5:38; 5:39-41; 5:42

REWARD (See SPIRITUAL INHERITANCE)
Degrees. 13:8; 20:23-28; 25:20-30
Described - identified as.
  Being filled. 5:6
  Children of God. 5:9
  Comfort. 5:4
  Great in the Kingdom of Heaven. 11:11
  Inheritance. 25:34
  Kingdom of Heaven. 5:3; 5:10-12
  Material & spiritual. 19:29
  Mercy. 5:7
  Presence of God & Christ. 10:40-42
  Receiving a hundredfold & eternal life. 19:27-30
  Reciprocal, equal. 10:40-42
  Recognition of men. 6:2
  Responsibility over many things. 25:20-23
  Ruler over God's property. 24:45-47
  Rulership & joy. 25:20-23
  Ruling & reigning. 19:28
  Sitting upon thrones. 19:27-28
  To see God. 5:8
  Three things. 5:3
  Wages paid. 20:8-16
Discussed. 19:27-30
For Apostles. To sit upon thrones. 19:27-28

How to secure - Basis.
  Accepting one's call & laboring. 20:1-7
  Based upon works. 16:27; 25:31-46
  By receiving ministers. 10:40-42
  God's grace. 20:1-7; 20:11-14
  Justice. God is just, not unjust, in r. 20:8-16; 20:11-14; 20:18
  Ministering & welcoming. 10:40-42
  Not works & energy. 20:11-14
  Seekers & achievers receive more & more. 13:10-11
  Use of gifts. 25:14-30
Results. Last shall be first; first shall be last. 20:16

RICH - RICHES
Compared to a camel. 19:24
Danger. Discussed. 19:23-26
Facts. Hoarding condemns. 19:21-22
Meaning. Who are the r. 19:23
Misconceptions. R. are a sign of God's blessings. 19:25
R. young ruler. 19:16-22
Saved - Salvation of. How a r. man can be saved. Discussed. 19:16-22
Some r. people who turned to Christ. Listed. 19:26

RICH YOUNG RULER
How a r. man enters heaven. 19:16-22

RIGHTEOUS - RIGHTEOUSNESS (See GODLY; JUSTICE)
Described.
  Golden rule. 7:12
  Summit of ethics. 7:12
Discussed. 5:6
Duty.
  Hunger and thirst for. 5:6
  To seek r. first. 6:33
Essential.
  To be clothed in. 22:11-14
  Wedding garment of r. essential. 22:11-14
Fulfilled in Jesus' baptism. 3:13
Need for.
  A religionist's r. is not enough to enter heaven. 5:20
  To be clothed in. 22:11-14
Self-r. Vs. another r. 5:3
Source of. Not inherited. 3:7-10

RITUAL (See RELIGION)

ROCK
Lord not a lifeless r., but a "living stone." 7:24-25
To build life upon. 7:24-27

ROOTS (See HERITAGE)
Honoring, relying upon. 23:29-33

RULES & REGULATIONS
Criteria to break. 12:3-4
Described as. Heavy burdens. 23:4
Placed upon men's shoulders. Four ways. 23:4

RUTH
Saved by God. 1:3

SABBATH - SUNDAY
Discussed. 12:1; 12:12
Laws governing.
  Broken by Christ. 12:1-8; 12:9-13

Jewish l. 12:1-8; 12:10
Not allowed to heal or help. 12:10
Meaning. 12:12
Messiah greater than Sabbath. 12:1-8
Purpose. Discussed. 12:5; 12:12
Working on S. Discussed. 12:5; 12:12

SACRIFICE
Duty.
  Mercy required, not s. Discussed. 12:7
  To s. all we are & have. 19:21-22; 19:23-26; 19:27-30
  To take precedence over common sense. 26:8-9
Vs. common sense. 26:8-9

SADDUCEES
Attacked - Opposed.
  Christ. 16:1-12; 22:23-33
  Cooperated with Pharisees. Discussed. 16:1-12; 22:34-40
  John the Baptist. 3:7-12
Belief about signs. 16:13-20
Liberal minded. Beliefs. 22:23-33; 22:23-28
Teaching. Errors of. 16:5-12

SALOME
Mother of James & John. 20:21

SALT
Discussed. 5:13

SALVATION
Deliverance. Receiving & rejecting men. 8:5-13
Described.
  Being made whole. 14:36
  Good ground. Fruit-bearing. 13:8, 23
Duty. (See Related Subjects)
  Two choices. 7:13-14
Error - Misconceptions.
  Man cannot save man. 19:26
  Waiting. Reasons. 8:25
Facts.
  Being s. is not assured. 18:13
  Jesus seeks every single person. 18:11; 18:12
  Not inherited. 1:7-10; 3:7-10
  Meaning. And results. 1:21
Rejected.
  Many called; few chosen. Reasons. 22:11-14
  Reasons. 8:23
Results.
  Christ heals soul & body. 14:36
  Discipleship. Of two blind men. 20:34
  Joy. Great rejoicing over. Reasons. 18:13
  Meaning & results. 1:21
Seeking.
  Response of Christ. Fourfold. 9:20-22
  Why not earlier. 8:25
Source - How one is s.
  A rich man enters heaven. 19:16-22
  By building wisely & not foolishly. 7:24-27
  Attitudes needed for s. 14:36
  Confessing vs. denying Christ. 10:32-33
  Confession of Christ. 16:13-17
  Enduring to the end. 10:22
  Faith of friends. 9:2
  God's great invitation. 22:1-14
  Having more righteousness than a religionist. 5:20
  How a rich man is s. 19:16-22

INDEX

Losing one's life means savings one's life. 16:25
Man cannot save man. 19:26
Peter's great confession. 16:13-20
Saved. Steps. Twofold. 19:26
Seeking after Christ. 5:6; 18:11-14
Steps. To being made whole. 8:2; 9:18-34; 14:34-36
Three attitudes. 5:3
Three steps. 8:19-20
Two choices. Broad and narrow. 7:13-14
What it takes to receive things of God. 8:2; 15:21-28
What s. takes. 9:27-31
Who shall enter heaven. 7:21-23
Willingness is not enough. 8:19-20
Who is s.
Desperate. How d. can be saved. 9:18-34; 14:15-21; 15:29-39; 20:29-34
Evil possessed. 8:28-34
Hopeless & desperate. 9:18-34
"Many" shall come. Predicted. 8:11
Most defiled. 8:1-4
Rude. 9:2
Sinner. 9:1-8; 9:9; 9:9-13
Socially rejected. 8:5-13

SAND
Building upon. What s. is. 7:26-27

SANHEDRIN (See **RELIGIONISTS**)
Discussed. 26:59
Opposed & condemned Christ. Predetermined, stacked guilt. 21:23; 26:57

SATAN
Defeated - destroyed. By Christ. House spoiled. 12:25-26; 12:29
Names & titles.
Adversary. 16:21-23
Beelzebub. 12:24
Power of. Broken by God's Word. 17:17-18
Work - strategy of.
How S. operates. 13:25, 38-39
Sow evil men among believers. 13:25, 38-39
Sow tares among wheat. 13:25; 38-39
Tempts. 4:1

SCATTERED
Meaning. 9:36

SCHOLAR
Attracted to Christ. 8:19-20

SCORN
Reasons. Threefold. 13:53-54

SCOURGE - SCOURGING
Discussed. 27:26-38
Of Christ. Discussed. 27:26-38

SCRIBAL LAW
Condemned by Christ. 5:17-18; 5:17-20; 5:17-48
Described. Six hundred laws. 22:36

SCRIBES
Accusations against. Nine a. 23:13-36
Authority of. Discussed. 7:29
Opposed Christ. (See **JESUS CHRIST**, Opposed; Response to; **RELIGIONISTS**, Opposed Christ)

Problem with.
Put tradition before God's commandments. 15:1-6
Spiritual blindness. 15:12-14
Worship is empty. 15:7-9

SCRIPTURE
Christ's use of. 4:4
Duty. To heed. 4:14
Fulfilled - Fulfillment. (See **JESUS CHRIST**, Prophecy Concerning; **PROPHECY**. Fulfilled)
Christ's person & work. 4:12-17; 5:17-18; 12:17-21
Misuse of. Adding to & taking away from. Discussed. 23:1

SEEK - SEEKING
Christ s. men.
His very purpose. 20:28
Savior. Compared to a Shepherd. Five facts. 18:12
Law of. 13:12
Meaning. 6:33
Men seek Christ.
By wise men. 2:1-11
Giving up all for Christ. 13:44; 13:45-46
Great application. 12:42
Must know about Christ before can s. 14:35
Reasons. 8:18-22
Steps to s. & being made whole. 14:34-36
Results. God meets need. 2:11

SELF - SELFISH - SELFISHNESS
Caused by. Wealth. Creates "big I." 19:23
Described. Big "I." 7:21
Growth of. Step by step. 8:28-31
Sins of. Listed. 18:3

SELF-CENTERED
Reaction to being offended. 18:15-17

SELF-CONFIDENCE
Errors of. 4:2-4; 4:5-7
Forgets human weakness & carnality. 14:28-31
Sin of. Over-confidence. Discussed. 26:33-34

SELF-DENIAL (See **CROSS**)
Discussed. 10:38
Duty.
To give is essential for salvation. 19:21-22; 19:23-26
Warning. Danger of not giving. 19:23-26
Essential.
For salvation. 19:21-22; 19:23-26
To follow Christ. 8:19-20
Meaning. Not shirking duties & families. 19:27
Results. Rewards - great & glorious. 19:27-30

SELF-DEPENDENCY
Inadequate to meet man's needs. 14:15-21

SELF-ESTEEM
Low self-image.
Causes of. 13:53-54
Nazareth. Reasons. 13:53-54

SELF-IMPORTANCE (See **PRIDE**; **BOASTING**)
Described. Favorite of God. 8:4

SELF-RIGHTEOUS - SELF-RIGHTEOUSNESS
Discussed. 19:16-22; 21:28-32
Great sin of the rich. Discussed. 19:16-22
Vs. Christ's righteousness. 7:22
What it takes to enter God's kingdom. Discussed. 21:28-32

SELF-SUFFICIENT
Blind to truth. 11:25-27
Described. As wise in own eyes. 11:25-27
Errors of. 4:2-4; 4:5-7

SENSATIONALISM - SPECTACULAR (See **SIGNS**)
Tempted to use. Christ is. 4:5-7

SENSES
Natural vs. spiritual s. 16:2-3

SEPARATE
Meaning. 13:49

SERMON ON THE MOUNT
Discussed. 5:1-7:29
Given to prepare the disciples. 5:1-2

SERPENTS
Discussed. 10:16
To be wise as s. 10:16

SERVANT - SLAVES
Ideal. Christ, the Chosen Servant of God. 12:14-21; 20:28
Questioning the origin of sin. 13:27

SERVANT, FAITHFUL & WISE
Parable of. 24:45-47

SERVE - SERVICE (See **BELIEVER**; **MINISTERS - MINISTERING**)
Duty. To s. while opportunity exists. 26:10-11
Failure in. Can know four things. 6:33
Meaning. 6:1
Need. Realistic view of the world. 7:3
Reward. Counted as the greatest, the chief by God. 20:23-28

SEVENTIETH WEEK
Of Daniel. Discussed. 24:15

SEX (See **IMMORALITY**; **ADULTERY**; **LUST**)
Purpose. Threefold. 5:27-20
Right vs. wrong use. 5:27-30

SHAMMAI SCHOOL
Conservative school of thought. 19:1-12

SHARING
Duty. To share the Old & New Testaments. 13:52

SHEBA, QUEEN OF
Example of seeking great wisdom. 12:42
Sought great wisdom. 12:42
To testify against this generation. 12:42

INDEX

SHEEP
  Describes. Lost world. 9:36
  Parable. Of lost s. Supreme example of caring. 18:11-14
  Types. Of believers. 25:31-33

SHEKINAH GLORY
  Discussed. 17:5-8

SHEPHERD
  Seeking a lost sheep. Five facts. 18:12
  Supreme example of caring. 18:11-14

SHOWBREAD
  Discussed. 12:3-4

SICKNESSES
  Borne by Christ. 8:16-17
  Cause. Ultimate c. 8:17

SIGNIFICANCE (See **PURPOSE**)

SIGNS
  Desire for.
    By Jews. Reasons. Problems. 12:38-40
    By men. Ways. Discussed. 16:2-3
  Discussed. 4:3-11; 12:38-40
  God works by faith, not s. 4:3-11; 12:38-40
  Of last day, that is, of today. Point to Christ. Three s. 16:2-3
  Vs. faith. 4:3-11; 12:38-40
  Warning. Beware of being blind to the s. 16:1-4

SIMON OF CYRENE
  Enlisted to carry the cross for Christ. 27:26-38

SIMON THE LEPER
  Discussed. 26:1-13; 26:6

SIN - SINS
  Acts - Behavior.
    Attitude toward. Several a. 9:12-13
    Childish: contrary, playful, mindless. 11:16-19
    Comfort, at ease, softness. Answer to. 11:8
    Criticism. 7:1-6
    Divisiveness. Steps to correcting. 18:15-20
    Greed. Love of money. 26:15
    Offending & leading others astray. 5:19; 18:5-10; 18:15
    Outward vs. inward. 23:27-28
    Over-confidence. 26:33-34
    Presuming upon God. Taking for granted. 26:40-41
    Selfishness. Listed. 18:3
    Sensual, senseless. 13:13-15
    Short of God's glory. 18:32-34
    Some are very evil. Discussed. 2:13-18
    Spectator only. 3:7-10
    State of world at the end time. 24:37-39
    What defiles a man. 15:1-20
  Caused by. Lack of logic, thought. 12:27-28; 13:13-15
  Deliverance.
    Cast out of life. Discussed. 12:43-45
    Steps to correcting divisiveness. 18:15-20
    What Jesus saves from. Four things. 1:21
  Described.
    As debts. Meaning. 6:12
    Sensual, senseless. 13:13-15
  Fact. Everyone sins—crosses over into s. 6:14
  Growth of. Step by step. 8:28-31
  List of. 15:19-20
  Meaning.
    Big "I." 7:21; 19:23
    Selfishness. 7:21; 19:23
  Results.
    Bankrupts. Puts in debt. 18:25
    Enslaves. 24:37-39
    Judicial blindness, hardness. 13:13-15
    Judgment of. 5:19
    Listed. 24:37-39
  Symbolic - Type of. Leprosy. 8:1-4
  Unpardonable s. 12:31-32
  Warning against. Offending a child. 18:5-10

SIN, UNPARDONABLE
  Discussed. 12:31-32

SINGLENESS OF EYE
  Meaning. 6:22

SINNER - SINNERS
  Attitude toward. Religionists feel they are more acceptable than s. 9:12-13
  Comfortable with Christ. 9:10-11
  Neglected. Many will not touch. 8:3
  State of. Spiritually sick. Three things. 9:12-13
  What it takes to enter heaven. 21:28-32

SLAVE
  Only s. ever brought to Christ. 8:8

SLAVERY
  Enforced labor. Discussed. 5:41

SLEEP - SLEPT
  Reasons for. 26:40-41

SLEEP, SPIRITUAL
  Meaning. 25:5
  Reasons for. 26:40-41

SLUMBER - SLUMBERED (See **SLEEP, SPIRITUAL**)

SODOM
  Discussed. 10:15; 11:23

SOLDIER
  Treatment of Christ before & during death. 27:26-38

SON OF MAN (See **JESUS CHRIST, NAMES - TITLES**)
  Meaning. 8:20

SONS, TWO
  Parable of. What it takes to enter heaven. 21:28-32

SORROWFUL
  Meaning. 26:37

SOUL
  Meaning. 16:25-28; 22:37
  Value of.
    Priceless. Giving up all to save. 13:45-46
    Worth more than the world. Reasons. 16:25-28

SOWER, PARABLE OF
  How men receive the gospel. 13:1-9

SPEAK - SPEECH (See **TONGUE**)
  To reflect the testimony for Christ. 26:73-73

SPECTACULAR, THE (See **SENSATIONALISM**)

SPIRIT
  Blind s. Defiles a man. 15:12-14

SPIRITUAL
  Things that lead away from the s. 16:17

SPIRITUAL BLESSINGS
  Described. Sixfold. 6:21-23
  Meaning. 6:19-20

SPIRITUAL BLINDNESS
  Judicial b. Reasons. 13:13-15
  Lost are blind. 9:27-31
  To God's purpose. 11:25-27
  To Messiah. 11:25-27
  To truth. 11:25-27
  Warning against. 16:1-4

SPIRITUAL DEATH
  Described. Dead men's bones. 23:27-28

SPIRITUAL EXPERIENCE (See **GLORY**)
  Described. 17:2; 17:3; 17:4; 17:5-8; 17:5
  God knows exactly what believers need. 17:4

SPIRITUAL FAMILY
  Discussed. 12:48-50

SPIRITUAL GROWTH - MATURITY
  Suffering, disability not to hinder. 12:9-10

SPIRITUAL HISTORY (See **HISTORY, SPIRITUAL**)

SPIRITUAL INHERITANCE (See **REWARD**)
  Described. Spiritual dimension. 21:43
  Discussed. 25:34-40
  Of believer. 25:34-40
  Of God's promises. 1:2
  Of Israel & of the church. 21:43

SPIRITUAL MINDED
  Vs. earthly minded. Example of disciples. 16:5-12

SPIRITUAL SENSES
  Natural vs. spiritual s. 16:2-4

SPIRITUAL STRUGGLE—WARFARE
  Discussed. 11:28-30
  Division within. 10:34-38

SPIRITUAL TREASURES (See **SPIRITUAL BLESSINGS**)
  Meaning. 6:19-20

SPIRITUAL TRUTH (See **TRUTH**, Spiritual)
  Hid from the wise, self-sufficient. 11:25-27

SPIRITUAL WORLD-DIMENSION
  Denied. 22:23-33; 22:29
  Nature. Discussed. 22:29
  Reality of. 22:29

SPITE
  Reasons. Threefold. 13:53-54

INDEX

STAR
Of Wise Men. Discussed. 2:2

STATE (See **CITIZENSHIP**)

STEALING
Example of. Judas embezzled the funds of the Lord. 26:15

STEDFASTNESS (See **ENDURANCE; PERSEVERANCE**)
Essential. For God's leadership. 2:12

STEWARDSHIP (See **GIVE - GIVING; TITHE**)
Of the Temple. Christ supported. Reasons. 17:25

STONE, THE
Symbolism.
  Of Christ. Discussed. 21:42; 21:44
  Pictures of. Fourfold. 21:44

STONY GROUND
How it receives the gospel. 13:5-6, 20-21

STORMS
Calmed by Christ.
  Power of Christ's presence. 14:22-33
  Power over fear & nature. 8:23-27
Of life. Listed. 7:24-25; 7:26-27

STRIVE - STRIVING
Of Holy Spirit. Not always s. with man. 12:14-16

STUDY
Challenge to. Devotion essential. Three e. 13:52

STUMBLING - STUMBLING BLOCK
Discussed. 18:5-10
Example of Christ. 17:27
Meaning. 5:29; 17:27
Steps to correcting offending brothers. 18:15-20
Warning against. 18:5-10
Ways offend others. 18:15

SUCCESS
Formula for; law of. 13:12

SUFFERING (See **PERSECUTION**)
Caused by. Ultimate c. 8:17
Duty. Not to keep one from worshipping. 12:9-10
Purpose.
  Why God allows suffering. 8:1-4
  Why God does not always heal. 8:1-4

SUNDAY (See **SABBATH**)

SURRENDER
Essential. To follow Christ. 8:19-20
Of resources. Essential to meet world's needs. 14:18-21
What is to be s. 6:9

SWAYING
Answer to. 11:7
Sign of weakness. 11:7

SWEARING
Discussed. 5:33-37; 23:16-22
Law governing. 5:33-37
Results. Weak self-image & spiritual. 5:44

SYNAGOGUE
Discussed. 4:23
Ruler. Discussed. 9:18-19

SYRIA
Discussed. 4:24

TALENTED, THE
How the t. enters heaven. 19:16-22

TALENTS (See **AMBITION—GIFTS**)
Duty. To surrender to Christ. 14:18-21
Parable of. Watch & work for judgment is coming. 25:14-30

TARES
Meaning. 13:24-30

TAX COLLECTOR
Discussed. 9:9-13

TAXES—TRIBUTE
Good citizenship. 17:24-27
Kind. Poll tax. Discussed. 22:17
Temple. Discussed. 17:24
Why Christ paid. Six reasons. 17:27

TEACHERS
Duty. Responsible for teaching the truth. 23:2
Fact.
  Can teach only so many. 10:2
  Either accept or reject the law. 5:19
Influence others. For good or bad. 5:19
Position. Highly esteemed. Sit in Moses' seat. 23:2

TEACHERS, FALSE (See **APOSTASY; DECEIVE; RELIGIONISTS**)
Described. As wolves in sheep clothing. 7:15
Discussed. 7:15-20; 23:1-12
Error. Fourfold. 7:15
Experience four things. 10:5
Nature.
  Deceptive. 7:15
  Discussed. 7:17
  Fourfold. 7:17
  Known by fruit. 7:16
Teaching of.
  Effective, but only half true. 7:17
  Four errors, four gospels. 7:18
Traits - marks. Discussed. 7:15; 7:16
Warning against. False religion. 7:15-20; 16:5-12; 23:1-12

TEACHING - TRAINING
Errors of. Threefold. 9:35
Method.
  Number ratio needs to be limited. 10:2
  Of Christ. 9:35
Parables. Reasons Jesus spoke in p. 13:10-17; 13:34-35
Training precedes service. 10:1

TEACHING, FALSE (See **APOSTASY; TEACHERS, FALSE**)

TEMPLE
Care - Treatment.
  Cleansed by Christ. 21:12-16
  Cleansed of commercialism. 21:12-16
  What the t. is to be. 21:12-16
Courts. Discussed. 21:12-16
Nature - Described as. House of prayer. 21:13

Purpose of. Discussed. 21:12-16
Supported by Christ. Reasons. Threefold. 17:25
Temple tax. Discussed. 17:24

TEMPTATION
Conquering - deliverance.
  By prayer. 6:13
  How to meet. 4:1-11
Danger. Twofold. 4:5-7
Kinds of t.
  Discussed. 4:2-4
  To be self-centered. 4:2-4
  To compromise. 4:8-10
  To meet one's needs in own strength. 4:2-4
  To test God. 4:5-7
  To use the spectacular. 4:5-7
Of Jesus Christ. 4:1-11
Origin - Source. Not of God. 4:1
Purpose. 4:1
When men are tempted. 4:5-7

TEST
Words vs. action. 9:4-7

TESTAMENT, NEW
Established between God & man. 26:26-30

TESTIMONY
Effect upon others. Warning. 18:1-4
Fact. Fine line between honoring Christ & self. 9:27-30

TETRARCH
Meaning. 14:1-14

THAMAR
Saved by God. 1:3

THINKING
Illogical. Exposed. 12:11

THIRST
For righteousness. 5:6

THORNS
Describes. World. 13:7, 22
Symbol. Of curse upon the earth. 27:29

THOUGHTLESS (See **MINDLESS**)

THOUGHTS (See **MIND**)

TIRED - TIREDNESS
Discussed. 11:28-30

TITHE - TITHING (See **STEWARDSHIP**)
Essential. To Jews. 23:23
Warning. Against t. for attention. 23:5

TOMB
Discussed. 27:65-66

TONGUE (See **WORDS**)
Idle words. Meaning. 12:36
What the t. does.
  Defiles a man. 15:10-11
  Determines one's destiny. 12:31-37
  Exposes the kind of person one is. Threefold. 12:34-35

TOUCH
Communicates two things. 8:14-15

INDEX

TRADITION
Of Jews.
Caused rejection of some. 9:20
Sabbath. Rules & regulations. 12:1-8
Stressed. 15:1-20; 15:6-9
Old vs. new. 9:16-17

TRAINING (See **DISCIPLES**, Training of)
Of disciples. Intensified. Launched a new phase. 16:13-20; 16:21-28
To precede service. 10:1-4; 10:1

TRANSFIGURED - TRANSFIGURATION (See **JESUS CHRIST**, Transfiguration)
Meaning. 17:2
Of Christ. 17:1-13
Strengthened to bear the cross. 17:1-13

TRANSFORMATION
Power of the gospel. 13:33

TREASURE, SPIRITUAL
Believers are considered t. 13:44
Christ is a t. 13:44
How handled in Jesus' day. 13:44
Parable of Hidden T. Giving all for Christ. 13:44

TRESPASS
Meaning. 6:14

TRIALS - TRIBULATION (See **LIFE**, Storms of)
Confronting. Terrible t. & death. 26:36-46
Deliverance through. Power over fear & t. 8:23-27
Listed. Manyfold. 7:24-25; 7:26-27
Questioning. Not q. 2:13-18

TRIBULATION, THE GREAT
Discussed. 24:1-31; 24:15-28; 24:29-31
Signs of.
Discussed. 24:1-31
Persecution - tragic sign. 24:9
Warning.
To believers. 25:1-46
Watchfulness essential. 24:42-51; 25:1-46
World to be destroyed. 24:29

TRINITY
First mention in New Testament. 3:16

TRIUMPHAL ENTRY
Demonstrated. Messiahship. 21:1-11
Fulfilled prophecy. 21:2-5

TROUBLEMAKER
Vs. peacemaker. 5:9

TRUST
Reasons to t. Twofold. 6:8

TRUTH
Fact. T. to be known someday. 10:26-27
Spiritual.
Blind & ignorant to. 12:11
Hid from the wise & self-sufficient. 11:25-27

UNBELIEF (See **REJECTION**)
Caused by.
Fear losing one's position, esteem, & livelihood. 23:1-12
Rebellion against the Lordship of Christ. 12:14-16
Faults - Problems with. 21:23-27
Deliberate, willful u. 13:10-17; 13:13-15
Inconsistent & illogical. 12:22-30; 12:26-28
Meaning.
Discussed. 17:19-20
Little faith. 6:30
Obstinate. Discussed. 12:24; 12:31-32; 13:13-17 21:23-27; 23:1-12
Sin common to false citizenship. 22:16-17
Rejected Christ. By hometown. 13:58
Results of.
Hurts several persons. 13:58
Rejects & loses. 13:12; 13:13-15
Strikes at core of Christ's nature. 21:23
Threefold. 13:58; 17:15-16
Types of. 13:4-7
Warning - Danger of. Leads to judicial blindness. 13:13-15
Why men reject. 8:23; 13:58; 19:22
Fear loss of position, wealth, etc. 21:25-27
Fear two things. 21:25-27
Threefold. 13:53-58

UNBELIEVERS
Described.
As goats. 25:33
As tares among wheat. 13:25, 38-39; 13:26
Hard hearted. 13:4
Problem of. Twofold p. with the death of Christ. 26:62-66
Ungodly vs. godly man. 14:1-14

UNFORGIVENESS
Caused by.
Bad feelings. 6:15
Not forgiving others. 6:14-15
Described. 18:22
Spirit & practice of forgiveness. 18:21-35

UNGODLY - UNGODLINESS (See **LOST, THE; UNBELIEVERS**)

UNITY (See **BROTHERHOOD; DIVISION**)
Basis. A forgiving spirit. 18:22
Steps to correcting divisiveness. 18:15-20

UNMERCIFUL SERVANT
Parable of. Spirit & practice of forgiveness. 18:21-35

UNPARDONABLE SIN
Discussed. 12:31-32

UNRIGHTEOUS (See **LOST, THE; UNBELIEVERS; UNGODLY**)

UNSAVED - UNRIGHTEOUS (See **LOST, THE; UNBELIEVERS**)
Being saved is not assured. 14:1-14; 18:13
Unsaved. Reasons. 6:31-32
Why men are unsaved. 19:22

URGENT - URGENCY
Essential. To follow Christ. 8:21-22
Duty. To grasp opportunity while one can. 26:10-11

VEIL
Of Temple. Torn from top to bottom at the cross. 27:51

VINEGAR
Christ offered on cross. To deaden pain. 27:26-38

VIRGIN BIRTH (See **JESUS CHRIST**, Birth)
Of Christ. Discussed. 1:16; 1:23

VIRGINS, TEN
Parable of. Warning. Watch for the Lord's return. 25:1-13

VISION, WORLD-WIDE
Equals success. Formula for s. 13:12
Greatest challenge known to man. 9:37-38
Of harvest of needful world. Ready for reaping. 9:37-38

VULTURES
Symbol of judgment. 24:28

WARNING
Against ruining life. Picture of a ruined life. 26:14-16

WATCH - WATCHFULNESS
Discussed. 24:42
Duty. For Lord's return. 24:42-51
Meaning. 24:42
Reasons do not w. 26:40-41
Warning to. 26:40-41

WAVERING
Answer. Discussed. 11:7
Sign of weakness. 11:7

WAYSIDE
Some sit by w. 13:4, 19

WEALTH - WEALTHY (See **RICH - RICHES**)
Dangers - Problems with.
Deceives. Four ways. 13:7, 22
Discussed. 19:23-26
Hoarding condemns. 19:21-22
Fact. Fourfold. 14:5
How a rich man enters heaven. 19:16-22
Misunderstanding of - Misconceptions.
Sign of God's blessings. 19:25
Seeking. Discussed. 18:1-4
What w. does. 19:23

WEARY - WEARINESS
Answer to. Rest of Christ. 11:28-30
Discussed. 11:28-30

WEDDING FEAST OF CHRIST
Garment of righteousness essential to attend. 22:11-14
God's great invitation to. 22:1-14

INDEX

WEEPING
Meaning. 8:12

WELCOMING
Reward for. Discussed. 10:40-42

WHEAT & TARES
Parable of. 13:24-30; 13:36-43

WHOLE - WHOLENESS
Meaning. Of both soul & body. 14:36

WICKED - WICKEDNESS (See **LOST, UNSAVED**)
Described. Short of God's glory. 18:32-34

WICKED HUSBANDMAN
Parable of. Israel's rejection of Christ. 21:33-46

WIDE GATE VS. NARROW GATE
Discussed. 7:12-14

WIDOWS
Courted in order to steal from. 23:14

WILDERNESS
Man wandering about in w. 18:11

WILL - WILLS
Four w. struggle for man. 6:10
Meaning. 16:24
Of God. Blind to. 11:25-27

WISDOM
Described as wise in own eyes. Self-sufficient. 11:25-27; 11:25
Duty. To seek w. diligently. 12:42
Of man. Blinded to truth. 11:25-27; 11:25

WISE MEN
Discussed. 2:1
Worshipped Jesus as King. 2:1-11

WISE VS. FOOLISH BUILDER
Describes life. 7:24-27

WITNESS - WITNESSING
Call to. Discussed 4:18-20
Challenge.
  If have not heard, cannot be saved. 14:35
  Laborers needed. Harvest plentiful. 9:37-38
  Must know about Christ before one can be saved. 14:35
  Neglected. Believers cloistered in the church. 5:13; 5:14
  Pharisees were strong in witnessing to their religion. 23:15
  Preparation. Threefold. 16:20
Commission.
  Great C. 28:16-20
  Sent forth. 10:5-15
Duty - Where to go.
  In home. 9:4-7; 9:10-11
  Three places. 5:14-15
  To friends first. 9:10-11
  To w. to family first. 9:4-7; 10:5-6
  To world. Reasons. 5:14
Example.
  Men's going out & bringing others. 14:35
  Supreme example of w. 18:11-14
How men receive the gospel. 13:1-9

How to go.
  Denying vs. confessing Christ. 10:32-33
  Method. Two by two. 10:3-4
  Rules governing. 10:5-15
  Wise as serpents; harmless as doves. 10:16

WOE
Meaning. 23:13

WOMEN
At burial of Jesus. Loyalty & affection. 27:61
At cross. Courage & love. 27:55-56
At resurrection. Witnesses to. 28:1
God's glorious mercy to. 1:3-6

WORD OF GOD
Adding to - Abuse of. Corrupted. Two ways. 12:1-2
Described. Instructions for building. 7:24-27
Fulfilled (See **PROPHECY**. Fulfilled; **SCRIPTURE**, Fulfilled)
  By Christ. 5:17-18
Power of. Breaks Satan's power. 17:17-18
Response to.
  Different ways the W. is received. 13:1-9

WORDS (See **TONGUE**)
Exposes one's heart. 12:34-35
Idle. Meaning. 12:36
Man's words determine his destiny. 12:31-37
Three things about man. 12:34-35

WORK - WORKS (See **GIVE - GIVING; LABOR; PROFESSION; SERVICE; EMPLOYMENT**)
Basis. Of judgment. 25:31-46
Call to. Rejected vs. accepted. 21:28-32
Duty.
  To do good to one's enemies. 5:44
  To do necessary w. 12:5
  To give precedence over religious law. 12:5
  To give to all who ask or take. 5:40; 5:41; 5:42
How to. Two descriptive ways. 6:3
Meaning. 16:25-28
Motive. Right vs. wrong. 6:1; 6:1-4
Of Christ. Discussed. 11:4-6
Purpose. To lead men to glorify God. 5:16
Results. Proves the believer's faith. 25:34-40
Weakness of. Unacceptable for salvation. 5:20

WORLD (See **CORRUPTION; INCORRUPTION**)
Created - Creation. God has given all provision for care. 21:33
Deliverance from.
  Answer to an evil generation. 12:38-45
  Forsaking. Losing life means one saves his life. 16:25-28
  God's great invitation to. 22:1-14
  Has some witness. 5:14-15
  Regeneration of. Discussed. 19:28
Duty to. Look after. Cultivate. 21:33
History of. Perceived by God. 21:33-46
Judgment of - End of. Predicted. 24:1-25:46
Nature.
  Corruptible vs. incorruptible. 6:19-20
  Sinful. Fact. 18:7-9

State of.
  At end time. As Noah's day, sensual. 24:37-39
  Earthly paradise. Inadequate. 14:34
  Inconsistencies of. 11:19
  Insecure. Reasons. 6:19-20
  Lost. Sheep without a shepherd. 9:36
  Neglected. Believers cloistered in church. 5:13; 5:14
Types of. Egypt. 2:13-18
Value of. Priceless. 13:1-58
Vs. Christ.
  Blind to Messiah. 11:25-27
  Christ ushered in a new age. 9:14-17
  Christ's vision of. 9:36-38
  Not approved by Christ. 10:34-37
  Opinion of Christ. 16:13-14
  Treatment of Christ. 26:55-56; 26:57-68
  Treatment of God's Son. Death of Christ. 27:26-44
Warning against. Christ's return in end time. 24:30
Worldly minded vs. godly minded. 6:19-24

WORLDLY - WORLDLINESS
Caused by. Man wrapped up in w. 6:31-32
Danger of. 19:23-26
Described as.
  A master. 6:24
  Evil. 6:21-23
  Five things. 6:21-23
  Foolish. Reasons. 6:19-20
  Thorns. 13:7, 22
Discussed. 13:7, 22
Problem of. Things that lead away from Christ. 16:17
Results - Effects of.
  Chokes the Word, spiritual growth. 13:7, 22
  Deceives. Reasons. 6:21-23
  Discussed. 6:19-20
  Loss of life. 6:19-20
  Loss of meaning. purpose. 6:19-20

WORLDLY WISE
Meaning. 11:25

WORRY (See **ANXIETY**)
Discussed. 6:25-34

WORSHIP
Duty. Not to let strife hinder. 12:9-13
Of Jesus Christ.
  As Lord. Example. 15:25
  By wise men. 2:1-11
  Stressed. 12:9-10
Meaning. 8:2

WRATH
To flee. 3:7

YOKE
Meaning. 11:29-30

YOUNG PEOPLE
Achieving, conscientious. 19:16-22
Rich young ruler. 19:16-22

ZACHARIAS THE MARTYR
Discussed. 23:35

OUTLINE BIBLE RESOURCES

This material, like similar works, has come from imperfect man and is thus susceptible to human error. We are nevertheless grateful to God for both calling us and empowering us through His Holy Spirit to undertake this task. Because of His goodness and grace, *The Preacher's Outline & Sermon Bible*® New Testament and the Old Testament volumes are now complete.

The Minister's Personal Handbook, The Believer's Personal Handbook, and other helpful **Outline Bible Resources** are available in printed form as well as releasing electronically on various software programs.

God has given the strength and stamina to bring us this far. Our confidence is that as we keep our eyes on Him and remain grounded in the undeniable truths of the Word, we will continue to produce other helpful Outline Bible Resources for God's dear servants to use in their Bible Study and discipleship.

We offer this material, first, to Him in whose name we labor and serve and for whose glory it has been produced and, second, to everyone everywhere who studies, preaches, and teaches the Word.

Our daily prayer is that each volume will lead thousands, millions, yes even billions, into a better understanding of the Holy Scriptures and a fuller knowledge of Jesus Christ the Incarnate Word, of whom the Scriptures so faithfully testify.

You will be pleased to know that Leadership Ministries Worldwide partners with Christian organizations, printers, and mission groups around the world to make Outline Bible Resources available and affordable in many countries and foreign languages. It is our goal that *every* leader around the world, both clergy and lay, will be able to understand God's Holy Word and present God's message with more clarity, authority, and understanding—all beyond his or her own power.

LEADERSHIP MINISTRIES WORLDWIDE
P.O. Box 21310 • Chattanooga, TN 37424-0310
(423) 855-2181 FAX (423) 855-8616
info@outlinebible.org
www.outlinebible.org – FREE download materials

LEADERSHIP MINISTRIES WORLDWIDE

Publishers of Outline Bible Resources

- **THE PREACHER'S OUTLINE & SERMON BIBLE® (POSB)** • KJV – NIV

NEW TESTAMENT

Matthew 1 (chapters 1–15)
Matthew 2 (chapters 16–28)
Mark
Luke
John
Acts
Romans

1 & 2 Corinthians
Galatians, Ephesians, Philippians, Colossians
1 & 2 Thessalonians, 1 & 2 Timothy, Titus, Philemon
Hebrews, James
1 & 2 Peter, 1, 2, & 3 John, Jude
Revelation
Master Outline & Subject Index

OLD TESTAMENT

Genesis 1 (chapters 1–11)
Genesis 2 (chapters 12–50)
Exodus 1 (chapters 1–18)
Exodus 2 (chapters 19–40)
Leviticus
Numbers
Deuteronomy
Joshua
Judges, Ruth
1 Samuel
2 Samuel

1 Kings
2 Kings
1 Chronicles
2 Chronicles
Ezra, Nehemiah, Esther
Job
Psalms 1 (chapters 1-41)
Psalms 2 (chapters 42-106)
Psalms 3 (chapters 107-150)
Proverbs
Ecclesiastes, Song of Solomon

Isaiah 1 (chapters 1-35)
Isaiah 2 (chapters 36-66)
Jeremiah 1 (chapters 1-29)
Jeremiah 2 (chapters 30-52),
  Lamentations
Ezekiel
Daniel, Hosea
Joel, Amos, Obadiah, Jonah,
  Micah, Nahum
Habakkuk, Zephaniah, Haggai,
  Zechariah, Malachi

Print versions of all Outline Bible Resources are available in various forms.

- **The Preacher's Outline & Sermon Bible New Testament** — 3 Vol. Hardcover • KJV – NIV
- **What the Bible Says to the Believer** — **The Believer's Personal Handbook**
  11 Chs. – Over 500 Subjects, 300 Promises, & 400 Verses Expounded - Italian Imitation Leather or Paperback
- **What the Bible Says to the Minister** — **The Minister's Personal Handbook**
  12 Chs. - 127 Subjects - 400 Verses Expounded - Italian Imitation Leather or Paperback
- **Practical Word Studies In the New Testament** — 2 Vol. Hardcover Set
- **The Teacher's Outline & Study Bible™ - Various New Testament Books**
  Complete 30 - 45 minute lessons – with illustrations and discussion questions
- **Practical Illustrations — Companion to the POSB**
  Arranged by topic and Scripture reference
- **What the Bible Says About Series – Various Subjects**
- **OBR on various digital platforms**
  See current digital providers on our website at www.outlinebible.org
- **Non-English Translations of various books**
  See our website for more information or contact our office

— Contact LMW for quantity orders and information —

LEADERSHIP MINISTRIES WORLDWIDE or Your Local Christian Bookstore
PO Box 21310 • Chattanooga, TN 37424-0310
(423) 855-2181 (9am – 5pm Eastern) • FAX (423) 855-8616
E-mail - info@outlinebible.org • Order online at www.outlinebible.org

LEADERSHIP MINISTRIES WORLDWIDE

PURPOSE STATEMENT

LEADERSHIP MINISTRIES WORLDWIDE exists to equip ministers, teachers, and laymen in their understanding, preaching, and teaching of God's Word by publishing and distributing worldwide *The Preacher's Outline & Sermon Bible*® and related **Outline Bible Resources**; to reach & disciple men, women, boys and girls for Jesus Christ.

MISSION STATEMENT

1. To make the Bible so understandable – its truth so clear and plain – that men and women everywhere, whether teacher or student, preacher or hearer, can grasp its message and receive Jesus Christ as Savior, and…

2. To place the Bible in the hands of all who will preach and teach God's Holy Word, verse by verse, precept by precept, regardless of the individual's ability to purchase it.

The **Outline Bible Resources** have been given to LMW for printing and distribution worldwide at/below cost, by those who remain anonymous. One fact, however, is as true today as it was in the time of Christ:

THE GOSPEL IS FREE, BUT THE COST OF TAKING IT IS NOT

LMW depends on the generous gifts of believers with a heart for Him and a love for the lost. They help pay for the printing, translating, and distributing of **Outline Bible Resources** into the hands of God's servants worldwide, who will present the Gospel message with clarity, authority, and understanding beyond their own.

LMW was incorporated in the state of Tennessee in July 1992 and received IRS 501 (c)(3) non-profit status in March 1994. LMW is an international, nondenominational mission organization. All proceeds from USA sales, along with donations from donor partners, go directly to underwrite translation and distribution projects of **Outline Bible Resources** to preachers, church and lay leaders, and Bible students around the world.

www.ingramcontent.com/pod-product-compliance
Lightning Source LLC
Chambersburg PA
CBHW080803020526
44114CB00046B/2747